Contract Law
Volume I

The International Library of Essays in Law and Legal Theory

Schools

Natural Law, Vols I & II *John Finnis*
Justice *Thomas Morawetz*
Law and Economics, Vols I & II *Jules Coleman and Jeffrey Lange*
Critical Legal Studies *James Boyle*
Marxian Legal Theory *Csaba Varga*
Legal Reasoning, Vols I & II *Aulis Aarnio and Neil MacCormick*
Legal Positivism *Mario Jori*
American Legal Theory *Robert Summers*
Law and Language *Fred Schauer*
Sociological Theories of Law *Kahei Rokumoto*
Rights *Carlos Nino*
Law and Psychology *Martin Levine*
Feminist Legal Theory *Frances Olsen*

Areas

Criminal Law *Thomas Morawetz*
Tort Law *Ernest Weinrib*
Contract Law, Vols I & II *Larry Alexander*
Anti-Discrimination Law *Christopher McCrudden*
Consumer Law *Iain Ramsay*
International Law *Martti Koskenniemi*
Property Law *Elizabeth Mensch and Alan Freeman*
Constitutional Law *Mark Tushnet*
Procedure *Denis Galligan*
Evidence and Proof *William Twining and Alex Stein*
Administrative Law *Denis Galligan*
Child Law *Harry Krause*
Family Law, Vols I & II *Harry Krause*
Welfare Law *Peter Robson*
Medicine and the Law *Bernard Dickens*
Commercial Law *Ross Cranston*
Communications Law *David Goldberg*
Environmental Law *Michael Blumm*
Conflict of Laws *Richard Fentiman*
Law and Religion *Wojciech Sadurski*

Legal Cultures

Comparative Legal Cultures *Csaba Varga*
Law and Anthropology *Peter Sack*
Hindu Law and Legal Theory *Ved Nanda*
Islamic Law and Legal Theory *Ian Edge*
Chinese Law and Legal Theory *Michael Palmer*
Japanese Law and Legal Theory *Kiochiro Fujikura*
Law and Development *Anthony Carty*
Jewish Law and Legal Theory *Martin Golding*
Legal Education *Martin Levine*

Future Volumes

Human Rights Law, Socialist Law and Legal Theory, Sociology of Law, Labour Law, Common Law and Legal Theory, Civil Law and Legal Theory, Law and Society, African Law and Legal Theory, Soviet Law and Legal Theory and Cumulative index.

Contract Law
Volume I

Edited by

Larry Alexander

University of San Diego

NEW YORK UNIVERSITY PRESS
REFERENCE COLLECTION

Manufactured in Great Britain

First published in the U.S.A. in 1991 by
NEW YORK UNIVERSITY PRESS
Washington Square
New York NY 10003

Library of Congress Cataloging-in-Publication Data
Contract law / edited by Larry Alexander.
p. cm. – (The International library of essays in law and legal theory).
Essays originally published in various publications.
Includes bibliographical references and index.
ISBN–0–8147–0602–9 (set) – ISBN 0–8147–0600–2 (cloth : v. 1) – ISBN 0–8147–0601–0 (cloth : v. 2)
1. Contracts. I. Alexander, Lawrence A. II. Series.
K840.C658 1991
346′.02–dc20
[342.62] 91-7406
CIP

Contents

Acknowledgements

The editor and publishers wish to thank the following for permission to use copyright material.

Columbia Law Review Association for article: Randy Barnett (1986), 'A Consent Theory of Contract', *Colum. L. Rev.* **86**, pp. 269–321. Copyright © 1986 by the Directors of the Columbia Law Review Association, Inc. All Rights Reserved. This article originally appeared at **86** *Colum. L. Rev.* 269 (1986).

Daniel D. Farber (1983), 'Contract Law and Modern Economic Theory', Original Publisher, *Northwestern University Law Review*, **78**, pp. 303–40. Copyright © Daniel D. Farber.

Harvard Journal of Law & Public Policy for article: Jules Coleman, et al (1989), 'A Bargaining Theory Approach to Default Provisions and Disclosure Rules in Contract Law', *Harvard Journal of Law & Public Policy*, **12**, pp. 639–709.

Harvard Law Review Association for article: Melvin M. Eisenberg (1982), 'The Bargain Principle and Its Limit', *Harvard Law Review*, **95**, pp. 741–802.

Michigan Law Review for article: Richard Craswell (1989), 'Contract Law, Default Rules, and the Philosophy of Promising', *Michigan Law Review*, **88**, pp. 489–530.

Northwestern University Law Review for article: Ian R. Macneil (1983), 'Values in Contract: Internal and External', *Northwestern University Law Review*, **78:2**, pp. 340–419. Reprinted by special permission of Northwestern University School of Law.

Sweet & Maxwell Limited for article: P. S. Atiyah (1978), 'Contracts, Promises and the Law of Obligations', *The Law Quarterly Review*, **94**, pp. 193–224.

University of Minnesota Law Review for article: F. H. Buckley (1988), 'Paradox Lost', *Minnesota Law Review*, **77**, pp. 775–828.

Christopher T. Wonnell (1990), 'The Abstract Character of Contract Law', *Connecticut Law Review*, **22**, pp. 437–97 and is reprinted by permission of the Connecticut Law Review. Copyright © Christopher T. Wonnell.

Yale Law Journal Company and Fred B. Rothman & Company for article: Charles J. Goetz and Robert E. Scott (1980), 'Enforcing Promises: An Examination of the Basis of Contract', *Yale Law Journal*, **89**, pp. 1261–322.

Every effort has been made to trace all the copyright holders, but if any have been inadvertently overlooked the publishers will be pleased to make the necessary arrangement at the first opportunity.

Series Preface

The International Library of Law and Legal Theory is designed to provide important research materials in an accessible form. Each volume contains essays of central theoretical importance in its subject area. The series as a whole makes available an extensive range of valuable material which will be of considerable interest to those involved in the research, teaching and study of law.

The series has been divided into three sections. The Schools section is intended to represent the main distinctive approaches and topics of special concern to groups of scholars. The Areas section takes in the main branches of law with an emphasis on essays which present analytical and theoretical insights of broad application. The section on Legal Cultures makes available the distinctive legal theories of different level traditions and takes up topics of general comparative and developmental concern.

I have been delighted and impressed by the way in which the editors of the individual volumes have set about the difficult task of selecting, ordering and presenting essays from the immense quantity of academic legal writing published in journals throughout the world. Editors were asked to pick out those essays from law, philosophy and social science journals which they consider to be fundamental for the understanding of law, as seen from the perspective of a particular approach or sphere of legal interest. This is not an easy task and many difficult decisions have had to be made in order to ensure that a representative sample of the best journal essays available takes account of the scope of each topic or school.

I should like to express my thanks to all the volume editors for their willing participation and scholarly judgement. The interest and enthusiasm which the project has generated is well illustrated by the fact that an original projection of 12 volumes drawn up in 1989 has now become a list of some 60 volumes. I must also acknowledge the vision, persistence and constant cheerfulness of John Irwin and the marvellous work done by Mrs Margaret O'Reilly and Mrs Sonia Bridgman.

TOM D. CAMPBELL
Series Editor
The Faculty of Law
The Australian National University

Introduction

This is the first volume of a two-volume collection of articles on theoretical aspects of contract law. This volume has two parts, the first part consisting of essays dealing with the question, 'Why enforce contracts?', the second part consisting of essays discussing the topic of interpretive and default rules. The second volume is divided into three parts: Defences to Breach of Contract; Remedies for Breach of Contract; and Contracts, the Distribution of Wealth, and Paternalism. This division into parts is, of course, somewhat artificial: theoretical essays in any area of contract law tend to have a direct bearing on the other areas, and most in fact discuss those other areas. Nonetheless, artificial and somewhat distorting though it may be, this division into parts is, I hope, like a Mercator projection, useful for its purposes.

The number of essays that deal with theoretical aspects of contract law far exceeds the number that can be included in even two large volumes, and many fine essays, some undoubtedly among the reader's favourites, are necessarily omitted. I should therefore say something about the criteria of selection that I employed, however imperfectly. First, in pursuance of the publisher's general plan for this series, I included only essays, not excerpts from books, and only unedited essays. Second, I included only essays in English. Third, I opted for more recent essays in preference to less recent essays even when the latter are more important in the development of a subject than the essay selected. I did so because the recent essays I selected summarize well the main points of the earlier pathbreaking ones, cite the reader to those earlier articles, and at the same time refer to and build upon work in the field subsequent to those earlier articles. In other words, one who stands on the shoulders of giants can see still further than the giants, and I deemed an essay's field of vision more important than its marginal contribution to a field. Thus the preference for recency. Finally, I believe that all of the essays I have selected are good of their type.

Despite the exclusion of many fine books and essays from these volumes, references to the best of these are included for the reader's benefit in two ways. First, as I noted, the essays I have selected, due to their recency and the fact that they are unedited, cite to most of the important books and essays that a reader of these volumes would want cited. Second, in the introductions to these volumes, in the course of briefly describing each work, I shall refer to other works in the area that I believe the reader will find useful, even if, as is usually the case, those same works are cited in the included essay.

Part I, Why Enforce Contracts?, begins with Randy Barnett's 'A Consent Theory of Contract', published in 1986. Barnett divides existing theories of contractual obligations into five types: the will theories, reliance theories, fairness theories, efficiency theories, and bargain theories. The first two theories he calls party-based, the second two, standards-based, and the last, process-based. Will theories focus on the promisor and her autonomy and justify legal enforcement of contracts on the ground that the promisor has freely chosen to be legally bound. But will theories, grounded in subjectivity, have difficulty justifying contract laws' attention to objectively manifested intentions, even in the face of evidence establishing contrary subjective intentions. Such attention is justified by considerations regarding protecting the security of transactions and reliance, but those considerations are external to will theories.

Reliance theories, on the other hand, focus attention on the promisee and his interests. But reliance theories are as one-sided and incomplete as will theories, though in the opposite direction. For only reasonable reliance is protected by contract law, and the criteria of reasonableness must come from something other than reliance itself. Both reliance and will theories need a broader moral framework than they themselves can provide, one that can take account of both parties to a contract.

The standards-based theories of fairness and efficiency evaluate the substance of contractual transactions by reference to their favoured standards. The fairness theories look to the contractual exchange and ask whether the parties have treated each other fairly according to whatever principles of fair exchange are endorsed by the theories. The efficiency theories ask whether contractual exchanges allocate resources efficiently. Both types of theory face the difficulty of identifying those bargains that are 'fair' or 'efficient'. Moreover, both types of theory employ patterned principles of distributive justice and authorize interference with individual preferences whenever those preferences dictate outcomes that depart from the preferred pattern.

The process-based theories focus on the manner in which the parties reach their agreement, the bargain theory of enforceable contractual obligation being a prime example. On that theory, promises are enforceable if supported by consideration, that is, if they are part of a bargained-for exchange. But the bargain theory fails to capture all and only the promises that we believe should be legally enforced. Moreover, all process theories, including the bargain theory, perforce rest on more fundamental substantive values that are obscured by their exclusive focus on process.

Barnett's own theory, one that he believes surmounts the difficulties of the others, is the consent theory of contract. One begins with a theory of moral rights, activities, and our own bodies, talents, and labour. Contract law is part of the more general subject of how these entitlements may be transferred, which includes the subject of gift as well. And at the core of the notion of enforceable transfer of an entitlement is the consent to the transfer by its holder.

Barnett believes that his consent theory of contractual obligation differs from the will theories to which it appears superficially to be related. It closes the gap between legal and moral obligation that mere promising leaves open. And it explains when and why contract law should and does preference objective manifestations of intentions over the actual intentions themselves. Barnett also believes that his consent theory retains the insights of the various theories he discusses – promise, reliance, fairness, efficiency, and bargain – without their shortcomings.

The next essay in Part I is F.H. Buckley's 'Paradox Lost'. Buckley's focus is on the relation of promising to legally enforceable contractual obligation. In contrast to Barnett's deontological natural rights/entitlements theoretical framework and that of Charles Fried, Buckley's framework is utilitarian. Buckley defends the proposition that the legal obligations flowing from promising are justified by the utility of the institution of promise keeping. Although, given this institution, it is analytic that promises are prima facie morally binding, the question Buckley addresses is why any given individual is bound by this institution.

Low-fidelity explanations of why we are bound by the institution of promise keeping are those that rest, not on the fact that adherence to the institution promotes overall justice or welfare, but on some special connection between the individual and the institution. Consent (to the institution) by the promisor, benefits received by the promisor, or reliance by the promisee are prototypical low-fidelity explanations, but each is unsatisfactory in accounting for why valid promises are binding. Buckley criticizes Barnett's theory as well as several others' theories in this section of the essay, which is the key section in Buckley's case for utility as the justification for why we are bound by the institution of promise keeping.

High-fidelity explanations for why we are bound by the institution of promise keeping rest on a general moral duty to support just institutions. The case for promise keeping's being a just institution might rest on an argument about rights or on an argument about consequences. Buckley finds the rights-based arguments for the duty to support the institution implausible because of their total disregard of consequences. And if irrespective of its consequences the institution of promise keeping does increase freedom along a certain dimension, so too do alternative institutions that we have no moral duty to support. On the other hand, Buckley argues that there are good consequentialist reasons for supporting the institution of promise keeping, and that the benefits of the institution, as opposed to particular enforceable promises within it, outweigh its costs.

The next essay in Part I moves us from consent and promise as the bases of contractual obligation to the domain of law and economics and efficient resource allocation theories. Daniel Farber's 'Contract Law and Modern Economic Theory' analyses both contractual freedom and its limits by reference to microeconomic models that take into account limited rationality, imperfect information, and transaction costs.

Farber begins his argument with the neo-classical economic model. Given a desirable distribution of initial endowments, fully informed and rational contractors, and costless transactions, the case for free exchange of goods follows. If we include within goods the good of a promised future performance, then the case for the ability to exchange contract rights is part of the more general case for free exchange of goods. Farber concludes that, given the neo-classical model's assumptions, a system of enforceable contracts, including contracts that are wholly executory, is necessary and sufficient for efficient resource allocation.

Farber contends that the neo-classical economic model supports the staple doctrines of contract law such as the requirement of consideration, the measure of damages, and extensive freedom with respect to items potentially subject to contract. But the neo-classical model is flawed because its assumptions of full rationality, perfect information, and no transaction costs are contrary to fact. Newer economic models that relax the assumptions of the neo-classical model and adopt more realistic assumptions explain and justify some recent and not-so-recent doctrinal restrictions on pure freedom of contract and its corollary of complete enforcement, such as restrictions that deal with warranty disclaimers, penalty clauses, and bankruptcy.

Another selection from the law and economics camp is Charles Goetz and Robert Scott's 'Enforcing Promises: An Examination of the Basis of Contract'. Goetz and Scott examine the current legal doctrines regarding contract enforceability through the prism of the economic analysis of promising. Specifically, they focus on the following two questions: Which system of promissory enforcement yields the maximum net social benefits from promise-making?, and Does such an optimal enforcement scheme explain current doctrine?

In exploring the first of these two questions, Goetz and Scott point out that promises and their value are distinct from the exchanges they announce. Promises signal future transfers. Promises typically carry both prospective benefits if kept and prospective harm if broken. But legal enforcement of regretted promises may deter socially useful future promising at the same time that it promotes reliability. Conversely, non-enforcement encourages promises but reduces their reliability. Finally, in a world where legal processes are costly and the information they require imperfect, the legal rules regarding contract enforceability will differ from those that would be optimal in the absence of such imperfections. Common law rules may be our best available proxies for theoretically optimal rules in the real world of imperfect and costly information and costly enforcement processes.

Goetz and Scott consider the alternative rules of expectation damages, true reliance damages, out-of-pocket loss damages, and complete non-enforcement in terms of how they would affect the mix of socially useful promises, regretted promises, promisee behaviour, and enforcement costs in a world where benefits and costs can be perfectly measured and process costs are absent. They then relax the assumptions of perfect measurement and zero process costs and conclude that existing common law rules of contract enforceability appear by and large to be economically warranted responses to measurement problems and process costs.

Ian Macneil's 'Values in Contract: Internal and External' represents a very different approach from the analyses of the preceding authors, who tend to focus on a very small number of values served by contractual enforceability. In this article, Macneil examines the social matrix required for the entire spectrum of contracting, from discrete exchanges to long-term contractual relations, and the numerous values reflected in the norms internal to contracting and in external social responses to contracting, including, but not limited to, the law's response.

The minimum social matrix necessary for even a simple exchange includes a means of mutual communication, a system of order that prevents theft, in modern times a system of money, and, with regard to promised exchanges, a system of promissory enforcement. Almost all exchanges, however, require additional relations and norms.

Macneil lists ten common contract norms as norms internal to all contracting: (1) role integrity, (2) reciprocity, (3) implementation of planning, (4) effectuation of consent, (5) flexibility, (6) contractual solidarity, (7) the restitution, reliance, and expectation interests, (8) creation and restraint of power, (9) propriety of means, and (10) harmonization with the social matrix.

When Macneil turns to the values associated with external social responses to contract, he first points out that since all contracts are linked with all other exchange relations, there really is no *external* social matrix nor are there any *external* (to contract) social values. All values are really internal, and any separation of contractual values into internal and external is artificial. Nonetheless, it is frequently heuristically useful to distinguish between values internal to a contractual relation and the external social responses to it.

Macneil also notes that the positive law is but one source among many of these 'external' contractual values. Customs, rules of private associations, and so forth are also important sources of external values. Turning his attention to the values in positive law, Macneil discusses the values of non-intervention by the law, such as autonomy, and the values associated with intervention, including both the imposition of various internal norms and also their transformation through intervention.

The final set of external responses that Macneil discusses is the conceptualizing about contracts engaged in by contract theorists, including Macneil himself. Here he points out the types of distortions produced by theories, such as Charles Fried's, that emphasize only one or a few of the norms associated with contract. He also analyses the ideological implications of his more inclusive set of values relative to those of less inclusive theories like Fried's or Marxism.

Macneil concludes his essay with an analysis of the current state and projected future of various contract norms. The bureaucratization of both the public and private spheres in response to technological imperatives has particularly jeopardized four internal values – reciprocity, solidarity, power, and propriety of means. For Macneil, changes in the direction of social and economic smallness are necessary for the preservation of robust contractual relations.

Patrick Atiyah's 'Contracts, Promises and the Law of Obligation' represents still another approach to contract enforceability, one which places the notions of benefits received and reliance at centre stage. Atiyah attacks the contractual paradigm of the exchange of bare promises, the legally binding bilateral executory agreement. This paradigm, the classical model of contract, is, for him, a relic of 19th-century values and concepts that place undue emphasis on individual free will and rationality.

Atiyah maintains that the classical model contains four presuppositions. First, it presupposes that contract law is about parties' intentions as opposed to what they have done (other than manifest those intentions through promises). Second, it presupposes that contracts are things, that they exist objectively. Third, it presupposes that the courts' primary job is to encourage desirable future behaviour rather than to settle disputes peacefully and fairly. And fourth, it presupposes that there is in fact *one* model of contract.

Atiyah rejects the classical model's centrality of the executory agreement on both descriptive and normative grounds. On the descriptive side, Atiyah points out that executory agreements are a relatively small part of the universe of enforced contracts and that they are somewhat less binding than the classical model would indicate. Usually there has been some detrimental reliance by the promisee. Or the promisor has received some requested benefit for which her promise both serves as evidence and assigns a value. And the trend, says Atiyah, seems to be in the direction of placing more emphasis on protecting reliance losses and on evidentiary uses of promises and away from emphasis on the binding nature of promises in themselves.

Still, there are some executory agreements that the law will enforce even if there have been no actions taken in reliance on the agreement and no tangible benefits received. Atiyah examines the normative case for the enforcement of executory contracts and rejects its assimilation to the case for free disposition of property. He also points out that deliberate lies are not actionable in the absence of reliance, nor are psychological harms generally compensable, making the case for enforceability of bilateral promises seem quite anomalous. He rejects the argument that enforcing all bilateral promises serves a prophylactic function with respect to promises that in fact induce reliance. And he argues that only a small percentage of executory contracts involve deliberate allocation of commercial risks. Finally, with respect to the purely moral case for enforcing contracts, Atiyah maintains that the moral strength of promises that are still executory is really no greater than the strength of the unrelied upon gratuitous promise and too slight to warrant legal enforceability.

The final essay in Part I is Melvin Eisenberg's 'The Bargain Principle and Its Limits'. Eisenberg, like Atiyah, attacks the general applicability of what Eisenberg calls the 'bargain principle', the principle that, in the absence of defective consent, bargain promises should be enforced to their full extent.

Eisenberg postulates two values – fairness and efficiency – as the sources of justification for the bargain principle. He argues that they fully support the principle in cases where contracts have been made in a perfectly competitive market and one party has performed. In such a situation, enforcing the other party's promise is fair because the promise represents the lowest price that we know the performing party would agree to accept for his performance – and in a perfectly competitive market, the performing party could have obtained other buyers of his performance had the promisor offered less – and because it represents the price the promisor has agreed to pay. It is efficient to do so because enforcing bargain promises aids planning regarding credit transactions, and because, in an efficient market, the contract price allocates resources to their most valued use.

Where markets are not perfectly competitive, however, the agreed upon price may not be ideal in terms of fairness and efficiency, and society may not want to enforce all bargains in such circumstances. The bargain principle must therefore be supplemented with a new paradigm, unconscionability. The latter includes four norms, although these do not exhaustively describe it: the norm against exploitation of distress, the norm against exploitation of transactional incapacities, the norm against unfair persuasion, and the norm against exploitation of price ignorance. In the situations which these norms of unconscionability govern, they supplant the bargain principle; for neither fairness nor efficiency support the bargain principle's application to unconscionable bargains.

Eisenberg next focuses on the purely executory contract and the question of when the remedy for breach of such a contract should be the expectancy measure of damages. His answer is that expectancy is the proper remedy in those cases where one of the three justifications for such a remedy exist, that is, where expectancy is a surrogate for costs, where expectancy promotes planning, or where expectancy vindicates a deliberate allocation of risk.

Eisenberg concludes his article by pointing out that the questions of when contracts are enforceable and what remedy should lie for breach are really at the deepest level the same question. Limiting the bargain principle to those cases where its justifications support it entails administrative costs, but failure to do so entails justice costs.

There are several additional modern works that the reader who is interested in the topics of Part I should consult. Because book excerpts are not included in these volumes, I list the following important modern books that deal with why contracts are enforceable. Charles Fried's promissory theory of contract, which is a prominent foil in many of the included selections, is found in his book, *Contract as Promise*. Important versions of the economic analysis of contract law can be found in Richard Posner's *Economic Analysis of Law* and in Anthony Kronman and Richard Posner's useful anthology, *The Economics of Contract Law*. Ian Macneil's theory of contract is fully set forth in *The New Social Contract: An Inquiry into Modern Contractual Relations*. Patrick Atiyah's reliance theory is elaborated in both *Promises, Morals, and Law* and in *The Rise and Fall of Freedom of Contract*. Grant Gilmore's *The Death of Contract* is also important.

There are also many fine essays that are relevant to Part I that I have had to omit for the sake of space. Among the most significant omissions are: Clare Dalton's 'An Essay in the Deconstruction of Contract Doctrine', representing a critical legal studies critique of liberal contract theory; Peter Benson's 'Abstract Right and the Possibility of a Nondistributive Conception of Contract: Hegel and Contemporary Contract Theory', putting forward a Hegelian approach to contractual obligations; and John Stick's reply to Benson, 'Contract and Hegel's Account of Abstract Rights: Some Brief Comments'. Full citations to these works are found in the Bibliography following this Introduction.

Part II, Interpretive and Default Rules, begins with Richard Craswell's 'Contract Law, Default Rules, and the Philosophy of Promising'. Craswell attempts to demonstrate that some of the theories about why and when contractual promises should be enforceable – theories that are the subject of Part I – may have little or no relevance to such issues as how the promises should be interpreted, what gap filling and default rules should exist, and what remedies should lie for breach of contract. Craswell's thesis thus contradicts, for example, Eisenberg's claim in Part I that theories of contractual enforceability and remedy at a deep level address the same question. This is not true, argues Craswell, for at least certain types of theories of enforceability, notably those like Fried's or Barnett's that ground enforceability on considerations such as commitment or autonomy that are neutral with respect to the content of promise. Thus, it is possible to combine a non-consequentialist theory of contract enforceability with a consequentialist theory of contractual interpretation, default rules, and remedies.

Jules Coleman, Douglas Heckathorn, and Steven Maser's 'A Bargaining Theory Approach to Default Provisions and Disclosure Rules in Contract Law' examines the question of what default rule should be applied to cover risks that the contracting parties failed to allocate. Part of their project in the essay is to justify the 'ex ante contract' default rule, the rule that fills gaps by recourse to what the parties would have agreed to had they adverted to the risk at issue. If the basis of contractual obligation is actual, not hypothetical, consent, how can the ex ante contract rule, which is bottomed on hypothetical consent, be justified? The authors' argument links what it would have been rational for the parties to have agreed to, to what they probably would have agreed to, but the real problem for them is how to link what the parties probably would have agreed to, to the default rules that they are deemed to agree to when they contract. The authors leave that problem in abeyance and turn their attention to elaborating a theory of rational bargaining, focusing on the particular problem of non-disclosure. Their hope is that by fleshing out the content of the rational bargain, they will have provided half of a theory of default rules, the other half being the linking up of the rational bargain to the parties' actual consent.

The authors point out that rational contractors must resolve three interrelated problems, the problems of co-ordination, division, and defection. They must seek advantageous opportunities for co-operation, they must reach agreement on division of the gains, and they must monitor each other's compliance. Each of these problems creates the possibility of contract failure, but at the same time the parties must not spend too many resources guarding against such failure or their costs will exceed their gains. The problems here are problems arising from lack of full information about each other and about external contingencies. Law can facilitate rational bargaining if it provides exogenous (to the parties) transaction resources to prevent contract failure and if the benefits of appealing to law to prevent contract failure exceed the costs of doing so.

The authors apply this theoretical framework to the problem of the legal treatment of non-disclosure in contracting. They analyse the famous case of *Laidlaw* v. *Organ*[1] by asking whether the undisclosed information there – that the US and Great Britain had signed the Treaty of Ghent concluding the War of 1812 – pertained primarily to efficient allocation or to distribution of gains, and by assessing the parties' bargaining resources and the role the courts could most usefully play in facilitating bargaining in the context of that case. The authors' focus is at all times on the question of what it would have been rational for *these* parties to have agreed to ex ante rather than on questions of global efficiency or fairness.

The last essay in Part II is Christopher Wonnell's 'The Abstract Character of Contract

Law'. Wonnell observes that the principles of contract law often abstract from particularities of person and subject matter, that is, from the question of who is entering into what kind of contract with whom. Legal historians have argued that abstract principles of contract law were largely a 19th-century phenomenon, heavily influenced by an ideology of *laissez-faire* and by economic models that themselves were highly abstract in character. On this theory, abstract principles served to disguise the bargaining power inequalities that could only be evidenced by taking a closer look at precisely who was contracting and with what subject matter.

Wonnell argues, to the contrary, that the abstract character of contract principles is a continuing source of social utility. Economic systems, whether centrally planned or market oriented, face the task of moving resources to their highest and best use. Determining the highest and best use of a commodity requires highly-concrete knowledge into that specific commodity's inputs, substitutes, complements, and end uses. However, the law best adapts to that need for concrete and particularistic knowledge, not by trying itself to become sufficiently concrete, but by creating a uniform framework for individuals to use whatever concrete information they may possess against the backdrop of prices generated by other individuals' use of that same framework.

Freedom of contract and sanctions for opportunistic breaches of contract are the primary legal institutions that allow resources to be moved in response to the pressures of each individual's concrete knowledge about resource use. For this purpose, general principles of contract law are sufficient, although for the sake of predictability such principles may need to be concretized for particular settings. True deviations from these abstract principles would only be justifiable if redistributive or paternalistic objectives could complement the law's pursuit of efficiency. However, attempts to introduce concreteness into contract law for the purpose of redistributing wealth are counterproductive, as parties respond to such attempts by refusing to use the concrete knowledge they possess.

Two abstract principles of contract law are that damages are compensatory and that non-breaching parties have a duty to mitigate those damages. The essay concludes by using these two principles as case studies to illustrate how the law can go wrong by trying to create exceptions from abstract principles for particular contractual contexts such as housing, employment, or insurance. In each case, the abstract principle directs the court toward the efficient outcome, while introducing the concrete context distracts the court into a counter-productive pursuit of redistributive objectives.

The reader interested in the topics covered in Part II should also consult two other recent essays, Ian Ayres and Robert Gertner's 'Filling Gaps in Incomplete Contracts: An Economic Theory of Default Rules', and Charles Goetz and Robert Scott's 'The Limits of Expanded Choice: An Analysis of the Interactions Between Express and Implied Contract Terms'. Both essays are in the law and economics camp. Their full citations are found in the Bibliography at the end of this Introduction.[2]

Notes

1 15 US (2 Wheat) 178 (1817).

2 I gratefully acknowledge the valuable assistance of Gay Morgan, Emily Sherwin, and Chris Wonnell in preparing these volumes and their Introductions.

Bibliography

Books

Atiyah, P.S. (1979), *The Rise and Fall of Freedom of Contract*, Clarendon Press, Oxford.
Atiyah, P.S. (1981), *Promises, Morals, and Law*, Clarendon Press, Oxford.
Fried, C. (1981), *Contract as Promise*, Harvard University Press, Cambridge, Mass.
Gilmore, G. (1974), *The Death of Contract*, Ohio State University Press, Columbus.
Kronman, A., and Posner, R. (eds) (1979), *The Economics of Contract Law*, Little, Brown & Co., Boston.
Macneil, I. (1980), *The New Social Contract: An Inquiry into Modern Contractual Relations*, Yale University Press, New Haven.
Posner, R. (1977), *Economic Analysis of Law*, Little, Brown & Co., Boston.

Articles

Ayres, Ian, and Gertner, Robert (1989), 'Filling Gaps in Incomplete Contracts: An Economic Theory of Default Rules', *Yale Law Journal*, **99**, 87.
Benson, Peter (1989), 'Abstract Right and the Possibility of a Nondistributive Conception of Contract: Hegel and Contemporary Contract Theory', *Cardozo Law Review*, **10**, 1077.
Dalton, Clare (1985), 'An Essay in the Deconstruction of Contract', *Yale Law Journal*, **94**, 997.
Goetz, Charles, and Scott, Robert (1985), 'The Limits of Expanded Choice: An Analysis of the Interactions Between Express and Implied Contract Terms', *California Law Review*, **73**, 261.
Stick, John (1989), 'Contract and Hegel's Account of Abstract Rights: Some Brief Comments', *Cardozo Law Review*, **10**, 1275.

Part I
Why Enforce Contracts?

[1]

A CONSENT THEORY OF CONTRACT

*Randy E. Barnett**

INTRODUCTION

> The mere fact that one man promises something to another creates no legal duty and makes no legal remedy available in case of non-performance. To be enforceable, the promise must be accompanied by some other factor. . . . The question now to be discussed is what is this other factor. What fact or facts must accompany a promise to make it enforceable at law?[1]

We look to legal theory to tell us when the use of legal force against an individual is morally[2] justified. We look to contract theory, in particular, to tell us which interpersonal commitments the law ought to enforce. Contract theory at present, however, does not provide a satisfactory answer to this question. The five best known theories or principles of contractual obligation—the will theory, the reliance theory, the fairness theory, the efficiency theory and the bargain theory—each have very basic shortcomings. A consent theory of contract avoids these difficulties while explaining contractual obligation in a plausible and coherent manner.

Theories are problem-solving devices. We assess the merits of a particular theory by its ability to solve the problems that gave rise to the need for a theory. We do not, however, assess a particular theory in a vacuum. No theory in any discipline, from physics to biology to philosophy, can be expected to solve every problem raised by the discipline.

---

* Assistant Professor of Law, Illinois Institute of Technology, Chicago-Kent College of Law. B.A. Northwestern University, 1974; J.D. Harvard Law School, 1977. An earlier version of this Article was presented to the Law and Society Association Annual Meeting, Denver, Colorado in June of 1983. I wish to thank the following people for their most helpful comments on various precursors of this Article: Larry Alexander, Douglas Baird, Mary Becker, Stuart Deutsch, Frank Easterbrook, Richard Epstein, George Fletcher, R.H. Helmholz, A.W.B. Simpson, Geoffrey Stone, Cass Sunstein, Lawrence H. White, Christopher Wonnell, and Richard W. Wright. I also thank my research assistants, Sharyl Schwartz and William Walsh. I am grateful to the University of Chicago Law School, where I began this paper as a Research Fellow, and to the Institute for Humane Studies at George Mason University and the Veritas Fund for the financial support that made my stay at the University of Chicago possible. Finally, I wish to thank my colleagues at I.I.T Chicago-Kent College of Law and my Dean, Lewis Collens, for providing me with an atmosphere conducive to productive research and unfettered speculation.

1. 1 A. Corbin, Corbin on Contracts § 110, at 490 (1963); see also Eisenberg, The Principles of Consideration, 67 Cornell L. Rev. 640, 640 (1982) ("A promise, as such, is not legally enforceable. The first great question of contract law, therefore, is what kinds of promises should be enforced.").

2. The view that morality plays an important role in legal theory is discussed infra notes 109–11 and accompanying text.

Rather, we *compare* contending theories to see which theory handles problems the best.

Our criteria for comparing theories include at least three factors: (a) the number of known problems the theory handles as well or better than its rivals, (b) the centrality of the problems that the theory handles well, and (c) the promise that the theory offers for solving future problems. When we assess legal theories, the better a particular theory explains cases where we are confident of the right outcome, the more confident we will be with the answers it suggests for those cases at the margin where our intuitions are less secure.

In Part I of this Article, the five most popular theories of contractual obligation will be assessed. Each of these theories accurately captures some aspect of contractual obligation. However, the current lack of a consensus concerning the proper basis of contractual obligation suggests that each approach has fundamental weaknesses. The theories can be grouped into three distinct types: party-based, standards-based, and process-based theories. At least part of each theory's weakness stems from deficiencies that are inherent in its type. The purpose of this comparative analysis will be to demonstrate the need for a more overarching approach that can capture the truths of these theories while avoiding their errors.

In Part II, a consent theory of contract[3] will be described and applied to the problems identified in Part I. A consent theory posits that contractual obligation cannot be completely understood unless it is viewed as part of a broader system of legal entitlements. Such a system, based in morality,[4] specifies the substance of the rights individuals may acquire and transfer, and the means by which they may do so. Properly understood, contract law is that part of a system of entitlements that identifies those circumstances in which entitlements are validly transferred from person to person by their consent. Consent is the moral component that distinguishes valid from invalid transfers of alienable rights.

A consent theory of contract explains why we generally take an "objective" approach to contractual intent and why we deviate from this approach in some situations. In addition, a consent theory validates the enforcement of certain commitments where no bargained-for exchange exists—such as those supported by "nominal considera-

3. I first discussed the consent theory of contract in Barnett, Contract Scholarship and the Reemergence of Legal Philosophy (Book Review), 97 Harv. L. Rev. 1223 (1984), where I also attempted to place recent developments in legal philosophy in a historical context to explain the resurgence of normative legal philosophy in general and entitlement theories in particular.

4. The theory presented by this Article is based in, and required by, the normative requirements of morality. See infra notes 109–28 and accompanying text. Nonetheless, readers who favor a positivist perspective may wish to consider the requirement of consent solely as a means of understanding past and present judicial decisions, and of reconciling apparently conflicting doctrines.

tion"—and thereby rescues these useful legal arrangements from their present uncertain status in contract law. By providing a clear, common-sense test of enforceability that avoids the need for courts to distinguish "reasonable" from "unreasonable" reliance in determining whether a contract was formed, a consent theory enables parties to calculate better who bears the risk of reliance and, hence, facilitates reliance on interpersonal commitments. Finally, a consent theory's account of contractual obligation explains and justifies the historically recognized defenses to contractual obligation.

I. Assessing Current Theories of Contractual Obligation

Five theories—the will, reliance, efficiency, fairness, and bargain theories[5]—are most commonly offered to explain which commitments merit enforcement and which do not. These theories of contractual obligation actually exemplify three types of contract theories. Will and reliance theories are *party-based*. Efficiency and fairness theories are *standards-based*. The bargain theory is *process-based*. At least some of each theory's weaknesses are characteristics of its type. For this reason, each type of theory shall be separately considered here.

The criticisms presented in this section are neither comprehensive nor particularly novel. Rather, the discussion will identify the main problems that most theorists have acknowledged attach to each theory. The object here is not to refute any of these approaches. Instead, the aim will be to demonstrate that none provides a comprehensive theory of contractual obligation.

Will, reliance, efficiency, fairness, and bargain are best understood as core concerns of contract law. A theory of contractual obligation is needed to provide a framework that specifies when one of these concerns should give way to another.[6] Their proper relationship cannot be explained by a theory based solely on any one concern or on some unspecified combination. In Part II, I will explain how a consent theory of contract provides this necessary framework.

A. *Party-Based Theories*

Theories described here as party-based are those that focus on protecting one particular party to a transaction. A more accurate (though more awkward) label is "one-sided party-based." Will theories

5. When an explanation of contractual obligation focuses exclusively on one of these factors, that factor may be identified as forming the basis of a distinct *theory*—as in "will theory." When two or more factors are combined, then they may more accurately be referred to as *principles*—as in "reliance principle"—or as *core concerns* of a more general theory of contractual obligation.

6. Cf. Eisenberg, supra note 1, at 642–43 (favoring an expansive conception of contractual obligation "that recognizes the enforceability of promises on the basis of various elements, and directs inquiry toward determining those elements while fashioning principles that reflect them in an appropriate way").

are primarily concerned with protecting the promisor. Reliance theories are primarily concerned with protecting the promisee. The undue emphasis that the will and reliance theories each place on one specific party creates insoluble problems for each approach.

1. *Will Theories*. — Will theories maintain that commitments are enforceable because the promisor has "willed" or chosen to be bound by his commitment. "According to the classical view, the law of contract gives expression to and protects the will of the parties, for the will is something inherently worthy of respect."[7] In this approach, the use of force against a reneging promisor is morally justified because the promisor herself has warranted the use of force by her prior exercise of will. A promisor cannot complain about force being used against her, since she intended that such force could be used when she made the commitment.[8]

Will theories depend for their moral force upon the notion that contractual duties are binding because they are freely assumed by those who are required to discharge them. Consequently, enforcement is not morally justified without a genuine commitment by the person who is to be subjected to a legal sanction. This position leads quite naturally to an inquiry as to the promisor's actual state of mind at the time of agreement—the so-called "subjective" viewpoint. After all, the theory can hardly be based on *will* if the obligation was *not* chosen by the individual but instead was imposed by law.

It has long been recognized that a system of contractual enforcement would be unworkable if it adhered to a will theory requiring a subjective inquiry into the putative promisor's intent.[9] Where we cannot discern the actual subjective intent or will of the parties, there is no practical problem, since we assume it corresponds to objectively manifested intentions. But where subjective intent can somehow be proved and is contrary to objectively manifested behavior, subjective intent should prevail if the moral integrity and logic of a will theory are to be preserved.

Of course, any legal preference for the promisor's subjective intent would disappoint a promisee who has acted in reliance on the appear-

---

7. Cohen, The Basis of Contract, 46 Harv. L. Rev. 553, 575 (1933).

8. See C. Fried, Contract as Promise 16 (1981) ("An individual is morally bound to keep his promises because he has *intentionally* invoked a convention whose function it is to give grounds—moral grounds—for another to expect the promised performance.") (emphasis added); see also Burrows, Contract, Tort and Restitution—A Satisfactory Division or Not?, 99 Law Q. Rev. 217, 258 (1983) ("It is the acceptance of an obligation that is vital; it is not enough to have represented that facts are true or to have merely declared that one is intending to do something, for in such situations, the will has not committed itself to do anything."). Anthony T. Kronman also categorizes Professor Fried as a "will theorist." See Kronman, A New Champion for the Will Theory (Book Review), 91 Yale L.J. 404, 404 (1981). For a comparison of Professor Fried's will theory with a consent theory, see infra notes 146–47 and accompanying text.

9. See, e.g., Cohen, supra note 7, at 575–78; Burrows, supra note 8, at 258.

ance of legally binding intent.[10] Permitting a subjective inquiry into the promisor's intent could also enable a promisor to fraudulently undermine otherwise perfectly clear agreements by generating and preserving extrinsic evidence of ambiguous or conflicting intentions. Such a strategy might create a de facto option in the promisor. The promisor could insist on enforcement if the contract continued to be in her interest, but if it were no longer advantageous, she could avoid the contract, by producing evidence of a differing subjective intent.[11]

Because the subjective approach relies on evidence inaccessible to the promisee, much less to third parties, an inquiry into subjective intent would undermine the security of transactions by greatly reducing the reliability of contractual commitments.[12] Not surprisingly, and notwithstanding the logic of obligation based on "will," the objective approach has largely prevailed.[13] The subjectivist moral component, on which a will theory focuses to justify legal enforcement, conflicts unavoidably with the practical need for a system of rules based to a large extent on objectively manifested states of mind. While a person's objective manifestations generally reflect subjective intentions, a will theorist must explain the enforcement of the objective agreement where it can be shown that the subjective understanding of a party differs from her objectively manifested behavior.

Some will theorists uneasily resolve this conflict by acknowledging that other "interests"—for example, reliance—may take priority over

10. See D. Hume, An Inquiry Concerning the Principles of Morals 30 n.5 (C. Hendel ed. 1957) (1st ed. 1751):

> If the secret direction of the intention, said every man of sense, could invalidate a contract, where is our security? And yet a metaphysical schoolman might think, that where an intention was supposed to be requisite, if that intention really had no place, no consequence ought to follow, and no obligation be imposed.

11. For an interesting example of a court suspecting a similar strategy by a party attempting to exploit the "mailbox rule," see Cohen v. Clayton Coal Co., 86 Colo. 270, 281 P. 111 (1929).

12. Note that neither the problem of reliance nor the problem of fraud would arise when a promisor, who manifested an intention to be bound, seeks to avoid liability by showing that the promisee did not actually or "subjectively" understand the promisor's actions to have this meaning. It provides few opportunities for fraud to permit the promisor to avoid liability by proving that the promisee understood the behavior as it was subjectively intended by the promisor and that consequently the promisee did not rely on the promisor's outward manifestation. Such a "subjective" inquiry, however rarely it might arise, is therefore quite properly permitted under a conventional objective approach. See, e.g., Embry v. Hargadine, McKittrick Dry Goods Co., 127 Mo. App. 383, 385, 105 S.W. 777, 779 (1907). As will be discussed below, see infra notes 156–60 and accompanying text, this position is also in harmony with a consent theory of contract.

13. See, e.g., Ricketts v. Pennsylvania R.R., 153 F.2d 757, 760–61 (2d Cir. 1946) (Frank, J., concurring); Restatement (Second) of Contracts § 2 comment b (1979); E. Farnsworth, Contracts § 3.6, at 114 (1982).

the will.[14] By permitting individuals to be bound by promises never intended by them to be enforceable, such a concession deprives a will theory of much of its force. Requiring the promisor's subjective will to yield always, or almost always, to the promisee's reliance on the promisor's objective manifestation of assent undermines the claim that contractual obligation is grounded in the individual's will[15] and bolsters the view that contractual obligations may be imposed rightfully on unwilling parties.[16] The inability of will theories to explain adequately the enforcement of objective manifestations of intention also accounts in part for the continued interest in reliance-based theories of contractual obligation.

2. *Reliance Theories*. — Theories that explain contractual obligation as an effort to protect a promisee's reliance on the promises of others have the apparent virtue of explaining why persons may be bound by the common meaning of their words regardless of their intentions. Thus, it has become increasingly fashionable to assert that contractual obligation is created by reliance on a promise.[17] A reliance theory is based upon the intuition that we ought to be liable in contract law for our assertive behavior when it creates "foreseeable" or "justifiable" reliance in others, in much the same way that we are held liable in tort law for harmful consequences of other acts.[18]

Reliance theories have nonetheless faced a seemingly insuperable

14. See, e.g., C. Fried, supra note 8, at 58–63 (acknowledging that a failure to agree subjectively deprives a contract of its moral force on a will- or promise-based theory, but asserting that recovery may be available on other principles of "fairness," "encouragement of due care," or concerns of "administration").

15. See Burrows, supra note 8, at 258; see also D. Hume, supra note 10, at 30 n.5 ("The expression being once brought in as subservient to the will, soon becomes the principal part of the promise . . . .").

16. See P. Atiyah, The Rise and Fall of Freedom of Contract 6 (1979); see also Feinman, Critical Approaches to Contract Law, 30 UCLA L. Rev. 829, 834 (1983) ("[C]ontract law is like tort law and judicial action is like legislative action: all necessarily involve public policy judgments in imposing legal liability."). But see Eisenberg, The Bargain Principle and Its Limits, 95 Harv. L. Rev. 741, 785 n.121 (1982) (taking issue with Atiyah's analysis of reliance-based obligation).

17. While the literature is replete with suggestions about "the reliance principle," a comprehensive reliance theory of contract has never been systematically presented. Such an approach clearly underlies Gilmore's seminal work, *The Death of Contract*. See, e.g., G. Gilmore, The Death of Contract 71–72, 88 (1974). Atiyah appears to call for a reliance theory, although he also acknowledges that "the voluntary creation and extinction of rights and liabilities" should remain one of the "basic pillars of the law of obligations." P. Atiyah, supra note 16, at 779; see also Feinman, Promissory Estoppel and Judicial Method, 97 Harv. L. Rev. 678, 716–17 (1984) ("reliance principle" undermines "classical" contract law doctrines); Henderson, Promissory Estoppel and Traditional Contract Doctrine, 78 Yale L.J. 343, 344 (1969) (rules of promissory estoppel create a contract grounded on effects of reliance).

18. See G. Gilmore, supra note 17, at 88 ("We may take the fact that damages in contract have become indistinguishable from damages in tort as obscurely reflecting an instinctive, almost unconscious realization that the two fields, which had been artificially set apart, are gradually merging and becoming one.").

difficulty. As Morris Cohen wrote as early as 1933: "Clearly, not all cases of injury resulting from reliance on the word or act of another are actionable, and the theory before us offers no clue as to what distinguishes those which are."[19] This deficiency has led necessarily to the employment of such phrases as "justifiable" reliance or "reasonable" reliance.[20] These adjectives, however, depend on (usually vague) standards of evaluation that are unrelated to reliance itself, because, whether justified or unjustified, reasonable or unreasonable, reliance is present in any event.

Furthermore, whether a person has "reasonably" relied on a promise depends on what most people would (or ought to) do. We cannot make this assessment independently of the legal rule in effect in the relevant community, because what many people would do in reliance on a promise is crucially affected by their perception of whether or not the promise is enforceable. A reliance theory, therefore, ultimately does no more than pose the crucial question that it is supposed to answer: is this a promise that should be enforced?

The analysis is no different if we ask whether the promisor knew or had reason to know the promise would induce others to act in reliance,[21] even though this formulation lessens a reliance theory's preference for the promisee's interests. Unlike the subject of the prediction required by foreseeability analysis in tort law—the physical consequences that follow from physical actions—the subject of the prediction required by forseeability analysis in contract law is the actions of a self-conscious person. A prediction that a promise can reasonably be expected to induce reliance by a promisee or third party will unavoidably depend upon whether the promisee or third party believes that reliance will be legally protected. The legal rule itself cannot be formulated based on such a prediction, however, without introducing a practical circularity into the analysis.[22]

Furthermore, if a promise is defined, as in the Restatement (Sec-

---

19. Cohen, supra note 7, at 579.

20. See, e.g., Eisenberg, supra note 1, at 656–59; Henderson, supra note 17, at 345.

21. See, e.g., Restatement (Second) of Contracts § 90(1) (1979). Section 90 qualifies reliance based recoveries at the level of formation, by requiring both a "reasonable" expectation of reliance and the imposition of sanctions only if "injustice" cannot otherwise be avoided, and, at the level of remedies, by limiting the remedy "as justice requires." Id. Traditionally, however, the legal method employs doctrinal and theoretical analysis (that is consistent with underlying notions of justice) *to discover* where justice resides in a particular case. See Barnett, Why We Need Legal Philosophy, 8 Harv. J.L. & Pub. Pol. 6–10 (1985). Section 90 obviously begs this question. While it may have been the victim of overly cautious draftsmanship, no more precise formulations have been offered to take its place.

22. This appears to be an example of what George Fletcher has characterized as a "paradox of legal thought." See Fletcher, Paradoxes in Legal Thought, 85 Colum. L. Rev. 1263 (1985). If so, it will be resolved only by finding a basis independent of foreseeability on which to distinguish legally protected from legally unprotected reliance. See id. at 1269 ("When a paradox is uncovered, we can restore consistency in our legal

ond) of Contracts, as "a manifestation of intention to act or refrain from acting in a specified way, so made as to justify a promisee in understanding that a commitment has been made,"[23] then it would seem that *every* promisor should reasonably expect to induce reliance. If so, "The real issue is not whether the promisor should have expected the promisee to rely, but whether the extent of the promisee's reliance was reasonable."[24] But this returns us once again to the difficulties of discerning "reasonable" reliance.

By providing an overly expansive criterion of contractual obligation, any theory that bases obligation on detrimental reliance begs the basic question to be resolved by contract theory: which *potentially* reliance-inducing actions entail legal consequences and which do not? A person's actions in reliance on a commitment are not justified—and therefore legally protected—simply *because* she has relied. Rather, reliance on the words of others is legally protected because of some as yet undefined circumstances.[25]

In short, a person, rather than being entitled to legal enforcement because reliance is justified, is justified in relying on those commitments that will be legally enforced. Reliance theories therefore must appeal to a criterion other than reliance to distinguish justified acts of reliance. Such a criterion has yet to be identified. It is suggested below[26] that a consent theory provides such a criterion.

3. *The Problem With Party-Based Theories.* — These difficulties reveal that reliance theories have much in common with will theories. Both sets of theories must resort to definitions of contractual enforcement that do not follow from either will or reliance, but are based on more fundamental principles that are left unarticulated. By failing to distinguish adequately between those commitments that are worthy of legal protection and those that are not, both the will and reliance theories have failed in their basic mission. Consequently, actual contract cases must be resolved ad hoc using vague concepts such as "reasonable-

---

structures . . . by finding or constructing a distinction . . . that dissolves the paradox.").

23. Restatement (Second) of Contracts § 2 (1979). Note that the Restatement's definition of promise differs from the definition of "consent" offered below, infra notes 121, 143–44 and accompanying text, in that consent is limited to a particular kind of commitment—a commitment to be legally bound.

24. Eisenberg, supra note 1, at 659.

25. Notwithstanding these weaknesses, the increased recognition of reliance-based recovery exemplified by § 90 of the Restatement may have been, on balance, more helpful than harmful to the cause of freedom of contract. Recovery purportedly based on reliance provides a gap-filling safety valve for cases involving nonbargained-for reliance and thereby enables the market oriented bargain requirement to survive. See E. Farnsworth, supra note 13, § 2.19, at 89 ("The failure of the doctrine of consideration to provide a more satisfactory basis for enforcing such promises might have brought greater pressure to reform the doctrine had it not been for the increasing recognition of reliance as an alternative ground for recovery.").

26. See infra notes 192–97 and accompanying text.

ness" or "public policy," or by employing clearer but formalistic criteria such as "consideration."

Each theory primarily focuses on protecting one side of a contractual transaction: will theories focus on respecting the intentions of the promisor, while reliance theories focus on correcting the injury to the promisee. As a result, neither can properly assess the *interrelational* quality of the process of contracting. The law of contract exists to facilitate transactions between persons. In such an enterprise, there is no obvious reason why either party should be automatically preferred. While subjective intentions and reliance costs are important to a proper understanding of contractual obligation, something more basic is missing in theories of contractual obligation the primary focus of which is on only one of these core concerns.

Ironically, though both will and reliance theories assume a strongly moralistic stance—protecting "autonomy" or remedying "injuries"—neither provides an adequate moral framework to explain the legal enforcement of contracts. Both theories fail in this way because both attempt to explain contractual obligation in a theoretical vacuum. In liberal political and legal theory, the interrelational quality of social life is facilitated by identifying the entitlements or property rights of individuals in society. Theories that focus exclusively on the will of promisors or the reliance of promisees fail to utilize this conceptual framework. Not surprisingly, attempts to explain contractual obligations arising between persons go awry when those attempts ignore the foundations of interpersonal legal relationships.

B. *Standards-Based Theories*

Standards-based theories are those which evaluate *the substance* of a contractual transaction to see if it conforms to a standard of evaluation that the theory specifies as primary. Economic efficiency and substantive fairness are two such standards that have received wide attention.

1. *Efficiency Theories.* — One of the most familiar standards-based legal theories is the efficiency approach associated with the "law and economics" school.[27] Economic efficiency is viewed by some in this school as the maximization of some concept of social wealth or welfare: "the term *efficiency* will refer to the relationship between the aggregate benefits of a situation and the aggregate costs of the situation . . . . In other words, efficiency corresponds to 'the size of the pie.' "[28] According to this view, legal rules and practices are assessed to see whether

27. For a brief discussion of the role this school has played in provoking recent jurisprudential developments, see Barnett, supra note 3, at 1229–33.

28. A. Polinsky, An Introduction to Law and Economics 7 (1983); cf. Cooter & Eisenberg, Damages for Breach of Contract, 73 Calif. L. Rev. 1432, 1460 (1985) ("Economists say that a contract is efficient if its terms maximize the value that can be created by the contemplated exchange.").

they will expand or contract the size of this pie.[29]

In its least assertive variation, an economic assessment of law does not constitute a distinct theory of contractual obligation. Rather, economic analysis of legal rules is simply viewed as a "value-free" scientific inquiry that is confined to accounting for or explaining the consequences that result from particular legal rules or schemes.[30] So viewed, economic analysis is not a competing theory of contractual obligation, but only one of many yardsticks for assessing competing legal theories.

Economic analysis may also be viewed as a normative theory of law[31]—that is, economic efficiency is seen as providing the best or only yardstick of law.[32] However, because standard economic analysis begins by assuming that some agreements are enforceable,[33] normative efficiency theories fail to provide a distinction between enforceable and

29. But cf. Coleman, Efficiency, Utility and Wealth Maximization, 8 Hofstra L. Rev. 509, 512 (1980) ("Economists as well as proponents of the economic analysis of law employ at least four efficiency-related notions, including: (1) Productive efficiency, (2) Pareto optimality, (3) Pareto superiority, and (4) Kaldor-Hicks efficiency.").

30. See id. at 548–49. One strain of this mode of economics—sometimes called "positive economics"—judges the efficacy of an economic explanation by its ability to generate hypotheses that can be verified by empirical research. For explanations of this methodology, see M. Friedman, The Methodology of Positive Economics, *in* Essays in Positive Economics 3 (1953); R. Posner, Economic Analysis of Law 12–13, 17–19 (2d ed. 1977). For applications of the methodology, see e.g., Posner & Landes, Legal Change, Judicial Behavior, and the Diversity Jurisdiction, 9 J. Legal Stud. 367 (1980); Priest, Selective Characteristics of Litigation, 9 J. Legal Stud. 399 (1980). For criticisms of the methodology, see O'Driscoll, Justice, Efficiency, and the Economic Analysis of Law: A Comment on Fried, 9 J. Legal Stud. 355 (1980); Rizzo, Can There Be a Principle of Explanation in Common Law Decisions? A Comment on Priest, 9 J. Legal Stud. 423 (1980).

31. See Coleman, supra note 29, at 549; see also Posner, A Reply to Some Recent Criticisms of the Efficiency Theory of the Common Law, 9 Hofstra L. Rev. 775 (1981) ("The normative branch of the theory asserts that [promoting efficient resource allocation] . . . is what judges *should* try to do in deciding common law cases."). But cf. id. at 779 (Posner's denial that normative analysis is his "primary interest").

32. See, e.g., R. Posner, supra note 30; R. Posner, The Economics of Justice (1981). Some normative analysts straddle this distinction by asserting that other concerns—for example, distributive concerns—are normatively important as well. See, e.g., Calabresi, About Law and Economics: A Letter to Ronald Dworkin, 8 Hofstra L. Rev. 553 (1980); Calabresi & Melamed, Property Rules, Liability Rules, and Inalienability: One View From the Cathedral, 85 Harv. L. Rev. 1089 (1972). But see Dworkin, Why Efficiency? A Response to Professors Calabresi and Posner, 8 Hofstra L. Rev. 563 (1980) (disputing the coherence of "mixing" efficiency with distributive concerns in a normative analysis).

33. What these economists sometimes refer to as "market transactions," see, e.g., Coase, The Problem of Social Cost, 3 J.L. & Econ. 1, 15 (1960) ("The argument has proceeded up to this point on the assumption . . . that there were no costs involved *in carrying out market transactions.*" (emphasis added)), are in fact contracts. See Cheung, Transaction Costs, Risk Aversion, and the Choice of Contractual Arrangements, 12 J.L. & Econ. 23 (1969) ("Every transaction involves a contract."); Furubotn & Pejovich, Property Rights and Economic Theory: A Survey of Recent Literature, 10 J. Econ. Literature 1137, 1141 (1972) ("[T]he standard competitive model envisions a special system where one particular set of private property rights governs the use of *all* resources, and where the exchange, policing and enforcement costs of contractual activities are *zero*.").

unenforceable commitments.[34] In a world of no transaction costs, it is asserted, individual economizing behavior would—by means of mutually advantageous exchanges of entitlements—ensure that legal entitlements are freely transferred to their highest value use.[35] Because such a hypothetical world presupposes enforceable exchanges of legal entitlements, it cannot (without much more) tell us why or when some promises are enforceable while others are not.

In a world of positive transaction costs,[36] economists who employ a model of "perfect competition" wish to assess the extent to which such costs block the movement of resources to their highest value use and the ways that legal rules and remedies—including those defining the background set of entitlements—can be altered to minimize such "inefficiency."[37] Such an analysis, based on detecting deviations from the background efficiency "norm" of initial entitlements and cost-free exchanges, must ultimately rest on no more than an assumption that such voluntary economizing exchanges are to some extent enforceable. Typically, then, efficiency analyses focus on the real world problems of forced exchanges (tort law) in an effort to make legal solutions to these nonmarket transactions approximate market solutions as closely as possible.[38] Efficiency analyses of voluntary exchanges (contract law) typically focus on issues other than the source of contractual obligation itself, such as appropriate remedies and other enforcement mecha-

34. Of course, one could try to define "market transactions" so narrowly that the concept of contract would be excluded. Cf. A. Kronman & R. Posner, The Economics of Contract Law 3 (1979) ("One can talk about the principle or system of voluntary exchange for quite some time before it becomes necessary to consider the role of contracts and contract law in facilitating the process."). Such a restricted definition, however, is not warranted. In fact, it is not clear that the market mechanism will have its supposed efficiency-producing effect without taking enforceable commitments into account in a much broader view of "market exchanges." See, e.g., Posner, Gratuitous Promises in Economics and Law, 6 J. Legal Stud. 411, 412 (1977) ("The approach taken here is that a gratuitous promise, to the extent it actually commits the promisor to the promised course of action . . . creates utility for the promisor over and above the utility to him of the promised performance."); see also infra notes 48–49 and accompanying text.

35. Cheung, The Structure of a Contract and the Theory of a Non-Exclusive Resource, 13 J.L. & Econ. 49, 50 (1970); see, e.g., Coase, supra note 33, at 15; cf. R. Posner, supra note 32, at 60 ("[T]he term 'value' in economics has generally referred to value in exchange . . . .").

36. See Coase, supra note 33, at 15:

> In order to carry out a market transaction it is necessary to discover who it is that one wishes to deal with, to inform people that one wishes to deal and on what terms, to conduct negotiations leading up to a bargain, to draw up the contract, to undertake the inspection needed to make sure that the terms of the contract are being observed, and so on. These operations are often extremely costly, sufficiently costly at any rate to prevent many transactions that would be carried out in a world in which the pricing system worked without cost.

37. See, e.g., R. Posner, supra note 32, at 70; Calabresi & Melamed, supra note 32, at 1097.

38. See, e.g., R. Posner, supra note 30, at 11.

nisms,[39] and assume, rather than demonstrate, the enforceability of all voluntary commitments.[40] How we recognize voluntary commitments that ought to be enforced, as opposed to mere social promises that are not enforceable, is not generally discussed.

Moreover, some normative efficiency theories[41] generate additional problems. If we are to enforce only those real world agreements that increase the overall wealth of society,[42] then it must be either claimed or assumed that a neutral observer (for example, an economist-judge) has access to this information—that is, knows *which* agreements increase wealth and which do not.[43] Two problems arise from this assumption or claim. The first concerns its truth. Can observers ever have information about value-enhancing exchanges independent of the demonstrated preferences of the market participants? More importantly, can a legal system practically base its decisions on such information? It has been persuasively argued that such knowledge is simply not available independently of the production of information by real markets.[44] If it is not available, then it cannot provide workable criteria

39. See Rea, Nonpecuniary Loss and Breach of Contract, 11 J. Legal Stud. 35, 36 (1982). But cf. Macneil, Efficient Breach of Contract: Circles in the Sky, 68 Va. L. Rev. 947, 968 (1982):

> [T]he economic model provides no basis for an a priori conclusion about the efficiency of passage of ownership at any given stage of a transaction. Moreover, the passage of ownership, a legal entitlement, cannot be separated analytically (except for analyzing transaction costs and the kinds of issues raised by Calabresi and Melamed) from remedies for breach of contract.

40. See supra note 33 and accompanying text.

41. See, e.g., R. Posner, supra note 32, at 88–115 (discussing the "ethical and political basis of wealth maximization"). Other economists would use a more restrictive Pareto criterion of efficiency. See Coleman, Efficiency, Exchange, and Auction: Philosophic Aspects of the Economic Approach to Law, 68 Calif. L. Rev. 221, 226–31 (1980).

42. Cf. Posner, supra note 34, at 415 ("The question whether it is economical for society to recognize a promise as legally enforceable thus requires a comparison of utility of the promise to the promisor with the social cost of enforcing the promise." (citation omitted)).

43. See, e.g., R. Posner, supra note 32, at 62 ("The purist would insist that the relevant values are unknowable since they have not been revealed in an actual market transaction, but I believe that in many cases a court can make a reasonably accurate guess as to the allocation of resources that would maximize wealth."); id. at 79 ("The 'interpersonal comparison of utilities' is anathema to the modern economist, and rightly so, because there is no metric for making such a comparison. But the interpersonal comparison of values, in the economic sense, is feasible, although difficult, even when the values are not being compared in an explicit market.").

44. See, e.g., Demsetz, Some Aspects of Property Rights, 9 J.L. & Econ. 61, 67–68 (1966); Rizzo, The Mirage of Efficiency, 8 Hofstra L. Rev. 641, 648–51 (1980); Coleman, The Normative Basis of Economic Analysis: A Critical Review of Richard Posner's *The Economics of Justice* (Book Review), 34 Stan. L. Rev. 1105, 1109 n.6 (1982). The seminal work in this area was done by Ludwig von Mises and F.A. Hayek. See, e.g., L. von Mises, Socialism 137–42 (rev. ed. 1951) (discussing why "artifical markets" are not possible); F. Hayek, The Use of Knowledge in Society, *in* Individualism and Economic Order 77, 77–78 (1948) ("The economic problem of society is thus not merely a problem of how to allocate 'given' resources . . . . It is rather a problem of how to secure the best use of

to distinguish enforceable from unenforceable promises.[45]

Assuming, however, that such knowledge is available, if we have direct access to information sufficient to know whether particular exchanges are value enhancing or not, why bother with contract law at all? Why not simply have a central authority use this knowledge to transfer entitlements independently of the parties' agreement, particularly given the fact that the need to reach agreements creates transaction costs? Or, why not let judges use this knowledge to ratify "efficient thefts"—that is, give thieves the option of obtaining title to property that they have taken from others without their consent, provided only that the thief pays court-assessed damages equal to the value to the victim of her property?[46] Normative economists are barred by their assumption about available information[47] from responding that we need the market to provide such information.

Observations provided by economic theory about the effects of certain contract rules or principles on the efficient allocation of resources may rightly influence our normative assessment of those rules

---

resources known to any of the members of society, for ends whose relative importance only these individuals know."); see also J. Gray, Hayek on Liberty 40 (1984) (explaining Hayek's thesis that the "impossibility of socialism . . . derives from its neglect of the *epistemological functions* of market institutions and processes" (emphasis in original)); D. Lavoie, Rivalry and Central Planning 48–77 (1985) (describing Mises' contribution to the "socialist calculation debate" of the 1930s).

45. Of course, after a forced exchange—whether a tort or breach of contract—has occurred, a court may have no choice but to assess values as best it can. See, e.g., Muris, Cost of Completion or Diminution in Market Value: The Relevance of Subjective Value, 12 J. Legal Stud. 379 (1983) (discussing compensation for subjectively measured damages that result from breaches of contracts); see also supra text accompanying note 38; infra note 130. At issue here, however, is not how best to rectify forced exchanges, but rather, why and which voluntary exchanges are legally enforceable. Therefore, it is appropriate to ask the normative-efficiency advocate whether a court system empowered to use an efficiency analysis can "outperform the market" in recognizing value-enhancing exchanges. There is no evidence that this is possible, and good reason to think that it is not. See supra note 44 and accompanying text.

46. Some economic analysts can be seen as coming perilously close to an "efficient theft" position when positing the legitimacy of "efficient breaches" of contract. For statements of the "efficient breach" position, see, e.g., A. Polinsky, supra note 28, at 29–32; R. Posner, supra note 30, at 88–93. But cf. Macneil, supra note 30 (criticizing an efficient breach analysis from an entitlements perspective).

47. See supra note 43 and accompanying text. An economist might argue that "marginal" value-enhancing adjustments can be made against a background of market institutions. See, e.g., R. Posner, supra note 32, at 111. This position has been criticized by Rizzo, supra note 44, at 651–54.

Normative theories can also be criticized as placing undue reliance on the "objective" as opposed to "subjective" concepts of cost. See, e.g., Rizzo, supra note 44, at 646 ("The difficulty in measuring what we have every reason to believe are relevant variables is not, however, an argument for disregarding them; rather, it demonstrates the essential limitations of the wealth-maximization criterion."). For an explanation of the difference between the two concepts of cost, see J. Buchanan, Cost and Choice 1–26 (1969); Thirlby, The Subjective Theory of Value and Accounting "Costs," *in* L.S.E. Essays on Cost 137 (J. Buchanan & G. Thirlby eds. 1981).

or principles, particularly when these effects are considered along with the effects such rules and principles would have on private autonomy, or "will," and on reliance. Most notably, the efficient allocation of resources may require a market composed of consensual exchanges that reveal and convey otherwise unobtainable information about personal preferences and economic opportunities.[48] Economic analysis may, therefore, suggest that demonstrated consent plays an important role in the law of contract, provided that efficient allocation of resources is a social activity that should be facilitated by a legal system.[49] From this perspective, the "transaction costs" created by a requirement of consent are no worse from an efficiency standpoint than any other cost of production. The costs of negotiating to obtain the consent of another may be resources well-spent because such negotiations serve to reveal valuable information.

Where the negotiating costs of obtaining consent become so high as to bar exchanges thought to be desirable by observers, at least three conclusions are possible. Each, however, argues against enforcing involuntary transfers. First, in the absence of a consensual demonstration of preferences, we do not really know if the exchange is worthwhile—value enhancing—or not.[50] Second, the inefficiency of government legal institutions that needlessly raise transaction costs may be principally responsible for making these consensual transactions prohibitively expensive. If so, then "government failure" and not "market failure" may be responsible for preventing the exchange and the appropriate response is to eliminate the true source of the ineffi-

48. See supra note 44 and accompanying text; cf. S. Cheung, The Theory of Share Tenancy 64 (1969) ("[C]ompetition conglomerates knowledge from all potential owners—the knowledge of alternative contractual arrangements and uses of the resource; and transferability of property rights ensures that the most valuable knowledge will be utilized."); Demsetz, supra note 44, at 65 ("[I]nsisting on voluntary consent tends to produce information accuracy when many costs and benefits are known only by the individuals affected.").

49. The political theory embodied in normative economic analysis has been questioned by Ronald Dworkin. See Dworkin, Is Wealth a Value?, 9 J. Legal Stud. 191 (1980); Dworkin, supra note 32. Other critical analyses can be found in Symposium on Efficiency as a Legal Concern, 8 Hofstra L. Rev. 485 (1980); A Response to the Efficiency Symposium, 8 Hofstra L. Rev. 811 (1980).

50. This is true for two related reasons. The first is the epistemological problem presented by the absence of consent. See supra note 44 and accompanying text. The second—which follows from the first—is the effect that scarcity of goods has on an efficiency analysis. Transaction costs include negotiating agreements (exchange costs) and obtaining legal enforcement (police costs). Both can be viewed as necessary information-revealing and security-enhancing components of a given transaction. Such costs will be positive in a world of scarcity. Suppose that they exceed the potential gain from a contract and the contract is therefore not made. Is this situation any more "nonoptimal" than is the situation where the cost of any other scarce factor input—such as land or labor—prevents a transaction? Cf. Demsetz, Information and Efficiency: Another Viewpoint, 12 J.L. & Econ. 1, 4 (1969) ("To make [such an] assertion is to deny that scarcity is relevant to optimality, a strange position for an economist.").

ciency.[51] Finally, when negotiation costs make consensual agreements too expensive a means of obtaining the vital information about value, several alternative ways exist to generate this information without negotiation—for example, by forming a new company or "firm," by merging one company with another, or by combining products into a single package.[52]

In this analysis, demonstrated consent can be seen as playing an important role in any effort to achieve economic or allocative efficiency. Efficiency notions alone, however, cannot completely explain why certain commitments *should* be enforced unless it is further shown that economic efficiency is the exclusive goal of a legal order. The attempt to provide such a normative theory of wealth maximization, in the area of contract law at least, is fundamentally flawed.[53] In short, while the requirement of consent is in general supported by efficiency arguments, the normative justification for a consent theory of contract must be more broadly based.

2. *Substantive Fairness Theories.* — Another standards-based school of thought attempts to evaluate the substance of a transaction to see if it is "fair."[54] Substantive fairness theories have a long tradition dating back at least to the Christian "just price" theorists of the Middle Ages[55]

51. Cf. Cheung, supra note 33, at 42 ("[T]ransaction costs also depend on alternative *legal* arrangements. For example, the varying effectiveness of law enforcement, or the varying corruptibility of courts, will affect the costs of transactions in the market place."); Coase, supra note 33, at 28 ("The kind of situation which economists are prone to consider as requiring corrective Government action is, in fact, often the result of Government action."); Demsetz, The Exchange and Enforcement of Property Rights, 7 J.L. & Econ. 11, 17 (1964) ("The value of what is being traded depends crucially on the rights of action over the physical commodity and on how economically these rights are enforced.").

52. See Coase, The Nature of the Firm, 4 Economica 386, 390–91 (1937); Demsetz, supra note 51, at 16.

53. For criticisms of normative economic analysis that extend beyond contract law, see Coleman, Economics and the Law: A Critical Review of the Foundations of the Economic Approach to Law, 94 Ethics 649 (1984); Coleman, supra note 44.

54. See, e.g., Eisenberg, supra note 16, at 754 ("[T]he new paradigm [unconscionability] creates a theoretical framework that explains most of the limits that have been or should be placed upon . . . [the bargain] principle, based on the quality of the bargain.").

This substantive fairness approach should be distinguished from approaches that focus on whether the contracting *process* is fair or unfair. See, e.g., Epstein, Unconscionability: A Critical Reappraisal, 18 J.L. & Econ. 293 (1975) (distinguishing procedural from substantive unconscionability); Leff, Unconscionability and the Code—The Emperor's New Clause, 115 U. Pa. L. Rev. 485 (1967) (same).

55. See R. Ely, Outlines of Economics 827 (5th ed. 1930). But medieval just price theory actually may have been more subjective and market oriented than most modern commentators assume. See Dempsey, Just Price in a Functional Economy, 25 Am. Econ. Rev. 471, 471, 474–76, 480–86 (1935) (more subjective); De Roover, The Concept of the Just Price: Theory and Economic Policy, 18 J. Econ. Hist. 418, 420, 421–34 (1958) (more market oriented).

and perhaps even to Aristotle.[56] Their modern incarnation in contract law can be found in nineteenth century discussions of the "adequacy of consideration"[57] and, more recently, in some treatments of "unconscionability."[58]

A substantive fairness theory assumes that a standard of value can be found by which the substance of any agreement can be objectively evaluated.[59] Such a criterion has yet to be articulated and defended.[60] Without such a criterion, substantive fairness theories fall back on one or both of two incomplete approaches. On the one hand, such theories tend to focus all their attention on a small fraction of commitments—those that are thought to be so "extreme" as to "shock the conscience" of the courts.[61] Most real world agreements are considered to be presumptively enforceable.[62] On the other hand, such theories tend to be-

---

56. See, e.g., Aristotle, Nichomachean Ethics 125 (M. Ostwald trans. 1962):

> Thus, if (1) proportional equality is established between the goods, and (2) reciprocity effected, the fair exchange we spoke of will be realized. But if there is no proportionality, the exchange is not equal and fair, and (the association of the two will) not hold together.

The doubt expressed in the text as to whether this committed Aristotle to a "just price" position reflects the fact that he may only be attempting here to explain exchange transactions as a modern day economist would, rather than normatively assess the "justice" of the exchange. Of course, such a distinction is itself foreign to Aristotle's system.

57. See, e.g., Richardson v. Barrick, 16 Iowa 407, 412 (1864); T.P. Shepard & Co. v. Rhodes, 7 R.I. 470 (1863).

58. See, e.g., Restatement (Second) of Contracts § 208 comment c (1979) ("Theoretically it is possible for a contract to be oppressive taken as a whole, even though there is no weakness in the bargaining process . . . .").

59. Cohen noted this problem with what he called "the equivalent theory" of contract. See Cohen, supra note 7, at 581 (Due to problems of measurement, modern law "professes to abandon the effort of more primitive systems to enforce material fairness within the contract. The parties to the contract must themselves determine what is fair."). As a purely descriptive matter, the idea that exchange occurs because goods are of "equivalent" or equal value captivated economists for centuries, see supra notes 55–56 and accompanying text, until it was shown to be quite false. In fact, exchange occurs because both parties ex ante perceive the value of the goods to be exchanged as unequal. Each subjectively perceives the good or service offered by the other to be of greater value (to an unknowable extent) than what they are willing to trade for it. See C. Menger, Principles of Economics 180 (J. Dingwall & B. Hoselitz trans. 1981).

60. According to a thoroughly subjectivist theory of economic value, such a criterion is impossible to develop. See, e.g., L. von Mises, Human Action 94–98, 242, 354 (rev. ed. 1963) (discussing the impossibility of measuring exchange value because of the subjectivity of value); see also J. Buchanan, supra note 47, at 23–26 (briefly tracing the history of "the *subjectivist economics* of the latter-day Austrians, notably Mises and Hayek").

61. On the evolution of the "conscience" conception of equitable relief, see Johnson, Unconscionability and the Federal Chancellors: A Survey of U.C.C. Section 2-302 Interpretations in the Federal Circuits During the 1980's, 16 Lincoln L. Rev. 21, 56 nn.341–42 (1985).

62. See Eisenberg, supra note 16, at 754 ("This new paradigm does not replace the bargain principle, which is based on sound sense and continues to govern the normal case."); see also Epstein, The Social Consequences of Common Law Rules, 95 Harv. L. Rev. 1717, 1748 (1982) ("Surely all transactions made in organized markets at competi-

come process based—looking for either information asymmetries or what is called "unequal bargaining power."[63]

The first of these responses attempts to find extreme instances of violations of a standard that cannot be articulated—or at least cannot be articulated for most transactions,[64] while the latter represents a retreat from the substantive fairness position altogether. Therefore, at best a substantive fairness approach attempts to deal with a qualitative issue by making either a quantitative or a procedural assessment, but *what* is being measured—the nature of the unfairness—is not disclosed.[65]

Most importantly for this discussion, however, the substantive fairness approach fails to address squarely the most central and common problem of contract theory: which *conscionable* agreements should be enforced and which should not? This after all, is, or ought to be, the starting point of a useful theory of contractual obligation that purports to discern which commitments merit legal enforcement.[66] In sum, the substantive fairness approach provides neither meaningful standards nor predictable results. Both the extreme indeterminacy and the focus on aberrant cases inherent in a principle of substantive fairness prevent it from providing the overarching account of contractual obligation that contract theory requires.

3. *The Problem With Standards-Based Theories.* — All standards-based theories face two problems, one that is obvious and another that is more subtle. The obvious problem, which has already been discussed, is identifying and defending the appropriate standard by which enforceable commitments can be distinguished from those that should be unenforceable. The more subtle problem arises from the fact that stan-

---

tive prices must go unquestioned, for to hold one of these exchanges suspect would be to strike down all identical transactions."). Even a severe critic of freedom of contract agrees that this is an aspect of current unconscionability doctrine. See Kennedy, Distributive and Paternalist Motives in Contract and Tort Law, with Special Reference to Compulsory Terms and Unequal Bargaining Power, 41 Md. L. Rev. 563, 621 (1982).

63. See E. Farnsworth, supra note 13, § 4.28, at 314–16.

64. Professor Eisenberg, for example, confines his analysis to the identification of circumstances or "norms" that, if present, would call the fairness of the resulting agreement into question. He discusses exploitation of distress, transactional incapacity, susceptibility to unfair persuasion, and price-ignorance. See Eisenberg, supra note 16, at 754–85. Eisenberg's resort to suspect circumstances finesses the issue of discerning the quality of "unfairness" of the substantive bargain that he is seeking to police. In a consent theory, the circumstances he lists would be analyzed as (controversial) contenders for defenses that undermine the normal moral significance of consent. See infra notes 210–14 and accompanying text.

65. See Epstein, supra note 54, at 306 ("It is difficult to know what principles identify the 'just term,' and for the same reasons that make it so difficult to determine the 'just price.' "); see also L. von Mises, supra note 60, at 727–30 (discussing the nature and deficiencies of "just price" theories).

66. See supra note 1 and accompanying text.

dards-based contract theories are types of what Robert Nozick has called "patterned" principles of distributive justice:

> [A] principle of distribution [is] *patterned* if it specifies that a distribution is to vary along with some natural dimension, weighted sum of natural dimensions, or lexicographic ordering of natural dimensions . . . .
>
> Almost every suggested principle of distributive justice is patterned: to each according to his moral merit, or needs, or marginal product, or how hard he tries, or the weighted sum of the foregoing, and so on.[67]

The problem created by such patterned theories of justice—including theories based on some notion of efficiency—is that they require constant interferences with individual preferences. "Render possessions ever so equal, man's different degrees of art, care, and industry will immediately break that equality."[68] The maintenance of a pattern, therefore, requires either that persons be stopped from entering the contracts they desire, or that those in power "continually (or periodically) interfere to take from some persons resources that others for some reason chose to transfer to them."[69]

Such interferences are at least presumptively suspect. They may sometimes even be objectionable according to the particular standard that is being used to justify the intervention. For example, inefficiency might be shown to be the ultimate result of interventions to achieve "efficiency" that thwart individual preferences in this way.[70] And a system in which judges may—in the absence of fraud, duress, or some other demonstrable defect in the formation process—second-guess the wisdom of the parties may create more substantive unfairness than it cures.[71] More fundamentally, a theory of rights might support the conclusion that such interferences are unjust and wrong.[72]

---

67. R. Nozick, Anarchy, State and Utopia 156–57 (1974).

68. D. Hume, supra note 10, at 25.

69. R. Nozick, supra note 67, at 163. See generally his discussion of "how liberty upsets patterns." Id. at 160–64.

70. See J. Gray, Indirect Utility and Fundamental Rights, Soc. Phil. & Pol'y, Spring 1984, at 73, 85 ("If direct utilitarian policy is counterproductive, we must accept practical constraints on it, and there is nothing to say that these will not include the distributive contraints imposed by principles conferring weighty moral rights on individuals."); see also Alexander, Pursuing the Good—Indirectly, 95 Ethics 315 (1985) (further elaborating this position).

71. Cf. Epstein, supra note 54, at 315 ("[W]hen the doctrine of unconscionability is used in its substantive dimension, . . . it serves only to undercut the private right of contract in a manner that is apt to do more social harm than good.").

72. See, e.g., R. Nozick, supra note 67, at 168 ("From the point of view of an entitlement theory, redistribution is a serious matter indeed, involving, as it does, the violation of people's rights."); Mack, In Defense of Unbridled Freedom of Contract, 40 Am. J. Econ. & Soc. 1 (1981) (each person should have liberty to enter into and right to insist on fulfillment of any rights-respecting contract); see also infra notes 93–120 and accompanying text.

C. *Process-Based Theories*

Process-based theories shift the focus of the inquiry from the contract parties and from the substance of the parties' agreement to the manner in which the parties reached their agreement. Such theories posit appropriate procedures for establishing enforceable obligations and then assess any given transaction to see if these procedures were followed. The best known theory of this sort is the bargain theory of consideration.

1. *The Bargain Theory of Consideration.* — The origin of the modern doctrine of consideration can be traced to the rise of the action of assumpsit.[73] When the voluntary assumption of obligation came to be viewed as the basis of contractual enforcement, no one seriously suggested that *every* demonstrable agreement could or should be legally enforced. The number of agreements made every day are so numerous that for reasons of both practice and principle some distinction, apart from that made by purely evidentiary requirements,[74] must be made between enforceable and unenforceable agreements.

The doctrine of consideration was devised to provide this distinction.[75] Where consideration is present, an agreement ordinarily will be enforced. And, most significantly, where there is no consideration, even if the commitment is clear and unambiguous, enforcement is supposed to be unavailable. In the nineteenth century, the "bargain theory of consideration" was promoted by some—most notably Holmes and Langdell—as a way of answering the problem of which commitments merit legal protection. Today it is probably the predominant theory of consideration and is embodied in section 71 of the Restatement (Second) of Contracts:

> (1) To constitute consideration, a performance or a return promise must be bargained for.
> (2) A performance or return promise is bargained for if it is sought by the promisor in exchange for his promise and is given by the promisee in exchange for that promise.[76]

This approach attempts to discern "mutuality" of inducement from the motives and acts of both parties to the transaction. It is not *what* is bargained for that is important; what solely matters is that each person's promise or performance is induced by the other's.

73. See E. Farnsworth, supra note 13, § 1.6, at 19–20.

74. These are rules that enable courts and other strangers to the transaction to evaluate the legitimacy of contracting parties' often conflicting claims, for example, a statute of frauds or a rule regulating the use of parol evidence. See, e.g., U.C.C. §§ 2-201, 2-202 (1977).

75. See A. Simpson, A History of the Common Law of Contract 316 (1975); see also Eisenberg, supra note 1, at 640 (answer to the question of what kinds of promises should be enforced "traditionally has been subsumed under the heading 'consideration' ").

76. Restatement (Second) of Contracts § 71(1), (2) (1979).

The difficulties presented by the doctrine of consideration depend on which way the concept is viewed. If the doctrine is interpreted restrictively, then whole classes of "serious" agreements will be thought to be lacking consideration. In his recent discussion of consideration, Charles Fried lists four kinds of cases—promises to keep an offer open, to release a debt, to modify an obligation, and to pay for past favors—where promisees have traditionally had considerable difficulty obtaining legal relief for nonperformance because bargained-for consideration is lacking,[77] although it is generally conceded that the parties may have intended to be legally bound and that enforcement should therefore be available.[78] To these may be added unbargained-for promises to assume the obligations of another,[79] to convey land, to give to charities, and those made by bailees and within the family.[80]

In each of these types of cases, a promise is made and then broken. The promisee then seeks to base his cause of action on the promise. In many of these cases, the promise is a serious and unambiguous one. In each situation, however, there is no "bargain" and therefore no consideration for the promise.

Such cases as these invite attempts by judges and others to expand the concept of consideration beyond the bargain requirement.[81] Any such attempt to capture these and other types of cases will, however, run afoul of an opposing difficulty. If the web of consideration doctrine is woven too loosely, it will increasingly capture "social" agreements where legal enforcement is not contemplated—for example, promises of financial assistance between family members.[82] Thus, any expanded concept of consideration threatens to undermine the doctrine's tradi-

77. See C. Fried, supra note 8, at 28.

78. That enforcement is deemed desirable in such cases is evidenced by statutes that have sometimes been enacted to provide a basis for liability. See id.; see, e.g., U.C.C. § 2-205 & comment 2 (1977) (Firm offer made binding in order "to give effect to the deliberate intention of a merchant . . . .").

79. See, e.g., U.C.C. § 3-408 & comment 2 (1977).

80. E. Farnsworth, supra note 13, § 2.19, at 90–91.

81. A well-known example of where the bargain requirement was stretched to the breaking point is, Allegheny College v. National Chautauqua County Bank, 246 N.Y. 369, 159 N.E. 173 (1927) (holding that college's promise to set up a memorial fund was consideration for a promise to make a "gift" to the college). E. Farnsworth, supra note 13, § 2.19, at 91, characterizes the consideration analysis in this case as "tenuous." Because of the presence of formalities and the recital of "moral" consideration, a consent theory might have reached the same result. See infra notes 176–81 and accompanying text. Then again, certain terms of the pledge at issue may indicate an intent that it be revokable. See *Allegheny College*, 246 N.Y. at 372, 159 N.E. at 174 ("This pledge shall be valid only on the condition that the provisions of my Will, now extant, shall be first met."). Such difficulties of interpretation are to be expected in a legal regime that so uncertainly enforces unbargained-for, but formal, promises, since the parties cannot be sure of the form that will effectuate their purpose. See infra notes 166–81 and accompanying text.

82. See, e.g., Richards v. Richards, 46 Pa. 78, 82 (1863) (enforcing such assurances would be "exceedingly hurtful to the freedom of social intercourse").

tional function: distinguishing enforceable from unenforceable agreements in a predictable fashion to allow for private planning and to prevent the weight of legal coercion from falling upon those informal or "social" arrangements where the parties have not contemplated legal sanctions for breach.[83]

Each strategy to deal with the problems generated by a doctrine of consideration, therefore, wreaks havoc in its own way with a coherent theory of contractual obligation. With a restrictive definition like that of bargain, serious promises which merit enforcement are left unenforced. With an expansive formulation, informal promises that are thought to be properly outside the province of legal coercion will be made the subject of legal sanctions. The most recognized problem with the bargain theory is that it appears to have erred too far in the direction of under-enforcement.[84] However, the bargain theory suffers in a more fundamental way from its purely process-based character.

2. *The Problem With Process-Based Theories.* — The problem with process-based theories is not simply that they must strike a balance between over- and under-enforcement. Such trade-offs cannot be completely avoided in any system that bases decision-making on rules and principles of general application.[85] The real problem with process-based theories like the bargain theory of consideration is that they place insurmountable obstacles in the way of minimizing such difficulties of enforcement.

First, a process-based theory's *exclusive* focus on the process that justifies contractual enforcement conceals the substantive values that must support any choice of process. By obscuring these values, process-based theories come to treat their favored procedural devices as ends, rather than as means. Then, when the adopted procedures inevitably give rise to problems of fit between means and ends, a process-based theory that is divorced from ends cannot say why this has occurred or what is to be done about it. This inherent weakness of process-based theories has plagued the bargain theory of consideration.[86]

83. See Cohen, supra note 7, at 573 ("Certainly, some freedom to change one's mind is necessary for free intercourse between those who lack omniscience."); Fuller, Consideration and Form, 41 Colum. L. Rev. 799, 813 (1941) ("There is a real need for a field of human intercourse freed from legal restraints, for a field where men may without liability withdraw assurances they have once given." (citation omitted)).

84. See Eisenberg, supra note 1, at 642.

85. See, e.g., Aristotle, supra note 56, at 141 ("[A]ll law is universal, but there are some things about which it is not possible to speak correctly in universal terms."); H.L.A. Hart, The Concept of Law 125 (1961) ("[U]ncertainty at the borderline is the price to be paid for the use of general classifying terms in any form of communication concerning matters of fact."). It is possible, however, that a presumptive approach to legal rulemaking minimizes this type of error. See infra notes 162–64 and accompanying text.

86. See Eisenberg, supra note 1, at 642 ("[S]uch an approach . . . tends to stifle judicial creativity and reconceptualization.").

The bargain theory, which was devised to limit the applicability of assumpsit,[87] fails to ensure the enforcement of certain reasonably well-defined categories of unbargained-for, but "serious" commitments.[88] Then, when courts are moved to enforce such commitments, the principal theory of consideration to which they adhere cannot account for these "exceptions" to the normal requirement of a bargain without appealing to concepts more fundamental than bargaining. Ironically, the rise of assumpsit—the source of the need for the consideration doctrine—was itself due to the inability of the then existing process-based writ system to accommodate enforcement of informal, but serious promises.[89]

Second, an exclusively process-based theory cannot itself explain why certain *kinds* of commitments are not and should not be enforceable. For example, it is widely recognized that agreements to perform illegal acts should not be enforceable. Similarly, slavery contracts are also thought to be unenforceable per se. If, however, agreements of these types were reached in conformity with all "rules of the game," a theory that looks only to the rules of the game to decide issues of enforceability cannot say why such an otherwise "proper" agreement should be unenforceable.

These two types of problems, however, are not confined to process-based theories. As was seen above,[90] party-based theories based on will and reliance are also plagued by an inability to account for and explain certain "exceptional" agreements that are enforceable without recourse to their animating principles. And theories based on principles of will, reliance, or efficiency have as hard a time as process-based theories explaining why certain agreements are unenforceable due to so-called "public policy" exceptions to their respective norms of contractual obligation.

Notwithstanding the weaknesses inherent in process-based theories, such theories offer significant advantages over both party-based and standards-based theories. By employing a neutral criterion for determining contractual enforcement, a process-based theory can better protect both the contractual intent and the reliance of both parties than one-sided party-based theories, provided it identifies features of the contractual process that normally correspond to the presence of contractual intent and substantial reliance. By identifying judicially workable criteria of enforcement, process-based theories can avoid the difficulties of extreme indeterminacy that were seen to plague standards-based theories.[91] They can, in short, better provide the tradi-

87. See supra note 73 and accompanying text.

88. See supra notes 77–80 and accompanying text.

89. See A. Simpson, supra note 75, at 136–96 (discussing difficulties in enforcing informal contracts prior to the development of assumpsit).

90. See supra notes 9–16, 19–25 and accompanying text.

91. See supra notes 31–45, 54–66 and accompanying text.

tionally acknowledged advantages of a system of generally applicable laws, such as facilitating private planning and helping to ensure equal treatment of similarly situated persons. Perhaps it is these advantages that have permitted a process-based theory like the bargain theory to survive its frequent detractors.

The significant administrative advantages of process-based theories suggest that the best approach to contractual obligation is one that preserves a procedural aspect of contract law, while recognizing that such procedures are *dependent* for their ultimate justification on more fundamental, substantive principles of right that occasionally affect procedural analysis in two ways. First, these principles might suggest specific improvements in procedures governing contract formation that are appropriate in the event that previously adopted procedures have created well-defined problems of under-enforcement. Second, these principles might serve to deprive certain procedurally immaculate agreements of their normal moral significance, thereby ameliorating identifiable problems of over-enforcement.[92] A consent theory of contract is such an approach.

II. A Consent Theory of Contract

A. *Entitlement Theory and Contract: The Central Importance of Consent*

1. *Entitlements as the Root of Contractual Obligation.* — The function of an entitlements theory based on individual rights is to define the boundaries within which individuals may live, act, and pursue happiness free of the forcible interference of others.[93] A theory of entitlements specifies the rights that individuals possess or may possess; it tells us what may be owned and who owns it; it circumscribes the individual boundaries of human freedom.[94] Any coherent theory of justice based on individual rights must therefore contain principles that describe how such rights are initially acquired, how they are transferred from person to person, what the substance and limits of properly obtained rights are, and how interferences with these entitlements are to

---

92. The relationship between procedural strictures and underlying principles is analogous to Ronald Dworkin's distinction between rules and principles, see R. Dworkin, Taking Rights Seriously 22–39 (1977), in that process rules of contract would be enforceable because of more fundamental principles and that such principles would also serve to define the outer limits of the rules.

93. The literature on entitlements or rights is vital and growing. I describe some of the factors that led to this growth in Barnett, supra note 3, at 1225–33. For a useful bibliography, see Nickel, Bibliographical Update/The Nature and Foundations of Rights, Crim. Just. Ethics, Summer/Fall 1982, at 64 (also citing other bibliographies). For a survey of the economic analysis of property rights, see Furubotn & Pejovich, supra note 33.

94. See Furubotn & Pejovich, supra note 33, at 1139 ("The prevailing system of property rights in the community can be described . . . as the set of economic and social relations defining the position of each individual with respect to the utilization of scarce resources." (citation omitted)).

be rectified.[95]

These constituent parts of an entitlements theory comport substantially with the traditional categories of private law. The issue of initial acquisition of entitlements in real and chattel resources is dealt with primarily in property law; tort law concerns the protection of and proper limits on resource use; and contract law deals with transfers of rights between rights holders.[96] Each category contains principles of rectification for the breach of legal obligations.[97]

Viewing contract law as part of a more general theory of individual entitlements that specifies how resources may be rightly acquired (property law), used (tort law), and transferred (contract law) is not new.[98] And, of course, the actual historical development of these legal categories has not perfectly conformed to the conceptual distinctions that an entitlements approach suggests. But this approach has long been neglected as a way of resolving some of the thorniest issues of contract theory and doctrine.

According to an entitlements approach, rights may be unconditionally granted to another (a gift), or their transfer may be conditioned upon some act or reciprocal transfer by the transferee (an exchange). Contract law concerns ways in which rights are transferred or alienated. Accordingly, the enforceability of all agreements is limited by what rights are capable of being transferred from one person to another. Whether a purported right is genuine or can be legitimately transferred is not an issue of contract theory only, but is one that may also require reference to the underlying theory of entitlements—that is, the area of legal theory that specifies what rights individuals have and the manner by which they come to have them. In this respect, the explanation of the binding nature of contractual commitments is derived from more fundamental notions of entitlements and how they are acquired and transferred.

---

95. Cf. R. Nozick, supra note 67, at 150–53 (providing a tripartite definition of justice consisting of justice in acquisition, transfer, and rectification).

96. See Epstein, The Static Conception of the Common Law, 9 J. Legal Stud. 253, 255 (1980).

97. Another possible category is restitution, which specifies circumstances not covered by either contract or tort when compensation for nongratuitous transfers of resources might be available. See Friedmann, Restitution of Benefits Obtained Through the Appropriation of Property or the Commission of a Wrong, 80 Colum. L. Rev. 504 (1980).

98. Several commentators have recently referred to its historical antecedents. A. Simpson, supra note 75, provides the most rigorous examination of the history of this approach and its operation and demise. See also P. Atiyah, supra note 16, at 89 ("In Blackstone's *Commentaries*, . . . contract and succession are both dealt with as a means by which the title to property gets transferred."); M. Horwitz, The Transformation of American Law 1780–1860, at 162 (1977) ("As a result of the subordination of contract to property, eighteenth century jurists endorsed a title theory of contractual exchange according to which a contract functioned to transfer title to the specific thing contracted for.").

The subjects of most rights transfer agreements are entitlements that are indisputably alienable. In such cases the rules of contract law are entirely sufficient to explain and justify a judicial decision. However, in rare cases—such as agreements amounting to slavery arrangements or requiring the violation of another's rights—contract law's dependency on rights theory will be of crucial importance in identifying appropriate concerns about the substance of voluntary agreements. For example, agreements to transfer inalienable rights[99]—rights that for some reason cannot be transferred—or to transfer rights that for some reason cannot be obtained, would not, without more, be valid and enforceable contracts.[100]

Although existing theories of contractual obligation have failed to recognize this dependent relationship explicitly, such a notion may sometimes be implicit. For example, it is difficult to understand how any theory based on the "will" of the individual or the rectification of "harm" to an individual caused by reliance makes sense without assuming a background of more basic individual rights. One would not care at all about an individual's expressed "will" or any reliance injury she might have sustained unless that person has a pre-contractual right to "bind herself" or a right to be protected from certain kinds of harm. Efficiency-based theories also depend on a (usually assumed) set of entitlements that form the basis of subsequent "efficient" exchanges.[101] The many gaps in these articulated theories of contract are, in practice, most probably filled by our shared intuitions about fundamental individual rights. Making this conceptual relationship explicit helps to clarify what continues to be a hazy understanding of contractual obligation.

As Part I demonstrated, a proper understanding of contractual obligation and its limits requires an appeal to something more fundamental than the concepts of will, reliance, efficiency, fairness, or bargain. A

99. Elaborating the important distinction between alienable and inalienable rights would require a more general discussion of rights theory than is possible here. See Barnett, Contract Remedies and Inalienable Rights, Soc. Phil. & Pol'y, Autumn 1986 (forthcoming); see also Kronman, Paternalism and the Law of Contracts, 92 Yale L.J. 763 (1983) (discussing implications for contract theory of the distinction between alienable and inalienable rights). A number of recent treatments of the issue of inalienable rights reinforce its significance for legal and moral theory. See J. Feinberg, Rights, Justice, and the Bounds of Liberty 238–46 (1980); D. Meyer, Inalienable Rights: A Defense (1985); H. Veatch, Human Rights: Fact or Fancy? ch. 3 (1986); Epstein, Why Restrain Alienation?, 85 Colum. L. Rev. 970 (1985); Kuflik, The Inalienability of Autonomy, 13 Phil. & Pub. Affs. 271 (1984); McConnell, The Nature and Basis of Inalienable Rights, 3 Law & Phil. 25 (1984); Rose-Ackerman, Inalienability and the Theory of Property Rights, 85 Colum. L. Rev. 931 (1985).

100. Other bases of obligation are possible besides contractual obligation, however, such as those recognized under the law of tort and restitution.

101. See Demsetz, Toward a Theory of Property Rights, 57 Am. Econ. Rev. 347, 347 (1967) ("Economists usually take the bundle of property rights as a datum and ask for an explanation of the forces determining the price and the number of units of a good to which these rights attach.").

framework or theory is needed to order these fundamental concerns, to show where each "principle" stands in relation to others. Recognizing the necessity of such an inquiry places the contract theorist in the realm of entitlements or rights theory. The legitimacy of principles of contract that determine which transfers of rights are valid depends upon the nature of individual entitlements and the extent to which rights have been or will be acquired by the parties to a transfer. The process of contractual transfer cannot be completely comprehended, therefore, without considering more fundamental issues, namely the nature and sources of individual entitlements and the means by which they come to be acquired.

2. *The Allocative and Distributional Function of Individual Rights.* — Any concept of individual rights must assume a social context. If the world were inhabited by one person, it might make sense to speak of that person's actions as "good" or "bad." Such a moral judgment might, for example, look to whether or not that person had chosen to live what might be called the "good life."[102] It makes no sense, however, to speak about this person's rights. As one court noted: "Unless and until one is brought into relation with other men, or property, or rights, he has no obligation to act with reference to them; and this is true whether the obligation be called legal, moral, or reasonable."[103]

From the moment individuals live in close enough proximity to one another to compete for the use of scarce natural resources, some way of allocating those resources must be found. In short, some scheme of specifying how individuals may acquire, use, and transfer resources must be recognized. Certain facts of human existence make certain principles of allocation ineluctable. For example, it is a fundamental human requirement that individuals acquire and consume natural resources, even though such activity is often inconsistent with a similar use of the same resources by others.

"Property rights" is the term traditionally used to describe an individual's entitlements to use and consume resources—both the individual's person and her external possessions—free from the physical interference of others.[104] That possession and use of resources is by

102. See, e.g., H. Veatch, For an Ontology of Morals (1971) (a critique of contemporary ethical theory from an Aristotelian perspective).

103. Garland v. Boston & M.R.R., 76 N.H. 556, 557, 86 A. 141, 142 (1913). As the court colorfully put the point in its discussion of duties of care: "The rule of reasonable care, under the circumstances, could not limit the conduct of Robinson Crusoe as he was at first situated; but as soon as he saw the tracks in the sand the rule began to have vitality." Id. at 563, 86 A. at 141; see also Demsetz, supra note 101, at 347 ("In the world of Robinson Crusoe property rights play no role.").

104. See, e.g., Furubotn & Pejovich, supra note 33, at 1139 ("[P]roperty rights do not refer to relations between men and things but, rather, *to the sanctioned behavioral relations among men that arise from the existence of things and pertain to their use.*" (emphasis in original)). Today, the term "property rights" tends to be limited only to rights to external resources. Traditionally, however, it was accorded the meaning employed in the

"right" suggests that any attempt at physical interference with possession and use may be resisted by force if necessary.[105] Additionally, if another interferes with a rightful distribution of resources, this violation may be rectified by *re*distributing resources.[106] Some rights to property can be exclusive and others less so. The exact contours of a proper theory of rights need not be specified here.[107] Only the recognition that *some* allocation of rights to resource possession and use is an unavoidable prerequisite of human survival and of human fulfillment is relevant to this discussion.

Although entitlements to resources can be acquired directly from nature by individual labor, in a complex society they will more likely be acquired from others.[108] Contract law, according to an entitlements approach, is thus a body of general principles and more specific rules the function of which is to identify the rights of individuals engaged in transferring entitlements, and thereby indicate when physical or legal force may legitimately be used to preserve those rights and to rectify any unjust interference with the transfer process.

---

text—the moral and legal jurisdiction a person has both over her body *and* over external resources. See, e.g., J. Locke, An Essay Concerning the True Original Extent and End of Civil Government, *in* Two Treatises of Civil Government ch. V, § 27 (1690) ("every man has a 'property' in his own 'person' "). This conception of property was so well accepted that some radical abolitionists in the 19th century referred to slavery as the crime of "manstealing." See, e.g., S. Foster, The Brotherhood of Thieves, or a True Picture of the American Church and Clergy 10 (1843), quoted in The Antislavery Argument 138 (W. & J. Pease eds. 1965). This broader view of property rights also prevailed in the Middle Ages. See McGovern, Private Property and Individual Rights in the Commentaries of the Jurists, A.D. 1200–1550, *in* Essays in Memory of Schafer Williams (tentative title) (S. Bowman & B. Cody eds.) (forthcoming).

105. See, e.g., R. Nozick, Philosophical Explanations 499 (1981) ("[A] right is something for which one can demand or enforce compliance."); Furubotn & Pejovich, supra note 33, at 1139 ("Property rights assignments specify the norms of behavior with respect to things that each and every person must observe in his interactions with other persons, or bear the cost for nonobservance.").

106. See, e.g., Nickel, Justice in Compensation, 18 Wm. & Mary L. Rev. 379, 381–82 (1976) ("[C]ompensation protects just distributions, and the rights they involve, by undoing, insofar as possible, actions that disturb such distributions.").

107. I have more fully discussed this issue elsewhere. See Barnett, The Justice of Restitution, 25 Am. J. Juris. 117 (1980) (defending the justice of restitutive rectification); Barnett, Pursuing Justice in a Free Society: Part One—Power vs. Liberty, Crim. Just. Ethics, Summer/Fall, 1985, at 50 (discussing the sources and proper content of a property rights theory) [hereinafter cited as Pursuing Justice]; Barnett, Restitution: A New Paradigm of Criminal Justice, 87 Ethics 279 (1977) (discussing the merits of various approaches to rectification); Barnett, supra note 21, at 6–15 (discussing the classical liberal account of law and rights); Barnett, Public Decisions and Private Rights (Book Review), Crim. Just. Ethics, Summer/Fall, 1984, at 50 (discussing the methodology of a property rights approach).

108. Cf. Baird & Jackson, Information, Uncertainty, and the Transfer of Property, 13 J. Legal Stud. 299, 299 (1984) ("Few of us who own property actually have reduced it to private property from a state of nature (or ownership in common). No matter what theory justifies initial ownership rights, our enjoyment of most property rests on our ability to acquire it from someone else.").

3. *Consent as the Moral Component of a Contractual Transaction.* — The areas of moral obligations and legal obligations are not coextensive.[109] A moral obligation is something we ought to do or refrain from doing. A moral obligation that is not also a valid legal obligation can only be legitimately secured by voluntary means. That is, one may have a moral obligation to do something, but unless there is also a valid legal obligation, one cannot legitimately be forced by another to do it. A moral obligation is only a legal obligation if it can be enforced by the use or threat of legal force.[110] This added dimension of force requires moral justification. The principal task of legal theory, then, is to identify circumstances when legal enforcement is morally justified.[111]

Entitlements theories seek to perform this task by using moral analysis to derive individual legal rights, that is, claims that may be justifiably enforced.[112] A theory of contractual obligation is the part of an entitlements theory that focuses on liability arising from the wrongful interference with a valid rights transfer. Until such an interference is corrected—by force if necessary—the distribution of resources caused by the interference is unjust. Justice consists of correcting this situation to bring resource distribution into conformity with entitlements.[113]

109. See L. Fuller, The Morality of Law 1–2 (rev. ed. 1969); R. Nozick, supra note 105, at 503 ("Political philosophy . . . is mainly the theory of what behavior legitimately may be enforced, and of the nature of the institutional structure that stays within and supports these enforceable rights . . . . In no way does political philosophy or the realm of the state exhaust the realm of the morally desireable or moral oughts.").

110. On the role that coercion ought to play in jurisprudential thought, see Nance, Legal Theory and the Pivotal Role of the Concept of Coercion, 57 U. Colo. L. Rev. 1 (1985).

111. One can distinguish between a *positive* legal obligation, which a particular legal system will enforce (whether or not it should), and a *valid* legal obligation, which is an obligation that it is morally appropriate to enforce. See, e.g., H.L.A. Hart, Positivism and the Separation of Law and Morals, 71 Harv. L. Rev. 593 (1958); Fuller, Positivism and Fidelity to Law—A Reply to Professor Hart, 71 Harv. L. Rev. 630 (1958). For an excellent discussion of this distinction, see J. Murphy & J. Coleman, The Philosophy of Law: An Introduction to Jurisprudence 7–68 (1984). In this section, the latter meaning is the one used.

112. See supra note 105 and accompanying text.

113. In certain rare circumstances, however, the protection of holdings might argue against such redistribution. The doctrine of adverse possession, for example, suggests that the justice of some present holdings of resources that did not originate by just means might nonetheless be considered rightful due to the passage of time. See Ballantine, Title by Adverse Possession, 32 Harv. L. Rev. 135, 136 (1918). Similarly, once so much time has passed since the initial "taking" that both the original wrongdoer and the original owner (or her discernible heirs) are no longer alive to claim ownership, then an innocent person in possession might be acknowledged as holding good title. Cf. Sher, Ancient Wrongs and Modern Rights, 10 Phil. & Pub. Affs. 3 (1980) (discussing the problems of rectifying past injustices). In the absence of an identifiable victim, the innocent recipient of property that was originally wrongfully acquired would, as against the world, have the best claim to title—or so the argument goes. Falling as it would within the realm of property law and outside the boundaries of contract law, a critical analysis of such an argument is beyond the scope of this Article.

To identify the moral component that distinguishes valid from invalid rights transfers, it is first necessary to separate moral principles governing the rightful acquisition and use of resources from those governing their transfer. Rights are the means by which freedom of action and interaction are facilitated and regulated in society,[114] and thus the rights we have to acquire previously unowned resources and to use that which we acquire must not be subject to the expressed assent of others. Although societal acquiescence may be a practical necessity for rights to be legally respected, no individual or group need consent to our appropriation of previously unowned resources or their use for our rights to *morally* vest.[115]

Similarly, principles governing rights transfer should be distinguished from principles governing resource use. Tort law concerns obligations arising from interferences with others' rights. A tortfeasor who interferes with another's rights (rather than obtaining a valid transfer of those rights to herself) is liable because of that interference, not because she consented to be held liable for her actions that impair another's rights. A tortfeasor can be said to "forfeit" (as opposed to alienate or transfer) rights to resources in order to provide compensation to the victim of the tort.[116]

In contrast, contract law concerns enforceable obligations arising from the valid *transfer* of entitlements that are *already vested* in someone, and this difference is what makes consent a moral prerequisite to contractual obligation. The rules governing alienation of property rights by transfer perform the same function as rules governing their acquisition and those specifying their proper content: facilitating freedom of human action and interaction.[117] Freedom of action and interaction would be seriously impeded, and possibly destroyed, if legitimate rights holders who have not acted in a tortious manner could be deprived of

---

114. See Barnett, Pursuing Justice, supra note 107, at 56–63.

115. The fact that society does not recognize a right cannot alone mean that morally such a right does not exist. Cf. R. Dworkin, supra note 92, at 184–85 (1977):

> In practice the Government will have the last word on what an individual's rights are, because its police will do what its officials and courts say. But that does not mean that the Government's view is necessarily the correct view; anyone who thinks it does must believe that men and women have only such moral rights as Government chooses to grant, which means that they have no moral rights at all.

Requiring societal acquiescence for the moral vesting of initially acquired rights would amount to a "consent theory" of property acquisition. See Rose, Possession as the Origin of Property, 52 U. Chi. L. Rev. 73, 74 (1985) ("According to this theory, the original owner got title through the consent of the rest of humanity . . . .").

116. See J. Feinberg, supra note 99, at 239–40 (distinguishing between alienating and forfeiting rights); Kuflik, supra note 99, at 275 ("To say that autonomy cannot be alienated is not to imply that in special circumstances it cannot be forfeited. A person may lose through misconduct what it would be wrong for him to transfer or relinquish through consent or agreement.").

117. See Barnett, Pursuing Justice, supra note 107, at 56–63.

their rights by force of law without their consent.[118] Moreover, the moral requirement of consent mandates that others take the interests of the rights holder into account when seeking to obtain the rights she possesses.[119] Wallace Matson succinctly describes the view of justice that makes consent the moral component of contractual transfer:

> [Justice is] . . . rendering every man his due. A man's due is what he has acquired by his own efforts and not taken from some other man *without consent*. A community in which this conception is realized will be one in which the members agree not to interfere in the legitimate endeavors of each other to achieve their individual goals, and to help each other to the extent that the conditions for doing so are mutually satisfactory . . . . Such a community will be one giving the freest possible rein to all its members to develop their particular capacities and use them to carry out their plans for their own betterment . . . . [T]his activity is The Good for Man . . . .[120]

---

118. See Baird & Jackson, supra note 108, at 299–300 ("Legal rules must confront the problems associated with the transfer of property from one individual to another. When we already *own* property, we want to ensure that we can control its disposition—that a new "owner" will not come into existence *without our consent*." (emphasis added)).

119. Cf. Demsetz, supra note 44, at 64 ("A property right system which requires the *prior* agreement of these input owners before they can be put to a particular task insures that these costs will be taken into account [by others]."). Moreover, as Joel Feinberg has noted:

> To have a right typically is to have the discretion or "liberty" to exercise it or not as one chooses. This freedom is another feature of right-ownership that helps to explain why rights are so valuable. When a person has a discretionary right and fully understands the power that possession gives him, he can if he chooses make sacrifices for the sake of others, voluntarily give up what is rightfully his own, freely make gifts that he is in no way obligated to make, and forgive others for their wrongs to him by declining to demand the compensation or vengeance he may have coming or by warmly welcoming them back into his friendship or love. . . . Without the duties that others have toward one (correlated with one's rights against them) there could be no sense in the notion of one's superrogatory conduct towards other people, for to help others when one has the right to decline is precisely what conduct "above and beyond duty" amounts to.

J. Feinberg, supra note 99, at 156–57.

120. Matson, Justice: A Funeral Oration, Soc. Phil. & Pol'y, Autumn 1983, at 94, 111–12 (1983) (emphasis added). He then contrasts this "bottom up" conception of justice with another:

> The other conception holds justice to be the satisfaction of needs so as to bring everyone as far as possible onto the same plateau of pleasurable experience. The view of human life underlying it is that life consists of two separable phases, production and consumption; the consumption phase is where The Good lies; there is ultimately no reason why any individual should have any more or less of this Good than any other individual; and the problem of how to secure the requisite production is merely technical. Society based on this conception must be structured as a hierarchy of authority, in order to solve the problem of production and to administer justice, i.e. to adjust the satisfaction quanta. Thus I have called this justice from the top down . . . .

Consequently, the consent of the rights holder to be legally obligated[121] is the moral component that distinguishes valid from invalid transfers of alienable rights in a system of entitlements.[122] It is not altogether novel to suggest that consent is at the heart of contract law,[123] although the claim that contractual obligation arises from a consent to a transfer of entitlements and is thereby dependent on a theory of entitlements is not widely acknowledged.[124] Yet it is certainly a com-

---

Id. at 112. For an example of the "top down" conception of justice applied to contract law, see Kronman, infra note 124.

121. Unlike "will" or "intent," the word "consent" can be used either subjectively to describe a state of mind or objectively to describe an interrelational act. Webster's New World Dictionary of the American language (1970) offers in part this definition:

> consent, *vi.*, . . . 1.*a*) to agree (*to* do something) *b*) give permission, approval, or assent (*to* something proposed or requested) 2. [Obs.] to agree in opinion—
> *n.* 1. permission, approval; or assent 2. agreement in opinion or sentiment [by common *consent*]

Id. at 302. Note that the first meaning for both the verb and the noun concerns an objective act, while the second meaning concerns a state of mind. The name "consent theory of contract" plays upon the objective-subjective ambiguity of "consent." While the focus of a consent theory may sometimes shift from objective to subjective consent, see infra notes 154–61 and accompanying text, the title is still apt, since even when operating at the objective level, the theory is concerned with the manifestation *of consent* and not a manifestation of some other intention. For clarity, "assent" will be used here to mean a subjective intent to be legally bound, and "consent" will generally be used to mean an objectively manifested intent to be legally bound, see infra notes 133–53 and accompanying text.

122. See Demsetz, supra note 44, at 62 ("A private property right system requires the prior consent of 'owners' before their property can be affected by others.").

123. See P. Atiyah, Promises, Morals, and Law 177 (1981) ("[P]romising may be reducible to a species of consent, for consent is a broader and perhaps more basic source of obligation."); Green, Is an Offer Always a Promise?, 23 Ill. L. Rev. 95, 95 (1928) ("[W]hen we are sophisticated enough to have ideas of ownership, societal or legal, ideas of right, as distinguished from ideas about situations of fact, an offer to sell may simply be an expression of consent or volition that ownership shall pass if and when the offer is accepted . . . .").

If promising is but a special instance of consent, it may well be that the traditional conception of contracts as *exclusively* concerning the matter of enforceable promises is what has blinded the profession to the more fundamental theoretical role of consent. For an example of the typical modern insistence on the promisory nature of contracts, see E. Farnsworth, supra note 13:

> The second limitation suggested by this definition is that the law of contracts is confined to *promises*. It is therefore concerned with exchanges that relate to the *future* because a "promise" is a commitment by a person as to his future behavior. Examples of exchanges that do not include such a commitment (and so do not involve a contract in this sense) are the transaction of barter . . . and the present (or "cash") sale . . . . Because no promise is given in either of these exchanges, there is no contract.

Id. § 1.1, at 4 (emphasis in original) (citations omitted). Because a consent theory embraces more than the enforcement of promises, the most appropriate terms to describe contracting parties might be "transferor" and "transferee." For convenience, however, the more conventional terms promisor and promisee will still occasionally be used here.

124. But see Cheung, supra note 33, at 23 ("The transactions conducted in the market place entail outright or partial transfers of property rights among individual con-

monly held and plausible conception of ownership that owning resources gives one the right to possess, use, and dispose of them free from the use or threat of force by others.[125]

In a modern society the chain between initial acquisition of resources and their ultimate consumption can be quite long and complicated. While controversies may exist, even among those who acknowledge the legitimacy of property rights in principle, about the proper mode of resource acquisition[126] and the proper manner of resource use,[127] a valid transfer of rights must be conditioned on some act of the rights holder. The allocative function that an entitlements theory is devised, in part, to fulfill suggests that the way rights are transferred is by consent.[128]

In sum, legal enforcement is morally justified because the promisor voluntarily performed acts that conveyed her intention to create a legally enforceable obligation by transferring alienable rights. Within an entitlements approach, contractual obligation, as distinct from other types of legal obligation, is based on that consent.

B. *Defining Consent*

1. *Consent and the Objective Theory of Contract.* — At first blush, a consent theory of contract may appear to some to be a version of a will theory. Understanding the fundamental differences between the two approaches, therefore, will assist an appreciation of the comparative virtues of the consent theory.

A will theory bases contractual obligation on the fact that an obligation was freely assumed. As was shown in Part I, a theory that bases

---

tracting parties."); Evers, Toward a Reformulation of the Law of Contracts, 1 J. Libertarian Stud. 3 (1977) (describing a "title-transfer theory" of contract based on property rights); Kronman, Contract Law and Distributive Justice, 89 Yale L.J. 472, 472 (1980) (Contracts "provide for the exchange of property."); Macneil, Relational Contract: What We Do and Do Not Know, 1985 Wis. L. Rev. 483, 523 ("[E]xchange relations . . . presuppose some idea of property . . . ."). For a recent attempt to employ the concept of property to explain the law of restitution and some issues of contract damages, see Friedmann, supra note 97.

125. See, e.g., Kronman, supra note 124, at 472. This idea is not a new one. See T. Aquinas, Summa Theologica, reprinted in 20 Great Books of the Western World 311 (1952) ("[T]he power of private persons is exercised over the things they possess, and consequently their dealings with one another as regards such things depend on their own will, for instance in buying, selling, giving and so forth.").

126. See, e.g., L. Becker, Property Rights: Philosophic Foundations 32–56 (1977) (critically assessing the labor theory of property acquisition); Epstein, Possession as the Root of Title, 13 Ga. L. Rev. 1221 (1979) (defending "first possession" as the means of acquiring property); Rose, supra note 115 (distinguishing the labor, consent, and first possession theories of property acquisition and discussing their respective merits).

127. See generally Coleman, Moral Theories of Torts: Their Scope and Limits. Part I, 1 Law & Phil. 371 (1982) (assessing competing moral theories of torts); Coleman, Moral Theories of Torts: Their Scope and Limits. Part II, 2 Law & Phil. 5 (1983) (same).

128. But see supra note 113.

contractual obligation on the existence of a "will to be bound" is hard pressed to justify contractual obligation in the absence of an actual exercise of the will. It is difficult to see why one is legally or morally committed to perform an agreement that one did not actually intend to commit oneself to and still hew to a theory that based the commitment on its willful quality. This subjective component creates a tension between a will theory and the inescapable need of individuals in society and those trying to administer a coherent legal system to rely on appearances—to rely on an individual's behavior that apparently manifests their assent[129] to a transfer of entitlements.

In contrast to a will theory, a consent theory's recognition of the dependence of contractual obligation on a rights analysis is able to account for the normal objective-subjective relationship in contract law. The concept of rights or entitlements is a social one whose principal function is to specify boundaries within which individuals may operate freely to pursue their respective individual ends and thereby provide the basis for cooperative interpersonal activity. Lawyers tend to concentrate on the function entitlements notions play in specifying the proper remedies for wrongful conduct, but given the uncertain justice of *any* legal remedy,[130] a vital function of a system of well-defined entitlements is the avoidance of disputes. And, while it is not unusual to discuss avoiding disputes by raising the cost of misconduct and thereby deterring "bad" persons,[131] it is frequently overlooked that an entitlements view must take a "good man" view of law at least as seriously as it does a "bad man" view.[132]

The boundaries of individual discretion that are defined by a sys-

---

129. See supra note 121.

130. Cf. Barnett, Resolving the Dilemma of the Exclusionary Rule: An Application of Restitutive Principles of Justice, 32 Emory L.J. 937, 979 (1983) ("One of the tragedies of justice is the necessity of objectifying the worth of subjectively valued rights, when rights are expropriated and not bargained for.").

131. The "bad man" view of law was made famous by Justice Holmes:

> If you want to know the law and nothing else, you must look at it as a bad man, who cares only for the material consequences which such knowledge enables him to predict, not as a good one, who finds his reasons for conduct, whether inside the law or outside of it, in the vaguer sanctions of conscience.

Holmes, The Path of the Law, 10 Harv. L. Rev. 457, 459 (1897). For commentators who employ a "bad man" view, see R. Posner, supra note 30, at 164–72; Becker, Crime and Punishment: An Economic Approach, 76 J. Pol. Econ. 169 (1968).

132. By focusing exclusively on the sanctions imposed for illegal conduct, a "bad man" view underestimates the epistemological function of general principles and rules of law. Properly crafted rules and principles supply vital information to "good" persons (and their legal counsel) who seek to avoid violating the rights of others without regard to the severity of the penalties that may attach to such conduct. See H.L.A. Hart, supra note 85, at 86–88 (distinguishing the "internal" from the "external" aspect of obligatory rules); F. Hayek, 1 Law, Legislation and Liberty 35–123 (1973) (describing the role of rules in creating and preserving a "spontaneous order" of human interaction); Hegland, Goodbye to Deconstruction, 58 S. Cal. L. Rev. 1203 (1985) (defending use of rules and principles against recent deconstructionist criticisms).

tem of clear entitlements serve to allocate decision-making authority among individuals. Vital information is thereby conveyed to all those who might wish to avoid disputes and respect the rights of others, provided they know what those rights are.[133] Potential conflicts between persons who might otherwise vie for control of a given resource are thus avoided. Therefore, an entitlements theory demands that the boundaries of protected domains be ascertainable, not only by judges who must resolve disputes that have arisen, but, perhaps more importantly, by the affected persons themselves before any dispute occurs.

In contract law, this informational or "boundary defining" requirement means that an assent to alienate rights must be *manifested* in some manner by one party to the other to serve as a criterion of enforcement. Without a manifestation of assent that is accessible to all affected parties, that aspect of a system of entitlements that governs transfers of rights will fail to achieve its main function. At the time of the transaction, it will have failed to identify clearly and communicate to both parties (and to third parties) the rightful boundaries that must be respected. Without such communication, parties to a transaction (and third parties) cannot accurately ascertain what constitutes rightful conduct and what constitutes a commitment on which they can rely. Disputes that might otherwise have been avoided will occur, and the attendant uncertainties of the transfer process will discourage reliance.

While this imperative of a system of entitlements may initially strike some as ad hoc, we react this way only because we are not used to thinking of contractual obligation as arising from the transfer of rights. The relationship between legal rules and entitlements theory is better understood in the realm of property law, where the boundary defining function of rights also necessitates an objective approach. No serious theory would suggest that persons initially acquire rights to (unowned) resources simply because they subjectively believe they have done so. Rather, rights to unowned objects are acquired by performing some demonstrable and meaningful act with respect to those objects. Depending on the theory of acquisition that is held and the conventions that are adopted, the act required might be possessing or staking out the resource, transforming it, or filing a claim to it with a claims office.[134] Each of these conventions objectively manifests ownership over a previously unowned or abandoned resource by conveying to others an unmistakeable claim to possess, control, and utilize the resource.[135]

133. See, e.g., Rose, supra note 115, at 78–79 ("Possession now begins to look even more like something that requires a kind of communication, and the original claim to the property looks like a kind of speech, with the audience composed of all others who might be interested in claiming the object in question.").

134. See, e.g., Baird & Jackson, supra note 108, at 301–11 (discussing the advantages and disadvantages of various conventions used to record and transfer interests in real and personal property).

135. See Rose, supra note 115, at 77 ("The clear-act principle suggests that the common law defines acts of possession as some kind of *statement*. As Blackstone said, the

The analysis for contract law is similar. Requiring the consent of the rights holder as a condition of a valid transfer of rights is absolutely vital to a regime of entitlements for the reasons discussed above.[136] But, whether one has consented to a transfer of rights under such a regime generally depends not on one's subjective opinion about the meaning of one's freely chosen words or conduct, but on the ordinary meaning that is attached to them. Language itself—the way that assent to a transfer is manifested—is as much a convention as those conventions governing rights acquisitions. If the word "yes" ordinarily means *yes*, then a subjective and unrevealed belief that "yes" means *no* is generally immaterial to a regime of entitlements allocation. Only a general reliance on objectively ascertainable assertive conduct will enable a system of entitlements to perform its allotted boundary-defining function.

Further, a legal theory that attempted to rest the rightful acquisition, use, or transfer of resources solely on subjective intentions could not provide a coherent set of rights or entitlements. There is nothing to prevent subjective intentions from conflicting with one another. Therefore, to the extent a theory attempts to derive rights from such intentions, it would produce "rights" that were necessarily in irreconcilable conflict with each other. Such a theory would then need to appeal to still other principles to resolve these conflicting claims of "rights," but any such appeal would mean that this type of legal theory was not a theory of rights at all.[137]

The function of a rights theory is to define the boundaries of permitted human action[138] and resolve competing claims.[139] A coherent rights theory will, therefore, allocate rights largely on the basis of fac-

---

acts must be a *declaration* of one's intent to appropriate." (citation omitted)). But cf. Helmholz, Adverse Possession and Subjective Intent, 61 Wash. U.L.Q. 331, 357 (1983) (Courts "regularly award title to the good faith trespasser, where they will not award it to the trespasser who knows what he is doing at the time he enters the land in dispute."). The tendency in the doctrine of adverse possession discussed by Helmholz may be analogous to those circumstances in a consent theory of contract, discussed infra notes 154–60 and accompanying text, where the presumptive significance of objective assent may be overcome by proof of the subjective understanding of the promisee.

136. See supra notes 109–28 and accompanying text.

137. That under a rights theory rights must be reconcilable is mentioned by R. Nozick, supra note 67, at 166 ("Individual rights are co-possible; each person may exercise his rights as he chooses."), and elaborated in Steiner, The Structure of a Set of Compossible Rights, 74 J. Phil. 767 (1977) (describing the logical requirement that a system of rights entails the compatible exercise—or "compossibility"—of designated rights). On the role that this formal requirement plays in the formulation of substantive rights, see Barnett, Pursuing Justice, supra note 107, at 58, 60.

138. See supra notes 93–94 and accompanying text.

139. Cf. J. Feinberg, supra note 99, at 152 ("[N]ot all claims put forward as valid really are valid; and only the valid ones can be acknowledged as rights."); id. at 155 ("To have a right is to have a claim against someone whose recognition as valid is called for by some set of governing rules or moral principles."); Steiner, supra note 137, at 768 ("Someone called upon to adjudicate between two persons whose actions are mutually obstructive and each of whom is able to show that his own action falls within the range

tors that minimize the likelihood of generating conflicting claims. In this regard, objectively manifested conduct, which usually reflects subjective intent, provides a far sounder basis for contractual obligation than do subjectively held intentions. Evidence of subjective intent that is extrinsic to the transaction and was unavailable to the other party is relevant, if at all, only insofar as it helps a court to ascertain the "objective" meaning of certain terms.[140]

What exact meaning must a court conclude was conveyed by a promisor to a promisee to find that a contractual commitment was incurred? If consent is properly thought of as "objective" or "manifested" assent, what is it that must be assented to for a contractual obligation to arise? It is not enough that one manifests a commitment or promises to perform or refrain from doing some act. Such a manifestation would be nothing more than a promise.[141] Contract theory searches for the "extra" factor that, if present, justifies the legal enforcement of a commitment or promise.

An entitlements theory specifies that consent to a transfer of rights is this factor.[142] The consent that is required is a *manifestation of an intention to alienate rights*.[143] In a system of entitlements where manifested rights transfers are what justify the legal enforcement of agreements, any such manifestation necessarily implies that one intends to be "legally bound," to adhere to one's commitment. Therefore, the phrase "a manifestation of an intention to be legally bound"[144] neatly captures what a court should seek to find before holding that a contractual obligation has been created.[145]

Charles Fried maintains that a promisor incurs a moral obligation

---

denoted by a claimed right, will . . . conclude that at least one of these two claimed rights is invalid.").

140. See, e.g., Kabil Dev. Corp. v. Mignot, 279 Or. 151, 157–58, 566 P.2d 505, 508–09 (1977) (discussed in Eisenberg, The Responsive Model of Contract Law, 36 Stan. L. Rev. 1107, 1119 n.36 (1984)).

141. See, e.g., Restatement (Second) of Contracts § 2 (1979) ("A promise is a manifestation of intention to act or refrain from acting in a specified way, so made as to justify a promisee in understanding that a commitment has been made.").

142. See supra notes 117–128 and accompanying text.

143. Such a manifestation of intention to alienate rights can be direct or indirect. The object of a direct rights transfer contract is to transfer alienable rights—for example, rights to external possessions. The object of an indirect rights transfer contract is to assure that someone else will exercise her inalienable rights—for example, the right to one's labor—in a particular way by requiring a transfer of alienable rights (for example, money damages) if there is no performance. See supra note 99; infra note 218; cf. Green, supra note 123, at 95 (distinguishing between a "self-executing offer" and "an offer to do or refrain from doing something").

144. Cf. Green, Is an Offer Always a Promise?, 23 Ill. L. Rev. 301, 302 (1928) (using the phrase, "an expression of will or consent to be answerable"); Lorenzen, Causa and Consideration in the Law of Contracts, 28 Yale L.J. 621, 646 (1919) ("Agreements which are physically possible and legally permissible should, on principle, be enforceable . . . if it was the intention of the parties to assume *legal* relations.").

145. Of course, a further requirement of contractual obligation in a system of enti-

because she intentionally invokes a social convention whose purpose is to cause others to expect the promised performance.[146] By contrast, a consent theory specifies that a promisor incurs a contractual obligation the legal enforcement of which is morally justifiable by manifesting assent to legal enforcement and thereby invoking the institution of contract. In the circumstances described by Fried, a promisor may have a moral obligation to do what she promised. Without more she would not have a legal obligation and a promisee would not have a legal right to performance.[147] She incurs a contractual obligation to perform only when she manifests to a promisee her intention to be legally bound. The basis of contractual obligation is not promising per se. The basis of contract is consent.

It is not paradoxical to adhere to an "objective" notion of consent that is based on just those ordinary words and deeds of persons that are commonly understood to reflect their subjective assent to be legally bound, notwithstanding that they may not have in fact meant to convey the commonly understood meaning.[148] A consent analysis is genuinely interested in the actual intentions of the parties, but we never have direct access to another individual's subjective mental state. We thus must always learn the meaning of terms by comparing (1) the conduct of persons with their words, or (2) their conduct and words in one context with those in another, or (3) one person's conduct and words with another person's conduct and words.[149] Even in a subjective theory, evidence of subjective assent must be manifested at some point—if only from the witness stand or in self-serving documents.

Therefore, the only difference in the treatment of evidence of subjective intent between subjective and objective approaches to contract concerns evidence of subjective intent that is *extrinsic* to the transaction. At the time of formation, such extrinsic evidence is unavailable to the other party who witnesses what did or did not appear to be an assent to a transfer of rights. Since, by definition, this information is unavailable to the other party at the time assent is manifested, its later use by a court (following a subjective approach) defeats the function that consent performs in clearly defining and communicating the boundaries of rightful conduct *at the time of the transaction*.[150] A truly subjective ap-

---

titlements is that the rights transferred be valid and alienable. See supra notes 99–100 and accompanying text.

146. See C. Fried, supra note 8, at 16.

147. Cf. 1 A. Corbin, supra note 1, § 110, at 490 ("To be enforceable, the promise must be accompanied by some other factor.").

148. Similarly, it is not considered paradoxical that the criminal legal system generally refuses to allow jury verdicts to be impeached by evidence of innocence not presented at trial.

149. This list may not be exhaustive.

150. Although a promisee may rightfully rely on the objective manifestation, if she does not in fact rely on this manifestation it would not serve the boundary defining purpose to enforce it. See infra notes 156–60 and accompanying text.

proach to contractual intent would admit this evidence and an objective one would exclude it.

The fact that objective consent generally takes precedence over subjective assent does not jeopardize the liberty interest that rights have been formulated to protect. No one suggests that an objective approach to either rights acquisition or resource use is inconsistent with the liberty interest that the scheme of private rights was intended to serve. Rather, these approaches to rights acquisition and resource use are favored precisely because they respect and protect the rights and liberty interests *of others*, whose plans and expectations would be severely limited if they were not entitled to rely on things as they appear to be and to take the assertive conduct of others at face value.[151]

The same is true in contract law. Volitional acts—words or deeds—that manifest assent to transfer entitlements presumptively bind the actor regardless of subjective intent. This "strict liability" theory of contract is appealing precisely because it too recognizes the legitimate rights and liberty interests in others.[152] Lon Fuller noted over forty years ago that a law of contract which seeks to secure a realm of private autonomy has a "bipartisan" quality and that this quality gives rise to an objective theory of contract.[153]

In a consent theory, then, contracts are interpreted with an eye

---

151. A correlative notion is the concept of legal as opposed to actual notice. Cf. 3 J. Pomeroy, Equity Jurisprudence § 842, at 292 (5th ed. Symons 1941) ("If ignorance of the law were generally allowed to be pleaded, there could be no security in legal rights, no certainty in judicial investigations, no finality in litigations." (footnote omitted)).

152. Cf. Epstein, A Theory of Strict Liability, 2 J. Legal Stud. 151, 168–69 (1973):

> The doctrine of strict liability holds that proof that the defendant caused harm creates [a] . . . presumption [in favor of the plaintiff] because [under the doctrine of strict liability] proof of the nonreciprocal source of the harm is sufficient to upset the balance where one person must win and the other must lose. There is no room to consider, as part of the prima facie case, allegations that the defendant intended to harm the plaintiff, or could have avoided the harm he caused by the use of reasonable care. The choice is plaintiff or defendant . . . .

153. In distinguishing his concept of "private autonomy" from a will theory, Fuller observed that:

> The principle of private autonomy, properly understood, is in no way inconsistent with an 'objective' interpretation of contracts. Indeed, we may go farther and say that the so-called objective theory of interpretation in its more extreme applications becomes understandable only in terms of the principle of private autonomy. . . . [This theory] rests upon the need for promoting the security of transactions. Yet security of transactions presupposes "transactions," in other words, acts of private parties which have a law-making and right-altering function.

Fuller, Consideration and Form, 41 Colum. L. Rev. 799, 808 (1941). Of course, the security of transactions is just one among many functions performed by the institution of rights. See also Raz, Book Review, 95 Harv. L. Rev. 916, 936 (1982):

> The objective test of contract formation is not an embarrassment to the view that the purpose of contract law is to support the practice of undertaking voluntary obligations. On the contrary, it is required by it. Paradoxical though it

towards honoring the actual intentions of the parties. But where the subjective intentions of one party have not been manifested to the other, only the "reasonable" or objective interpretation of the commitment will establish the clear boundaries required by an entitlements approach.

There is nothing novel or revolutionary about contract law's concern for the protection of reliance by promisees. One of the most important functions of the institution of property rights is to legally protect certain expectations of the rights holder so that she may rely on the continued use of certain resources. For example, an owner of real property relies upon her title when she invests in building a house or a factory upon it, because she expects that her title will be honored by a legal system in the future. She also relies upon her title when she leaves town on vacation, expecting her property to still be hers when she returns.

In a consent theory, reliance on the words or deeds of another is "justified" only (1) when and to the extent that such words or deeds have a commonly understood meaning within the relevant context or when a special meaning can be shown to have been understood by both parties to this transaction, and (2) when this meaning indicates a consent to transfer legitimately acquired and alienable rights. The hard work facing any legal system based on entitlements includes determining what constitutes "valid" title and what acts constitute "consent." Only when these concepts are properly defined can we "expect" the legal system to act in a predictable enough manner to make our reliance "reasonable" or "justified."

2. *The Proper Limits of the Objective Approach.* — A consent theory also explains the limits of the objective approach—why the objective interpretation of a party's acts will yield, at times, to proof of a different subjective understanding of one or both parties.[154]

To find the presence of consent, what matters is the meaning that is generally attached to some given word or conduct indicating assent—a meaning to which both parties have access. In contract law, this generalized meaning therefore becomes the *presumptive* meaning.[155] The presumption can be rebutted, not by reference to the promisor's subjective intent in performing the consenting acts, but either by proof of any special meaning that the parties' behavior reveals they held *in common*, thereby negating the social function of accepting the generalized

sounds, it is in order to protect the practice from abuse and debasement that the law recognizes the validity of contracts that are not voluntary obligations.

154. See Eisenberg, supra note 140, at 1117-27 (discussing what limits should properly be placed on the applicability of the objective approach).

155. See Restatement (Second) of Contracts § 201 comment a (1979) ("Words are used as conventional symbols of mental states, with standardized meanings based on habitual or customary practice. Unless a different intention is shown, language is interpreted in accordance with its generally prevailing meaning.").

meaning,[156] or by the promisor's proof that the listener did not actually understand the "reasonable" meaning to be the intended meaning.[157] A promisee is not "justified" in relying on the ordinary meaning of a promisor's words or deeds where a special meaning can be proved to have been actually understood by both parties. Similarly, the enforcement of the "reasonable" meaning serves no constructive purpose where it was not the promisee's actual understanding.[158] The boundary-determining function[159] of a rights analysis simply does not require that such reliance be protected or such a meaning enforced.[160]

This also explains why the misuse of a particular term by party *A* who was unaware of its ordinary meaning would not bind *A* if it could be shown that *B*, the other party, was made aware of this mistake by the circumstances of the transaction.[161] Proof of this occurrence would show that the normal boundary-defining function of an objective approach designed to protect parties in *B*'s position had been satisfied by *B*'s actual knowledge of *A*'s meaning. A consent theory, therefore, explains both why parties are free to shift away from the ordinary meanings of words or deeds either intentionally or inadvertently, and why, if a shift by both cannot be shown, the ordinary or "objective" meaning will govern.

Persons generally use conventional words and actions to convey their intentions with a considerable degree of accuracy. Because of this, the outcomes of cases decided by an objective approach based

---

156. See, e.g., Weinberg v. Edelstein, 201 Misc. 343, 345, 110 N.Y.S.2d 806, 808 (Sup. Ct. 1952) (A court cannot "rely upon naked dictionary definitions" but must determine meaning according to "the practices and customs of the trade."); Restatement (Second) of Contracts § 201 comment a (1979). But cf. id. § 201 comment c ("But parties who used a standardized term in an unusual sense obviously run the risk that their agreement will be misinterpreted in litigation.").

157. Permitting a promisor to contest whether a promisee had in fact relied upon the objective meaning is quite consistent with the boundary-defining function of contract law in a consent theory. Assuming that a promisor can prove such an allegation, the reliance that the objective approach is designed to protect is nonexistent, and permitting such proof would provide few opportunities for fraud. In this regard a consent theory conforms to the conventional interpretation of the objective theory. See, e.g., Embry v. Hargadine, McKittrick Dry Goods Co., 127 Mo. App. 383, 392, 105 S.W. 777, 780 (1907) (holding that defendant is liable for breach of contract if a reasonable person would have understood him as having accepted plaintiff's offer and plaintiff in fact so understood defendant).

158. See E. Farnsworth, supra note 13, § 7.9, at 483–92.

159. See supra notes 139–40 and accompanying text.

160. Cf. E. Farnsworth, supra note 13, § 7.9, at 484 ("Since a contract involves two parties, however, the search for meaning begins with the meaning attached by both parties to the contract language; each needs the other's assent."); U.C.C. § 1-201(3) (1978) (" 'Agreement' means the bargain of the parties in fact as found in their language or by implication from other circumstances including course of dealing or usage of trade or course of performance as provided in this Act.").

161. See, e.g., Restatement (Second) of Contracts § 153 (1979) (specifying when mistake of one party makes a contract voidable).

upon the ordinary and natural meaning of words and other assertive conduct will differ from those decided by a subjective approach only in unusual circumstances. Most cases would come out the same in either event. But unlike a will theory, a consent theory, because it is based on fundamental notions of entitlements, can explain both why we generally enforce the objective manifestation of consent when it differs from subjective intent and the exceptions where evidence of subjective intent will prevail.

C. *Determining Contractual Obligation in a Consent Theory*

1. *The Presumptive Nature of Consent.* — Richard Epstein has suggested that legal principles used to determine obligation can best be thought of as presumptive in nature.[162] That is, legal principles which attempt to describe in a general fashion what obligations will result from certain actions ought not to be applied in an "absolute" fashion. Rather, legal principles ought to state a "prima facie case" of legal obligation that describes the normal or presumptive connection between specified acts and their legal consequences.[163] Any such presumption of obligation, however, may be "rebutted" if other facts are proved to have existed that are generally recognized by a legal system as undermining the normal significance of the prima facie case. Such responses or "defenses" to the prima facie case are themselves only presumptively compelling. They in turn may be rebutted by still other facts alleged by the person seeking relief. In this way the principles or elements that determine legal obligation come in "stages."[164]

In a consent theory, absent the assertion of a valid defense, proof of consent to a transfer of alienable rights (plus breach) is legally sufficient to obtain a judgment for breach of contract. Consent is prima facie binding because of its usual connection with subjective assent (thereby protecting the private autonomy of the promisor) and because people usually have access only to the manifested intentions of others

162. See Epstein, Pleadings and Presumptions, 40 U. Chi. L. Rev. 556 (1973) (describing the operation of staged pleadings in legal analysis); cf. Eisenberg, supra note 1, at 641 ("Putting the problem in the language of civil procedure, the principles that address the enforceability of promises should determine whether breach of a given type of promise gives rise to a legal complaint. Issues concerning the quality of individual promises should then be matters of defense.").

163. An approach that constructs presumptively applicable legal rules—the prima facie case—based on "normal" circumstances and then allows certain defenses based on "abnormal" circumstances that undercut the appropriateness of the prima facie case would serve to minimize (though perhaps not entirely eliminate) the problem of the "open texture" of general rules that was noted supra note 85 and accompanying text.

164. Cf. Epstein, Defenses and Subsequent Pleas in a System of Strict Liability, 3 J. Legal Stud. 165 (1974) (offering an expanded description of those circumstances that rebut the normal presumption embodied in the prima facie case of tort that persons will be held strictly liable for the injuries they cause); Epstein, supra note 152, at 166–74 (having volitionally caused harm to another, *A* is prima facie liable for the injury, but, if *A* successfully pleads a valid defense, *B* may not be entitled to a judgment).

(thereby protecting the reliance interest of the promisee and others as well as the "security of transactions"). The next two sections will discuss the prima facie case of consent and the role that defenses to consent play in a consent theory.

2. *Establishing the Prima Facie Case of Consent.* — There are two ways to manifest one's intention to be legally bound. The first is to deliberately "channel" one's behavior through the use of a legal formality[165] in such a way as to explicitly convey a certain meaning—that of having an intention to be legally bound—to another. This is the formal means of consenting. The second is by indirectly or implicitly conveying this meaning by other types of behavior. This is the informal means of consenting.

a. *Formal Consent.* — For a considerable part of the history of the common law, the principal way of creating what we now think of as a contractual obligation was to cast one's agreement in the form of a sealed writing.[166] Actions based on informal promises were subject to the defense of wager, and this seriously undermined a promisee's ability to obtain enforcement.[167] The rise of the action of assumpsit can be understood as the way common law judges responded to competitive pressures[168] to escape this (and other) procedural barriers to the enforcement of informal promises.

As was noted above,[169] however, the emergence of assumpsit as the principal action of contractual enforcement required the development of a doctrinal limitation on the enforcement of commitments—that is, the doctrine of consideration.[170] This development eventually resulted in the ascendancy of the bargain theory of consideration, which had the unintended consequence of creating doctrinal problems for the enforcement of formal commitments where there was no bargained-for consideration. Notwithstanding their ancient history, formal commitments, such as those under seal, came to be thought of as "exceptions" to the "normal" requirement of consideration. Expressions such as "a seal imports consideration" or is "a substitute for consideration" became commonplace.[171]

---

165. See Fuller, supra note 153, at 801 (The use of legal formality "offers a legal framework into which the party may fit his actions, or, to change the figure, it offers channels for the legally effective expression of intention.").

166. See A. Simpson, supra note 75, at 88–90.

167. Id. at 137–44.

168. See Helmholz, Assumpsit and *Fidei Laesio*, 91 Law Q. Rev. 406 (1975) (describing the competition between the common law courts and the ecclesiastical courts in the enforcement of informal promises).

169. See supra notes 73–75 and accompanying text.

170. The Statute of Frauds, passed in 1677, was another such limitation. See A. Simpson, supra note 75, at 599–600.

171. See, e.g., In re Conrad's Estate, 333 Pa. 561, 563, 3 A.2d 697, 699 (1938); Aller v. Aller, 40 N.J.L. 446 (1878); cf. Crane, The Magic of the Private Seal, 15 Colum. L. Rev. 24, 25–26 (1915) ("The books frequently spoke of a seal as implying a considera-

Despite such cases and restatements,[172] formal promises have had an uncertain place in the law of contract[173] because they lacked a theoretical underpinning. In a climate of opinion dominated by notions of "bargain" and "induced reliance," where there is no bargain and no demonstrable reliance to support enforcement, the presence of a meaningful formality may not be enough to satisfy a court.[174] Not even the renowned contract writings of Lon Fuller[175] were able to change the formal contract's orphan status.

A consent theory of contract, however, provides the missing theoretical foundation of formal contracts and explains their proper place in a well-crafted law of contract. The voluntary use of a recognized formality by a promisor manifests to a promisee an intention to be legally bound in as unambiguous a manner as possible. As one court noted:

> If a party has fully and absolutely expressed his intention in a writing sealed and delivered, with the most solemn sanction known to our law, what should prevent its execution where there is no fraud or illegality?[176]

Formal contracts ought to be an "easy" case of contractual enforcement, but prevailing theories that require bargained-for consideration, induced reliance, or even economic "efficiency" would have a hard time explaining why.[177] In a consent theory, by contrast, there need be no

---

tion; but the correct statement of the rule is that a sealed instrument required no consideration." (footnote omitted)).

172. See, e.g., Restatement (Second) of Contracts § 95 (1979) (specifying conditions necessary for a sealed writing to be binding without consideration).

173. See C. Fried, supra note 8, at 28–29 ("[T]he trend away from the seal as an anachronistic relic and the narrow, episodic nature of the statutory exceptions leaves the doctrine of consideration as very much the norm.").

174. It is difficult to determine how much of this decline is due to theoretical reasons and how much is due to the uncertain significance of certain formalities claimed to constitute seals. Compare Chancellor Kent's opinion in Warren v. Lynch, 5 Johns. 239, 245–46 (N.Y. 1810) ("A scrawl with a pen is not a seal, and deserves no notice . . . . The calling a paper a deed will not make it one, if it want the requisite formalities . . . . The policy of the rule consists in giving ceremony and solemnity to the execution of important instruments, by means of which the attention of the parties is more certainly and effectually fixed, and frauds less likely to be practiced upon the unwary.") with 1892 N.Y. Laws, ch. 677 § 13 ("The private seal of a person . . . to any instrument or writing shall consist of . . . the word 'seal,' or the letters 'L.S.,' opposite the signature."). See also Eisenberg, supra note 1, at 660 (describing the erosion of "the elements of ritual and personification"); Fuller, supra note 153, at 823 (questioning "whether with our present-day routinized and institutionalized ways of doing business a 'blanket formality' can achieve the desiderata which form is intended to achieve.").

175. See Fuller, supra note 153, at 822–23 ("The desiderata underlying the use of formalities will retain their relevance as long as men make promises to one another.").

176. Aller v. Aller, 40 N.J.L. 446, 451 (1878); see also Handbook of the National Conference of Commissioners on Uniform State Laws and Proceedings 194 (1925) ("I don't see why a man should not be able to make himself liable if he wishes to do so." (statement of S. Williston)).

177. For example, when there is no separate consideration for making an offer irrevocable for a certain period of time, a bargain theory of consideration would have a

underlying bargain or demonstrable reliance for such a commitment to be properly enforced.

The same holds true—as Lon Fuller again recognized—for nominal consideration and for false recitals of consideration.[178] A consent theory acknowledges that, if properly evidenced, a recital by the parties that "consideration" exists may fulfill the channeling function of formalities, whether or not any bargained-for consideration for the commitment in fact exists. If it is widely known that the written phrase "in return for good and valuable consideration" means that one intends to make a legally binding commitment, then these words will fulfill a channeling function as well as, and perhaps better than, a seal or other formality.[179] The current rule that the falsity of such a statement permits a court to nullify a transaction because of a lack of consideration[180] is therefore contrary to a consent theory of contract.[181]

b. *Informal Consent.* — Consent to transfer rights can be express or implied. Formal contracts expressing consent to transfer alienable rights pose no problem for a consent theory. The enforcement of informal commitments where evidence of legally binding intentions is more obscure, however, has plagued contract law for centuries.[182] In such agreements courts must infer assent to be legally bound from the circumstances or the "considerations"[183] or "causa"[184] that induced the parties' actions.

---

difficult time explaining the enforceability of such "firm offers" as are recognized by U.C.C. § 2-205 (1977), which requires neither consideration nor detrimental reliance for enforcement to be obtained.

178. See Fuller, supra note 153, at 820 ("The proper ground for upholding these decisions would seem to be that the desiderata underlying the use of formalities are here satisfied by the fact that the parties have taken the trouble to cast their transaction in the form of an exchange.").

179. See Eisenberg, supra note 1, at 660–61 ("[I]t can be safely assumed that parties who falsely cast a nonbargain promise as a bargain do so for the express purpose of making the promise legally enforceable.").

180. See Restatement (Second) of Contracts § 71 comment b (1979); see, e.g., Schnell v. Nell, 17 Ind. 29, 32 (1861) ("The consideration of one cent is, plainly, in this case, merely nominal, and intended to be so."); Shepard v. Rhodes, 7 R.I. 470, 475 (1863) (Consideration of one dollar was "a mere *nominal* consideration." (emphasis in original)).

181. But see Restatement (Second) of Contracts § 87(1)(a) (1979) (qualifying the prohibition of § 71 to permit recitals of purported consideration to render a "firm" offer enforceable as an option contract).

182. See Lorenzen, supra note 144, at 646 (criticizing limits placed by Anglo-American law on ways in which "intent to assume an obligation" can be shown).

183. On this archaic usage of the word "consideration," see A. Simpson, supra note 75, at 321 ("Pleadings in assumpsit had always included matters of inducement.").

184. For the possible parallels between consideration and the civilian concept of "causa," see Mason, The Utility of Consideration—A Comparative View, 41 Colum. L. Rev. 825, 825–31 (1941); cf. Lorenzen, supra note 144, at 646 ("There is in reality no definable 'doctrine' of *causa*.").

(i) *Bargaining as Evidence of Consent.* — Within a consent theory, bargained-for consideration would perform a channelling role.[185] The fact that a person has received something of value in return for a "promise" may indeed indicate that this promise was an expression of intention to transfer rights.[186] Moreover, in some circumstances where gratuitous transfers are unusual, the receipt of a benefit in return for a promise should serve as objective notice to the promisor that the promise has been interpreted by the other party to be legally binding.[187]

Although the existence of a bargain or other motivation for a transaction may be good evidence of the sort of agreement that has been made, in a consent theory the absence of consideration does not preclude the application of legal sanctions if other indicia of consent are present. To return to the examples given by Fried,[188] if it can be proved that a party voluntarily consented to be legally bound to keep an offer to transfer rights open, to release a debt, to modify an obligation, or to pay for past favors, these commitments are enforceable (provided that other contract requirements such as acceptance are met).

Where bargaining is the norm—as it is in most sales transactions—there is little need for the law to require explicit proof of an intent to be legally bound, such as an additional formality,[189] or even proof of the existence of a bargain. In such circumstances, if an arms-length agreement to sell can be proved, there presumptively has been a manifestation of intent to be legally bound. For this reason, the Uniform Commercial Code's stricture that "[a] contract for the sale of goods may be made in any manner sufficient to show agreement, including conduct by both parties which recognizes the existence of such a contract"[190] is entirely consonant with a consent theory.

185. Cf. Restatement (Second) of Contracts § 75 comment a (1979) ("Since the principle that bargains are binding is widely understood and is reinforced in many situations by custom and convention, the fact of bargain . . . tends to satisfy the cautionary and channelling functions of form.").

186. Cf. P. Atiyah, supra note 123, at 184 ("[A] very common justification for treating a promise as binding is that the promise is evidence, is an admission, of the existence of some other obligation already owed by the promisor. By making an explicit promise, the promisor concedes or admits the existence and extent of the preexisting obligation.").

187. The duties, if any, that receipt of a nongratuitous benefit imposes on the recipient are beyond the scope of this Article, except to note that such receipt may manifest the recipient's intent to be legally bound to a contemporaneous commitment.

188. See supra note 77 and accompanying text. Note that in most of these cases formalities adequate to indicate consent were present.

189. See Fuller, supra note 153, at 806 (The channelling function of formality "has no place where men's activities are already divided into definite, clear-cut business categories . . . . It is for this reason that important transactions on the stock and produce markets can safely be carried on in the most 'informal' manner."). Formality might well be required, however, if it were the trade custom or if the transaction was particularly large or unusual in some other respect.

190. U.C.C. § 2-204 (1977).

In a legal system animated by a consent approach, the recognition that "consideration" is only presumptive evidence of consent and that consent can be shown by other means might produce results that correspond remarkably to current practice. To avoid unnecessary confusion and error, however, it is important to understand the theoretical framework.[191]

(ii) *Reliance as Evidence of Consent.* — A consent theory also identifies those circumstances where the presence of reliance provides an adequate substitute for the traditional requirement of consideration. If the primary function of consideration is to serve as one way of manifesting assent to be legally bound, and not as a requirement of a prima facie case of contractual obligation, then asserting the equivalence of reliance and consideration[192] is less problematic. Expenditures made by a promisee in reliance on the words and conduct of the promisor may prove as much about the nature of this transaction as the existence of consideration, especially where the reliance is or should be known to the promisor.[193]

Suppose that *A* makes a substantial promise to *B*—for example, a promise to convey land. The promise is clear, but it is ambiguous as to its intended legal effect. Does *A* intend to be bound and subject to legal enforcement if she reneges, or is she merely stating her current view of her future intentions? Now suppose that *B* announces to *A* his intention to rely on *A*'s promise in a substantial way—for example, by building a house on the land—and that *A* says nothing. Suppose further that *B* commences construction and observes *A* watching in silence. It would seem that under such circumstances *A*'s ambiguous legal intent has been clarified. By remaining silent in the face of reliance so substantial that *B* would not have undertaken it without a legal commitment from *A*—*A* could not reasonably have believed that *B* intended to make a gift to her of the house—*A* has manifested an intention to be legally bound.[194]

In this manner, a promisor's silence while observing substantial reliance on the promise by the promisee can manifest the promisor's as-

---

191. As Fuller, supra note 153, at 824 concludes:

> [A]n original attack on these problems would arrive at some conclusions substantially equivalent to those which result from the doctrine of consideration as now formulated. What needs abolition is not the doctrine of consideration but a conception of the legal method which assumes that the doctrine can be understood and applied without reference to the ends it serves. When we have come again to define consideration in terms of its underlying policies the problem of adapting it to new conditions will largely solve itself.

192. See, e.g., P. Atiyah, supra note 123, at 184–89.

193. See id. at 192–95 (discussing the evidentiary value of reliance on a promise).

194. See, e.g., Greiner v. Greiner, 293 P. 759 (Kan. 1930); Seavey v. Drake, 62 N.H. 393 (1882); Roberts-Horsfield v. Gedicks, 94 N.J. Eq. 82, 118 A. 275 (1922). In each of these cases, the promisor remained silent in the face of substantial reliance on a promise to convey land. The courts granted relief despite the lack of bargained-for consideration.

sent to the promisee.[195] In a consent theory, if consent is proved, then enforcement is warranted even if a bargain or a formality is absent.

As was discussed above,[196] when we seek to discern "reasonable" (or prudent) reliance on a promise, a conclusion cannot be reached that is independent of the perceived enforceability of the promise, which brings us full circle to the question of enforceability with which we started. A theory based only on reliance cannot, therefore, answer this question. By contrast, in a consent theory, reliance is legally protected (and therefore deemed to be justified) only if it is reliance on a manifested intention to be legally bound.[197] Reliance on a commitment that is something less than a manifested intention to be legally bound is not legally protected and is undertaken at the promisee's own risk.

The only assessment of "reasonableness" that is required in a consent theory of contractual obligation is an assessment of the "reasonable," or probable, *meaning* of the promisor's words and conduct. However difficult such an interpretive inquiry into meaning might sometimes be, it is not plagued with the same kind of circularity that attaches to an assessment of "reasonable reliance." Interpretation of meaning in the contractual context is a matter of determining either (a) the usual nonlegal meaning of words, (b) the special meaning of legal terms of art or formalities that have been freely employed by the parties,[198] or (c) some other special meaning jointly understood by the parties.[199] In any event, this is the sort of inquiry all of us routinely engage in every day when we communicate.[200]

By providing a clearer criterion of enforceability *that is available to the parties*, a consent theory encourages informed action. Once the legal standard for contractual enforcement is known to be consent, who is to

195. Cf. McCormick on Evidence § 270, at 799 (3d ed. 1984) ("If a statement is made by another person in the presence of a party to the action, containing assertions of facts which, if untrue, the party would under all circumstances naturally be expected to deny, his failure to speak has traditionally been receivable against him as an admission." (footnote omitted)).

196. See supra notes 20–25 and accompanying text.

197. This is subject to the qualification that courts will enforce subjective agreement where it is proved. See supra note 156 and accompanying text.

198. An ideal formality is an act that is so bizarre that it has no "normal" meaning other than the legal one, so that no "reasonable" person who did not intend the legal effect would ever have performed the act. Lighting a candle and dripping the wax on a document and then impressing in the wax one's seal was an act of a suitably bizarre nature. When a "sealed" document could be executed by preprinting the letters "L.S." after the place for a signature, the act quite obviously lost this character. See supra note 174.

199. This meaning would include any special usages employed within a particular community. See, e.g., Weinberg v. Edelstein, 201 Misc. 343, 345, 110 N.Y.S.2d 806, 808 (Sup. Ct. 1952).

200. See H.L.A. Hart, supra note 85, at 123 ("General terms would be useless to us as a medium of communication unless there were . . . familiar, generally unchallenged cases.").

say what conduct is then "reasonable" or prudent? It may be prudent to rely on a commitment that is known to be unenforceable, given other things that the promisee may know about the promisor, or it may not. This is not for a court to decide. It should by now be clear, however, that a consent theory would identify instances of contractual obligation that a bargain theory would ignore and thereby would better protect and facilitate reliance: one need not have relied on a bargain to be protected in a consent theory.

Once it is determined that reliance is protected because (and therefore when) it is based on consent, a court must still decide *how much* reliance is to be protected—that is, what is the extent of liability for consequences caused by a breach of an admittedly enforceable obligation?[201] The standard approach is to adopt a "foreseeability"[202] assessment of liability that is much the same kind of prudential or predictive judgment that is employed in assessing the existence of reliance-based obligation: what would a promisor have reasonably expected a promisee to have done in reliance on the contract? But much the same problem exists for this issue of liability that was seen above with respect to the issue of obligation.[203] Here, as there, what most persons will do depends on their perception of what the legal rule is concerning the extent of liability, and therefore such a prediction cannot itself determine the legal rule.

Just as a consent theory addresses the problem of obligation by employing the criterion of "consent to obligation," it would handle the problem of extent of liability by employing the criterion of "consent to liability." This is much the same answer as was suggested by Justice Holmes in *Globe Refining Co. v. Landa Cotton Oil Co.*[204] and has been called the "tacit-assent" test.[205]

201. See Eisenberg, supra note 1, at 651 ("[T]he determination of what *kinds* of promises the law should enforce is tightly linked with the *extent* to which various kinds of promises should be enforced." (emphasis in original) (footnote omitted)).

202. See, e.g., Hadley v. Baxendale, 9 Ex. 341, 355, 156 Eng. Rep. 145, 151 (1854).

203. See supra notes 19–25 and accompanying text.

204. 190 U.S. 540, 545 (1903) (knowledge of extent of liability " 'must be brought home to the party sought to be charged, under such circumstances that he *must know* that the person he contracts with reasonably believes that he accepts the contract with the special condition attached to it' " (emphasis added) (quoting British Columbia Saw-Mill Co. v. Nettleship, 3 L.R.-C.P. 499, 509 (1868)); see also Hooks Smelting Co. v. Planters' Compress Co., 72 Ark. 275, 286–87, 79 S.W. 1052, 1056 (1904) (employing tacit assent test); O. Holmes, The Common Law 236–37 (M. Howe ed. 1963) ("[N]otice, even at the time of making the contract, of the special circumstances out of which special damages would arise in case of breach, is not sufficient unless the assumption of that risk is to be taken as having fairly entered into the contract."); C. McCormick, A Handbook on the Law of Damages § 141, at 578–79 (1935) (citing other cases that follow *Globe* in employing a tacit assent test).

205. See E. Farnsworth, supra note 13, § 12.14, at 875 (describing the tacit assent test and noting that it has been rejected by most jurisdictions); U.C.C. § 2-715 comment 2 (1977) ("The 'tacit agreement' test for the recovery of consequential damages is re-

While some have objected to the often fictional nature of such "tacit" consent,[206] the source of this problem lies not with a consent theory. It lies instead with the centuries-old judicial reluctance to enforce express clauses that specify the extent of liability where such clauses differ from the standard for damages that the courts would apply on their own.[207] With this as the legal background, why would rational economizing parties negotiate such a clause unless they strongly disagreed with that background *and* could devise a way to subvert it? By recognizing contracting parties' right to consent to extent of liability as well as to obligation, we can anticipate fictional "tacit" assent to be supplanted by actual agreements—whether implied or expressed—when parties disagree with the background rule established by the courts.[208]

To the extent, however, that parties *can* freely "opt out" of complete liability for all forseeable consequential damages, the adopting of a consent theory in this area is less pressing than it is at the level of obligation. For most parties know that they are entering into a contract and, if so, they can and do provide for clauses that limit by consent the consequences for which they may be liable. In contrast, if a consent theory is not employed to assess the existence of an obligation, parties who do not know that they are contracting cannot always or easily take steps to avoid an obligation that might be imposed upon them.

In sum, bargained-for consideration and nonbargained-for reliance are equivalent to the extent that the existence of either in a transaction may manifest the intentions of one or both of the parties to be legally bound. In any case, the absence of either bargained-for consideration or reliance will not bar the enforcement of a transfer of entitlements that can be proved in some other way—for example, by a formal written document or by adequate proof of a sufficiently unambiguous verbal commitment.[209]

---

jected."). But see Murrow v. First Nat'l Bank, 261 Ark. 568, 550 S.W.2d 429 (1977) (retaining tacit-assent test).

206. See, e.g., C. McCormick, supra note 204, § 141, at 580 ("It adds the fiction of a tacit promise to the original fiction of 'contemplation'. . . .").

207. See Note, Liquidated Damages Recovery Under the Restatement (Second) of Contracts, 67 Cornell L. Rev. 862, 866 (1982) ("Where the actual damage resulting from a breach was small or nonexistent, some courts used equitable principles to avoid enforcing a liquidated damage clause." (citation omitted)); see also A. Simpson, supra note 75, at 118–25 (describing the decline of conditioned penal bond).

208. See, e.g., A. Polinsky, supra note 28, at 25 (contract law provides gap-filling terms that minimize the costs of transacting by accommodating the intentions of most parties); R. Posner, supra note 30, at 69 (One economic function of contract law "is to reduce the complexity and hence the cost of transactions by supplying a set of normal terms that, in the absence of a law of contracts, the parties would have to negotiate expressly.").

209. It is not being suggested here that such prophylactic measures that serve an evidentiary function—such as a statute of frauds, a parol evidence rule, or certain formal requirements—are inappropriate in a consent theory. Cf. Lorenzen, supra note 144, at

3. *Contract Defenses: Rebutting the Prima Facie Case of Consent.* — Consent, either formal or informal, is required to make out a prima facie case of contractual obligation. This means that, in the absence of an "affirmative" defense to the prima facie case of contractual obligation, the manifested intention of a party to transfer alienable rights will justify the enforcement of such a commitment. Traditional contract defenses can be understood as describing circumstances that, if proved to have existed, deprive the manifestation of assent of its normal moral, and therefore legal, significance. These defenses may be clustered into three groups, each of which undermines the prima facie case of consent in a different way.

The first group of defenses—duress, misrepresentation, and (possibly) unconscionability[210]—describes circumstances where the manifestation of an intention to be legally bound has been obtained improperly by the promisee. The manifestation of assent either was improperly coerced by the promisee[211] or was based on misinformation for which the promisee was responsible.[212] The second group—incapacity, infancy, and intoxication—describes attributes of the promisor that indicate a lack of ability to assert meaningful assent. The third group—mistake, impracticability, and frustration—stem from the inability to fully express in any agreement all possible contingencies that might affect performance. Each describes those types of events (a) whose nonoccurrence was arguably a real, but tacit assumption upon which consent was based, and (b) for which the promisee should bear the risk of occurrence.[213] Each type of defense thus is distinguished by the way it undermines the normal, presumed significance of consent. But all valid contract defenses describe general circumstances where the appearance of assent tends to lack its normal moral significance.

These traditional contract defenses would function in a consent theory, as they do currently, to preserve the actual voluntariness of rights transfer, in those rare cases where consent has been improperly coerced or where we are willing to acknowledge other circumstances,

---

644 (The law may "require certain formalities for the prevention of fraud, or as a guarantee, so far as it is legally possible to provide such, that the contract in question represents the serious and deliberate will of the parties. But within the limits so outlined it is submitted the will of the parties to assume legal relations should control.").

210. For analyses of unconscionability that would place it in this category of defenses, see Epstein, supra note 54; Leff, supra note 54.

211. See generally Philips, Are Coerced Agreements Involuntary, 3 Law & Phil. 133 (1984) (distinguishing coerced and involuntary agreements).

212. Cf. Epstein, Privacy, Property Rights, and Misrepresentations, 12 Ga. L. Rev. 455, 466 (1978) ("False words . . . undermine the voluntariness of the individual's conduct . . . .").

213. In this third group of defenses, the consent was not improperly induced by the promisee, and the person giving consent was capable of doing so. This, in part, may help explain why courts are quite receptive to arguments by the promisee that the promisor assumed the risk of the mistake, impracticability, or frustration. See E. Farnsworth, supra note 13, §§ 9.3–.4, 9.6–.7, at 659–61, 666, 684–86, 692–94.

such as misinformation, that vitiate the presence of consent. This refusal to enforce some instances of apparent assent does not, however, reflect a retreat to a subjective will theory. It remains true that an objective manifestation of intent to be legally bound is sufficient to give rise to an enforceable commitment. The only qualification is that this objective manifestation must have been voluntary.[214]

A consent theory explains both the modern reception of the objective theory in the prima facie case of contractual obligation and the traditional defenses to the prima facie case which are based on circumstances that in some significant fashion rebut the usual voluntary nature of consent. When such circumstances are proved to have existed, even a manifested assent to be legally bound does not justify enforcement.

Conclusion: A Consent Theory in Perspective

A consent theory of contractual obligation views certain agreements as legally binding because the parties bring to the transaction certain rights and they manifest their assent to the transfer of these rights. This approach accurately captures what is at stake when individuals seek to exchange or bestow entitlements that they have acquired or will acquire. It provides a coherent account of both the traditional common law preference for an objective interpretation of contracts and its exceptions.

A consent theory dictates both that a showing of consent is sufficient (prima facie) to obtain enforcement and that defenses that show circumstances which undermine the moral significance of objective consent are warranted. A consent theory also provides a focus for contemporary dissatisfaction with the doctrine of consideration, while putting into better perspective the recognized need to enforce some gratuitous commitments and to protect some acts of reliance that were not bargained for. What of the five "principles" of contract discussed in Part I? A consent theory specifies the proper relationship among these core concerns of contract law. In this way, it helps determine which principle or concern should be given priority in different situations.

A consent theory's concern with the issue of individual *will* and *autonomy* is reflected in the manner by which consent is determined—the theory looks for a manifestation of intention to be legally bound. Contractual enforcement, therefore, will usually reflect the will of the parties. Unlike a will theory, however, a consent theory explains the enforcement of manifestations of assent that are contrary to the actual intent of one party. A consent theory, like a reliance theory, legally

214. See Cohen, supra note 7, at 578.
A developed system of law . . . must draw some distinction between voluntary and involuntary acts. . . . The whole of the modern law of contract, it may be argued, thus does and should respond to the need of greater or finer discrimination in regard to the intentional character of acts. The law of error, duress and fraud in contract would be unintelligible apart from such distinction.

protects a promisee's *reliance* on a promisor's consent even in some instances where a promisor did not subjectively intend to be bound. A consent theory differs from a reliance theory by offering a workable criterion independent of reliance itself[215] to distinguish legally protected from legally unprotected reliance.

A consent theory facilitates *efficient* resource distribution by legally protecting consensual exchanges. Such consensual exchanges produce vital and otherwise unavailable information about value and thereby enable resources to gravitate to their highest value user. However, a consent theory refuses to approve nonconsensual transfers regardless of the alleged "efficiency" of such transfers. A consent theory also avoids the extreme indeterminacy of a substantive fairness approach, while protecting that concept of *fairness* that is not a phantom—procedural fairness—by its reliance on generally formulated principles of contract formation and avoidance.

Finally, though a consent theory acknowledges that, under certain circumstances, by *bargaining* and incurring unbargained-for *detrimental reliance* parties can manifest assent to transfer rights, it also recognizes the dependent relationship between contract theory and entitlement theory. In this way, a consent theory avoids the dangers of basing contractual obligation entirely on either bargain or reliance.

How does a consent theory fit into the typology of contract theories suggested in Part I? A consent theory of contract is an entitlements theory and therefore it bases legal obligation upon the rights of the parties. In contrast to one-sided party-based theories, a consent theory stresses the interrelational function of contract law. The criterion of enforceability—a manifested intention to be legally bound—respects the interests of both parties. A corollary of the manifestation requirement is that the meaning of a promisor's conduct is interpreted from the perspective of (reasonable) promisees. Requiring that it is an intention to be legally bound that must be manifested protects the autonomy of promisors.

Further, a consent theory acknowledges that substantive concerns arising at the level of entitlements—for example, a distinction between alienable and inalienable rights—can affect the enforceability of certain commitments. Yet a consent approach eschews the sorts of substantive inquiries into and interference with ordinary contractual arrangements that substance-based theories demand. Finally, a consent theory supports the traditional recognition that certain processes—such as bargaining or using a seal—give rise to a heavy presumption of enforceability. Unlike a process-based theory, a consent theory clearly specifies its dependence on underlying notions of entitlements that enable a legal system to choose which processes to recognize and to know when procedural requirements should be overridden.

215. See supra notes 197–200 and accompanying text.

In describing the acceptance of new scientific theories, Thomas Kuhn has noted that the fact that new theories cannot initially answer all questions that may be put to them does not prevent them from supplanting old theories.[216] Rather, new theories are accepted because they explain known truths and resolve previously vexatious anomalies, and provide promising new areas of research.[217] By these criteria, a consent theory should be considered a potentially valuable approach to explaining contractual obligation.

Still, the theory must be further extended and elaborated before it can be fully evaluated. For example, the recognition that contractual obligation is dependent on a deeper notion of individual entitlements promises an explanation of why some rights might by their nature be inalienable and therefore why some consensual agreements might be unenforceable. This understanding may also assist in determining which form of contract remedies—specific performance or monetary damages—is appropriate if a contract is breached.[218]

The purpose of this Article is not to end discussion of contract theory or doctrine, but rather to permit the ongoing discussion of contractual obligation to emerge from its longstanding intellecutal cul-de-sac and begin traveling a more productive course. If the "death of contract" movement is a product of a disillusionment with and abandonment of both the will theory of contract as a distinct source of contractual obligation and the bargain theory of consideration as the means of formally distinguishing between enforceable and unenforceable exercises of the will, the "resurrection of contract" is a recognition of contract law's proper function as a transfer mechanism that is conceptually dependent on more fundamental notions of individual entitlements. A better understanding of contractual obligation should ultimately result in rules and principles of contract that better facilitate the important social need to make and rely upon enforceable commitments. These and other promises of the consent theory await future performance.

216. T. Kuhn, The Structure of Scientific Revolutions 157–59 (2d ed. 1970).

217. Id. at 169.

218. See, e.g., Barnett, supra note 99 (discussing how a consent theory of contract and a proper distinction between alienable and inalienable rights suggest that the rules governing choice of remedies should vary depending on which of three kinds of contracts has been breached: a contract for external resources, a contract for personal services, or a contract for corporate services).

[2]

Paradox Lost

F.H. Buckley*

The fundamental question of contract theory is why a promise gives rise to a legal obligation. Without promising, the scope of contract law shrinks to immediate transfers of property; and without a justification for promissory institutions, a considerable part of contract law is of dubious normative content. An analysis of some special feature of contract law, such as consideration requirements, could not aspire to great moral status if promissory institutions could be abolished without apparent loss.

This Article defends a utilitarian theory of promising, under which legal and moral obligations to perform promises are justified by the felicific consequences of a convention of promise keeping. Utilitarian theories, once accepted as providing the most plausible normative support for the economic analysis of law, fell into disfavor about ten years ago.[1] The rejection of utilitarianism now seems premature because many of the criticisms leveled at it do not withstand close scrutiny.[2] This Article does not seek to defend utilitarianism in general, however, but rather to demonstrate the inadequacy of rival, nonutilitarian theories. It does so through an analysis of contract theory, for if utilitarianism alone offers a persuasive account of so fundamental a legal institution as contract law, lawyers will find rival theories difficult to accept.

The first rival theory, identified most closely with John

* Associate Professor, Faculty of Law, McGill University. I am indebted for comments on earlier drafts of this Article to Richard Epstein, Serge Gaudet, Esther Goldberg, Mane Hajdin, David Stevens, and the participants at conferences at the University of Sherbrooke and George Mason School of Law. Special thanks also go to my research assistants, Jason Mogg and Kevin Woodall.

1. For a discussion of the movement away from utilitarianism, see R. POSNER, THE ECONOMICS OF JUSTICE 48-60 (1981), which is based on Posner, *Utilitarianism, Economics, and Legal Theory*, 8 J. LEGAL STUD. 103 (1979).

2. The clearest rebuttal of the anti-utilitarian position is found in D. PARFIT, REASONS AND PERSONS 3-114 (1984). For a shorter statement of many of these arguments, see Smart, *An Outline of a System of Utilitarian Ethics*, in UTILITARIANISM; FOR AND AGAINST 1 (J. Smart & B. Williams eds. 1973).

Rawls, is referred to as a low-fidelity theory because it does not invest promising with a moral status. Under this theory promissory obligations ultimately rest on morally compelling connecting factors between individuals and morally neutral institutions.[3] The institution of promising is not ethically desirable in itself. Rather, the connecting factors alone have moral force.

Under high-fidelity explanations, in contrast, the duty to support promising arises as a consequence of the institution's desirability. Examples of high-fidelity theories include both utilitarianism and neoformalism,[4] which is utilitarianism's second rival. Neoformalism defends promising on the basis of the moral value of a right to promise. As a high-fidelity explanation of promising, neoformalism seeks to provide a justification for the institution of promising and is not simply a theory that, on principles of rights, promises made in a promissory society are binding. Although neoformalists are rights theorists, not all rights theorists are neoformalists, for in promissory matters a rights theorist might subscribe to a low-fidelity theory.

Neoformalism today attempts to recapture private law institutions from a perspective of rights. Like the earlier formalists, neoformalists analyze legal institutions with little regard to their end-state consequences. Unlike their predecessors, however, the neoformalists' defense of contract law is more self-consciously philosophical, with principles of moral choice derived from deontological theories which exclude evidence of the remote consequences of acts. The neoformalists' readiness to bring forward the Kantian heavy artillery may be seen as a compliment to the strength of their adversaries, the nihilists and consequentialists, for whom no justification, or only one that looks to end states, is possible.

Neoformalist theories attempt both to explain and to justify legal rules and institutions by reference to the moral values they serve. The two endeavors are quite different, for the

3. *See* J. RAWLS, A THEORY OF JUSTICE 342-50 (1971).

4. Neoformalism is a term used in this Article. The leading example of the neoformalist analysis of contract law is C. FRIED, CONTRACT AS PROMISE (1981), which applies a general theory of promissory obligations to the broad contours of contract law. A chapter on lying in C. FRIED, RIGHT AND WRONG 54-78 (1978) provides an excellent analysis of misrepresentation from the perspective of a rights theory. In addition, the libertarian theory of contracts may be neoformalist in its insistence on the respect to be accorded a right to promise. *See, e.g.*, Barnett, *A Consent Theory of Contract*, 86 COLUM. L. REV. 269, 291-300 (1986).

descriptive exercise of identifying the values courts find underlying contract law differs from the justification of the institution's ways to man. The descriptive project is a crucial part of any theory of contracts, for if the institution that is defended does not resemble the accepted regime of contract law, some otherwise valid contracts will not generate an obligation of performance. This would be a serious failure, for a normative theory would be unattractive if adherence to it came at the cost of jettisoning one class of binding agreements.[5] However, the discovery of that value which underlies every valid contract does not of itself generate a moral theory of contracts. Unless it is assumed that the value is ethically desirable, its explanatory power is on the same moral plane as my decision to organize my library by author and not by subject matter. Thus, a justification of promising must be a normative theory which at the same time can account for the circumstances when promises are in fact binding.

While promissory theories would be unpersuasive if they claimed that valid promises did not oblige, they need not seek to explain every kind of bargaining activity. Promissory theorists are therefore free to focus on contract as promise.[6] Even

5. *See* Barnett, *supra* note 4, at 270 (criteria for selecting a theory include whether it handles known problems as well as or better than its rivals).

6. As a matter of strategy, a combatant may pick the terrain, eschewing war on all fronts. In a defense of contract law, promissory theorists may legitimately narrow their focus to contract as promise, seeking to justify the legal enforcement of promises in the promisor's moral obligation to perform. This is not to say that all contracts reduce to forward-looking promises. Even nonpromissory societies may know the bare gift or simultaneous exchange, by which property (shorn of any warranty rights) may be transferred in the immediate present. Contract law would then largely be limited to the conditions that determine the validity of consent, without any need for promises of future performance.

In the same way, an analysis of contract as promise does not deny the existence of nonpromissory, cooperative norms in many bargains, particularly those involving relational contracts. *See, e.g.*, Goetz & Scott, *Principles of Relational Contracts*, 67 VA. L. REV. 1089, 1090-92 (1981). For a discussion of nonpromissory norms in contract, see I. MACNEIL, THE NEW SOCIAL CONTRACT: AN INQUIRY INTO MODERN CONTRACTUAL RELATIONS (1980) (contract as the relations among parties in the process of future change); Macneil, *Values in Contract: Internal and External*, 78 NW. U.L. REV. 340 (1983) [hereinafter Macneil, *Values in Contract*] (contract as the relations among people in the course of projecting exchanges into the future); Macneil, *The Many Futures of Contracts*, 47 S. CAL. L. REV. 691 (1974) (relational norms aim at protection of relationship between parties). The promissory skeptic might then ask whether promises can be viewed in isolation from broader social conventions. But if admittedly not everything in contract is promise, so too not everything is background convention, social norm, firm, or relationship, with one kind of

when restricted to contract as promise, however, promissory obligations cannot be understood except by reference to a preexisting convention or institution that permits obligations to be incurred in this way. Although the moral status of promissory obligations distinguishes promising from more trivial institutions, conceding a moral value to the imperative does not explain how an individual may have an obligation to perform a promise. If commands are issued by a convention, how do they command *me*? A justification of promissory institutions requires a principle of fidelity by which the convention's moral imperatives ought to be regarded as binding on a particular individual.

This Article argues that a principle of fidelity can be derived only by assuming the moral worth of the convention, but it does not seek to demonstrate that promissory institutions ought to exist.[7] Instead, it assumes that promising is morally desirable and asks what conclusions follow therefrom.[8] Part I examines promising as a convention, following the well-known discussion of conventional rules by John Searle and John

---

monism replacing another. The contract theorist may then select promising for analysis, and ask what values attach to it.

Macneil, from whose holistic perspective it is unrealistic to examine institutions in fractions, criticized C. FRIED, CONTRACT AS PROMISE (1981) for its focus on promising. *See* Macneil, *Values in Contract*, *supra*, at 409. If everything is connected in this way, however, the only kind of knowledge is of everything at all times and in every place, and the work of analysis, which considers discrete institutions and transactions, would be impossible.

Read uncritically, Macneil's studies might lead one to wonder how promising is possible at all. This kind of mistake, not accurately attributed to Macneil, seems a species of what Austin termed the *ivresse des grandes profondeurs*. *See* J. SEARLE, SPEECH ACTS 176 (1970) (discussing Austin's theory of speech acts).

7. Promising ends at the border of the doctrine of illegality. A further question therefore remains of where, on the continuum between individual liberty and paternalism, promises ought not to be performed. I offer no solution to that problem, nor do I purport to meet the arguments of extreme paternalists who, by expanding the realm of illegality, would ban promising altogether.

Lawyers have recently given much attention to paternalism. *See, e.g.*, Epstein, *Why Restrain Alienation?*, 85 COLUM. L. REV. 970 (1985); Jackson, *The Fresh-Start Policy in Bankruptcy Law*, 98 HARV. L. REV. 1393 (1985); Kronman, *Paternalism and the Law of Contracts*, 92 YALE L.J. 763 (1983); Sunstein, *Legal Interference with Private Preferences*, 53 U. CHI. L. REV. 1129 (1986). For a useful introduction to recent philosophical studies of the subject, see PATERNALISM (R. Sartorius ed. 1983).

8. This device owes much to H.L.A. Hart (although its origin is Kantian). *See* Hart, *Are There Any Natural Rights?*, 64 PHIL. REV. 175 (1955) (promissory institutions presuppose a range of unfettered action).

Rawls.[9] Because promising is conventional, the obligation to perform a promise must rest on a principle of fidelity to promising by which the convention's rules bind individuals. Two kinds of duties of allegiance are distinguished. Under low-fidelity obligations, the principle of allegiance requires a morally compelling connecting factor between the individual and a convention. High-fidelity duties, on the other hand, base fidelity requirements on the duty to support just institutions, dispensing with special connecting factors.

Part II considers whether principles of low fidelity to promising may satisfactorily be generated through connecting factors. Various explanations of promissory institutions, based on different connecting factors, are examined from this perspective. Although voluntary consent by the promisor, acceptance of benefits, and promisee reliance might all be proffered as possible links between individuals and institutions, none of these provides an adequate account of promising. A successful defense of fidelity requirements must therefore assume the moral value of promissory institutions.

Part III examines what the values of the institution might be in high-fidelity theories. The first high-fidelity theory discussed is neoformalism, which prizes the institution for permitting individuals to exercise a right to promise. Like low-fidelity theories, neoformalism is unpersuasive. While promising might at first seem desirable from a libertarian perspective, the institution is neither a necessary nor a sufficient condition of a free society. As a consequence promissory institutions cannot be justified on abstract libertarian norms but must instead be defended for the special values of a regime of promising. Neoformalism, however, is unable to identify the ethically desirable attributes of promising and therefore must be rejected. Given

---

9. J. SEARLE, *supra* note 6, at 33-53. Rawls first set forth his analysis of conventional rules in Rawls, *Two Concepts of Rules*, 64 PHIL. REV. 3 (1955), which argued that utilitarian theories of promising were more plausible on a conventional account of the institution. By contrast, this Article suggests that *only* utilitarianism offers a persuasive theory of promissory institutions. Rawls later abandoned his utilitarian explanation of promising in J. RAWLS, A THEORY OF JUSTICE 342-50 (1971).

Hume's category of "naturally unintelligible" rules would seem to have anticipated Searle's constitutive rules. D. HUME, A TREATISE OF HUMAN NATURE, bk. III, pt. II, § 5, at 516-25 (L. Selby-Bigge ed. 1967); *see* J. MACKIE, HUME'S MORAL THEORY 96-99 (1980). Kelsen suggested a similar distinction, noting that promissory obligations depend on a higher norm which permits the parties to create obligations by promising. Kelsen, *La théorie juridique de la convention*, 1940 ARCHIVES DE PHILOSOPHIE DU DROIT 33, 47.

the failure of neoformalism, contract theorists must choose between consequentialism, which accords a moral status to the consequences of adopting a promissory regime, and nihilism, which does not. This Article concludes that only utilitarianism provides a satisfactory defense of the institution of promising.

I. OBLIGATIONS OF FIDELITY

It sometimes helps to begin by asking what the questions are. Thus, it is a false start to ask why promises should be performed, for the proposition that promises are prima facie morally binding is analytic. As a matter of definition, then, a promise ought to be kept unless it is trumped by an overriding ethical concern, as under the doctrine of illegality in contract law. Instead of asking why promises should be performed, the primary question for promissory theory is why a convention that issues moral obligations is rightly regarded as binding upon an individual. Answering this question requires both an explanation of how promising is conventional and a general theory of fidelity to conventions.

A. Promising as Convention

The device of describing promising as a convention, even if widely accepted in analytic philosophy, no doubt remains counterintuitive. In fact, if convention is used to mean a societal institution that could easily be dismantled,[10] promising is not conventional.[11] In another sense of the term, however, promising is conventional. Here a convention is a set of rules that creates the very possibility of the activity in question, and an institution is conventional if it cannot exist without these rules. Games provide the clearest examples of such rules: one can swing at a ball without making contact, but only in a game does this count as a strike. Without the rules of the game, the activity of striking out, hitting a home run, or stealing second would not be possible. For this reason, Searle described these rules as *constitutive rules* (C-rules).[12] To say that a rule is conventional, then, does not mean that it relates to a particular society, but rather that the rule cannot be imagined without the convention. Searle distinguished C-rules from *regulative rules* (R-rules), which prescribe activity without regard to the con-

10. *See* Midgley, *The Game Game*, 49 Phil. 231, 252 (1974).

11. The frequent use by philosophers of game as a synonym of convention may bring this meaning to mind.

12. J. Searle, *supra* note 6, at 33-42.

ventions of a society.[13] For example, normative R-rules indicate whether a particular activity is right or wrong but do not define the activity. The distinction between the two kinds of rules is not always sharp, and promissory C-rules may overlap with R-rules. Thus, physical duress may void a contract but might also be wrong even without the convention.

Like R-rules, C-rules also regulate (otherwise they would not be rules). In addition to prescribing conduct, however, C-rules create the very possibility of the activity.[14] Moreover, C-rules may specify not only the consequences of breach but also what kind of conduct is within or without the convention. For example, promissory conventions may stipulate when an utterance successfully constitutes a promise and when it misfires and does not impose an obligation.

Those rules whose compliance require the use of a language constitute a special kind of C-rules, for language is itself a convention. For example, prohibitions of lying are C-rules because they depend on a language under which assertions are ordinarily taken as truthful.[15] Without the convention, the act of asserting would not be possible. Similarly, promising requires a language (or some other convention) that specifies what counts as a promise.

Some resistance to this analysis may come from those who suspect that it represents a downgrading of promissory obligations. Conventional explanations are indeed objectionable if they mistake an R-rule for a C-rule, for such a mistake could

---

13. *Id.*

14. The distinction between the two kinds of rules may have little to do with their prevalence in various societies. For example, an R-rule may not be incorporated into the operating norms of every society. Even when an R-rule is not incorporated, however, it is still meaningful to speak of the rule being breached, with the failure of the society's norms to incorporate it going at best to an excuse for decidedly wrongful behavior. The excuse could even be rejected and the R-rule thought categorical, giving rise to an absolute prohibition at all times in every society. Similarly, a C-rule may be universal if all societies have adopted the convention. Unlike R-rules, however, a plea that the convention does not figure in one's society is not an excuse but rather a denial that the activity took place.

15. *See* C. FRIED, RIGHT AND WRONG 57 (1978) (every assertion intended to "be understood as an intended move within the assertion game"); Khatchadourian, *Institutions, Practices and Moral Rules*, 86 MIND 479, 482-84 (1977). A language without such a convention might be imagined, although only with some difficulty. *But see* Winch, *Nature and Convention*, 60 PROC. ARISTOTELIAN SOC'Y 231, 242 (1959-1960) ("[T]he notion of a society in which there is a language but in which truth-telling is not regarded as the norm is a self-contradictory one.").

change the nature of the prohibition. If the obligation is contingent upon a society's adoption of a particular convention, then the most heinous act could be rendered benign simply by swapping conventions. We would therefore insist that rules against murder, for example, do not rest on conventions about bodily integrity.

To say that promissory obligations are conventional, however, does not mean that they must be of a lower normative force. A convention's C-rules may endow its outputs with a moral status, and this in fact is how promising works. Promising prima facie provides a sufficient moral reason to perform. Asking why this is so, as Rawls noted, is like wondering why batters do not get four strikes.[16] Thus, it is a manifest contradiction for a person to say, "I promise to do *X* but am under no obligation to do so." Such a person either is not promising, or does not understand what promising means. Promissory conventions are therefore to be distinguished from nonmoral games whose imperatives are of a "have-to" kind.[17] (If you want to get on base, this is what you have to do.) Unlike the rules of baseball, which tell us only how to play the game, promissory obligations are both have-to and ought-to in nature. Nonperformance of a promise is not merely unconventional but also morally wrong.

B. Rules of Fidelity

The moral status of promissory obligations rests on a rule of fidelity to the convention. Unless it can be connected to people, contract law must be, as an institution without members, a matter of moral indifference. To make this more concrete, consider the parallel to political allegiance. Suppose that Norway may be characterized as a just society. From this, it does not follow that a Canadian has a duty of allegiance to Norway.[18] Similarly, a society may have a convention that wearing a hat gives rise to a peculiar moral consequence. If, hatted, I visit the society, a resident might claim that the convention is invoked. But I may legitimately object that the convention does not bind foreigners. Everyone would agree that a principle of allegiance

16. Rawls, *supra* note 9, at 64.

17. For the distinction between have-to and ought-to rules, see Cameron, *'Ought' and Institutional Obligation*, 46 PHIL. 309 (1971).

18. For this reason Simmons argues that "we need a principle of political obligation which binds the citizen to one *particular* state above all others." A.J. SIMMONS, MORAL PRINCIPLES AND POLITICAL OBLIGATIONS 31-32 (1979) (emphasis in original).

is needed to bind the foreigner. If so, however, a principle of allegiance is also required to bind a resident of the society. (When does one stop being a foreigner?) In the same way, it is impossible for a promisor to derive a moral obligation to perform merely by doing that which constitutes promising according to the convention. Instead, one must ask what it is about a convention that makes it *my* convention to follow. If no principle of fidelity explains why the promisor is rightly regarded as bound by the convention, she is not obliged to perform.

Rules of fidelity differ from the convention's membership C-rules because no convention in itself requires allegiance without an outside principle of fidelity. In some cases a reference to membership C-rules may adequately explain why a rule should be followed. If the door to a private club bears the sign, "Members only," and I (as a nonmember) enter anyway, the doorkeeper has an easy answer if I ask, "Why can't I go in?" So too, the laws of Norway define citizenship in that country, and promissory C-rules tell us who is a promisor. This will not, however, generate a principle of fidelity if the C-rules (including membership rules) may be legitimately challenged. For example, one might claim that the club's membership policies wrongly exclude academic lawyers and assert a right to enter. In the same way, Canadians may resist the application of Norwegian laws whatever the citizenship laws of that country. These cases require a principle of fidelity separate from institutional membership rules.[19]

19. *See* Khatchadourian, *supra* note 15, at 486-96. Searle's derivation of an *ought* from an *is* seems vulnerable. In an abbreviated form, Searle's argument is that, from the statement, (1) "Jones uttered the words 'I hereby promise to pay you, Smith, five dollars,'" it follows as a tautology both that (2) Jones promised to pay Smith five dollars, and (3) Jones ought to pay Smith five dollars. *See* J. SEARLE, *supra* note 6, at 177. Hence an evaluative conclusion (3) is derived from a nonevaluative premise (1). *See id.* at 175-98. Searle emphasized that his thesis concerned the philosophy of language and not ethics, or "oughts" and not "moral oughts." *Id.* at 176-77. In either case, however, it must be assumed that Jones is bound by the convention for the derivation to work. While Searle appeared to think that such membership questions could be resolved solely through the C-rules, this will not suffice to generate fidelity rules. Even if a convention points to me, I can still ask, "And am I bound?" As Hare noted, what links me to a convention must be something outside the convention. Hare, *The Promising Game*, 18 REV. INT'L DE PHIL. 398, 408-12 (1964).

Hare's reference to a need for "subscribing members" to a convention will not, however, commend itself to one who rejects contractarian explanations of an obligation of allegiance. *Id.* at 411. For reasons discussed in Part II, Searle is correct in arguing that the act of promising need not amount to an affirmation of the value of the institution. *See* J. SEARLE, *supra* note 6, at 194-95; *see*

1. Hybrid Rules

Fidelity rules are a species of a more general kind of rule that regulates relationships between conventions and people. These are *hybrid rules* (H-rules), which are exclusionary when they prescribe who may not participate in a convention and inclusionary when they specify who must do so. H-rules are neither constitutive nor regulative but resemble both. They are regulative insofar as they do not create a convention and conventional insofar as they cannot be understood without one. These exclusionary and inclusionary rules are not R-rules because they cannot be understood by one not familiar with the convention (for example, no admittance to *what*?). But H-rules are not C-rules either, for a breach of the rule leaves the game intact (for example, girls playing minor league hockey). When played in violation of an exclusionary H-rule, a game is still a game. Nonobservance of an H-rule, therefore, is different from nonobservance of a C-rule. This may seem unduly dogmatic, because it is undoubtedly possible to play baseball without complying with all of its C-rules, for example, by ignoring the infield fly rule (or playing with designated hitters). The relevant question, however, is not "What is baseball?," but rather "What are its rules?" Some rules are H-rules *about* baseball rather than C-rules *of* baseball.[20]

2. High and Low Fidelity

Fidelity duties vary in their content, and the requirements of an inclusionary H-rule may depend on the nature of the institution. It might involve a subscription for membership or financial support for well-organized institutions. Other institutions might demand adherence in less exacting ways, such as through requirements of noninterference.

In the case of promising, it is helpful to distinguish two different kinds of fidelity to an institution. Duties of high fidelity arise when the institution is so morally desirable that societies without the institution are less just. In such cases every individual, no matter how remote from the institution, owes it allegiance. If the institution already exists, it should be granted such support as it requires, and conscientious objection should be prohibited. If the institution does not exist, it should be fos-

---

also Zemach, *Ought, Is, and a Game Called "Promise,"* 21 PHIL. Q. 61 (1971) (discussing Searle's views on the act of promising).

20. I am indebted to Mane Hajdin for pointing out this distinction to me.

tered.[21] A justification of a duty of high fidelity requires a universalizable defense of an institution so good that nonsupport is everywhere prohibited. Duties of high fidelity then arise naturally in that they are imposed with or without voluntary acceptance of the institution.[22]

By contrast, the principle of low fidelity only binds individuals to an institution by virtue of the particular connecting factor between the two. One example of this is political allegiance to a particular state, in which duties of fidelity may depend on residence or citizenship. Without the requisite nexus, no duty to support the institution arises. If the connecting factor legitimately could be erased, conscientious objectors might then opt out of the institution. Although other variants exist, the leading low-fidelity theory of promising is that of Rawls.[23]

What may serve as a connecting factor in a regime of low fidelity depends on the institution in question. In the case of promising, one frequently mentioned candidate is a voluntary act by the promisor from which attornment to the institution's jurisdiction may be implied. Because the act is consensual, the requirement is referred to as an obligation, the term duty being reserved for imperatives that arise without our consent.[24] Describing a low-fidelity inclusionary requirement as an obligation may, if one is not careful, lead to confusion, for promising, as a voluntary act, also generates obligations. It is therefore necessary to distinguish between the obligation of low fidelity and the promissory obligation created by the promise. The first kind of obligation might be thought to be owed to institutions and the second to people, if requirements to an institution made sense. It is, however, more accurate to think of fidelity obligations as different in kind from promissory obligations, being rather an element in the justification of institutional rules. Through fidelity requirements, a promisor is estopped from asserting an otherwise available defense to the imposition of a promissory obligation.

Whether a duty is one of high or low fidelity may depend

21. For example, Rawls's duty of justice, premised on a just society, requires that we both support and comply with just institutions which exist and apply to us and also further just arrangements not yet established, at least when this can be done at little individual cost. J. RAWLS, *supra* note 3, at 115, 334.

22. *See id.* at 115.

23. *See id.* at 115-16, 342-45 (discussing principle of fairness or fidelity to promising).

24. *Id.* at 114-15, 343-44.

on the normative value of the underlying institution. A duty of high fidelity might then arise from a more ethically desirable institution, with an ethically neutral one generating only an obligation of low fidelity. For example, if truth-telling conventions were so valuable as to support high-fidelity duties, the inclusionary rule that prohibits cheating at cards would likely be one of low fidelity. In other cases the distinction may turn on the scope of the institution itself. Thus, although allegiance to the just state of Norway is a low-fidelity duty based on a particular connecting factor (such as domicile), a Rawlsian duty to support just societies in the abstract may be one of high fidelity.[25]

The justice of the institution is not wholly irrelevant to a low-fidelity theory, for at some point its actual injustice would break any bonds of allegiance. In addition, even just institutions may give rise to a principle of low and not high fidelity. Because political allegiance to the just state of Norway requires a connecting factor, the duty is one of low fidelity. Furthermore, the existence of the right kind of connecting factor is a necessary but not a sufficient reason for low-fidelity requirements. For example, one may be bound to two different institutions by separate connecting factors, and allegiance to both may not be feasible. In such cases the dispute may perhaps be resolved by reference to institutional values.[26] Thus, while institutional value implies a high-fidelity theory, low fidelity does not necessarily imply a morally neutral institution. Nevertheless, because the justice of the institution need not be of great concern under low-fidelity theories, such theories will be deemed to refer to morally neutral institutions.

Clearly, theories of high and low fidelity cannot explain every question of fidelity. For example, the distinction between the two kinds of duties may have little to do with the kind of support appropriate to a particular institution. If low-fidelity obligations have a lesser stature than high-fidelity duties, this is not because low-fidelity obligations are necessarily less onerous, but only because they depend on a special connecting factor. Low-fidelity obligations may vary in intensity, from require-

25. *Id.* at 115.

26. For example, suppose that as an academic lawyer I feel that I ought to support an association of law teachers from whose activities I derive benefits (the receipt of benefits constituting the connecting factor). If two such associations exist, I may decide that my obligation of allegiance is owed to the one that best accords with principles of justice, whether or not I derive more benefits from it.

ments of mere noninterference to duties such as enlisting in an army during wartime. In addition, when a right of conscientious objection is asserted, those realms of low fidelity, which rightfully forbid defection once the connecting factor has been established, resemble high-fidelity regimes. When the connecting factor is an indelible mark, individuals already bound to a low-fidelity duty differ little from their high-fidelity brethren.

Among defenses of promising, low-fidelity theories are today ascendant.[27] It was not always so. Earlier writers assumed that a justification of the institution of promising had to be based on an affirmation of the libertarian values or the goals of promissory regimes.[28] A preference for low-fidelity imperatives may then be rooted in a rejection of the values that seem implicit in ethical defenses of the institution. In addition, reasons of economy suggest that institutional values need not be considered if promising may be adequately explained from a low-fidelity perspective. Such theories would then rest not on the ethical value of institutions, but on the connecting factors which bind them to us.

II. LOW-FIDELITY REQUIREMENTS

Low-fidelity explanations of promising may be either promisor- or promisee-based, depending on the connecting factors that give rise to requirements of allegiance. Promisor-based theories focus on the voluntariness of the promisor's conduct in invoking a regime with its own ethical imperatives. An obligation of low fidelity to the institution of promising may thus arise either through consent to the imposition of an obligation or through voluntary acceptance of benefits from promis-

27. One example of this is Rawls's uncharacteristically fatalistic attitude toward institutions (other than the most general features of a just society): one takes them as one finds them. *See* J. RAWLS, *supra* note 3, at 348-49. Provided that they are not actually unjust, they may be accepted without the need to inquire whether any better institution exists. In addition, critics of promissory institutions are today more prominent than their defenders, whether they subscribe to low- or high-fidelity theories. For an overview of promissory nihilism, see C. FRIED, *supra* note 6, at 1-6.

28. "[D]ans sa mystique, l'autonomie de la volonté consacrerait la liberté, pour les parties, de contracter *à leur guise*, et sur *tout ce qui les intéresse*, puisque le Code civil les assimile au législateur." R. SAVATIER, LA THÉORIE DES OBLIGATIONS § 91, at 142 (1967) (emphasis in original); *see also* C. BEAUDANT, LE DROIT INDIVIDUEL ET L'ÉTAT 146 (2d ed. 1891); G. RIPERT, LA RÉGLE MORALE DANS LES OBLIGATIONS CIVILES § 22, at 38 (4th ed. 1949); Kelsen, *supra* note 9, at 48 ("on doit finalement constater que le principe politique de l'autonomie en matière de contrats repose sur une conception individualiste ou libérale de la vie").

ing. In promisee-based theories, on the other hand, the inclusionary duties rest on reliance by the promisee. In each case the question is why one should support an institution that has no moral significance in itself.

To be successful, a low-fidelity theory must show why allegiance is owed. This alone is not sufficient, however, for the institution that the theory describes also must resemble the accepted regime of promising. A connecting factor that cannot explain why some valid promises are binding cannot provide an adequate justification of promising. The theory, through its connecting factors, must then be able to account for both the H-rules of fidelity and the C-rules of promissory obligations.

Low-fidelity theories are generally unsatisfactory on both grounds. Neither consent nor benefits theories offer a compelling account of fidelity requirements, and only promisee reliance provides a plausible connecting factor between individuals and the institution. Even reliance theories, however, fail to describe promissory C-rules in an acceptable manner because they must gerrymander promises that are not relied on outside of the institution. None of these low-fidelity theories covers all of the contours of promising, for nothing is like promising save promising.

A. Promisor-based Theories: Consent

Two kinds of theories may base fidelity to promissory regimes on consensual values. An institution that permits an obligation to result from a consensual act may be thought just, insofar as freedom to choose through promising is considered morally desirable. This explanation, called a will theory because of its focus on voluntariness, endows the C-rules of promising with an ethical content. Because the will theory assumes the moral value of the institution, it must be a high-fidelity theory. As a consequence, will theories cannot be justified from a low-fidelity perspective.

A low-fidelity consent theory must then base a principle of allegiance on the promisor's consent to the imposition of the obligation. Consent theories are, however, subject to two fatal objections. First, it is not possible to demonstrate that promisors actually do consent in a meaningful way to the institution's C-rules. Moreover, even if they did, consent theories would be circular since they cannot explain how consent to promissory institutions could impart an obligation without a prior convention of promising.

1. Reality of the Consent

No promisor formally subscribes to the institution of promising, as a partner may to a firm, and so an act of tacit consent must suffice. The duty to support a promissory regime thus resembles the model of political allegiance provided by social contract theorists. The parallel between fidelity to promising and allegiance to a state is closest when the consent to both is thought to arise solely from residence in regimes in which promissory institutions may be found. Thus, John Locke believed that a foreign visitor to England tacitly consented to obey its laws merely by travelling through the country.[29]

Although tacit, the consent must be real if it is to support a promise of allegiance. It is difficult, however, to see how such a theory can withstand David Hume's attack on contractarian explanations of allegiance. As Hume noted, the contractarian justification of political allegiance is quite implausible if the consent is implied from forms of participation over which the individual has little control.[30] Consent must presuppose rejectability. As for promissory allegiance, mere residence in a promising society is even less likely to provide evidence of tacit consent to the institution, it being harder still to leave promissory societies than political states.

On the other hand, a stronger case for promissory allegiance might be thought to arise if the requisite consent could be found in promising itself. Here the act of promising is seen as a voluntary adherence to an institution whose C-rules determine when obligations arise and are extinguished. By promising, the promisor assumes an obligation to the promisee; in promising, the promisor incurs an obligation of fidelity to the institution.[31] So regarded, the obligation to support promising

29. Locke, *An Essay Concerning the True, Original Extent and End of Civil Government*, in SOCIAL CONTRACT 1, 70-71 (E. Barker ed. 1970).

30. Hume argued:

> Can we seriously say, that a poor peasant or artisan has a free choice to leave his country, when he knows no foreign language or manners, and lives, from day to day, by the small wages which he acquires? We may as well assert that a man, by remaining in a vessel, freely consents to the dominion of the master; though he was carried on board while asleep, and must leap into the ocean and perish, the moment he leaves her.

Hume, *Of the Original Contract*, in SOCIAL CONTRACT 145, 156 (E. Barker ed. 1970). For other critiques of contractarian explanations of political allegiance, see J. RAWLS, *supra* note 3, at 336-37; Murphy, *Consent, Coercion, and Hard Choices*, 67 VA. L. REV. 79 (1981); Simmons, *Consent, Free Choice, and Democratic Government*, 18 GA. L. REV. 791 (1984).

31. *See* Barnett, *supra* note 4, at 305 (under consent theory promisor's in-

regimes is positional, attaching to one who voluntarily occupies the position of promisor pursuant to a convention whose membership rules impose obligations to perform on those who take on that position. The principle of fidelity to promising is then similar to the obligation of an elected representative to perform the functions of a political office for which he has campaigned. In both cases voluntary behavior that fulfills the conditions for the application of C-rules explains why it is right that such rules are binding.

This amended contractarian theory of promising still leans heavily on tacit consent. While little sense can be made of consent to a promising regime unless a realistic possibility exists of rejecting promising, it is not easy to see how this might conscientiously be done. Could all promissory language systematically be pruned from one's vocabulary? Eliminating gerunds would likely be harder, while the subjunctive might perhaps be done away with a little more easily. Even that would not suffice for nonverbal conduct signifying consent. Thus, the possibility of opting out of promising entirely seems a little farfetched.[32] Yet contractarian theories of promising must assume that it is possible because the consent to promising would otherwise be entirely fictitious.

If consent to promising is the moral glue that holds together all contracts, it is curious that there has been so little concern to obtain such consent. One might propose, in the in-

---

vocation of institution provides justification for legal enforcement of contracts). This would also appear to have been Searle's view of how one is bound to adhere to a promissory regime. *See* J. SEARLE, *supra* note 6, at 194-95 (promising invokes undertaking to use the word *promise* in accordance with its literal meaning). A contractarian explanation of allegiance would be plausible if, as Searle thought, a promisor must intend that his utterance will place him under an obligation. *See id.* at 60. If this were the case, a false promise by one who lacks the requisite state of mind might not be binding. The objective theory of contract, however, which dispenses with such spiritual acts, better accords with our understanding of what constitutes a promise. Under the objective theory, a court "exercises its jurisdiction for the enforcement of the truth, and makes a man's acts square with his words, by compelling him to perform what he has undertaken." Laver v. Fielder, 32 Beav. 1, 13, 55 Eng. Rep. 1, 5 (M.R. 1862); *see* J. AUSTIN, HOW TO DO THINGS WITH WORDS 10 (2d ed. 1975) ("Accuracy and morality alike are on the side of the plain saying that *our word is our bond.*") (emphasis in original).

32. *See* Hanfling, *Promises, Games and Institutions*, 75 PROC. ARISTOTELIAN SOC'Y 13, 22 (1974-1975) (nonrejectable institutions like promising must be distinguished from rejectable games). Principles of fidelity to the institution still stand in need of justification, however, because a nonconscientious rejection is always possible, with rebels opting out of performance if not out of promising.

terest of resolving moral ambiguities, promissory registration legislation under which only promises by current registrants are binding. The registration system would be expensive, but such prudential or utilitarian concerns would have little importance next to the higher moral purpose served by the scheme. The plan would be equitable, just, and entirely silly. That no sensible person would accept it may put the concern to find a consent to promising in its proper place. This in turn suggests not that such consent may be presumed, but rather that some other justification for promising must be sought.[33]

One further attempt at a hypothetical consent must also be rejected. If real consent were possible and a meaningful possibility of rejecting the convention existed, contractarian theories would be unstable insofar as free riders might opt out for strategic reasons. This is to be deprecated if the convention is thought beneficial, and in a hypothetical agreement all members would then consent to the imposition of duties of allegiance. In this way lapsed contractarians may reduce consent to a subservient role. The state is not just because it is chosen; rather, it is chosen because it is just. But if it is assumed that the state is just, consent is superfluous and fidelity may instead be based on a duty to support just institutions. Actual consent is unnecessary if it suffices that one ought to consent. The result, expressly adopted by Rawls in the case of political allegiance, is a duty of high fidelity.[34] So too, it is difficult to see how a moral obligation to support a convention of promising can be derived from a hypothetical consent to a beneficial institution unless the benefits are endowed with a moral status.[35]

2. Circularity

Even if a meaningful possibility of consent existed, a con-

33. Even if a consent to promising were somewhere to be found, this might not suffice to justify the institution. Such a consent would demonstrate a preference for promissory over nonpromissory regimes but nothing more than that. In particular it would not in any way show that the institution's C-rules are preferred to any other set of promissory rules that might be imagined and is not now available.

34. J. RAWLS, *supra* note 3, at 334-37.

35. This forms the basis of Dworkin's argument that hypothetical consent to wealth maximization norms is not equivalent to real consent. Dworkin, *Why Efficiency?*, 8 HOFSTRA L. REV. 563, 574-79 (1980). In the same way, Gauthier's contractarian justification of dispositions of constrained maximization cannot be qualified as a theory of ethics unless the consequences of such dispositions are regarded as good. *See* D. GAUTHIER, MORALS BY AGREEMENT 167-70 (1986).

tractarian explanation of high fidelity to promising would still be objectionable as circular. The theory requires something like a promise to obey promises, and it founders in its inability to explain why the first promise is binding.[36] Suppose that two members of a nonpromising society, aware of this difficulty, seek to craft their own promises. So long as the society has some concept of moral duty, they might stipulate that a person who breaches a promise is to be considered as acting wrongly. They might then agree upon their own private contract regime, with C-rules as detailed as any of those found in a promising regime. In these circumstances Joseph Raz argues that they have consented to the rules of promising and that the promisor is required to perform.[37] But is she? Assume that the parties specify that a certain verbal formulary signifies that an obligation has been undertaken. This might be a statement such as "Let me be bound to perform." Even here, however, it is meaningful to ask whether the private convention morally binds its participants. Without a convention to uphold private conventions, they are not bound. But what is the prior convention, if not the institution of promising? The convention was constituted by its two participants through a promise to adhere to its norms. If that promise were not binding, the convention would not be, either. A promissory regime therefore cannot be crafted from a private convention.

If contractarian explanations of high-fidelity duties are necessarily circular, can a principle of consent sufficient to support an obligation of low fidelity be extracted from adherence to a convention of promising that already exists? It is unnecessary to wonder how the institution may arise if it is already present in society. Nevertheless, a justification of an institution

36. The circularity of contractarian explanations of how promising may arise was noted by Hume. *See* Hume, *supra* note 30, at 160-61. To avoid this difficulty, Locke, while seeking a connecting factor of consent to explain political allegiance, turned to natural law theories to justify allegiance to such institutions as promising and property. *See* P. RILEY, WILL AND POLITICAL LEGITIMACY 72-73 (1982); J. TULLY, A DISCOURSE ON PROPERTY 48-50 (1980). In the same way, Rawls's theory of justice cannot plausibly rest on a contractarian foundation. At times Rawls does speak of the deliberation in the original position in terms of a choice among alternatives. J. RAWLS, *supra* note 3, at 11-13, 41-42, 45. In the end, however, the procedure would seem not consensual but rational, with a single version of the theory deduced from abstract principles. *See* M. SANDEL, LIBERALISM AND THE LIMITS OF JUSTICE 132 (1982) (stating that "what begins as an ethic of choice and consent ends, however unwittingly, as an ethic of insight and self-understanding").

37. *See* Raz, *Promises and Obligations*, in LAW, MORALITY, AND SOCIETY, 210, 214-15 (P. Hacker & J. Raz eds. 1977).

that relies on a feature of the institution for support is still circular, unless that feature can be independently established as a criterion of value. Suppose that a promissory regime is not deemed just in itself, as low-fidelity theorists would have it. Why then does a promisor's consent to the institution represent a choice that her society must respect? The assumption must be that in choosing promising the promisor provides a justification for imposing a promissory regime. This assumption presupposes that the choice itself imports a binding commitment. Yet this is true only if one is bound to perform that which one has consented to do. This defense of contractarianism must then be circular and must reduce to a will theory which justifies contract law on the basis of the intrinsic value of the convention. Because it relies on the value of the convention, this explanation of promissory allegiance must rest on high-fidelity theories which dispense with connecting factors.

B. PROMISOR-BASED THEORIES: BENEFITS

1. Principle of Fairness

The second low-fidelity explanation of promising grounds a duty of allegiance on the promisor's receipt of a benefit. H.L.A. Hart regarded this social quasi contract as the only intelligible foundation of political obligation. "[W]hen a number of persons conduct any joint enterprise according to rules and thus restrict their liberty, those who have submitted to these restrictions have a right to a similar submission from those who have benefited by their submission."[38] In these circumstances both groups are bound in a mutuality of restrictions, with the former accorded a moral right to support from the latter.

One difficulty with Hart's theory is that the obligation of fidelity arises whatever the moral quality of the institution or its benefits. A burglar may thus be subject to an obligation to a thieves' society that bribes police officers. To rescue his explanation of inclusionary rules from a duty to support immoral institutions, Hart relies on a category of morally unperformable obligations: although the obligation of fidelity arises, it may be one that ought not to be performed.[39] Similarly, promissory C-rules might provide that immoral promises

---

38. Hart, *supra* note 8, at 185. For a similar argument, see W. ROSS, THE RIGHT AND THE GOOD 27 (1930). Plato's *Crito* likely advanced the earliest such theory. *See* PLATO, *Crito*, in THE COLLECTED DIALOGUES OF PLATO 27, 37 (E. Hamilton & H. Cairns 2d ed. 1961).

39. Hart, *supra* note 8, at 185-86.

generate unperformable obligations.[40] Hart's benefits theory, however, does not describe how one ordinarily thinks of political allegiance. Even with a receipt of benefits, no obligation arises to support a wholly evil society. At some point, for example, a state may be so unjust that any obligation of fidelity is extinguished, with the only possible requirement being a duty of rebellion.[41]

Rawls's benefits theory, called the *principle of fairness*, provides a less counterintuitive explanation of duties of fidelity.[42] Unlike Hart's theory, the principle of fairness presupposes that the institution satisfies Rawlsian principles of justice. But notwithstanding the requirement that the underlying institution be just, the principle of fairness is a low-fidelity theory of promise keeping. This is because ethically neutral institutions may satisfy the principle of justice, provided that basic liberties are not infringed and that any resulting changes in social and economic inequalities respect Rawls's difference principle.[43] The more trivial the institution, then, the more easily are principles of justice satisfied: how, after all, can tiddlywinks be troublesome under the difference principle? To say that promising is just is therefore not to say that it is necessarily morally preferable to regimes without promising, as in a high-fidelity theory of justice. In the same way, Rawls is careful to note that his theory of justice is compatible with both private and socialized property regimes.[44] Even if one could argue that promising served efficiency goals, this would not provide an ethical

40. That is to say, an obligation that ought not to be performed. That *ought* and *obligation* statements should be distinguished in this way may be seen in how we think about contradictory promises. If I promise Smith to do *X* and Jones to do *not-X*, the two obligations both stand. I do not, for example, absolve myself from one of the obligations through a cancelling out of the promises. On the other hand, I cannot say that I ought to perform both promises, if ought implies can. On ought and obligation statements, see G. WARNOCK, THE OBJECT OF MORALITY 94-96 (1971); Beran, *Ought, Obligation and Duty*, 50 AUSTRALASIAN J. PHIL. 207, 207-09 (1972); Brandt, *The Concepts of Obligations and Duty*, 73 MIND 374, 376-80 (1964).

41. *See* M. WALZER, OBLIGATIONS—ESSAYS ON DISOBEDIENCE, WAR, AND CITIZENSHIP 3-23 (1970); Pitkin, *Obligations and Consent—II*, 60 AM. POL. SCI. REV. 39, 41-42 (1966).

42. J. RAWLS, *supra* note 3, at 342-50. Earlier versions of Rawls's theory, then called the *principle of fair play*, may be found in Rawls, *Justice as Fairness*, 67 PHIL. REV. 164, 180-84 (1958); Rawls, *The Justification of Civil Disobedience*, in CIVIL DISOBEDIENCE: THEORY AND PRACTICE 241 (H. Bedau ed. 1969); Rawls, *Legal Obligation and the Duty of Fair Play*, in LAW AND PHILOSOPHY 3 (S. Hook ed. 1964).

43. J. RAWLS, *supra* note 3, at 75-83.

44. *Id.* at 274.

defense of the institution, for Rawlsian principles of justice are always prior to those of efficiency.[45]

Rawls does not specify the sort of benefits he has in mind, but clearly not every kind will suffice. They must not be too general, for if they had no reference to promising they could as easily support a principle of nonfidelity. Neither may they be too specific. In a bilateral contract, the benefit that comes first to mind is the promisee's reciprocal promise to perform or his immediate performance. Basing allegiance on such benefits, however, is more properly a reliance theory which justifies inclusionary H-rules on the basis of anticipated harm to promisees.[46] The benefits must then arise from promising itself. This, seemingly, is what Rawls has in mind, for the principle of fairness is stated as a rule of adherence to an institution and not merely an obligation to an individual promisee.

Thus, Rawls's argument is that an individual who has accepted benefits from an ethically neutral (although not unjust) institution is bound to support it. Benefits that derive from an institution that is ethically neutral share the institution's neutrality. If benefits were morally desirable in themselves, they would provide a sufficient reason to adhere to promising regimes. In that case the principle of fairness would simply rest on the natural duty to support a just regime of promising. Because the duty would be one of high fidelity, it would then be unnecessary to look for connecting factors. For this reason Rawls does not seek to base obligations of political allegiance on a receipt of benefits any more than on social contract theories. His natural duty of allegiance to just societies arises involuntarily, for the institution itself is deemed just.[47]

Because the benefits of promising are ethically neutral, the principle of fairness cannot be defended for its effect on the production of public goods. A benefits theory does indeed promise greater stability for the institution than consent theories because beneficiaries are not permitted to free ride. If beneficiaries do not support an institution, their free riding may encourage other defections from it until it may at last disappear. When present participants in the institution are injured thereby, this may be objectionable under reliance theories of promising. Aside from this, however, the collapse of the institution is of no moral concern if it is ethically neutral.

45. *Id.* at 79-80.

46. *See infra* text accompanying notes 67-75.

47. J. RAWLS, *supra* note 3, at 335-36.

Free-rider arguments have force only if it is assumed, from a high-fidelity perspective, that promising should be preserved. The survival of promissory institutions is therefore no part of the purpose of the principle of fairness, nor is it justified if that is its result.

2. Promissory C-rules

If the receipt of benefits grounds the obligation, as Rawls argues, promises are not binding when no benefits have been received. As such, Rawls's explanation of promising is inconsistent with the institution's C-rules. So long as the theory is not tautological, it should be possible to posit persons who have not derived benefits from promising, such as recent arrivals from a nonpromissory regime. Even though they have received no benefits from promising, we would fault them if they promised and failed to perform. If they objected, we would simply tell them that their moral or cultural education was incomplete.

3. Valuation Problems

A further difficulty of benefits theories is their reliance on strong assumptions as to how the benefits may be identified. For example, from a high-fidelity perspective, the advantages of promising seem entirely obvious, for promising leads to a greater likelihood of reciprocal reliance by contractors. But these prospective gains will not suffice to ground the principle of fairness, under which the benefits must have been received in the past. The difficulty of identifying the benefit (not morally good in itself) that is received by living in a promising society is analogous to the problem that arises in restitution when unsolicited services are provided. While the donor of the services may have incurred a detriment, absent something that looks like solicitation or consent it is not clear that such services are of any value to the recipient. As a consequence officious gifts ordinarily do not ground restitutionary claims.[48]

48. Because valuations of property and services are subjective, the risk is that the transformation will not be Pareto superior. The policy against recovery in restitution is therefore strongest when the donor of the benefit might easily have eliminated this risk by seeking instructions from the beneficiary. *See, e.g.*, J.L. Carpenter Co. v. Richardson, 118 Conn. 322, 172 A. 226 (1934) (mechanic performed additional work on motor boat that owner had left simply for a tune-up). But recovery is more likely to be permitted when the valuation problems are of diminished importance. Thus, restitution is nearly always granted for a mistaken payment of money. *See* 3 G. PALMER, THE LAW OF RESTITUTION §§ 14.18-.19 (1978).

How much harder it must be to derive a principle of fidelity to promising, whose benefits are so much less focused than goods or services in restitution. Did I receive a benefit from promissory institutions? Perhaps, instead of owing allegiance, I might simply repay it, if I only knew to whom.

Given such valuation problems, Robert Nozick argues that obligations of political allegiance may disappear altogether.[49] A similar difficulty besets benefits theories of promising. Suppose one argues that she derives no benefit from the institution. She may regard promising as less desirable than life in nonpromissory regimes. We cannot easily contradict her, so long as no moral value is ascribed to promising. This kind of objection could be handled without difficulty on a high-fidelity theory of promising under which a subjective estimate of value can be trumped by an objective measure of the benefit of an institution. But how could this be done on a low-fidelity theory? In political philosophy, as in law, valuation uncertainties may prevent the resolution of substantive issues.

4. Voluntary Acceptance

The objection based on valuation uncertainties may tell more against benefits theories of political than of promissory obligation. The benefits of promising, although not uncontestable, at least seem less controversial than the benefits of actual governments. If promising offers prospective benefits, a present promisor might even be seen to have received benefits from past promisors through their performances, which renders her present promises more creditable.

Even if promisors are assumed to have derived a benefit from the institution, however, it is difficult to see how the mere receipt of benefits gives rise to duties of allegiance unless the benefits are voluntarily accepted. Without such acceptance a fidelity requirement may not be extracted merely by officiously providing a person with a benefit, even if its desirability is conceded. Consider, for example, the case of a community about to decide whether to take measures to reduce air pollution. Assume that the scheme's expected value exceeds its expected costs and that for each member of the community it represents a Pareto superior transformation. All recipients are asked to contribute to the expense. Despite one person's objection, the measure is carried out and air pollution is reduced without his

49. *See* R. NOZICK, ANARCHY, STATE, AND UTOPIA 93-94 (1974).

support. The dissenter's failure to contribute to the scheme would justify his exclusion from its benefits. But if the benefits are nonexcludable (as is likely the case with air pollution measures), no inclusionary rule arises even if the scheme is deemed beneficial for each member of the society. In the same way, no obligation of support arises through the receipt of the nonexcludable benefits of Eastern Standard Time, the market for corporate control, and French literature. Without having voluntarily accepted benefits, one does not owe loyalty.[50] Rawls therefore excluded from the principle of fairness those nonrejectable benefits which come whether we will them or not.[51] If these benefits, like clean air, cannot be rejected, it follows that they cannot feasibly be accepted by their recipients without express consent.

A further difficulty of benefits theories of promising then is that the benefits do not seem voluntarily accepted. Clearly the general benefits of living in a promissory society do not constitute an act of acceptance. At best the acceptance might be found in the act of promising itself, in the knowledge that promises are more likely to be relied on by virtue of performance by prior promisors. Such past performances are public goods, inasmuch as they facilitate future reliance by other promisees. If these benefits are accepted by promisors in their promises, this may be thought sufficient to support the principle of fairness. These benefits, however, are scarcely more

50. *See* A.J. SIMMONS, *supra* note 18, at 122 (Canadians do not owe allegiance to the United States simply because they, as well as Americans, derive benefits from law enforcement in the United States); *see also* Arneson, *The Principle of Fairness and Free-Rider Problems*, 92 ETHICS 616, 619 (1982) ("One cannot voluntarily accept a good one cannot voluntarily reject.").

It may be objected that such institutions seem less like active schemes of social cooperation than the town meeting on air pollution. If principles of fairness were restricted to community meetings or joint enterprises, however, they could scarcely explain the obligation to support a regime of promising. There is, moreover, no compelling reason why a benefits theory should be so limited, as long as some meaningful way exists of exhibiting an obligation of fidelity to the institution. *See* A.J. SIMMONS, *supra* note 18, at 104 (benefits theories extend to broad range of schemes, programs, enterprises, and institutions).

51. J. RAWLS, *supra* note 3, at 111-12. Greenawalt has argued that voluntary acceptance is not required if the recipient is delighted to receive a benefit, understands the cooperative scheme by which it is supplied, and thinks he or she received a fair share. *See* Greenawalt, *Promise, Benefit, and Need: Ties that Bind Us to the Law*, 18 GA. L. REV. 727, 757 (1984). But if the recipient's actual feelings are what matters, it is odd that fair-minded people should owe obligations when ingrates do not. If the recipient's actual feelings do not matter, Greenawalt's theory is no different than that of Simmons.

rejectable than the general material benefits available to those who live in a promising society.[52]

Assuming, however, that it were possible to reject promising, finding a voluntary acceptance of benefits in the act of promising would greatly narrow the difference between benefits theories and contractarian explanations of promising.[53] The more that voluntariness is emphasized, the more closely the acceptance of benefits looks consensual. Consent theories, however, do not adequately explain promising.[54] Furthermore, to distinguish the principle of fairness from contractarian accounts of promising, it is necessary to posit a case in which benefits are voluntarily accepted but not consented to. John Simmons attempts to give an example of this in a community meeting to consider a clean water proposal.[55] One holdout announces that he wants nothing to do with the plan and votes against it. The proposal nonetheless carries at the meeting, and the community implements the plan. Unlike clean air, clean water need not be accepted because it is available only to those who take it from a particular well. This the holdout does, at night so no one will see him. It is presumed that the benefits of clean water cannot be excluded, in that the community cannot prevent him from drawing water from the well. Enough exists for everyone, and no one misses what he takes. He has not consented to the scheme, but Simmons concludes that an obligation of support arises from the acceptance of benefits.[56] Nozick's argument that a mere receipt of benefits without consent does not ground allegiance is thus alleged to be refuted.

Simmons's example is not well chosen, however, for the holdout's removal of the water when he said he would have nothing to do with the plan seems fraudulent. This example does not support a principle of fidelity, but only, if at all, a duty of nonfraudulent bargaining. In addition, even without the holdout's misrepresentation of his intentions, Simmons's example is flawed by its failure to distinguish between the allocational and distributional effects of free riding in the consumption of public goods.[57]

---

52. *See supra* notes 29-33 and accompanying text.

53. *See* A.J. SIMMONS, *supra* note 18, at 124 (if principle of fairness binds only those who have undertaken to support institution, it collapses into theory of consent).

54. *See supra* notes 29-37 and accompanying text.

55. A.J. SIMMONS, *supra* note 18, at 126-27.

56. *Id.* at 127.

57. A similar difficulty arises in Klosko's argument for a principle of fair-

When an individual refuses to participate in collective action, two allocational consequences are possible. First, the probability increases that the scheme will not be undertaken by the remaining participants. Alternatively, if the scheme is implemented, there is a probability that it will not be on such a large scale as it would have been had the individual joined in.[58] This is undesirable if, on a high-fidelity perspective, the scheme is one that should be supported. These ex ante considerations, however, do not ground an obligation of fidelity if it is assumed that the plan is ethically neutral.

In addition, if allocational considerations could support fidelity requirements on the receipt of rejectable goods (like clean water), they would also do so when nonrejectable goods (like clean air) were received. Allocational issues must be determined at the time of the meeting to approve the plan, not at the later time when the holdout receives the benefits. If what is important is the provision of public goods, fidelity becomes important only at the meeting, when support is requested and when the plan will succeed or fail. Thus, no difference exists between the benefits of nonrejectable clean air and those of rejectable clean water. A defection at the meeting might be fatal to either plan if it encourages more attempts at free riding and the scheme eventually collapses. The defection might be principled, based on a preference for an alternate scheme of pollution control or perhaps for an entirely different cooperative scheme. But even in the hardest case, that of the defector angling for a free ride, rejectable benefits cannot be distinguished from nonrejectable ones. An obligation of fidelity must arise in both cases or in neither. If the obligation arises in both cases, with no need for rejectability, the class of institutions to which fidelity is owed would be impossibly broad. If neither

---

ness on the receipt of public goods that are "presumptively beneficial." Klosko, *Presumptive Benefit, Fairness, and Political Obligation*, 16 PHIL. & PUB. AFF. 241 (1987); Klosko, *The Principle of Fairness and Political Obligation*, 97 ETHICS 353 (1987) [hereinafter Klosko, *The Principle of Fairness*]. What Klosko means by presumptively beneficial goods are those needed to maintain a minimally acceptable life. In such cases "the indispensability of the goods overrides the outsider's usual right to choose if he wishes to cooperate." Klosko, *The Principle of Fairness*, *supra*, at 355. If these benefits are deemed morally good, the principle of fairness would collapse into a high-fidelity theory. *See* Simmons, *The Anarchist Position: A Reply to Klosko and Senor*, 16 PHIL. & PUB. AFF. 269, 272 (1987). If not, Klosko's argument is subject to the criticisms made in the following paragraphs.

58. *See* Stigler, *Free Riders and Collective Action: An Appendix to Theories of Economic Regulation*, 5 BELL. J. ECON. & MGMT. SCI. 359, 359-60 (1974).

case generates fidelity requirements, then benefits theories must fail.

Arguments for fidelity requirements on distributional theories are equally troubling. If the holdout makes clear at the meeting that he will not contribute to the plan but will accept its benefits, the other participants will have been put on notice of his plans and will only proceed on that basis. If exclusion from benefits were feasible, the holdout's refusal to participate in the plan would certainly justify his exclusion from the benefits. If not feasible under present technology, the participants might invest in the production of new technology that would exclude the holdout. They might also seek to exclude him from the benefits of other public goods to which he cannot claim an entitlement. They cannot, however, claim that they are entitled to his support at the meeting.

Moreover, if distributional theories do not require the holdout to support the plan at the meeting, nothing much changes after the meeting when he takes water from the well. The participants will have already reacted to his defection, and the well will never run dry. This suggests that issues of distributional fairness, like those of allocational efficiency, should be determined at the time of the meeting. If they were not, the holdout would be wrong to take water from the well even if he has warned the participants of his plans and the supply of water is inexhaustible.

The principal reason why distributional arguments are unpersuasive, however, is that they suffer from an impoverished view of social relations. Public goods are too many and too varied to speak of fidelity requirements on their receipt. Like Blanche Dubois, we rely on the kindness of strangers, and in unforeseen ways assist others, as Frank Capra showed us in *It's a Wonderful Life*.[59] These benefits must not be trivialized; if they could be measured, they could well be as important as the benefits of promising. Beyond kindness is the spillover effect of ubiquitous public goods, like Richard Arneson's case of the well-dressed person who walks down the street, providing pleasure to those who see her.[60] Such benefits may be voluntarily accepted so long as the viewer permits his gaze to settle on the well-dressed person, but he could hardly be expected to choose

59. Liberty Films, Inc. 1946.

60. Arneson, *supra* note 50, at 621; *see also* Simmons, *Voluntarism and Political Associations*, 67 VA. L. REV. 19, 29 (1981) (receipt of spillover benefits does not ground fidelity requirements).

between looking away and owing an obligation. No one could seriously suggest that a Rawlsian meter is running.[61]

Benefits theories of fidelity to institutions are beset by other difficulties, notably because of their static character. Once benefits are received, one is bound forever and subsequent rejection of the institution is wrongful. Even the abandonment of promising by all other members of society would not loosen one's ties to the institution if the obligation is owed to past promisors.[62] A dynamic account of how new institutions replace old ones would always begin with some first act of disloyalty, and each new institution, unless it arose out of thin air, would be founded on treachery. Even the features of an institution would remain immobile. Either institutions would never evolve or a theory based on loyalty would periodically require disloyalty. If applied consistently, the principle of fairness would inevitably offend under any regime of freedom of association that might reasonably be desired. For example, suppose that, of two similar institutions, one provides greater benefits. Surely recipients of benefits from the less desirable institution would not be barred from adopting the first. Although I derive benefits from the English language, I am free to enjoy them without moral scruples and may even without any sense of guilt abandon English for Norwegian the moment I find greater benefits in doing so. It is absurd to suggest that when taking benefits from such institutions, one should calculate nicely whether such benefits have in fact been supported (and, if so, to the requisite extent). One has the right to shop around, to be fickle. So long as two institutions are ethically indistinguishable, no obligation of fidelity to either arises through a receipt of benefits.

The receipt of benefits, therefore, does not suffice to ground a duty of fidelity to promising. This is not to say that every morally desirable enterprise should be supported without regard to the voluntary acceptance of benefits. The absence of a connecting factor may absolve one from obligations of alle-

61. This analysis does not mean to imply that public goods are never valuable. In fact, it is the low-fidelity theorist who refuses to ascribe moral worth to them. This Article suggests that public goods may be morally desirable, and if so they are best defended from a high-fidelity perspective. In such cases they should be supported by all, without regard to the degree to which past benefits were shared.

62. *See* R. SARTORIUS, INDIVIDUAL CONDUCT AND SOCIAL NORMS 104 (1975) (criticizing fidelity requirements, based on past receipt of benefits even though others generally do not cooperate).

giance to just institutions. The lawyer who derives benefits from a local bar association may feel obligated to support it. She would owe no such obligation to an association of dentists even if both are desirable institutions. As promising illustrates, however, duties of fidelity do not always require a special connecting factor. As a consequence the receipt of benefits is neither a sufficient nor a necessary condition for an obligation of fidelity to promising.

5. Gratitude Theories

A final attempt at a benefits theory bases obligations of fidelity on gratitude for receipt of a benefit. It is, of course, difficult to speak of an obligation of gratitude, which in part is simply a feeling rather than an action. In some cases the debt of gratitude may even be requited with an expression of a feeling of gratitude. As Simmons notes, people have less control over their feelings than over their actions, so an obligation to feel grateful sounds odd.[63] Moreover, even when gratitude might lead one to some more positive action, it does not seem correct to label this an obligation. What distinguishes a gift, for which gratitude is appropriate, from mere self-seeking cooperative behavior is that a gift excludes obligations of reciprocity.[64]

In addition, if gifts alone call for gratitude, the idea of gratitude is not easily extended to institutional benefits. What is needed are actual givers, quite apart from the institution itself: the gift without the giver is bare. Institutional benefits, however, are scarcely gifts. In the case of promising, the institutional benefits are derived from past performances by other promisors through which one's promise becomes more worthy of belief. But if past promisors are the donors, their self-interested performances generally are not gifts to anyone.[65] Without the instinct of charity, institutions such as promising are not suitable objects for gratitude.

Furthermore, a gratitude theory of fidelity to promising cannot succeed because gratitude is not an impersonal virtue, but is rooted in the relationships that it permits to flourish. It is part of a gift ceremony in which both donor and recipient

63. A.J. SIMMONS, *supra* note 18, at 166-67.

64. *See* Lyons, *The Odd Debt of Gratitude*, 29 ANALYSIS 92, 92 (1969); Smith, *Is There a Prima Facie Obligation to Obey the Law?*, 82 YALE L.J. 950, 953 (1973).

65. *See* A.J. SIMMONS, *supra* note 18, at 187-89 (criticizing gratitude accounts of political obligations); Berger, *Gratitude*, 85 ETHICS 298, 300 (1975) (no gratitude owed for contractual performance).

demonstrate their bonds to each other. For this reason a want of gratitude is most objectionable when the relationship is most prized, as with family ties. Similarly, the recipient who may rightly reject the relationship does not have to show gratitude for the gift.[66] What then is important is whether the relationship should be upheld. Thus, gratitude for the benefits of a promising regime is appropriate only if a case can be made for promising on other grounds, as when the institution is thought just in itself. Although this might justify duties of high fidelity, it does not support low-fidelity obligations.

C. Promisee-based Theories: Reliance

1. Duty of Respect

Reliance theories of promising are based on the foreseeable harm to promisees if promises are not kept. Because he trusted the promisor and acted upon the promise, the promisee is worse off on breach than he would have been had the promise never been made.[67] Under these circumstances the requirement of allegiance reduces to a duty to prevent harm from coming to those who rely on a person who breaches her promise.

Reliance theories are circular when applied in defense of high-fidelity duties. If the institution does not exist, it cannot be justified through promissory reliance, for promisees would not have relied in the same way on promises without the obligations generated by the institution.[68] Promisees would simply adjust their actions in accordance with their lessened expectation of performance and would have only themselves to blame for overreliance. Breach would not be an occasion for moral concern unless it were thought ethically desirable to resolve informational disparities concerning the likelihood of performance. This, however, would require endowing the institution of promising with moral status without regard to whether reliance

66. *See* L. HYDE, THE GIFT: IMAGINATION AND THE EROTIC LIFE OF PROPERTY 70-73 (1979) (gifts should be refused when acceptance would establish inappropriate relationship to giver).

67. "My statement is like a pit I have dug in the road, into which you fall." C. FRIED, *supra* note 6, at 10.

68. This circularity has been described as a "secret paradox of the common law," *see* P. ATIYAH, PROMISES, MORALS, AND LAW 38 (1981) (arguing that this secret paradox is largely historical), but this difficulty with reliance theories was well known to some of their earliest proponents. *See, e.g.*, Fuller & Perdue, *The Reliance Interest in Contract Damages: 1*, 46 YALE L.J. 52, 59-60 (1936).

interests are affected.[69]

Although reliance theories do not support high-fidelity duties, they do generate low-fidelity duties to support the institution. A convention requires a minimal respect, if not allegiance, so long as any harm may come to another through an assumption that one is acting according to it. When driving in a foreign country, for example, I should learn on which side of the road to drive, and not merely for my own sake. So too, a visitor to Canada from a nonpromissory society has a duty of fidelity to ensure that no one mistakenly believes she is promising. Thus, an inclusionary H-rule of *respect* arises, under which one is bound to take reasonable care to inform oneself of a society's conventions and to ensure that other members of society are not misled as to one's participation in them. This duty of respect can be distinguished from the more exacting requirements of allegiance. The duty is not imposed on everyone, but only on those in sufficient proximity to the society in which the convention is found to give rise to a risk of harm. The duty is therefore one of low fidelity.

In the case of promising, the duty of respect requires one to tread warily around the institution's borders, lest others come to harm. Breach of the duty may invoke a tortious regime of sanctions premised on promisee reliance. In other cases the sanctions may be found within promissory C-rules, and transgressors may become promisors.[70] If one were bound to take care to learn the convention, one would also know when it binds one. A duty to respect the institution by performing promises or abstaining from promising thus arises. Because opting out of promising in a promissory society is virtually impossible,[71] the duty to perform or abstain generally collapses into a duty of performance.

69. An institution of quasi promising may survive despite a lack of moral sanctions. Promisors might have strong prudential reasons to perform, insofar as a reputation for trustworthiness raises the inference that cooperative behavior will be repeated in the future. MacCormick is undoubtedly correct in pointing out that, for this reason, a reliance theory of quasi promising need not presuppose a convention that promises are regarded as binding. MacCormick, *Voluntary Obligations and Normative Powers I*, 46 ARISTOTELIAN SOC'Y 59, 62-69 (Supp. 1972). But if promises do not create an obligation, a reliance theory cannot be advanced to explain why they ought to do so. In addition, as MacCormick notes, the likelihood of reliance is far greater given the existence of a convention of morally binding promises. *Id.* at 72.

70. The result is, of course, an objective theory of contracts, in which promissory obligations may attach to fraudulent or negligent promisors. *See supra* note 31.

71. *See supra* notes 29-33 and accompanying text.

This reliance-based explanation of low fidelity avoids the circle into which high-fidelity duties lead. The perform or abstain requirement assumes the existence both of the convention and of an obligation to prevent other parties from being harmed by relying on one's participation in it. Moreover, it is usually beside the point to argue that such promisee reliance as arises in a society is undesirable. Even if greater self-reliance by the promisee might be preferred, this ordinarily is irrelevant if his behavior was reasonable by his society's conventions. Under the duty of respect, one generally takes one's conventions as one finds them.[72]

A promise thus may be extracted from patterns of reliant behavior. Suppose, for example, that a practice has developed whereby a friend drives me home from work each night. My friend has never formally undertaken to do so, but he and I both know that I have come to expect a ride and that by waiting for him I miss the last bus home. One day he leaves early without telling me. I might legitimately be upset by my friend's behavior and complain that he broke a tacit promise to give me a lift (or at least to warn me to find alternative transportation home). In contrast to this example, however, other examples of reliance clearly do not import an obligation. The burghers who set their watches by Immanuel Kant's walks relied on him but could not have been heard to complain if Kant had altered his habits. Reliance, therefore, may not be a sufficient condition for a promissory obligation.

It is necessary to find some way to distinguish these two kinds of reliance so that only the first gives rise to a promise. It might then be suggested that questions about fidelity should focus on the something else that differentiates the first example from the second.[73] But this mistakes a justification of an inclusionary H-rule with a description of the institution's C-rules. The difference between justified and unjustified reliance may simply be that, under promissory C–rules, one act counts as a promise while the other does not. An explanation of this difference may refer to the institutional values of promissory regimes, which prescribe its contours. Once a convention ex-

72. In an extreme case, the convention may be so unjust that opting out is permitted in spite of reliance. In other cases the more proper course is to warn those who might rely, rather than to instill self-reliance the hard way.

73. *See, e.g.*, P. ATIYAH, *supra* note 68, at 64-68, 127-29 (extra element as compliance with socially accepted values).

ists, however, an inclusionary rule can be found in a duty of respect.

2. Promissory C-rules

Notwithstanding that reliance theories provide an explanation for requirements of low fidelity, these theories remain implausible insofar as they fail to offer a satisfactory account of the contours of promising. Duties of respect do not oblige without promisee reliance, and for this reason reliance theorists cannot explain why a promise remains binding even if the promisee has not relied in any way. To meet this objection, reliance theorists may prefer to focus on the vindication of the promisee's reasonable expectations. Here too, however, the theory remains unpersuasive. If it simply means that, on every promise, the promisee ought to have expected performance, the theory is tautological. If instead it limits promissory obligations to cases in which the promisee did expect performance, the theory does not offer an adequate account of promising. Reliance theorists like Patrick Atiyah must therefore gerrymander their C-rules, redrawing the boundaries of the convention so that promises do not take without reliance.[74] But this is plainly wrong. A promisor's obligation to perform is not excused, either in morals or in law, if the promisee did not believe her.[75] For this reason, reliance theories do not provide a satisfactory explanation of promising, as they can of quasi-promissory institutions like estoppel.

The unrelied-on promise provides another insight into inclusionary H-rules. Without fidelity requirements a conscientious objector to promising might promise and fail to perform in an effort to destroy the institution. This would be wrong under an H-rule of respect, but respect requirements cannot explain why promises are binding even when there is no reliance. This portion of promissory C-rules then requires its own H-rule. Once again, unless the C-rule is linked to people, its obligations do not bind individuals.

III. HIGH-FIDELITY REQUIREMENTS

Given the failure of low-fidelity theories, the only plausible

74. *See id.* at 52-59; *see also* Mack, *Rights, Liberties, and Expectations: A Reply to Sterba and Markie*, 89 ETHICS 301, 303 (1979) (promises binding only with reliance by promisee).

75. *See* Markie, *Mack on Promises and Natural Rights*, 88 ETHICS 263, 264 (1978) (promises binding even without reliance).

justification for promissory institutions is a high-fidelity one in which the source of the allegiance requirement is found in natural duties to support just institutions. Although some just conventions do not command fidelity without a connecting factor, others may bind individuals even if nothing links them to the convention. This is because the institution itself may deserve support, either for the good that results from it on a consequentialist theory or for some intrinsic feature of the convention on a rights theory.

A. Forms of Justification

1. Argument from Inevitability

A justification for a high-fidelity obligation requires that an ethical case be made for the institution. At first glance it might be thought odd to search for a justification for a normative convention: how does one part of our moral language support another part? What might be behind this concern is that a moral justification for morality cannot be given. Prudential, nonmoral reasons for moral rules are possible in terms of consequences not deemed good in themselves. But if morality is good for a particular reason, why is that reason good? On the other hand, if a justification of morality as a whole must be circular, a noncircular justification may be possible for certain features of a moral system, like promise keeping. A morally desirable institution could then be justified by its more fundamental good consequences. Must we suppose that in ethical spheres there is only the good (which cannot be justified) and that which is justified (which cannot be good)?

A more serious critique of promissory theory claims that the institution is so necessarily a part of our society that no justification is required. This objection from inevitability argues that nonpromissory societies cannot exist and concludes that promising must be accepted as a necessary social convention.[76] This argument does not generate an ethical defense of fidelity requirements, for that would amount to drawing an evaluative conclusion from a descriptive premise. It suggests, however, that inclusionary H-rules are not required when defection is impossible.

The challenge of such arguments, therefore, is to produce an intelligible account of a rebellion against promising. Admit-

76. *See, e.g.*, Hanfling, *supra* note 32, at 26-27; Midgley, *supra* note 10, at 252; Pitkin, *supra* note 41, at 48.

tedly, refraining from promising in a promissory society would be extraordinarily difficult. Suppose, however, that defectors consider nonpromissory regimes to be in every way superior to promissory societies. Thinking that promising is evil, they might promise and systematically refuse to perform in an effort to hasten the convention's fall. This behavior would be wrongful if it could be established that they owed the institution allegiance. Whether the rejection of promising is wrongful or not, however, it remains intelligible. Nor could defectors be granted the right to opt out of the convention and yet be told that their promises ought to be performed. Every promissory ought thus requires a principle of fidelity for both rebels from and supporters of the institution. If the promisor is bound to perform, this must be by virtue of an inclusionary H-rule. Such a rule may arise because of the moral value of the institution even if the promisor thinks it unjust.

In addition, the argument that promising is a necessary convention is undercut by the fact that a society without promising does exist. Tonga is a Pacific monarchy that lies east of Fiji and south of Samoa. Several scholars have documented its customs, which are worthy of study even apart from the undoubted incentive to conduct a field trip there.[77] One of the more idiosyncratic customs in Tonga is the meaning of promises. Although several Tonganese words mean something like promising, none give rise to a moral obligation to perform.[78] Nevertheless, Tongan society places great importance on the maintenance of personal relationships and on reciprocal acts of assistance. A Tonganese promise is a recognition of solidarity, with the intention to assist in the future evidencing a

77. Tonga first came under European influence in the eighteenth century. Captain Cook visited it in 1773 and, with a Westerner's ignorance of native feeling, named it the Friendly Islands. He was apparently unaware that the Tongans were plotting to assassinate him and his crew and that they were saved only because of tribal disagreements as to whether this should be done by day or by night. S. LĀTŪKEFU, CHURCH AND STATE IN TONGA 12 (1974). He may also not have noticed the Tongan penchant for cannibalism and the strangling of widows. *Id. See generally* Korn & Korn, *Where People Don't Promise*, 93 ETHICS 445 (1983); K. Morton, Kinship, Economics, and Exchange in a Tongan Village (Sept. 1972) (Ph.D. dissertation, University of Oregon, available from University Microfilms International, Ann Arbor, Michigan).

78. Korn & Korn, *supra* note 77, at 446-47; *see also* H. MAINE, ANCIENT LAW 312 (15th ed. 1894) ("No trustworthy primitive record can be read without perceiving that the habit of mind which induces us to make good a promise is as yet imperfectly developed, and that acts of flagrant perfidy are often mentioned without blame and sometimes described with approbation.").

present desire to maintain a relationship.[79] But the future is uncertain, and if performance becomes difficult it may be omitted without moral sanction.[80] The greater probability of future breach in Tonga must then be balanced against the less easily quantifiable benefits of living in a society whose institutions suggest a heightened concern for present expressions of sympathy and concern. Compared to the advantages of promising, those advantages may not seem compelling, but at least a nonpromissory society exists.

A second argument from inevitability is that an inquiry into the values of promissory regimes is unnecessary because of the institution's evident desirability. Under this theory nonpromissory institutions are regarded as so repellant that everyone would reject them, with no need to explore the basis for doing so. For example, imagine a nonpromising society called the Kingdom of Natural Duty. Here promising is excluded not through some feature of the language, as in Tonga, but because of the breadth of preexisting natural duties. If contract is to be squeezed out in this way, putative promisors cannot be allowed any room to maneuver, with all their waking moments filled in the performance of some duty. In the land of Natural Duty, that which is not prohibited is made compulsory. Contract is eliminated because it is meaningless to say that one assumes an obligation to do that which one already has a duty to perform.

Promising regimes clearly are incompatible with realms of Natural Duty, for if all future actions are accounted for, nothing remains to promise. From this, Hart concludes that the existence of a promissory regime implies a range of personal liberty as to future action.[81] Because he believes promising to be a universal practice, Hart describes the promisor's ability to arrange future affairs as a natural right.[82]

Hart's argument is subject to the same weaknesses as other attempts to derive moral conclusions from empirical premises. In addition, were it (wrongly) taken as a defense of promising, it would be quite misleading. If promising implies liberty, it does not follow that liberty implies promising.[83] A rejection of

79. Korn & Korn, *supra* note 77, at 448-49.

80. *Id.* at 449.

81. *See* Hart, *supra* note 8, at 183-84.

82. *See id.* at 184 (promisor's ability to create future obligation follows from natural right of freedom).

83. One may even be troubled by the restrictions on choice that arise through the act of promising. *See* M. ROTHBARD, THE ETHICS OF LIBERTY 133-48 (1982) (because promises restrict liberty, no contract should be enforced ex-

the realm of Natural Duty need not lead to promising. One might also end up in Tonga. In both Tonga and the Kingdom of Natural Duty, the law of civil obligations is restricted essentially to tort. Despite this similarity, the two societies differ in the scope of their tortious regimes, with considerably fewer requirements in Tonga than in the land of Natural Duty. While in Tonga the scope of tort law can be more expansive than that found in promissory societies, it may also be less so. (The Gulag is after all a promissory society.) Nonpromissory regimes need not, therefore, place as many restrictions on human choice as do Western states, and promissory regimes cannot be justified as essential to liberty. Instead, a defense of promising requires a discriminating analysis of the institution's advantages.

2. Rights and Consequentialist Theories

High-fidelity explanations of natural duties of fidelity seek to justify promising from the perspective of either theories of rights or of consequences. Neoformalism, an example of a rights theory, values promising for the choices it facilitates, whatever the consequences. Consequentialist theories value promising for its consequences, taking into account how they are produced. With respect to promissory institutions, the most plausible version of consequentialism is utilitarianism.

Although neoformalism focuses on the choices involved in promising, such theories are devoid of content if they totally ignore consequences. Choosing in total ignorance of conse-

---

cept transfers of property); Macneil, *Values in Contract*, *supra* note 6, at 356-59 (enforcing promises that reduce future options is inconsistent with valuing free choice). The paradox of freedom that free choice in promising gives us the liberty to bind ourselves is the basis for the tension in the commercial exchanges of Venice and the matrimonial ones of Belmont, for, like Antonio's bond, Portia's promise was also a sale of her person. *See* W. SHAKESPEARE, THE MERCHANT OF VENICE, act III, sc. ii, 16-18 (W. Merchant ed. 1967); M. SHELL, MONEY, LANGUAGE, AND THOUGHT 81 (1982) ("The beautiful marriage bond is not far removed from the ugly bond that made it possible in the first place."). In the end the tensions remain, and for want of a resolution in tragedy we are given the palliative of comedy (mistaken identity of Portia–Balthasar).

These concerns dissipate when it is realized that promises are but one kind of bonding technique and that self-control theories provide numerous examples of unobjectionable methods by which an individual may restrict future choices. If promises are suspect for this reason, alarm clocks are dangerous as well. On self-control theories, see T. SCHELLING, CHOICE AND CONSEQUENCE 57-112 (1984) (describing theories of self-command and their relation to ethics and law); Schelling, *Enforcing Rules on Oneself*, 1 J.L. ECON. & ORG. 357, 361-73 (1985) (describing self-imposed rules designed to improve individual behavior).

quences would be like pushing a button without knowing where the current leads. Unlike the consequentialist, however, a neoformalist deliberately cuts off evidence of remote consequences when rights are concerned. Once the immediate consequences are known and the act can be identified, a choice that respects the rights of moral actors is preferred to one that produces a better end state but that violates those rights. The priority of rights over good end states is lexicographic in that no end state, however desirable, outweighs the observance of a right. Without the possibility of a trade-off between rights and consequences, evidence of probable end states is entirely irrelevant when a right is invoked.

Notions of the right and the good seem to color our ethical intuitions of many moral issues, and we may then be led to search for some overarching theory that unties these two strands of our moral ideas.[84] It may be suggested, for example, that rights may be relaxed in the face of monstrous consequences.[85] If so, this may be thought to involve something less than a total abandonment of rights theories, which might continue to serve for less dramatic moral questions. Alternatively, the consequentialist need not be indifferent to procedural rules with a rights component in selecting end states. In choosing a course of action, one also selects the path that leads there. If this involves abridging some right, the consequentialist must take that into consideration.[86] Moreover, the violation of a right should be weighed not merely from the perspective of the party directly injured, but more generally in terms of the precedent value of the breach. For example, a breach of promise may render the institution of promising more unstable for other parties in the future. In this way end states that would otherwise be desirable might be qualified as bad for their spillover effects.

These attempts at synthesis may seem to be headed in the right direction, being better able to accommodate ordinary feel-

---

84. For several suggestions as to how this might be accomplished, see R. NOZICK, PHILOSOPHICAL EXPLANATIONS 494-98 (1981). The same author's *Anarchy, State, and Utopia*, however, was nonconsequentialist in its approach to questions of political obligation. *See* R. NOZICK, *supra* note 49, at 26-53.

85. For example, this is suggested by Fried in his concept of catastrophic cases, those "extreme situations in which the usual categories of judgment (including the category of right and wrong) no longer apply." C. FRIED, *supra* note 15, at 10.

86. "Mattering as a means is a way of mattering." D. PARFIT, *supra* note 2, at 46. A society whose citizens act rightly may also be taken as one of the ends posited as good by consequentialist theories. *Id.* at 48-49.

ings of justice than unreconstructed rights or consequentialist theories might. But what works in practice may not work in theory. The first suggestion—rights theories for ordinary cases, consequentialist for exceptions—simply raises the question of how the border between the two kinds of moral questions is established. If rights are like tunnels, so that only small cars pass through, the distinction between the two kinds of theories is moved back one step, where the height is established and where only one kind of theory is possible. As for the second suggestion, a consequentialist theory of rights must always refer to end-state consequences if rights are abridged, for information about the consequences of an ascription of rights cannot be shut out. Thus, every moral theory must be either a rights or consequentialist one insofar as it would exclude or admit evidence of remote consequences in moral decisions.

B. Neoformalist Theories

The case for a natural duty of fidelity therefore must rest on either a rights or a consequentialist ethical theory. Neoformalist explanations of promising, based on concepts of rights, are considerably less persuasive than consequentialist theories for two reasons. Neoformalism cannot plausibly indicate when a regime of contracts ends, at the border of the doctrine of illegality. In addition, neoformalism cannot explain why promising, of all institutions, should be valued.

1. Limits of Contract

The first objection to neoformalism is that it fails to account for the circumstances when promises ought not to be performed, as under the doctrine of illegality. Of course, a rights theorist need not argue that every promise should be performed, in the way that Kant believed that lying was never justified.[87] When promises impose burdensome costs on third parties, for example, they might simply not count as promises, thus eliminating the apparent counterexample. But what of the promise that is unobjectionable when made and whose external costs become apparent only at the time of performance? From a neoformalist perspective, how can present promissory

87. *See* I. Kant, *On a Supposed Right tp Tell Lies from Altruistic Motives*, in Critique of Practical Reason and Other Writings in Moral Philosophy 346, 347-48 (L. Beck trans. 1949). For a recent statement of Benjamin Constant's argument that lying to liars or murderers is justified, see C. Fried, *supra* note 15, at 69-78.

rights be trumped by remote consequences? If the change of circumstances affected only the two parties, it might be argued that the problem could be resolved through a hypothetical consent to efficient breaches. Relating the changed circumstances to the original promise seems a little artificial, however, and in any event this move seems even more fictitious when third parties suffer the disastrous consequences. Performance of such promises may be forbidden by consequentialist theories, but from the perspective of rights, an implied consent to avoid unpleasant consequences does not seem possible without abandoning neoformalism. It is, however, easy to imagine examples in which this feature of rights theories is uncomfortably absolutist.

The major weakness of any rights theory of ethics now becomes visible. It is not that rules are established in spite of their consequences, but that they are prescribed in ignorance of them. A disregard of known consequences might seem, at an intuitive level, a part of the price paid to protect rights. This kind of thinking may lead one, like Charles Fried, to propose a measure of consequentialism in extreme cases, in which the cost of respecting rights is too high.[88] Such suggestions, however, reveal a misunderstanding of the distinction between the two ethical theories. In excluding as irrelevant any evidence of remote results of an ascription of rights, neoformalism requires ethical decisions to be made at a time when extreme consequences cannot be distinguished from moderate ones. The theory of rights must be formed in the face of unknown consequences. From behind the veil of ignorance, the moral actor is permitted to anticipate the worst.

2. Fidelity to a Convention

The second objection to neoformalism is its failure to provide a justification of promising that takes account of its conventional nature. What must be shown is why this convention is desirable. Two such arguments must be considered. Promising may first be thought to provide greater freedom by expanding the domain of alternatives. On the other hand, adopting the institution might be seen to offer a more focused set of advantages under which the kind of alternatives available under the institution matter. Both of these explanations ultimately reduce to consequentialism.

88. *See supra* note 85.

At first glance it might seem easy enough to ground a neoformalist defense of promising in the greater range of action in promissory than in nonpromissory societies. There is one thing that can be done in promissory but not in nonpromissory societies, and that is to make a promise. The expansion of the domain of alternatives in this way offers more choices, with the case for promising resting on a simple affirmation of libertarian values.

This argument has a superficial appeal. While liberty may mean many different things, in part it does implicate the number of available alternatives.[89] With only one member in the class of alternatives, no real choice is possible. Suppose, for example, that one cannot leave his house because a large boulder blocks the only exit. Surely he need not know whether the rock was placed there by human hand or by nature before he can say whether his liberty has been restricted.[90] On the other hand, not every increase in the domain of alternatives results in an expansion of liberty. The mugging victim has alternatives (the highwayman's "your money or your life"), but neither is very pleasant. When the alternative is undesirable or not pre-

89. Thus, Locke believed that "the end of law is not to abolish or restrain, but to preserve and enlarge freedom." Locke, *supra* note 29, at 33. For discussions of the relation between liberty and the domain of alternatives, see Jones & Sugden, *Evaluating Choice*, 2 INT'L REV. L. & ECON. 47, 47-57 (1982); Beavis & Rowley, *Evaluating Choice: A Note*, 3 INT'L REV. L. & ECON. 79, 79-81 (1983); Jones & Sugden, *Evaluating Choice: A Reply*, 3 INT'L REV. L. & ECON. 85, 85-87 (1983).

90. From a utilitarian perspective, the distinction between negative freedom, by which only actual coercion restricts liberty, and positive freedom is suspect. Theories of positive and negative freedom are most closely associated with I. BERLIN, TWO CONCEPTS OF LIBERTY 7-19 (1958), although they may be traced back to Saint Augustine's distinction between the freedom to choose and the freedom to choose rightly. ST. AUGUSTINE, ENCHIRIDION § 30 (E. Evans trans. 1953) (Benedictine Folio ed. 1701). For arguments that the man confined to his house by the boulder is free, see F. HAYEK, THE CONSTITUTION OF LIBERTY 12-13 (1960) (distinguishing freedom of choice from range of physical possibilities); Miller, *Constraints on Freedom*, 94 ETHICS 66, 68-70 (1983) (distinguishing between freedom and ability to do an act).

In this Article positive freedom is identified with the size of the domain of alternatives and with the quality of the choices offered. *See, e.g.*, Regan, *Paternalism, Freedom, Identity, and Commitment*, in PATERNALISM, *supra* note 7, at 113, 116-21 (discussing freedom-maximization principle). More frequently, however, positive freedom is taken to refer to the deliberative quality of the choice, *see* Sunstein, *supra* note 7, at 1132-38 (paternalistic regulation does not curtail but enhances liberty if process norms are served), or to self-realization norms, *see* C. TAYLOR, *What's Wrong with Negative Liberty*, in PHILOSOPHY AND THE HUMAN SCIENCES 211, 215-16 (1985) (directing action toward goal of self-realization does not curtail but enhances liberty).

ferred to existing alternatives, its effect on the realm of liberty is at best neutral. In addition, Nozick clearly is right in suggesting that two choices may both be described as free even if the relevant domains differ in size.[91] Liberty is not measured simply by counting up alternatives with no consideration of the kinds of choices available.[92]

The mere expansion of the domain of alternatives through the adoption of a convention of promising is then not enough to justify the institution from a libertarian perspective. It is true that, before the institution existed, one could not promise. And before Abner Doubleday, one could not play baseball. But surely no burst of liberty occurred when baseball was invented. A neoformalist justification of an institution therefore requires not only that new forms of activity be made possible when a convention is adopted by a society, but also that the convention increases liberty in a significant way.

In addition, a rights theorist cannot prefer promising to other conventions on the basis of its consequences. If, for example, promises are thought to generate more wealth than baseball, this merely provides a prudential reason for valuing the former institution more than the latter. From a rights perspective, the explanation of the importance of promising must focus on abstract rights and ignore end-state considerations. Imagine, therefore, that the consequences of adopting promissory institutions are not benign; instead, a realm of spontaneous disorder ensues. We must understand that, even here, the neoformalist's support for promising continues unabated, lest rights be thought parasitic upon ends.

Neoformalist theories therefore must explain, without reference to its consequences, why promising should be valued over other conventions. One response to this challenge might be to argue that a priority attaches to promissory institutions because they permit obligations to be incurred. There are, however, a variety of ways, not now available, in which obligations could arise. The easiest example of this is vows, conceived of as

91. *See* R. NOZICK, *supra* note 49, at 263-64.

92. It may be objected here that the weighing of two sets of alternatives is a hopeless task. In many cases this may be so, such that both states might be qualified as free. But in other circumstances it is not implausible to suggest that some alternatives may be thought trivial and others significant. In dwelling on the choices open to one chained to a column, Lord Byron did not persuade us that the Prisoner of Chillon was in any sense free. *See* Regan, *supra* note 90, at 119-20 (ranking of qualities of alternatives may be amenable to acceptable intuitive judgments).

promises to oneself, not to God. Although vows could easily give rise to moral or legal obligations,[93] given the right kind of institutions, they currently do not. Suppose, for example, that someone writes a note to herself in which she vows not to start smoking. In spite of the note, she smokes. She may be mildly reproved for this, but she will not be faulted more because she wrote the note. As a consequence promising cannot be prized as an obligation-creating institution without a further explanation of why that kind of obligation is valuable.

There is, moreover, a further reason why no unique advantage attaches to promising as an obligation-creating institution. This is because promises are *content independent*, conferring a moral quality to the object of the promise because of the promise and not because of the object itself.[94] The fact of promising, not the substance of the promise, creates the moral obligation. Promising is not justified by its obligations; rather, the obligations are justified by the promises behind them.

The neoformalist may also attempt to explain the particular advantages of promising by assimilating the institution to property law: the obligation is reified and made the subject of transfer to the promisee.[95] When I promise, I sell you the right to my performance. Nonpromissory regimes are then seen as ones in which such forms of property are inalienable, and the

93. On the Roman law of vows, see 12 G. BAUDRY-LACANTINERIE & L. BARDE, TRAITÉ THÉORIQUE ET PRATIQUE DE DROIT CIVIL § 28 at 36 n.3 (3d ed. 1906); *see also* R. WORMS, DE LA VOLONTÉ UNILATÉRALE CONSIDÉRÉE COMME SOURCE D'OBLIGATIONS 41-79 (1891) (discussing promises to a city and to a god). Vows as self-control tactics are discussed in T. SCHELLING, *supra* note 83, at 99-107.

94. H.L.A. Hart introduced the concept of "independence of content" in Hart, *Legal and Moral Obligation*, in ESSAYS IN MORAL PHILOSOPHY 82, 102 (A. Melden ed. 1958); *see also* Raz, *Voluntary Obligations and Normative Powers* (pt. 2), 46 ARISTOTELIAN SOC'Y 79, 95-98 (Supp. 1972) (discussing arguments that justify norms).

95. The justification of legally binding promises on the analogy of property transfers is most clearly made by Grotius, who argued that the right to a property transfer or to performance of some action by the promisor may itself constitute property and that private ownership entails full rights of alienation. 2 H. GROTIUS, 2 DE JURE BELLI ET PACIS ch. XI, I, 3, at 33 (W. Whewell trans. 1853) (1625); 1 *id.* at ch. VI, I, 1, at 340; *see also* Benson, *The Executory Contract in Natural Law: A Theory of the Right in Contract* 26-32 (unpublished manuscript on file at Minnesota Law Review) (explaining Grotius's analogy equating a perfect promise with the transfer of property). I understand Kant to have adopted a similar explanation of promissory obligations. *See* I. KANT, THE PHILOSOPHY OF LAW 65, 104-05 (W. Hastie trans. 1887) (promises give one possession of will of another); *see also* Barnett, *supra* note 4, at 291-300 (contractual obligations arise from consent to transfer of alienable entitlements or rights).

justification of promising comes down to a rejection of paternalism, in the form of restrictions on alienation.

The analogy to property is not entirely unreasonable. Balance sheets would look quite different if promises were discounted from assets and liabilities. It remains unclear however, why such assets must be alienable on a theory of rights. What is needed is a counterargument to the paternalist who would prevent the alienation of promissory obligations. If some restrictions on choice are to be permitted, the theory must distinguish proper from improper paternalism. Here, however, neoformalism seems bound to a treadmill, beyond a bare assertion that these kinds of assets ought to be alienable. Moreover, even the neoformalist libertarian who rejects any form of paternalism seems not to have a convincing argument for the superiority of promising to other institutions—baseball, for example.[96] The ability to imagine one institution as a property right more easily than another hardly moves the argument forward. For example, other rights (the right to associate with eight other people on a team) are better suited to baseball than promising. There are even property regimes, in which baseball teams are sold, better suited to baseball than promising. What is missing then is an explanation why *this* kind of property should be alienable.[97] And that question logically cannot be answered merely through an analogy to property.

The last attempt at a neoformalist justification of promising focuses upon the virtue of trust fostered by the institution. Fried has argued that a respect for informed human choice mandates upholding the institution of truth telling,[98] and in *Contract as Promise* he applies the same analysis to promising.[99] His defense of promising is, however, less plausible than

96. Some libertarians, like Murray Rothbard, would indeed prefer baseball, for legally binding promises are troubling under the paradox of freedom. *But see supra* note 83 (self-control tactics also permit individuals to fetter themselves, and these tactics cannot reasonably be thought objectionable).

97. This was the basis upon which Mill rejected the Kantian analysis of promising, under which the duty to perform rested on a perceived inability to make a universal law of promise breaking, because the institution then would not survive. *See* I. KANT, FOUNDATIONS OF THE METAPHYSICS OF MORALS 18-19 (L. Beck trans. 1959). But all that this shows, as Mill noted, is that the consequences of the adoption of such a rule would be undesirable. *See* J.S. MILL, *Utilitarianism*, in 10 COLLECTED WORKS OF JOHN STUART MILL 203, 207 (J. Robson ed. 1969).

98. C. FRIED, *supra* note 15, at 63 ("The foundational values of freedom and rationality imply the foundational value of truth, for the rational man is the one who judges aright, that is, truly.").

99. C. FRIED, *supra* note 6, at 16-17.

his theory of truth telling, for it is harder to ascribe a foundational status to promissory trust. If moral choice must be informed to be meaningful, it is not clear why such knowledge must extend to future action by others. Are Tongans, lacking these foundations, unfree and irrational or less responsible in their moral choices? Surely notions of moral praise or blame are not inappropriate in nonpromissory societies.

The problem with the argument from trust is similar to that faced by neoformalists in their analogies to property regimes. It provides no explanation of why *this* kind of trust should be promoted, as opposed to the reliance that arises between teammates in baseball (Tinker to Evers to Chance). Doubtless, promissory trust produces more material wealth, but this kind of prudential reason counts as nothing in neoformalism, which must look to something intrinsic to promissory conventions as opposed to baseball conventions. What then is that essence of promising, shorn of its consequences, which leads one to prefer it to baseball? Trust arises through patterns of cooperative behavior, which in turn may be a by-product of almost any convention. How then is trust assayed, so that between conventions the quality (or quantity) of various kinds of trust can be compared? By dollars? To be sure, promissory trust is more important than baseball trust. But does this refer to anything more than the consequences of favoring one institution over another?

Furthermore, the adoption of promising in a nonpromissory regime might lead in part to unpleasant consequences. Might not some negative externalities arise with so fundamental an institution? The claim that Tongan society better promotes communitarian virtues should not be rejected out of hand. More trust may come only at a cost, as other features of society change in the new regime. In particular, if the abstract value of a regime of trust stems from the interpersonal relationships that it permits to flourish, it must be relevant to ask whether the adoption of promising might in some way weaken ties to one's fellowman.[100]

100. There is another reason why a rights theory of the contours of contract law is unstable. As consequences become less remote, the parties might be expected through private contracting to alter the C-rules of the neoformalist regime if it departed from consequentialist norms. Indeed, the parties could not be prevented from doing so under any theory whose primary tenet is the value of human choice. Imagine, therefore, how rights theorists would select the kinds of conduct to be actionable for misrepresentation. For example, where on the continuum between fraud and nondisclosure is conduct

C. Consequentialist Theories of Promising

1. Utilitarian Explanations

Consequentialist theories of promising must ground fidelity requirements on the superiority of promissory to nonpromissory societies. In examining end-state justifications of the institution, one manner of proceeding would be first to identify what counts as a good consequence and then to examine how it figures in a promissory regime. Although this might seem the most direct path, the circuitous route sometimes leads more quickly to one's goal. Thus, this Article questions the consequences of adopting the institution and assumes that they are morally desirable. There may be many other plausible concepts of the good, but I seek only those that might justify promising and contract law.

While the best known variant of consequentialism is utilitarianism, a consequentialist position is not necessarily utilitarian. For example, a complete contingent theory might rank all possible end states without inquiring as to their place in the felicific calculus. Alternatively, other goods, such as end states characterized by particular virtues, may be the desiderata. A consequentialist thus may prefer a choice leading to an end state that leaves its members with less average or total utility than is available through another choice.[101]

Apart from spillover effects, the direct product of promising is the disclosure of information concerning the promisor's likelihood of performance. The assumption of a moral obligation, like that of a legal obligation when civil remedies for breach are attached, may assist in resolving the informational disparity between promisor and promisee as to performance.[102] Higher quality promises may be made when the consequences of breach are more painful to the promisor. In this way a promisee who is not satisfied by the promisor's statement of intention may ask, "But do you *promise*?," thereby raising the stakes on breach. Promising operates, both on moral and legal levels, as a bonding technique. Without it, substitutes for prom-

---

wrongful? Suppose that the choice of fraud standards is to be made at a time before the consequences are known, but that the parties are subsequently told the economic consequences of their decision. Must any attempt on their part to reallocate disclosure duties now be resisted?

101. *See* D. PARFIT, *supra* note 2, at 26-27 (pluralist consequentialism appeals to several different concepts of what constitutes a good outcome).

102. For a discussion of this signalling explanation of guarantees as a response to informational asymmetries, see Akerlof, *The Market for "Lemons": Quality Uncertainty and the Market Mechanism*, 84 Q.J. ECON. 488, 499 (1970).

ising may arise, such as third-party guarantees and performance bonds.[103] Stable firms may also make more creditable promisors if they have acquired a reputation for performance.[104] But these devices will not wholly take the place of promising in promissory regimes.

The advantage to promisees of information concerning the possibility of performance is that it permits greater reliance (or trust). The promisor will respond to the possibility of sanctions for breach by decreasing both the number of promises made and their breadth, revealing regret contingencies through the conditions attached to the bargain.[105] A better quality of promise results, and promisees may more safely arrange their affairs in the expectation of performance, facilitating future planning. If promissory regimes are defended, it therefore must be for such beneficial reliance. The possibility of beneficial reliance is not, however, a connecting factor of the type that would support a low-fidelity theory. The inclusionary duty arises from the general benefit that accrues to society from the capacity to rely on promises, not from actual reliance by a particular promisee. In this way the duty presupposes the moral value of the institution.

But why stop there? Beneficial reliance itself seems at best an instrumental good, desirable only insofar as it promotes some higher good. Apart from a belief that welfare gains will result, it is not easy to see what it is about promising that might attract. Why would we promote reliance if we thought, in a

---

103. The use of performance bonds as a substitute for the enforcement of promises is proposed in M. ROTHBARD, *supra* note 83, at 133-40 (discussing libertarian theories under which courts should recognize property transfers but not enforce promises through damages remedies). Such bonds implicate a hostage strategy in resolving informational asymetrics between promisor and promisee. *See* Kronman, *Contract Law and the State of Nature*, 1 J.L. ECON. & ORG. 5, 12-18 (1985) (discussing varieties of hostage techniques).

104. *See* Klein & Leffler, *The Role of Market Forces in Assuring Contractual Performance*, 89 J. POL. ECON. 615, 618-25 (1981). An investment in reputation is warranted only when (1) promisor and promisee are repeat players or information about the former's cooperative strategy will be conveyed to other parties with whom she will bargain in the future, and (2) all such bargains are characterized by a temptation to defect (such as arises in prisoners' dilemma games). A cooperative strategy in a prior game may then communicate that defection strategies are unlikely to be adopted in future games. *See* Scott, *Conflict and Cooperation in Long Term Contracts*, 75 CALIF. L. REV. (1987).

105. For a discussion of considerations in devising efficient sanctions for breach, see Goetz & Scott, *Enforcing Promises: An Examination of the Basis of Contract*, 89 YALE L.J. 1261, 1274-86 (1980) (optimal damages rule will seek to maximize beneficial reliance while minimizing detrimental or mistaken reliance).

particular instance, that it would lead to a net loss of utility? A defense of promissory institutions therefore appears to rest on utilitarian foundations.

Under such a theory, it is not necessary to deny that negative externalities arise, but only to assume that they are exceeded by the benefits of promising. A utilitarian defense of promising does not require that communitarian virtue in Tonga be denied. In fact, a better strategy for the utilitarian might be to insist on such values, for they must on his estimate be exceeded by the values of promissory societies. The greater its costs, the greater its virtues.

Utilitarian theories also offer a creditable explanation of fidelity to a just institution. Even if promising is desirable, this does not suffice to bind one to the institution unless one's defection would weaken it. If an ethical case could be made for an institution, an individual ought then to support it when fidelity to it makes a difference. Moreover, the appropriate question here is not whether a single breach matters, but whether a rule absolving promisors from performing (or a disposition not to perform) threatens the institution. For example, promissory skeptics sometimes argue that "desert island promises" do not bind promisors.[106] These are promises made to a dying person at a time when no one else is around to hear them or to know if they are performed. Yet even here a rule that these promises are not binding would lead to fewer such promises being believed in the future. This is because a moral theory that accords a right of defection in particular circumstances affects the behavior of parties who later find themselves in that situation. On a utilitarian theory, desert island promises continue to have a moral force, provided that a rule of enforceability in these circumstances is itself justified on utilitarian grounds.

2. Nihilist Objections to Utilitarian Theories

With the failure of low-fidelity theories and of neoformalism, only consequentialist explanations of promising offer a plausible alternative to promissory nihilism. In particular, utilitarian theories provide the strongest defense of promising. In what remains, this Article considers three objections to the utilitarian analysis of promising. The most serious objections reduce to nihilism, against which no defense is offered save to recognize it as such.

106. Arguments for and against the binding quality of desert island promises are discussed in P. ATIYAH, *supra* note 68, at 59-63.

The first objection is that high-fidelity duties require too much of an individual. Utilitarian theories of promising prohibit not merely free riding but also conscientious objection. If the institution deserves support without a connecting factor, then even a principled attempt to secede from promissory societies is wrongful. But is this too hard? Must an individual be prevented from severing links with existing societies and institutions so as to work out private utopian dreams?[107] Could Roman tax collectors legitimately have been sent out to Saint Paul of Egypt, among his society of lions?

The context of questions of political allegiance may be too rich to permit their easy resolution through the single touchstone of a duty to support just institutions. Much may depend on the kind of individual and his reasons for seceding, as well as the nature of the institution and the kind of fidelity it requires. It is also difficult to imagine how a theory of political allegiance could mandate fidelity without some kind of connecting factor such as residence in a territory. If the nexus could be erased legitimately, a right of conscientious objection in political regimes must be conceded. In contrast to political allegiance, however, duties of fidelity that do not depend on a connecting factor may more easily be imagined for promissory institutions. One reason for this is that promising's demands on an individual seem less intrusive than the demands of a modern state. In addition, we are likely to have less concern for the scruples of an anarchist or visionary in matters of promissory rather than political allegiance. This may be due to nothing more than a stronger intuition that the institution of promising is morally desirable.

The second objection to utilitarianism assumes that promissory institutions can be justified only through the independent desirability of the bargained-for result. This objection asserts that, so long as any value is thought more desirable than the bargained-for result, it is fair game to substitute a duty aimed at fostering the higher value for the promissory obligation. This might be termed the fallacy of content dependency, although it is really a species of promissory nihilism.[108] It takes

107. *See* R. NOZICK, *supra* note 49, at 309-12 (rejecting idea of one best society for all individuals).

108. A prominent example of this kind of nihilism is found in P. ATIYAH, *supra* note 68, at 193-94, which suggests that promises are admissions of preexisting or noncontractual obligations. "[T]he modern social group has much more difficulty in recognizing the right of individuals to create obligations in circumstances where the group itself does not recognize the existence of obli-

doctrines of illegality as the norm, not the limiting case, with the content of every promise held to be of no moral worth except insofar as it accords with public goals such as distributive justice. Utilitarianism may seem particularly susceptible to the objection from content dependency. With its instinct that moral issues may require trade-offs, utilitarianism may appear to lack the barriers to paternalism of libertarian rights theories under which public purposes might never trump private rights.

The problem with content dependency, however, is that it misconceives the nature of the institution of promising. Promissory institutions and norms of distributive justice are not mutually exclusive, but if both are supported, the social planner must be denied the right to substitute his goals for those of the promisor and promisee. This is because promises are necessarily content independent.[109] Thus, any perspective which asserts that some justification beyond the fact of promising is required for enforceability denies that a moral case can be made for promising. From a utilitarian perspective, then, it is the institution and not the individual promise that is content dependent. Although the institution must be one that promises greater utility than would obtain in a nonpromissory regime, the institution so approved is one of private obligations whose content is left to individual choice.[110]

The third objection to utilitarianism focuses on the procedural rules of promising. Not all promises are binding, but only those that satisfy a threshold level of procedural fairness. If procedural norms are not respected, the moral imperative does not arise. A further kind of promissory nihilism then suggests that theories based on the moral value of promissory institutions are rendered doubtful by the difficulty in providing a principled distinction between procedural fairness and unfairness. If no such distinction is possible, the contractual output may always be of dubious ethical value, and some other societal goal, such as distributive justice, could be substituted.[111] Again,

gations." *Id.* at 194. This explanation of promising is criticized in Cartwright, *An Evidentiary Theory of Promises*, 93 MIND 230 (1984).

109. *See supra* text accompanying note 94.

110. "La morale nous commande de ne pas traiter le contrat comme un fait social dont le juge a le droit de tirer telle ou telle conséquence . . . ." G. RIPERT, *supra* note 28, § 22, at 39.

111. What lies at the heart of this objection may be a confusion between two quite separate questions: ought the contract be performed? and can a fairer set of terms be imagined? These are separate questions, however, and an affirmative answer can be given to both. In other words even if a neutral arbitrator might have crafted slightly different terms, the contract may still be

this attack seems most directed at utilitarian accounts of promising, for the conclusion that greater utility is derived from promising rests on pragmatic assumptions of individual rationality. The utilitarian, although perhaps not the rights theorist, might excuse performance if in one readily identifiable kind of promise the promisor systematically ended up worse off as a result of judgment biases.

If this objection were taken at face value, it would be destructive of any contractual values. If contracts entered into with a gun at one's head cannot be distinguished from those in which the parties have the slightest disparity in wealth, the enforcement of contracts is never justified. Promising is fraud. This kind of paradox mongering therefore must be rejected, not only under utilitarian, but also under any ethical theory of promising.[112]

There are two further reasons why such arguments cannot plausibly support promissory nihilism. First, save in theories that impeach all moral choice, cases involving the impairment of individual judgment form the exception and not the rule, and such exceptions are readily distinguishable. Although categories of rationality and irrationality shade together, the distinction between the two may be understood even if rigid borders cannot be laid out. Prophylactic arguments for total nonenforceability are therefore unconvincing. Second, even if subject to judgment biases, systems of individual choice still lead to greater utility than realms of Natural Duty. Some recent defenses of paternalism assume that restrictions on choice are justified on utilitarian grounds.[113] But on such theories, the case for interfering with individual preferences is not made merely by demonstrating individual judgment errors. Instead, the real issue is who, as between the individual and the paternalist, has better information about the individual. Normally,

---

considered enforceable in its unamended state so long as promissory institutions are on balance beneficial and the cost of correction is excessive. It is then unnecessary, to meet this objection, to deny that questions of fairness are meaningful if the procedural requirements of a binding contract are satisfied.

112. *See* G. RIPERT, *supra* note 28, § 22, at 38-40. Attacks that question the ability of promisors to make *any* rational choices must also be rejected. The claim that individuals act against self-interest through irrationality (for example, intransitive preferences) may be restricted in scope to certain kinds of bargaining contexts in which a degree of paternalism may seem warranted. If so, a range of unimpeded promising is still preserved. But if it is suggested that irrationality invades *all* of our choices, such arguments are destructive of any ethical theory founded on individual responsibility, in addition to promising.

113. *See, e.g.*, Sunstein, *supra* note 7, at 1140-41.

this must be the individual, for the paternalist's opinion about how to maximize an individual's utility is parasitic upon the individual's preferences. The paternalist is permitted to second-guess individual choice in the restricted sphere in which this is done, not because the result better accords with the paternalist's preferences, but because the individual's utility is maximized thereby. The paternalist's authority stems from a knowledge of individual preferences, and this is derivative of observed human choice. So, far from extinguishing individual choice, this kind of paternalism must be founded on it.[114]

CONCLUSION

Among ethical issues promissory theory is of cardinal importance to lawyers, for the moral value of virtually all of contract law rests on it. The most plausible theory of promising is consequentialist, basing a duty to support the institution on the desirable results of its adoption. Although promising's consequences are several, utility appears the ultimate good. Other consequences, such as promisee reliance, appear instrumental only. Thus, the institution rests most easily on utilitarian theories.

Two other explanations of promising must be rejected. The first of these, described as neoformalism, bases promissory institutions on an abstract right to promise. A justification of promising that ascribes value to the institution without knowledge of its consequences is unconvincing. Neoformalism is flawed in assuming that promising may be preferred to competing conventions by virtue of its prudential and economic consequences without endowing these consequences with a moral status.

That leaves low-fidelity theories, which would find a justification for promise keeping in morally binding connecting factors between individuals and a convention. On these theories, a duty of performance would be imposed upon promisors because of their consent to the institution, their receipt of benefits from

114. The tension between legal rules and private orderings is also visible in canons of interpretation. Goetz and Scott have noted that rules of interpretation constrain private choice first by offering parties a restricted list of implied terms and then by erecting interpretive barriers should they wish to contract around them. *See* Goetz & Scott, *The Limits of Expanded Choice: An Analysis of the Interactions Between Express and Implied Contract Terms*, 73 CALIF. L. REV. 261, 288-91 (1985). But rules of interpretation are also informed as to their content by private bargains, with an evolutionary process by which standard terms develop and achieve legal recognition. *See id.*

it, or reliance by promisees on the promise. None of these theories provides an adequate explanation of allegiance to promissory institutions. As a result only utilitarianism offers a creditable alternative to promissory nihilism.

In rejecting consequentialism rights theorists may adopt either low-fidelity requirements or neoformalism. In neither case have they yet provided a persuasive justification of legally and morally binding promissory obligations. This Article has shown why they cannot do so.

[3]

The Yale Law Journal

Volume 89, Number 7, June 1980

Enforcing Promises: An Examination of the Basis of Contract*

Charles J. Goetz† and Robert E. Scott‡

The obligation to keep promises is a commonly acknowledged moral duty.[1] Yet not all promises—however solemnly vowed—are enforceable at law.[2] Why are some promises legally binding and others not? Orthodox doctrinal categories provide only modest assistance in answering this persistent question. Conventional analysis, for example, has distinguished promises made in exchange for a return promise or performance from nonreciprocal promises.[3] Indeed, common law "bar-

* We would like to thank Michael Dooley, Stanley Henderson, Arthur Leff, Douglas Leslie, Alan Schwartz, Paul Stephan, and the participants in the University of Virginia Faculty Workshop and the University of Chicago Law and Economics Workshop for their helpful comments on earlier versions of this Article.

† Professor of Law, University of Virginia School of Law.

‡ Professor of Law, University of Virginia School of Law.

1. Pound, *Promise or Bargain?* 33 TUL. L. REV. 455, 455 (1959) ("From antiquity the moral obligation to keep a promise [has] been a cardinal tenet of ethical philosophers, publicists, and philosophical jurists.") [hereinafter cited as *Promise or Bargain?*]; *see id.* at 457-63. *See generally* Pound, *Individual Interests of Substance—Promised Advantages,* 59 HARV. L. REV. 1, 3-11 (1945). In terms of moral obligation, promises have been clearly distinguished from other representations or predictions. "A promise is not, therefore, merely an assurance one gives to help another, just as it is not merely an expression of a resolution to perform an action. It is, in addition, to *underwrite* any endeavor the other party to the transaction may choose to launch. . . ." A. MELDEN, RIGHTS AND PERSONS 46, 47-54 (1977). The peculiar status of promissory representations forms the basis of the law of contract.

2. The hint of this restraint is revealed in the common definition of contract as a promise that is legally enforceable. *See, e.g.,* 1 RESTATEMENT OF CONTRACTS § 1 (1932) [hereinafter cited without cross-reference as RESTATEMENT 1ST]. This definition of contract is retained in the *Second Restatement.* RESTATEMENT (SECOND) OF CONTRACTS § 1 (Tent. Draft Nos. 1-7, 1973) [hereinafter cited without cross-reference as RESTATEMENT 2D].

3. *See* RESTATEMENT 2D § 75. The traditional distinction between bargained-for and gratuitous promises suggests that only two categories can be identified. Actually the institutional environment is more accurately described as having three distinct contexts. Explicitly bargained-for promises are only a part of a larger exchange context in which the opportunity for interactive communication remains. We define nonreciprocal promises as being limited to those contexts in which the promisee has no realistic ability to obtain adjustments in promise-making through bargaining. *See* p. 1301 & note 38 *infra.*

gain theory" is classically simple: bargained-for promises are presumptively enforceable; nonreciprocal promises are presumptively unenforceable. But this disarmingly simple theory has never mirrored reality.[4] Contract law has ventured far beyond such narrow limitations, embracing reliance and unjust enrichment as additional principles of promissory obligation.[5]

Thus, a promise may be enforceable to the extent that the promisee has incurred substantial costs, or conferred benefits, in reasonable reliance on the promise.[6] Promissory estoppel under Section 90 of the *Restatement of Contracts* is the primary enforcement mechanism when action in reliance follows the promise.[7] If the change of position by the promisee precedes the promise, its nexus with the promise is more subtle. For example, a promise is enforceable when it follows a nondonative material benefit conferred by the promisee. Unjust enrichment principles are typically invoked to enforce such "past consideration" promises.[8] Despite this expansion of liability, "gratuitous" promises of gifts or unilateral pledges to confer benefits remain legally unenforceable.[9]

4. Professor Grant Gilmore has argued provocatively that a clearly defined "bargain theory" of contract never really existed in the first place. The "theory," he argues, was simply the creature of nineteenth-century formalism. *See* G. GILMORE, THE DEATH OF CONTRACT (1974).

5. The first breach in the armor of classical bargain theory is credited to Professor Corbin. *See id.* at 62-66. *See generally* 1 A. CORBIN, CONTRACTS §§ 109, 110 (1963). Subsequently, the pioneering scholarship of Lon Fuller and Stanley Henderson has demonstrated that the environment of promissory liability differs markedly from conventional assumptions. *See, e.g.*, Fuller & Perdue, *The Reliance Interest in Contract Damages* (pt. 1), 46 YALE L.J. 52 (1936); Henderson, *Promises Grounded in the Past: The Idea of Unjust Enrichment and the Law of Contracts*, 57 VA. L. REV. 1115 (1971) [hereinafter cited as *Unjust Enrichment*]; Henderson, *Promissory Estoppel and Traditional Contract Doctrine*, 78 YALE L.J. 343 (1969) [hereinafter cited as *Promissory Estoppel*].

In addition to Professor Gilmore's essay, the development of contract theory is thoughtfully explored by Lawrence Friedman, *see* L. FRIEDMAN, CONTRACT LAW IN AMERICA (1965), and by Patrick Atiyah, *see* P. ATIYAH, THE RISE AND FALL OF FREEDOM OF CONTRACT (1979).

6. *See* pp. 1345-54 *infra*. Under classical common law doctrine, a mere promise could be elevated to a legally binding contract only by the formality of a seal or a bargained-for exchange of consideration for the promise. L. FULLER & M. EISENBERG, BASIC CONTRACT LAW 124 (1972).

7. *See* note 106 *infra*. The inclusion of section 90 in the *Restatement 1st* is generally identified as the initial doctrinal recognition of the inadequacy of the simple bargain model in explaining the enforcement of promises. Professor Gilmore suggests that Corbin's "revolutionary" attack on bargain theory predates the *Restatement* by several decades. G. GILMORE, *supra* note 4, at 58. Following the adoption of the *Restatement*, scholarly attention turned to describing the emerging principle. *See* Boyer, *Promissory Estoppel: Principle From Precedents* (pts. 1 & 2), 50 MICH. L. REV. 639, 873 (1952); *Promissory Estoppel*, *supra* note 5; Shattuck, *Gratuitous Promises—A New Writ?* 35 MICH. L. REV. 908 (1937).

8. *See* pp. 1349-54 *infra*.

9. *See* pp. 1339-45 *infra*.

Enforcing Promises

These often overlapping, yet seemingly unconnected, principles of bargain, detrimental reliance, and unjust enrichment characterize all legally enforceable promises. They, in turn, are linked with corresponding sanctions that determine the level of enforcement for a given set of promises.[10] Contract damage rules embrace a variety of remedial choices. But the principles determining this choice of remedies are largely unarticulated. In most cases *A* can seek the value of what he expected from *B*'s promise. Such standard "compensatory" recovery puts *A* in the economic position he would have occupied had *B* fulfilled his obligation.[11] There are alternatives to the compensation rule, however. Thus, *A* may seek restitution of any benefit conferred on *B* as a result of *B*'s promise.[12] Alternatively, *A* may seek to recover identifiable costs incurred in reliance on *B*'s promise.[13] Recovering conferred benefits and reliance expenditures has the stated objective of returning the parties to the same economic position they occupied before the promise was made.

How can these interlocking doctrinal patterns be explained? Damage and liability rules have both redistributive and behavior-adaptive functions. In an earlier paper we commented on the apparently random—and arguably regressive—distributive effects of the basic contract remedial options.[14] The adaptive effects of contract rules seem to offer greater explanatory possibilities.[15] A liability or damage rule induces

10. *See* Farnsworth, *Legal Remedies for Breach of Contract*, 70 COLUM. L. REV. 1145 (1970); Fuller & Perdue, *supra* note 5; Goetz & Scott, *Liquidated Damages, Penalties and the Just Compensation Principle: Some Notes on an Enforcement Model and a Theory of Efficient Breach*, 77 COLUM. L. REV. 554, 558-62, 568-77 (1977); Shattuck, *supra* note 7.

11. *See* Goetz & Scott, *supra* note 10, at 558-59. Notwithstanding the universality with which the goal is articulated, scholars have long doubted the rigor of the law's commitment to compensation. We have previously suggested that "a strong argument can be made that the theory of damages is designed to err toward undercompensation." *Id.* at 558 n.19.

12. *See* p. 1337 *infra;* Childres & Garamella, *The Law of Restitution and the Reliance Interest in Contract*, 64 NW. U.L. REV. 433 (1969); Dawson, *Restitution or Damages?* 20 OHIO ST. L.J. 175 (1959).

13. *See* p. 1337 *infra*. The definitive work in this area remains Fuller & Perdue, *supra* note 5.

14. Goetz & Scott, *supra* note 10, at 566-68.

15. A wealth of theories has been advanced to explain the enforcement of promises. The "intuitionist" theory of the inherent moral force of promises formed the basis of obligation for the social contract theorists of the 17th and 18th centuries. Although the intuitionist perspective is appealing, it fails to explain the simple fact that no legal system attempts to enforce all promises. The 19th-century response to the morality of promising was the "will" theory of contract. The law of contract was conceived of as merely executing and protecting the will of the parties. The 19th-century formalists, typified by Langdell and Pollock, used the notion that the essence of contract is the agreement of wills—or the meeting of minds—to craft the classical bargain theory of consideration.

The obvious limitations of the will theory have produced a reaction among 20th-

contracting parties to adapt their behavior in ways that will affect social welfare. The rules of promissory liability can, therefore, be examined usefully in terms of these welfare effects. It is important to emphasize that the proper focus here is on prospective effects, that future promising is the behavior to be influenced by the rules summarized above. If only promises already made were considered, ease of measurement is a primary factor that might commend the compensation rule over any more complex damage measure.[16] With respect to past promises, choosing among reliance, compensatory, or punitive remedies involves primarily a distributional issue; the damage rule allocates the gains or losses from any particular broken promise between the promisor and promisee. But, considered prospectively, rules of promissory liability have efficiency consequences as well: they frequently alter the actual magnitude of the gains or losses to be divided between the parties. Whether a particular type of promise will be enforceable, and to what extent, are choices that may powerfully modify the nature and amount of future promising. We will evaluate these choices by separating the enforcement question into two parts:

First, which system of promissory enforcement yields the maximum net social benefits from promise making?

Second, does such an optimal enforcement scheme explain current doctrinal patterns?

Part I of this Article considers the first of these questions by developing an analytical model that examines both the function of promises and the impact of liability on the making of promises. Clarifying the function of promising is a necessary first step in deriving an optimal enforcement model. It is critically important to realize that a promise is conceptually distinct from the actual transfer that it announces. As advance information signaling a future transfer, a typical promise prospectively carries *both* benefit if kept and harm if broken. This entanglement of benefits and harms substantially complicates the en-

century contract scholars that leads toward an instrumentalist view of promissory liability: promises are enforceable because enforcement secures socially desirable ends. *See, e.g.*, Atiyah, *Contracts, Promises and the Law of Obligations*, 94 LAW Q. REV. 193, 197-98 (1978); Patterson, *An Apology for Consideration*, 58 COLUM. L. REV. 929, 941 (1958); *Promise or Bargain?, supra* note 1, at 463. Although evaluation of promises in terms of their welfare effects dominates current contract jurisprudence, alternative evaluations based on shared ethical norms or common moral intuitions continue to be asserted. *See* J. RAWLS, A THEORY OF JUSTICE 342-50 (1971); Havighurst, *Consideration, Ethics and Administration*, 42 COLUM. L. REV. 1, 9 (1942). Such claims have not proved very helpful, however, in explaining the observable limits that the law sets on enforcing the sanctity of promises. And if moral force is attached to promises merely because people rely upon them, the argument is subject to the claim that such reliance is dependent upon legal enforceability.

16. *See* Goetz & Scott, *supra* note 10, at 566-68.

Enforcing Promises

forcement question. Thus, the enforcement of promises may have harmful consequences by deterring socially useful future promising. Alternatively, nonenforcement encourages more promises but also reduces the reliability of the announcement; the promisor's intent to perform is not tested against a potential penalty for its nonperformance. The value of social welfare is maximized by a system of legal rules that provides the optimal balance between the beneficial and the harmful effects of promising.

In Part II, we discuss the practical compromises necessary to implement efficient regulation of promises in a world of costly legal process and imperfect information. We examine common law rules of liability as proxies for theoretically optimal rules rendered impractical by the inherent difficulties of measuring the true social effects of promising. We conclude that a substantial congruence exists between traditional contract rules and optimal promissory enforcement. Indeed, this congruence offers a persuasive explanation for the peculiar patterns of promissory liability observed in actual practice.[17]

I. Optimal Enforcement of Promises

Attempts have been made to explain the overlapping patterns of promissory liability in terms of the economic implications of promise-making. Bargained-for promises support value-enhancing exchanges. Such promises are thus seen as fully enforceable under the compensation rule in order to protect and encourage value-maximizing resource allocation.[18] Measuring damages in terms of expectation rather than reliance is said to encourage more efficient breach decisions once the contract is made.[19] A nonreciprocal promise, on the other hand, is

17. A recent scholarly debate has centered on the hypothesis that the common law can be explained in terms of principles of economic efficiency. *See, e.g.*, R. POSNER, ECONOMIC ANALYSIS OF LAW 404-05, 439-41 (2d ed. 1977); Rubin, *Why is the Common Law Efficient?* 6 J. LEGAL STUD. 51 (1977); Priest, *The Common Law Process and the Selection of Efficient Rules*, 6 J. LEGAL STUD. 65 (1977); Michelman, *A Comment on* Some Uses and Abuses of Economics in Law, 46 U. CHI. L. REV. 307 (1979). We take no position on the extent to which economic efficiency is a dominant or merely subsidiary element in explaining the development of common law doctrine in general. Our intent is the more modest one of measuring a relatively narrow segment of legal doctrine against some underlying economic optimality considerations.

18. *See* RESTATEMENT 2D § 76, Comment b ("Bargains are widely believed to be beneficial to the community in the provision of opportunities for freedom of individual action and exercise of judgment and as a means by which productive energy and product are apportioned in the economy.") The assumption that enforcement of bargains promotes allocative efficiency is widespread. *See* Hays, *Formal Contracts and Consideration: A Legislative Program*, 41 COLUM. L. REV. 849, 852-53 (1941); Llewellyn, *What Price Contract?—An Essay in Perspective*, 40 YALE L.J. 704, 716-18 (1931); Patterson, *supra* note 15, at 945-48.

19. R. POSNER, *supra* note 17, at 88-93.

frequently labeled as a "sterile transaction," which does not facilitate the movement of resources to more valued uses.[20] On this basis, enforcement is justified only as a deterrent to the harm caused by any detrimental reliance on the promise.[21] In sum, these lines of analysis suggest that full enforcement of bargains consolidates benefits while protection of reliance-based promissory interests minimizes harms.

But existing explanations of the legal enforcement of promises are incomplete and perhaps misleading. A principal limitation has been the failure to consider the effects of various levels of legal enforcement on the making of promises. Inquiry has generally focused instead on the effects of legal sanctions on decisions to breach or perform, assuming that the promise has already been made.[22] Yet, a decision to enforce promises, and the subsequent choice of remedy, does not merely mold the performance behavior of contracting parties; it also shapes both the nature and amount of promise-making activity.

Appropriately calibrated enforcement rules can be used to achieve the optimal number and type of promises based on the degree and form of adaptation by promisor and promisee. Thus, the effects of legal enforcement on promise-making are critical factors in evaluating the seemingly disparate liability and damage rules of contract. In Part I we examine these effects by first describing the reactions of both the promisee and promisor to the risks inherent in promising. We then specify an enforcement model that encourages the socially optimal interaction between the promising parties.

A. *The Function of Promises: Adaptation by the Promisee*

In analyzing the promisee's reactions to a promise, it is critically important to bear in mind the conceptual distinction between the promise itself and the future benefit that it foretells. By communicating a

20. *See* C. Bufnoir, Propriété et Contrat 487 (2d ed. 1924); Fuller, *Consideration and Form*, 41 Colum. L. Rev. 799, 815 (1941); *cf.* R. Posner, *supra* note 17, at 69 (gratuitous, nonreciprocal promises not part of "process by which resources are moved").

21. *See* R. Posner, *supra* note 17, at 69-70; Fuller, *supra* note 20, at 811.

22. *See generally* Shavell, *Damage measures for breach of contract*, Bell J. Econ. (forthcoming 1980); W. Rogerson, Economic Efficiency and Damage Measures in Contract Law (unpublished paper on file with *Yale Law Journal*).

In order to increase its accessibility to a legal readership, this Article uses relatively nontechnical terms to present an underlying economic model that typically would be articulated by economists in highly formal mathematical terms. The formal model developed in the economic literature by Shavell and extended by Rogerson differs conceptually from ours in some important areas. For instance, we focus upon the influence of potential remedies on the quality and quantity of promises, rather than upon the optimal enforcement of a promise, the character of which is already determined. In addition, our definition of reliance damages differs because we incorporate the notion of "reasonableness." Hence, the implicit model underlying this Article is somewhat more complex conceptually than are those cited above.

Enforcing Promises

promise, the promisor informs the promisee about the proposed future receipt of a benefit. The promise itself is merely the production of a piece of information about the future. Normally, advance knowledge of a future transfer will increase the benefit to the promisee because he can more perfectly adapt his consumption decisions to the impending change in wealth. For instance, a person informed of a $25,000 bequest to be made one year hence may revise some of the plans that he otherwise would have followed in the interim twelve months. Because of the revisions in plans, the individual can achieve a higher intertemporal level of satisfaction than if the wealth were transferred without any advance notice. Such adaptive gain from the information embodied in a promise may appropriately be termed "beneficial reliance." The problem occurs, however, when the transfer foretold by the promise is not actually performed. In this case, the information conveyed by the promise turns out to have been misleading and the promisee's induced adaptation in behavior makes him worse off than he would have been without the expectation of a future benefit. Losses incurred by ill-premised adaptive behavior are commonly termed "detrimental reliance." Because the role of promises as units of information is so fundamental to the entire analysis developed below, we will use an economic indifference curve model to give more rigorous content to such key legal concepts as reliance and the reasonableness of the promisee's adaptation process.

1. *Reliance Reactions of a Promisee*

Figure 1 will be used to develop a very simple intertemporal allocation model, one in which a person must allocate his income between two periods, present and future. *A*, the potential promisee, begins with $100, which he can divide between consumption now and consumption in the future. In Figure 1, his possible choices are represented by the straight line budget constraint indicating all combinations of present and future consumption that sum to $100. His preferences about alternative combinations of present and future consumption are summarized by the indifference curves, which define a kind of topographic map of the desirability of different present-future consumption patterns.[23] On these assumptions, the highest preference level consistent with the scarce resources is point e_1, where indifference curve I_1 is

23. Indifference curves may be thought of as a topographical map of a "preference mountain," on which higher "elevations" represent the greater preferences of outcomes. The points in any single indifference curve constitute equally preferred outcomes. An individual thus will be indifferent between any two points on an indifference curve. In the model represented by Figure 1, the higher an indifference curve lies to the northeast, the more utility the individual derives from the outcomes represented by the curves.

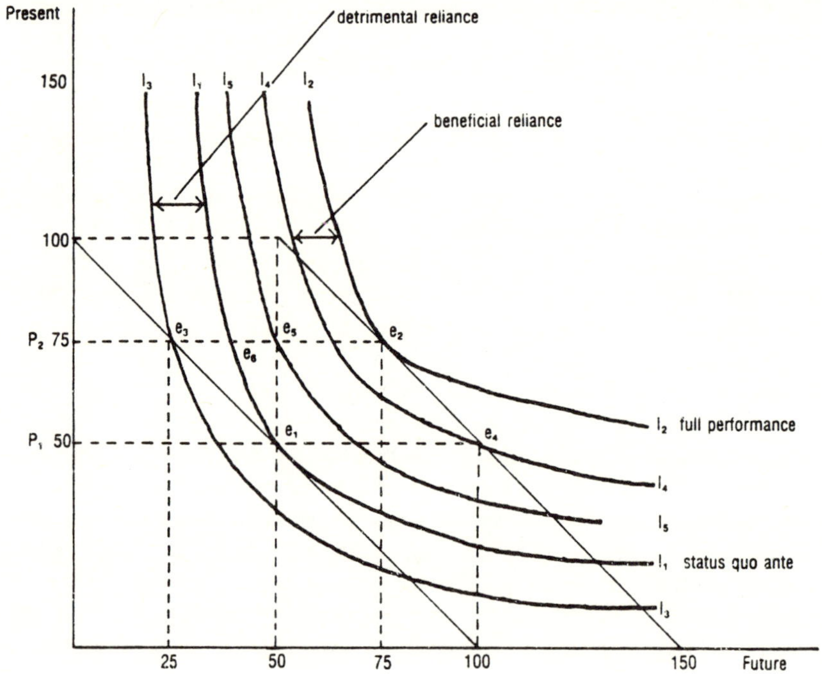

Figure 1

tangent to the budget constraint. This involves spending \$50 now and a planned expenditure of \$50 in the future.

Suppose now that *B* promises *A* a transfer of \$50 to be made in the future period and that *A* believes the promise. Even neglecting the possibility of borrowing against his future wealth, *A*'s budget constraint will shift out to the dotted line in Figure 1.[24] The new constraint indicates that, although no more than \$100 can be spent in the present, the two-period consumption levels may now total \$150 rather than \$100. Based on the new information, *A*'s best two-period plan would be point e_2. *A* is thus led to revise his current consumption upward to \$75 and to project \$75 worth of future consumption.[25] But what happens if

24. For simplicity, we assume that the interest rate on money is zero in order to produce a one-to-one tradeoff between present and future consumption. The introduction of interest is irrelevant to this analysis because it merely alters the rate of tradeoff, reflected in the slopes of the budget lines.

25. The promisee's consumption of all goods with nonzero income elasticities will be modified. His intertemporal consumption stream will be adjusted to the higher wealth level created by the gift.

Enforcing Promises

the promise is broken when the second period actually arrives? *A* has already expended \$75 and has only \$25, rather than the prospective \$75, left to spend. In terms of Figure 1, breach of the promise pushes *A* leftward from his anticipated outcome of e_2 back to his original budget constraint at e_3. As indifference curve I_3 indicates, *A* is worse off at the post-breach result e_3 than he was at e_1, the pre-promise point on indifference curve I_1. In sum, *A* has been misled by the promise into making what is now recognizable as a mistake; the consequences of that detrimental reliance are captured in the difference between indifference curves I_1 and I_3.

Because detrimental reliance is widely regarded as a basis for damage computation, an advantage of the Figure 1 model is that it clearly illustrates why it is a mistake to use *A*'s observable action in reliance on a promise as the measure of his damages. Under the facts assumed, *A*'s observable reliance is the \$25 extra he spends in period 1. If, however, he were awarded this \$25 as damages for breach, his ultimate position would be at e_5 on indifference curve I_5. He would have spent \$75 in the first period and, including the \$25 damages, would have available \$50 for the final period. But since return to the status quo ante requires only that indifference curve I_1 be achieved, the true reliance damages are equal only to the lesser amount indicated by the horizontal distance between e_3 and e_6 in Figure 1. The common-sense explanation for this, of course, is that detrimental adaptation in behavior is usually only a partial rather than a total loss. In this case, *A* did get some benefit from the excessive \$25 consumption, even though not as much as he would have if the consumption had been postponed to the optimal time. Reliance is, simply, the opportunity cost of the broken promise. Thus, true damages are measured by the difference between the value of the stream of consumption choices not taken—indifference curve I_1—and those choices induced by the promise—indifference curve I_3. Because it is important to distinguish compensation based on observable reliance from true reliance damages, we shall refer to the former as "reimbursement damages" in the discussion below.

Even where the precise meaning is imperfectly captured, the notion of detrimental reliance tends to be better understood than that of beneficial reliance. This is unfortunate because the production of beneficial reliance is perhaps the principal social rationale of promising; the risk of detrimental reliance is merely the unavoidable concomitant cost. Figure 1 aptly illustrates the beneficial consequences of promising when the promise is performed. Assume, for instance, that the \$50 in our hypothetical is merely transferred to *A* in period two without any advance warning. Not knowing about the wealth increase, *A* will have committed himself to plan e_1. When period two arrives, *A* will unexpectedly find himself with $100 to spend. At this point, the best available choice is at e_4, which is on a lower indifference curve than e_2, the point that would have been achievable had *A* obtained advance knowledge of the transfer. In common-sense terms, the difference between I_2 and I_4 illustrates the benefits to *A* of being able to adjust, because of the promise, to revised expectations about the future.

2. *The "Self-Protection" Reaction to Uncertain Promises*

Conceptualizing beneficial and detrimental reliance in the context of a simple model such as Figure 1 does have one major limitation. We have assumed implicitly that the promisee places total credence in the promise. Against the background of the Figure 1 model, however, it is possible to consider at least heuristically the imperfect credibility situation. When the promisee does not completely believe a promise, the results illustrated in Figure 1 can be understood as extreme or limiting cases of reliance.

What happens if the promisee knows that the probability of the promisor's performance is less than certain? In this case, the beneficial results of any adaptive behavior when the promise is performed must be weighed against the detrimental results of the same adaptive behavior if the promise is breached. A prospective gain from an adaptive action is balanced against the risk of loss.[26] Whatever the reasons for the riskiness attached to the performance prospects of any promise, the promisee can protect himself against prospective losses from detrimental reliance by limiting his behavior adjustments. In practice, the attempt to do this is frequently manifested in intermediate courses of action taken by promisees who do not completely ignore the implications of a promise in their planning but do not react as fully as if performance were certain. The price for this self-protection against the risk of detrimental reliance is, therefore, the value of the prospective beneficial reliance that would accrue from full adaptation to the advance knowledge of a promissory performance.[27]

26. In formal statements of this balancing process, the promisee is usually regarded as weighting the alternative consequences by the probabilities of performance and nonperformance. It should be noted that the promisee's central concern is whether the preannounced transfer will take place, not whether the performance is a purely voluntary one as opposed to one motivated by legal or other sanctions. Thus, because legal sanctions presumably affect the expected performance probability of many promises, the extent of the reliance experienced can be modified by the legal treatment of promises.

27. An important observation with regard to the promisee's adjustments to uncertain

The possibility of self-protection adjustments by promisees undermines the common assumption that detrimental reliance is the only behavior modified by the enforcement choice. This assumption often leads to characterizing certain "gratuitous" promises as incapable of inducing any reasonable reliance. Once the legal rule is announced, detrimental reliance on such announcements would, it is argued, not be reasonable. But the problem is quite simply that policies that reduce the reliability of promises are likely to reduce both beneficial and detrimental reliance. Thus, legal rules that encourage self-protective adaptation by the promisee achieve desired reductions in detrimental reliance only at the cost of concomitant reductions in beneficial reliance.

B. *Making Promises: Actions of the Promisor*

Understanding the behavior of the promisor is the next important step in our analytic model. How do promisors act and how do prospective sanctions modify their behavior? The initial phase of our analysis employs some strong simplifying assumptions. First, we assume that although future events may be uncertain, retrospective information is perfectly accurate. Second, we also posit that legal process costs are negligible, so that the theoretical gains from an otherwise beneficial regulatory rule are never counterbalanced by implementation costs. These assumptions are relaxed below when we discuss the practical compromises that may be dictated in a more realistic setting.

Potential promisees view promises as beneficial actions and as desirable economic goods. One can thus consider a promisor's willingness to make promises in much the same manner as his willingness to pursue any other economic goal. To predict the level of promise-making activity, the costs of promising must be examined.

1. *The Costs of Promising: The Regret Contingency*

Derivation of the promisor's cost of promising requires consideration of a number of potentially confusing factors. Therefore, we shall begin with the simplest possible environment. First we shall assume

prospects is that even very uncertain promises may produce substantial detrimental reliance if their prospective beneficial reliance is high. The mere improbability of performance does not destroy the informational significance of the promise. Recognition of this fact suggests that the legal concept of "reasonable" reliance is more complex than is sometimes realized. For example, it is perfectly reasonable and rational to rely detrimentally, to some extent, on many promises even though there is a substantial probability of nonperformance.

that the cost of communicating the promise is negligible.[28] Second, we assume that no legal mechanism exists to enforce promises. Absent a legal compulsion, the promisor remains free to refuse performance. If he does, the making of the promise will have generated costs in the amount of the detrimental reliance imposed on the promisee.

The option of nonperformance also imposes costs on the promisor in two situations. The first case is when the promisor exhibits some welfare interdependence with the promisee; that is, he is to some extent altruistic and cares about costs incurred by the promisee.[29] Then, the detrimental reliance costs imposed by nonperformance become, to some degree, costs to the promisor himself. Intrafamilial promises and promises between close friends are most likely to exemplify this phenomenon. In addition, and closely related, guilt may accompany the promisor's imposition of harmful results on others. In any event, this class of breach-related costs, which arise out of an altruistic or ethical sense, may be termed "self-sanctions."

The second extra-legal sanction arises when nonperformance would produce some post-breach reaction, either from the promisee or others, that is costly to the promisor. The resulting costs may range from hostile, retributive behavior to a mere loss of others' esteem to foreclosure of future beneficial dealings.

What are the effects of these extra-legal sanctions for breaking promises? To the extent that such sanctions are effective, their prospect acts as a "cost" of promising and deters promises that are worth less to the promisor than the prospective cost. Thus, extra-legal sanctions are a supplement to, or substitute for, legal sanctions.[30] Given the

28. On these facts, the cost of promising may be zero. One key question to ask, of course, is whether the act of promising has foreclosed any future opportunities to the promisor or made such opportunities more expensive.

29. The economic terminology for such relationship is "interdependent utility functions." The intrafamilial promise offers an obvious illustration of how such interdependency can increase the utility of any given transfer. *See* Posner, *Gratuitous Promises in Economics and Law*, 6 J. LEGAL STUD. 411, 412, 418-19 (1977).

30. Although the existence of extra-legal sanctions may properly affect the choice of legal measures, extra-legal sanctions have several disadvantages as mechanisms for inducing optimal promise-making. First, extra-legal penalties are highly circumstantial, are difficult to calibrate, and vary widely in their efficacy from individual to individual. Second, a sanction must constitute a cost to the person on whom it is imposed; it is not necessary, however, that no one benefit from the sanction. When damages or performance are extracted from a promisor, the resources are transferred to someone else who benefits thereby. Consequently, there may be no net social cost associated with the sanction; at least, the net loss is less than the gross loss imposed on the promisor. By contrast, many forms of extra-legal sanction represent a cost to one party without counterbalancing benefit to another. Prospects of retributive reaction or guilt, for example, tend to be inefficient sanctions in the sense that they could be replaced by resource transfers from promisor to promisee so that the promisee is made better off while the promisor is made no worse off than under the extra-legal sanction.

existence of extra-legal sanctions, under what circumstances might a promisor fail to perform his promise? When a promise is made in good faith, the promisor presumably believes that he is likely to perform. Still, many good-faith promisors would acknowledge the possibility that events may arise that cause them to regret having made the promise. Thereafter, if it were costless to do so, they would indeed breach the promise. Such contingencies may involve a wide range of factors, from changes in personal conditions to disappointment about external considerations that orginally made the promise seem desirable. The term "regret contingency" will be used to denote the future occurrence of a condition that would motivate breach if breach were a costless option for the promisor. Assuming any reliance, the occurrence of a regret contingency necessarily implies that either the promisor or promisee must bear a cost.

When a regret contingency arises, the promisor's options are either to bear the loss attributable to performance, which now costs more than it is worth, or to breach and accept the cost of any corresponding sanction. Presumably the promisor would adopt the cheaper of these regret costs. In any event, someone will suffer a net loss whenever a regret contingency arises, whether in the form of regret costs to the promisor, uncompensated detrimental reliance to the promisee, or both.[31]

2. *Adaptation by the Promisor: Precautions and Reassurance*

By what means does the promisor adapt to the prospective costs of promising?[32] The promisor can substantially influence the probability of a regret contingency, and thus its prospective costs, by adjusting his behavior ex ante. One means of mitigating potential costs is by altering the form of the promise. For instance, the promisor may condition performance on the proviso that certain circumstances—potential regret contingencies—not arise. Alterations in the form of the promise will generally entail a cost to the promisor either in terms of direct resource

31. The regret contingency is a key concept because much of the discussion below will involve either how society can adjust to an optimal volume of exposure to regret contingencies or how to achieve the objective that any given volume of such risk exposure be borne in a least-cost manner.

32. The prospective cost of promising is based on a two-step estimation process by the promisor. First, what is the probability that a regret contingency will arise? Second, if one does arise, what is the magnitude of the accompanying regret costs? The promisor uses the probability of the regrettable outcome to discount the costs of that outcome. Because the future consequences of promises are frequently uncertain, it should be emphasized that the adjective "prospective" is used in a particular sense. Specifically, it indicates that a set of alternative future consequences have been weighted by their probabilities, adjusted for any risk preference, and reduced to a single-valued equivalent.

cost—time and trouble—or in the possibility that the benefit of the promise-making to the promisor will be diminished. The second means of avoiding regret costs is simply to make fewer promises. The costs of this option are forgone benefits from unmade promises.

The costs that result from restrictions in the scope or number of one's promises can be termed "precautionary costs." It is useful to distinguish these further as either quality precautions or quantity precautions. Quality precautions involve adjustments restricting the scope of promises and impose a cost of decreased reliability. Quantity precautions, which consist of reductions in the number of promises made, result in a loss of benefits from promising. A rational promisor will pursue precautionary adjustments up to the point at which marginal precautionary costs are exactly balanced by marginal reductions in regret costs.

Precautionary adjustments by the promisor decrease the value of the promise. Conversely, when the promise is worth more to the promisor than its prospective cost, the promisor may engage in "reassurance." Reassurance includes such actions as the offer of guarantees, verbal persuasions, and the development of a reliable reputation, designed to convince the promisee that the promise is valuable. Reassurances increase the value of the promise to the promisee. Indeed, promisees may regard voluntary reassurance measures as substitutes for sanctions. Reassurance usually entails some cost to the promisor and, hence, will be pursued up to the point at which marginal reassurance costs are exactly balanced by increases in resulting benefits to the promisor.

Precautionary and reassurance reactions by promisors are triggered by variations in the cost of promising. It should be apparent, therefore, that an additional legal sanction will raise prospective costs, thereby precipitating adjustments of the scope and volume of promises. The net effects of these changes can be evaluated by combining the descriptive models of promisee and promisor reaction developed above.

C. *Optimizing Promisor-Promisee Interaction*

To what extent do legal sanctions optimize the interactions between promisor and promisee? In the present context, optimization is defined as maximizing the net social benefits of promissory activity—that is, the benefits of promises minus their costs.[33] This approach is equivalent

33. The adjective "prospective" should be applied to such costs and benefits, and this sense is intended below even when the term is not explicitly used. Strictly speaking, the maximization of prospective benefits need not produce results that, viewed retrospectively, will have truly maximized the net benefits ultimately realized. This is not a serious

Enforcing Promises

to the balancing of prospective costs and benefits under the widely accepted Learned Hand test for the required duty of care in potential tort-producing activities.[34] Indeed, there are strong theoretical parallels between the production of dangerous, but useful, products and the making of promises.[35]

The role of damages or sanctions in generating socially optimal behavior can be focused more sharply by observing the distinction between internal and external effects.[36] Because self-interested maximiz-

objection, however, because the prospective benefits criterion amounts to one under which people are induced to maximize benefits to the extent possible within the limits of the information at their disposal at the time the relevant decisions are made. There is no reason to believe that, as a practical matter, any other criterion can function as well.

34. Under the Hand definition, an actor is guilty of negligence if the loss caused by the accident multiplied by the probability of its occurrence exceeds the burden of taking adequate precautions. United States v. Carroll Towing Co., 159 F.2d 169, 173 (2d Cir. 1947).

35. The optimization process can be analyzed most clearly in terms of marginal effects—that is, the incremental variations in costs and benefits associated with a proposed change in legal treatment. If the marginal benefits attributable to a rule adjustment exceed the marginal costs, then the adjustment is beneficial, and vice versa. The system is optimized when no changes exist for which the marginal net benefits are positive. It is not necessary, therefore, to know the absolute levels of costs and benefits associated with alternative legal rules as long as the increases or decreases in the levels of costs and benefits can be estimated.

Social optimization implicitly presumes that the welfare of promisors and promisees is given equal weight ex ante. In the extreme, this assumption implies that even a promise with a high prospect of net cost to the promisee is optimal if the promisee's costs are outweighed by sufficient benefits to the promisor. In particular classes of cases, such results may be quite discomforting; their possibility constitutes one of the caveats applicable to any efficiency analysis of legal policy. In situations in which such cases arise, supplemental norms may be applied. One such case may be that of the bad-faith promisor who does not intend to perform, but who seeks nevertheless to benefit by making the promise. Here, standard intentional fraud analysis, providing for damages at least equalling the amount of detrimental reliance necessary to make the victimized promisee whole, would be appropriate. Indeed, it might be socially desirable to increase the sanction and extract any unjust gains from the bad-faith promisor.

The most commonly adopted measure of damages for fraud is the "benefit of the bargain" rule. Similar to the compensation principle, the rule puts the plaintiff in the same financial position as if the fraudulent representation had in fact been true. *See* Auffenberg v. Hafley, 457 S.W.2d 929, 938-39 (Mo. App. 1970); Lawson v. Citizens & S. Nat'l Bank, 255 S.C. 517, 180 S.E.2d 206 (1971).

Punitive damages are available when the defrauder has been guilty of morally reprehensible conduct. This generally requires more aggravated conduct than a mere intentional misrepresentation of fact or intentional lie; rather, the fraud must be gross, oppressive, or violative of a position of trust and confidence. *See, e.g.*, J. Truett Payne Co. v. Jackson, 281 Ala. 426, 203 So. 2d 443 (1967); Fowler v. Benton, 245 Md. 540, 552-53, 226 A.2d 556, 564, *cert. denied*, 389 U.S. 851 (1967).

When the plaintiff has transferred property or conferred benefits upon the defendant, he is entitled to a disgorgement of the property or its value. *See* Brooks v. Conston, 364 Pa. 256, 72 A.2d 75 (1950), RESTATEMENT OF RESTITUTION § 202 (1937).

36. Internal effects are those costs and benefits felt by the individual actor. External effects are those consequences of an act that are felt only by individuals other than the actor. Only if a party makes decisions as if he were experiencing all of the consequences of his behavior, external as well as internal, will his behavior be socially optimal.

ing behavior entails consideration of only internal costs and benefits, unfettered individual behavior is incompatible with social optimization in circumstances in which significant external costs or benefits are present. Individuals will oversupply activities with external costs and undersupply those with external benefits. By imposing costs and creating incentives, the law can cause individuals to consider external effects in their decisionmaking and thus "internalize" them.

Inducing optimal promise-making therefore requires that the promisor's costs of promising be adjusted to reflect any external effects on the promisee.[37] But this adjustment process is complex. Changes in the costs and benefits of promising are highly interactive in two senses. First, an individual's adjustments may substitute one category of his costs for another. Second, the actions of one party may produce reactions by the other and, in turn, feedback responses to the first party. The role of legal damages in optimizing this interaction depends upon whether a promise is reciprocal or nonreciprocal. Nonreciprocal or gratuitous promises, which are not conditioned upon performance of a return promise, do not typically enjoy the presumption of enforceability attached to reciprocal or bargained-for promises. As the analysis below reveals, the critical variable that distinguishes these categories of promises is whether the parties can interactively influence the nature and amount of promise-making through bargaining. It is the existence of effective impediments to interaction in the case of nonreciprocal promises that seems to explain why the law treats these two types of promises in such different fashions.[38]

1. *Nonreciprocal Promises*

Consider the case of a gratuitous promisor who has adjusted his promise-making to an arbitrarily assumed level of extra-legal sanction so that he cannot further improve his situation. In addition, assume that social considerations effectively prevent the promisee from influencing the promisor's calculations through bargaining. Under these conditions, when does the intervention of the law lead to optimal

37. As long as the effects of the announcement of the promise itself are carefully distinguished from those of any actual resource transfer, the value of the performance per se to the promisee can be ignored.

38. Barriers to effective interaction between parties to promises may arise from many different sources. Ordinary transaction-costs impediments may exist as a result of the time and trouble involved in negotiating. Alternatively, there may be something inherent in the very relationship of the parties that renders interaction impractical, such as a social taboo, a status relationship, or an institutional environment that obstructs meaningful communication. *See* Leff, *Injury, Ignorance and Spite—The Dynamics of Coercive Collection*, 80 YALE L.J. 1, 41 (1970).

results? We shall first discuss the conditions under which nonenforcement of such a nonreciprocal promise will produce suboptimal reassurance and precautionary adjustments. We then derive an optimal damage formula for those cases in which some level of enforcement is suggested.

a. *Legal Enforcement and Reassurance*

Legal enforcement of a particular class of nonreciprocal promises increases the reliability of the promises. This added reassurance increases social benefits in three situations. First, legal enforcement increases the net benefits of promissory reassurance if a legal sanction such as money damages displaces existing extra-legal penalties such as guilt or social pressure. If the total level of the sanction stays the same, the promisor's costs, benefits, and behavior all remain unchanged, while the promisee's benefits are increased by the receipt of the damages. The promisee's self-protection costs also fall. Because the consequences of a regret contingency are reduced by a prospect of legal compensation, the promisee can spend less on mitigating the risk of uncompensated detrimental reliance. In the event of breach, damage payments reduce the cost of nonperformance to the promisee. Thus, his beneficial reliance on the promise will increase. In essence, the substitution of one type of sanction for the other provides the promisee with the benefits of more reassurance against the regret contingency at no additional cost to the promisor. Hence, the imposition of legal sanctions may increase net reassurance benefits, if extra-legal sanctions are replaced by legal enforcement.[39]

Second, legal enforcement may increase net reassurance benefits regardless of the degree of substitutability of sanctions. Such an opportunity arises when a gratuitous promisor assesses the risk of a regret contingency at zero, because he is certain he will perform. In this case, if the law intervenes by raising the sanction for breach, the promisor's prospective regret and precautionary costs remain at zero. The prospect of sanctions is largely irrelevant to such a promisor. If the promisee knew that the risk of a regret contingency were in fact zero, he too would be unaffected by a stronger sanction. He would be perfectly assured already and, consequently, would incur no self-protection costs. Generally, however, a promisee's subjectively perceived risk of a regret contingency will be greater than the actual zero risk known to the

39. In the case of nonreciprocal promises, no basis appears for predicting when legal enforcement will successfully replace extra-legal sanctions. To the extent that sanctions are cumulative rather than substitutable, the net reassurance benefits of legal sanctions will be reduced.

promisor. Therefore, the increased sanction provides greater reassurance and permits a promisee who was originally engaging in excessive self-protection to decrease his self-protection costs.[40]

Third, even the gratuitous promisor who is not totally certain of future performance may prefer more enforcement. This will occur, for instance, when the promisor cares about the welfare or the reaction of the promisee. Then, the net benefit of promising to the promisor may be enhanced by the provision of additional reliability to the promisee through legal enforcement. Although enforcement puts such promisors at additional risk, the greater reassurance to the promisee may generate increased benefits to the promisor that outweigh any increased costs.[41]

Under what circumstances, then, will legally induced increases in the reliability of nonreciprocal promises be socially optimal? When the mutual interests of both parties are furthered by more assured promises, the promisor will voluntarily seek legal mechanisms for providing additional reassurance. However, often it will not be in the self-interest of the promisor to undertake voluntarily a more reliable promise. Even when some benefits to the promisor are produced by additional reassurance, the external benefits from performance may be inadequately communicated to the promisor by self-sanctions. As a general empirical premise, therefore, enforcement will be more likely to optimize promissory reassurance when extra-legal sanctions are relatively ineffective. The social desirability of enforcement, however, ultimately depends upon whether those gains are offset by corresponding costs. Before proposing a sanction for particular nonreciprocal cases, therefore, we must consider the societal effect of the promisors' precautionary adjustments triggered by legal liability.

b. *Legal Enforcement and Precautionary Action*

Although legal enforcement of nonreciprocal promises will initially increase the reliability of such promises, it may induce both qualitative and quantitative precautionary action by promisors. The net societal

40. As has been noted in different terms, the value of the transfer to the promisee is enhanced because the information content of the promise is improved and the beneficial reliance is increased. *See* Posner, *supra* note 29 (discussing the enforceability of gratuitous promises). The Posner analysis, though persuasive, is limited by its pristine premises.

41. Based on essentially this line of reasoning, Posner is critical of the abandonment of the formal promise under seal as a means of permitting a promisor to opt for legal enforcement of his gratuitous promise. *Id.* at 419-20. Reintroducing measurement costs may conceivably explain the abandonment of the seal. However, as a theoretical principle, an opportunity for the promisor voluntarily to adopt an enforceable form of promise does hold out the opportunity for gains to both parties.

effect of legal enforcement of a class of promises depends on the relative social value of these interacting adjustments.

Qualitative precautionary adjustments by promisors to increased sanctions may be thought of as merely the converse of reassurance. These precautionary moves entail a lessening of the scope of the promise and a shifting of the risk of potential regret contingencies to the promisee, while reassurance enhances the value of the promise and constitutes an assumption of risk by the promisor. These qualitative dimensions of a promise encompass two conceptually distinct effects: first, risk minimization by providing the promisee with better information on which to determine his degree of reliance; and, second, risk allocation by dividing the costs of regret contingencies between promisor and promisee. Analysis of these two factors suggests that legal sanctions can be used to induce risk-minimizing precautionary adjustments by both parties, but are much less successful in directing risk-bearing choices.

By providing the promisee with information concerning regret contingencies, precautionary adjustments by the gratuitous promisor improve the accuracy of the promisee's degree of reliance. Without a legal sanction, the benefits generated by the information effect of precautionary adjustments may not be maximized. The promisor is motivated to make precautionary adjustments only to the extent that his increased precautionary costs are outweighed by decreases in his regret costs. For instance, when only minimal extra-legal sanctions are imposed on breach, the savings in regret costs are relatively trivial, and precautionary moves by the promisor are not likely to be cost-effective. Under these circumstances, the promisee will be insufficiently forewarned about the risks of breach and will consequently overrely, failing to protect himself adequately against the prospect of breach.

Thus, where the external costs of a nonreciprocal promise are unlikely to be conveyed to the promisor, legal enforcement can induce the promisor to make optimal precautionary adjustments. Alternatively, the promisee must optimize self-protection and reliance in the light of the information he now possesses about the reliability of the promise. Paradoxically, if promises are unenforceable, the promisee has the correct incentives to protect himself to the optimal level against risks. Because the promisee bears all risks of breach, in this environment, he will rely on a promise only to the extent that the prospective cost of reliance is outweighed by prospective benefits. In contrast, if a promise is legally enforceable, and the regret costs shift to the promisor, the promisee may engage in a greater than optimal level of reliance. Because the reduction of regret costs becomes an external benefit of the promisee's actions, the promisee may ignore these costs in determining the extent of his reliance. In order to discourage the promisee from overrelying, the promisor must not be held liable for damages when the promisee knew or should have known that the marginal cost of self-protection was lower than the corresponding marginal reduction in prospective regret costs. This rule gives meaning to the concept of "reasonable reliance" and avoids not only an underinvestment in self-protection by the promisee, but also an overinvestment in precautionary adjustments by the promisor. It fills essentially the same function as does the rule of contributory negligence in tort.[42]

In addition to these risk minimization effects, legally induced qualitative precautionary moves reallocate the risk of regret to the promisee. What can be said of the risk allocation implications of these qualitative adjustments? The allocation of risk to a least-cost risk bearer by the manipulation of legal liability may have efficiency consequences that justify the costs of such adjustments. However, in the case of most nonreciprocal promises, the risk of a regret contingency ultimately will be borne by the promisee in spite of the promisor's risk-bearing advantages. Initially, the imposition of a legal sanction allocates some or all of the risk of a regret contingency to the promisor. But so long as the promisor is free to make qualitative adjustments, by conditioning his promise, he can shift that risk back to the promisee. In some cases, of course, the promisee may be the least-cost risk bearer. However, because it is the enforcement of the promise that removed the risk from the promisee initially, legally induced precautionary moves to shift it back again cannot be regarded as efficiency gains attributable to the liability rule. Thus, in terms of risk allocation, qualitative adjustments have only distributional consequences; their implementation costs may be regarded as net social losses.[43]

This analysis suggests that qualitative precautionary adjustments by

42. Imposition of a legal sanction equal to full detrimental reliance would, in the absence of a mitigation limitation, encourage overinvestment in reliance by promisees. Indeed, it has been suggested that enforcement of promises under a reliance scheme would create a moral hazard in terms of the promisee's adjustments. In other words, a promisee might be tempted to extend his reliance beyond any objectively reasonable point; if the promise is kept, he reaps the benefits, while if it is broken, the promisor bears the full costs under the liability rule. *See* Shavell, *supra* note 22. Optimal legal sanctions can respond to the problem of over-investment in reliance by structuring a compound liability rule under which the behavioral adaptations of both parties are scrutinized. Of course, the implementation costs of such a rule may be substantial. *See* pp. 1289-90 *infra*.

43. If promises are unenforceable, however, promisors may also engage in qualitative reassurance adjustments. This also entails social costs of implementation. These costs will be reduced under an enforcement rule.

Enforcing Promises

the gratuitous promisor have mixed effects. Increasing these adjustments by legally enforcing nonreciprocal promises is optimal, therefore, only when gains in promisee reliance from improved information exceed the net implementation costs of reallocating the risk of regret to the promisee. This implies, as an empirical generalization, that enforcing nonreciprocal promises will improve outcomes when there exists a substantial prospect of beneficial information exchanges through qualitative adjustments. Conversely, in contexts in which self-sanctions are already effective and the prospects of improved information are poor, the social gains from enforcement are negligible and may be exceeded by implementation costs. Nonenforcement of such nonreciprocal promises is thus the optimal choice.

c. *An Optimal Damage Formula*

The effect of a decision to enforce legally any particular class of nonreciprocal promises depends upon the nature of the sanction imposed for breach. Promisors will respond to higher levels of sanction by increasing their qualitative and quantitative precautions, reducing both the reliability of a given volume of promises and the number of promises actually made.

A necessary starting point in determining an optimal damage rule is to specify the external effects of a nonreciprocal promise as the supply of such promises is increased by one marginal unit. The external effects are the prospective detrimental reliance incurred if the promise is broken and the prospective beneficial reliance enjoyed if the promise is performed. Proper reflection of external effects therefore requires not only that the promisor be charged for the harm expected from broken promises, but also that he be rewarded for the prospective benefits of performance. It is helpful to state this condition symbolically. Let p be the promisor's reasonable, subjective assessment of the probability that he will perform a promise under an existing legal rule calling for damages of D in the event of breach. For the damage rule to deter all promises with net social costs and encourage those with net benefits, the amount of damages awarded must satisfy the following equation:

$$(1 - p)D = (1 - p)R - pB$$

where R and B are the values of detrimental and beneficial reliances, respectively. Assuming that all broken promises are litigated, the left-hand side of the equation represents the expected value of the prospective legal sanction. Because only broken promises are affected by the law, the probability $(1 - p)$ of the promise being broken is used to "discount" the damages D. The values for R and B on the right-hand side of the equation should be understood as those resulting from optimal self-protection by the promisee. Thus, promisees will appropriately minimize the value of the right-hand term, which is the net social cost of the promise. In calculating this prospective net reliance, the magnitudes of the potential detrimental and beneficial reliances are each discounted by their probabilities. When the equation is satisfied through the imposition of optimal damages D, the promisor's internal cost-benefit calculus will reflect the external effects of his promise-making. If the external effects are thus accounted for, the promisor's maximization of his internal net benefits is consistent with supply of the socially optimal quantity and quality of promises. We call this damage rule the "prospective net reliance" formulation.

In some cases, the prospective beneficial reliance from a promise will exceed its prospective detrimental reliance. Because the net external effect of such a promise is beneficial, it would be optimal to reward the making of such promises. However, in the nonreciprocal setting no practical legal mechanism exists for rewarding promises. This limitation renders true optimization impossible; the situation is necessarily second-best. At minimum, promises with prospects of net beneficial reliance should not be the subject of damages if breached. Only promises with prospective net detrimental external effects should be enforceable.

The prospective net reliance formulation developed above can be used to analyze the optimal level of enforcement. By dividing both sides of the original equation by the probability of breach $(1 - p)$, the following damage rule emerges:

$$D = R - \left[\frac{p}{(1-p)}\right] B.$$

The optimal damage rule thus subtracts from the promisee's reliance cost a fraction of his potential beneficial reliance. This fraction is the ratio of the ex ante subjective probability of performance to that of nonperformance. It determines the extent to which the prospect of beneficial reliance when the promise was made is credited against the promisee's prospective detrimental reliance. Because this ratio may be thought of as an index of the promisor's good faith, we call it the "good-faith ratio." A damage offset based on the good-faith ratio and on the amount of potential beneficial reliance will encourage the optimal quantity and quality of promises by reflecting in the promisor's decision calculus both the harmful and beneficial effects of his promise-making. This optimal legal sanction is likely to be unattainable in an environment of costly legal process and imperfect information.[44] But specifying an optimal sanction permits more rigorous evaluation of the error produced by any practical adjustment attributable to process costs. In addition, the good-faith ratio and the damage offset suggest a possible explanation for the language of the *Restatement of Contracts*, which conditions both the enforceability and the magnitude of reliance-based sanctions upon the "requirements of justice."[45] This language may reflect the view that the prospective beneficial effects of a promise should be considered in effecting a remedy for nonperformance.

The rule suggested by the formula above will admittedly result in a large quantity of uncompensated damages from broken nonreciprocal promises. Although greater damages would deter many injurious transactions, a stricter standard also would deter beneficial transactions in even greater magnitudes. Viewing an already-broken promise, the affected promisee would always prefer the highest possible damage award. But from the ex ante standpoint, a promisee would not wish to discourage a promise that creates a prospect of gain outweighing the risk of uncompensated loss. Such promises are "good bets" for the promisee over the long run, even though some of the promises will result in uncompensated harm. The penalty formulation developed above awards damages both to protect promisees from "bad bet" promises and to avoid deterrence of promises that are "good bets."

Under this prospective net reliance damage formula, the gratuitous promisor also has an incentive to undertake cost-effective qualitative precautions to modify prospective reliance induced by any promise actually made. A properly calibrated legal sanction will induce the promisor to convey to the promisee socially beneficial information about the risk of regret contingencies. In essence, such a promisor is encouraged to make cost-effective adjustments in both the quality and the quantity of his promises because the legal rule converts social benefits into savings for him. If, in addition, the law recognizes only the amount of damages that constitutes a "reasonable"—*i.e.*, cost-effective—reliance by the promisee, then the promisee will also have an incentive to minimize net social costs. Thus, the rule penalizes each party for failing to take cost-effective steps to minimize the social costs of promising. Damages exceeding those described above will tend to induce the promisor to invest too much in precautionary adjustments. This phenomenon is analogous to the excessive level of prudence anticipated if tort victims were awarded a multiple of their true damages.

44. *See* pp. 1289-90 *infra*.
45. Restatement 1st § 90; Restatement 2d §§ 89B(2), 89D, 90(1), 217A(1).

2. *Reciprocal Promises*

Promising is reciprocal when the parties can adjust interactively to the nature and amount of promise-making. The prospective net reliance formulation is equally applicable to reciprocal as well as to nonreciprocal promises. But the net reliance damage rule seems in sharp conflict with accepted legal doctrine in the reciprocal promise context, in which damages for breach are typically based on the promisee's full-performance expectation rather than on his detrimental reliance. Upon analysis, the apparent conflict can be dissipated; moreover, reciprocal promises are easier than nonreciprocal promises for the law to address.

This conclusion is buttressed by two independent lines of argument. First, in the case of reciprocal promises, a plausible empirical generalization is that a promisee's acceptance of one promise frequently requires his foregoing a potential substitute promise. The forgone value of the best substitute promise available—the opportunity cost—is key in determining the promisee's detrimental reliance when an accepted promise is subsequently broken. In a well-organized market, alternative promises will be close, if not perfect, substitutes. In that case, detrimental reliance is equal to the full performance value of the breached promise.[46] Similarly, beneficial reliance will be small, because the promisor's pledge, even if performed, will not constitute a very substantial improvement over the potential beneficial reliance from substitute promises. This empirical generalization implies that, in the damage formula developed above, full performance expectation E can be substituted for detrimental reliance R because $E \approx R$. Furthermore, because $B \approx 0$, the term of $\left[\frac{1-p}{P}\right]$ B drops out. We are left with $D \approx E$; thus, expectation damages are a good proxy for the prospective net reliance damage formulation developed above.[47]

Second, a fundamental theoretical difference exists between reciprocal and nonreciprocal promises. In the case of a reciprocal promise,

46. The correlation between detrimental reliance and full performance expectation whenever there is a competitive market for the broken promise was first observed by Fuller and Perdue. *See* Fuller & Perdue, *supra* note 5, at 62-63.

47. Nothing in the logic of this argument limits its applicability to reciprocal promises. Although the argument's empirical premise tends to have greater validity with respect to bargained-for promises, classes of nonreciprocal promises may exist for which forgone substitute promises also yield a close convergence between reliance and expectation. The implications of using expectation as a proxy for reliance on reciprocal promises will become apparent when we introduce practical problems of measurement below. *See* pp. 1288-1321 *infra*.

the principal objective of a promisor is to obtain consideration in the form of a return promise. The value of the return promise elicited is the main element of the promisor's benefit. Therefore, changes in the qualitative aspects of the promise are reflected in commensurate shifts of benefits to the promisor; a higher quality promise motivates a more valuable return promise, and vice versa. In contrast to the case of nonreciprocal promises, qualitative adjustments are internalized in the promisor's cost-benefit calculus by generating a more or less valuable consideration for his promise. Hence, the bargaining process accomplishes an important part of the behavioral regulation that, for nonreciprocal promises, must be performed by the legal system.

Furthermore, the bargaining process, not available by definition in the nonreciprocal context, can facilitate the optimal allocation of risk for reciprocal promises. Precautionary action is subject to a test of the ability of the promisee to bribe the promisor to make an unconditioned promise. Within any scheme of enforcement, then, the parties can reallocate the risks of regretted promises by buying or selling protection through the terms of their agreement. The least-cost bearer of any risk will presumably agree to absorb that risk in exchange for an enhanced return promise.

For much the same reasons, the consequences of excessive damages for breaching reciprocal promises are also mitigated, as long as the rule providing for excessive damages is understood in advance. The parties can always bargain out from the rule, for instance by a limited damages agreement. Thus, when transactions costs are zero, the particular damage rule selected for reciprocal promises is irrelevant. Although the existence of transactions costs renders bargaining over damage rules costly in practice, the feedback adjustment of the return promise markedly reduces the potentially inefficient effects of legal rules. While in the nonreciprocal case, excessive damages overdeter the promisor from promissory activity, in the reciprocal relationship, the promisee will regard the excessive damages as a quality improvement and will offer an enhanced return promise. The enhanced return promise will tend to offset the deterrence effect of the damages. However, some inefficiencies remain. Legally mandated "overinsurance" induces a moral hazard because the promisee will not exercise optimal self-protection. Furthermore, there is a cheaper allocation of risk than the legally mandated level of reassurance provided to—and paid for by—the promisee.[48]

48. There is a close conceptual analogy between excessive contractual damages and specific guarantees or minimum quality requirements imposed by law on consumer

The result may be even more costly, however, when the law provides a suboptimal level of enforcement. The extreme case of a complete refusal to enforce reciprocal promises provides an instructive illustration.[49] The initial impact of the rule, which is to underdeter promisors, will be counterbalanced by reductions in the value of return promises. Promisors may then substitute extra-legal forms of reassurance for legal sanctions. Creating adequate extra-legal enforcement mechanisms is likely to be less efficient than legally sanctioned reassurance. If so, the inefficiency consequences of underenforcement may be more serious than those of overenforcement.

In sum, the theoretical damages principles developed in connection with nonreciprocal promises apply to reciprocal promises as well. The difference in their legal treatment may be due to a close empirical identity of reliance and expectation in reciprocal promises. However, modification of the return promise is a powerful additional adjustment mechanism, which exists, by definition, only for reciprocal promises. By internalizing many of the promissory interactions among contracting parties, the return promise reduces the stress placed on legal rules for optimally influencing the behavior of promisors and promisees.

D. *Summary and Implications*

The preceding analysis suggests that the function of promises can be observed more precisely by conceptually distinguishing the effects of the advance information from the actual transfer. Information from promises induces reliance whenever the promisee attaches a positive probability to performance. Reliance responses are beneficial when a promise is kept and detrimental when it is broken. The principal normative justification for permitting promises to be made freely is the belief that, on balance, promissory benefits exceed harms. Legally enforcing promises can sometimes increase this net social gain by encouraging cost-reducing behavior by both promisors and promisees.

The treatment of promises when performance or nonperformance is certain is simple: such promises can be fully enforced so as to maximize benefits or minimize costs respectively. In the sure performance case,

products. Because the product is required to be "better," it can command a higher price, which overcomes at least in part the reluctance of producers to supply a more expensive output. Nevertheless, a suboptimal result exists because consumers and producers could, if permitted, work out a mutually advantageous trade of less quality for less money.

49. In contrast to bargained-for limitations of standard damage measures, attempts to contract for supranormal remedies may run afoul of the rule against penalties. *See* Goetz & Scott, *supra* note 10, at 558-62.

Enforcing Promises

enforcement, without deterring the promisor, increases the reliability of the promise to the promisee. In the certain nonperformance case, maximum deterrence of promises serves to prevent a bad-faith promisor from enriching himself at certain cost to the promisee.

The more important case of promises for which performance is potentially uncertain is more complex, because each promise carries both potential benefits and harms that must be balanced. Future contingencies may materialize rendering performance of such promises unattractive to the promisor. The risk of this regret contingency can be allocated several ways. On the one hand, nonenforcement of promises induces self-protective reductions in reliance by the promisee. These, in turn, may trigger reassurance reactions from the promisor. On the other hand, enforcement of promises increases promisee reliance, but also induces precautionary adjustments by the promisor. The social cost of the regret contingency is minimized when the optimal interactive adaptations are encouraged.

An examination of the function of legal rules in optimizing the interactions between the promisor and promisee explains the traditional distinction between nonreciprocal and reciprocal promises. In the case of reciprocal promises, the bargain mechanism provides a feedback of costs and benefits to the promisor and promisee. Thus, the liability rules for reciprocal promises do not directly influence promise-making; instead, they affect the costs of contracting between bargainers. For nonreciprocal promises, however, enforcement substantially shapes the adaptive responses of both parties.[50] For example, enforcement of nonreciprocal promises will optimize social benefits when extra-legal sanctions are minimal and the promisor can be encouraged to adapt the form of the promise to the risk of regret. Calibration of the optimal damages for such enforceable promises requires a consideration of both the beneficial and the detrimental reliance prospectively induced by the promise. Such a prospective net reliance formulation encourages promisors accurately to internalize social effects and thereby induces appropriate qualitative and quantitative adjustments.

But the practical implications of this ideal enforcement scheme must be considered. When nonenforcement is optimal, no measurement difficulties impede its implementation. When enforcement is indicated, implementation of the optimal rule is more difficult. A standard expectation-interest sanction may impose supra-optimal damages and deter socially valuable promise-making by inducing excessive precautionary behavior in promisors. The traditional reliance damage formulation—

50. *See* pp. 1307-08 *infra*.

return of the promisee to the status quo ante—most clearly approximates the optimal level of enforcement.[51] However, despite the language usually invoked, the status quo ante goal is rarely achieved by courts awarding so-called reliance damages. This systematic disparity between principle and practice isolates a central dilemma of promissory liability. True reliance damages, which include the value of opportunities forgone as well as the costs of actions taken, are extraordinarily difficult to measure accurately. Courts have generally responded to this largely unarticulated measurement conundrum by simply reimbursing the promisee for the gross value of any actions taken or actual expenditures incurred in reliance on the promise.[52] The recovery of such expenditures, which we have termed "reimbursement damages," should be distinguished from the theoretical objective of reliance damages.

We have developed the preceding model under an assumption of perfect measurement in order to evaluate the effects of legal rules on promissory behavior. Existing patterns of promissory liability often appear to produce substantial error costs in failing to regulate this conduct efficiently. Can this systematic error be explained? The complexity of the preceding analysis suggests that measurement of the true social cost of promising is likely to be itself a very costly activity. Enforcement costs increase the risk that the promisee's true reliance losses will not be fully recouped.[53] Moreover, process costs necessary to ascertain and implement the optimal level of enforcement may be so high that they exceed the error costs attributable to simpler rules of thumb such as no enforcement, full enforcement, or reimbursement. In Part II we relax the assumptions of perfect measurement and zero process costs to evaluate the efficiency of the rules of promissory obligation from a more practical standpoint.

II. Efficient Rules of Promissory Obligation

The second aspect of the promissory enforcement question asks whether the optimal enforcement model when adjusted for enforcement costs explains current patterns of promissory liability. We address this question first by describing the legal costs necessary to enforce promises and examining the relationship of these costs to different substantive rules. We then evaluate the rules of promissory liability by examining three basic categories of promises: fully bargained-for reciprocal prom-

51. *See* p. 1298 *infra*.

52. *See* pp. 1292-93 *infra*.

53. *See* Goetz & Scott, *supra* note 10, at 558 n.19; Schwartz, *The Case for Specific Performance*, 89 YALE L.J. 271, 274-78 (1979).

Enforcing Promises

ises within the common law "consideration" model; nonreciprocal promises distinguishable by the parties' inability to adjust interactively the nature and amount of promising; and, finally, the intermediate category of unilateral promises in a reciprocal context, which, under the narrow common law standard, may be unenforceable despite the possibility of bargaining.

A. *Problems of Proof, Process, and Error Costs*

In Part I we developed damage rules that encourage the socially optimal production of beneficial reliance on future promises. Except when a nonenforcement rule is appropriate, imposition of such an optimal sanction necessitates that the detrimental reliance losses from the broken promise be ascertained. Unfortunately, promissory reliance is peculiarly impervious to accurate measurement and proof when it diverges from full performance expectation.[54] Because true reliance cost is equal to the opportunity cost of the promise, measurement of the loss requires a comparison of the promisee's behavior in response to the promise with his prospective conduct in the absence of the promise: the promisee's detrimental reliance cost is the difference in satisfaction between these two positions. This calculation entails identifying the value of alternative opportunities forgone because of the promise and the benefits retained from the actions taken in reliance. Generally, these values can be determined solely by evaluating the subjective claims of the promisee. Only when a competitive market generates prices indicating the value of foregone opportunities will there be reliable evidence of the position the promisee would have occupied had no promise been made.[55]

Furthermore, an optimal legal sanction may also include a discount for the effects of extra-legal factors—such as reputational losses or social restraints on breach—that independently reward the performing promisor for taking into account some of the social effects of promising.

54. The process costs of measuring reliance include both direct costs of litigation and the effects of "error," which are social costs that arise when the procedural mechanism fails to apply accurately the substantive rule. *See* Posner, *An Economic Approach to Legal Procedure and Judicial Administration*, 2 J. LEGAL STUD. 399, 400-02 (1973); Scott, *Constitutional Regulation of Provisional Creditor Remedies: The Cost of Procedural Due Process*, 61 VA. L. REV. 807, 810, 844-46 (1975).

Reliance expenditures are extraordinarily difficult to measure even in business contexts. Such expenditures often consist of overhead expenditures and joint costs not readily allocable to particular contracts. *See, e.g.*, Reiss & Weinsier, Inc. v. United States, 116 F. Supp. 562 (Ct. Cl. 1953); Houston Ready-Cut House Co. v. United States, 96 F. Supp. 629 (Ct. Cl. 1951).

55. Presumably, in a competitive market the prevailing market price reveals the opportunities forgone in reliance on the broken promise.

Thus, any theoretically precise reliance-based damage calculation may require an additional computation of the prospective beneficial effects that performance of the promise would have conveyed.[56] In addition to computing the magnitude of both detrimental and beneficial reliance, this "good-faith" calculation requires ascertaining the promisor's subjective probability of performance at the time the promise was made.

Adjustment of the damage formula may be necessary if measurement costs prohibit even the approximation of true reliance losses. The award of reliance-based reimbursement damages does not—despite its stated purposes of restoring the status quo ante—accurately measure true reliance.[57] In fact, there is no a priori reason to believe that a reimbursement award is preferable in any particular case to nonenforcement or full performance compensation.[58] In sum, the administrative and error costs of attempting to apply a theoretically optimal net reliance standard suggest that it may be worthwhile to adopt a surrogate measure that is cheaper to apply.

The ease of administration of rules regulating promising are in part a function of the clarity of the substantive rule. Clarity is enhanced by use of a substantive rule that reduces the number and complexity of facts to be determined. A clear rule, such as nonenforcement or full performance compensation, yields benefits of reduced litigation costs and increased procedural accuracy. The primary cost of a clear rule is that it regulates promissory conduct imprecisely.[59] Full performance compensation, for example, may deter some promises with positive expected benefits that an optimal rule would encourage. But a rule that better reflects true promissory reliance requires resolution of more

56. *See* p. 1283 *supra*.

57. In order to approximate the status quo ante position of the promisee, the damage rule must measure two additional variables: the cost of forgone opportunities and the gain to the promisee from the induced action. Mere recovery of the out-of-pocket costs of the induced action will overvalue the harm induced by actions taken and undervalue the hidden losses incurred from forbearance. Yet, only when there is a competitive market for such promises can either of these variables be measured confidently. *See* pp. 1296-97 *infra*.

58. When forbearance is significantly greater than out-of-pocket expenditures, a reimbursement award will be substantially lower than the value of true reliance. Alternatively, when the induced actions involve substantial expenditures that produce difficult-to-measure benefits to the promisee, a reimbursement award may substantially exceed the value of detrimental reliance.

59. A clearer enforcement/nonenforcement rule may be both overinclusive and underinclusive. For example, full performance enforcement may restrain some socially beneficial promises by imposing an excessive sanction. Alternatively, nonenforcement may fail to charge promisors for the social costs of nonperformance. *Cf.* Ehrlich & Posner, *An Economic Analysis of Legal Rulemaking*, 3 J. LEGAL STUD. 257, 267-71 (1974) (explaining how precision of legal rules generates costs of overinclusion and underinclusion).

factual issues and thereby reduces the rule's clarity. Thus, a particular rule is efficient when both substantive and procedural components are constructed so as to provide the cost-minimizing balance between accuracy and clarity.[60]

A theory of promissory liability that minimizes these costs remains elusive. The foundations for such a theory were established by Professor Lon Fuller over fifty years ago.[61] Fuller's claim for the preeminence of reliance, however, seems inconsistent with established bargain theory. For example, a gratuitous promise, unsupported by consideration, is commonly presumptively unenforceable. Yet that same promise, if a product of a bargained-for exchange, is fully enforceable without any evidence of reliance. Fuller explained this apparent anomaly by suggesting that gratuitous promises are unenforceable because reliance is lacking, while the bargained-for promise is fully enforceable in order to facilitate likely reliance.[62] Our analysis of the information function of promises confirms the inadequacy of these explanations. Gratuitous promises can induce reliance, whose costs are ignored under nonenforcement.[63] Furthermore, facilitation of likely reliance by awarding full compensation for executory bargains may deter the future production of socially useful promises.[64]

However, the rules of promissory liability can be reconciled with the reliance principle. The existing tension between bargain and reliance is a product of the failure to discriminate adequately between ideal and pragmatic objectives. For example, common law bargain theory and the doctrine of consideration, as well as the modern concept of promissory estoppel, can be examined best as cost-minimizing surrogates for true reliance. Introducing the complexities of measurement and proof indicates that the traditional choice between reliance damages and the alternatives of nonenforcement and full performance compensation should be recast as an attempt to select from potential contract rules the best achievable approximation of the optimal enforcement standard.

60. *See id.* at 262-71.

61. *See* Fuller & Perdue, *supra* note 5; Fuller, *supra* note 20. Three critical insights can be extracted from Fuller's exploration of the remedial and formal structures of contract: first, reliance is the organizing principle that supports all contractual obligation; second, typical contractual remedies—such as compensatory damages—serve as cost-reducing administrative surrogates for reliance; and third, a direct relationship can be identified—through the formal structure of promissory liability rules—between process considerations and the substantive rules of contract.

62. *See* Fuller, *supra* note 20, at 815-18.

63. *See* pp. 1267-70 *supra*.

64. *See* pp. 1285-86 *supra*.

B. *Reciprocal-Bargain Promises: The Consideration Model*

First, we examine reciprocal promises reached by bargaining, for which the common law developed the consideration doctrine.

1. *The Functions of Bargain*

Evaluating contract rules as cost-reducing surrogates for the theoretically optimal enforcement rule reemphasizes the importance of the distinction between reciprocal and nonreciprocal promises. Promises that satisfy the reciprocal exchange requirement of consideration are presumptively enforceable. Breach entitles the promisee to full performance compensation. The enforceability of reciprocal promises is supported by a rich normative literature emphasizing the social utility of bargains.[65] But more importantly, as suggested above, the bargain mechanism can reduce discrepancies between optimal and actual enforcement rules.

We have pointed out the identity between detrimental reliance and full-performance expectation whenever markets for promises are competitive.[66] Furthermore, bargaining tends to produce the optimal amount of promissory reliance even when the legal rule deviates from the optimal reliance principle. By modifying contractual terms, the parties can vary the standard liability rule in order to maximize net reliance benefits.[67]

What effects can be predicted from full enforcement of reciprocal bargain promises? As the model developed in Part I suggests, application of sanctions for breach imposes the risk of the regret contingency

65. *See, e.g.*, 1 A. SMITH, THE WEALTH OF NATIONS 12-15 (Everyman's Library ed. 1937); Patterson, *supra* note 15, at 945; *Promise or Bargain?*, *supra* note 1, at 463-65.

66. The competitive market offers one polar case in which the promisees' detrimental reliance is precisely equal to full performance expectation. *See* Goetz & Scott, *Measuring Sellers' Damages: The Lost Profits Puzzle*, 31 STAN. L. REV. 323, 333-35 (1979) (measuring damages in competitive markets). The other pole is represented by the classic bilateral exchange in which the promise made to one or both parties is singular or unique. An example drawn loosely from the facts of Hamer v. Sidway, 124 N.Y. 538, 27 N.E. 256 (1891), may illustrate this point. Suppose William II promises his Uncle William to refrain from smoking and drinking, while the uncle promises in return to pay his nephew $5000 for each year in which the youth remains an abstainer. Subsequently, Uncle William reneges on his promise. Because no alternative market existed in which William II could have obtained a promise of money in exchange for his own promise, he has not forgone any alternative promise and his "immediate reliance" is zero. Nonetheless, receipt of even a singular bargain promise does induce a "consequential reliance" of alterations in consumption, whose magnitude is unpredictable.

67. The bargaining context invites a promisee to obtain any promise with a positive expected value. Legal liability, like any other risk in an executory exchange, can be optimally allocated between the parties.

Enforcing Promises

on the promisor. As the promisor's potential liability is increased, he is encouraged to take precautionary action to minimize the expected liability, by conditioning promises more carefully in negotiations. The promisee, in turn, may bargain for a less restricted promise by paying explicitly for the additional reassurance provided by a compensation award.

Alternatively, a rule denying enforcement of a bargained-for promise reduces precautionary costs incurred by promisors seeking to minimize the risks of regret, because it shifts that risk to the promisee. The promisee may adapt to this increased uncertainty by discounting the price he is willing to pay for the promise. If the promise is actually worth more than the promisee estimates, the promisor will incur costs up to the expected value of the promise in order to assure the promisee of the true worth of the promise. These additional reassurance costs induced by the promisee's adaptive behavior could include the voluntary assumption of legal liability through collateral guarantees or performance bonds.

Thus, because bargainers will attempt to allocate the risk of regret optimally themselves, the effects of enforcement rules depend on the transaction costs of risk allocation. Evaluation of these costs requires an analysis of how bargainers adapt to the risks of regret contingencies. If in certain transactions precautionary efforts by promisors would be more expensive than reassurance, nonenforcement enables the parties to shift the risk of regret more cheaply. Alternatively, when reassurance is more costly, fully enforcing promises induces cheaper precautionary conduct. If each type of transaction can be identified ex ante, specifying the cost-effective rule in advance produces the outcome that the parties would reach if they bargained over legal liability for breach.

2. *The Design of the Bargain Paradigm*

The classical bargain model can be examined on the basis of these assumed variations in precautionary and reassurance costs. Not all promises made in a bargaining context are presumptively enforceable. Indeed, the reciprocal bargain or consideration model is considerably more limited than the larger exchange context that it occupies. For example, promises made during preliminary negotiations[68] and prom-

68. In the words of the *Restatement 2d*: "A manifestation of willingness to enter into a bargain is not an offer if the person to whom it is addressed knows or has reason to know that the person making it does not intend to conclude a bargain until he has made a further manifestation of assent." RESTATEMENT 2D § 25; *see* 1 A. CORBIN, *supra* note 5, §§ 26-27, at 95-100.

ises to discharge contractual obligations[69] are traditionally unenforceable even though they are made in the context of a bargain. This failure to impose liability in certain exchange contexts can be contrasted with the wholly executory completed bargain, which is fully enforceable when supported by consideration. In each case, the liability rule can be explained by its impact on transactional efficiency.

Under traditional bargain theory, promises made during preliminary bargaining are not enforceable until the bargain is sealed by an agreed exchange. Complex rules of offer and acceptance have been developed in order to distinguish enforceable bargained-for promises from unenforceable preliminary negotiations. Suppose *A* promises to sell, and *B* to buy, 1000 widgets "at cost plus a nice profit." Subsequently, in a disagreement over the price, *A* refuses to deliver the widgets to *B*. Because the price term was not determined, the bargain remains incomplete. Hence *A*'s promise will probably be characterized as an unenforceable preliminary promise.[70] If, instead, a ten percent profit were negotiated, both promises would be fully enforceable. But assume that after the widgets have been delivered *A* promises *B*, "Your obligation will be cancelled. I will release my right to the $1000 that you owe me." As with the preliminary negotiation, this discharge promise is unenforceable. The rights that were created by the bargain cannot be extinguished by agreement without consideration.[71]

Freedom from liability upon entry and exit from bargaining, coupled with full enforcement of wholly executory promises once agreement has been achieved, is the basic design of the bargain model of traditional contract law.[72] This pattern typically has been explained in terms of differences in the magnitude of either actual or likely reliance. Neither explanation is persuasive. Disregarding the effect of the rule itself,

69. On promises to discharge contractual obligations, the *Restatement 2d* states the following: "A promise to discharge [a] duty must, like any other promise, be supported by consideration in order to be enforceable." RESTATEMENT 2D, Introductory Note, §§ 343-347, at 5 (Tent. Draft No. 13, 1978); *see* 5 A. CORBIN, *supra* note 5, § 1236; RESTATEMENT 1ST § 406.

70. *See* C.H. Leavell & Co. v. Grafe & Assocs., 90 Idaho 502, 414 P.2d 873 (1966); RESTATEMENT 2D § 32, Comment 7, Illustration e.

71. RESTATEMENT 2D § 343, Illustration 1 (Tent. Draft No. 13, 1978).

72. There are some imperfections in the symmetry of the common law design. The traditional preexisting-duty rule held that when a promisee agreed in exchange for a promised benefit to do what he was already legally obligated to do, the exchange lacked consideration and the return promise was unenforceable. *See* 1 A. CORBIN, *supra* note 5, §§ 171-192; Patterson, *supra* note 15, at 936-38. Because this rule was both overinclusive and underinclusive with respect to the coercive conduct it purported to attack, the modern view finds promises that modify a prior agreement presumptively enforceable absent unfair pressure or bad faith. *See* U.C.C. § 2-209(1), Comment 2; RESTATEMENT 2D §§ 76A, 89D, Comment b.

Enforcing Promises

there is no a priori reason to believe that reliance on either a preliminary or a termination promise will be less prevalent than reliance on the main promise itself. The enforcement choice, however, will affect the expected costs of bargaining between *A* and *B*. Enforcement of preliminary or termination promises will increase the cost of promising to promisors. Potential promisors will be willing to incur greater precautionary costs to avoid the risks of liability. Alternatively, a nonenforcement rule increases the cost of promises to promisees. Consequently, the amount of bargaining devoted to assurances of performance will be increased. The enforcement pattern could be explained if, during entry into, and exit from, bargaining, reassurance were cheaper than precaution. Then, the risk of a regret contingency could be allocated more cheaply by adjusting reliance once the promise is made rather than restricting the promise itself.

The design of the consideration model can be explained if the categories of bargaining risks are conceptually distinguished. Each bargainer, being both a promisor and promisee, faces two sets of parallel risks. As a promisor, the bargainer confronts the risk of liability should he fail to keep his promise. He also faces the risk of detrimental reliance should the promise made to him in return be broken. Based on the common empirical assumption that bargainers are generally risk-averse, the consideration model is justifiable in economic terms. Because the outcomes of negotiations are uncertain and gains and losses are indefinite, risk-averse parties will choose to forgo uncertain gains rather than incur equally uncertain losses of the same magnitude. In other words, risk-averse bargainers will prefer to bear uncertain risks as promisees rather than as promisors. Moreover, because a promisee can control reliance costs more easily than can a promisor, the risk of detrimental reliance is lower if borne by the promisee rather than the promisor. An enforcement rule would encourage excessive precautionary adjustments by risk-averse bargainers, because the uncertain consequences of nonperformance could not be controlled. Therefore, negotiations by such bargainers to reallocate risks through precautionary action would be more costly than the reallocation of identical risks through reassurance.[73]

73. The basic economic justification for such a scheme is that it saves most parties the costs of negotiating the preferred allocation of risks. Considerable flexibility to rearrange the risks of liability are retained by individual bargainers. Generally, the parties can elect to incur liability during preliminary exchanges by signaling their intention to be bound. *See* U.C.C. § 2-204(3) (requiring reasonably certain basis for granting remedy); RESTATEMENT 2D §§ 25, 32, Comment b (same). Alternatively, bargainers can choose a nonenforcement regime by indicating an intention not to be bound. *See* RESTATEMENT 2D § 21B, Comment b.

But bargainers prefer the risk of uncompensated reliance only on the periphery of bargaining. The crucial distinction between the periphery and the core of bargaining is the shift toward greater certainty of outcome. The impetus to bargain is the assumption that expected gains will exceed expected losses. Thus, when the transaction is finally negotiated, the expected value of gain outweighs the risk of liability upon breach.[74] Thus, after agreement, bargainers prefer to bear remaining risks as promisors rather than as promisees, thereby mutually enhancing the expected benefits to each. Consequently, expenditures required for reassurance under nonenforcement would exceed the investment in precaution required by full enforcement.[75]

The reluctance to enforce peripheral promises, on entry or exit, can also be explained on process grounds, even if the parties intend to be legally bound. The more incomplete and uncertain the details of an exchange, the greater the adjudicatory and error costs in resolving subsequent disputes. A greater allocation of resources to negotiation of the details of an agreement saves the parties expected litigation costs in case of subsequent dispute. If both litigation and negotiation costs were fully borne by bargainers, it would be efficient to permit them to negotiate to the point at which marginal expenditures in negotiations equalled marginal reductions in expected litigation costs. However, because litigation costs are partially subsidized by taxpayers, parties will engage in a suboptimal amount of negotiation and thereby generate an overinvestment in litigation. The refusal of the common law rules to enforce indefinite bargains can be seen as an attempt to compensate for this process distortion.[76]

In sum, the design of the consideration model can be explained persuasively by an analysis of efficient risk allocation. Manipulation of the liability rule shifts the risk of a regret contingency between prom-

74. Changed conditions producing regret will not necessarily induce the promisor to breach. Breach occurs only when the cost of performance exceeds liability for nonperformance. Breach is motivated, at least in part, by a belief that the promisee is better able to salvage or minimize the effects of the changed conditions than is the promisor. For example, a seller-promisee can generally resell unwanted goods more cheaply than a buyer-promisor who no longer wants to retain them. *See* Goetz & Scott, *supra* note 66, at 344 (optimal liability rule would make choice between performance and breach a matter of indifference).

75. Discharge negotiations seem characterized by less ambiguity and uncertainty than are preliminary negotiations. This intuition is confirmed by the fact that the nonenforcement rule has been applied much more hesitantly in the discharge context.

76. *See* 1 A. Corbin, *supra* note 5, §§ 95-97; Restatement 1st § 32; 1 S. Williston, Contracts §§ 37-48 (3d ed. 1957). Although the Uniform Commercial Code shifts the presumption in favor of party autonomy, it retains the injunction against enforcing indefinite bargains unless "there is a reasonably certain basis for giving an appropriate remedy." U.C.C. § 2-204(3).

Enforcing Promises

isees and promisors. These varying liability patterns can induce interactive adaptations by the parties to allocate the social costs of promising efficiently. This cheapest-risk-allocation design is buttressed by process considerations that justify imposing promissory liability only if agreement upon the basic transaction has been reached.

3. *Remedies for Nonperformance of Bargained-for Promises*

The impact of any enforcement rule ultimately depends on the character of the remedy for nonperformance. Full enforcement compensation is the standard recovery for breach of reciprocal-bargain promises, whenever such an award can be determined accurately. The stated objective of this compensation rule is to place the promisee in the same economic position he would have occupied had the promise been performed.[77] As we have argued above, this rule, by imposing a sanction in excess of the social costs of breach, overdeters socially useful promising, except in competitive markets in which expectation is equivalent to reliance. The bargain context, however, enables the parties to vary, with low transactions costs, the legal rule by agreement and thereby mitigate the effects of any remedial distortion. Moreover, the disparity between compensatory recovery and optimal reliance damages is usually more than offset by gains in the clarity of the rule. Suppose *A* promises *B* $5,000 in exchange for *B*'s agreement to paint *A*'s portrait. After the painting is completed, *A* reneges. Because the market for similar promises is likely to be thin, the immediate reliance or opportunity cost of *A*'s promise may vary unpredictably from the $5,000 contract price. Furthermore, *A*'s promise and breach will have produced a detrimental adjustment in *B*'s pattern of consumption. The amount of such consequential reliance is even more difficult to measure. Full performance compensation in this example is precisely and objectively measured by the $5,000 face value of *A*'s promise. The administrative advantages of this clear rule outweigh the potential costs of distortion.

When the promisee's expectation includes the consequences of performance, the damage rule becomes more complicated. Suppose *A* promises to sell *B* the raw materials for manufacturing 1,000 widgets at the current market price of $5,000. *A*'s breach causes *B* to lose two weeks of production of widgets. The $5,000 contract price no longer approximates *B*'s expectations from performance. In this situation, *B* will not be entitled to recover his lost profits from *A* unless they were

77. 5 A. Corbin, *supra* note 5, § 992.

foreseeable when the contract was made and can be proved with reasonable certainty.[78] If *B*'s expectation is unforeseeable or difficult to establish, reimbursement damages may be awarded rather than full performance compensation.

It is tempting to conclude that reimbursement recoveries are always preferable to full-performance damages as a more accurate approximation of the optimal reliance-based sanction. However, as suggested above, reimbursement recoveries are limited on practical grounds to the amount of the expenditures induced by the promise.[79] Courts have not even attempted to ascertain the value of forgone opportunities; expenditures have been reduced to their net value only when a salvage market exists. Thus, a reimbursement remedy is not necessarily a more accurate proxy for the optimal reliance-based sanction than full-performance compensation.

Following a total breach by the promisee, the value of a partial performance by the promisor can also be recouped through a reimbursement recovery.[80] The intricate patterns of recovery in partial performance cases can be explained by variations in magnitude of the costs of proof and valuation.[81] Courts usually award whichever recovery of reimbursement and compensation is readily measurable in monetary terms. In the more common cases in which neither compensation nor reimbursement is easily measured, the promisee may elect either compensation or reimbursement damages for partial performance so long as he is not made better off than his original expectation.[82]

Although objectively measurable recovery has the advantage of re-

78. *See* Farnsworth, *supra* note 10, at 1158-59 (also requiring effort to mitigate damages); Note, *Lost Profits as Contract Damages: Problems of Proof and Limitations on Recovery*, 65 YALE L.J. 992, 997-98 (1956) (relating causation to foreseeability and certainty).

79. *See* Royce Chem. Co. v. Sharples Corp., 285 F.2d 183 (2d Cir. 1960); L. Albert & Son v. Armstrong Rubber Co., 178 F.2d 182 (2d Cir. 1949); Gruber v. S-M News Co., 126 F. Supp. 442 (S.D.N.Y. 1954).

80. 5 A. CORBIN, *supra* note 5, § 1104; RESTATEMENT 1ST § 347.

81. The relation between process costs and the choice of remedies can be illustrated by returning to the example that was described above. Suppose *A* promises to sell *B* the raw materials for manufacturing 1,000 widgets at the current market price of $5,000. *A* reneges. If *B* has paid the agreed price, he is entitled to a $5,000 restitutionary reimbursement even though performance by *A* would have yielded a loss to *B*. *See* Bush v. Canfield, 2 Conn. 485, 488 (1818). Conversely, if *A* were to deliver the raw materials and *B* were to breach his promise to pay $5,000, reimbursement of expenditures would be denied to *A*; rather, *A* would be limited to his $5,000 expectancy even when the value of the raw materials delivered was significantly greater. *See* Oliver v. Campbell, 43 Cal. 2d 298, 306, 273 P.2d 15, 20 (1954).

82. A court will not "knowingly put the plaintiff in a better position than he would have occupied had the contract been fully performed." Fuller & Perdue, *supra* note 5, at 79; *see* Farnsworth, *supra* note 10, at 1178-79.

Enforcing Promises

ducing process costs, ease of measurement does not fully explain the selection of damage rules. In addition to the uncertainty of the loss, findings of remoteness and unforeseeability are used to limit consequential recoveries.[83] Courts appear unwilling to inflict socially harmful overdeterrence when the gains from awarding compensation are attenuated. Furthermore, the damage limitations of uncertainty and unforeseeability are not uniformly applied. The doctrines have been rigorously applied in cases in which liability appeared disproportionate to the gains the promisor anticipated from the contract, but have been rarely invoked when recoveries were of more limited magnitude.[84]

These limitations on consequential losses are consistent with the assumption of risk aversion discussed above. If a risk-averse promisor faces potential consequences of breach that are disproportionately large as well as unpredictable, he will increase his precautionary efforts. Limitation of the legal sanction divides the risk of regret between promisors and promisees. Promisors continue to bear the risk of the known and ascertainable consequences of concluded bargains, while promisees bear the risk of uncertain and unforeseeable consequences. A partial reallocation of the risk will reduce promisors' precautionary costs and increase their investment in reassurance. However, the expenditures on reassurance should be less than the investment in precaution under a fully compensatory scheme. First, risk-averse bargainers will choose to forgo gains rather than risk losses of equal magnitude. The cost to the promisee of forgoing profitable but unforeseeable actions in reliance on a promise will be lower than the cost to the promisor of bearing the risks that the promisee will engage in such action and that a regret contingency will arise. Thus, bargainers will prefer to bear the risk of uncertain and potentially severe consequences as promisees rather than as promisors. Second, because the consequences of breach are better known to the promisee, he is better able to select the optimal mix of promisor reassurance and self-protection through

83. *See* Fuller & Perdue, *supra* note 5, at 373-77 (analyzing other factors that limit recovery); *cf.* Note, *supra* note 78, at 997-1000 (criticizing rules limiting recoveries).

84. *See* Fuller & Perdue, *supra* note 5, at 375-76. *Compare* Dieffenbach v. McIntyre, 208 Okla. 163, 254 P.2d 346 (1952) (denying recovery for anticipated profits to plaintiff who received some damages) *with* Smith v. Onyx Oil & Chem. Co., 120 F. Supp. 674 (D. Del. 1954), *modified*, 218 F.2d 104 (3d Cir. 1955) (allowing recovery for anticipated profits to plaintiff who otherwise would recover nothing).

In addition to the disproportionate verdict problem, the bad faith or willfulness of the promisor's breach has been a relevant variable influencing the application of the uncertainty and foreseeability limitations. *See* Bauer, *The Degree of Moral Fault as Affecting Defendant's Liability*, 81 U. PA. L. REV. 586, 592 (1933); Fuller & Perdue, *supra* note 5, at 374-75. Imposition of full enforcement sanctions on the bad-faith promisor is consistent with the optimal enforcement model developed above. *See* note 35 *supra*.

limited reliance. In addition, the limitation on the award of damages for unascertainable consequences of breach induces the promisee to disclose to the promisor information that the promisor may not have concerning the consequences of breach. This information would not be disclosed to the promisor under a full-performance compensation rule and benefits from promise-making would not be maximized. Thus, the limitation on damages for unforeseeable consequences of breach increases the efficiency of promissory activity by stimulating the provision of information between bargainers.[85]

4. *The Implications of the Consideration Model*

Dissatisfaction with the mechanical rules of the common law has induced courts and commentators to offer more flexible alternatives.[86] For example, detrimental reliance has been urged as a basis for imposing discretionary liability for broken promises made in a bargaining context.[87] The current liability design of the consideration model appears to rest on crucial assumptions about bargainers' risk preferences and relative abilities to minimize risks. The indeterminacy of these empirical assumptions may explain the rigidity of the common law pattern. Liability based on future actions such as those in reliance increases bargaining uncertainty, the cost of which reduces the social value of the exchange. Whenever the outcome of private bargaining is unpredictable, liability rules that clearly specify the consequences of alternative actions will minimize uncertainty. By sharply distinguishing fully enforceable bargains from unenforceable promises, the formal rules of consideration permit bargainers to choose the outcome that minimizes expected bargaining costs.

The preceding analysis explains only the basic design of the consideration model. It does not help identify where to draw the line between enforcement and nonenforcement. At common law the category of enforceable bargained-for promises was rigidly narrow. The reluctance of common law courts to impose liability for a broader category of bargain promises perhaps can be explained by the frequent

85. Hadley v. Baxendale, 9 Exch. 341, 156 Eng. Rep. 145 (1854); *see* U.C.C. § 2-715(2)(a). Denial of lost profits as too uncertain or remote is generally accompanied by the recovery of reimbursement damages for expenditures incurred in pursuing the venture, on the presumption that the promisee would at least have covered his losses. *See, e.g.*, C.C. Hauff Hardware, Inc. v. Long Mfg. Co., 260 Iowa 30, 35, 148 N.W.2d 425, 428 (1967). In any event, the burden of reducing recovery below plaintiff's expenditures must lie on the defendant. *See, e.g.*, L. Albert & Son v. Armstrong Rubber Co., 178 F.2d 182, 189 (2d Cir. 1949).

86. *See, e.g.*, Knapp, *Enforcing the Contract to Bargain*, 44 N.Y.U. L. Rev. 673 (1969).

87. *See, e.g.*, Restatement 2d §§ 89B(2), 89C(c), 89D(c), 90.

distortion between the standard compensation rule and the optimal reliance sanction. Because nonenforcement eliminates distortions in measurement, it may be the preferable treatment for bargain promises when full enforcement provides no compensating advantages. We suggest below, however, that the recent expansion of promissory liability is consistent with the judgment that, for certain types of bargain promises, a larger core of liability can be defined without causing a significant increase in enforcement costs. Our analysis of this development can be clarified by first examining promise-making outside the exchange model.

C. *Nonreciprocal Promises*

Promises that are not conditioned upon a return promise are, unlike bargained-for promises, generally unenforceable.[88] Although unbargained-for promises are frequently made in exchange contexts, we consider here only the case of promises made outside a bargain setting. Such nonreciprocal promises typically include promises of gifts, charitable subscriptions, and other unilateral pledges to confer benefits.

The substance rather than the form of bargain triggers the distinction between reciprocal and nonreciprocal promises.[89] For example, social engagements, domestic bargains, and sham exchanges may use the bargain form for an essentially gratuitous promise. Courts typically explain the nonenforceability of social promises with the tautology that no legal obligation was intended.[90] In the case of intraspousal bargains, this rationale is reinforced by an expressed deference to the marital relation. For sham exchanges, courts generally find "nominal consideration" insufficient to support the gift promise, whose enforceability depends on the reality, not the form, of bargain.[91] Enforcement of such purely formal bargains could entail high process costs, inasmuch as such frequently trivial promises would be relatively expensive to adjudicate. However, it is no less expensive to litigate most small contracts. Non-

88. "[A] mere promise, without more, lacks a consideration and is unenforceable," Stonestreet v. Southern Oil Co., 226 N.C. 261, 263, 37 S.E.2d 676, 677 (1946), though it "cannot be broken without a violation of moral duty," Mills v. Wyman, 20 Mass. (3 Pick.) 207, 210 (1825).

89. Obviously, any distinction between bargaining and nonreciprocating contexts is an arbitrary one. The test that we propose is whether the promisee has a realistic opportunity to affect the nature and supply of promising by altering the "price" of the promise. *See* note 38 *supra*.

90. 1 A. CORBIN, *supra* note 5, § 34; RESTATEMENT 2D § 21B, Comment c & Illustration 5.

91. Lawhead v. Booth, 115 W. Va. 490, 177 S.E. 283 (1934); RESTATEMENT 2D § 76, Comment b & Illustration 5, Comment c.

enforcement of these promises can be more plausibly related to the same empirical assumptions that support the general unenforceability of nonreciprocal promises.

1. *The General Policy of Nonenforcement*

The hypothetical case of *Mortensen v. Central National Bank*[92] provides a convenient vehicle for evaluating the practical legal questions implicit in the treatment of nonreciprocal promises. Assume that on September 15, 1978, 72-year-old Mary Guillette wrote a letter to her nephew, James Mortensen, promising him a $10,000 Persian rug that he had long admired. The letter indicated that the rug would be shipped to Mortensen "sometime after I return from Florida in the spring, but no later than June 1." Guillette died in Florida on January 1, 1979, shortly after assuring Mortensen, "I'm looking forward to sending you the rug as soon as possible; you can count on it." Subsequently, Central National Bank, as the executor of Guillette's estate, refused to deliver the rug to Mortensen.

In practice, Mortensen's right to enforce his aunt's promise would depend crucially on whether the promise, which lacks the requisite bargained-for consideration, induced Mortensen to act visibly in detrimental reliance.[93] In fact, as shown above, detrimental reliance is likely to occur even if no visible evidence of it exists.[94] Between the date of the promise and that of the repudiation, Mortensen will have modified his consumption habits in adjustment to his suddenly increased expected wealth. If this expectation is disappointed, Mortensen's excessive consumption will have produced a permanent net loss in welfare; this loss is his reliance injury. Courts rarely acknowledge the existence of such uncompensated reliance when they refuse to enforce gratuitous promises.[95] The absence of bargained-for consideration triggers instead a presumption of nonenforcement.

The optimal enforcement model identified a series of interactive adaptations induced by legal enforcement of nonreciprocal promises. A legal sanction initially increases the reliability of a promise above the level the promisor voluntarily provided. But enforcement also triggers

92. The facts are drawn loosely from a case on which one of the authors consulted; it was ultimately resolved by settlement.

93. *But see* pp. 1305-07 *infra* (requirements for enforcement under § 90).

94. *See* pp. 1267-70 *supra.*

95. *See, e.g.*, Stonestreet v. Southern Oil Co., 226 N.C. 261, 263, 37 S.E.2d 676, 677 (1946) ("It is said that when one receives a naked promise and such promise is not kept, he is no worse off than he was before the promise was made. He gave nothing for it, loses nothing by it, and upon its breach he suffers no recoverable damage.")

Enforcing Promises

precautionary adjustments by promisors. Whether these interactions are optimal depends upon the promisor's certainty regarding performance, the effectiveness of extra-legal sanctions, and the capacity of qualitative adjustments to minimize the social costs of the regret contingency.

In this hypothetical case, Guillette intended to perform up until the time of her death. When the promisor is subjectively certain of performance, full enforcement offers the social benefits of increased beneficial reliance without countervailing precautionary costs. Even slightly uncertain promisors may obtain benefits through enforcement that exceed any increased precautionary or regret costs.[96] Thus, the certainty of performance seems critical in distinguishing the enforcement of sham bargains from the legal treatment of other nonreciprocal promises. At common law, the formal contract under seal provided a means for promisors to assure enforcement of gratuitous promises.[97] A sham bargain performs a similar function in encouraging deliberation, preserving evidence, and identifying the promisor's intention.[98] Although devices such as seals and sham bargains entail significant administrative costs, the voluntary use of these formal mechanisms suggests that the benefits to both parties of the additional reassurance from legal enforcement outweighs the transactions costs.[99]

The aggravated process costs of regulating social, rather than commercial, conduct seems to underlie nonenforcement even when the promisor is certain of performance. These additional costs may outweigh the gains in reliability under an enforcement rule. Enforcement of nonreciprocal promises in which formality suggests certainty requires

96. *See* pp. 1271-74 *supra.*

97. Dean Pound suggested that the seal fell victim to the "informality of pioneer America." *Promise or Bargain?, supra* note 1, at 468. The status of the seal is tenuous in many jurisdictions. *See* RESTATEMENT 2D, Introductory Note §§ 95-110. It is easy, however, to overlook alternative legal mechanisms that accomplish similar results. In particular, the decline of the seal has been paralleled by a corresponding increase in the use of *inter vivos* trusts and a relaxation in the delivery requirements for the validity of *inter vivos* gifts of personal property. Symbolic transfers, including informal writings, have been sustained when intent was clear and physical transfer was not easily accomplished. *E.g.*, Hawkins v. Union Trust Co., 187 A.D. 472, 473, 175 N.Y.S. 694, 695 (1919).

98. For the classic discussion of the rationale of legal formalities, see Fuller, *supra* note 20; *cf.* RESTATEMENT 2D § 76, Comment c. The sham bargain offers formal advantages that justify a distinction from the treatment accorded a simple donative promise. Although the evidentiary basis may not be any stronger, the fact that the promisor went to the trouble of constructing the sham exchange is substantial evidence of deliberation and intention.

99. One of the functions of legal formality, defined by Fuller as the cautionary function, is to deter inconsiderate action. Fuller, *supra* note 20, at 800. Professor Melvin Eisenberg argues that the information and process costs of ensuring a form adequate to guard against both improvidence and false claims are significant. *See* Eisenberg, *Donative Promises*, 47 U. CHI. L. REV. 1, 8-18 (1979).

additional procedural safeguards to protect against careless promise-making and false claims.[100] The problem of false claims is exacerbated by the context of many nonreciprocal promises. Many donative promises are oral[101] and the claims are often lodged against the promisor's estate.[102] The concern over resulting fraudulent claims is reflected by the more rigorous evidentiary rules governing the actual transfer of these property rights. Testamentary dispositions and *causa mortis* gifts require objective evidence of the transfer not required for *inter vivos* dispositions.[103]

If the gratuitous promisor is at all uncertain about future performance, nonenforcement can be explained by two empirical assumptions unrelated to process costs:

First, extra-legal sanctions against breach are effective in most nonreciprocal settings.

Second, even when extra-legal sanctions are not fully effective, the prospect of increasing the exchange of information through qualitative adjustments is small in most donative contexts.

Donative promises generally are more likely to be performed than are other promises and thus offer prospective benefits that outweigh prospective harms. Extra-legal sanctions are likely to be effective in the donative context because promisors generally care about the welfare of promisees. In contemplating a promise, the promisor may regard costs suffered by the promisee as equivalent to costs suffered by himself. Then, the promisor will have already taken into account the prospective detrimental reliance of the promisee. Thus, the need for a legal sanction to reflect the promisee's interests is obviated.

Furthermore, the supply of donative promises is likely to be very sensitive to the attachment of legal liability. Social considerations frequently will deter the qualitative precautionary option of attaching

100. *See, e.g.*, Haase v. Cardoza, 165 Cal. App. 2d 35, 38, 331 P.2d 419, 421 (1958) (informal promise not enforceable if utterly alone, without past consideration or reliance); Overlock v. Central Vt. Pub. Serv. Corp., 126 Vt. 549, 553, 237 A.2d 356, 358 (1967) (rigorous exactions required for enforceability because reliance unbargained-for and promise gratuitous).

101. *E.g.*, Haase v. Cardoza, 165 Cal. App. 2d 35, 331 P.2d 419 (1958); Dewein v. Estate of Dewein, 30 Ill. App. 2d 446, 174 N.E.2d 875 (1961).

102. *E.g.*, Dewein v. Estate of Dewein, 30 Ill. App. 2d 446, 174 N.E.2d 875 (1961).

103. Although *causa mortis* gifts do not require the same formality as testamentary dispositions, such transfers are policed more carefully than are *inter vivos* gifts. *See, e.g.*, Foster v. Reiss, 18 N.J. 41, 112 A.2d 553 (1955). On the other hand, when a gratuitous promise is in writing, courts have often manipulated the delivery requirements of the law of gifts in order to enforce the transfer. *See, e.g.*, Faith Lutheran Retirement Home v. Veis, 156 Mont. 38, 473 P.2d 503 (1970) (written promise is symbolic delivery executing gift); Hawkins v. Union Trust Co., 187 A.D. 472, 175 N.Y.S. 694 (1919) (delivery of letter evidencing gift sufficient to complete gift).

Enforcing Promises

explicit conditions to the promise. It seems implausible, for example, for Guillette to promise to "deliver the rug unless I decide to take a final Caribbean cruise." The only alternative to announcing a narrow promise may be forgoing any announcement at all. If donative promises are not enforced, promisees will adapt to the risk of a regret contingency by self-protective limitations on their beneficial reliance. These adjustments generally will be more precise and less costly in reduced reliance than the solely-quantitative precautionary adjustments available to promisors reluctant to impair the social relationship. Thus, the legal enforcement of donative promises may produce an excessively costly precautionary reduction in the quantity of future promising.

Although theoretically plausible, these two assumptions require empirical verification. The uncertainty surrounding the determination of the optimal legal sanction for nonreciprocal promises is reinforced by the parties' inability to bargain over legal liability. Without the bargain mechanism to reveal the value of a promise to the promisee, judicial efforts to approximate optimal enforcement are necessarily crude. In the next two sections, we evaluate whether these key empirical assumptions explain those circumstances in which courts have deviated from the general policy of nonenforcement for nonreciprocal promises.

2. *Change of Position in Reliance: Enforcement Under Section 90*

Although promissory estoppel is used most frequently in the context of bargained-for promises, the doctrine was first applied to nonreciprocal promises.[104] Conventional analysis has long assumed that promissory estoppel is a readily available means of enforcing relied-upon nonreciprocal promises.[105] Nevertheless, in the above hypothetical, Mortensen's prospects of obtaining enforcement are unlikely to improve under the provisions of section 90 of the *Restatement of Contracts*.[106] Thus, even if Mortensen could indicate specific actions in-

104. *See Promissory Estoppel, supra* note 5, at 346-54.

105. *See, e.g.*, Devecmon v. Shaw, 69 Md. 199, 14 A. 464 (1888); Ricketts v. Scothorn, 57 Neb. 51, 77 N.W. 365 (1898).

106. Section 90 is quoted below in a form that indicates the language of both the 1932 original *Restatement 1st* and its 1965 revision, the *Restatement 2d*. Bracketed words appear in the *Restatement 1st* but have been deleted in the current version. Italicized words are those added by the *Restatement 2d*.

> A promise which the promisor should reasonably expect to induce action or forbearance [of a definite and substantial character] on the part of the promisee *or a third person* and which does induce such action or forbearance is binding if injustice can be avoided only by enforcement of the promise. *The remedy granted for breach may be limited as justice requires.*

Most of the decided cases have used the language of the *Restatement 1st* in evaluating

duced in reliance on the promise, such as execution of a contract to sell the rug, the reliance would likely be found insufficiently "foreseeable" and "reasonable" to justify enforcement.

The existence, foreseeability, and reasonableness of claimed actions in reliance are difficult factual issues that the plaintiff must establish for the promise to be enforced under section 90.[107] Furthermore, under section 90 the plaintiff must demonstrate that "justice" requires the enforcement of the promise. Although in bargaining contexts courts have responded to this invitation to the exercise of judicial discretion with complex analysis, in nonreciprocal situations courts have followed clearer rules. Litigation to enforce nonreciprocal promises under section 90 has centered on charitable subscriptions, employee retirement benefits, and donative intrafamilial promises. An examination of recent decisions reveals distinct patterns of enforcement among each type of promise.

Courts generally refuse to enforce intrafamilial promises under section 90, even when the promisee claims he has incurred costs from tangible actions in reliance.[108] Indeed, in the only recent case in which

section 90 claims. But several courts have explicitly adopted the more flexible standard of the *Restatement 2d*. *See* Chapman v. Bomann, 381 A.2d 1123, 1127 (Me. 1978); Warder & Lee Elevator, Inc. v. Britten, 274 N.W.2d 339, 342-43 (Iowa 1979).

107. Under the terms of the *Restatement 1st*, the promisee would be obliged to establish the "definite and substantial character" of his reliance. Although this condition has been deleted in the *Restatement 2d*, a showing that the promise did actually induce reliance is still required. Courts have not been persuaded by the argument that changes in the promisee's consumption behavior create a presumptive case for the existence of detrimental reliance. For example, in Baggs v. Anderson, 528 P.2d 141 (Utah 1974), the court held that the requirement of substantial change in position because of reliance "is not satisfied by the mere fact that [the promisee] indulged in the pleasant and euphoric assumption that he would not have to meet his obligations and that he bought a more expensive car and moved to a more expensive apartment." *Id.* at 144.

In practice, a promisee will probably be required to indicate specific and identifiable instances of foreseeable reliance. *See, e.g.*, Corbit v. J.I. Case Co., 70 Wash. 2d 522, 539, 424 P.2d 290, 301 (1967). Thus, a plaintiff will tend to be disadvantaged if his behavioral adaptations in reliance on the promise were many, small, and diffuse rather than few, large, and identifiable. RESTATEMENT 2D § 90, Comment b. The specific-foreseeability requirement can be justified as a control on the "reliance shopping" behavior that might otherwise be anticipated. *Id.*

Finally, assume that facts reveal that the promisee knew that the gratuitous promise was not legally enforceable. Thus, it could be argued that reliance was unreasonable because the promisee knew that no legal rights were conveyed by the promise. From the perspective of true reliance this argument seems irrelevant. If a promise carries a substantial nominal value, considerable reliance would be expected even if the promisee were aware of the restrictive legal rules governing nonreciprocal promises. Hence, even assuming nonenforceability upon the death of the promisor, the value of the promise would merely be discounted by the probability of nonperformance. Nonetheless, such reliance is likely to be characterized as unreasonable and, therefore, unworthy of section 90 enforcement. *See, e.g.*, Union Tank Car Co. v. Wheat Bros., 15 Utah 2d 101, 387 P.2d 1000 (1964).

108. *E.g.*, Bush v. Bush, 278 Ala. 244, 246, 177 So. 2d 568, 570 (1964); Dewein v. Estate of Dewein, 30 Ill. App. 2d 446, 449-50, 174 N.E.2d 875, 877 (1961).

Enforcing Promises

enforcement has been granted, specifically foreseeable action in reliance was used merely to buttress a promise grounded on formal evidence of an exchange after fifteen years of services rendered by the promisee.[109] In contrast, as provided by the second *Restatement*, courts tend to enforce fully charitable subscriptions regardless of reliance.[110] The frequent argument that the societal interest in eleemosynary activities explains the distinctive legal treatment of charitable promises is not convincing.[111] The social benefit from promise-making would be similarly impaired if enforcement led to restraints on future charitable promises.

Variations in legal process costs, including the risk of false claims, may explain the divergent enforcement patterns in these cases. Furthermore, the differing contexts of nonreciprocal promises suggest important differences in the ability of the parties to adjust the scope and volume of promises. Although charitable promises are formally nonreciprocal, they often are exchanged implicitly for recognition and esteem.[112] Hence, charitable promises are to some extent susceptible

109. *In re* Estate of Bucci, 488 P.2d 216 (Colo. App. 1971). In *Bucci*, after fifteen years of living with and being cared for by the plaintiff, the plaintiff's grandfather promised to give the plaintiff $17,000 to allow plaintiff to purchase a house, when the grandfather sold a certain tract of land or within three years, whichever came first. In reliance upon the promise, the plaintiff withdrew $2,000 of her savings and secured an option on the house. The grandfather died within three years without selling his land. The court held the promise enforceable on two grounds. First, "natural love and affection" constituted sufficient consideration to support the promise based on the 15 years of care and prior services performed. *Id.* at 218-19; *see* pp. 1310-12 *infra*. Second, the administratix of the estate was estopped from denying liability because of the promisee's detrimental reliance on the promise. The court concluded that the plaintiff would not have entered into the option contract without the assurance of completion provided by the promise. 488 P.2d at 219.

110. RESTATEMENT 2D § 90(2) ("A charitable subscription or a marriage settlement is binding under Subsection (1) without proof that the promise induced action or forbearance.")

Salsbury v. Northwestern Bell Tel. Co., 221 N.W.2d 609 (Iowa 1974), is illustrative of the cases that have supported a conclusive presumption of reliance. In *Salsbury*, the defendant telephone company promised to donate $15,000 to a newly formed college. The college failed and the defendant did not pay its pledge. The court held the promise enforceable without proof of detrimental reliance, on the basis of public policy. Requiring evidence of reliance, the court reasoned, may result in the enforcement of fewer charitable promises. *Id.* at 612-13; *cf.* Hirsch v. Hirsch, 32 Ohio App. 2d 200, 289 N.E.2d 386 (1972) (consideration for pledge to eleemosynary institution is accomplishment of purposes for which institution is organized).

Not all courts, however, have adopted the conclusive presumption of reliance. *See, e.g.*, Mount Sinai Hosp., Inc. v. Jordan, 290 So. 2d 484 (Fla. 1974). In *Mount Sinai*, the court refused to enforce the decedent's charitable pledge because the hospital did not "affirmatively show actual reliance of a substantial character." *Id.* at 487.

111. *See, e.g.*, Danby v. Osteopathic Hosp. Ass'n, 34 Del. Ch. 427, 434-35, 104 A.2d 903, 907 (1954); RESTATEMENT 2D § 90, Comment f.

112. The exchange model of charitable donations is not wholly explanatory. When the donation is purely altruistic, as in a gratuitous promise to make a charitable gift, the context may seem directly analogous to the intrafamilial donation. Enforcing such prom-

to bargaining.[113] Intrafamilial donations, on the other hand, are peculiarly resistant to interactive adjustment and epitomize the nonreciprocity of donative promises. When the nature and amount of promising can be adjusted, the choice of liability rule has less impact. As the importance of specifying the optimal enforcement choice is reduced, the value of a certain, clear rule increases.

The choice between the equally clear rules of full enforcement and nonenforcement, however, must rest upon other factors. First, self-sanctions are probably less effective in the charitable than in the intrafamilial setting, because extra-legal sanctions are often limited to the goodwill value of the promisor's word.[114] Second, in the extrafamilial context, promisors are not as disabled by social considerations from making qualitative precautionary adjustments. Thus, in general, enforcement may induce cost-effective precautionary adjustments that increase the net beneficial reliance on charitable promises. Excessively costly self-protection by promisees may be reduced both because qualitative precautions improve the information concerning future regret contingencies and because legally imposed reassurance improves the promise's overall reliability.

Other types of nonreciprocal promises are more difficult to categorize. For example, promises relating to employee retirement benefits occur in a wide variety of promissory settings.[115] For purely gratuitous promises, enforcement efforts on grounds of either promissory estoppel or unjust enrichment have been largely unsuccessful.[116] However, when inferences of reciprocity can be drawn, pension promises have been enforced even though they are not strictly bargained-for.[117]

ises is partially explicable in process terms. The costs of identifying a narrow category of unenforceable promises would substantially increase process costs. A clear and certain rule is advantageous when the judgment whether to perform the promise is frequently made by risk-averse executors and administrators. But, more important, the enforcement choice may also be consistent with the judgment that self-sanctions are significantly reduced in these essentially arms-length transactions.

113. There are a number of mechanisms by which a promise can be solicited from a reluctant charitable donor by adjusting the cost of the subscription. For example, the common practice of commemorating the charitable donor by publicizing his name is one of the key strategies of charitable solicitation. *See, e.g.*, Allegheny College v. National Chautauqua County Bank, 246 N.Y. 369, 375, 159 N.E. 173, 175 (1927) (promisor imposed condition that "gift" be known as "Mary Yates Johnston Memorial Fund").

114. Of course, when a recurring pattern of similar promises exists, the loss of goodwill from nonperformance may be as substantial as other disincentives to breach. An interesting question for further empirical inquiry is whether the magnitude of reputational losses provides a reliable basis for distinguishing variations in the enforcement of promises made in commercial environments.

115. *See Unjust Enrichment, supra* note 5, at 1172-74; *Promissory Estoppel, supra* note 5, at 371.

116. *See, e.g.*, Pitts v. McGraw-Edison Co., 329 F.2d 412, 415-16 (6th Cir. 1964).

117. *E.g.*, Hurd v. Hutnik, 419 F. Supp. 630, 644-45 (D.N.J. 1976); Wickstrom v. Vern E. Alden Co., 99 Ill. App. 2d 254, 261-64, 240 N.E.2d 401, 405-07 (1968).

Enforcing Promises

The nonenforcement and full-enforcement options can be compared usefully with the intermediate scheme proposed by section 90(1) of the second *Restatement*.[118] This reformulation of section 90 eliminates the threshold requirement that action in reliance be definite and substantial and instead limits the degree of enforcement "as justice requires." The optimal damage formula proposed in Part I may explain the nature and role of this limited sanction. As we showed earlier, if the ex ante probability of a promisor performing a promise were high, the prospective beneficial reliance from the promise could exceed prospective detrimental reliance, in which case the overall ex ante prospects would represent a net social benefit. Section 90(1) can thus be read to authorize award of optimal damages based upon this calculation of the promisee's prospective net reliance. This may necessitate damages in amounts less than both full performance and full detrimental reliance.

The justification for abandoning the clearer alternatives of nonenforcement and full enforcement is the error cost of using remedies that do not accurately shape optimal promise-making. The advantage of an optimal net reliance rule is lost, however, if the rule cannot be applied accurately without substantial process costs. The problem in implementing a section 90(1) enforcement rule for nonreciprocal promises lies in the difficulty in determining true reliance on the basis of observable facts. Indeed, the intermediate sanction of reimbursement is as much an approximation of an optimal reliance rule as are the more extreme alternatives. Although relying upon crude liability options may be unsatisfying, incurring the costs necessary to apply more complex rules of recovery and to resolve more factual issues would not necessarily improve the outcomes.

The inclination of courts to ground legal rules in fact-specific contexts illustrates the risks of stipulating one rule for all actions for reliance-based recovery. Section 90 was drafted to address a variety of recurring circumstances in which promises outside the perimeters of traditional bargain theory have been enforced. Although within these specific factual contexts the effects of the enforcement choice could be more carefully observed, as a rule of general application, section 90 demands a degree of precision beyond current empirical understanding. Furthermore, a broad general rule blurs distinctions between bargaining and nonreciprocal environments that may legitimately influence judicial decisions.[119]

118. *See* note 100 *supra*.

119. Arguably, distributional goals explain the judicial discretion invited by the concern for the requirements of justice found in section 90. These goals are, perhaps, more effectively implemented by general statements of principle than by adherence to specific

3. *Moral Obligation: Promise for Benefit Received*

Conferral of benefits on the promisor by the promisee prior to a nonreciprocal promise may affect the decision whether to enforce the subsequent promise. Under the common law material benefit rule, a promise may be enforced if the benefits were conferred after either an express or an implied request of the promisor.[120] When the services were requested, the subsequent promise functions as a mechanism for valuing the implied preexisting bargain.[121] Alternatively, when unsolicited benefits create no quasi-contractual obligation, subsequent promises are ordinarily not enforced.[122] More recently, the material benefit rule was reformulated to reflect the broader instinct for enforcement suggested by case law development. Thus, section 89A of the second *Restatement* provides that a subsequent promise recognizing a prior benefit is enforceable unless "the promisee conferred the benefit as a gift or for other reasons the promisor has not been unjustly enriched."[123]

Discussion of the enforceability of the subsequent promise implies that the original conferral of benefits was not sufficient to support restitution for unjust enrichment. The subsequent promise may, however, fill the interstices between contract and quasi-contract by minimizing the prospect of reward for forcible imposition of "benefits." By removing these objections to a quasi-contractual liability, the subsequent promise justifies recovery of the conferred benefits.[124] But consider the effect of such an enforcement rule on future promising. When a promisor is uncertain about future performance, enforcement will deter socially beneficial promises, thus undermining the policy of

rules designed to regulate future conduct. But neither has a distributional principle that clarifies the enforcement choice under section 90 been identified nor have courts engaged in the kind of factual inquiry necessary to support principled redistributive outcomes. *See* pp. 1320-21 *infra*.

120. *See* 1 S. WILLISTON, *supra* note 76, §§ 144-147. The material-benefit rule requires a finding that it is reasonable to suppose that the promisee expected to be compensated in some way for the conferred benefits, thereby creating a "moral obligation." Manwill v. Oyler, 11 Utah 2d 433, 436, 361 P.2d 177, 178-79 (1961). As Henderson has suggested, liability imposed under this formulation is haphazard and imprecise. *See Unjust Enrichment, supra* note 5, at 1120-26.

121. 1 S. WILLISTON, *supra* note 76, § 146; *see* Jacobs v. Brock, 66 Wash. 2d 878, 883-86, 406 P.2d 17, 20-22 (1965).

122. *See* Perreault v. Hall, 94 N.H. 191, 193-94, 49 A.2d 812, 813-14 (1946); Pershall v. Elliott, 249 N.Y. 183, 187-88, 163 N.E. 554, 556 (1928).

123. RESTATEMENT 2D § 89A. As the Reporter conceded, this section "fairly bristles with unspecific concepts." Braucher, *Freedom of Contract and the Second Restatement*, 78 YALE L.J. 598, 605 (1969); *see Unjust Enrichment, supra* note 5 (charting case-law development underlying § 89A formulation).

124. *See* RESTATEMENT 2D § 89A, Comment b; *Unjust Enrichment, supra* note 5, at 1165-76.

Enforcing Promises

restoring a benefit unjustly retained.[125] A broader justification for enforcement can be identified. The emphasis on isolated cases involving the provision of emergency[126] or mistaken[127] services has blurred the true significance of the liability principle incorporated in section 89A. The concept of unjust enrichment can be examined most usefully as a symbol for the detrimental reliance resulting from an abortive exchange relationship.[128]

How do past events illuminate the detrimental reliance resulting from the broken promise? The application of section 89A sharpens the distinction between reciprocal and nonreciprocal settings. A subsequent promise is typically enforced when it recognizes a benefit conferred in the context of an exchange.[129] Alternatively, enforcement is denied if the benefits were donated or provided to satisfy existing contractual obligations.[130] Examination of the prior events that induced the promise may rebut the assumption of benevolence and instead suggest that the promise was made in a reciprocal context.

If the promise can be located in a bargaining context, the detrimental reliance on the promise can be approximately measured by the price paid in conferred benefits. Indeed, partial performance of this newly discovered bargain provides the strongest basis for the claim of unjust enrichment if the return promise is found enforceable.[131] Identification of the promise within an exchange also reduces the risk of false claims and process errors resulting from the absence of formality.[132] Furthermore, the assumption of reciprocity implies that the promisor can adjust to legal liability by attaching more explicit conditions to the promise. In general, when such qualitative precautionary adjustments

125. *See* p. 1275 *supra*. In the case of the certain promisor, for whom the probability of performance is either zero or one, use of the subsequent promise as a device for clarifying a prior unjust enrichment will have no deterrent effects on future promising. The bad-faith promise can be enforced fully under any circumstances. The more interesting question concerns the promisor who is certain that future performance will be forthcoming. When nonenforcement of such promises is justified on process grounds, the prior benefits may provide formal support for an otherwise gratuitous undertaking.

126. *E.g.*, Webb v. McGowin, 232 Ala. 374, 168 So. 199 (1936); Boothe v. Fitzpatrick, 36 Vt. 681 (1864); *see* RESTATEMENT 2D § 89A, Comment d.

127. *See* Drake v. Bell, 26 Misc. 237, 55 N.Y.S. 945, *aff'd on other grounds*, 46 A.D. 275, 61 N.Y.S. 657 (1899); RESTATEMENT 2D § 89A, Comment c.

128. *See Unjust Enrichment*, *supra* note 5, at 1158.

129. *See, e.g.*, Holland v. Martinson, 119 Kan. 43, 237 P. 902 (1925); Reece v. Reece, 239 Md. 649, 212 A.2d 468 (1965); Jacobs v. Brock, 66 Wash. 2d 878, 406 P.2d 17 (1965).

130. *See, e.g.*, Collord v. Cooley, 92 Idaho 789, 792, 451 P.2d 535, 538 (1969); Youngberg v. Holstrom, 252 Iowa 815, 819-21, 108 N.W.2d 498, 500-01 (1961); Jensen v. Anderson, 24 Utah 2d 191, 468 P.2d 366 (1970); RESTATEMENT 2D § 89A, Comments e & f.

131. *See* Fuller, *supra* note 20, at 812; Fuller & Perdue, *supra* note [illegible], at [illegible]; *Unjust Enrichment*, *supra* note 5, at 1136-37, 1147-49, 1157-59, 1178-83.

132. *See Unjust Enrichment*, *supra* note 5, at 1159-65.

are feasible, the promisor has more accurate knowledge of future contingencies and, hence, can avoid risk more cheaply than can the promisee.[133]

The prior benefits principle of section 89A reflects an expanding enforcement of promises outside the consideration model even more clearly than does the promissory estoppel concept of section 90. Classic bargain theory delimited the borders of enforcement too narrowly to incorporate the full regulatory benefits of the exchange context. Courts are expanding liability under a variety of guises in order to reach the perimeters of exchange. Only when the effects of enforcement cannot be internalized by individual bargaining is the policy of nonenforcement clearly retained.

D. *Unilateral-Bargain Promises: The Expansion of Bargain Theory*

Reciprocal-bargain promises and nonreciprocal promises represent the polar extremes of promissory settings. The recent expansion in promissory liability has been concentrated in the intermediate contexts, in which bargaining and exchange remain a realistic, if not realized, prospect. Indeed, the main source of tension between traditional bargain theory and the optimal enforcement of promises lies in the incongruence between the narrowly drawn consideration model and

133. For promises judged enforceable under the prior benefits principle, section 89A invites a limitation of remedy when the face value of the promise is disproportionate to the benefit conferred. "A promise is not binding under Subsection (1) [of § 89A] . . . (b) to the extent that its value is disproportionate to the benefit." RESTATEMENT 2D § 89A. Framing the question of remedy in terms of disproportion may seem puzzling. A reimbursement recovery equal to the value of the conferred benefits is not necessarily an accurate approximation of the true reliance induced by the promise. The disproportion principle is more plausibly examined as a means of resolving the peculiar problem of mixed motivations. If limiting recovery to the reasonable value of the promisee's services successfully separates the hybrid elements of gift and bargain, the harmful consequences of overenforcement of nonreciprocal promises are reduced. Limiting enforcement to that portion of the promise that is subject to an exchange can be explained, therefore, as a further illustration of the distinction between nonreciprocal and reciprocal contexts.

Courts' traditional reluctance to assess the adequacy of consideration can be reconciled with the disproportion principle of section 89A by locating the promissory context on a continuum between the poles of benevolence and bargain. As promises approach the pure bargain, the uncertainty costs of judicial review of relative values increase. Even when both parties concede that a transaction is part bargain and part gift, common law consideration rules support full enforcement. *See, e.g.*, RESTATEMENT 2D § 81, Comment c; *id.* § 75, Comment c ("Even where both parties know that a transaction is in part a bargain and in part a gift, the element of bargain may nevertheless furnish consideration for the entire transaction.") The lesson of the expanding liability reflected in section 89A is that the exchange environment extends beyond the classic bargain model. In the prior benefits transaction, the elements of bargain are somewhat attenuated, as are the costs of judicial assessment of disproportion. Limiting recovery to the value of services exchanged is efficient when the resulting increase in uncertainty is outweighed by a reduction in the damaging effects of excessive enforcement on nonreciprocal transactions.

Enforcing Promises

this broader exchange context. Courts have responded to this tension by using alternative theories of liability to enforce a much wider range of bargain promises, such as subsequent promises to renew an antecedent legal obligation barred by bankruptcy or the statute of limitations.[134] In addition, reliance-based theories have often been employed when rules of consideration deny enforcement.[135] We designate representations lacking any legally enforceable consideration as "unilateral-bargain" promises. Much of the uncertainty concerning the enforcement of such promises arises because the doctrinal support for enforcement has emerged from the gratuitous context. However, although the boundaries have been redefined, the distinction between the enforcement of nonreciprocal and reciprocal promises remains largely undisturbed.

Enforcement rules for unilateral-bargain promises may never be as precisely defined as the provisions regulating other promissory categories. Nevertheless, under recurring circumstances, patterns of enforcement emerge from which individual variables can be isolated. The examination of cases in which courts have recently expanded liability is necessary to isolate the key elements in the enforcement decision.

1. *Reduced Transactions Costs*

We have suggested that the classic consideration model can be explained by analysis of the transactions costs of exchange. When outcomes are uncertain, the risk of legal liability may be perceived as a greater threat than the risk of uncompensated reliance from a broken promise, because each actor can exercise greater control over his own detrimental reliance than over the potential losses of his promisee. Thus, all other things equal, forgoing an uncertain gain by reducing

134. *See* A. CORBIN, *supra* note 5, § 222 (observing this practice); G. GILMORE, *supra* note 4, at 55-65 (describing the historical use of alternative theories of obligation); 1 S. WILLISTON, *supra* note 76, § 158 (observing practice). The rhetoric of the cases typically explains enforcement of such promises on the basis of the moral obligation created by the original bargain. *See, e.g.*, Stanek v. White, 172 Minn. 390, 391, 215 N.W. 781, 781 (1927). The same pattern—enforcing subsequent promises arising out of a completed exchange—is found in those decisions renewing contractual obligations voidable by fraud or infancy. *See* 1 A. CORBIN, *supra* note 5, § 228 (fraud); S. WILLISTON, *supra* note 76, § 151 (infancy).

135. In addition to the obvious use of promissory estoppel to enforce promises inducing post-promise reliance, many of the enrichment cases enforcing promises following the conferral of benefits are usefully examined in terms of a presumption that such promises are most likely to induce post-promise reliance. *See Unjust Enrichment*, *supra* note 5, at 1181. Although the cases examined in this section are largely limited to promissory estoppel claims, many of the prior-benefit cases can be categorized on similar bases. Only a few courts have discussed the relationship of the reliance element. *E.g.*, General Bronze Corp. v. United States, 338 F.2d 117, 122-25 (Ct. Cl. 1964).

reliance will be preferred over suffering an equally uncertain loss of similar magnitude. This assumption helps explain both the offer and acceptance and discharge rules of consideration and the remedial limitations on liability.

Examining the disposition of promissory estoppel claims in bargain settings reveals patterns of enforcement that parallel the design of the consideration model. Promises made in either preliminary or termination negotiations are generally unenforceable under section 90.[136] Alternatively, reliance theories have been used successfully to enforce promises made in the context of an ongoing exchange transaction. Indeed, promises that modify an existing agreement have long been enforced, despite the common law preexisting duty rule, if there is evidence of reasonable reliance.[137] Although the decisions in such "waiver by estoppel" cases often focus doctrinally on equitable estoppel, the impact reliance has on the imposition of liability is clear.[138]

Similarly, courts have enforced a variety of collateral promises reinforcing completed but defective exchanges.[139] For example, in *Wheeler v. White*,[140] after an agreement had been signed, the promisor represented that funds for a projected shopping center would soon be available and convinced the promisee to demolish existing buildings. Although the original agreement was judged indefinite, the subsequent promises of performance were found enforceable under section 90.[141]

By enforcing such promises, the courts have not ventured far beyond the assumptions underlying the consideration model. The requirements for recovery under section 90 have been strictly construed whenever the outcome of bargaining is uncertain, but have been liberally interpreted when the essence of the bargain has been established. When agreements are unclear, risk-averse bargainers prefer to bear the risks

136. *See, e.g.*, Coley v. Lang, 339 So. 2d 70, 74 (Ala. App. 1976) (preliminary negotiations); Malaker Corp. Stockholders Protective Comm. v. First Jersey Nat'l Bank, 163 N.J. Super. 463, 473-74, 395 A.2d 222, 227 (App. Div. 1978) (same); McMath v. Ford Motor Co., 77 Mich. App. 721, 725-27, 259 N.W.2d 140, 142-43 (1977) (termination negotiations).

137. But for the preexisting-duty rule, which requires modifying promises to have a separate consideration, such promises would be fully enforceable at common law without the need to establish reliance. *See* note 72 *supra* (discussing evolution of rules).

138. *See, e.g.*, Albanese v. N.V. Nederl. Amerik Stoomv. Maats., 279 F. Supp. 635 (S.D.N.Y. 1967) (basing defendant's liability on plaintiff's reliance); Shell Oil Co. v. Kelinson, 158 N.W.2d 724, 729 (Iowa 1968) (same); *cf. Unjust Enrichment*, *supra* note 5, at 1173-74 (reliance theory grounded in notion of promissory estoppel has been "marginally successful").

139. *See, e.g.*, Travelers Indem. Co. v. Holman, 330 F.2d 142, 151 (5th Cir. 1964) (enforcing misleading promise that insurance policy covered specified damages); Alaska Airlines, Inc. v. Stephenson, 217 F.2d 295, 298 (9th Cir. 1954) (enforcing promise that business expenses ancillary to employment contract would be covered).

140. 398 S.W.2d 93 (Tex. 1965).

141. *Id.* at 95-97.

of regret contingencies as promisees, and the nonenforcement rule is optimally retained. When the bargain is clear but fails technically, however, parties may prefer pursuing gains to avoiding losses. Enforcement under section 90 allocates the risk of regret to promisors and thereby shifts resources to more efficient precautionary conduct.

These reflections of the assumptions underlying the consideration model also appear in the remedies provided under the doctrine of promissory estoppel. Generally, full-enforcement compensation has been awarded whenever such damages would have been available under the certainty and foreseeability limitations of bargain theory.[142] Reimbursement has been awarded when the harmful consequences of nonperformance were not reasonably foreseeable and the claim for greater damages was too speculative.[143] Although the rhetoric of some of these decisions suggests that reimbursement damages are the preferred recovery under promissory estoppel, the outcomes imply that courts are animated by the same concerns that have produced the design of the consideration model.

2. *Accuracy: Promises Made in Competitive Markets*

Traditional bargain theory does not distinguish between exchange transactions in established markets and exchanges of unique promises.[144] Because detrimental reliance and full expectancy are equivalent in competitive markets, however, when a promise made in a competitive market induces reasonable reliance, full enforcement is a more accurate approximation of the true detrimental reliance caused by the promise regardless of whether the promise was bargained-for. Enforcement of competitive promises that reasonably induce reliance is efficient, however, only if marginal gains in accuracy exceed marginal increases in the process costs of enforcement. Thus, courts can be expected to expand liability when competitive markets are readily identifiable.

The expanding use of promissory estoppel to impose liability outside traditional boundaries is substantially explained by such net gains in the accuracy of the measurement of damages.[145] For example,

142. *See, e.g.*, Drennan v. Star Paving Co., 51 Cal. 2d 409, 414-17, 333 P.2d 757, 760-61 (1958) (subcontractors' bid); Southwest Water Servs., Inc. v. Cope, 531 S.W.2d 873 (Tex. Civ. App. 1975) (fixed water rates).

143. *See, e.g.*, Associated Tabulating Servs., Inc. v. Olympic Life Ins. Co., 414 F.2d 1306, 1311 (5th Cir. 1969) (new business profits); Goodman v. Dicker, 169 F.2d 684, 685 (D.C. Cir. 1948) (same).

144. *See* note 66 *supra* (discussing unique-bargain promises).

145. Similar inferences can be drawn from an examination of prior-benefits cases. *See, e.g.*, Husted v. Fuller, 361 F.2d 187 (7th Cir. 1966) (subsequent promise to refund forfeited

in a number of cases involving bids by subcontractors, courts have imposed liability for reasonable reliance on a firm offer even though the promise was not supported by bargained-for consideration.[146] The Uniform Commercial Code enforces similarly firm written offers by merchants,[147] and the second *Restatement* generalizes the rule to include all offers reasonably inducing reliance before acceptance, when "necessary to avoid injustice."[148] This discretionary provision can be interpreted as mandating enforcement only when enforcement is an accurate proxy for detrimental reliance. In each of these circumstances, the existence of a competitive market is the variable that best explains the enforceability of firm offers.

It is useful to examine the market for substitute promises in other reliance cases. Courts have generally circumvented the Statute of Frauds only in the presence of clear and substantial evidence of an "unconscionable injury" induced by detrimental reliance on an oral promise.[149]

earnest money enforced). The plaintiff in *Husted* was a businessman, and the promise could reasonably be inferred as having induced a forbearance on his part from alternative financing opportunities.

Because the theory of enforcement for prior-benefits promises focuses attention on prepromise facts, however, the cases rarely explore postpromise circumstances with sufficient detail to permit accurate judgment about the congruence between postpromise reliance and enforcement.

146. *See, e.g.*, Drennan v. Star Paving Co., 51 Cal. 2d 409, 333 P.2d 757 (1958). Since *Drennan*, promissory estoppel has been consistently employed to deny subcontractors the power to withdraw their bids after general contractors have relied on them by incorporating the bids into their prime bid for the construction job. *See, e.g.*, S.M. Wilson & Co. v. Prepakt Concrete Co., 23 Ill. App. 3d 137, 318 N.E.2d 722 (1974); Constructors Supply Co. v. Bostrom Sheet Metal Works, Inc., 291 Minn. 113, 190 N.W.2d 71 (1971). Traditionally, firm offers were not enforced unless they were supported by bargained-for consideration. *See, e.g.*, James Baird Co. v. Gimbel Bros., Inc., 64 F.2d 344 (2d Cir. 1933); Board of Control v. Burgess, 45 Mich. App. 183, 206 N.W.2d 256 (1973).

147. *See* U.C.C. § 2-205 (written offers by merchants, if announced as irrevocable, are binding without consideration for up to three months). The limited scope of § 2-205 increases the likelihood that the firm promises captured by its provisions will have been made in a competitive market.

148. *See* Restatement 2d § 89B(2) ("offer which the offeror should reasonably expect to induce action or forbearance of a substantial character on the part of the offeree before acceptance and which does induce such action or forbearance is binding as an option contract to the extent necessary to avoid injustice").

149. *See* Monarco v. Lo Greco, 35 Cal. 2d 621, 220 P.2d 737 (1950). *But see* FMC Fin. Corp. v. Reed, 592 F.2d 238, 243 (5th Cir. 1979) (following Mississippi law; holding that Statute of Frauds cannot be circumvented by doctrine of collateral estoppel).

The most familiar factual pattern of these estoppel cases involves oral promises of employment followed by acts of reliance by the promisee. But mere change in job or residence is generally held insufficient unless the forgone alternatives resulted in "unconscionable injury." Such injury has been found in cases in which the promisee relinquished pension benefits and sold a custom home, *see* Lucas v. Whittaker Corp., 470 F.2d 326 (10th Cir. 1972), or resigned from lifetime employment, *see* Ruinello v. Murray, 36 Cal. 2d 687, 227 P.2d 251 (1951). These examples suggest that the notion of unconscionable injury in these cases is usefully examined as a symbol of forgone substitute

Enforcing Promises

In the highly competitive commodities markets, however, oral promises by farmers to deliver their crops to grain elevators have been readily enforced.[150] Courts have also generally been reluctant to allow promissory estoppel to undermine the parol evidence rule.[151] However, in *Ehret Co. v. Eaton, Yale & Towne, Inc.*,[152] the promisee, a sales representative for a manufacturer, obtained enforcement of a promise of "extremely fair treatment" in sharing future commissions despite a fully integrated written agreement to the contrary.[153] The existence of a developed market for the promisee's services helps to explain the court's decision in *Ehret* to enforce the promise.[154]

Competition for the promisee's services explains the enforceability under section 90 of certain preliminary negotiations and indefinite agreements. Thus, detrimental reliance has been found an adequate basis for enforcing promises to lease business facilities,[155] to provide a construction job,[156] and to award a construction contract.[157] These cases are closely linked to decisions enforcing promises of insurance[158]

promises roughly equal in value to the oral one in question. In turn, these cases have provided the support for codifying the reliance principle as a means of enforcing oral promises within the Statute of Frauds. *See* RESTATEMENT 2D § 217A. Section 217A is complementary to section 90 and varies in its form only by identifying five specific "considerations" for determining whether justice can be avoided only by enforcement.

150. In the grain elevator cases, the operators typically use the farmers' oral promises in reselling their produce on the futures market. *See, e.g.*, Jamestown Terminal Elevator, Inc. v. Hieb, 246 N.W.2d 736 (N.D. 1976). *But see* Sacred Heart Farmers Coop. Elevator v. Johnson, 305 Minn. 324, 232 N.W.2d 921 (1975) (holding oral promisor not bound).

151. A number of courts have rejected the proposition that action in reliance might properly permit courts to avoid the application of the parol evidence rule. *See, e.g.*, Mack v. Jorgensen Co., 467 F.2d 1177 (7th Cir. 1972); Clark Oil & Ref. Corp. v. Leistikow, 69 Wis. 2d 226, 230 N.W.2d 736 (1975).

152. 523 F.2d 280 (7th Cir. 1975).

153. *Id.* at 282.

154. The plaintiff, Ehret Company, had an exclusive sales contract with the defendant and had invested up to 10 years of development work to adapt the defendant's products to its customers' needs. *See id.* at 281-83.

155. Mooney v. Craddock, 530 P.2d 1302 (Colo. App. 1974).

156. Hunter v. Hayes, 533 P.2d 952 (Colo. App. 1975).

157. Swinerton & Walberg Co. v. City of Inglewood-Los Angeles County Civic Center Auth., 40 Cal. App. 3d 98, 114 Cal. Rptr. 834 (1974).

158. Promises to procure insurance are the most common circumstances in which the amount of reliance greatly exceeds the face value of the promise. *See, e.g.*, Spiegel v. Metropolitan Life Ins. Co., 6 N.Y.2d 91, 160 N.E.2d 40, 188 N.Y.S.2d 486 (1959) (promise to pay life insurance premium of $39.75 causing reliance equal to $10,650, proceeds of policy). Consequently, some courts have been reluctant to use section 90 to enforce the full amount of the resulting loss. *See, e.g.*, Dillown v. Phalen, 106 Ohio App. 106, 153 N.E.2d 687 (1957). Nonetheless, a number of courts have explicitly used promissory estoppel to enforce a broken promise to insure. *See, e.g.*, Graddon v. Knight, 138 Cal. App. 2d 577, 292 P.2d 632 (1956); East Providence Credit Union v. Geremia, 103 R.I. 597, 239 A.2d 725 (1968). Furthermore, liability is often imposed on the additional basis of negligent failure to perform services gratuitously undertaken. *See, e.g.*, Colonial Sav. Ass'n v. Taylor, 544 S.W.2d 116 (Tex. 1976); RESTATEMENT (2D) OF TORTS § 323 (1965). The *Restatement of*

and gratuitous bailments,[159] for which a similar promise would have been available to the promisee.[160] In this case, the opportunity cost of acceptance of a promisor's representations that designated property would be insured or safeguarded is equal to the entire loss if the risk materializes after the promise is broken.[161]

At the other extreme are cases in which the exchange is negotiated between two unique bargainers. These disputes often materialize as breakdowns in preliminary negotiations,[162] indefinite agreements,[163] or franchise terminations.[164] Notwithstanding several celebrated decisions,[165] promissory estoppel has rarely been applied to enforce incomplete agreements reached by unique bargainers. Under this circumstance, full enforcement is not an accurate proxy for true reliance. Thus, when the exchange is isolated from a competitive market, enforcement is often denied in spite of the existence of credible evidence of detrimental reliance by the promisee.[166] Isolated decisions to enforce

Torts retains the distinction between nonfeasance and misfeasance and expresses no opinion as to whether the nonfeasance of a gratuitous promise is sufficient to establish liability under section 323. *Compare* Siegel v. Spear & Co., 234 N.Y. 479, 138 N.E. 414 (1923) (nonfeasance sufficient to establish liability) *with* Comfort v. McCorkel, 149 Misc. 826, 268 N.Y.S. 192 (Sup. Ct. 1933) (defendant guilty of nonfeasance not liable to plaintiffs).

159. *See, e.g.*, Abresch v. Northwestern Bell Tel. Co., 246 Minn. 408, 75 N.W.2d 206 (1956) (promise); Siegel v. Spear & Co., 234 N.Y. 479, 138 N.E. 414 (1923) (bailment); RESTATEMENT (2D) OF AGENCY § 378 (1958) (codifying enforceability of gratuitous bailments). The formulation of the reliance principle under section 378 is carefully tied to the availability of substitute promises on the market. This approach is consistent with the argument that enforcement is properly related to the existence of a competitive market for the promise in question.

160. *See, e.g.*, Lincolnland Properties, Inc. v. Butterworth Apartments, Inc., 65 Ill. App. 3d 907, 382 N.E.2d 1250 (1978) (promise to release mortgage enforced when competitive financing available); Homestead Supplies, Inc. v. Executive Life Ins. Co., 81 Cal. App. 3d 978, 147 Cal. Rptr. 22 (1978) (promise to offer insurance at quoted rates enforceable when competitive alternatives forgone).

161. *See* Industro Motive Corp. v. Morris Agency, Inc., 76 Mich. App. 390, 256 N.W.2d 607 (1977).

162. *See, e.g.*, Slater v. George B. Clarke & Sons, Inc., 186 F. Supp. 814 (D. Del. 1960); Hoffman v. Red Owl Stores, Inc., 26 Wis. 2d 683, 133 N.W.2d 267 (1965).

163. *See, e.g.*, Dovenmuehle, Inc. v. K-Way Assocs., 388 F.2d 940 (7th Cir. 1968); United Elec. Corp. v. All-Serv. Elec., Inc., 256 N.W.2d 92 (Minn. 1977); Silberman v. Roethe, 64 Wis. 2d 131, 218 N.W.2d 723 (1974).

164. *See, e.g.*, Chrysler Corp. v. Quimby, 144 A.2d 123 (Del. 1958). Other terminations subsequent to promises have been litigated. *See, e.g.*, McMath v. Ford Motor Co., 77 Mich. App. 721, 259 N.W.2d 140 (1977) (employment discharge); Aubrey v. Workman, 384 S.W.2d 389 (Tex. Civ. App. 1964) (release from secondary lien).

165. *See, e.g.*, Goodman v. Dicker, 169 F.2d 684 (1948); Wheeler v. White, 398 S.W.2d 93 (Tex. 1965); Hoffman v. Red Owl Stores, Inc., 26 Wis. 2d 683, 133 N.W.2d 267 (1965).

166. *See, e.g.*, Slater v. George B. Clarke & Sons, Inc., 186 F. Supp. 814 (D. Del. 1960); Baggs v. Anderson, 528 P.2d 141 (Utah 1974); Clark Oil & Ref. Corp. v. Leistikow, 69 Wis. 2d 226, 230 N.W.2d 736 (1975).

The unique promise made in a noncompetitive environment presents the best example of a reciprocal promise for which the original form of an optimal damages formula would be appropriate. Breach of such a promise would ideally entail damages in the

Enforcing Promises

such promises can be explained only by analyzing factors other than accuracy and transactional efficiency.

3. *The Probability of Nonperformance: Bad Faith*

When the behavior of the promisor at the time of promising clearly indicates that the probability of performance is zero, tort doctrines of fraud are adequate to protect the promisee fully.[167] However, in several celebrated cases, promissory enforcement seems to derive from more subtle inferences that the promisor did not intend to perform. In *Chrysler Corporation v. Quimby*,[168] the promisee was asked to buy out other interests in an automobile franchise as a condition for award of the franchise upon the death of the current operator. After the promisee acquired sole control, Chrysler terminated the promisee's franchise and awarded the dealership to another individual, as apparently had been contemplated from the outset.[169] Although the final terms of the agreement had not been resolved, the court awarded full performance damages to the plaintiff for detrimental reliance on Chrysler's promise.[170]

Although the deceit in *Quimby* is clear, the evidence of bad-faith conduct in *Hoffman v. Red Owl Stores, Inc.*[171] is less certain. In *Hoffman*, the promisee was awarded reimbursement damages following the breakdown of extensive negotiations for award of a grocery store franchise. During the negotiating period, the promisee performed several acts in clear preparation for receipt of the franchise, including sale of his bakery business and purchase and resale of a small grocery store. Negotiations were subsequently discontinued when the promisor suddenly increased the capital contribution required of the promisee.

difficult-to-measure middle range, between zero and expectation damages. But measurement costs may dictate a choice between the two extreme remedies.

The decision whether to grant zero or full damages may then be influenced by an empirical asymmetry in the costs to the parties of adjusting enforcement levels. Specifically, it may be cheaper for the parties to bargain out of an excessive enforcement scheme than to create additional enforcement mechanisms when inadequate ones existed. Hence, when some tentative initial allocation of legal rights must necessarily be avoided, erring on the side of excess enforcement has cost-minimization advantages over comparable errors on the side of inadequate enforcement. *See* p. 1286 *supra*.

167. *See* W. Prosser, Handbook of the Law of Torts 728-31 (4th ed. 1971). It has long been established that a promise carries an implied representation of present intention to perform. A promise made without a present intention to perform is a sufficient basis for a tort action of fraud. *See, e.g.*, Kauffman v. Bobo & Wood, 99 Cal. App. 2d 322, 221 P.2d 750 (1950); Sabo v. Delman, 3 N.Y.2d 155, 143 N.E.2d 906, 164 N.Y.S.2d 714 (1957).

168. 144 A.2d 123 (Del.), *modified and aff'd*, 144 A.2d 885 (1958).

169. *Id.* at 128.

170. *Id.* at 132-36.

171. 26 Wis. 2d 683, 133 N.W.2d 267 (1965).

The court expressly declined to enforce the promise on grounds of fraud, finding insufficient evidence to infer that the promisor "made any of the promises . . . in bad faith with [a] present intent that they would not be fulfilled."[172] Nonetheless, the sudden change in contract terms suggests that at some point in the negotiations Red Owl determined not to perform the promise. Although the mere failure promptly to withdraw a rash promise may not constitute fraud, it may help explain the court's use of promissory estoppel to enforce indefinite preliminary negotiations.

The historical nexus between promissory estoppel and equitable estoppel may blur the independent significance of bad-faith conduct, especially when the inferences of bad faith are based on post-promise factual representations concerning future performance. In *Goodman v. Dicker*,[173] for example, the promisor followed a promise to award a franchise with the representation that the promisee's application had been accepted. The court, without distinguishing promise from misrepresentation, held that the defendants were estopped by their statements from refusing to grant the franchise. Because doctrines of fraud and deceit are commonly invoked in equitable estoppel cases, their independent significance may not be clear when promissory reliance is at issue.[174] However, the "requirements of justice" language of section 90 offers courts opportunities to broaden the traditional scope of enforcement for bad-faith representation. When none of the enforcement alternatives carries either a presumption of accuracy or an obvious transactional advantage, the court's assessment of performance probabilities may often prove decisive.

4. *Certainty and Distributional Effects*

When considerations of accuracy, transactional efficiency, and bad faith are eliminated, a significant difference remains between the enforcement theories of bargain and reliance. Bargain rules are more certain; reliance rules invite greater flexibility and discretion. Because reliance-based enforcement requires evidence of future facts unknown at the time of bargaining, the availability of such enforcement doctrines increases bargainers' uncertainty as to the risks of legal liability. Un-

172. *Id.* at 695, 133 N.W.2d at 273.

173. 169 F.2d 684 (D.C. Cir. 1948).

174. The equitable roots of promissory estoppel explain, in part, the continuing confusion between equitable estoppel and promissory reliance that is evident in the case law. *See, e.g.*, Schmidt v. McKay, 555 F.2d 30 (2d Cir. 1977); C. & K. Eng'r Contractors v. Amber Steel Co., 23 Cal. 3d 1, 587 P.2d 1136, 151 Cal. Rptr. 323 (1978).

Enforcing Promises

certainty imposes a social loss that reduces the value of exchange. The inefficiency of a discretionary rule of promissory estoppel may be worth incurring if it results in the achievement of socially desirable distributional goals.[175] However, examination of reliance cases does not yield discernible distributional policies.

Evidence of relative ability to sustain losses or of the reasons for breach is required before the losses, or gains, from the breach can be distributed according to any fairness norms. None of the litigated cases reveals careful exploration of the distributional consequences of alternative decisions. Furthermore, in most cases the redistributional effects of varying rules are difficult to predict. Absent a clear commitment to promissory redistribution, the uncertainty induced by broadly conceived discretionary rules is unjustified. Systematization of the expansion of the bargain model calls for developing clearly articulated liability rules paralleling those that have emerged from the rules of consideration. Such rules can be generally sketched from current patterns of enforcement.

Conclusion

Examination of the economic implications of promising reveals a tension between ideal and practical objectives. Because uncertainty cannot be eliminated, it may be tempting to resist systematization of expanding areas of liability.[176] The suggestion that the results in individual cases can safely be predicted by employing a handful of simple economic tools is misguided. Economic concepts are useful, however, in specifying the effects of legal objectives and in observing and isolating systemic patterns of enforcement. The indeterminacy of empirical parameters necessitates the use of assumptions that only crudely approximate the true theoretical objectives. Often the effects of using estimates are unclear, as undetermined factors affect the behavior under examination.[177] Nonetheless, systematic collection and observation of data increases understanding of the regulation of behavior by legal rules.

We have assumed that the economic objective of regulating promises is to maximize the net beneficial reliance derived from promise-making activity. In general, this objective is best achieved by a scheme of

175. For a discussion of the legitimacy of using contract law to achieve distributional ends, see Kronman, *Contract Law and Distributive Justice*, 89 YALE L.J. 472 (1980).

176. *See* G. GILMORE, *supra* note 4, at 102-03.

177. *See* Leff, *Law and*, 87 YALE L.J. 989, 1005-11 (1978).

promissory enforcement that induces adaptive behavior by the party better able to minimize the risk that future contingencies may materialize and cause the promisor to regret the announcement. Optimal adaptation requires a reduction in the prospective reliance on promising whenever this investment produces a greater decrease in expected harms from nonperformance. Both legal and extra-legal sanctions impose these social costs on the promising parties. Optimal legal sanctions are, therefore, a function of both the magnitude of these extra-legal factors and the parties' relative advantage in risk avoidance. The ideal liability choice ranges from zero enforcement to liability equal to the reasonable detrimental reliance caused by breach. However, because promissory reliance is peculiarly impervious to measurement, alternative rules are often applied as proxies for true reliance.

Promissory liability rules can be examined by classifying promises in three categories along principles of reciprocity and bargain. First, reciprocal promises are distinguishable from nonreciprocal promises on the basis of the ability of bargainers to adjust the volume and form of promising by varying the price of the promise. When such adjustments are not possible, promises are not enforced. Nonenforcement of gratuitous promises is justified because in the nonreciprocal setting, self-sanctions against breach are frequently effective, and promisees are often better able than promisors to adapt to the risks of regret. Second, the narrow consideration model defined by common law delineates a subdivision within the category of reciprocating promises. Enforcement is narrowly limited by assumptions that costs of promise-making are best reduced by precautions at the core of bargaining, and by reassurances on the periphery.

However, courts have used alternate theories of liability to expand enforcement appropriately beyond the confines of the consideration model. Promises have been enforced when increased accuracy, transactional efficiency, or bad faith justified the imposition of liability. These alternative bases of liability have been recently generalized into broad grants of judicial discretion. Although discretion permits the pursuit of distributional goals, it increases the uncertainty facing future bargainers. Absent careful articulation of distributional objectives, the social cost of uncertainty requires the development of clear rules for recoveries grounded on reliance.

[4]

CONTRACT LAW AND MODERN ECONOMIC THEORY

*Daniel A. Farber**

As generations of law professors have realized, Contracts is an ideal course for the Socratic method. The fundamental questions addressed in the course are easy to understand: Why enforce contracts? Why not enforce promises of gifts? Why limit freedom of contract? Yet, as many first-year students have discovered, the answers to these fundamental questions are surprisingly elusive. Despite the pleasures of the Socratic dialogue, ultimately the Contracts teacher also is apt to become frustrated; the Socratic admission of ignorance seems a bit inadequate as a final conclusion. Like Plato, many Contracts teachers wish to find some more positive answers, a desire all the more understandable because the questions are so much more mundane than those that plague philosophers.[1]

In their search for answers to these questions, many scholars recently have turned to economic theory.[2] This Article differs somewhat from previous ventures in this vein. Generally, scholars previously have borrowed particular techniques (such as the use of indifference curves)[3] or concepts (such as transaction costs)[4] from the field of economics and applied them in an *ad hoc* manner to a single legal prob-

---

* Professor of Law, University of Minnesota.

Several groups of individuals contributed to the production of this Article. My colleagues at the University of Minnesota Law School, Bob Hudec, John Matheson, Leo Raskind, and Andy Schoettle, provided many useful criticisms and suggestions, as did my former colleague, Mary Lou Fellows. Craig Swan of the Minnesota Economics Department, Tom Ulen of the Illinois Economics Department, and Paul Fellows of the Iowa Finance Department, provided valuable technical advice. My research assistant, Tom Pender, provided exceptional help in analyzing the economics literature, as well as insightful comments on earlier drafts. Finally, Dean Robert Stein provided generous financial support.

1 *See, e.g.*, 1 F. COPLESTON, A HISTORY OF PHILOSOPHY 98-108 (1963).

2 A 1979 bibliography lists 160 articles in this genre. C. VELJANOVSKI, BIBLIOGRAPHY IN LAW & ECONOMICS (1979) (Centre for Socio-Legal Studies, Wolfson College, Oxford) (on file with the author). For a collection of recent work, see THE ECONOMICS OF CONTRACT LAW (A. Kronman & R. Posner eds. 1979).

3 Birmingham, *Damage Measures and Economic Rationality: The Geometry of Contract Law*, 1969 DUKE L.J. 49; Goetz & Scott, *Liquidated Damages, Penalties and the Just Compensation Principle: Some Notes on an Enforcement Model and a Theory of Efficient Breach*, 77 COLUM. L. REV. 554 (1977).

4 *See, e.g.*, R. POSNER, ECONOMIC ANALYSIS OF LAW ch. 4 (2d ed. 1977); Posner & Rosenfield, *Impossibility and Related Doctrines in Contract Law: An Economic Analysis*, 6 J. LEGAL

lem.[5] This Article, on the other hand, will attempt to examine links between contract law and some important models of the economy as a whole. No attempt will be made to explain the fine detail of contract law. Instead, the Article will focus on basic doctrines such as consideration and freedom of contract.

Perhaps the most basic feature of contracts is that, unlike barter transactions, they involve exchanges over time. Consequently, understanding contract law requires an examination of the reasons for enforcing promises to take future actions. The Article begins with a critique of a recent economic analysis of this problem.[6] The essential weakness in that analysis is its attempt to examine the issue in isolation from more general economic theory. In order to develop a more satisfactory analysis, the Article then will discuss in some detail the standard neoclassical microeconomic model.[7] As will be shown, justifications for enforcing promises flow quite naturally from certain features of this model. These features, however, may be unfamiliar to many readers, because they are generally covered only in advanced courses in microeconomic theory. The discussion will draw on some relatively sophisticated aspects of general equilibrium theory that have not been easily available to legal readers in the past.[8] The treatment, however, will be primarily nonmathematical[9] and should be understandable to readers with a minimal knowledge of economics.

The Article then will explore the implications for contract law of this standard neoclassical model. The neoclassical model provides strong justifications for many aspects of classical contract law, such as enforcement of executory contracts,[10] refusal to enforce promises to make gifts,[11] and protection of the expectation interest in awarding

---

STUD. 83 (1977); Priest, *Breach and Remedy for the Tender of Nonconforming Goods Under the Uniform Commercial Code: An Economic Approach*, 91 HARV. L. REV. 960 (1978).

5 *E.g.*, Goetz & Scott, *Enforcing Promises: An Examination of the Basis of Contract* (pt. 2), 89 YALE L.J. 1261 (1980); Kronman, *Specific Performance*, 45 U. CHI. L. REV. 351 (1978); Leff, *Injury, Ignorance and Spite—The Dynamics of Coercive Collection*, 80 YALE L.J. 1 (1970). Often, these scholars have emphasized the costs and limitations inherent in the legal system itself.

6 *See infra* text accompanying notes 17-37.

7 *See infra* text accompanying notes 38-74.

8 *See infra* text accompanying notes 53-73.

9 This is true with the exception of a brief criticism of a damage formula proposed by some writers. *See infra* text accompanying notes 17-37.

10 An executory contract is an exchange of promises that the parties have not yet started to perform. Such contracts are enforceable. RESTATEMENT (SECOND) OF CONTRACTS § 75 (1981); 1 A. CORBIN, CONTRACTS § 142 (1963).

11 A promise to make a gift generally is not enforceable. It is not a contract, since it does not involve an exchange. *See* RESTATEMENT (SECOND) OF CONTRACTS § 71 (1981); A. CORBIN, *supra* note 10, § 114. If, however, the promisee was harmed by reasonably relying on the promise and if the promisor should have anticipated the possibility of this reliance, then the promise (although still not a contract) will be enforced at least to the extent necessary to avoid injustice. RESTATEMENT (SECOND) OF CONTRACTS § 90(1). Although reliance-based recovery has received a great

damages for breach.

The microeconomic theory discussed in the first part of the Article provides an intellectually elegant treatment of a large number of economic and legal problems. This intellectual elegance is purchased, however, at the cost of considerable oversimplification. Important aspects of the real world simply find no place in the model. Economic theorists have devoted a great deal of attention in recent years to developing more realistic models.

Consequently, the Article next addresses the implications of these recent attempts to improve upon the neoclassical model. A large literature has developed concerning the effects of imperfect information and transaction costs on economic institutions.[12] Looking outside their own field, some important economic theorists also have begun to consider the economic implications of modern research in psychology.[13]

These newer models point toward justifications for some important rules of contract law such as various restrictions on freedom of contract. From a neoclassical economic perspective, most restrictions on freedom of contract make very little sense. Given the assumptions of the neoclassical model, this is hardly surprising. The model assumes that individuals have perfect information, that they are completely rational, and that there are no impediments to entering into transactions.[14] It would be surprising if such superhumans were *not* able to manage their own affairs without the intervention of the government. In the newer models, however, individuals are assumed to have imperfect information, to possess limited rationality, and to encounter substantial transaction costs. The result is that individuals' ability to order their affairs through voluntary arrangements such as private contract is limited and government intervention through the courts is justified. After examining the newer models in some detail, the Article then discusses the economic basis of two specific common law restrictions on freedom of contract.[15] One rule prohibits penalty clauses; the other limits enforcement of personal-injury disclaimers. The newer microeconomic models provide support for these rules.

The Article concludes with a tentative attempt at a broader theory of the limits on freedom of contract. It will suggest that various legal rules fit together to form a safety net protecting against catastrophic losses. Complementing the general principle of freedom of contract is an opposing principle of mandatory loss sharing, a kind of compulsory insurance. If individuals were able to engage in perfect planning, this

deal of attention from scholars, its practical significance seems to be limited. *See* Goetz & Scott, *supra* note 5, at 1302-09.

[12] *See infra* text accompanying notes 107-14.

[13] *See infra* note 134.

[14] *See infra* note 40 and accompanying text.

[15] *See infra* text accompanying notes 124-62.

safety net probably would not be justified. Limited rationality, imperfect information, and transaction costs, however, limit the ability of individuals to plan for the future. As a result, individuals face unexpected, unpleasant surprises that they are unable to protect against by contract. The safety net provides protection against such surprises for individuals and, consequently, for society.

The trend in this century has been towards greater government intervention in the marketplace. Recently, however, a sharp reversal in this trend has taken place. This reversal in policy often has been justified on the basis of economic theory.[16] This Article should demonstrate that contemporary economic theory and *laissez faire* need not be synonymous.

Contract Law and the Neoclassical Model

The Goetz & Scott Theory of Contract

In a recent article, Professors Goetz and Scott have attempted to provide a unified theory of contract law.[17] Although their article is of considerable interest in its own right, it also provides a good illustration of some of the pitfalls of attempting *ad hoc* economic explanations of legal rules outside the context of a general economic theory.

Goetz and Scott view promises as signals of future conduct.[18] These signals allow promisees to increase their present consumption, knowing that they will receive increased wealth in the future. Goetz and Scott call this "beneficial reliance."[19] These signals also can be misleading, for a promise later may be broken, leaving the promisee worse off than before the promise was made. Goetz and Scott call this "detrimental reliance."[20] In their view, "perhaps the principal social rationale of promising"[21] is to produce beneficial reliance.

Because promises convey both benefits and possible harm, Goetz and Scott draw an analogy between promises and potentially defective consumer goods.[22] They then argue that the harm done by "defective" promises should be made a cost of promising, just as tort liability makes the harm caused by defective goods a cost of production. Goetz and Scott argue that awarding damages based only on detrimental reliance would deter the making of valuable promises by failing to give promisors credit for producing valuable beneficial reliance.[23] Based on

16 This recent phenomenon is associated with the University of Chicago Economics Department and, to a lesser extent, with its Law School.

17 Goetz & Scott, *supra* note 5.

18 *Id.* at 1264.

19 *Id.* at 1267.

20 *Id.*

21 *Id.* at 1269.

22 *Id.* at 1275.

23 *Id.* at 1281-83.

this argument, they derive the following damages rule:

$$D = R - [p + (1 - p)]B.$$[24]

In this equation, D stands for damages, R stands for detrimental reliance, B stands for beneficial reliance, and p stands for the "promisor's reasonable, subjective assessment of the probability that he will perform a promise under an existing legal rule calling for damages D in the event of breach."[25]

Goetz and Scott apply this formula both to contracts and to other kinds of promises. As applied to contracts, they argue, the formula can be simplified. Because the promisee could have entered into an alternative contract, detrimental reliance equals the performance value of the alternative contract. In a well-functioning market, the performance value of the alternative contract should equal that of the breached contract. Hence, R is approximately equal to E, the full-performance expectation. Similarly, the beneficial reliance attributable to any given contract is small, because the promisee could have obtained the same benefit from alternative contracts. Hence, B is approximately equal to zero. The formula given above then simplifies to D = E. "[T]hus," Goetz and Scott conclude, "expectation damages are a good proxy for the prospective net reliance damage formulation developed above."[26]

This analysis assumes that maximizing the welfare of the two parties to the contract is socially desirable. That assumption, however, need not be true. For example, when one of the parties decides to perform on her contract because of the threat of damages, she diverts resources from other possible uses, thereby possibly injuring third parties. Without applying the more sophisticated economic analysis discussed below,[27] one cannot assume that benefits to the original parties resulting from performance of the contract will exceed the harm done to these third parties. Thus, in order to justify their assertion that contract enforcement is desirable, Goetz and Scott need the help of more general economic theories. As the Article will show later, however, these theories themselves require that contracts be enforceable, thus obviating the need for the Goetz & Scott theory.[28] In short, the Goetz & Scott theory justifies contract enforcement only when combined with other theories that are quite capable of justifying contract enforcement on their own.

Another weakness in the Goetz & Scott theory is its narrow view

---

[24] *Id.* at 1282.

[25] *Id.* at 1281.

[26] *Id.* at 1284.

[27] *See infra* text accompanying notes 38-50. Effects on third parties can be ignored in the standard neoclassical model unless they take place outside the price system. Goetz and Scott, however, do not rely explicitly on this theorem of the neoclassical model, and, as shown later, the validity of this theorem itself depends upon the existence of enforceable contracts.

[28] *See infra* text accompanying notes 54-72.

of the benefits of contract. Recall that, according to Goetz and Scott, the primary benefit of promising is that it allows optimal allocation of resources between present and future consumption.[29] Their damages formula is intended to provide an incentive for promisors to give useful signals, in order to enable the promisee to increase present consumption. Contracts, however, actually perform far more important functions than the allocation of present and future consumption. Insurance contracts and contracts for future delivery of goods are important examples of contracts serving other functions.[30]

A related problem is that the Goetz & Scott damages formula is really only an equilibrium condition. The "formula" gives D as a function of p, B, and R. Damage awards, however, will affect p, the probability of performance.[31] The probability of performance, in turn, affects the reliance measures, B and R, since promisees presumably rely more heavily as performance becomes more likely. Consequently, rather than being a formula for finding the optimum D, the equation really describes an equilibrium relationship between B, R, p, and D.[32] Multiple equilibria may well exist, but Goetz and Scott do not explain how to choose among them.

An example may help to clarify this point. Consider a society of individuals who are risk-averse and therefore would like to purchase insurance.[33] Assume that in this society, all of the insurance companies issue what purport to be unconditional contracts, but the insurance companies intend to perform only one percent of the time.[34] Now, consider the application in this context of the Goetz & Scott damage formula ($D = R - [p \div (1 - p)]B$). R, the detrimental reliance, is very small. By entering into one insurance contract, a consumer has forgone other possible insurance contracts, but those alternative contracts

29 *See supra* text accompanying note 21.

30 *See infra* text accompanying notes 60-63.

31 Goetz and Scott acknowledge this in passing. *See* Goetz & Scott, *supra* note 5, at 1270 n.26.

32 A similar problem is posed by Goetz and Scott's treatment of good faith. If a promisor makes a promise with *no* intention of performing, Goetz and Scott consider the promise to be made in bad faith and would award full expectation damages. *Id.* at 1287. Suppose, however, that the promisor would perform if threatened with such damages. Then the promise is no longer made in bad faith. Hence, D changes. Given the new level of D, the promisor again may decide never to perform. The promisor then is in bad faith, and D changes again. No equilibrium value of D may exist.

33 A risk-averse individual prefers a certain loss to a lottery that involves a loss of uncertain magnitude but the same expected value as the certain loss. For instance, a risk-averse individual would be willing to pay more than $100 to avoid a lottery situation involving a 90% probability of zero loss and a 10% probability of a $1,000 loss. Thus, the individual would be willing to pay an insurance premium over $100 in exchange for the insurance company's promise to reimburse any $1,000 losses that occur. *See* K. ARROW, ESSAYS IN THE THEORY OF RISK-BEARING ch. 3 (1971); R. POSNER, *supra* note 4, at 75-76.

34 Since p is not equal to zero, Goetz and Scott apparently would not consider this to be bad faith. Goetz & Scott, *supra* note 5, at 1287. *See supra* note 32.

would have been just as worthless as the actual contract. Thus, the benefits forgone by entering into this particular contract are themselves very small. The second term of the formula can be ignored because p is so close to zero.[35] Clearly, D will be quite small. The small amount of damages gives no incentive for the insurance companies to adhere more closely to their contracts.

This result, however, is not economically desirable. Consumers would prefer protection for the face amount of the policy but are unable to obtain such protection through any one policy because of insufficient legal enforcement.[36] On the other hand, as Goetz and Scott point out, in a competitive market their formula is also satisfied when D = E,[37] where E represents the expectation interest (in this case, the face amount of the policy). Under these new conditions, breach would

---

[35] Furthermore, B, the beneficial reliance, is probably small also. Consumers probably will not rely on promises that they know are so unlikely to be kept.

[36] A risk-averse consumer would not be able to obtain coverage equally satisfactory to her by purchasing a policy with a face amount one hundred times the value of the loss she is insuring against. If she bought such a policy, the expected value of her compensation should the loss occur would equal the value of the loss. This expected value, however, would be the sum of a 99% probability of zero compensation and a 1% chance of compensation equal to one hundred times the loss. This would be inferior, from the risk-averse consumer's perspective, to a policy that provided a 100% probability of exactly covering the loss. Faced with only a 1% chance that the insurance company will adhere to its contract, a risk-averse consumer would need a policy with a face amount well in excess of one hundred times the loss to make her indifferent between that policy and one that covers the loss with certainty. The expected value of the policy with a 1% chance of performance would have to exceed the expected value of one with certain performance. This larger expected value would translate actuarially into a larger insurance premium. Thus, the consumer would have to pay more to get equivalent coverage and might rationally choose to underinsure.

The consumer also could attempt to adjust to a 1% probability of performance by purchasing one hundred policies, each having a face value equal to the loss against which the consumer wants to insure. Here again, however, a risk-averse consumer would prefer to have the loss covered with certainty; therefore, she would need more than one hundred policies with a 1% probability of performance in order to be equally satisfied with her coverage. Buying more than one hundred policies would result in coverage with a larger expected value and therefore would require larger total premiums for coverage than if the consumer could buy insurance with certain performance. The consumer thus would pay more for equivalent coverage or would underinsure.

Professors Kahneman and Tversky, whose work on prospect theory is discussed later in this Article, *see infra* text accompanying notes 135-43, compare the desirability of what they call probabilistic insurance with that of insurance providing certain coverage. In experiments, they found that consumers preferred probabilistic insurance over insurance offering certain coverage. Kahneman & Tversky, *Prospect Theory: An Analysis of Decision Under Risk*, 47 ECONOMETRICA 263, 269-70 (1979). As the authors note, this finding conflicts with what expected utility theory predicts. *Id.* at 270. The author's expected utility analysis is not relevant to the probabilistic insurance under discussion here for two reasons. First, the consumer in their example gets a refund of the premium if the insurance does not cover the loss; this increases the relative desirability of their probabilistic insurance. Second, their consumer is indifferent between certain coverage and no coverage at all, while the consumer under discussion here prefers the certain coverage. *See supra* text accompanying note 33.

[37] *See* Goetz & Scott, *supra* note 5, at 1284.

no longer profit the insurance company, and p would rise from .01 to 1. Thus, the Goetz & Scott formula gives different levels of damages to correspond with different levels of p, the probability of performance. Goetz and Scott fail to provide any basis for setting p.

In short, the Goetz & Scott theory is incomplete in two respects. First, it assumes that optimizing the welfare of the two parties to the contract will optimize social welfare. This assumption can only be justified in the context of a more powerful economic theory. Second, their damages formula requires a prior choice of the optimal level of contract performance. This choice also requires a more general theory of the function of contracts in the economy. As the next section will demonstrate, a more satisfactory account of the economics of contract can be derived from modern welfare economics.

Neoclassical Welfare Economics and Contract Law

The two fundamental theorems of neoclassical welfare economics provide the theoretical basis for assertions that the free market is economically efficient.[38] The two theorems assert that, given certain assumptions, a free market will possess equilibria having certain desirable qualities.[39] The crucial question here is the extent to which the existence of enforceable contracts is necessary to obtain these equilibria. In order to answer that question, however, an explanation of the fundamental theorems is necessary.

Assuming that trades between parties are both voluntary and are made with full knowledge,[40] every trade logically must be to the benefit of both parties. Even if every trade benefits both parties, however, the cumulative effect of these trades conceivably might not be beneficial. Both real life and game theory present numerous situations in which individually rational choices lead to social catastrophe.[41] Furthermore,

---

38 A market that is economically efficient allocates each resource to its highest-valued use (as measured by willingness to pay). In a society with an efficient market, for instance, each parcel of land is used for the purpose that maximizes the value of its output and each worker works in the type of employment that maximizes the value of what she produces. One way to understand heuristically why a free market might be thought capable of achieving this result is to realize that in a free market resources are sold to the highest bidder. Producers in different industries and within the same industries bid against each other for resources. The producer to whom a particular resource is worth the most because of its contribution to final output will be willing to bid the most for that resource. *See* E. BROWNING & J. BROWNING, PUBLIC FINANCE AND THE PRICE SYSTEM 7-10 (1979); R. POSNER, *supra* note 4, at 10-12.

39 As explained in more detail later, *see infra* notes 44-49, the desirable qualities are that equilibria are economically efficient and that they span the range of possible wealth allocations.

40 *See* C. FERGUSON & J. GOULD, MICROECONOMIC THEORY 12, 224-25 (4th ed. 1975).

41 For instance, game theory has developed the well-known Prisoners Dilemma model. Assume that two individuals have robbed a bank and are questioned separately by the district attorney. The district attorney does not have enough evidence to convict them of bank robbery but does have enough evidence to convict them of a lesser offense. He tells each prisoner that if only one confesses and testifies against the other, the one who confesses will go free while the one

even if trades are beneficial, government intervention might produce even better results than trade among individuals. As the following discussion will explain in more detail, the two fundamental theorems of neoclassical economics preclude the possibility that society as a whole might not benefit by individually rational choices and the possibility that government intervention might create even better results than unimpeded exchanges.

The easiest economic model to understand involves a pure exchange economy. In such an economy, goods are not produced but are simply given to individuals as part of their initial endowment. Goods can change hands only by voluntary exchange. This model places a number of technical restrictions on the nature of the goods and individual preferences, but these restrictions limit the applicability of the model only slightly.[42] The critical question is whether individuals could exchange their way into an equilibrium state—that is, a state in which

---

convicted will serve a long sentence for bank robbery. If neither confesses, they both will be prosecuted for the lesser offense. If both confess, they will receive sentences longer than those they would receive for the lesser offense but shorter than sentences given to nonconfessing convicted bank robbers. For each prisoner, the individually rational choice is to confess regardless of what the other prisoner does. If the other prisoner confesses, his partner had better confess in order to receive the more lenient sentence given to confessing bank robbers. If the other prisoner does not confess, his partner, by confessing, can go free rather than be punished for the lesser offense. If both prisoners pursue their individual well-being, both will confess. These individually rational decisions, however, do not achieve the best possible result for both, since both would be better off if neither confessed. Since the circumstances prevent their entering into an enforceable agreement not to confess, they will achieve that mutually preferable outcome only if they trust each other enough not to confess. That outcome is inherently unstable since if one trusts the other not to confess, the other can confess and go free. For expositions and applications of this model, see R. LUCE & H. RAIFFA, GAMES AND DECISIONS 94-97 (1957); F. SCHERER, INDUSTRIAL MARKET STRUCTURE AND ECONOMIC PERFORMANCE 160-64 (2d ed. 1980); Birmingham, *Legal and Moral Duty in Game Theory: Common Law Contract and Chinese Analogies*, 18 BUFFALO L. REV. 99, 103-10 (1969); Davis & Whinston, *The Economics of Urban Renewal*, 26 LAW & CONTEMP. PROBS. 105, 107-12 (1961).

This model captures the key elements of some social problems. For instance, improvements in the appearance of one landlord's property may allow higher rents for that landlord and also higher rents for landlords of neighboring properties. If the cost of improving landlord *A*'s property exceeds the present value of the resulting higher future rents on *A*'s property, then *A* has no incentive to improve her property even if the cost is less than the sum of the present value of resulting higher future rents on *A*'s property plus those resulting on neighboring properties. The result of the individually rational behavior of not improving property, however, is not the best outcome, since all landlords would prefer the outcome in which all improve their property. The high cost of agreeing to and enforcing a contract to improve their properties may prevent that outcome. *See* Davis & Whinston, *supra*. Many environmental problems can be subjected to a similar analysis.

The Prisoner's Dilemma also captures the essence of the arms race. Both Russia and the United States may prefer mutual reductions in strategic weapons; but in the absence of mutual trust or an enforceable agreement, both countries find it individually "rational" to continue the arms race. F. SCHERER, *supra*, at 41.

42 For a discussion of the necessary restrictions on characteristics of goods, see W. HILDEBRAND & A. KIRMAN, INTRODUCTION TO EQUILIBRUM ANALYSIS 36-37 (1976). For restrictions

no one has any incentive to engage in any further trades. General equilibrium theory leads to the important conclusion that such an equilibrium does indeed exist. This equilibrium can be described by a set of prices at which, for each good, the quantities supplied and the quantities demanded are equal.[43]

The fundamental theorems of welfare economics describe some important characteristics of this competitive equilibrium state. The first fundamental theorem of welfare economics asserts that, given certain assumptions, the competitive equilibrium is Pareto-optimal. A state of affairs is Pareto-optimal when any one individual's welfare can be improved only at someone else's expense.[44] Thus, the first theorem asserts that a competitive equilibrium is economically efficient.[45]

The problem with using Pareto-optimality as a normative guide is that infinitely many Pareto-optimal states may exist, each corresponding with a different initial endowment of goods.[46] For example, a state in which one individual owns all the goods is Pareto-optimal because no other individual can be helped without decreasing the welfare of this individual.[47] Hence, calling a state Pareto-optimal or economically efficient is not necessarily much of an endorsement for that state, even if it is economically efficient. One might well ask whether competitive

---

on the nature of preferences, see K. ARROW & F. HAHN, GENERAL COMPETITIVE ANALYSIS 19-22 (1971).

43 It is not necessary to consider in any detail the mathematical proof that an equilibrium exists, but some knowledge of the form of proof is useful in understanding the limitations of the conclusion. Essentially, the proof proceeds as follows: For any set of relative prices of the goods, we identify those goods that are in excess demand. Goods are in excess demand if buyers wish to purchase more of such goods at the current price than sellers are willing to supply. We then construct a function that increases the relative price of those goods that are in excess demand. Intuition tells us that such a process ultimately would lead to elimination of excess demand and hence to a balance between supply and demand. This result is proved mathematically by demonstrating that the adjustment process has a fixed point—a set of prices at which adjustment no longer occurs. Since the adjustment process changes the relative prices whenever there is excess demand, no excess demand exists at the fixed point. Therefore, the fixed point represents an equilibrium. Mathematically, the existence of a fixed point is demonstrated by using any one of several theorems from topology.

It is very important to note that the existence of such a fixed point does not mean that if the economy begins with some other set of prices, the adjustment process ultimately will lead it to the equilibrium. The theorem says only that there exists a set of prices that, once obtained, would not be subject to further change. *See* K. ARROW & F. HAHN, *supra* note 42, at 25-29; J. QUIRK & R. SAPOSNIK, INTRODUCTION TO GENERAL EQUILIBRIUM THEORY AND WELFARE ECONOMICS 70-76 (1968); H. VARIAN, MICROECONOMIC ANALYSIS 138-44 (1978).

44 J. HENDERSON & R. QUANDT, MICROECONOMIC ANALYSIS: A MATHEMATICAL APPROACH 286-87 (3d ed. 1980); J. HIRSHLEIFER, PRICE THEORY AND APPLICATIONS 524 (2d ed. 1980).

45 J. HENDERSON & R. QUANDT, *supra* note 44, at 292-93; J. QUIRK & R. SAPOSNIK, *supra* note 43, at 124-40; H. VARIAN, *supra* note 43, at 145-47.

46 J. HENDERSON & R. QUANDT, *supra* note 44, at 312; J. QUIRK & R. SAPOSNIK, *supra* note 43, at 146; H. VARIAN, *supra* note 43, at 147.

47 This assumes the absence of satiation. In other words, it assumes that the individual in question always prefers having more of a good and is never indifferent to the loss of goods.

equilibria restrict the range of possible distributions of wealth. For example, one might wonder whether individuals always have unequal incomes in a competitive equilibrium. If so, some forms of egalitarianism and the free market might be considered incompatible. The second fundamental theorem of welfare economics, however, asserts that no such incompatibility exists between egalitarianism and the free market. The second fundamental theorem asserts that, given any Pareto-optimal allocation of goods, a set of prices and initial endowments exists for which that allocation is an equilibrium.[48] This means that, through the political process, society can choose the Pareto-optimal allocation that corresponds to its preferences about the distribution of wealth. By rearranging individuals' initial endowments through an appropriate system of taxes and transfer payments,[49] the government could assure that a competitive equilibrium having the desired distributional characteristics would be reached.

Together, the two fundamental theorems make a strong case for the free market. The first theorem says that the free market will reach economically efficient results. The second theorem says that these results can be squared with society's preferences about the distribution of income without interfering with the competitive process; the government need only change the initial allocation of goods and then let the market go to work. To the extent that any rigorous, theoretical basis exists for economists' general preference for the free market, it is to be found in these two theorems.[50]

So far, the discussion has been concerned with pure exchange economies. Extending these theorems to economies in which production takes place is more complex and requires additional restrictive assumptions;[51] however, it introduces no fundamentally new concepts.

---

48 J. QUIRK & R. SAPOSNIK, *supra* note 43, at 140-44; H. VARIAN, *supra* note 43, at 147-49.

49 These taxes and transfer payments must be "lump-sum," meaning that they must not depend upon the behavior of individuals or firms. If, for instance, a tax on consumption of some good were used to redistribute purchasing power, this tax would reduce efficiency by distorting consumer choices. Desire to purchase the taxed good would be too low and desire to purchase untaxed goods too high, as compared to true consumer preferences. In a simple economy with no production, in which consumers received their initial endowments as the Hebrews received *manna* from heaven, lump-sum taxes and transfer payments might be achieved by making them a function of individuals' initial endowments. If the economy were more complex—for instance, if it included production—lump-sum taxes and transfer payments would become more difficult. *See infra* note 51. For an introductory treatment, see P. SAMUELSON, ECONOMICS 593-603 (11th ed. 1980). The problem of how to combine individual preferences about income distribution into a social choice itself involves great difficulties.

50 J. HIRSHLEIFER, *supra* note 44, at 526-29; H. VARIAN, *supra* note 43, at 154-55.

51 *See* H. VARIAN, *supra* note 43, at 158-68. The second theorem's assumption of the availability of the necessary lump-sum taxes and transfer payments, *see supra* note 49, becomes more problematical when applied to a production economy. Assume that society desires to equalize economic welfare by transferring purchasing power from the rich to the poor. If the rich recognize that taxes depend on their income or wealth, they may choose to change the amount they earn (for

The same theorems hold true for the more realistic economy in which goods are produced as well as exchanged.

Nonetheless, some of the important limitations on these theorems should be noted. First, the equilibrium state may never actually be reached. A difficult analysis is required to determine whether equilibrium eventually will result if the economy begins in a state of disequilibrium.[52] Second, some of the assumptions underlying the theorems are clearly unrealistic. Not all markets are competitive. Many economic actors lack the perfect information postulated by the theory. Other assumptions less relevant to contract law also may fail. Third, these results are inherently keyed to general equilibrium analysis. In other words, they are keyed to the economy as a whole rather than to some individual market. If the assumptions fail for some sectors of the economy, free markets in other sectors may not be optimal.[53] Despite these limitations, many economists believe that the two theorems provide appropriate guidance for formulating social policy.

The discussion so far supports the desirability of a policy of free exchange. Contracts, however, involve future performances; the only transactions considered so far are cash sales or barter transactions. The forgoing model makes no reference to the passage of time and cannot describe agreements to make exchanges in the future. Extending the model to include future transactions, however, is quite straightforward. Only the definition of what constitutes a "good" needs some modification. Instead of defining goods as physical objects or services, a "good" is defined to be a contract right. More precisely, each good consists of the enforceable right to obtain delivery at a given date and place. The good also consists of specifications of the cost and of any conditions on the right to delivery. An example of such a good is the enforceable right to obtain from a certain individual an umbrella for $10 on July 4, 1983 if it rains on that day. Redefining the term "goods" does not af-

instance, by decreasing their work hours). If the poor perceive their transfer payments to be inversely related to their labor income, they too may choose to work fewer hours. These alterations of time allocation would be inefficient, since they would reflect a relative valuation of produced goods and leisure time distorted by the taxes and transfer payments. It is hard to imagine an equalizing transfer system that does not make one's tax or transfer payment a function of one's income or wealth. *See* E. BROWNING & J. BROWNING, *supra* note 38, at 217-19, 315-17 (1979). Essentially, the tax would have to be imposed as a complete surprise on a one-shot basis.

52 H. VARIAN, *supra* note 43, at 188-93.

53 The theory of second best holds that if an economy does not attain efficiency in one market, it is not necessarily desirable for that economy to attain efficiency in all other markets. For instance, assume that an economy has just two sectors—one perfectly competitive and the other monopolistic. If the latter for some reason cannot be made competitive, the allocation of resources in the society as a whole may be improved by making the competitive industry less competitive. For a clear summary of the theory of second best, see F. SCHERER, *supra* note 41, at 24-29. In a large multimarket economy, inefficiency in one market may often be safely ignored in evaluating the efficiency of other, unrelated markets. J. HENDERSON & R. QUANDT, *supra* note 44, at 317.

fect the mathematical model, so the same fundamental theorems remain valid.[54] Hence, if individuals are allowed to trade freely in these enforceable contract rights, a Pareto-optimal equilibrium exists. Furthermore, as described earlier, the distributional aspects of the equilibrium can be manipulated simply by changing the initial endowment of goods. Thus, given the existence of enforceable contracts, the free market at least theoretically can attain economic efficiency.

Some penalty for breach of contract clearly is necessary in order to ensure economic efficiency. The individual who is paid to deliver an umbrella under certain future contingencies clearly would prefer to keep the money without ever delivering the umbrella.[55] Hence, some system of sanctions[56] must exist so that the purchaser of the right to future delivery actually receives the required umbrella or its equivalent.[57]

The discussion so far has indicated that, given the existence of a sufficiently broad range of enforceable contracts, certain economically desirable consequences will follow. The existence of such contracts conceivably might be a sufficient but not a necessary condition for the existence of Pareto-optimal equilibria. Suppose, for instance, that the creation of enforceable contracts for future performances were not allowed. Would an equilibrium still exist and, if so, would it be optimal?

Unless enforceable contracts are allowed, the economy will progress through a series of temporary equilibria on successive dates. That is, on any given day the quantities supplied and demanded for any given resource will be equal, but the equilibrium will shift over time.[58] For three reasons, such equilibria generally are not Pareto-optimal.[59]

The first reason relates to risk. Risk-averse individuals benefit from the existence of insurance contracts.[60] Such contracts by their nature must be contingent upon future events[61] and therefore require the existence of enforceable contracts.[62]

---

54 H. VARIAN, *supra* note 43, at 175-76.

55 Sanctions also may be needed even if payment has not been made in advance. Consider an insurance company that bills at the end of the coverage period. If no sanctions exist, the profit-maximizing strategy for the company is to bill all customers who have not had losses and to make no payments to customers with losses. Of course, the customers' best strategy is not to pay the bills.

56 Conceivably, a society could have such a rigorous set of informal sanctions or could inculcate such strong ethical values that no legal sanctions would be required. In some unusual situations, breach might not be profitable for other reasons. For example, goods might have no market or use other than that for which they were contracted, and might be expensive to store or destroy.

57 For further discussion of the measure of damages, see *infra* text accompanying note 84.

58 K. ARROW & F. HAHN, *supra* note 42, at 49; Grandmont, *Temporary General Equilibrium Theory*, 45 ECONOMETRICA 535, 542 (1977).

59 H. VARIAN, *supra* note 43, at 178.

60 *See supra* note 33.

61 Such contracts also may be contingent upon current events not yet known to the parties.

62 Similar problems involving risks also may require the existence of capital markets in which

Second, some individuals may prefer to consume more than their current wealth; others may prefer lower consumption now in return for higher consumption later. Loan contracts are necessary to allow individuals to choose when to consume their wealth.[63]

The final reason why temporary equilibria are not Pareto-optimal relates to the problem of individual expectations. If the economy changes over time, individuals surely will not be ignorant of this fact. Presumably, they will attempt to make predictions about the future of the economy. The model therefore must be expanded to allow individuals to form expectations about future economic conditions. In other words, the model must account for the fact that individuals will enter into exchanges that reflect what they expect will happen to the economy in the future. These individual expectations, however, may well be inconsistent with what actually occurs in the future, because if all individuals act according to their own expectations, the future may turn out differently than any of them anticipated. Individual planning thus may be ineffective.[64] Hence, unless special assumptions are made about individual expectations, the market solution generally is not Pareto-optimal. Pareto-optimality potentially could be obtained by a government agency having complete control of the economy and thus more ability than individuals to make appropriate plans for the future.[65]

---

individuals may trade portfolios of investments. Competitive capital markets allow an optimal allocation of risk while economizing on the need for state-contingent futures markets in commodities. If a consumer wants to guarantee that she will be able to buy a given consumption bundle at some future date, competitive securities markets can provide financial instruments with pay-out structures contingent upon changes in prices of the relevant goods and resources. Securities markets then can provide a form of insurance and allow money to reach its full potential for economizing on transaction costs. *See* K. ARROW, *supra* note 33, ch. 4.

63 *See* J. HENDERSON & R. QUANDT, *supra* note 44, at 326-33; J. HIRSHLEIFER, *supra* note 44, at 488-96; Samuelson, *An Exact Consumption-Loan Model of Interest with or without the Social Contrivance of Money*, 66 J. POL. ECON. 467 (1958).

64 Grandmont, *supra* note 58, at 542. In economics, prophecies are not necessarily self-fulfilling. For instance, if consumers expect electricity prices to remain at current levels, they may switch to electric cars. The resulting increased demand for electricity then may lead to the construction of new electric generating plants with costs, and therefore electricity prices, far in excess of current levels. Consumer planning thus will be ineffective, since consumers will not be able to consume the combinations of automobile travel and other goods and services upon which they had planned. They will have to reduce either their automobile travel or their consumption of other goods and services, or both. Many consumers will regret having bought electric cars. If only one individual had expected constant electricity prices and had bought an electric car, individual expectations would have been consistent with what actually happened in the future, since that one individual's increased electricity purchases would not have had an appreciable effect upon electricity prices. The general principle involved is called "the fallacy of composition." *See* P. SAMUELSON, *supra* note 49, at 11-12.

65 J. HIRSCHLEIFER, *supra* note 44, at 530-31; H. VARIAN, *supra* note 43, at 178; Polemarchakis, *Incomplete Markets, Price Regulation, and Welfare*, 69 AM. ECON. REV. 662 (1979). For instance, in the electricity example, *see supra* note 64, the government could improve upon the market result by regulating the number of electric cars purchased. At some number of

An example of the expectations problem is provided by the famous Cobweb Model. This Model describes the behavior of a market in which individuals make production plans based upon the output and prices of the preceding period. For example, wheat farmers may well decide, based upon the past year's high prices, to increase their production. As a result of the simultaneous decision of many farmers to increase production, the supply expands in the following year, forcing the price down and thus frustrating the expectations of the individual farmers. Each year, the market is brought into equilibrium by price changes necessary to balance supply and demand.[66]

Such a market is capable of behaving in a variety of different ways over time. Output may converge toward an ultimate equilibrium; the market may cycle through the same range of prices over successive time periods; or it may go through ever-increasing fluctuations. An equilibrium will exist in each given year.[67] The equilibria, however, will not correspond to the preferences of the individuals within the economy, who have no reason to desire these fluctuations of supply. If individuals are risk-averse, they will suffer a welfare loss even if, on the average, the level of production is optimal.[68] In such a situation, government intervention to stabilize supply potentially could increase consumer welfare.[69] This situation, therefore, is not Pareto-optimal.

On the other hand, if farmers not only sell their current output in a spot market but also can sell enforceable contracts for future delivery, a Pareto-optimal equilibrium can be reached. After a year of high prices, farmers initially may attempt to offer contracts for larger outputs in the succeeding year, but they will quickly find that these contracts outstrip demand at the anticipated higher price. This will lead them to change

electric cars, the cost of using electric cars will equal the cost of using gasoline-engine cars. If consumers, or the government, have no other reasons than cost for preferring one fuel source to the other, this is the efficient number of electric cars for the government to allow. Since no consumer would then regret his choice of engine type, the result would be Pareto optimal. Whether in reality governments have better information or decisionmaking abilities than individuals is, of course, another question.

66 For graphical treatment and more detailed discussion of the Cobweb Model, see J. HENDERSON & R. QUANDT, *supra* note 44, at 166-69; P. SAMUELSON, *supra* note 49, at 381-83.

67 J. HENDERSON & R. QUANDT, *supra* note 44, at 167-69.

68 People who are risk-averse prefer a certain return to an uncertain return having the same expected value. *See supra* note 33. Hence, risk-averse consumers would prefer to have food prices fixed at the average level. Furthermore, if farmers are risk-averse, fluctuating prices, resulting in fluctuating returns, will be less desirable than certain prices if the prices average out over time; some may leave farming for some other business, thus reducing the food supply. This assumes that costless ways of insuring against these price changes do not exist. *See supra* note 62.

69 *See* P. SAMUELSON, *supra* note 49, at 399. For a related discussion of whether economic welfare is increased by cartels that adjust supply to stabilize price in reaction to demand fluctuations, see F. SCHERER, *supra* note 41, at 214-20. The discussion in the text is limited to the simplified Cobweb Model and is not meant to take any position on the complex problems of agricultural policy.

both their asking price and their output plans. Thus, the existence of a market for contracts for future delivery can compensate for imperfections in the process of forming expectations.[70]

In such a market, individuals may buy and sell options for future purchases. In some cases, the option may specify a price of zero for its exercise. Such an "option" is simply a contingent promise to make a future delivery. For example, a fire insurance contract may be viewed as the cash sale of an option to receive a specified amount of money if a house burns during a given time period. In a recent article, Professor Eisenberg has designated such agreements "half-completed-bargain promises."[71] Rather than paying cash, a buyer might exchange a contingent promise of his own for the seller's promise. Eisenberg argues that such wholly executory exchanges—exchanges of two future rights—have a lesser claim to enforcement than half-completed contracts.[72] Economically, however, the two kinds of contracts are equivalent. A purchase of a promise serves the same function of risk allocation whether the purchase is made with cash or on credit.[73]

Thus, the existence of a system of enforceable contracts is both necessary and sufficient to establish the conditions for an optimal competitive equilibrium. This provides a powerful theoretical basis for the enforcement of contracts. This basis for contract enforcement has the advantage over the Goetz & Scott theory discussed earlier[74] of being directly connected to some of the central concepts and results of modern economic theory.

---

[70] The futures market reduces the price expected by farmers until it is consistent with the price that consumers are willing to pay. This consistency of expectations allows the long-run equilibrium price and quantity to be reached as quickly as possible. *See* Grandmont, *supra* note 58, at 544, 547.

[71] Eisenberg, *The Bargain Principle and its Limits*, 95 HARV. L. REV. 741, 743 (1982).

[72] *Id.* at 800-01.

[73] Suppose that only half-executed contracts were enforced. Would efficiency suffer? Not in a world without transaction costs. In such a world, someone wishing to make a purchase on credit of goods for future delivery could enter into a pair of transactions: (1) a loan to obtain the cash, and (2) a cash payment for goods with a later delivery date. In the real world, however, transfers of cash are not costless. For instance, positive interest rates and liquidity constraints create transaction costs. These transaction costs would be increased pointlessly by requiring exchanges to be made for spot cash in order to be fully enforceable. Generally speaking, individuals will structure the form of exchange and the medium of payment in order to minimize their transaction costs. A rule limiting their choices can only force them to use less efficient forms of exchange and more costly forms of payment. Just as individuals can set their own prices, they are also competent to decide whether an exchange should involve a credit card, an electronic funds transfer, cash, a check, a promissory note, a secured debt, or an ordinary unsecured debt. For a general discussion of the importance of a medium of exchange that optimizes transaction costs, see J. HIRSHLEIFER, *supra* note 44, ch. 8.

[74] *See supra* text accompanying notes 17-37.

Legal Implications of the Neoclassical Model

The neoclassical model provides guidelines for contract enforcement that neatly track the rules of "classical" contract law.[75] To begin with, the neoclassical model supports the enforcement of contracts for future performances as a means of attaining several economic goals: spreading or shifting risks,[76] optimizing choices between present and future consumption,[77] and eliminating disruptions caused by mistaken expectations.[78] Enforcement of contracts serves these functions even when exchanges are wholly executory.[79] Thus, the neoclassical model supports enforcement of all promises given in exchange for some consideration.

The doctrine of consideration bars enforcement of promises outside of the exchange context.[80] In particular, promises to make a gift are generally unenforceable. This rule is quite consistent with the neoclassical model. In order to account for gifts, the model can be modified to provide for interdependent utilities.[81] In the modified model, one person's utility (a measure of his satisfaction) can depend both upon his own level of consumption and upon that of some other

---

75 The "classical" system of contract law is analyzed in G. GILMORE, THE DEATH OF CONTRACT (1974). Briefly, the classical system was the set of rules embodied in the First Restatement and propounded by Williston. *See* RESTATEMENT (FIRST) OF CONTRACTS (1932). It stressed the importance of clear rules concerning exchanges and tended to devalue more "equitable" concepts such as reliance and good faith that have become important in recent years.

76 *See supra* text accompanying notes 60-62.

77 *See supra* text accompanying note 63.

78 *See supra* text accompanying notes 64-70.

79 *See supra* text accompanying notes 71-73.

80 Consideration for a promise exists if the promisor made it in exchange for a bargained-for performance or promise by the other party. A promise made in the absence of consideration is, with some exceptions, not enforceable. RESTATEMENT (SECOND) OF CONTRACTS § 71 (1981); 1 A. CORBIN, *supra* note 10, §§ 109-124. One exception allows enforcement if the promisee reasonably and foreseeably relied on the promise. *See supra* note 11. A second group of exceptions arises out of the Uniform Commercial Code (UCC). The UCC altered the rule that a pre-existing duty cannot function as consideration for a new promise by allowing contract modification even if the modification seems to benefit or harm one party without an offsetting change in the other party's obligation. J. MURRAY, CONTRACTS §§ 88-89 (2d rev. ed. 1974); U.C.C. § 2-209(1). The UCC also permits a waiver of one party's right to sue the other for an alleged breach of contract, even if the waiving party receives nothing in exchange for the waiver. J. MURRAY, *supra*, § 89; U.C.C. § 1-107. In addition to these reliance and UCC exceptions to the requirement of consideration, some courts are willing to enforce a promise to perform a "moral obligation" without consideration. RESTATEMENT (SECOND) OF CONTRACTS §§ 82-86; J. MURRAY, *supra*, §§ 94-101.

81 The necessary modifications actually involve some significant complications. To begin with, interdependencies may or may not be Pareto-relevant. This means that at the competitive equilibrium there may be no possibilities for gifts that benefit both parties, even in the presence of interdependent utility functions. *A* may prefer that *B* not starve, but if *B* always chooses a non starvation consumption bundle, then *A*'s preference does not lead to any possible Pareto-improvement of the competitive equilibrium. Even if interdependence is still present at the competitive equilibrium, it may not be Pareto-relevant: *A* may want *B* to consume more, but not as strongly as *A* wants to increase his own consumption. *See* D. COLLARD, ALTRUISM AND ECONOMY 21

individual. This provides a motive for making gifts. The consideration doctrine requires that a gift be made in cash or present goods, rather than by giving the individual a right to a future performance.[82] In a frictionless market, however, no reason exists to make a gift in the form of a future right instead of giving the cash value of that right. Unlike exchanges of future rights, gifts of those rights serve no economic function in the neoclassical model. Hence, refusing to enforce them carries no economic cost.[83]

(1978); D. Johnson, The Fundamental Economics of the Charity Market 70 (1968) (Ph.D. diss., University of Virginia).

Further complications relate to the precise form of the interdependency. An interdependency is commodity-related if *A*'s utility depends upon the composition of *B*'s consumption bundle. If *A*'s utility depends upon *B*'s utility, the interdependency is utility-related. D. COLLARD, *supra*, at 7-8, 122-39. This distinction is crucial in evaluating the welfare economics of competitive equilibria in the presence of interdependencies.

The first theorem of welfare economics, which is that all competitive equilibria are Pareto-optimal, does not hold true in the presence of Pareto-relevant interdependencies of either type, but this results only from the definition of competitive equilibria. They are defined as including only the results of exchanges, therefore excluding gifts. For an excellent treatment of this point, see *id.* at 23-25. The first theorem is invalid then only because it does not take into account gifts of goods and services in the case of commodity-related interdependencies or wealth in the case of utility-related interdependencies. Collard shows that the first theorem does hold for "net competitive equilibria," which include the voluntary transfers needed to reach Pareto-optimality. *Id.* at 24.

The second theorem of welfare economics, which is that all Pareto optima are competitive equilibria, holds in the case of utility-related but not commodity-related interdependencies. For utility-related interdependence, the key idea is that any Pareto optimum can be arrived at through the competitive process if the process starts out from the appropriate initial distribution of wealth. Rader, *The Second Theorem of Welfare Economics When Utilities Are Interdependent*, 23 J. ECON. THEORY 420 (1980). The distribution of wealth can be reached through a mix of voluntary and involuntary lump-sum transfers. D. COLLARD, *supra*, at 25. The involuntary transfers are needed to avoid "free riders" when the redistribution is a "public good," benefiting not only donors but also others who have the same preferences. *Id.* at 30-35; E. BROWNING & J. BROWNING, *supra* note 38, at 186-88. For commodity-related interdependence, the second theorem does not hold because any attainable Pareto optimum cannot be a competitive equilibrium. Pareto optima in the face of commodity-related interdependence require that different individuals face different price ratios, since gifts involve subsidized prices to particular individuals. D. Johnson, *supra*, at 69-74. This violates one of the requirements for competitive equilibrium. F. SCHERER, *supra* note 41, at 597. In practice, it would be difficult to reach a Pareto optimum in the case of commodity-related interdependence because potential donors of the relevant commodities know that they cannot prevent the donees from converting the gifts to cash or from reducing the amount of the commodities that they otherwise would have purchased. *See* D. COLLARD, *supra*, at 125, 131; D. Johnson, *supra*, ch. 6.

82 An enforceable gift of future rights presumably could be sold to a third party for its present discounted value. If the donee does not sell the rights, they become an addition to the donee's portfolio of assets and immediately increase his wealth by their present discounted value. The donor's wealth is reduced by this same amount at the time of the gift, whether the donee sells the rights or not. In view of this result, the donor has no reason to avoid making the gift in the form of cash or some other already-existing asset. Perhaps the best way to see this point is to consider a gift of the donor's promissory note. Given perfect markets, such a note is worth no more to either the donor or the donee than its cash market value at the time of the gift.

83 Imperfect information and transaction costs provide possible rationales for gifts of future rights. For instance, if the donor is unsure of his longevity, he may be uncertain of the size of the

Besides supporting enforcement of contracts, the neoclassical model suggests a measure of damages. Consider the market for insurance. With fully enforceable contracts, an individual might choose to buy, for example, $100,000 of fire insurance. If damages for breach are any amount less than $100,000, a profit-maximizing insurance company would never pay on a policy. Of course, nonlegal motives for performance (such as morality) may exist. Thus, if ninety-nine percent of insurance companies perform anyway, the expected payout on a policy is $99,000, assuming that consumers cannot identify "honest" companies. The marginal consumer, however, is unwilling to pay the same premium for less coverage. Hence, premiums must fall. At the lower premium, honest companies cannot continue to offer the same level of coverage, so the level of coverage must fall. Now policies offer only ninety-nine percent coverage. The same process repeats. Consumers receive, on the average, less than ninety-nine percent coverage, since one percent of the companies breach. As a result, the coverage level sinks to roughly ninety-eight percent. In theory, this process could continue until the level of coverage reached zero. The conclusion is that if damages are less than the full-performance value of the contract, markets can collapse even if the vast majority of firms are trustworthy.[84] Hence, expectation-based damages are necessary.

Another classical contract doctrine receiving strong support from the neoclassical model is freedom of contract. In the neoclassical model, contracts represent rational attempts to maximize individual welfare. Intervening in market transactions can make some individuals better off only by injuring others. This is a necessary implication of the Pareto-optimality of market equilibrium. If the distribution of wealth is fair (by whatever criteria are used), tampering with the market will result in a shift away from the fair distribution. On the other hand, if wealth distribution is unfair, government taxes and transfer payments appear to be a more effective means of changing it than government intervention in market transactions.[85]

gift that he wants to make. By delaying performance until his death, he can fashion a gift that is smaller in present value the longer his life turns out to be. As compared to an immediate gift, this type of gift functions partly as an annuity paid by the donee. It is not clear, however, that the donee is the most efficient bearer of the risk of the donor's longevity. A risk-averse donee would prefer that the donor give him the expected present discounted value of the future rights immediately and that the donor then purchase an annuity in the market. Transaction costs provide a possible explanation for gifts of future rights if, for instance, the donor's lack of liquidity makes a cash gift difficult. This implies that the donor cannot readily borrow against his assets or that the donee can borrow more readily against the enforceable gift of future rights. In spite of these possible rationales for gifts of future rights—imperfect information and transaction costs—the economic functions of gift promises seem much less significant than those of exchange promises.

84 This is an example of the "lemons" problem discussed *infra* text accompanying note 113.

85 *See* A. POLINSKY, AN INTRODUCTION TO LAW AND ECONOMICS 105-13 (1983). Part of the argument against using regulation to redistribute income is that the distributive effects are often perverse. For instance, minimum wage legislation may help high-wage union members at the

In short, the neoclassical model and the classical rules of contract law are highly consistent. This may be coincidence; it may be due to some tendency of the judicial process toward economic efficiency;[86] or it may derive from the common roots of the neoclassical model and the classical rules of contract law in nineteenth century liberalism.[87] As we shall see, post-neoclassical models have some rather different implications for the legal system than the neoclassical model.

Beyond the Neoclassical Theory

Flaws in the Neoclassical Model

This Article has demonstrated the integral role played by contracts for future performances in the neoclassical theory that has dominated microeconomics in this century. This model not only explains the functions of contract, but also provides a powerful argument for freedom of contract. Under the basic neoclassical model, intervention in the market can never improve economic efficiency and is generally an inefficient means of pursuing other goals such as income redistribution. One of the achievements of the past thirty years has been to provide a rigorous mathematical basis for this position. At the same time that economists have been exploring the ramifications of the neoclassical theory, however, they also have begun to appreciate its limitations.

Several reasons exist for dissatisfaction with the neoclassical microeconomic model. To begin with, the model fails to address important aspects of economic reality, such as the dynamic processes of economic growth and technological change.[88] The failure to deal with economic growth is especially significant. Economic growth builds on prior growth, like compound interest, while an increase in static efficiency is a one-time gain. Thus, given sufficient time, even a small increase in economic growth can compensate for a decrease in static

expense of black teenagers by preventing the latter from "buying" (by working at a low wage) the on-the-job training they need to compete with presently-employed workers. M. Friedman & R. Friedman, Free to Choose 237-38 (1980). Similarly, housing code enforcement has been interpreted as a means of increasing the supply of middle-income housing by reducing the supply of low-income consumers. *See* R. Posner, *supra* note 4, at 356-59.

For a philosophical argument in favor of using contract law to redistribute income, see Kronman, *Contract Law and Distributive Justice*, 89 Yale L.J. 472 (1980). Although Professor Kronman makes a number of valid points, he seems to overlook the troublesome possibility of perverse distributional effects.

86 The thesis that the judicial process does have an inherent tendency toward economic efficiency provides the foundation for a "positive" economic theory of law. *See* R. Posner, *supra* note 4, at 17-19. For an introduction to the evolutionary theory supporting this thesis, see *id.* at 439-41; Epstein, *The Social Consequences of Common Law Rules*, 95 Harv. L. Rev. 1717, 1743 n.88 (1982).

87 *See* P. Atiyah, The Rise and Fall of Freedom of Contract 398-409 (1979).

88 For a survey of the literature, see Nelson, *Research on Productivity Growth and Productivity Differences: Dead Ends and New Departures*, 19 J. Econ. Literature 1029 (1981).

efficiency. Consequently, the value of the neoclassical model as a guide in setting social policy is diminished by the fact that the considerations for which the neoclassical model accounts are probably less significant than the dynamic considerations that the model overlooks.[89]

In addition to its failure to address some extremely important issues such as economic growth, the neoclassical microeconomic model has also been a disappointment empirically. Some of the major facts of economic life seem incompatible with the neoclassical model. For example, unemployment is impossible within the terms of the model. The model predicts that if employment falls below the desired level, unemployed workers will bid down the wages until they are low enough that the marginal worker will be indifferent between receiving the going wage and enjoying the "leisure" of unemployment. Thus, the only individuals who should be unemployed are those who preferred not to work at the going wage.[90] Although the Great Depression is the most striking empirical refutation of this prediction, the behavior of wages in more recent recessions has also been inconsistent with the predictions of neoclassical microeconomics. Wages in recessionary periods have stubbornly refused to fall as required by the theory.[91]

Empirical tests of other features of the neoclassical model also have been disappointing. According to the model, the prices firms charge for their goods should reflect their marginal cost of production. A wealth of empirical studies on this subject have failed to confirm this proposition. Typically, firms set prices based upon a mark-up over their average costs.[92] Furthermore, the marginal cost curves themselves do not have the U-shape so familiar to students of microeconomics.[93] Instead, a large number of studies have found either very shallow or flat marginal cost curves.[94] Indeed, considerable doubt exists whether firm managers even have the goal of maximizing profits that the theory postulates. From the manager's point of view, maximizing profits may

---

89 *See* F. SCHERER, *supra* note 41, at 407; Nelson, *Assessing Private Enterprise: An Exegesis of Tangled Doctrine*, 12 BELL J. ECON. 93, 104 (1981). For example, the efficiency losses due to monopoly would be acceptable if, as Schumpeter suggested, monopoly led to more rapid technological innovation. J. SCHUMPETER, CAPITALISM, SOCIALISM, AND DEMOCRACY 88, 103 (1942). *See also* F. SCHERER, *supra* note 41, at 423-32.

90 *See* R. DORNBUSCH & S. FISCHER, MACROECONOMICS 364-65, 375-79 (2d ed. 1981); P. SAMUELSON, *supra* note 49, at 325-27; J. TOBIN, ASSET ACCUMULATION AND ECONOMIC ACTIVITY 34-37 (1980).

91 R. GORDON, MACROECONOMICS 166, 238-40 (2d ed. 1981); R. DORNBUSCH & S. FISCHER, *supra* note 90, at 380-81; J. TOBIN, *supra* note 90, at 2-3.

92 F. SCHERER, *supra* note 41, at 185-89; J. TOBIN, *supra* note 90, at 35.

93 A U-shaped curve means that the unit cost of producing goods falls until a certain volume of production is reached and then rises again once that volume is exceeded. For examples of U-shaped marginal cost curves, see J. HENDERSON & R. QUANDT, *supra* note 44, at 85; J. HIRSHLEIFER, *supra* note 44, at 305; P. SAMUELSON, *supra* note 49, at 428-29.

94 *See* E. MANSFIELD, MICROECONOMICS: THEORY AND APPLICATIONS 185-91 (abr. 3d ed. 1979)(summarizing numerous studies).

simply be one of several goals, including expanding the firm's size and maximizing her own salary and job security.[95] Numerous studies show that firm size itself is a product of a dynamic process called "random walk" rather than the kind of static equilibrium found in the neoclassical model.[96]

The empirical problems are not limited to the prices firms charge for their goods. Consumers also fail to behave as predicted by the theory. Although the neoclassical model makes very weak assumptions about the behavior of consumers under conditions of certainty, the model's assumptions about consumer choice between risky alternatives are more stringent.[97] The predicted results have not materialized. For example, one basic postulate of the model is transitivity. The model postulates that if an individual finds A equivalent to B, prefers B to C, and finds C equivalent to D, then that individual should prefer A to D.[98] In fact, experiments have failed to confirm this prediction. In these "preference reversal" experiments, the subjects are offered the choice between two gambles. The subjects are also asked to state the amount of money that each gamble is worth to them. Surprisingly, in many cases the subjects prefer to take gambles that have a lower cash equivalent than the gambles they reject. Despite strenuous efforts, economists have been unable to invalidate these results.[99]

Perhaps the most obvious flaw in the neoclassical model, however, is that its basic assumptions are incorrect. One critical assumption is that individuals have perfect information about the goods offered on the market and the prices of those goods. Thus, they know exactly what they are paying for and what alternative purchases would cost.[100] This is, on its face, a highly unrealistic assumption. The model also assumes that entering into contracts is costless.[101] In reality, transaction costs are significant. For example, common experience suggests that the cost of making and closing a house sale can approach ten percent of the purchase price of the house. Economists have attempted to modify these unrealistic assumptions of the neoclassical model. As shown in the next section, the modified theories provide new functions

---

95 F. SCHERER, *supra* note 41, at 29-41.

96 *See id.* at 92-100, 146, 289-95.

97 J. HENDERSON & R. QUANDT, *supra* note 44, at 52-60.

98 *Id.* at 53.

99 *See* Grether & Plott, *Economic Theory of Choice and the Preference Reversal Phenomenon*, 69 AM. ECON. REV. 623 (1979). It is not necessary, however, to search the literature for esoteric psychological experiments to find instances of irrational behavior under conditions of uncertainty. For example, despite the well-documented benefits of seat belts in reducing the probability of death or serious injury from automobile accidents, less than 20% of the population uses them. Arnould & Grabowski, *Auto Safety Regulation: An Analysis of Market Failure*, 12 BELL J. ECON. 27, 27 (1981).

100 J. HENDERSON & R. QUANDT, *supra* note 44, at 136-37.

101 J. HIRSHLEIFER, *supra* note 44, at 234.

for contract, but they also may provide new justifications for limiting freedom of contract.

Recent Developments in Economic Theory

Attempts to perfect the neoclassical theory have focused on modifying the model's assumptions of zero transaction costs and perfect information. In the newer models, contracts can serve as a means of minimizing transaction costs or avoiding problems associated with imperfect information. The role of contract in these new models can be illustrated by the example of an individual who wishes to build a new house. In a world of perfect information and zero transaction costs, the individual might proceed as follows. Every hour of construction would be the subject of separate bidding by contractors. The contract for each hour would state the operations to be performed during that hour in such detail that the tasks would be entirely specified. Each time segment would be contracted to the firm making the lowest bid on that segment.

In the real world, of course, such a procedure would be impossible. Transaction costs make it infeasible to write the series of detailed contracts or to conduct the numerous auctions that this procedure would require.[102] Furthermore, the costs of monitoring the contractors' performance make it impractical to tie compensation to the precise physical tasks performed.[103] Obviously, the transaction costs of moving workers and materials on and off the job site on an hourly basis also would be prohibitive. Instead, the individuals would enter into contracts for the entire job with a single contractor, allowing that contractor to subcontract out parts of the work. Entering into a single contract economizes on transaction costs and reduces the individual's information requirements. Similar factors motivate firms to enter into long-term contractual relations.[104] Even when they use no formal legal contract, individuals and firms often may rely on informal, implicit con-

102 *See* Williamson, Wachter & Harris, *Understanding the Employment Relation: The Analysis of Idiosyncratic Exchange*, 6 BELL J. ECON. 250, 264-67 (1975); Williamson, *Transaction-Cost Economics: The Governance of Contractual Relations*, 22 J. LAW & ECON. 233 (1979).

103 Williamson, Wachter & Harris, *supra* note 102, at 262-64. The literature on principals and agents deals with the problem of achieving optimal incentive and risk-sharing when costs of monitoring performance are high. This approach is relevant to contracting between two parties when one party, the principal, provides an input that will have a productivity dependent upon some external variable (such as market conditions) and upon the inputs (usually called "effort") of the other party, the agent. The agent's effort cannot be fully specified in the contract and is often costly to monitor. The classic example is the employer who hires a worker to run a machine. The problem is to determine terms that will most efficiently allocate the market risks while leading to an optimal level of effort by the employee and minimizing the expense of supervision. *See* Harris & Raviv, *Some Results on Incentive Contracts with Applications to Education and Employment, Health Insurance, and Law Enforcement*, 68 AM. ECON. REV. 20 (1978); Shavell, *Risk Sharing and Incentives in the Principal and Agent Relationship*, 10 BELL J. ECON. 55 (1979).

104 *See* Goetz & Scott, *Principles of Relational Contracts*, 67 VA. L. REV. 1089 (1981); Macneil,

tracts to allocate risks, reduce transaction costs,[105] and to reduce the need to search for new partners.[106]

Most of the rigorous mathematical modeling in the last decade has focused on the problem of imperfect information rather than on the problem of transaction costs. In the past, the neoclassical model's assumption of perfect information often was considered unimportant. Recent work, however, has indicated that introducing information costs into the neoclassical model can drastically change the results that it predicts. In particular, consideration of information costs undermines the strong support for the principle of freedom of contract that the neoclassical model otherwise provides. The new models addressing the problem of imperfect information can be divided into two groups. The first group of models incorporates imperfect price information. The second group of models incorporates imperfect information about the quality of products.[107]

Imperfect information about prices can have drastic effects on the performance of markets. This is made clear by a model developed by Professor Diamond.[108] In this model, information about prices must be obtained through a costly search process.[109] The model assumes that all individuals have the same demand curve and have search costs greater than zero. It also assumes that all firms have identical cost curves. Given these assumptions, even if the search costs are extremely small and the number of firms is extremely large, the firms will not charge the competitive price. This is because each firm can profitably raise its price by an amount less than the search cost of the individual with the lowest search cost so long as the current price is below the price a monopolist would charge for the goods.[110] Raising the price by

---

Economic Analysis of Contractual Relations: Its Shortfalls and the Need for a "Rich Classificatory Apparatus," 75 Nw. U.L. Rev. 1018, 1025-39 (1981).

105 The main reasons costs are reduced by using a general contractor are: (1) the general contractor has more expertise and can supervise more effectively, (2) because the contractor is frequently in the market, he can locate subcontractors with good work records more cheaply. Consequently, those subcontractors have an incentive to do good work in order to keep their good reputation and to get repeat business. This in turn reduces the need for detailed specifications and close supervision.

106 The late Professor Okun and others have argued that such implicit contracts characterize large segments of the economy. A. Okun, Prices & Quantities: A Macroeconomic Analysis 83-92, 138-48 (1981). *See also* R. Gordon, *supra* note 91, at 190-92, 243-44.

107 For an introductory survey of these models, see H. Varian, *supra* note 43, at 231-47.

108 Diamond, *A Model of Price Adjustment*, 3 J. Econ. Theory 156 (1971). *See also* Scitovsky, *Ignorance as a Source of Oligopoly Power*, 40 Am. Econ. Rev. 48, 50 (1950). For a summary, see Stiglitz, *Equilibrium in Product Markets with Imperfect Information*, 69 Am. Econ. Rev. 339, 339-40 (1979).

109 It is easiest to think of this as the cost in time and effort of shopping among different stores.

110 The monopoly price is the price that a profit-maximizing firm would charge if it had no competition. For an explanation of how a monopolist sets this price, see F. Scherer, *supra* note 41, at 14-16.

this amount will not induce any customer to search for another seller. Hence, all firms will raise their prices by small steps until they have reached the "monopoly" price, at which point further price increases are no longer profitable. If free entry into the market is possible, new firms will then enter to obtain this monopolistic profit until the monopolistic profit has been entirely dissipated. The result will be that firms will charge consumers monopoly prices but the firms will receive no higher profit than they would have received if consumers had perfect information in a freely competitive market.[111] In this model, a monopoly would be a Pareto improvement over free competition. A monopolist would charge the same price as the multitude of firms but at least the monopoly profits would not be dissipated by an excessive number of firms.

This model demonstrates that introducing even very small search costs can radically change the conclusions of the neoclassical model. Of course, the Diamond model is itself highly simplified. Economists have devoted a considerable amount of time to introducing more sophisticated assumptions concerning price search. These more sophisticated models lead to a variety of results. In some models, the equilibrium price returns to the competitive level; in other models, the equilibrium price is the monopoly price, a range of prices exist at equilibrium, or no equilibrium can be found.[112] The existence of search costs clearly does not make it impossible for the free market to reach a Pareto-optimal equilibrium, but, equally clearly, no reason exists for confidence that such a result will occur.

Imperfect information about product quality also can be inconsistent with Pareto-optimality. Consider the market for used 1978 Honda Civics. Assume that the cars in the best condition are worth $4,000, while those in the worst condition are worth nothing. Now, make two additional assumptions: (1) sellers know the value of their cars and will not sell at a price below that value; and (2) buyers cannot determine the condition of specific cars prior to sale but do know the average value of the cars on the market. Given these assumptions, the price for used cars must be zero and no sales will be made. The proof is simple. Suppose the price were $3,000. No car worth more than $3,000 would be offered for sale, but the owners of cars worth less than $3,000 would find it profitable to sell. Consequently, the average worth of cars on the market would be less than $3,000. Knowing this, buyers would be unwill-

[111] The absence of supercompetitive profits often seems to be taken as an indication that markets are operating properly. *See, e.g.*, E. FARNSWORTH & W. YOUNG, CONTRACTS: CASES & MATERIALS 516 (3d ed. 1980); W. HAWKLAND & M. BENFIELD, SALES: CASES & MATERIALS 115-17 (1980). Actually, normal profit levels only indicate free entry.

[112] For surveys of the literature, see Schwartz & Wilde, *Intervening in Markets on the Basis of Imperfect Information: A Legal & Economic Analysis*, 127 U. PA. L. REV. 630, 640-51 (1979); Stiglitz, *supra* note 108.

ing to pay $3,000. As a result, contrary to the assumption, $3,000 could not be the equilibrium price. The same argument applies to any possible equilibrium price above zero. This is Akerlof's famous "market for lemons."[113]

Of course, this is an extremely simplified model. Recent researchers have experimented with more sophisticated models in which buyers are assumed to use a variety of costly methods of ascertaining product quality, and sellers are given more complex characteristics. In general, markets no longer break down entirely under these more complex assumptions, but neither do they necessarily attain Pareto-optimal results.[114] At least in theory, then, government intervention in the marketplace appears to have a potential for increasing welfare when product information is costly.

These models also have significant implications for freedom of contract. The assurances provided by the two fundamental theorems of welfare economics[115] concerning the desirability of the free market do not appear to be justified under more realistic assumptions. Free markets may well be characterized by excessive prices, an excessive number of firms, or suboptimal product quality. Skepticism about the performance of the free market appears even more justified when one examines the economy as a whole rather than these models of particular markets. The attempts of individuals to adapt to a world of search costs and imperfect product information may optimize the welfare of those individuals but may create adverse effects upon others.[116] For example, Professor Okun argued that the use of cost-of-living clauses in contracts is a functional adaptation to uncertainty about price levels, but that widespread use of such clauses in inflationary periods accelerates inflation to the detriment of society as a whole.[117]

Many of these concerns about the free market are of dubious relevance to contract law. Courts are ill-suited to regulate the effects of

---

113 Akerlof, *The Market for "Lemons": Quality, Uncertainty and the Market Mechanism*, 84 Q.J. ECON. 488 (1970).

114 *See* Farber, *Reassessing the Economic Efficiency of Compensatory Damages for Breach of Contract*, 66 VA. L. REV. 1443, 1457-63 (1980); Riley, *Informational Equilibrium*, 47 ECONOMETRICA 331, 353 (1979); Rothschild & Stiglitz, *Equilibrium in Competitive Insurance Markets: An Essay on the Economics of Imperfect Information*, 90 Q.J. ECON. 629 (1976); Satterthwaite, *Consumer Information, Equilibrium Industry Price, and the Number of Sellers*, 10 BELL J. ECON. 483 (1979); Stuart, *Consumer Protection in Markets with Informationally Weak Buyers*, 12 BELL J. ECON. 562 (1981); Wilson, *The Nature of Equilibrium in Markets with Adverse Selection*, 11 BELL J. ECON. 108 (1980).

115 *See supra* text accompanying notes 38-51.

116 For example, use of long-term contracts can potentially decrease the number of market transactions so sharply that information about current prices becomes greatly restricted. *See* Wilson, *Adaptation to Uncertainty and Small Numbers Exchange: The New England Fresh Fish Market*, 11 BELL J. ECON. 491-92, 499-504 (1980).

117 A. OKUN, *supra* note 106, at 99-103, 278-96, 334-35.

search costs on prices.[118] Other problems, such as those addressed by Okun, are more properly the concern of macroeconomic planners than of jurists. On the other hand, as Professor Eisenberg has recently argued, courts may be justified in refusing to enforce contracts on the grounds of unfairness when search costs are extraordinarily high or when some other radical breakdown in the market has taken place.[119] A classic example is the sale of durable goods to consumers at phenomenal prices under circumstances where competition is clearly ineffective, such as the door-to-door sale of goods to customers who do not speak English.[120] In such extreme circumstances, as Eisenberg points out, courts have been increasingly reluctant to give effect to contracts with unfair terms.[121]

The radical market breakdowns discussed by Eisenberg, however, fail to account for some significant common law restrictions on freedom of contract. For example, penalty clauses generally are invalid even in competitive markets.[122] Similarly, disclaimers of liability for personal injury are generally unenforceable in consumer contracts.[123] As a practical matter, these restrictive rules apply to far more transactions than the few extreme cases of radical market failure considered by Professor Eisenberg. The next section will consider whether these restrictive legal rules serve any economic function.

Legal Restrictions on Contract Terms

Warranty Disclaimers.—One of the best-established restrictions on freedom of contract is the rule restricting the enforceability and scope of warranty disclaimers. All goods carry an implied warranty of suitability for their ordinary uses.[124] Defects in the goods resulting in injury or property damage when the goods are put to their ordinary use constitute a breach of this implied warranty. Under a long-standing common law rule,[125] now embodied in the Uniform Commercial

---

118 *See* Schwartz & Wilde, *supra* note 112, at 666-82.

119 Eisenberg, *supra* note 71, at 754-85 (1982). An earlier comment by Professor Kornhauser suggested that information costs might justify judicial or legislative supervision of contract terms. Comment, *Unconscionability in Standard Forms*, 64 CALIF. L. REV. 1151, 1167-79 (1976).

120 *See* Eisenberg, *supra* note 71, at 763-85.

121 For examples of such judicial intervention, see Williams v. Walker-Thomas Furniture Co., 350 F.2d 445 (D.C. Cir. 1965); American Home Improvement v. MacIver, 105 N.H. 435, 201 A.2d 886 (1964); Frostifresh Corp. v. Reynoso, 52 Misc. 2d 26, 274 N.Y.S.2d 757 (Dist. Ct. 1966), *rev'd as to damages*, 54 Misc. 2d 119, 281 N.Y.S.2d 964 (App. Term 1967).

These cases seem to give additional legal protection to impoverished individuals by preventing sharp reductions in their already limited assets. To some extent, the unconscionability doctrine may be part of the social safety net discussed *infra* text accompanying notes 162-76.

122 *See infra* text accompanying notes 147 & 148.

123 *See infra* text accompanying notes 125 & 126.

124 *See* U.C.C. § 2-314(2)(c).

125 The leading case is Henningsen v. Bloomfield Motors, Inc., 32 N.J. 358, 161 A.2d 69 (1960).

Code,[126] attempts to disclaim liability for personal injury resulting from such product defects are ineffective.[127] In a world of perfect information, such a restriction on freedom of contract would make very little sense. Having complete knowledge of the products and warranty terms offered on the market, consumers would choose the combination of product, warranty term, and price best suited to their needs. Competition would force sellers to offer those terms sought by consumers.[128] If any justification for the legal restrictions on warranty disclaimers exists, therefore, it must be based on the absence of perfect information.[129]

The absence of perfect information, however, would not necessarily result in overuse of disclaimers. If competition over warranty terms were effective, disclaimers could serve a variety of useful functions. Warranties provide a form of consumer insurance against accidents. Some consumers may not wish to purchase such insurance coverage. They may already have other insurance, they may be more willing than the average consumer to take risks, or they may be especially careful and thus less likely than the average consumer to become involved in an accident.[130] On the other hand, sellers would have a strong incentive to offer full warranties as an option. By providing additional warranty coverage, a seller could provide a signal to consumers about product quality. If consumers find it difficult to assess the quality of a product before purchasing that product, the seller could use the warranty as an inexpensive means of overcoming consumer ignorance.[131] Given effective competition, warranty coverage would be an available option, which some consumers might waive.

---

[126] U.C.C. § 2-719(3) makes limitations on damages for personal injury prima facie unconscionable. U.C.C. § 2-302 also has been construed to make warranty disclaimers of such liability unconscionable. J. WHITE & R. SUMMERS, THE LAW UNDER THE UNIFORM COMMERCIAL CODE § 12-11 (2d ed. 1980). Finally, under the Magnuson-Moss Act, if a seller makes any express warranty, it cannot disclaim implied warranties. 15 U.S.C. § 2308 (1976).

[127] Because the duty to provide a safe product is not disclaimable, it is often dealt with under tort law rather than contract law. RESTATEMENT (SECOND) OF TORTS § 402A (1965)(see especially comment e); W. PROSSER, HANDBOOK OF THE LAW OF TORTS 634-36, 656-58 (4th ed. 1971). *See also* Epstein, *supra* note 86, at 1739.

[128] Priest, *A Theory of the Consumer Product Warranty*, 90 YALE L.J. 1297, 1347 (1981).

[129] Widespread agreement now exists that neither monopoly nor less extreme forms of economic concentration in themselves would result in unfair warranty terms. *See* Priest, *supra* note 128, at 1299-1302, 1320-25; Schwartz, *A Reexamination of Nonsubstantive Unconscionability*, 63 VA. L. REV. 1053, 1071-76 (1977).

[130] *See* Priest, *supra* note 128, at 1307-19. Other authors have argued that use of disclaimers to sort out low-risk consumers involves a welfare loss, because these consumers must forgo full insurance in order to signal their low-risk status. *See* Ordover, *Products Liability in Markets with Heterogeneous Consumers*, 8 J. LEGAL STUD. 505, 518-20 (1979); Rothschild & Stiglitz, *supra* note 114, at 637-38.

[131] *See* Grossman, *The Informational Role of Warranties and Private Disclosures About Product Quality*, 24 J.L. & ECON. 461 (1981); Spence, *Consumer Misperceptions, Product Failure, and Product Liability*, 44 REV. ECON. STUD. 561 (1977).

Unfortunately, several significant barriers exist to effective competition over warranty terms. First, consumers find it difficult to understand the legal language used in warranties.[132] Second, apart from the difficulty of interpreting the language of the warranty, assessing its value may also be quite difficult. In order to determine the value of warranty coverage for a particular product, one would need to determine the accident rate associated with that product and the extent of loss associated with each possible accident. The accident rate will be affected by the design of the product, the manufacturer's quality control and sources of materials and parts, and the level of care of the particular consumer using the product. Gathering such information about a particular product is likely to be quite difficult and costly. Gathering information about a sufficient number of firms to allow comparison is obviously an even more costly and difficult undertaking. If consumers cannot accurately determine the value of warranties, a "lemons" problem arises.[133] As in the Akerlof model, one would expect to find a suboptimal level of quality in the warranties offered.

In addition to these information costs, consumers also may face special difficulties in processing the information they do have available. An area of study known as "cognitive psychology" recently has received increasing attention from economists.[134] Psychologists have developed a large body of experimental data suggesting that the ability of most individuals to process information about risks is limited in three respects.[135] First, individuals are extremely unsophisticated about statistical theory. They tend to assign far too much weight to small samples.[136] In general, they tend to assume that the data they possess represents the real situation; thus, they overlook other evidence sug-

---

[132] For an excellent discussion of this problem, see Davis, *Protecting Consumers from Overdisclosure and Gobbledygook: An Empirical Look at the Simplification of Consumer-Credit Contracts*, 63 VA. L. REV. 841 (1977).

[133] *See supra* text accompanying notes 113 & 114. On the effects of imperfect warranty information, see Gerner & Bryant, *Appliance Warranties as a Market Signal?*, 15 J. CONSUMER AFF. 75, 79 (1981); Goldberg, *The Economics of Product Safety and Imperfect Information*, 5 BELL J. ECON. & MGMT. SCI. 683 (1974). The analogy between unfair contract terms and defective goods is nicely drawn in Leff, *Contract as Thing*, 19 AM. U.L. REV. 131 (1970).

[134] *See* Arnould & Grabowski, *supra* note 99, at 29, 34-35, 45; Arrow, *Risk Perception in Psychology and Economics*, 20 ECON. INQUIRY 1 (1982); Simon, *Rational Decision Making in Business Organizations*, 69 AM. ECON. REV. 493, 506-07 (1979).

[135] *See* R. NISBETT & L. ROSS, HUMAN INFERENCE: STRATEGIES AND SHORTCOMINGS OF SOCIAL JUDGMENT (1980); Hershey & Schoemaker, *Risk Taking and Problem Context in the Domain of Losses: An Expected Utility Analysis*, 47 J. RISK & INS. 111 (1980); Tversky & Kahneman, *Judgment Under Uncertainty: Heuristics and Biases*, 185 SCIENCE 1124 (1974) [hereinafter cited as Tversky & Kahneman, *Judgment Under Uncertainty*]; Tversky & Kahneman, *The Framing of Decisions and the Psychology of Choice*, 211 SCIENCE 453 (1981) [hereinafter cited as Tversky & Kahneman, *The Framing of Decisions*].

[136] R. NISBETT & L. ROSS, *supra* note 135, at 77-82; Tversky & Kahneman, *Judgment Under Uncertainty*, *supra* note 135, at 1125.

gesting the unreliability of their data.[137] In short, they fail to anticipate properly the likelihood of future surprises.[138]

Second, substantial evidence exists that individuals tend to underestimate the likelihood that low probability events will occur.[139] For example, when asked about the probability of their being involved in an automobile accident in the next year, the majority of individuals selected odds of one in one hundred or greater. The real figure is one in ten.[140]

Finally, individual decisionmaking appears to be quite sensitive to the way in which the question that they are deciding is framed.[141] For example, one experiment showed that doctors assess the desirability of an operation differently when told that the survival rate is eighty-five percent than when they are told the death rate is fifteen percent.[142] In another experiment, use of seat belts varied depending on whether individuals were told the probability of an accident per trip or the probability of experiencing an accident in their lifetime.[143]

This failure of individuals to assess risk accurately could be expected to lead consumers to undervalue sharply the benefits of warranty coverage. Apart from individuals' cognitive limitations, emotional factors also may play a part. Considering the hazards associated with purchase of a product might be a substantial source of cognitive dissonance that consumers would prefer to avoid.[144]

Despite the barriers to acquiring and processing information about product warranties, some consumers may manage to acquire and process such information effectively. Professor Priest recently has argued that these consumers provide a sufficient check on the market and that

---

137 R. NISBETT & L. ROSS, *supra* note 135, at 25, 41, 142-46; Tversky & Kahneman, *Judgment Under Uncertainty*, *supra* note 135, at 1124-30.

138 This is particularly serious because individuals also tend to be unable to make accurate predictions. Not only do they predict less accurately than simple regression formulae, but even experts refuse to modify their predictions when informed of the improved results they could reach with the regression formula. *See* R. NISBETT & L. ROSS, *supra* note 135, at 140-41. Kenneth Arrow has recently suggested that this cognitive defect causes excessively rapid price movements in certain futures markets. Arrow, *supra* note 134, at 4-6.

139 H. KUNREUTHER, DISASTER INSURANCE PROTECTION: PUBLIC POLICY LESSONS 12-17 (1978); Arnould & Grabowski, *supra* note 99, at 29, 34-35. One explanation for this finding is that probabilities must be high enough to cross an attentional threshold before individuals consider them. H. KUNREUTHER, *supra*, at 182-84; Kahneman & Tversky, *supra* note 36, at 263, 275, 282-83.

140 Arnould & Grabowski, *supra* note 99, at 34.

141 Kahneman & Tversky, *supra* note 36; Tversky & Kahneman, *The Framing of Decisions*, *supra* note 135.

142 Arrow, *supra* note 134, at 7.

143 Arnould & Grabowski, *supra* note 99, at 35. *See also* H. KUNREUTHER, *supra* note 139, at 174-75.

144 *See generally* Akerlof & Dickens, *The Economic Consequences of Cognitive Dissonance*, 72 AM. ECON. REV. 307 (1982).

manufacturers will tailor warranty terms to meet these consumers' needs.[145] Several economic theorists have pointed out, however, that these "marginal" consumers may or may not be representative of the average consumer. For example, consumers who take the trouble to shop for good warranty terms may be less careful when using goods or have less insurance than other individuals. Contract terms tailored to the needs of the marginal consumer thus may not be well suited to the needs of the vast number of consumers.[146]

Penalty Clauses.—Under a long-established common law rule, contract clauses fixing damages for breach are enforceable only if they constitute a reasonable attempt to estimate actual damages.[147] Clauses intended to penalize breach are unenforceable.[148] Yet, penalty clauses seem to be a potentially useful way of protecting plaintiffs who have unusual losses that cannot be proven in court or who are unable easily to detect breaches by the other party.[149] Effective competition presumably would prevent the use of such clauses as a means of exploiting the weaker party to the contract.[150]

Informational asymmetries may partly explain why the courts refuse to enforce these clauses. Consider a contract in which a manufacturing company hires a construction company to build an addition to its factory. Suppose the manufacturer wishes to include a penalty clause in the contract in order to increase the likelihood of performance or to compensate itself for losses that it could not prove in court in the event of breach. The manufacturer needs to determine the probability of breach in order to determine the proper price at which to bargain. The construction companies with which the manufacturer might contract, however, have better information about the probability than does the manufacturer. For any given price and penalty package that the

145 Priest, *supra* note 128, at 1347.

146 In the standard neoclassical model, which assumes homogeneous goods and contract terms, this problem cannot arise. The average consumer in the neoclassical model would always be willing to pay more for a warranty term than the marginal consumer. In a world of imperfect information and heterogeneous contract terms and goods, however, the average consumer might well prefer more warranty coverage than the marginal consumer, even though the average consumer would be required to pay a higher price than the marginal consumer is willing to pay for these terms. *See* Spence, *Monopoly, Quality, and Regulation*, 6 BELL J. ECON. 417, 428-29 (1975); Trebilcock & Dewees, *Judicial Control of Standard Form Contracts*, in THE ECONOMIC APPROACH TO LAW 93, 110, 117 (P. Burrows & C. Veljanovski eds. 1981). For a discussion of a similar problem in the context of termination clauses, see Goetz & Scott, *supra* note 104, at 1089, 1131-34.

147 RESTATEMENT (SECOND) OF CONTRACTS § 356(1) (1981); J. MURRAY, MURRAY ON CONTRACTS 473-76 (1974). For the sale of goods, this common law rule has been codified as U.C.C. § 2-718(1).

148 RESTATEMENT (SECOND) OF CONTRACTS § 356.

149 *See* Goetz & Scott, *supra* note 3, at 578-79 (1977); Farber, *supra* note 114, at 1477; Klein, *Transaction Cost Determinants of "Unfair" Contractual Arrangements*, 70 AM. ECON. REV. 356 (1980).

150 Goetz & Scott, *supra* note 3, at 589-92; Klein, *supra* note 149, at 360.

manufacturer offers, that package will be most attractive to those construction companies that are least likely to breach the contract. From the manufacturer's point of view, however, it is paying an excessive price to the low-risk builder, since the builder is receiving a higher price than he otherwise would command in return for agreeing to pay a penalty in the event of a breach that is likely never to occur.[151] On the other hand, the construction company cannot assess the reasonableness of the damages specified in the penalty clause without knowing how much it would be required to pay if damages were judicially determined. The manufacturer, however, is in a much better position to know its potential provable damages than are the construction companies that are bidding on the job.[152] Under these circumstances, bargaining between the parties over the penalty and price package is likely to be quite difficult.[153]

In addition, the generally low probability of breach may explain the court's refusal to enforce penalty clauses. As discussed in connection with warranty disclaimers, cognitive psychology has shown that individuals are likely to lack the ability to assess accurately the probability of such events.[154] A construction company that has been successful in the recent past is likely to be overly optimistic in assuming that it will not encounter difficulties in its next contract.[155] The construction company is also likely to overlook the possibility that a penalty clause will give the manufacturer an incentive to provoke a breach.[156] Most lawyers seem to agree that businessmen give insufficient attention to the prospect of future difficulties in their business re-

151 The manufacturer would like to give a price bonus that compensates the construction company only for (1) the expected amount of penalty payments at the optimal level of risk and (2) the cost of attaining that risk level. If the construction company can reach a lower level of risk or can reduce risk more cheaply than the manufacturer realizes, it will enjoy a price bonus greater than the cost that it will incur as a result of the penalty clause. From the manufacturer's perspective this is an undeserved windfall to the construction company.

152 Although the rule in Hadley v. Baxendale, 9 Ex. 341, 156 Eng. Rep. 145 (1854), allows recovery only for reasonably foreseeable kinds of damage, it does not require that the amount of damage be foreseeable. RESTATEMENT (SECOND) OF CONTRACTS § 351 comment b (1981).

153 Conceivably, competitive bidding might cure these problems; however, the bidding system would have to be rather complicated. Both price and penalty would have to be specified in each bid, and the system would have to be designed to allow simultaneous competition between construction companies (to eliminate the first informational problem discussed in the text) and among manufacturers (to eliminate the second). Transaction and search costs seem likely to impede effective competition in practice.

154 *See supra* text accompanying notes 134-43.

155 There seems to be a tendency among businessmen to overestimate the predictive value of recent business performance. *See* Arrow, *supra* note 134, at 5-6. *See also* Goetz & Scott, *supra* note 3, at 555 n.7 (quoting C. MCCORMICK, HANDBOOK ON THE LAW OF DAMAGES § 147, at 601 (1935)) (on excessive business optimism).

156 *See* Clarkson, Miller & Muris, *Liquidated Damages v. Penalties: Sense or Nonsense?*, 1978 WIS. L. REV. 351, 375-77.

lationships and pay slight attention to the details of their contracts.[157]

Furthermore, penalty clauses involve several potential externalities. First, they arguably provide an incentive for litigation. Plaintiffs have a greater reason to sue because the potential recovery is greater than it would be if only actual damages could be recovered. Defendants have a corresponding reason to resist more vigorously. The result would be more lawsuits and more hotly contested lawsuits. Since the parties pay only a small part of the costs of the court system, this imposes an externalized cost on the public.[158] Second, penalty clauses can increase the probability of business failures. In a frictionless world this might be of little concern, but in reality the bankrupted party may well be involved in a web of long-term business relations with others, and these too will be disrupted by the business failure.[159] Furthermore, if these other contracting parties fail to include penalty clauses in their own contracts, they will be disadvantaged in receiving a share of the assets in bankruptcy, which are generally distributed on a pro rata basis.[160] Finally, if the use of penalty clauses were widespread, a wave of business failures triggered in a recession by penalty clauses could have a severe effect on investor confidence. It may be in the public interest to nurse marginal firms through recessionary periods rather than forcing them out of business, as penalty clauses would tend to do.[161]

Thus, economic theory suggests strong, though hardly conclusive, reasons for doubting that the free market would subject penalty clauses and warranty disclaimers to sufficient control. Analysis of the individual clauses disfavored by the common law does not entirely explain, however, why those clauses, rather than other contract terms, have been singled out for special regulation. The next section will propose a tentative explanation.

Contract Law and the Safety Net.—One of the most powerful principles of contract law is freedom of contract—the power of parties to allocate risks between themselves. A number of contract rules, however, reveal a countervailing principle of loss spreading. The rules against penalty clauses and warranty disclaimers for personal injury prevent catastrophic losses from being imposed on one party to the

[157] *See* Beale & Dugdale, *Contractual Remedies*, 2 BRIT. J.L. & SOC'Y 45 (1975); Macaulay, *Non-contractual Relations in Business: A Preliminary Study*, 28 AM. SOC. REV. 55, 58 60 (1963).

[158] Rubin, *Unenforceable Contracts: Penalty Clauses and Specific Performance*, 10 J. LEGAL STUD. 237, 244-45 (1981).

[159] Those most obviously affected are customers and suppliers with explicit or implicit long-term contracts, the business's employees, and its major creditors. Each of these groups, in turn, is involved in a similar set of relationships of its own. *See also infra* note 169. The strength of these externalities is illustrated by the pressure for a governmental "bail-out" of the Chrysler Corporation when it neared bankruptcy. N.Y. Times, Jan. 8, 1980, § 4, at 1, col. 3.

[160] *See* 11 U.S.C. § 726(b) (Supp. V 1981).

[161] *See* F. SCHERER, *supra* note 41, at 369. *See also infra* note 164.

contract. Bankruptcy laws further restrict the extent of the losses that a party can suffer.[162] Even outside of bankruptcy, the *Hadley v. Baxendale*[163] rule and the certainty rule of contract damages[164] tend to result in undercompensation to plaintiffs,[165] thus requiring losses at least partially to be borne by both parties. Rules of commercial impracticability under the Uniform Commercial Code also tend to restrict exposure to extreme risks.[166] It is difficult, if not impossible, for the parties to negotiate their way around these rules.

There seems to be a consistent principle in these rules. In addition to the principle of freedom of contract, contract law seems to embody an insurance principle limiting individual catastrophic losses. The social policy of risk sharing, which Calabresi has noted in tort law,[167] also seems to play a role in contract law.

In order to understand the social functions of risk sharing, it may be helpful to consider a problem faced by many primitive societies. Hunter-gatherer societies often face uncertain, fluctuating food supplies. In response, these societies commonly impose mandatory sharing rules. During scarcity periods, successful hunters are not allowed to profit from the scarcity but rather must share their food with some less successful members of the society. As Posner has pointed out, this system makes economic sense given the difficulty of establishing insurance markets and the large degree of uncertainty faced by members of these primitive societies.[168] The problems of these primitive societies seem at first glance quite different than those of modern technological economies. Nevertheless, modern societies are faced with a number of similar risks. Various kinds of surprises buffet the economy, such as oil embargoes, wars, shifts in consumer tastes, technological uncertainty, recessions, and inflation. These economic shocks play the same role in our society that drought and game migration play in hunting societies.

---

162 The general policy of the bankruptcy laws is to give the debtor a fresh start. *See* 11 U.S.C. § 727 (Supp. V 1981); Local Loan Co. v. Hunt, 292 U.S. 234, 244 (1934).

For other economic analyses of bankruptcy law, see Symposium, *The Economics of Bankruptcy Reform*, 41 LAW & CONTEMP. PROBS. 1 (1977).

163 *See supra* note 152.

164 The certainty rule disallows damages that cannot be proved with reasonable certainty. RESTATEMENT (SECOND) OF CONTRACTS § 352 (1981).

165 *See* Farber, *supra* note 114, at 1443 n.2, 1445 n.13.

166 U.C.C. § 2-615 provides that a seller of goods is excused from performance "if performance as agreed has been made impracticable by the occurrence of a contingency the non-occurrence of which was a basic assumption on which the contract was made."

In addition to the legal rules mentioned in the text, various forms of welfare payments, such as public assistance and unemployment compensation, clearly have a similar purpose of loss spreading. *See also supra* note 121 (discussion of the possible function of the unconscionability doctrine).

167 G. CALABRESI, THE COSTS OF ACCIDENTS 39-67, 278-85 (1970).

168 *See* R. POSNER, THE ECONOMICS OF JUSTICE 152-62 (1981).

Our response, like theirs, has been to create a mandatory risk sharing system—a social safety net.

Strong reasons exist not to allow individuals or firms to bargain their way out of this social safety net. First, when individuals or firms suffer catastrophic losses, externalities are likely to occur. In the case of individuals, the externalities are most immediately felt by other family members. To the extent that individuals have a claim on charity or the welfare system, the externality is felt by larger segments of society. As mentioned earlier, because of the involvement of business in a web of long-term business arrangements, business failures also have such negative externalities.[169] Furthermore, like other insurance systems, the safety net also involves a problem of "adverse selection."[170] At any given time, those individuals with the lowest risk in the participating group would have an incentive to opt out of the insurance system, since there seems to be no feasible way of adjusting premiums to risk levels. The result of low-risk individuals opting out could be the collapse of the insurance system.[171] Finally, developments in cognitive psychology suggest that individuals' ability to assess risks accurately is limited. In particular, individuals fail to anticipate that their recent experience may under-represent the likelihood of catastrophe and that the future may have major surprises in store.[172]

To take an extreme case, consider the former laws that allowed imprisonment for debt. The neoclassical model would have favored such laws, just as present-day scholars argue for freedom of contract with respect to debtor protection.[173] Indeed, John Quincy Adams made the standard neoclassical argument that abolishing debtors' prison would only injure the least creditworthy debtors, who would be unable to obtain loans unless creditors could rely on the sanction.[174] Acceptance of this argument could have had serious economic effects. For example, given the extent of optimism in the 1920's, it is easy to imagine that large numbers of individuals at that time would have agreed to the possibility of debtors' prison in order to obtain additional funds for speculation. Obviously, these individuals would have failed to give

169 *See supra* text accompanying note 159. For the suggestion that full enforcement of contracts could lead to a string of successive business failures and that market solutions to this problem are improbable, see Kennedy & Michelman, *Are Property and Contract Efficient?*, 8 HOFSTRA L. REV. 711, 747 (1980).

170 For further elaboration on this concept, see *supra* note 114 and sources cited therein.

171 This is Posner's explanation for why primitive societies make their sharing rules mandatory. *See* R. POSNER, *supra* note 168, at 155-56.

172 *See supra* text accompanying notes 134-43.

173 *See, e.g.*, R. POSNER, *supra* note 4, at 86-88; Epstein, *Unconscionability: A Critical Reappraisal*, 18 J.L. & ECON. 293, 305-15 (1975). For historical surveys, see McGovern, *Forfeiture, Inequality of Bargaining Power, and the Availability of Credit: An Historical Perspective*, 74 NW. U.L. REV. 141, 143-44 (1979).

174 S. BEMIS, JOHN QUINCY ADAMS AND THE UNION 256-57 (1956).

sufficient weight to the possibility of a complete economic collapse. Furthermore, the macroeconomic myopia of these individuals would affect not only themselves and their families, but also the economy at large. As difficult as it was for the country to recover from the Depression of the 1930's, imagine how much more difficult it would have been if hundreds of thousands of investors and businessmen had been imprisoned for failure to pay their debts.[175] While this is an extreme example, the same considerations may underlie the common law rules against enforcing warranty disclaimers and penalty clauses.

The "safety net" clearly has an important function in our society. Although it decreases economic efficiency in the short run, this effect appears to be outweighed by its contribution to long-run, dynamic efficiency.[176]

Conclusion

This Article has explored the implications for contract law of two different economic theories. The Article first explained the neoclassical economic model and its implications. The most important of those implications were that contracts should be enforceable and that the government should not attempt to regulate the terms of contracts.[177] This endorsement of freedom of contract is, of course, most congenial to conservatives. In addition to this ideological appeal, however, the neoclassical economic model also has considerable intellectual attraction. It describes aspects of reality that clearly play an important role in the economy.[178] Moreover, its intellectual elegance and mathematical sophistication plainly add to its appeal.

The more recently developed models that the Article considered next do not possess the same degree of intellectual elegance as the neoclassical economic model. By attempting to account for factors ignored in the neoclassical model, such as information costs, these newer models provide a richer and more complex view of reality. Unfortunately, this increased richness results in a loss of conceptual simplicity and mathematical elegance. Nonetheless, by providing a fuller description of the functions of contract, these models do provide additional reasons

[175] On the role of the investor in recoveries from recessions, see R. GORDON, *supra* note 91, at 102, 166, 432-34.

[176] Obviously, this judgment cannot be made with any great degree of certainty. The "safety net" also appears to reflect strongly held beliefs about equity. Both considerations of efficiency and equity, perhaps along with simple paternalism, probably played a role in the creation of the "safety net." *See* P. ATIYAH, THE RISE AND FALL OF FREEDOM OF CONTRACT 602-781 (1979). For an interesting philosophical discussion of social protection against economic losses, see McClennen, *Some Decision-Theoretic Reflections on Welfare Protection*, 9 HOFSTRA L. REV. 1453 (1981).

[177] *See supra* text accompanying notes 75-85.

[178] For instance, people and firms often do act in a rational, wealth-maximizing fashion and supply and demand have some tendency to balance.

for a general policy of enforcing contracts.[179] Unlike the neoclassical economic model, however, they also support recognition of exceptions to the general policy of enforcement. In particular, these models seem to justify some of the well-established legal rules denying enforcement to particular contract clauses.[180]

The picture that begins to emerge from these newer theories is that of a world in which market transactions are only one among a group of important economic institutions. This Article has suggested that among these other institutions is a legal "safety net." This safety net tends to spread losses and prevent individuals from bargaining their way into potentially catastrophic losses. Although no definitive new model has arisen to supplant the neoclassical model, the newer theories hold considerable promise for clarifying many issues of interest to legal scholars.[181]

Economic theory cannot provide the final answers to legal problems, if only because economic theory itself has no final answers.[182] Nor, except to a limited extent, can it resolve the ultimate normative issues underlying many disputes about law.[183] Nonetheless, economic theory can provide an illuminating perspective on how legal rules relate to the functioning of the economic system.[184] Understanding the functions served by legal rules is the first step toward evaluating them.[185]

---

179 *See supra* text accompanying notes 102-06.

180 *See supra* text accompanying notes 124-61.

181 These models clearly tend to support conclusions drawn by some legal scholars about the inadequacy of the neoclassical model with respect to long-term contractual relations, and the consequent desirability of judicial intervention to ensure good faith. I. MACNEIL, THE NEW SOCIAL CONTRACT: AN INQUIRY INTO MODERN CONTRACTUAL RELATIONS (1980); Speidel, *Court-Imposed Price Adjustments Under Long-Term Supply Contracts*, 76 NW. U.L. REV. 369, 404-22 (1981).

182 Indeed, the excitement of economic theory today stems precisely from its being in a state of flux. For an excellent critique of conventional economic theory, which appeared while this Article was in press, see L. THUROW, DANGEROUS CURRENTS: THE STATE OF ECONOMICS (1983).

183 With the significant exception of Judge Posner in THE ECONOMICS OF JUSTICE, *supra* note 168, at 60-76, 88-115, it is difficult to find anyone who seriously argues that economic efficency is either the ultimate or the exclusive measure of value.

184 This Article has not attempted any serious investigation of the causal connection, if any, between the economic utility of legal rules and their adoption by the legal system. It does not seem unreasonable to assume, however, that the stable features of a society serve *some* function, and are not simply accidental. *See* Leff, *Economic Analysis of Law: Some Realism About Nominalism*, 60 VA. L. REV. 451, 463-69 (1974).

185 Although this Article has argued that various restrictions on freedom of contract serve useful functions, it does not follow that better means of achieving those functions could not be devised.

[5]

VALUES IN CONTRACT: INTERNAL AND EXTERNAL

*Ian R. Macneil**

* This Article is a revision of a paper prepared for the Conference on Philosophical Jurisprudence of Contract Law at the Westminster Institute for Ethics and Human Values, Westminster College, London, Canada, November 20-21, 1981 and May 15, 1982.

I am greatly indebted to Nancy C. Macneil for her extensive editorial help. Roderick W. Macneil made a number of penetrating and helpful suggestions, as did Michael Timmers. The interchanges with my colleagues in a seminar at Northwestern University School of Law and at the Westminster Conference were also very helpful.

I. INTRODUCTION

Comprehending values in the universe of contract involves understanding at least three intersecting dimensions in that universe. First is the dimension of contract itself—hereafter called the contract dimension—which I take to be the relations among people in the course of projecting exchange into the future.[1] So viewed, *all* contracts are rela-

[1] When one struggles against ancient concepts—and their labels—it seems almost impossible to avoid being misunderstood, even by very perceptive people. For example, Michael Elliott, in a review of my book, I. MACNEIL, THE NEW SOCIAL CONTRACT: AN INQUIRY INTO MODERN CONTRACTUAL RELATIONS (1980) [hereinafter, I. MACNEIL, THE NEW SOCIAL CONTRACT], combines sharp criticism with exceptional graciousness in asking why my thesis (which in essence is summarized by the definition of contract in the text) "is limited to explaining *future-looking* relations? Cannot the theory of the relational contract be extended to the spontaneous exchange, to the money-for-immediate-goods transaction, to the jostling of shoulders in the street, or to sexual coupling?" Elliott, Book Review, 44 MOD. L. REV. 345, 347 (1981)(emphasis in original). Of

tional. Nevertheless, some contracts, called here "contractual relations," are far more relational than others. They lie towards one end of a relational spectrum of contractual behavior, opposite from the nonrelational end where the discrete transaction is found.[2] It is not, in my view, possible to understand either contractual relations or discrete transactions without understanding the other—or, in other words, without understanding the whole spectrum of the contract dimension. For that reason, in order to treat values in any part of the contract dimension intelligently, it is necessary to consider both discrete transactions and contractual relations not only as separate subjects, but as part of the overarching contract dimension as well.[3]

The second dimension in the universe of contract is that of value-arenas. These value-arenas include values reflected in the goals and means of people engaged in contract, in internal principles and rules governed by contract behavior (these are virtually inseparable from the first), and in external social responses to contract.[4] The latter include,

course Mr. Elliott is correct, and I never have had any other intention, but obviously had not made that clear. All the events he describes occur in relations with a past (and usually a future). One does not go into the street without being aware of the *future* possibility of jostling shoulders. (Only the relative paucity of exchange in jostling shoulders might lead one to think it noncontractual, but one would not conclude this from its lack of future.) Furthermore, as will be seen, the "money-for-immediate-goods-transaction" is ripe with futurity if looked at in the whole, rather than merely at the instant the exchange occurs. The last thing in the world I had in mind was excluding from the universe of contract immediate sales of goods, but I underestimated the obscuring power of ancient concepts, and indeed of ancient controversies. For one such skirmish, see Goble, *Is an Offer a Promise?*, 22 ILL. L. REV. 567 (1928); Williston, *Is an Offer a Promise?*, 22 ILL. L. REV. 788 (1928); Green, *Is an Offer Always a Promise?*, 23 ILL. L. REV. 95 (1928); Williston, *An Offer Is a Promise*, 23 ILL. L. REV. 100 (1928); and Green, *Is an Offer Always a Promise?*, 23 ILL. L. REV. 301 (1928). This sequence is reproduced in that ancient book, so well known to first year law students in the 1930's, 1940's, and 1950's, SELECTED READINGS ON THE LAW OF CONTRACTS 203-28 (1931).

2 When the term "contractual relations" is used, as it is here, to refer to contracts towards the relational end of the spectrum, the term of course fails to exhaust the universe of contract.

3 Throughout the Article, the words "contract" and "contracts" are used generically to encompass *the entire spectrum* of contract, from the most discrete, including immediate barters or sales, to the most relational. In this usage, the most immediate exchange of existing goods is a contract, *see supra* note 1, as is a marriage or other such small relations, and the relations of everyone inside corporations—employees (managerial and non-managerial), stockholders, and directors—as well as outside them, no matter how big the corporations are.

4 If one presses the term contract to encompass all exchange relations interlinked up to and including the world economy, all contracts are part of larger contracts up to and including that world economy. There is then no internal or external. Nonetheless, for many purposes, both real and analytical, it is necessary or desirable to stop somewhere along the line and consider a particular contract as a semi independent relation with internal and external aspects.

The difficulty of distinguishing internal from external is illustrated by private "positive law." Leagues impose law on professional athletic teams; trade associations impose law on businesses; the American Association of University Professors imposes law on universities; churches impose law on families. Such law is either internal or external, depending upon how one wishes to look at it. The same is true of more horizontal impositions, such as customs, and not only those horizontal impositions of people or groups closely related to a particular contract, such as trade customs,

inter alia, current social mores, public opinion, responses of the Fourth Estate— which includes the modern media—conceptualizing by people who think, speak, and write about contract, and political responses short of positive law, as well as the positive law of the sovereign.

The third dimension is the level of values being discussed. Are they, for example, utilitarian values, or are they values reflecting some other, perhaps deeper, level of morality than mere utility? If they reflect some other level of morality, what is that morality and what is its source?[5]

The Article will be organized around only two of the three dimensions: the overarching contract dimension and value-arenas of contracts. The third dimension will be omitted. Moreover, no effort will be made to erect a comprehensive "system" of values.[6]

II. The Contract Dimension

I have explored the contract dimension at length elsewhere[7] and

---

but also horizontal impositions of broader origin, such as customs of civilized intercourse in the particular society.

5 I wish to disclaim any idea that the theory of relational contract developed in this Article is a comprehensive "system" of values based on utilitarianism, natural law, or any other dogma.

In his review of THE NEW SOCIAL CONTRACT, *supra* note 1, Elliott states that "the message of the book is . . . that the presence of contract defines 'society,' and that the norms of contract are not so much reflective of social formations as identical with them." *Id.* at 351. Later, he refers to a "new and all inclusive social theory." *Id.* He is correct in divining my thoughts, except that the words "identical" and "all inclusive" go too far. Two factors in my "system" preclude claims to such comprehensiveness. First, as will be seen, one of the contract norms inserts into *all* contracts an historical element. *See infra* note 17 and *infra* text accompanying notes 180-205. Since I offer no theory or system of history, much less a comprehensive one, this leaves the system I suggest a less than comprehensive system. Second, one of the relational norms, called "supracontract norms," invites the introduction of additions to my system; thus, to whatever extent every contract is relational, another potential incompleteness exists in the "system."

I believe my system to be further incomplete, because it does not offer an "all inclusive" theory of personality, which would also be necessary to complete it. Among many omissions is the following: is there a basic human need for being treated as a whole person in relations with others? My relational contract theory does not deal with that issue. Yet, to the extent such a need exists, application of my theory may call for an answer to that question. For example, such a need would affect the very possibility of discreteness being successful in particular circumstances, to say nothing of suggesting limits on the viability of the bureaucratic approach to life. In my own ideological "powering" of the theory, *see infra* text accompanying notes 238-44, I add such a need, but that addition is not part of the overall theory itself as described in THE NEW SOCIAL CONTRACT.

This disclaimer of completeness is made for at least the foregoing reasons. Moreover, I do not believe that useful, complete, and internally logical systems can ever be developed respecting human behavior or human societies. To that can also be added an immense distrust of any closed system of social analysis.

6 *See* discussion *supra* note 5.

7 This Article continues work on discrete and relational contract conducted over a period of years. The following will be referred to occasionally: I. Macneil, Exchange Revisited: Individual Utility and Social Solidarity (1982)(unpublished manuscript)[hereinafter, I. Macneil, Exchange

will limit the re-exploration here as much as possible. Nonetheless, it is important to stress the highly relational character of *all* contracts in real life. Exchange of any importance is impossible outside a society. Even the purest discrete exchange necessarily postulates a social matrix providing at least the following: (1) a means of communication understandable to both parties; (2) a system of order so that the parties exchange instead of killing and stealing; (3) typically, in modern times, a system of money; and (4) in the case of exchanges promised, an effective mechanism to enforce promises.[8]

This social matrix is, of course, the minimum necessary for exchange; it takes great imagination to produce examples of exchange, in any society, with as few relations as the minimum. Consider what *seems* a very discrete transaction—the purchase of gasoline at a service station along a superhighway.

> [E]xcept for the expectation of the driver that the station would have gasoline available and the expectation of the station that any driver stopping would have some means of paying, the exchange has no past. There are no precedent relations between the parties. Nor will there be any future relations between the parties. As to the present, two general characteristics dominate the transaction: it is short; it is limited in scope. A few minutes measure its duration, and no one, even the most gregarious, enters into anything approaching a total human relationship in such a situation. In such a transaction the measured exchange, gallons/dollars, is what matters. Without it, the pleasantries, the little extras of service and courtesies have no real meaning; with it those immeasurables are an added fillip and no more.[9]

Although this transaction is very discrete, relations exist beyond the four minima.[10] Customs dictating which side of the pump a car going a particular direction should use, that the driver should move his car

---

Revisited]; Macneil, *Efficient Breach of Contract: Circles in the Sky*, 68 VA. L. REV. 947 (1982) [hereinafter, Macneil, *Efficient Breach*]; Macneil, *Economic Analysis of Contractual Relations: Its Shortfalls and the Need for a "Rich Classificatory Apparatus,"* 75 NW. U.L. REV. 1018 (1981)[hereinafter, Macneil, *Economic Analysis*]; I. MACNEIL, THE NEW SOCIAL CONTRACT, *supra* note 1; Macneil, *Contracts: Adjustment of Long-Term Economic Relations Under Classical, Neoclassical, and Relational Contract Law*, 72 NW. U.L. REV. 854 (1978)[hereinafter, Macneil, *Adjustment*]; Macneil, *The Many Futures of Contracts*, 47 S. CAL. L. REV. 691 (1974)[hereinafter, Macneil, *Many Futures*]; Macneil, *Restatement (Second) of Contracts and Presentiation*, 60 VA. L. REV. 589 (1974) [hereinafter, Macneil, *Presentiation*].

[8] *See* I. MACNEIL, THE NEW SOCIAL CONTRACT, *supra* note 1, at 11.

[9] Macneil, *Many Futures*, *supra* note 7, at 720-21.

[10] The only minimum element perhaps slightly hidden in this transaction is that of promise. The gasoline purchase, however, inevitably involves some credit: Either the tank is filled before payment or after; in either case credit, and with it promise, occurs. This may be obscured by the fact that the sources of "enforcement mechanisms" are customs and laws *against theft* rather than laws purporting to enforce promises. The time involved in the transaction is so short that a failure to pay or a failure to deliver paid-for gasoline would be viewed as deliberate from the start, and hence a theft, rather than a breach of a promise initially intended to be kept. (An implied promise is nevertheless present, at least in the mind of the innocent party.)

while he goes to a restroom, and that he should not smoke around the gas tank, and, on the other side, customs dictating that the station attendant should clean the windshield and ask to check "under the hood," for example, are all integral parts of the relations between the parties. Moreover, the example omits relational characteristics present in many purchases of gasoline, such as brand loyalty and the use of credit cards. In addition, regulations in modern industrial societies add many other relations to the transaction. For example, the station operator maintains restrooms regulated by the oil company franchisor and sells gasoline meeting a range of legal standards. Thus, it is readily apparent that even a transaction deliberately chosen for its discreteness is deeply embedded in a wide range of interconnected relations.[11]

Perhaps even more important, the vast majority of exchange behavior takes place in far more relational patterns. These relations may be informal—for example, the relations between a regular customer to a supermarket who comes to know its manager, meatman, and checkout clerks—or they may be formal—for example, the relations between corporate bond trustee and holders of the bonds. Most common of all is a mixture of both formal and informal relations. But whatever the mixture of formal and informal, many important relational elements will be present.[12]

The foregoing is a simple description of contract behavior, and it will be noted that nothing has been said so far of values.[13] This brings us to the next dimension,the various arenas in which values emerge.

---

[11] It is, of course, possible to conjure up somewhat more discrete exchanges—for example, a purchase of a nonbrand-name item in a foreign country one expects to leave immediately and never visit again. Nonetheless, it is amazing how relational even those exchanges can be. On a visit to Poland several years ago, my wife and I discovered that every Polish shopkeeper has a relative in the United States—most of them in Chicago—a fact that established relations even over the smallest and otherwise discrete purchase.

[12] These relational elements are summarized for modern contractual relations in I. MACNEIL, THE NEW SOCIAL CONTRACT, *supra* note 1, at 23-35. They include the following: primary personal relations; multiple participants; some utility that is difficult or impossible to measure or specify; internal sources of solidarity among participants; extended periods of commencement, duration, and termination; much planning of very different kinds from that of discrete transactions—planning for change, for example—but often incorporating very precise and binding planning as well; circumstances where future cooperation will be essential to the relation; sharing as well as dividing of benefits and burdens; obligations—general as well as specific—arising from the relation itself and also arising externally; in some ways not transferable to others, but transferable "en masse" (as in the case of the work force in a corporate takeover); different attitudes of participants to conflicts of interest, unity, time, and trouble; and complex power relations, including hierarchical.

[13] This is not true, of course, to whatever extent expressing a description itself is inherently prescriptive and hence constitutes a conclusion about values. As will be seen, I agree with the many social analysts, Marxist and non-Marxist, who argue that no social action, including simple description of even the obvious, is value-free, an apolitical act. My writing this description of contract is a social act, and inevitably a conscious ideological act, since I cannot avoid knowing—indeed hoping—that it might influence people's thinking in ways that ultimately could affect polit-

This Article will treat each of the three arenas identified earlier: contract behavior, internal principles and rules of that behavior, and external social responses. For reasons that will become apparent, the first two of these are so closely intertwined that they should, and probably must, be considered together. The many components of the third arena, external social responses, were stressed earlier, but in this Article space allows for treatment only of two: the positive law of the sovereign and conceptualizing about contracts.

III. Values in Context: Contract Behavior and its Internal Principles and Rules

The New Social Contract[14] sets out three classes of contract norms: common contract norms, discrete norms, and relational norms. These norms constitute "an abstract summary of the varied and specific norms appearing in myriad varieties of contracts."[15]

The common norms are essential to *any* behavior we might be willing to call contractual and they become, by conversion of is to ought,[16] principles of right action as well. Similarly, *given a discrete transaction*, the discrete norm reflects both behavior and the oughts growing out it, just as, *given relational contracts*, the relational norms reflect both behavior and the oughts emerging from it. So stated, however, these norms appear to be ahistorical.[17] To the extent the appear-

ical action. So, might it be added, are both the expressions and investigations of every positivist who ever lived.

It should be noted that the foregoing acceptance of subjectivity in all social analysis is not an acceptance "of the Marxist insight that engaging in political philosophy with knowledge of one's class position in class society inevitably reproduces the idea of the dominant class." Hyde, *Book Review*, 57 N.Y.U. L. Rev. 1031, 1058 (1982). Were that insight sound how does one explain the writings of the bourgeois Karl Marx? (Hyde's statement reminds me of the remark of Vishinski—born an aristocrat—to Aneurin Bevan—born a proletarian: "We are both traitors to our classes.") The observer's subjectivity may or may not lead to reproducing the idea of the dominant class.

The word "ideology," along with its various derivatives, is used extensively throughout this Article. It is a word of multiple meanings and of usage ranging from the simple, even simple-minded, to the most exquisitely sophisticated. One spectrum of meaning relates to the neutrality of the word itself. At one end it may be used in a relatively neutral descriptive sense, see R. Geuss, The Idea of a Critical Theory: Habermas and the Frankfurt School 4-12 (1981); at the other its very definition may encapsulate a comprehensive sociopolitical theory, complete with ideas of cognitive falsity and correctness. *Id.* at 12-22. My usage is, I hope, not simple-minded, but it is not intended to be very sophisticated, and it lies towards a neutrally descriptive usage. I recognize that even definitions—or perhaps particularly definitions—carry ideological content; by use of the word, I want merely to convey the notion expressed in the second preceding paragraph.

14 *Supra* note 1.

15 I. Macneil, The New Social Contract, *supra* note 1, at 39.

16 Rejection of the possibility of such a conversion is often attributed to Hume. For a recent questioning of this conventional wisdom, see Milton, *David Hume and the Eighteenth-Century Conception of Natural Law*, 2 Legal Stud. 14 (1982).

17 The appearance is misleading because when one of the common norms—harmonization of

ance reflects reality, they can have only circumscribed analytical value, if one believes, as I do, that norms and values cannot sensibly be discussed in any ultimate or global sense outside a particular historical context.[18]

Given the intertwining of these norms in behavior, principle, and rule, they encompass the two merged value-arenas of contract behavior and internal principles and rules. The common contract norms are then, in my view, *the* values in the internal (as opposed to external) arenas of contracts whether the contracts are discrete or relational. It is therefore necessary to describe them here briefly and also to suggest some modifications from their earlier statement in *The New Social Contract*.

A. *Common Contract Norms*

The ten common contract norms are (1) role integrity (requiring consistency, involving internal conflict, and being inherently complex), (2) reciprocity (simply stated as the principle of getting something back for something given[19]), (3) implementation of planning, (4) effectuation of consent, (5) flexibility, (6) contractual solidarity, (7) the restitution, reliance, and expectation interests (the "linking norms"), (8) creation and restraint of power (the "power norm"), (9) propriety of means,[20] and (10) harmonization with the social matrix.[21] Although all the com-

---

the contract with the social matrix in which it occurs—is applied, it removes the ahistoricity of all the norms whenever considered other than entirely abstractly. I. MACNEIL, THE NEW SOCIAL CONTRACT, *supra* note 1, at 57-59. *See infra* text accompanying notes 180-205.

18 Historical as opposed to ahistorical analysis is discussed *infra* text accompanying notes 180-205.

19 In THE NEW SOCIAL CONTRACT, the term used for this concept was "mutuality." There, the mutuality norm was developed in terms of "evenness" in exchange—a kind of limiting factor: "Some evenness of exchange, some mutuality, is a sine qua non norm without which contractual relations will not work." I. MACNEIL, THE NEW SOCIAL CONTRACT, *supra* note 1, at 46. While I have no reason to retreat from this notion per se, it now seems to me too limiting and too negative.

20 The closest I have come to articulating this key norm before this Article has been references to procedural justice in Macneil, *Adjustment*, *supra* note 7, at 898 and in I. MACNEIL, THE NEW SOCIAL CONTRACT, *supra* note 1, at 70. Not only is the term "procedural justice" far too narrow and culture-limited, but also in both instances I referred to it only as an example of a supracontract norm—that is, a particularly relational norm—not a common contract norm. The norms of role integrity and solidarity also imply propriety of means, but I did not see that in them from the start. A paper prepared for the Westminster Conference, *see supra* note *, B. Reiter & E. Belobaba, Good Faith in Contracts, finally triggered full recognition of this essential norm. (Although the paper was a joint work, the parts referred to here will appear in final form in 17 VAL. U.L. REV. 208 (1983) with Reiter as the sole author. For this reason the paper is hereinafter referred to as Reiter, *Good Faith*.) It may be noted that to the extent that Reiter's concept of good faith—relevant-community standards of appropriate behavior—embodies obligations to use only proper *means*—avoiding deceit, for example—the addition of propriety of means as a common contract norm incorporates good faith directly into relational contract theory.

21 Reiter, *Good Faith*, *supra* note 20, may be suggesting that the substantive aspects of good faith—relevant-community standards of appropriate behavior—are an additional common con-

mon contract norms are essential elements of contract behavior and constitute the values of such behavior, two of them call for special notice: contractual solidarity and reciprocity.

As students of man in society, we are faced with an illogicality. Man is both an entirely selfish creature and an entirely social creature,[22] in that man puts the interests of his fellows ahead of his own interests *at the same time* that he puts his own interests first. Such a creature is schizophrenic, and will, to the extent that it does anything except vibrate in utter frustration, constantly alternate between inconsistent behaviors—selfish one second and self-sacrificing the next. Man is, in the most fundamental sense of the word, irrational, and no amount of reasoning, no matter how sophisticated, will produce a complete and consistent account of human behavior, customs, or institutions.[23] Two principles of behavior are essential to the survival of such a creature: solidarity and reciprocity. Man, being a choosing creature, is easily capable of paralysis of decision when two conflicting desires are in equipoise.[24] The two principles of solidarity and reciprocity, neither of which can operate through time without the other,[25] solve this problem.[26] Getting something back for something given neatly re

tract norm. In terms of substantive norms, however, I have found nothing in the content of good faith requiring additional contract norms. I believe that, apart from the propriety of the means aspect of good faith, *see supra* note 20, the essence of good faith in any society is adherence to the common contract norms. If a person has sufficiently met those norms in any given instance—something that can never be determined except in a particular historic social context—the person has acted in good faith; if the person has not met those norms, he has not acted in good faith. (This is not, of course, to pass judgment on the usefulness in various circumstances of organizing the examination of social and legal phenomena one way or another.)

22 For lack of better words, these conflicting traits will, when considered in collective terms, sometimes be encompassed in the words "individualism" and "communalism."

23 It is the existence of this duality—which leads, *inter alia*, to the fact that we *can* choose—and the irrationality of it that enables us to think in terms of "ought"—of "right" and "wrong." After all, we do not say that quasars "ought" to follow certain paths or that sharks "ought not" to eat fish—or even people—because the kind of irrationality found in our own existence does not, so far as we know, exist in quasars or sharks. The fundamental rights and wrongs of human existence appear to derive from man as a biological phenomenon blessed or cursed with this peculiar social-antisocial irrationality. Ramifications of this aspect of human nature in terms of exchange, utility, and solidarity are discussed in I. Macneil, Exchange Revisited, *supra* note 7.

For a recent discussion of a somewhat similar "obstinate dualism" in the personality of Sigmund Freud, see Freud's words in Simon-Miller, *Ambivalence and Identification: Freud on Literature (Part I)*, 28 LITERATURE & PSYCHOLOGY 23, 26 (1978):

> My emotional life has always insisted that I should have an intimate friend and a hated enemy. I have always been able to provide myself afresh with both, and it has not infrequently happened that the ideal situation of childhood has been so completely reproduced that friend and enemy have come together in a single individual.

Id. (quoting S. FREUD, INTERPRETATION OF DREAMS (1900)).

24 Hamlet is the classic, or at least the modern classic, example of a person trapped by two conflicting desires

25 The need for reciprocity is as great but not as apparent in mechanical solidarity the massing of likes—as it is in organic solidarity—the linking of the diverse.

26 The problems of potential paralysis of decision are never solved and the tensions of selfish-

leases, or at least reduces, the tension in a creature desiring to be both selfish and social at the same time;[27] and solidarity—a belief in being able to depend on another—permits the projection of reciprocity through time.[28]

While all the contract norms operate in the behavior and in the internal principles and rules of all kinds of contracts, some assume special importance in discrete transactions and others assume special importance in contractual relations. In addition, a contextual transformation or merger of some of these norms may occur. For these reasons, analysis of the differences between discrete transactions and contractual relations is aided by outlining the common norms constituting the basis of the discrete norm and those constituting the bases of the relational norms.

B. *Common Contract Norms and the Discrete Norm: Enhancing Discreteness and Presentiation*

As will be seen, the discrete norm is the product of the intensification of two common contract norms: implementation of planning and effectuation of consent.

> Discreteness and presentiation are themselves not the same phenomenon, in spite of their merger in discrete contracts. Discreteness is the separating of a transaction from all else between the participants at the same time and before and after. Its ideal, never achieved in life, occurs when there *is* nothing else between the parties, never has been, and never will be. Presentiation, on the other hand, is the bringing to the future into the present. Underlying both is the ideal of 100 percent planning of the future.[29]

The closer the parties are to behaving and governing themselves in accordance with this discrete norm, the more they will choose planning that is completely binding (or as close to completely binding as they

ness and sociality are never finally resolved until death, if then. Rather, they are always in the process of being solved and resolved in an ever unfolding process of behavior.

[27] My wife and I recently saw a poignant illustration of the intense strength of the reciprocity norm while eating lunch in a small park outside a McDonald's restaurant in Chicago. An elderly derelict was digging through the many trash barrels, salvaging and ravenously gobbling down the bits of sandwiches and other food left by the more affluent. A young woman, watching this, quietly went over and handed him her own unopened lunch. She turned and walked away. Instead of eating the lunch, he began digging away in the small bundle of his belongings, pulled out a pretty scarf he had salvaged from somewhere, and started to follow her to make a reciprocal gift. But she, young and swift, and perhaps somewhat embarrassed by her own generosity, walked away too fast for him to catch her. It was with real disappointment that he gave up, returned the treasure to the bundle, and ate his gift lunch. Here was someone about as isolated from his society as one can be who nevertheless felt intensely the need to reciprocate, even though the other person clearly never dreamed of such reciprocation.

[28] Countless biological and other needs can be satisfied only if reciprocity can be projected through time; truly immediate reciprocity is rare.

[29] I. Macneil, The New Social Contract, *supra* note 1, at 60.

can get), thereby bringing the future into the present as much as is humanly possible.

C. *Common Contract Norms and the Relational Norms*

The relational norms of role integrity, preservation of the relation, harmonization of relational conflict, and supracontract norms[30] are also intensifications of particular common contract norms. These are primarily role integrity, contractual solidarity, and harmonization with the social matrix. In addition, relational contexts affect the nature of other common norms. For example, flexibility in relations is at least partially an internal, rather than an entirely external norm as it is (in theory) in discrete transactions. Hence, flexibility comes into partial conflict with the planning and consent norms in ways not occurring in discrete transactions. Reciprocity also becomes an important internal

---

[30] I have stated in an earlier article that

> As contractual relations expand, those relations take on more and more the characteristics of minisocieties and ministates. . . . In the case of huge bundles of contractual relations, such as a major national or multinational corporation, they take on the characteristics of large societies and large states. But whether small or large, the whole range of social and political norms become pertinent *within* contractual relations. In ongoing contractual relations we find such broad norms as distributive justice, liberty, human dignity, social equality and inequality, and procedural justice, to mention some of the more vital.

Macneil, *Adjustment*, *supra* note 7, at 898.

The term "supracontract norms" was adopted not because these norms "are beyond the bounds of contractual relations, but because they are not *particularly* contractual." I. MACNEIL, THE NEW SOCIAL CONTRACT, *supra* note 1, at 70. Use of the term enabled me to avoid facing the full implications of "promulgation of a new and all inclusive social theory." Elliott, *supra* note 1, at 351. The brashness of promulgating such a theory, especially "in the absence of a critical examination of competing theoretical explanations," *id.*, is more than I want to admit to, then or now. To the extent that I have moved in the direction of promulgating "a new and all inclusive social theory," my only excuse is that these various norms seemed from the start a sound analysis of *mini*-contract, where I *have* examined competing theoretical explanations. *See* Macneil, *Presentiation*, *supra* note 7. Once I had applied my "contract theory" at the mini-contract level, there was no stopping it; I found that it applied to ordinary forward contracts as well as to such arrangements as collective bargaining, franchises, and corporate structures and their countless interlinkages with society. Nor could I find a place to stop there. See, for example, the discussion of homeowners associations—supposedly contractual—and cities—supposedly sovereign, in Ellickson, *Cities and Homeowners Associations*, 130 U. PA. L. REV. 1519 (1982). The "contract theory" has carried me to all aspects of political and sovereign life. As an acquaintance recently said, when I asked him what he did: "I am in the family business now, and no longer practicing law But what's the difference? I used to think business, law, and politics were different, but now I think they are all the same."

Once contract is perceived to encompass all aspects of life, there can be no supracontract norms that are not *particularly* contractual. Norms such as "distributive justice, liberty, human dignity, social equality and inequality, and procedural justice," I. MACNEIL, THE NEW SOCIAL CONTRACT, *supra* note 1, at 70, are then contract norms; to the extent they are essential to contractual behavior, they are common norms, not just relational norms. If the reader keeps in mind that their existence as possible common contract norms prevents relational contract theory as I have expressed it from being "all inclusive," I shall be content.

matter lest the relation break down.[31] Power also is an important internal matter in relations.[32]

D. *Commentary*

The level of values I have been discussing—values of contract behavior and of internal principles and rules—is an extremely important one. It is also one too often partially or entirely overlooked in contract scholarship,[33] which tends to focus either on the next level—the response, especially the legal response, of external society to contract—or on only the discrete transactional aspects of this level. The importance stems from the fact that this is the real operating level—the real life level of exchange relations. Consequently, this is the level at which implementation of values undoubtedly has by far the greatest impact upon the lives of the participants and everyone affected by their activities. The norms generated internally in billions of contractual relations are the most important in determining the value patterns of the overall society in which they occur. A more complete analysis of those norms is, therefore, appropriate before considering the next value-arena.

1. *Common Contract Norms*.—It should be noted that since the common contract norms are present in all contracts, they give rise to whatever values emerge from all contract behavior and our assessment of it. Those norms and their interplay permit the widest possible range of "successful" human activity and interaction.[34]

The only time these norms are not present and therefore do not give rise to oughts is when contract is not operating. Nevertheless, they do not necessarily blossom fully in all contractual relations at all times. Contractual relations fall along a "success spectrum." Those contractual relations operating effectively will reveal the common contract

---

[31] It may, of course, also be an external norm. See the discussion concerning sovereign imposition of the reciprocity norm, *infra* text accompanying notes 99-124.

[32] There is a fundamental difficulty in the very idea of internal norms in discrete transactions; the instantaneous nature of the theoretical discrete transaction precludes any norm from being internal, because such a transaction has no insides due to the absence of relation. Thus an "internal" norm of any kind in a purely discrete transaction—if one can contemplate such a fictional transaction—exists solely because of external forces. Even so, the parties behave *as if* the norm were internal to a relation between them, because of those external pressures. For that reason, the discussion in this Article proceeds as if discrete transactions could have internal norms. This is not unrealistic, since no real life transaction is truly discrete. All transactions are relational in considerable degree. *See supra* text accompanying notes 7-11.

[33] This is the case whether the scholarship is that of legal academics, modern philosophers, or social scientists—especially economists.

[34] I have no doubt that those norms operated in the bands of Genghis Kahn, the feudalism of Anglo-Norman England, and the most vicious of early capitalist factories. They also operated in Athens of the Golden Age (among both freemen and slaves), in Sweden of the Middle Way, and in the Quaker's Peaceable Kingdom. Today they operate in IBM, a liberal arts college, a small family business, a Polish state enterprise, and a Russian collective farm.

norms in robust condition, while those in varying degrees of trouble will reveal the common contract norms in varying degrees of disarray, both as they affect contract behavior and as they affect the internal rules and principles of that behavior. Uganda, both before and after Idi Amin, offers an excellent example of how contract norms disappear as a large contractual relation—the nation and its economy—falls apart; at a more microcosmic level, most any failure of a marriage will illustrate the point.

Lest the foregoing be taken as unthinking adoption of an exclusively consensus theory a comment concerning conflict versus consensus is in order here. In a review of the *New Social Contract*, Foster says:

> As political theory, the book is flawed by its Durkheimian premise of social solidarity. The state as an instrument of class domination and control, or as a bureaucratic organization resting on legitimated domination are theories pushed to one side. Like Durkheim, Macneil appears to see the State as representing the collective organ of moral conscience. Conflict is then a disfunctional disruption of this collective morality. The law's function is to restore the harmony of society. This may be a defensible theorectical position but it needs more explicit argument than Macneil offers. His political values slip into the book as if they were non-problematic and shared by everyone; a not unusual error of consensus theorists.[35]

The relational contract theory set out in the *New Social Contract* is far from incompatible with theories of the state as an instrument of class domination and control or as a bureaucratic organization resting on legitimated domination. Indeed, I accept such theories of the state to a considerable extent myself. Those theories are incompatible with the theory of "the State as representing" *a* "collective organ of moral conscience" *only* if one believes that a conflict theory and a consensus theory must be incompatible. This I do not believe.[36] Nor do I view conflict as entirely dysfunctional, as Foster implies. A propensity for conflict is a fact of human nature and no more dysfunctional than any other limiting factor in our nature, such as our inability to understand completely both ourselves and the world around us or our restricted range of ways to communicate with one another. In this sense, our propensity to conflict is simply something to which we accommodate ourselves, just as is our propensity to cooperate. Whether actual conflict is functional or dysfunctional in any given circumstance cannot be

35 Foster, Book Review, 9 BRIT. J.L. & SOC'Y 144, 147 (1982).

36 This belief is, of course, a political value. As already noted, and as will be developed at greater length further on, I believe that all writers, not excluding Foster, slip their political values into their writing as if those political values were nonproblematic and shared by everyone.

Although I believe the state has a role respecting the common conscience, it should be apparent from THE NEW SOCIAL CONTRACT that I consider the modern bureaucratic state a relatively poor provider on that score. Indeed, another political value I hold is that the scarcity of nonbureaucratic producers of a common conscience is perhaps our major modern social problem.

answered abstractly. Nevertheless, I would have thought that it is a truism that uncontrolled conflict is the antithesis of continuing social behavior. In this sense, wherever there is continuing social behavior among a particular group, the very existence of the group shows that consensus is resolving the problems raised by conflict sufficiently to allow that existence.[37] Elsewhere, I have discussed the fact that this kind of consensus is only a tension between conflict and cooperation.[38] It does not eliminate conflict in some magical way, as Foster seems to imply.

It is Gurvitch, I believe, who has captured most clearly the spirit of the relation between conflict and consensus in contractual relations:

> The jural bond established by a contract consists simultaneously of (a) a convergence of wills of the contracting parties with a view to establishing a mutual obligation valid in the future *(rapprochement)* and (b) the opposition of two or more wills seeking exactly opposite aims and establishing opposing duties (to give something or to receive it, etc.: separation). Again, the contracting parties are in a harmony of rights and interests in so far as execution of the contract is concerned *(rapprochement)* and in a conflict of rights and interests insofar as material clauses and manner of carrying them out are concerned (separation). That is why it is impossible to characterize unequivocally, as has often been erroneously attempted, the contractual relationship, whether as a *consensus* of wills and duties (Durkheim), or as their conflict and delimitation (Tonnies). The secret of contractual bonds, as well as of exchanges in general, various sorts of obligations and the like, lies in the intercourse of *rapprochement* and separation.[39]

Both the possibility of high conflict levels in contractual relations and the vast range of character of successful, that is surviving, contractual relations mentioned earlier[40] raise questions about the usefulness of the "oughts" arising out of the common contract norms. These norms seem to provide so little basis for moral discrimination among such a wide range of behavior that few would be content solely with the

---

37 Consensus must not be confused with cheerful willingness or anything like it. For example, consensus, uneasy though it may be, governs relations of prisoners and guards alike in a prison at any time until a riot erupts. Indeed, consensus governs even after a riot breaks out, unless the prisoners or guards, or both, go truly berserk, as occasionally happens. For a recent discussion of significant differences for social theory between conformity resulting from commitment and conformity resulting from coercion, calculation, and the like, see DiTomaso, *"Sociological Reductionism" from Parsons to Althusser: Linking Action and Structure in Social Theory*, 47 AM. SOC. REV. 14 (1982).

38 I. Macneil, Exchange Revisited, *supra* note 7 (unavailable to Foster when he reviewed THE NEW SOCIAL CONTRACT).

39 G. GURVITCH, SOCIOLOGY OF LAW 172-73 (1947). For a vivid account of contractual relations with very high conflict levels but which nonetheless survived tenaciously for generations until destroyed, mainly by external forces, in the Civil War, see J. OAKES, THE RULING RACE—A HISTORY OF AMERICAN SLAVEHOLDERS 179-91 (1982) [hereinafter J. OAKES, RULING RACE].

40 *See supra* note 37.

resulting broad-brush naturalistic morality they suggest.[41]

Nevertheless, we should not sneer at norms purporting to reflect nothing more than successful social behavior. The brute social human may not provide all the norms of our higher aspirations, but what he provides is much more than the normative zero that the mythical Hobbesian individual human provides.[42] What social man provides is also in many ways more useful for analysis than more controversial higher levels dependent upon greater ideological consensus.[43] It is true

---

41 Professor Fried's comments are pertinent here: "The persistence of this view that naturalism is fallacious is in large part due to the fact that the attempts to show that one can derive an "ought" from an "is" rely on some very fishy, fancy, and suspiciously "ought"-like "is"es from which to launch the derivation." Fried, *Biology and Ethics: Normative Implications*, in MORALITY AS A BIOLOGICAL PHENOMENON: THE PRESUPPOSITIONS OF SOCIOBIOLOGICAL RESEARCH 186 (G. Stent ed. 1980).

I see nothing fancy or fishy about deriving "ought" from the "is" of human behavior, but I certainly agree that it is easy to slip one's favorite oughts through the back door into is and then out the front door as ought. It may be noted that it is just as easy to do the same thing with formal models; indeed, it is easier. I would argue that *all* jurisprudents are naturalists, the formalistic ones being closet naturalists. *See* Macneil, *Lon Fuller: Nexusist*, 26 AM. J. JURISPRUDENCE 219 (1981)[hereinafter, Macneil, *Lon Fuller*].

For a useful recent bibliography of "naturalist" philosophy, see Silver, *Men, Monkeys, and Morals: A Property Rights Theory of Social Justice*, in SOCIAL JUSTICE 121, 143 n.60 (R. Braham ed. 1981).

42 T. HOBBES, LEVIATHAN (Everyman's ed. 1914).

The word "social" is used loosely in the sentence in the text as well as elsewhere throughout this Article to convey the idea of the essential psychic and other interconnectedness of humans with other humans, i.e. the opposite of the Hobbesian lone individual. It is not intended to differentiate, for example, the interconnectedness involved in small or other groups from that involved in the whole society, a distinction made, for example, in Garet, *Community and Existence: The Rights of Groups*, 56 S. CAL. L. REV. 1001 (1983).

43 For recent contrasts in legal scholarship, see Kennedy, *Distributive and Paternalist Motives in Contract and Tort Law, With Special Reference to Compulsory Terms and Unequal Bargaining Power*, 41 MD. L. REV. 563 (1982)[hereinafter Kennedy, *Paternalist Motives*], and R. POSNER, THE ECONOMICS OF JUSTICE (1981).

James Bayley, after accepting that some morality, such as truth telling, can be derived from our "social nature," rejects the idea that justice can be derived from our social nature. Bayley, *Human Nature and Justice*, in SOCIAL JUSTICE, *supra* note 41, at 1, 9-10. He sees circular reasoning in trying to do so because "we cannot know what justice is until we know what our nature is, and we cannot properly shape our nature until we know what justice is." *Id.* at 10. Also, he sees justice as more regulatory than subservient to social nature, since justice, but not our social nature, precludes slavery and wars of conquest.

If, however, we define justice as the total of the moralities we can derive from human nature, without an additional regulatory aspect, there is no problem with the idea of a "social nature justice" such as that encompassed by the common contract norms. Even slavery and wars of conquest can at least tentatively be judged by such a standard. Where conquering or enslaving someone violates the common contract values—because of lack of reciprocity, for example—the action may be criticized on the ground that such behavior would clearly be immoral as to persons conceded to be members of the same exchange relation. To the response, "The victims are being treated as strangers because they *are* strangers," morality based on our social nature may have no answer. Nonetheless, it can supply some minimal standards of morality for anyone responsive to a sense that no other human is a total stranger. That this is not a totally satisfactory answer hardly

that ideology will affect agreement and disagreement about the content of such naturalistic norms, but surely less so than for norms starting from liberal idealism or Marxist determinism. If, for example, reciprocity is accepted as a fundamental norm for all social behavior, we can move some distance towards establishing quite a decent social morality. I do not, however, want to press the morality of the common contract norms too far at this point. I am still talking about *internal* behavior and norms, and it is therefore not yet necessary to deal with problems relating to the interface of given contractual relations with some larger society and its moralities.[44]

A significant difference between the discrete and relational norms and the common contract norms should now be stressed. I have claimed that contractual behavior cannot exist without the common contract norms. Relative dearth of the discrete or the relational norms does not destroy contractual relations.[45] Rather, dearth of the discrete or relational norms causes, respectively, the relation to become less discrete (more relational) or less relational (more discrete).

2. *The Discrete Norm*.—What does the existence of the discrete norm at the level of behavior and internal principles and rules imply about the values underlying that behavior? You will recall that the norm calls for enhancing discreteness and presentiation. I have described it in that way in a deliberate attempt to strip from it as much value as possible. Nevertheless, some of its values, at least, are immediately apparent.

a. Values of the Discrete Norm.—First, the discrete norm is a "norm of precision, a focusing norm. It enables people to deal precisely with one thing at a time—to keep their eyes on the ball—a vital factor in much human endeavour."[46] It is a value that everyone resists in some aspects of life, and that some people resist in all aspects of life to the extent it is possible to resist the value and still survive.[47] It is, thus, far from "neutral" or universal.

Second, where the norm governs, "following through" on planning irrespective of the consequences is what matters. Although *pacta sunt*

---

needs to be said, but it may well go as far towards establishing a "universal morality" as our peculiar social-antisocial characteristics permit.

44 The norm of harmonization with the social matrix, however, *is* that interface.

45 If the common contract norms underlying the discrete or relational norms disappear, then, of course, contractual behavior will disappear.

46 I. MACNEIL, THE NEW SOCIAL CONTRACT, *supra* note 1, at 63.

47 The value of precise focus is resisted even past the point at which it is possible to resist and still survive by many of those under the influence of various kinds of drugs and other psychological problems.

servanda[48] usually is thought to mean that choice-generated consent is binding, it must never be forgotten that it means equally *planning est servanda*. This planning value is both enhanced and limited by the other intensified common contract norm, that of implementing consent; consenting, where the norm of discreteness and presentiation operates, means what it says—the consenter is well and truly stuck. The emphasis on consent, however, is also a limiting factor, because together the participants can consent to change; thus, the norm of enhancing discreteness and presentiation does not prevent the parties from creating a new and different discrete presentiation any time they wish. Thus, the norm as it works in discrete transactions contains the seeds of its own destruction.

Third, discreteness "fits very well the concepts of efficiency developed in the neoclassical microeconomic model. Indeed, that is a tautology, since the discrete transaction is the basis of the model."[49] Thus, whatever are the values of patterning real contracting on the efficiency paradigm also are values of the discrete norm. I am not at all sure that these values differ in any respect from the other values discussed here. Nonetheless, given the prevalence of efficiency theory in economic analysis of law, this "efficiency value" should be mentioned.

Fourth, because the discrete norm is, in part, a great intensification of the norm of consent, and because of the origin of consent in choice, the discrete norm appears to promote the value of freedom of individuals to choose. This is what Charles Fried calls the liberal ideal, the ideal which "makes what we achieve our own and our failures our responsibility too."[50] But, the appearance that the discrete norm promotes the value of the autonomy of individuals—that is, the purported value of what Professor Fried calls the promise principle—is misleading.

Placing value on allowing people to make choices—to act free of restraint[51]—leads to placing value on not freeing persons of the consequences of their choices. Freeing them of such consequences would undo the choice and in significant ways would retroactively deprive them of the power of choice.[52] Consider, for example, a child required by a limited supply of money to make a choice on Saturday afternoon

48 Agreements are to be observed. This phrase, from Justinian, was the motto of Edward I, who took feudal obligations very seriously indeed.

49 I. MACNEIL, THE NEW SOCIAL CONTRACT, *supra* note 1, at 63 (citing Goldberg, *Toward an Economic Theory of Contract*, 10 J. ECON. ISSUES 45 (1976)).

50 C. FRIED, CONTRACT AS PROMISE: A THEORY OF CONTRACTUAL OBLIGATION 8 (1981) [hereinafter, C. FRIED, PROMISE].

51 It is only *social* restraint that concerns us here, not questions concerning how the remainder of the environment both provides opportunities for choice and constrains it.

52 Of course, one cannot really be deprived of choice retroactively, but the existence of the likelihood of such subsequent interference at the time putative choices are made constitutes an effective restraint on the power to choose.

between going to the movies and going to a video game arcade. The child goes to the movies. Then he goes to his parents and asks for money to play video games, saying that he regrets the choice he made. His freedom-loving parents will say: "You made a choice, and we will, in effect, deprive you retroactively of the power to act like a free being if we relieve you of the consequences of your choice by giving you the money you ask. We think it more important not to do that than to assauge your present unhappiness for having made a decision you have come to regret."

It does *not*, however, automatically follow that placing value on effective choice leads to placing value on consent to bind oneself in the future. Indeed, on the face of it, the individualistic premise suggests the opposite. The only way an autonomous individual *can* bind himself in the future is by invoking the power of the society of which he is a member—that is, by calling upon it to bind him, to deprive him of choice in the future. Even though the individual may have asked society to deprive him of his future choice, this social tying down of the individual appears to conflict with placing value on choice.

Consider, for example, the child just mentioned. It is the next Friday afternoon and his sister asks him if he will promise to go to the movies with her on Saturday. He promises. On Saturday, however, he decides he wants to go to the video game arcade instead, and goes to seek his parents' advice. They reply: "You chose to express promissory words to your sister. The consequence of that choice is that you can only go to the video game arcade by failing to do what you promised, and that will make your sister angry at you. As lovers of freedom we think it most inappropriate for us to relieve you of that consequence. So, if you go to the video game arcade, don't expect us to calm Sis down." The child responds: "Is that all? You are the law in this family. If I break my promise, isn't it up to you to do something about it?" The parents reply: "No. There is only one basis for law-making in this liberal family: the necessity to restrain each of its members from using his freedom to limit the freedom of the other members. We regret having to make laws even for this purpose, but there is no alternative. Sis might have claimed that your words infringed on her freedom and thereupon might have invoked that principle, but she has not. Nor are you invoking it, because you, who are free to choose between which of the two consequences of your prior choice you wish to suffer, are asking us to limit your freedom to choose by adding some legal sanctions in favor of one of the two choices now facing you. You are, in short, asking us to use our lawmaking power to tie you down, to make you unfree, to enslave you. This we will not do." The child gives up and either goes to the movies, suffering the loss of the preferred video games, or enjoys the latter and endures a disappointed and angry sister.

Had the child been of an age to read Charles Fried, he would have discovered the only justification for enforcing promises—for converting choice into consent—consistent with the value of autonomy: "The restrictions involved in promising are restrictions undertaken just in order to increase one's options in the long run, and thus are perfectly consistent with the principle of autonomy—consistent with a respect for one's own autonomy and the autonomy of others."[53] Following this line, the child might have said: "By adding sanctions to enforce my promises, you will increase my options in the long run. Thereby you will make me even more autonomous. This belief of yours in autonomy yields a second legal principle: restraint is justified if it will increase options and make the individual more autonomous over time. You should therefore add legal sanctions to my promise to Sis."

Professor Fried's (and the child's) argument is one based on empirical consequences, not a deduction from the principle of autonomy. As such, it is always subject to challenge on the ground that in various particular circumstances the claimed increase does or does not, will or will not, occur. Thus, the parents' reply should be: "Maybe adding legal sanctions to your words will make you more autonomous by increasing your options in the long run and maybe it won't. That is an empirical question worth exploring in the circumstance of this family."

The parents are right; it certainly is not correct that surrendering autonomy by asking the legal system to add sanctions to the surrender will always increase options—sometimes it will and sometimes it will not. To the extent promises do in fact "increase one's options in the long run," giving effect to consent may be consistent with placing a value on free choice.[54] To the extent that promises reduce one's op-

53 C. FRIED, PROMISE, *supra* note 50, at 14.

54 It only "may be consistent" rather than "is consistent" because the phrase is ambiguous. Does it mean options in a total environmental sense, or only in terms of fewer long run social restraints on choice? What morality of autonomy results depends on the answer. The former meaning measures freedom in terms of the variety of choices actually available. A well educated, prosperous 20th century Russian is, under such an approach, far freer than were almost all 19th century frontier Americans. The social restraint meaning measures freedom not in terms of total number and variety of choices that might be available in the long run, but rather in terms of what part of those that might otherwise be available are precluded by social restraint. (This distinction is partially, but only partially, artificial, because it is never possible to analyze society separately from its environment except artificially.) Of the two, the social restraint analysis is far more consistent with the "liberal ideal" espoused by Professor Fried. Indeed, the multiplication of available choices in the total environment may in fact reduce autonomy, since *having* to choose is an important restriction on autonomy. The tyranny of choice can be immense.

My colleague, Anthony D'Amato, suggested to me that Professor Fried is making the following argument: Enabling a person to bind himself in the future adds to his total number of choices, simply because he can now choose to be bound in the future in addition to all other courses otherwise available to him. I do not read Professor Fried that way. Moreover, the route is fraught with problems. Since this additional choice is not, as Professor Fried demonstrates, something the individual can achieve by himself, such an argument depends on someone else—society—supplying a particular opportunity, namely the opportunity to be bound. But why should society supply this particular choice? The liberal ideal hardly requires society—consisting of autonomous indi-

tions in the long run, giving effect to consent is clearly inconsistent with placing a value on free choice.[55]

Because planning merges with choice in consent, and because both planning and consent are important in the discrete norm, the question whether the discrete norm places value on choice in any given circumstances depends on whether the consent has a net overall freeing effect or a net overall enslaving effect. This is not something that can be ascertained by ahistorical abstract analysis of the kind adopted by Professor Fried, but only by examining particular circumstances in their historical context.

Fifth, in one sense the discrete norm is conservative; it "presupposes the status quo and goes on from there."[56] But this is only part of its effect. Discreteness involves sharp focusing, it is consent-oriented, and it is related to efficiency in the technical sense; therefore, continual following of the discrete norm may be the path of great social and economic change. Indeed, the common view, accurate or not, of the putative heyday of discreteness in contract—the early-middle of the industrial revolution in Great Britain and America—is that dependence on the discrete norm led to significant social and economic change. Because of the opposing effects of the discrete norm on social change, however, we are again unable to make sound conclusions in the abstract about the values actually implemented, but must instead depend upon empirical study of particular historical contexts.

Sixth, the discrete norm looks equalitarian because choice appears to dominate. That appearance, however, is deceptive; the discrete norm is inequalitarian in its immediate effect to whatever the degree the status quo is inequalitarian, and generally more so. By presupposing the status quo, the discrete norm

> inevitably aids the already powerful and tends to make them more powerful . . . The norm also aids the powerful in capturing a larger part of the exchange-surplus than the less powerful. . . . [It is important] that we recognize the existence of this power bias of the discrete norm and not pretend an equality in it that does not exist.[57]

This immediately inequalitarian character of the discrete norm has stimulated many attacks on the norm on many intellectual, social, and political fronts. Nevertheless, the same comments may be made here

---

viduals, it will be recalled—to use its resources to add to the total supply of choices available to individuals, and certainly not to add any particular kind of choice to the individual's life. To argue that society should make available *this* particular kind of choice—the power to bind oneself by promise—requires going back to Professor Fried's empirical argument about the individual's long run options.

55 For a discussion of the effect of freedom of contract *(power* of contract) in either increasing or decreasing freedom in the society, see MAX WEBER, LAW IN ECONOMY AND SOCIETY 188 (M. Rheinstein trans. 1954).

56 I. MACNEIL, THE NEW SOCIAL CONTRACT, *supra* note 1, at 64.

57 *Id.* at 64.

that were made respecting the consent principles and conservatism. Whether, in a macro sense, the internal governance of contracts by the discrete norm is any more equalitarian than more relational alternatives is a matter for empirical historical investigation, and cannot be determined by abstract reasoning.

Seventh, and finally, the discrete norm requires the sacrifice of relational values of many kinds, because it focuses sharply on money and other easy-to-quantify subjects of exchange, it ignores the identity of the parties, and it uses precise promise as a touchstone. All of these aspects of the discrete norm not uncommonly conflict with such particularly relational values as preservation of the relation and harmonization of relational contract. Furthermore, they may conflict with role integrity as it appears *in relations*, as well as with various supracontract norms.

b. Relationship Between Values of the Discrete Norm and Values of the Other Common Contract Norms.—Although the discrete norm reflects the great intensification of two of the common contract norms—implementation of planning and effectuation of consent—the other eight do not—indeed, cannot—disappear if the contract is to be viable. Thus, everything that has been said about the values of the discrete norms must be read against a backdrop of the other common contract norms, but a backdrop itself vitally affected by the presence of the discrete norm. What follows is a brief discussion of the other eight common contract norms as they relate to the discrete norm.

In the face of discreteness, role integrity is maintained by each participant's "operating within rigid rules of property and law under which he will maximize his utility, but only to the extent that the other consents."[58] Reciprocity is served by the *mutual* consent process leading to the formation of the deal. After that, reciprocity drops out. Where discreteness prevails, however, there is theoretically no "after that" because the whole approach to the transaction is complete presentiation. Flexibility is achieved, not within the discrete transaction, where all is rigid presentiation, but outside it, in the repeated use of numerous discrete transactions. Contractual solidarity is maintained only through external forces, such as the law of contract, implementing the presentiated discrete transaction. The linking norms are served by equating restitution and reliance with expectation, and by the protection of expectation by the external forces fostering solidarity.[59]

In addition, propriety of means is established where the discrete

[58] *Id*. at 65.

[59] These three contract interests become identical in discrete transactions. For example, where a person enters a futures contract for the purchase of a commodity in six weeks, his expectation is exactly equal to whatever the market does during that period; his reliance is identical because had *this* seller not contracted with him, some other seller would have; and his restitution interest is

norm prevails by whatever the parties consent to in the agreement process. Where the agreement process does not explicitly deal with means, the discrete norm calls for whatever means are effective to accomplish the substantive results agreed upon. The free use of the full force of positive law in the event of backsliding clearly falls within this norm where discreteness prevails. The power norm is served by the existence of enforceability of the terms consented to as well as the limitation of all enforcement to such terms. There are no open-ended obligations.

Finally, the discrete norm must be harmonized with the social matrix, since it can be implemented only if the larger society in which it occurs is either willing to have it implemented or is unwilling to have it implemented but is unable to prevent implementation. The latter pattern cannot occur respecting any projection of the discrete transaction into the future, since such projection is dependent on the larger society's providing enforceability, the discrete transaction's version of contractual solidarity.[60]

From the foregoing discussion, it is apparent that the intensification of the planning and consent norms in discrete transactions affects the other common contract norms, often drastically. While this brief treatment of this interplay fails to show any need to add to or change items in the list of discrete values, it does sharpen the relief respecting some of them. For example, the fact that contractual solidarity exists in the discrete transaction only because of external force brings into sharp focus the questions raised earlier concerning the antichoice characteristics of the consent (promise) principle.

3. *The Relational Norms*.—The five norms of enhanced importance in ongoing contractual relations are role integrity, preservation of the relation, harmonization of relational conflict, propriety of means, and supracontract norms. Once again it should be stressed that, except to the extent that they are also common contract norms, the relational norms are not essential to contract behavior, they are simply essential to *relational* contract behavior, just as the discrete norm is essential to discrete transaction behavior. Their disappearance from any given contractual relation thus may or may not end all contract behavior among the parties to the contract. All contractual behavior between the participants is in danger of ending only if the relational norms are

identical, because he has conferred on the seller an opportunity for speculation exactly equal in value to his own.

60 Only contractual relations can supply their own *internal* enforcement mechanisms enabling the projection of exchange into the future; the discrete transaction is dependent on something external—law, for example—for such enforcement. (Law is what usually first comes to mind, at least to the mind of lawyers.) It is this, among other things, that precludes the real life existence of a truly discrete transaction with a future.

so eroded that the common contract norms underlying them are unfulfilled.

a. Values of the Relational Norms.—Role integrity, a common contract norm, becomes a very complex value in contractual relations, involving as it does intricate linkings of habit, custom, internal principles and rules, social exchange and other social principles, dependence, expectations, and much else. Moreover, relational roles tend to be long term and to involve primary relations and diverse obligations. Role integrity becomes "more than simply keeping the rule honest; . . . maintaining its integrity in the sense of keeping it together in a coherent piece is a major job of social engineering. Particularly is this so in the face of . . . internal conflicts in roles."[61]

The norm of preservation of the relation "is an intensification and expansion of the norm of contractual solidarity . . . [It] involves preservation of particular memberships in relations—individual preservation—as well as preservation of the larger relation—collective preservation."[62] (Preservation of the larger relation and individual preservation of membership can easily come into conflict.)

The peaceable value, harmonization of relational conflict, is almost distinguishable from its underlying role of preserving relations; peace is valued in its own right. One reason for its importance in modern contractual relations, at least, is that conflict exists between the need for measurement and specificity, for precision and focus, and for adherence to planning, and the need for flexibility to meet countless kinds of changed circumstances.

An aspect of harmonization of relational conflict is the necessity of dealing with whole persons, since contractual relations are characterized by whole person—primary—relations. Thus, unless it is possible simply to eliminate someone from a contractual relation, harmonization of relational conflict involving that someone necessarily requires harmonization with the whole person.[63] The disgruntled employee, for example, is a potential or actual saboteur. This type of conflict is very different from conflict in a discrete transaction, where only the particular discrete dispute needs resolving and only for its own sake.

Propriety of means, also a common contract norm, becomes very complex in contractual relations. Every social relation generates norms concerning the ways by which ends may be achieved and the ways by which ends, no matter how legitimate may not.[64] The more complex

[61] I. MACNEIL, THE NEW SOCIAL CONTRACT, *supra* note 1, at 66 (footnote omitted).

[62] *Id.*

[63] Even elimination of a participant will not suffice to harmonize relational conflict if remaining participants are concerned either about the eliminated participant or about being eliminated themselves.

[64] Means and ends often are inseparable, or indeed indistinguishable, and nowhere is this

the social relation, the more complex such principles and practices of decorum become. Thus, just as role integrity becomes complex in contractual relations, so does propriety of means.

Finally, since the scope of supracontract norms is open-ended, it is not feasible to deal with their values in the Article, except to stress again their importance in keeping relational contract theory from being a closed, ahistorical system of analysis.

b. Relationship Between Values of the Relational Norms and Values of the Other Common Contract Norms.—Just as the discrete norm must be analyzed against a backdrop of the other common contract norms, so must the relational norms. Since two of the relational norms—role integrity and propriety of means—are themselves common contract norms, examination of this interplay of common contract norms with relational norms has, in effect, already started.

Because contractual relations cannot continue without reciprocity, the preservation norm requires continual maintenance of adequate reciprocity. There is no magic formula, such as promise in the discrete transaction, to resolve the reciprocity issue for all time. The question, "What have you done for me lately?" is always in the background, if not the foreground, of ongoing contractual relations. The relational norms are relatively neutral respecting implementation of planning and effectuation of consent. As will be seen in the discussion of the values of relational norms relative to the discrete norm, these common contract norms may be intensified or weakened depending upon the nature of the relation. Flexibility—adaptability to change—in no way conflicts with the relational norms. Indeed, it is essential to implementing all of them. Relations cannot be preserved, nor conflict in relations harmonized, without adequate attention to the demands of change. Furthermore, roles cannot survive with total rigidity.[65] Finally, various supracontract norms very often require adaptability to change.

The connection between contractual solidarity and the relational norms is that one of the relational norms—preservation of the contractual relation—is simply the intensification of the common contract norm of contractual solidarity. In contractual relations, the linking norms—restitution, reliance, and expectation—do not necessarily collapse into one, as in the discrete transaction. They may therefore come into conflict with each other, thereby calling into play the relational norms of preservation and conflict resolution to harmonize the conflicts. In addition, since no relation can endure without both the crea-

---

more true than in complex contractual relations. Witness the tenacious hold on existence of any large bureaucratic structure; the "means"—the bureaucracy— often outlasts the accomplishment of the "ends"—whatever the bureacracy was originally created to do.

[65] The education of Inspector Javert in Hugo's *Les Miserables* provides an example. *See* VICTOR HUGO, LES MISERABLES (C. Wilbur ed. 1931).

tion and the restraint of power, and since those two aspects of the power norm are in internal conflict, the relational norms of preservation and conflict resolution are necessarily consistent with this common contract norm. The relational norms are also consistent with the common contract norm of harmonizing with the social matrix. Roles, for example, that do not fit adequately within the social matrix simply will not work.[66] For similar reasons, preservation of the relation and harmonization of relational conflict require adherence to the supracontract norms prevailing in the internal relation and the larger society.

In sum, relational norms are always consistent with the common contract norms. Indeed, relations being a more open social approach to exchange than discrete transactions, relational norms often tend to harmonize more with human relations than does the more refined norm of discreteness and presentiation.

c. Are the Values of the Relational Norms Contrary to the Values of the Discrete Norm?—The answer to the question whether the values of the relational norms are contrary to the values of the discrete norm varies with both context and the value in question. Nothing in the relational norms necessarily precludes precision and focus. Consider rigidly disciplined organizations such as crack military outfits; they achieve very sharp precision and focus within very relational frameworks. NASA with its space shots is another example. Yet, nothing in the relational norms themselves requires a great deal of precision and focus, as many a successful marriage attests.

Planning, too, may or may not be elevated to extremely high levels in relations. "The greatest blossoming of discreteness and presentiation the world has ever seen is not to be found" in private contract "at all, either in the past or in the present. Rather it is alive and well—or perhaps alive and malignly sick—in the detailed rules of bureaucracies, whether private or public."[67] On the other hand, unlike the discrete

[66] This is not to say that particular application of relational norms within a relation may not come into conflict with the external social matrix. Indeed, even a Charles Manson can emerge, and survive for some time, in a role very much in discord with much of the surrounding society. Nonetheless, it will be noted that Manson, Jim Jones, and other such messianic leaders work very hard to keep their contractual relations as separate as possible from any larger society by, among other means, convincing their followers that the larger society is The Enemy. As Hitler attests, this is true even when they are operating on a very large scale. Messianic leaders do this precisely because the leaders' desired roles cannot survive in the larger context.

[67] I. MACNEIL, THE NEW SOCIAL CONTRACT, *supra* note 1, at 77. I was probably wrong not to exclude discreteness here, at least without more extensive analysis. Discreteness may be different in a discrete transaction generated by consent than it is when generated by bureaucratic rules in a complex relation. While its inclusion here may not have been astute or neat, however, I do not think any harm is done in terms of discussing values. If there is a difference in the discreteness of the two situations, as I believe there is, the difference originates in the presence of consent of the "governed" in the one form and its absence in the other. The discussion of consent below ensures

norm, the relational norms do not require such extensive planning, again a fact that many families illustrate.

On the face of it, the relational norms appear to be contrary to notions of economic efficiency; but the basic failure of the microeconomic model to take always-present relational factors into account renders such conclusions highly suspect.[68]

The relational norms often operate contrary to the value of autonomy, at least autonomy viewed as of any instant. The relational norms may, for example, lock people into relations that they wish to escape, as in a conscript army. On the other hand, people may voluntarily observe the relational norms, as in the case of a student adapting to the many norms of university life. Certainly voluntary, but even involuntary, adherence to relational norms may increase long run options, an assumption underlying required grade school education, for example.[69] Thus, the impact of relational norms on the choice-value is equivocal, as was true of the impact of implementing consent.[70] The impact of neither norm on the autonomy of the individual can be stated abstractly but can be determined only by examining particular circumstances in historical context.

The relational norms, like the discrete norm, are equivocal in their effect in creating or preventing change. They may operate either to bring about or to stifle change, depending upon the particular circumstances in their particular historical setting. For an example of relational norms effecting social change at the macro-level, consider early Maoist China where all the relational norms, including the supracontract norms of Maoism, dominated every interaction among individuals. Since these norms were operating in a revolutionary society, they were norms of great change. The same norms (other than some of the Maoist supracontract norms) operating in a period of social stability in China, as certainly has happened in the past, would strongly favor the status quo.

---

that the difference in the two kinds of discreteness does not lead to the omission of treatment of the key differential value—choice.

68 Macneil, *Economic Analysis*, *supra* note 7, at 1041-63. Oliver Williamson has done extensive work on this subject from the standpoint of the institutional economist. *See* Williamson, *Transaction-Cost Economics: The Governance of Contractual Relations*, 22 J.L. & ECON. 233 (1979)[hereinafter Williamson, *Governance*]; Goetz & Scott, *Principles of Relational Contracts*, 67 VA. L. REV. 1089 (1981). A specific example of the failure of typical neoclassical analysis to take into account the effect of relational norms is discussed in Macneil, *Efficient Breach*, *supra* note 7, (analyzing these issues in terms of remedies for breach of contract).

For a discussion of recent formal-empirical work supporting the long-term efficiency of relational norms such as reciprocity, see Hofstadter, *Metamagical Themas: Computer Tournaments of the Prisoner's Dilemma Suggest How Cooperation Evolves*, 248 SCI. AM. 18 (1983)(describing the work of Robert Axelrod, soon to be published under the title THE EVOLUTION OF COOPERATION).

69 The same problem of definition discussed earlier, *supra* note 54, arises here. Once again, the focus is on *social* restraint on choice.

70 *See supra* note 55 (citing Max Weber).

The relational norms also have an equivocal effect on the sixth value discussed relative to discreteness: equality. Just as it is not possible to decide abstractly whether discreteness fosters or impedes equality, neither is it possible to decide abstractly whether the relational norms foster or impede equality. Once again, we must examine the circumstances in an historical context.

Virtually by definition, the relational norms have an opposite impact from that of the discrete norm on relational values: the relational norms foster relational values while the discrete norm does not. Probably the only exception to this statement is that short-term discreteness is sometimes beneficial to long-term relational patterns. Nonetheless, one is forced to use rather extreme circumstances to illustrate the latter situation. For example, when a group of soldiers scatters in the face of unexpected incoming artillery fire, each soldier typically is reacting in an extremely selfish, discrete manner. Nevertheless, if the soldiers did not scatter, the whole unit—that is, the contractual relation—might be destroyed.

In sum, the relational norms are equivocal respecting all of the first six values discussed in relation to the discrete norm, whereas two of those values—precision and focus and adherence to planning (presentiation)—always are present when the discrete norm prevails. But both kinds of norms—discrete and relational—are equivocal respecting the other four of those six values—economic efficiency, choice, status quo as opposed to change, equalitarian values. Thus, the only clear, ever-present clash between relational norms and the discrete norm concerns the seventh value discussed in relation to the discrete norm: the sacrifice or nonsacrifice of relational values.[71]

Summary. At the level of contract behavior and internal principles and rules, all common contract norms are essential to the processes of projecting exchange into the future; no exchange activity can continue for long absent any of them. Nevertheless, some of these norms may become exaggerated relative to others, as occurs inevitably in discrete transactions and very often in relations; such exaggeration also may considerably alter the nature of other common contract norms.

[71] The discussion in the text encompasses the micro-level, not the macro-level. There never has been a society in which the discrete transaction was anything more than a relatively small part of the total pattern of exchanges. Such transactions are possible only in a setting of contractual relations, not as the primary organizing technique of the economy. Thus, in a macro sense, the discrete norm is always complementary to the relational norms, since its existence always depends on them. So too, some discreteness and presentiation is essential to all human behavior and, hence, to cooperation; in modern societies, tremendously high levels of discreteness are required inside complex relations. There remains, however, a residual incompatibility between discreteness and some aspects of relations. This incompatibility is traceable, I believe, to the basic nature of man; our consciousness intracts with the passage of time only in uneasy ways.

IV. Values in Context: External Social Responses

A. *Introduction*

1. *Internal-External; Sovereign-Nonsovereign*.—Although a distinction between internal and external social response to contracts causes relatively little trouble for traditional analyses of contract,[72] it causes problems for relational contract theory. Since all contracts are linked horizontally and vertically with other exchange relations until the entire world economy is encompassed, there is no such thing as an external social matrix, nor are there social values external to any contract. All values are internal. Thus, there is never any point at which separation of the internal from the external can be other than partially arbitrary.

Nevertheless, in many circumstances it may be very helpful to say: "This is the end of the inside of the relations between the parties, and this is where the external society begins." The nuclear family is illustrative. Because of the deep core of relations among mother, father, children, and other members of the immediate household, it is feasible and useful to think in terms of the bounded nuclear family. We then can consider as external the parents' employment and other economic and social relations, and the children's school and other economic and social relations, as well as the family's relations with other family members, friends, church, and government, even though all are really integral aspects of the nuclear family. As long as we remember that our separation of the internal from the external is somewhat artificial and arbitrary, we can proceed with caution to speak in such terms. We can then logically consider the subject of external social values.

Before turning to the substance of values in external social responses to contracts, it should be stressed that such values may originate not only in the positive law of the sovereign, but also from many other sources, of which only one source is conceptualizing about contract. Thus, an exhaustive examinination of external social values would by no means be limited to the positive law of the sovereign and conceptualizing about contract. It would also have to include private law, such as that imposed on professional football teams by league rules, on businesses by trade associations, on colleges and universities by the American Association of University Professors, and on family life by churches. Futhermore, it could not stop with relatively hierarchical or vertical impositions such as those listed. It also would have to deal with more horizontal imposition of external values, such as those

[72] It would be more accurate to say that the trouble has been largely resolved during the long history of discrete contract scholarship and discrete contract law, at least within the limited terms of that system of law and scholarship. Nevertheless, traditional contract theorists still sometimes feel the need to work out the relations between the internal and the external of discrete contract law. *See* C. Fried, Promise, *supra* note 50.

arising from customs—not only those customs of closely related people or groups, such as customs of a trade, but also customs of broader origin, such as those of civilized intercourse in the particular society.

One Article cannot discuss imposition of external social values by all the important horizontal and nonsovereign sources. The following discussion will thus be limited to imposition of external social values by a sovereign, or, in other words, to sovereign positive law.[73] Considerable danger lies in such limitation. Beginning and ending with this traditional subject creates the potential for a vastly distorted picture, not only of contract, but also of the sovereign positive law itself when it is erroneously perceived as the *only* imposer of external social values.[74] The danger is unavoidable, however, if the Article is not to be prolonged unduly.

2. *Prohibition, Nonintervention, and "Total" Control.*— One sovereign norm governing contracts may be that particular contracts ought not to exist. Under Nazi laws, for example, a Jewish-Aryan marital relation was anathema. To the extent that a sovereign prohibition is successfully implemented, there is, of course, no contract left to be subjected to sovereign values. While such restrictions on forming or continuing certain kinds of contracts raise a host of questions, I do not intend to explore those questions here. To the extent the sovereign prohibitions succeed, there is no interaction to discuss. To the extent they are only partially implemented, the values of the sovereign "prohibition" are transformed into different kinds of values than the value of absolute prevention (even though the desire for prevention may remain the motivating force).

Thus, the following discussion assumes that, whatever else is involved, the sovereign is not actually stamping out the pertinent contract. Having made this assumption, a broad range of possible postures by the sovereign remains, reflecting a wide spectrum of values. At one end of the spectrum is complete nonintervention. The value reflected by nonintervention is total autonomy of the internal participants. A noninterventionist sovereign imposes externally none of the contract norms—common, discrete, or relational.

At the other end of the spectrum is as complete sovereign control

[73] "Legal" may be read for the phrase "sovereign positive law," as long as it is kept in mind that "legal" is limited to sovereign-generated law. I believe, however, that this is far too narrow a definition to be useful. I find it generally far more helpful in discussions such as these to define law in Fullerian terms: the purposive enterprise of subjecting men to the guidance of rules. L. FULLER, THE MORALITY OF LAW (2d ed. 1969).

The discussion also will be limited to imposition of the contract norms themselves, ignoring the imposition of supracontract norms not fitting easily into the other contract norms.

[74] The final section of this Article, which deals with conceptualizing about contract by people who think, speak, and write about the subject, is a partial antidote to this danger. *See infra* text accompanying notes 125-237.

of the relation as possible. When this end is reached, however, the external and internal merge so much that separating them at all may make little sense, or may make sense for only very limited purposes; examples of such extensive mergings are socialist state enterprises, our complex public-private space program, and military procurement.[75] Examples falling short of such a merger are wartime price, quantity, and quality controls, or perhaps the extremely close regulation of employment relations in some Western mixed economies.

The common contract norms impose limits on how far the sovereign *can* go in imposing total control over contractual behavior. Sovereign prevention of the operation of those norms will destroy contract, just as does their disruption by internal forces. One example of how sovereign prevention of the common contract norms destroys contract is the generally conceded inefficiency of slave labor camps; the levels of reciprocity in such camps are simply too low for effective contractual relations to exist.[76]

The class of sovereign norms that will now be treated is identical to the internal norms of contract behavior, principles, and rules discussed earlier. Furthermore, we are interested in their imposition (or nonimposition) by the sovereign only to the extent that such imposition (or nonimposition) does not result in such great erosion of the *internal* norms of contract behavior, principles, and rules, as to cause the disapperance of contract.[77]

B. *External Social Responses: Values in Sovereign Positive Law*

1. *Values of Nonintervention*.—The value reflected in complete nonintervention by sovereign positive law is total autonomy of the internal participants. The noninterventionist sovereign imposes exter-

[75] Nongovernmental examples of efforts at "total" control abound: 18th century Presbyterian ministers in small Scottish communities, Portnoy's mother, and the Chinese Communist party's interference with the family at the height of the cultural revolution. Portnoy's mother is, of course, *internal* insofar as the original Portnoy family is concerned; I am thinking of her as part of the society external to Portnoy's relations with, say, his wife. The example is a useful one, because it demonstrates how artificial is the separation of internal and external.

[76] For another example, see *infra* text accompanying notes 85- 91 (discussing Edward G. Budd Mfg. Co. v. NLRB, 138 F.2d 86 (3d Cir. 1943)).

[77] Two factors make possible the apparent anomaly that external imposition of contract norms can destroy contract. One factor is the transformation that occurs when norms are imposed rather than generated internally; the other factor is that the vigorous imposition of the discrete norm, or of one or more of the relational norms may erode one or more of the common norms to such an extent that contract is not possible. Consider, for example, the mythical world of 1985, where the society has elevated the norm of preservation of the employment relation so high that every person has the right *not* to work for any reason that suits him, but without losing his job and while preventing anyone else from doing it; the result is putative contractual relations that are not contract at all, but rather are anarchic nonfunctioning economic structures. A. BURGESS, 1985 (1978).

nally none of the contract norms—common, discrete, or relational.[78] The effect is to separate the sovereign altogether from the contractual relation in question. An example of sovereign nonintervention is the great reluctance of American courts to interfere in any way at all in the internal affairs of churches. This reluctance is based on the constitutional provision that "Congress shall make no law respecting establishment of religion or prohibiting the free exercise thereof."[79] Another example (in theory) is to be found in the treatment of British collective bargaining agreements as "gentlemen's agreements" not enforceable in the courts. Yet another results from the doctrine of *pari delicto* when applied to illegal contracts.[80] To the extent such a value prevails, it is as if the relation were occurring in some other society.[81]

Because of the confusing nature of the term "freedom of contract," it is important to note that the value of sovereign nonintervention is *not* the same as the value of freedom of contract. Freedom of contract is almost always used to mean freedom to bind oneself by contract—that is, to cause the sovereign to confer power on the other contractor to enforce the contract against one's self.[82] This is sovereign intervention, not sovereign nonintervention.

2. *Transformation of Norms When Imposed.*—Sovereign imposition of norms on contract, in contrast to their generation within the contract, results in a transformation of the contract's values.[83] That is, the values of imposing contract norms—whether common, discrete, or relational—are not identical to the values reflected by their internal generation. Not only is an imposed norm theoretically different—respecting consent, for example—but it will be practically different as well.[84]

---

78 The common norms must be served internally or the relations between the participants will never exist.

79 U.S. CONST. amend. I. *See* Laycock, *Towards a General Theory of the Religion Clauses: The Case of Church Labor Relations and the Right to Church Autonomy*, 81 COLUM. L. REV. 1373 (1981).

80 One of the most delightful examples is Everet v. Williams (Exch. 1725), in which one highwayman sued another highwayman for breach of an agreement to split the loot of their joint endeavours. Not surprisingly, the court would have none of it. *See* Note, *The Highwayman's Case*, 9 L.Q. REV. 197 (1893); Riddell, *A Legal Scandal Two Hundred Years Ago*, 16 A.B.A. J. 422 (1932)

81 *See* Ellman, *Driven from the Tribunal: Judicial Review of Internal Church Dispute*, 69 CALIF. L. REV. 1378 (1981). Of course, as long as the contractual relation does occur in the society the policy cannot prevail completely. Thus, American courts have been unable to avoid being drawn into disputes concerning ownership of church property. *See, e.g.*, Jones v. Wolf, 443 U.S. 595 (1979).

82 See the discussion of choice and consent, *supra* notes 50-55 and accompanying text.

83 *See supra* note 77 (noting that efforts to impose common contract norms by positive law can so destroy internal operation of common contract norms as to destroy the contract).

84 Because the internal-external dichotomy is somewhat artificial, so is the distinction between the effects of internal generation and external imposition. More important, whether the norm

The foregoing may be illustrated by *Edward G. Budd Manufacturing Co. v. NLRB*,[85] where the National Labor Relations Board (NLRB) ordered reinstatement of an employee whom the Board found had been fired because of his work on behalf of the CIO union complaining in the case.

> The case of Walter Weigand is extraordinary. If ever a workman deserved summary discharge, it was he. He was under the influence of liquor while on duty. He came to work when he chose and he left the plant and his shift as he pleased. In fact, a foreman on one occasion was agreeably surprised to find Weigand at work and commented on it. Weigand amiably stated that he was enjoying it. He brought a woman (apparently generally known as "Duchess") to the rear of the plant yard and introduced some of the employees to her. He took another employee to visit her and when this man got too drunk to be able to go home, punched his time-card for him and put him on the table in the representatives' meeting room in the plant in order to sleep off his intoxication. Weigand's immediate superiors demanded again and again that he be discharged, but each time officials intervened on Weigand's behalf because as was naively stated he was "a representative" [of a company union]. In return for not working at the job for which he was hired, the petitioner gave him full pay and on five separate occasions raised his wages. [Only one of these was a general pay increase given other employees.][86]

When the employer suspected that Weigand had joined the CIO union, it fired him. In spite of the foregoing description of Weigand, the Court of Appeals enforced the NLRB's order of reinstatement. One may either be outraged at the imposition of such an employee on a business, or think the order served the employer right, or both.[87] But it is clear that the NLRB's and the court's imposition on the employer of Weigand as an employee reflects very different values from the employer's original retention of him. The upper management originally viewed him as supplying services sufficiently valuable to warrant his retention, thereby satisfying the norm of reciprocity as they saw it.[88] Once Weigand "joined the other side" and hence no longer served his

---

arises from internal generation or external imposition is only one of many factors affecting the broad key issue. That key issue is: *how* are the norms generated and implemented? The text here deals with one particular external imposer—the sovereign. Moreover, it is a sovereign acting through modern bureaucratic processes, which may have considerably different effects from, for example, the processes of a sovereign acting through moral revolutionary suasion.

85 138 F.2d 86 (3d Cir. 1943).

86 *Id.* at 90 (citation to record omitted).

87 It is not clear whether the employer's original antiunion action would preclude it from firing Weigand for future misconduct such as that described.

88 One of the interesting aspects of the case is that *inside* the employment relation, upper management was originally imposing on the lower operating management exactly the same thing that the NLRB and court subsequently imposed on the company—namely, a relation lacking adequate levels of reciprocity *as to this individual employee*. This illustrates the point made *supra* note 78, concerning the artificiality of distinguishing external imposition of norms from their internal generation.

theretofore useful function for management, they, entirely correctly, no longer believed that any individual reciprocity would be achieved. While the voluntary retention of Weigand reflected the reciprocity norm as applied to a single employee, the sovereign imposition of Weigand as an employee reflected at least three, and perhaps four, norms. These were the reciprocity norm applied collectively, the contractual solidarity norm,[89] the restraint of power norm,[90] and perhaps some unidentified supracontract norms. The result, however, unless Weigand mended his ways or was successfully fired for not doing so, was not a contractual relation between the employer and Weigand as an individual. Rather, it was a private welfare scheme imposed on the employer as a means of policing the National Labor Relations Act.[91]

The foregoing is merely illustrative. It is not feasible to deal at length here with all the transformations that contract norms—whether common, discrete, or relational—undergo when those norms are imposed by government compared to internal generation. Instead, only sovereign imposition of the discrete norm and limited aspects of the imposition of other norms will be explored, and those relatively briefly.

3. *Imposition of the Discrete Norm*.—Sovereign reinforcement of discreteness and presentiation, through classical and, to a lesser extent, neoclassical contract law appears to elevate consent to a position of high value.[92] But this appearance is deceiving. Professor Fried has recently done contract scholarship the great service of recognizing—from the standpoint of an advocate of the will or consent theory of contract—the limitations of consent. Unlike earlier advocates of the objective theory of contracts such as Williston, Professor Fried is more than willing to recognize gaps in contracts and then refrain from trying to cram those gaps into the promise principle.[93] Since, however, classical contract law did far overstep the promise principle in the imposition of discrete values,[94] it is apparent that sovereign law following the objec-

89 This is difficult to see vis-a-vis Weigand himself, since the employer can hardly have had any faith in its solidarity with Weigand. The court, however, is viewing the problem in terms of solidarity respecting the employer and the worker collectively. Rightly or wrongly, the court sees prevention of the alleged discrimination against an employee for union activities as the key to that principle of collective solidarity, a principle imposed by the National Labor Relations Act.

90 Discussing the normal power of an employer to fire and the restraint of that power by the Act, the court says: "[A]n employer may discharge an employee for a good reason, a poor reason or no reason at all so long as the provisions of the National Labor Relations Act are not violated." Edward D. Budd Mfg. Co. v. NLRB, 138 F.2d at 90.

91 The scheme will "work" as long as the overall levels of reciprocity between *all* the employees and employer (and other norms) are met.

92 As already noted, implementing consent does *not* necessarily mean the elevation of choice to a position of particular value.

93 C. FRIED, PROMISE, *supra* note 50, at 57-73.

94 Macneil, *Presentiation*, *supra* note 7.

tive theory[95] was, in considerable measure, either anticonsent or neutral respecting it. Rigorous application of the parol evidence rule appears to be a good example of how sovereign law following the objective theory can be anticonsent.[96] Nonetheless, it is often difficult to tell whether sovereign law implements consent or not. It is possible to argue, for example, that a rigorously exclusionary parol evidence rule prevents perjury and will more often lead to implementing consent than a looser rule leaving perjury a lively possibility.

Another example of an apparently anticonsent doctrine that nevertheless possibly implements consent is found in U.C.C. § 2-302, which provides relief from the enforcement of unconscionable provisions in contracts for the purchase and sale of goods. The word "unconscionable" appears to allow relief from terms to which consent has been given. Nevertheless, the official comment to the section suggests something else: "The principle is one of the prevention of oppression and unfair surprise . . . and not of disturbance of allocation of risks because of superior bargaining power."[97] Thus, the relief is given when the appearance of consent is a false one, when consent to the terms is not "real." To the extent § 2-302 is so applied, it does not frustrate consent at all. Indeed, it implements what the court views as genuine consent.

It may be noted how the *imposition* of the discrete norm, as distinct from its *internal* growth, may transform it. For example, as between parties to a relatively discrete transaction, the norm of discreteness may be served by their implementing promises made over the telephone, even though those promises might be contrary to the formal documents exchanged between them. The parties thereby implement the norm of consent. On the other hand, where there is a dispute, the norm of consent may be disserved when the discrete norm is imposed by government, because the sovereign lacks information available to the participants—for instance, whether the alleged telephone conversation actually took place.

The common difficulty of ascertaining whether imposition of the discrete norm is proconsent, neutral, or anticonsent adds to the difficulty of ascertaining whether that imposition is prochoice, neutral, or antichoice. Consent originates in choice coupled with the chooser's own invocation of society's enforcement of his choice. Provision of such enforcement by society, however, might or might not have the long run effect of implementing the value of choice. Thus, when the sovereign value is anticonsent, when freedom of contract is not allowed

---

95 It must be remembered that for all its current disrepute and downgrading, the objective theory of contracts was, and indeed still is, very powerful.

96 *See* Calamari & Perillo, *A Plea for a Uniform Parol Evidence Rule and Principles of Contract Interpretation*, 42 IND. L.J. 333 (1967).

97 U.C.C. § 2-302, Comment 1 (1978).

to prevail, no general conclusion can be reached about whether this value is prochoice or antichoice over any substantial period of time. Nor does a proconsent position necessarily mean that a prochoice value is being implemented. Each set of circumstances must be examined to ascertain whether the anticonsent position "has a net overall freeing effect or a net overall enslaving effect."[98]

4. *Imposition of Reciprocity, the Power Norm, Preservation of the Relation, and Propriety of Means*.—Much of the Western nations' imposition of sovereign values on contract has concerned four values, two of them common contract norms, one a particularly relational norm, and one which is both. These four values are reciprocity, creation and restraint of power, preservation of relations, and propriety of means. Two aspects of sovereign imposition of these values will be explored: their relation to choice, and their bureaucratic effect.

a. Relation to Choice.—Once again, it is not possible to make valid generalizations about the ultimate effect of sovereign imposition of these values on choice. One could argue, for example, that the federal government's increasing intervention into every kind of contractual relation over the past forty years, including its intervention through all its macroeconomic policies, has been a vital factor in a mind-boggling proliferation of choice relating to employment, consumption, and lifestyle. One could also counter that such intervention has helped set the country on a largely technologically-determined historical course in which all such choices are highly superficial; one could counter further that such patterns have gone far to erode the availability of significant choice.[99] Rather than engage in such highflown discussion, however, this section will simply examine some key values the sovereign has sought to impose and their relatively immediate effect on choice.

Reciprocity. A vast array of legislative, administrative, and judicial law of the last fifty years is aimed at imposing levels of reciprocity other than those it is believed would occur in the absence of that law. Nowhere is this more evident than in the area of employment. The government has, for example, imposed the minimum wage, protected and encouraged labor monopolies to raise wages of selected workers,

[98] *Supra* text accompanying note 55. Arguments that "restraint equals freedom" are always looked upon with suspicion, and properly so. That does not, however, mean that they are always specious, as arguments for governmental implementation of consent illustrate. Consent itself is fundamentally antichoice; autonomy principles can justify the government enforcing consent with legal sanctions only on the basis of its long-term freeing effect. Such arguments may or may not be sound in any given circumstances. *See supra* text accompanying notes 51-55.

[99] Both these arguments reflect the ambiguity of the idea of increasing "one's options in the long run." *See supra* notes 51-55.

levied social security taxes, and prohibited discrimination respecting wages (and other conditions of employment) on a wide variety of grounds, including race and sex.

Such sovereign efforts to impose reciprocity are intended to limit the choice of one participant in contract, the one whose share in the fruits of the contract are being reduced. It should also be noted, however, that the imposition of reciprocity often deprives other participants of choice as well, since they might well choose *not* to have the reciprocity adjusted in their favor because of various costs to them of doing so. For example, payment of Social Security taxes is mandatory[100] in very considerable measure because many workers, as well as employers, would opt out if given the chance. Furthermore, such opting out would not be limited to the workers least favored by the system. Proponents of the system argue that workers in general place insufficient utility on saving for old age compared to spending their wages immediately.[101] The minimum wage also illustrates that imposed levels of reciprocity restrict choice, of employees as well as of employers. Even if the widespread view that the minimum wage laws eliminate hundreds of thousands, perhaps millions, of jobs is incorrect,[102] every evasion of those laws proves that they aim to limit choice of participants on *both* sides.[103]

Power. To put this norm in context, it should be recalled that the most fundamental sovereign *creation* of power affecting contracts is first, sovereign enforcement of liberty and property rights among the populace and their organizations, and second, sovereign enforcement of contracts. While such creation of power carries with it built-in restraints,[104] over the past century or so sovereign restraints on liberty, property, and contract-enforcement power have become increasingly specific. While relatively little of such regulation seems to be aimed at changing the fundamental nature of liberty, property rights, or contract-enforcement power, its total effect has been to change them

100 Social Security taxes are not, however, mandatory for current federal employees—one of the still largely ignored scandals of modern American government.

101 The "long run argument" that the workers' lifelong autonomy is increased by forcing them to "save" for their old age is, of course, made by proponents of the system. The argument is often made that workers "cannot afford to save" for their old age. If, however, they can bear a nonredistributing tax accomplishing such savings that phrasing is specious. *See* Kennedy, *Paternalist Motives*, *supra* note 43, at 628.

102 To the extent that the minimum wage laws do eliminate jobs they provide an example of how government imposition of contract norms destroys contract. Where the work, if paid for at the minimum wage level, will yield either a loss, no return, or too little return for the employer, the reciprocity is so low for the employer that it simply will not enter such contracts.

103 This is clear in the short run; as usual, arguments can be made concerning the ultimately liberating effect of such laws.

104 These restraints occur partly because the very nature of both liberty and property, indeed of society, precludes unlimited power in anyone.

drastically.[105]

As it did for sovereign imposition of reciprocity, employment law provides a good example of sovereign imposition of the power norm. Since the power norm operates both to create and to restrain power, it is necessary to deal with both aspects.

Much regulation aims to restrain the power of employers over their employees.[106] Other legislation, such as the National Labor Relations Act,[107] aims largely to increase the power of employees over their employers.[108] A restraint of employer power obviously reduces the employ*er's* choice, at least in the short run. It may also reduce the employ*ee's* choice, just as happens when the sovereign alters levels of reciprocity. To the extent, for example, that employment safety regulations force marginal employers out of business, they deprive existing or potential employees of a choice to work for those employers, albeit under less safe conditions. Those regulations also may deprive employees, who continue on the job, of choice. Just as employees may not like the form that enhanced levels of reciprocity takes, they may not like the results of every sovereign restraint of employer power even though they retain their jobs. Employ*ee* disregard for safety practices, for example, is an endemic problem in industry. In addition, legislation such as title VII of the Civil Rights Act of 1964[109] poses the special problems of restraining employer power and restraining the power of some, but not all, employees. The most vigorous opponents of title VII have probably not been employers, but employees organized into trade unions, particularly in the construction industry.

When the sovereign creates countervailing power, it also reduces the choices available to the parties. For instance, the NLRA's good faith bargaining requirements reduce the choices of both the employer

---

105 See, for example, Professor Atiyah's insights into the "property" effect of rent legislation and council housing. P. ATIYAH, THE RISE AND FALL OF FREEDOM OF CONTRACT 727-29 (1979)[hereinafter P. ATIYAH, FREEDOM OF CONTRACT].

106 Examples: Occupational Safety and Health Act of 1970, P.L. 91-596, 84 Stat. 1590 (1970); Employee Retirement Income Security Act of 1974, P.L. 93-406, 88 Stat. 829 (1974) (The complexity of this legislation is reflected in the difficulty of citing it to the United States Code; the list of U.S.C. sections for it and its amendments covers close to half a printed page); Civil Rights Act of 1964, tit. VII, P.L. 88-352, 78 Stat. 241, 42 U.S.C. §§ 2000a-2000h-6 (1981).

107 29 U.S.C. §§ 151 - 169 (1935).

108 There is much practical and theoretical difference in the effect on choice between restraining the power of one side and adding to the power of the other. A focus solely on the net difference in power between parties rather than on the power extant on both sides leads improperly to equating the two techniques. Such a focus is typical of analyses based on beliefs in the powerlessness of some classes or groups. Such beliefs are rejected here; even the most oppressed exercise some power over their oppressors, see J. OAKES, RULING RACE, *supra* note 39, and a focus only on the net difference in power distorts our understanding of the relationship between the two groups. *See* I. MACNEIL, THE NEW SOCIAL CONTRACT, *supra* note 1, at 126-27.

109 Civil Rights Act of 1964, tit. VII, P.L. 88-352, 78 Stat. 241, 42 U.S.C. §§ 2000a-2000h-6 (1981).

and the union, the exclusive bargaining agent of the employees. Such requirements, taken out of context, seem intended to affect both parties equally. In context, however, their purpose is to increase choice on one side of the relation—the worker's side—by improving its bargaining position. In many respects they achieve this effect, but only by substantially reducing and transforming worker choice. The system requires both a monopolization of the labor supply and a monopolization of the bargaining process by the union. Such monopolies cannot exist without depriving employees and potential employees of choice. Even in the short term, however, the processes of collective choice replace in altered form some of this reduced individual choice.[110]

Preservation of Relations. Much sovereign imposition of values has effectuated the relational norm of preservation of the relation. Some of this has been done indirectly, as has often been the case respecting employment,[111] but some has been done directly, as in the case of the Automobile Dealer's Day in Court Act.[112] Nevertheless, at the same time that such increased impositions have occurred in employment and franchising, very considerable reductions in the imposition of this norm have occurred respecting family relations.[113]

The contrast between the decreasing sanctity of marriage and the increasing sanctity of franchises as reflected in the government's imposing continuation of the relation over the objection of one party is interesting in terms of choice. In the case of franchising, the reduction of choice is one sided; regulations restricting the freedom of franchisors to terminate dealerships do not reduce choice for all participants. Rather, franchisees generally welcome the imposition of the norm on the rela-

---

[110] The extent and nature of the replacement are, of course, the subject of lively debate, not only in abstract terms, but respecting particular relations.

As the discussion of contract in employment suggests, different techniques for imposing the reciprocity and power norms have different effects on choice. Quite a wide range of regulation—for example, Truth-in-Lending legislation—with roots in these norms is aimed at making choice more effective. Any comprehensive discussion of the subject of regulation would have to treat the effect of a wide range of regulatory techniques, of which those discussed in the text are but a tiny part.

[111] For example, legislation encouraging unionization invariably also leads to pressures on employers to provide more job security than they would provide in the absence of the pressure.

Direct intervention in the employment relation also occurs, as in the case of legislation prohibiting firing employees on grounds of race, religion, and age.

[112] 15 U.S.C. §§ 1121-1125 (1981). This act restricts the freedom of automobile manufacturers to terminate dealerships.

[113] For a fine discussion of the contrast, *see* M. GLENDON, THE NEW FAMILY AND THE NEW PROPERTY (1981). For an excellent discussion of the latter phenomenon respecting dyadic spousal relations only—that is, excluding the effect of children—see Shultz, *Contractual Ordering of Marriage: A New Model for State Policy*, 70 CALIF. L. REV. 204 (1982). (The omission of children from the analysis is a significant limitation even in analyzing the dyad, because the dyad is potentially a triad.)

tion, because it increases their choice.[114] On the other hand, marriage is an area where sovereign regulation in favor of preservation of the relation would often reduce the choice of all the internal participants.[115]

Propriety of Means. A great deal of government intervention in contractual relations has taken the form of changing the means by which the parties conduct themselves, rather than the substance of their conduct. This type of intervention frequently takes the form of imposing procedural requirements. These requirements have generally been of the "due process" nature, which presumes a high adversarial level among the participants. These impositions may come about in a range of ways. Perhaps most common are those following automatically from the creation by law of substantive rights—in other words, the imposition of legal duties—where none existed before. Such substantive legal rights carry with them the full panoply of judicial, and often administrative, enforcement replete with rights to due process, often to the highest of constitutional requirements. Imposition of due process requirements may also be created specifically, as in the Wisconsin Dealership Practices Act which requires ninety days' notice of termination by the franchisor, regardless of the validity of the franchisor's cause for terminating.[116] Due process requirements also may be imposed indirectly, as in the case of labor laws protecting collective bargaining, since collective bargaining invariably leads to formalized grievance procedures, usually (in the United States) including arbitration if all other procedures fail.

The effect of due process on choice is clear enough respecting the party upon which it is imposed, at least in the short run: it curtails choice whenever that side would not have introduced such process on its own initiative, which is commonly the case. The long run curtailment is not, however, always so clear; in labor relations, for example, many employers may come to prefer grievance procedures as an effective way of curbing the discretion of lower-level managers—for exam-

[114] In neoclassical economic theory, this is presumably not true. Such imposition increases franchisor costs. If franchisees could waive rights against termination, they could, in theory, bargain away those rights for better terms on items they valued more, such as better discounts on goods purchased from the franchisor. A host of informational and institutional barriers, however, stands in the way of such bargaining. These barriers seem to lead to a near unanimity among franchisees about the value of these statutory rights. Such unanimity among workers about the value of Social Security, however, seems unlikely. The same may be said regarding much safety legislation, and most certainly, about the value of job security acquired through unionization.

[115] Children, who have no opportunity to choose to live with both parents in a single dwelling where the parents want to split, might find their choice implemented by sovereign imposition of this norm; but their choice, too, would be overruled by governmentally coerced continuance if they would prefer to see the parents separate.

[116] WIS. STAT. ANN. § 135.04 (West 1973). The statute allows fewer than ninety days' notice for a limited number of causes.

ple, foremen. Once again, choice may also be curtailed in the group for whose benefit the procedures are putatively required. Certain kinds of costs are inherent in the shift from less formal to more formal means—costs in reduction of trust and in flexibility, for example. Not everyone in a protected group would necessarily choose to incur those costs in order to secure the often uncertain benefits of "due process." For example, under the National Labor Relations Act, a union may, if it acts in good faith, refuse to take a grievance to arbitration, and in doing so, the union may deprive the grieving employee of the right to judicial relief that might have been available in the absence of grievance-arbitration provisions in the collective bargaining agreement.[117]

In sum, the effect on choice, even immediate choice, of sovereign imposition of these four values is immensely complex. The sovereign often intentionally reduces choice of a party which is reciprocating too little, is too powerful, is terminating relations, or is following arbitrary or other procedures viewed as inadequate by the sovereign. By doing so, however, the sovereign also may consequentially reduce the choice of the putative beneficiaries of the enhanced levels of reciprocity, the redressed power balances, the preserved relations, and the due process.[118] Sovereign imposition of these values also may transform the nature of choice from, for example, individual choice, to choice exercisable only through group political processes and structures. For a complete understanding of the impact of such impositions on choice, it is necessary to look at long run effects as well as immediate restrictions and transformations.

b. Bureaucratization—Transformation of the Propriety of Means.—One of the most important effects of sovereign imposition of the four values discussed—reciprocity, the power norm, relational preservation, and "due process"—is that it bureaucratizes the relations affected. This is especially so in relations which otherwise would be relatively little bureaucratized. Consider, for example, what has happened to many small, originally nonunionized businesses in the last fifty years or so. Ownership and management were initially vested in the sole proprietor; one or more intermediate levels of management may or may not have existed between the proprietor and the employees engaged directly in production. Division of labor could be quite complex, as in a machine shop, with lathes, drill presses, punch machines, various cutting tools, and so on, but an individual laborer did not necessarily always work at the same task or machine. Obviously, such an

[117] Vaca v. Sipes, 386 U.S. 171 (1967). The gain-loss tradeoff is, however, complicated, because without the union, the employee might very well have had no substantive rights to enforce judicially. For the latest Supreme Court case on this subject, see Bowen v. United States Postal Serv., 103 S.Ct. 588 (1983).

[118] The effects on choice discussed in the text are viewed in the relatively short term.

organization had many bureaucratic elements; in particular, it had extensive division of labor and rational planning and execution of functions. Moreover, the authority structure was based not on traditional or feudal notions, but on the concept of property, of ownership. The reification of human authority into modern property rights was itself a move away from feudal relational patterns toward more discrete social patterns. It was also a step on the road to the concept of authority being legitimized by substantive detailed rules and the correct following of detailed procedures, the mature bureaucratic pattern. Nonetheless, modern property rights are far more general than bureaucratic rights and confer legitimate arbitrary power on their holder[119]—in this case, to direct, to hire and fire, and to determine levels of reciprocity, who will or will not exercise power and what that power will be, and how long relations shall continue.[120]

Now consider the same business in a modern context. It is still a sole proprietorship, with the same levels of intermediate management and division of labor, but now it is subject to the national or state labor relations act, and, as a result, it is unionized. It must comply with complex income tax laws, including obligations to withhold taxes, and Social Security laws. In addition, it must comply with ERISA and OSHA, among much other regulation. All other things being equal, this business is inevitably far more bureaucratized than it was in 1933. Completely apart from technological changes, the division of labor will be far sharper and more permanent than before unionization, not only because of job classification and restrictive work provisions common in collective bargaining agreements, but also because of the mores and personal psychology arising from the existence of such bureaucratic requirements. Rational planning and performance of work will be far more extensive now, partly because of the increased sharpness and permanence of the division of labor. Also, the multiplication of goals in conducting the work increases the need for rational planning and performance; whereas the firm's original goal was to produce the final product and sell it at a profit, now it must add the goal of following the additional rules of the game. These rules are not general principles of safety, for example, but are detailed ways of behaving safely. Further,

[119] This power is legitimate not in any absolute sense, but by the standards of a property-type social system.

[120] This is not to suggest that the owner of a 1933 machine shop was free of restraints—of course he was not. He was free only of many of the *kinds* of restraints endured by truly bureaucratic managers. He was, of course, subject to restraints resulting from the property and liberty rights of others, including his employees, as is his 1983 successor.

This section of the Article discusses the bureaucratic impact of sovereign law on rights of property and liberty. For an interesting analysis of forces moving in the opposite direction, from property and liberty rights and impacting on sovereign law, see Cameron & Midgley, *Contract, the Rule of Law, and the Liberal-Democratic State: The Case of Britain and North Sea Oil*, 10 INT'L J. SOC. L. 239 (1982).

a change has taken place in the source of legitimacy of authority. Although the sole proprietor remains endowed with the general authority arising from rights of ownership, that authority is now hedged about with a host of rules—both substantive and procedural—arising both from the collective bargaining agreement and from sovereign regulation. His authority is thus a combination of "dos" and "don'ts" very similar to those of more prototypical bureaucrats in large organizations—public or private.[121]

In addition to the foregoing factors, the policing of business needed to ensure compliance with regulation increases bureaucratization. By and large, norms can be imposed by large bureaucratic organizations, such as government, only by detailed rules.[122] Detailed rules require administration not only by the ruler, but also by the organization being ruled. Such internal administration adds to the need for rational planning and performance respecting activities collateral to what once appeared to be the sole function of the organization—producing and selling the goods or services it produces.

The example of the machine shop reveals how a theretofore small, relatively unbureaucratic organization has, by virtue of the sovereign imposition of these four norms, merged into larger bureaucratic organizations—union and government—and has thereby become heavily bureaucratized.

Where the contractual relation upon which government imposes these norms is heavily bureaucratized from the start—for example, General Motors—the imposition will generally increase the degree of bureaucratization, unless a saturation level of bureaucratization, if there is such a thing, already exists. In any event, the imposition will add new levels in the bureaucracy. This occurs both internally and externally. For example, sovereign imposition of affirmative action programs results not only in the creation of agencies in the sovereign to enforce the policy, but also in the appointment by the institutions subject to the regulation of their own affirmative action officers. Large employers may even create whole affirmative action offices.[123]

---

[121] Obviously, there is a continuum, not a discontinuity, between the bureaucratization of the sole proprietorship and that of the large private or public bureaucracy. Furthermore, the 1983 owner of a small business is still viewed as an owner and not a mere manager, as he would be if the firm were a corporation of which he was the president and a small stockholder. Nevertheless, erosion of ownership through regulation can go so far as to change the psychology of the business altogether. For a description of how legislation caused rapid bureaucratization of employment discipline, see Henry, *Factory Law, the Changing Disciplinary Technology of Industrial Social Control*, 10 INT'L J. SOC. L. 365 (1982).

[122] Moral suasion, such as patriotism, "jawboning," Chairman Mao's Little Red Book, and the like, have effect in imposing such rules, but that effect is limited, especially in a pluralistic society.

[123] Heavily bureaucratized institutions like universities may nevertheless have relatively unbureaucratized activities or parts of activities. For example, faculty hiring in many universities is quite unbureaucratic at key levels, such as the departmental. Government regulation of these

Thus, whether we like it or not, one set of values of sovereign imposition of such norms in a modern technological society inevitably is the value of conducting affairs bureaucratically and of multiplying levels in bureaucratic structures.[124] To the extent this occurs, there is a marked change in what means are proper and what means are improper; nonbureaucratic means of conduct no longer are proper. This is significant not only respecting the means considered purely as means, but also, as the foregoing discussion suggests, in terms of the effect the change in the standards of means-propriety has on the various substantive norms.

C. *External Social Responses: Conceptualizing*

We now turn to the values reflected in the ways in which people organize their thoughts about contract.[125] The scope of this subject may be sensed by examining Patrick Atiyah's *The Rise and Fall of Freedom of Contract*, "a splendid *big* book. . . . of legal history as intellectual history."[126] Even so comprehensive a book as Atiyah's, however, deals with but limited aspects of contract conceptualizing and its significance. It is thus clear that the discussion here must be, and is, closely limited to some key questions.

1. *Diversity in Both Discrete and Relational Conceptualizing.*— Even those who conceptualize contracts as discrete transactions differ among themselves, not only in the nature of their theories, but also respecting the scope accorded the theories by those adhering to them. Fried is not a Posner, neither is a Williston, nor Williston a Corbin, nor

---

activities, such as government-imposed affirmative action, tends to bureaucratize them. For a case where the court struggled quite valiantly, although probably in vain in the long run, to limit the bureaucratization effect while providing for procedures needed in a race discrimination case, see Gray v. Board of Higher Educ., 692 F.2d 901 (2d Cir. 1982)(court adopted the American Association of University Professors' view of the proper conduct of tenure reviews). *See also* Comment, *Balancing Academic Freedom and Civil Rights: Toward an Appropriate Privilege for the Votes of Academic Peer Review Committees*, 68 IOWA L. REV. 585 (1983).

124 In I. MACNEIL, THE NEW SOCIAL CONTRACT, *supra* note 1, I explored some of the values underlying the bureaucratic way of life in a fanciful postscript describing a mystical land of Post-Technique. The postscript was far more a cry of pain than serious scholarly analysis. There are many such cries of pain to be heard. Some, such as H. JACOBY, BUREAUCRATIZATION OF THE WORLD (1973), are far more scholarly; many, such as the frustration expressed by Moslem terrorists or in newspaper columns like Action Line, are far less scholarly. Most of the *values* underlying bureaucratization can be determined only in particular contexts, although some of them, such as the willingness to fragment the human personality, are present in all contexts. Even those "universal values" still can be judged only in context, however, because to some degree they are simply part of human nature. Time itself, for example, fragments the human personality. Thus, in order to inquire about the values underlying such fragmentation in bureaucratic structures we must ask such questions as how much? for what purpose? for how long?

125 The term "contract" encompasses contract behavior, internal principles and rules of contract, and external responses, including, but not limited to, positive law.

126 Black, *Book Review*, 79 MICH. L. REV. 929 (1981).

Corbin a Farnsworth, and yet all of them are not improperly described as, in whole or part, scholars who conceptualize contracts as discrete transactions.[127] Moreover, the discrete theorists differ widely in the extent to which they tend to think of contract as meaning contract *law*, rather than contract behavior in which contract law is but one of many environmental factors. Because of this fractionation, it is feasible to examine here the work of only one proponent or school of discrete contract conceptualizing. Since I have elsewhere addressed various aspects of the efficiency school,[128] and since Professor Fried has recently focused so extensively on promise, his work will serve to illustrate discrete conceptualizing.

While the work of scholars who conceptualize about contracts as discrete transactions is quite diverse, all those scholars nonetheless center their thinking on discreteness in some form or other. This provides a single central core enabling us reasonably to view them as a single group. Scholars who conceptualize about contracts in the relational mode, however, are more difficult to classify. There is simply no single core to holistic or relational conceptualizing about contract—no analog to the single focus of discreteness. The only thing remotely like a core for relational theorists is the rejection of discreteness as the center, or at least sole center, around which the *concepts* of contract and contract law turn. Going on from that negative core, relational contract theorizing can span from Mao to Adam Smith, to mention but two of many diverse relational theorists. This is quite vividly demonstrated by Professor Fried's list of authors of an "insidious set of criticisms" denying "coherence or independent viability of the promise principle": Atiyah,[129] T. Friedman, Gilmore, Horwitz, Kennedy, Kronman, and me.[130] To this list of his intellectual opponents, Professor Fried later adds Fuller, Kessler, and Durkheim.[131] Anyone the least bit familiar with the writings of these individuals will recognize this as a bizarre set of bedmates. Indeed, the only thing linking them all is that each rejects some aspect of discrete conceptualizing—and even that generalization may have to be stretched in order to include

127 This grouping would be most difficult to defend respecting Corbin and Farnsworth, who are discrete theorists primarily in terms of their overall system of thinking about contract law. *See* Macneil, *Presentiation*, *supra* note 7. Were it not for the very considerable relationizing of contract law and theory that has occurred since the heyday of Corbin, Farnsworth would seem far more relational in outlook than he does today.

128 Macneil, *Economic Analysis*, *supra* note 7; Macneil, *Efficient Breach*, *supra* note 7.

129 For an infinitely more subtle understanding of Atiyah, one recognizing what I suspect is Atiyah's genuine pain at the present state of "freedom of contract," see Mensch, *Book Review*, 33 STAN. L. REV. 753 (1981).

130 C. FRIED, PROMISE, *supra* note 50, at 3.

131 *Id.* at 76. He also lists a number of philosophers, but as I am only modestly familiar with the work of but one, MacCormick, the comments following might or might not apply to all, or even to any, of them.

Gilmore.[132]

Even though the work of nondiscrete theorists, unlike discrete theorists, lacks a common single affirmative conceptual core, they and

[132] Professor Fried often attributes sweeping ideas to groups of individuals with, at best, only general citations to their work, and without paying attention to the often great differences among them. For example, he attributes to Friedman, Gilmore, and me without citation, the point "that the search for a central or unifying principle of contract is a will-o'-the-wisp, an illusion typical of the ill-defined but much excoriated vice of conceptualism." *Id.* at 3. The reader is therefore left to assume that this is the overall thrust of each of the writers cited. This may be a fair summary of the central theme of G. GILMORE, THE DEATH OF CONTRACT (1974). At any rate, let us assume it is, if only for the purpose of showing the distortion created by Professor Fried's "lumping."

Professor Fried's attribution certainly is not accurate, without a great deal of explanation, respecting L. FRIEDMAN, CONTRACT LAW IN AMERICA (1965). Friedman makes singularly clear that there *is* a central or unifying principle in contract, which he identifies as the market principle. *Id.* at 184. Furthermore, he does not suggest that that principle has disappeared from contract law. Quite the contrary, he claims that it remains the underpinning of classical and neoclassical contract legal doctrine, and he launches specific attacks against that legal doctrine. *Id.* at 184-215. What Friedman does do—and not unnaturally, in view of what we see all around us—is stress how the applicability of the market principle in real life contracts and contract law (as distinct from formal legal doctrine) has shrunk over the periods of time he considers in the book. This may entitle him to be classified as a member of the Death of Contract school, but it certainly does not justify the statement that he sees no central or unifying principle in the concepts of contract or contract law.

Professor Fried also misrepresents my work. In contrast to the "Wisconsin school," which has, by and large, stressed the nonunity of contract as it actually occurs in everyday life and everyday courts, I have spent virtually my entire academic career searching for and identifying unifying principles—in both contract behavior and contract law of all kinds. At first, the three Fullerian principles of restitution, reliance, and expectation seemed to be enough. Macneil, *Power of Contract and Agreed Remedies*, 47 CORNELL L.Q. 495 (1962). (Professor Fried dislikes these, too, as a single contract unifying principle.) The more I struggled, however, the less adequate they seemed. Although THE NEW SOCIAL CONTRACT did not appear in time for Professor Fried to cite it, my search for unifying principles was well underway in work published years before that book, and my opposition to the Death of Contract idea is clearly set out in those of my works Professor Fried does cite.

It is true that I consider the search for a *single* central or unifying contract principle to be a will-o'-the-wisp, and that Fried's statement might therefore be said to be literally correct as applied to me. This might be adequate were it not for Professor Fried's lumping of Gilmore, for whom (it is assumed that) there is no unifying principle; Friedman, for whom *the* unifying principle is the market principle, which continues to prevail in doctrine but relatively little in real life law, and Macneil, who insists upon the existence of unifying principles in all contracts and all contract law. It is highly misleading to treat in one category the true Death of Contract advocate and the believer in unifying contract principles simply because the latter insists that there is more than one unifying principle.

The foregoing also bears on Professor Fried's categorization of all three writers as considering contract unity "an illusion typical of the ill-defined but much excoriated vice of conceptualism." C. FRIED, PROMISE, *supra* note 50, at 3. It may be that Gilmore and Friedman would consider this accurate as to them (and an unintended compliment), but certainly anyone who has conceptualized contract as much as I have can consider it nothing but a grotesquely inaccurate description of his work. This description is particularly crude, because current attacks on conceptualism are so closely associated with two schools. One is the "sociological" school. For a recent discussion, see Tushnet, *Post-Realist Legal Scholarship*, 1980 WIS. L. REV. 1383 (also published at 15 J. SOC. PUB. TCHRS. L. (n.s.) 20 (1980)) [hereinafter Tushnet, *Scholarship*]. The other is the "critical" school. I belong to neither school.

their work do not completely defy classification. Two large classes may be identified: core-denial theorists[133] and relational or holist theorists.

Both Grant Gilmore[134] and the Wisconsin sociological school illustrate conceptualization denying an indentifiable core in contract. As the closing pages of his *The Ages of American Law* suggest, Gilmore was far more concerned about the dangers of "all-purpose theoretical solutions to our problems" than he was about seeking new conceptualizations.[135] Nor has the Wisconsin sociological school demonstrated much desire to seek cores of contract behavior.[136] (This is not surprising, given the considerable theoretical disarray of western sociology.[137])

The other class of conceptualization, relational or holist analysis, can be divided into at least two subclasses: narrow dogmatic and pluralist dogmatic.[138] The most obvious examples of the first subclass are various Marxist and other radical conceptualizations. For example, Tushnet recently defined the "essential contribution of Marxism" to legal analysis to be the showing "that the fundamental forms of life are those implicated in the *material social relations of production*—and that those relations, because they contain contradictions, allow contradictory ways of thinking to develop."[139] Many persons claiming to be Marxist, however, would assert that Marxism also shows the inevitability of a ruling class and a dynamic struggle between that class and all other classes, a struggle the ruling class is doomed to lose sooner or later because of historic forces pushing towards social equality. Each Marxist writer, then, bases his economic, social, and, therefore, his legal and contractual analysis on the variant of Marxist dogma to which

---

133 Gilmore's phrase, Death of Contract, is so overused and misused that this phrase is less likely to confuse the reader.

134 This is more apparent in G. GILMORE, THE AGES OF AMERICAN LAW (1977), perhaps, than in G. GILMORE, THE DEATH OF CONTRACT, *supra* note 132.

135 G. GILMORE, THE AGES OF AMERICAN LAW, *supra* note 134, at 109-11. I share this concern, in spite of my penchant for conceptualizing, but I see the dangers elsewhere than in conceptualizing itself: The dangers lie in conceptualizing that is too narrow, too perfectionist, or both.

136 *See* Tushnet, *Scholarship*, *supra* note 132. This is not to say, as noted in the earlier discussion of L. FRIEDMAN, CONTRACT LAW IN AMERICA, *supra* note 132, that the Wisconsin school rejects the idea of cores in traditional contract doctrine.

137 In contrast to the Wisconsin school, Phillip Selznick, in LAW, SOCIETY, AND INDUSTRIAL JUSTICE (1969), has conceptualized, in the context of industrial relations, about cores of contract behavior. This scholarship, however, lies outside the behavioral, statistical mainstream of American sociology, in which, of course, he has also done work. (This is the mainstream of which most American—but not British—law and sociology, including that of the Wisconsin school, is an offshoot.) My own debt to Selznick is acknowledged in Macneil, *Many Futures*, *supra* note 7.

138 All social analysis is, in my view, dogmatic. That is, I reject the idea that social analysis can be either "neutral" or positive in any sense even remotely like positive physical sciences, except for very limited purposes. I might add that although I question much of the detail of his argument, I agree with Adelstein that the closest physical science analog to any realistic social science is evolutionary biology, not physics. Adelstein, *Institutional Function and Evolution in the Criminal Process*, 76 NW. U.L. REV. 1 (1981).

139 Tushnet, *Scholarship*, *supra* note 132, at 1399 (emphasis added).

he adheres.[140]

The difference between narrow dogmatic holist analysis and pluralist dogmatic holist analysis lies in the absence from the latter of a single dominant dogma. The analysis of contracts in this Article and in my earlier work illustrates the latter. It is founded on a belief in some fundamental nature of man, both as a biologically separate individual and yet as an integral part of a biological society. It is also founded on a belief in the limited, but nonetheless real, capacity of men to understand in quite an objective sense what is "really" going on in the social as well as the physical world about them.[141] These beliefs are obviously dogmatic beliefs; the only thing separating them from a "narrow" dogma is that far more, and far more diverse, connections to reality lead, for example, from the premises in the mind of the believer in pluralism than lead from the premises in the mind of a Marxist.[142]

A caveat is in order. Much current Marxist writing shows so much dogmatic diversity that it is increasingly difficult to consider it Marxist. For example, in the article quoted above, Tushnet gave semiology and phenomenology equal billing to Marxism.[143] Moreover, Tushnet and other apparent Marxists[144] have given so much autonomy to various social structures and groups— for example, lawyers and bureaucrats— in their social analysis, that the classic dialectic of the class struggle is becoming virtually unrecognizable. In short, many "Marxists" are coming perilously close to adopting a form of multidogmatic pluralism as their mode of analysis.

Consider, as an example of the move in the direction of convergence, the withdrawal of E.P. Thompson from serious scholarship in favor of the political struggle against what he views as almost certain nuclear Armageddon. I cannot help but wonder if his withdrawal is entirely unrelated to the crisis likely to be generated in a Marxist upon confessing the following about the rule of law—and drastic ideological ruling class law at that: "The imposing of effective inhibitions upon power and the defence of the citizen for power's all-intrusive claims,

140 I do not use the adjective "narrow" pejoratively here. Moreover, a "narrow dogma" by no means precludes analyses of incredible breadth and perspective; witness the writings of Marx himself.

141 For a recent effort to distinguish three kinds of "understanding" in social science reportage, explanation, and evaluation—see 1 W. RUNCIMAN, A TREATISE ON SOCIAL THEORY: THE METHODOLOGY OF SOCIAL THEORY (1983)[hereinafter W. RUNCIMAN, SOCIAL THEORY].

142 Particular dogmas, narrow or pluralist, vary in the degree to which they adopt rationality as a value for its own sake. *See infra* text accompanying notes 169-71 & 218-19. Narrow dogmatists do not necessarily adopt that value more intensely than do pluralist dogmatists.

143 Tushnet, *Scholarship*, *supra* note 132.

144 I am never sure these days who is and who is not a Marxist. My purpose in using the term "Marxist" is solely for tentative identification, with no thought of thereby either praising or denigrating the work or the person.

seems to me to be an unqualified human good."[145] While I have emphasized Thompson's assessment of the rule of law, most striking is the phrase "effective inhibitions." The nature of the class struggle becomes murky indeed once such a phrase appears. Horwitz's angry response to such heresy[146] suggests how much anguish, how much struggle between Marxist and Englishmen, may have gone on in Thompson's breast in coming to these conclusions.

On the other hand, it is certainly possible for putative pluralists to omit so much from their analysis that they become more narrowly dogmatic than many Marxists. This is especially true when these putative pluralists are compared with Marxists such as Tushnet,[147] Thompson,[148] and Kinsey,[149] who concede a great deal of autonomy to various parts of what used to be dismissed as the superstructure of society. Nevertheless, a gulf between Marxist pluralists and non-Marxist pluralists will continue, at least until Marxists add more to their *basic* concepts than such subjects as semiology and phenomenology together with rather grudging respect for the superstructure. While only blind pluralists could deny the importance of the material social relations of production, non-Marxists would want to add other basic concepts as of *equal* importance.[150] For example, as a non-Marxist pluralist I would, at the economic level alone, insist on the inclusion of two further factors of importance equal to the material social relations of production: the material social relations of consumption and technological determinism.[151]

Another difference standing as a barrier between even pluralistic

---

145 E. THOMPSON, WHIGS AND HUNTERS: THE ORIGIN OF THE BLACK ACT 266 (1975)(emphasis added)[hereinafter, E. THOMPSON, WHIGS].

146 Horwitz, *Book Review*, 86 YALE L.J. 561 (1977).

147 M. TUSHNET, THE AMERICAN LAW OF SLAVERY 1810-1860: CONSIDERATIONS OF HUMANITY AND INTEREST (1981) [hereinafter TUSHNET, SLAVERY].

148 E. THOMPSON, WHIGS, *supra* note 145.

149 Kinsey, *Marxism and the Law: Preliminary Analyses*, 5 BRIT. J.L. & SOC. 202 (1978).

150 Equal not in the sense that at all times and places each concept is equal as a determinant, but in the sense that at *some* time (for long enough periods not to be labeled "ahistorical") and *some* significant place any one may be as important or more important than another "equal."

151 I mean equal here as defined *supra* note 150. In my view, technological determinism has been an "equal" factor since man started making tools; it is now, I suspect, far more important than all the other factors put together—including the social relations of production, which it largely determines, rather than vice versa. The social relations of consumption have perhaps in the past not been an equal factor, but rather a factor largely dependent on the social relations of production. They have now, however, become increasingly independent and, in the developed world at least, perhaps a good deal more important than the material social relations of production.

I would have included the existence of bureaucracy as a third additional factor, but for the fact that it overlaps all three of the basic factors mentioned. A reading of H. COLLINS, MARXISM AND LAW (1982)[hereinafter COLLINS, MARXISM AND LAW], will provide a good basis for assessing how close, yet how far away, modern Marxist analysis is from non-Marxist pluralist dogma.

Hunt has suggested that a kind of merger has already occurred at certain levels, but a very

Marxists and other pluralists is a way of thinking about social analysis, a way of relating dogmatic premises to the "facts" and vice vera. As a non-Marxist, I must confess to having a great deal of difficulty in understanding this difference in general—it is pretty rarefied stuff—but it is there, and in particular contexts I can see the differences, albeit with difficulty. What matters, however, is not my tenuous grasp on the difference, but rather the fact that it exists and is clearly perceived by Marxists as existing.[152] As long as it either exists or is perceived to exist, Marxist and non-Marxist pluralistic analysis will remain partially distinct.[153]

The foregoing excursus on the variants of holist social analysis is designed in part to suggest the absurdity of the idea, found in the work of Professor Fried, that we can talk intelligently about values in terms of a gross dichotomy between discrete and relational (holist) conceptualizing. To make any significant sense, comparison must start with particular kinds of discrete and relational conceptualizing.[154] Since it is too large an enterprise to compare multiple examples of each type, this Article will compare the values of one of each. Professor Fried's model of discreteness will be compared with the relational conceptualizing set out in this Article and my previous work.[155] For the sake of simplicity,

---

different merger from that suggested here. Hunt, *Dichotomy and Contradiction in the Sociology of Law*, 8 BRIT. J.L. & SOC. 47 (1981).

152 *See, e.g.*, Howe & Sica, *Political Economy, Imperialism, and the Problem of World System Theory*, 1 CURR. PERSPS. SOC. THEORY 235 (1980).

153 This part of the Article was written before I had seen H. COLLINS, MARXISM AND LAW, *supra* note 151. After reading his clear and concise, sympathetic yet critical, discussion of the basic tenets of Marxism and their relation to law, I still have some difficulty in knowing just what it is that separates Marxist pluralists from non-Marxist pluralists. Perhaps it is "nothing" but a belief or a nonbelief in the Grail; if so, the nothing is a mighty barrier to an intellectual merger.

154 It may be possible after comparing a range of variants from each end of the spectrum to generalize about some or even all conceptualizing at one end or the other. I rather doubt, however, that it would be possible to generalize respecting the relational end; in any event, the merest attempt would be a daunting endeavour indeed.

155 Two reasons lead me to select this particular body of relational conceptualizing: I know it better than other pluralistic conceptualizations; and using my own work permits me to clarify my position and, I hope, reduce some of the confusion that has arisen concerning values in my particular conceptualizing.

As mentioned *supra* note 137, Selznick developed a similar overarching system in the context of industrial relations over a decade ago, but he did not (and has not, so far as I know) developed it beyond that context. Obviously, many people writing about industrial relations long ago developed ideas to which relational contract theory is closely related. Foster, *Book Review*, *supra* note 35, mentions Kahn-Freund and Freedland in addition to Selznick, to which I would add at least Shulman and Fuller. Such ideas have influenced thinking about contracts and contract law other than industrial relations, but in non-Marxist legal writing, not, so far as I know, in any systematic and comprehensive way apart from relational contract theory.

Moves in the direction of nonradical holist thinking are, of course, occurring in many disciplines. In economics, the JOURNAL OF ECONOMIC ISSUES, the journal of the Association for Evolutionary Economics, attests to the existence of a more holistic movement than that of mainstream economics. For a perceptive analysis of the margins of the mainstream and this smaller stream,

the term "relational contract theory" in what follows is limited to this particular relational contract theory.

2. *Neutral-Ahistorical Values and Historical-Political Values.*— The thesis expressed earlier—that all conceptualizing is a political act—requires two steps in analyzing the values of any conceptualizing.[156] First, one must determine what values are reflected when the conceptualizing is looked at discretely—that is, out of historical context and as if the conceptualizing were a politically neutral act.[157] Second, one must determine what values are reflected by the political act of the particular articulation in the historical context in which it occurs.

For a number of reasons, the values revealed at these two steps may differ greatly in any given situation. For instance, ignorance (including in that term ordinary lack of clairvoyance and naivete) as well as deliberate misleading may cause values as articulated in a particular conceptualization to differ greatly from the values that would be implemented should the conceptualization ever affect human institutions in any significant way.[158] If we attribute purpose to acts of conceptualiz-

see Dugger, *The Transaction Cost Analysis of Oliver E. Williamson: A New Synthesis?*, 17 J. ECON. ISSUES 95 (1983)[hereinafter Dugger, *Williamson*]. Anthropology, in spite of various inroads, has never abandoned holistic approaches in the same way that economics abandoned political economy. For both an example and a current review, see Prattis, *Synthesis, or a New Problematic in Economic Anthropology*, 11 THEORY & SOC'Y 205 (1982)[hereinafter, Prattis, *Synthesis*].

In law, Patrick Atiyah has announced an intention to work along such lines, P. ATIYAH, FREEDOM OF CONTRACT, *supra* note 105, at 778-79. In addition, Melvin Eisenberg states that he is attempting a reconceptualization of "contract law through the development of principles that are intellectually coherent, yet sufficiently open-textured to account for human reality and to unfold over time." Eisenberg, *The Bargain Principle and its Limits*, 95 HARV. L. REV. 741 (1982). He cites Eisenberg, *"Donative Promises,"* 47 U. CHI. L. REV. (1979), and the article quoted as the first two in the effort. With the publication of the third article in the series, Eisenberg, *The Principles of Consideration*, 67 CORNELL L. REV. 640 (1982), it is becoming increasingly apparent that Eisenberg is not attempting to develop a real relational or holist approach. Rather, it is apparent that he intends to remain within the relatively discrete structure of neoclassical contract law, albeit of his own expanded variety. The fact that Eisenberg excludes from his synthesizing effort Eisenberg, *Private Ordering Through Negotiation: Dispute-Settlement and Rulemaking*, 89 HARV. L. REV. 637 (1976), which is a significantly relational approach to contracts, reinforces these conclusions.

156 This in itself is a value-laden conclusion, and those who reject the possibility of even partially objective social analysis will presumably reject this too. On the subject of objectivity, see W. RUNCIMAN, SOCIAL THEORY, *supra* note 141.

157 One does not have to believe in any positivism in order to make this effort worthwhile; even a single-minded dogmatist believing all social analysis to be purely normative, purely political, could approach conceptualizing this way, for the sole purpose of uncovering the political purposes of those engaging in the activity, including his own.

158 By no means all such differences between values as articulated and as implemented should bring condemnation upon the head of the conceptualizer; where there is ignorance, it may be inevitable and totally excusable. We live in a world where rationality is bounded, H. SIMON, MODELS OF MAN (1957), and where our clearest thinking often turns out to have been misguided. For example, those who advocated the progressive income tax at the turn of the century surely should not be condemned for their conceptualizing because the values they articulated have in the mature income tax system been largely replaced by different—and in many ways unworthy—

ing, however, it is essential to try to identify what the conceptualizer thinks he is doing, as well as what we think he is doing in terms of historical effect.

3. *Values in Discrete Conceptualizing: Professor Fried's Contract-as-Promise*.—Professor Fried's theoretical purpose is "to show how a complex legal institution, contract, can be traced to and is determined by a small number of basic moral principles."[159] Indeed, it is a small number—to wit, one: the moral obligation of promise. Promise, and promise only, is the moral basis of contract law.[160] The moral position of other principles in his analysis is unclear to me. It appears that those principles that he treats—restitution, reliance, good faith, conscionability, absence of duress, fairness, and "decency and common sense"[161] as well as those he does not—for example, many principles putatively implemented by the law of the modern welfare state—are, in his analysis, without any moral basis, at least in the world of contract. Nevertheless, whether this appearance is correct is relatively unimportant for present purposes. What is important is that promise, and promise alone is *the* dogmatic base upon which Professor Fried analyzes contract. Everything else becomes something to be fed into that dogma, in the same way that a traditional Marxist feeds all other facts and principles into the dogma of the materialist social relations of production, the ruling class notion, and the class struggle.

The question is what values are reflected in conceptualizing contract in this manner? Before answering this question, certain points made throughout this Article require reiteration. In addition, those points must be linked to Professor Fried's conceptualization, which I shall often refer to as "contract-as-promise." I am not discussing now the values emerging from contract behavior or from internal principles and rules governing contract. Nor am I discussing what values are reflected in various kinds of law imposed on contract by government. Furthermore, I am not discussing what values are imposed on contract in other ways by the external social matrix, with one exception: values emerging from a particular way of organizing our thoughts about contract.[162]

values. Only with the benefit of hindsight can we see that their political acts turned out to have had significantly different values from those articulated.

159 C. FRIED, PROMISE, *supra* note 50, at 1 preface. A second purpose is to display for students the underlying structure of the basic legal institution of contract as Professor Fried sees it. *Id.*

160 "The promise principle, which in this book I argue is the moral basis of contract law, ..." *Id.* at 1.

161 *Id.* at 6.

162 This distinction between what I am and am not discussing is especially important respecting Professor Fried's work, because he himself confuses conceptualizing about law with law itself. For example, Professor Fried at one point refers to "Maine's classic thesis in *Ancient Law* that modern *law* has moved away from status relations to relations founded on promise, that is, relations de-

a. Contract-as-Promise Viewed Ahistorically.—

The Discrete Norm. The most obvious values reflected by contract-as-promise are those of the discrete norm: precise focus, following through on planning, and efficiency. Contract-as-promise also reflects the value of consent, but may or may not reflect the value of choice. It also may or may not reflect the value of equality. It is clear, however, that contract-as-promise sacrifices relational values. Since the same can be said of virtually any discrete conceptualizing, these statements are but a start at analyzing contract-as-promise. To differentiate contract-as-promise from other discrete conceptualizations requires further consideration.[163]

---

fined by the will of the parties." *Id.* at 76. He then says that "[m]any have sounded this retreat from Maine's *conception*." *Id.* (emphasis added). This simply makes no sense. Maine meant just what he said in his famous statement that the progress of law is from status to contract. He was talking about the progress of law, not the progress of his own conceptions; he was talking about the history of law, not the history of conceptions—his or those of anyone else. Professor Fried twists Maine's statement about law into one about conceptualizing, about how a particular person, Maine himself, structured his own thoughts about law.

This kind of confusion can lead to serious error of analysis. Such confusion is demonstrated by the fact that Professor Fried cites I. MACNEIL, CONTRACTS: EXCHANGE TRANSACTIONS AND RELATIONS 346-502 (2d ed. 1978), as proof of my part in the "retreat from" Maine's nonexistent thesis about his own conceptions. These pages in my casebook deal with illegality, the limited legal power of contract, legislative and administrative control of contract, governmental imposition of contractual relations, and government use of private contract to achieve special public goals. They consist almost entirely of legal materials showing massive government interference with freedom of contract in America. They are in a casebook for law students who, upon graduation, will be dealing with these aspects of law more regularly than they will with any other aspect of law governing contractual behavior. In short, they show what scholars of virtually all philosophical and political outlooks, except Professor Fried, seem to recognize: that since the time of Maine the "progress," i.e. movement, of law in Western states has been from contract to status. However one may feel about this "progress," it is as real as the "progress" of the automobile in the same period. (Modern statuses are not, of course, identical to the more primitive statuses Maine had in mind. *See* Rehbinder, *Status, Contract, and the Welfare State*, 23 STAN. L. REV. 941 (1971).)

None of the foregoing is intended to deny that descriptions of law are themselves aspects of intellectual history and political statements, as already suggested, *supra* note 13. No doubt Maine's statement about the history of law is properly viewed as "political" as well as an effort to state an objective fact; so too is my inclusion of materials in a casebook "political." What the political thrust of such statements or inclusions is, however, calls for analysis, not for casually drawn conclusions.

[163] It is not possible to reject one of these discrete values entirely and still have a discrete transaction. For example, Professor Fried "rejects" efficiency as the basis for contract in favor of promise and its allegedly special morality. This permits him to select promise over efficiency in the rare instances where the two clash in a discrete model. In his neoclassical contract model, however, the value of technical efficiency coincides with the value of promise virtually all the time. This makes it impossible for Professor Fried to "reject" efficiency without rejecting promise at the same time. His purported rejection of efficiency is no more than a statement of distaste for some of the inevitable practical and intellectual consequences of adopting promise as *the* contract principle.

Dominance of Choice. Professor Fried believes that promise is *the* moral principle of contract, because choice is the dominant value in his hierarchy of values. His touchstone is always the autonomy of the individual. As shown earlier, however, consent does not necessarily achieve that goal. Nevertheless, Professor Fried's belief in the importance of choice is both genuine and carefully implemented. He does not, for example, ignore the limitations of objective manifestations of consent in effectuating choice. Consequently, he delivers a devastating attack on the objective approach to contracts. Repeatedly, he avoids pressing promise to unrealistic lengths, keeping it as close to the exercise of choice as possible. Thus, unlike Williston, whose extreme objective theory was intended to be a system of social control aimed at achieving precision and implementation of the forms of planning irrespective of the effect on choice, Fried is willing to sacrifice such discrete values when choice will be adversely affected. Thus, at the articulation level, the ahistorical level, Professor Fried values choice in contract—real choice, not just consent—more than most modern contract theorists, even the so-called Chicago School theorists, who often sacrifice choice in favor of choice-destroying consent.

Sacrifice of Relational Values. All discrete conceptualizations of contract sacrifice relational values. Contract-as-promise is no exception: to the extent it is given primacy, inconsistent relational values are sacrificed.[164] Professor Fried, however, carefully limits the promise principle and states that nothing about it "entails that all disputes between people who have tried but failed to make a contract or who have broken a contract must be decided solely according to that principle."[165] Thus, he avoids complete sacrifice of relational values, but sacrificed in considerable measure they are. The very nature of any conceptualization with a single focus, such as contract-as-promise, assures the sacrifice of other values. This is especially the case when the single value is elevated to a special position as the only *moral* value. Moreover, Professor Fried in dealing with the relation between his promise principle and many competing values severely limits the range of those competing values. He considers restitution, reliance, good faith, conscionability, absence of duress, fairness, "decency and common sense."[166] Professor Fried thus omits many of the values that modern liberal governments attempt to impose on contracts of all sorts, such as levels of reciprocity, limitations of power, preservation of rela-

[164] *See* Rosett, *Partial, Qualified, and Equivocal Repudiation of Contract*, 81 COLUM. L. REV. 93 (1981).

[165] C. FRIED, PROMISE, *supra* note 50, at 27.

[166] Curiously, none of these, not even decency, is a "moral" value in the world of contract-as-promise!

tions, and approved processes.[167] In sum, contract-as-promise sacrifices a great many relational values, although not as completely as does, for example, neoclassical microeconomics, especially when it omits transaction costs.

Rationality for the Sake of Rationality. There is, I believe, also another value reflected in contract-as-promise. Professor Fried deliberately creates a closed logical system of contract conceptualization, one bounded by promise, even though doing so leads him to omit vast areas of everyday contract and contract law, even when those terms are narrowly defined. The logic of his starting point, individual autonomy, could equally well have led him to (or dropped him off at) *all* the common contract norms.[168] Moreover, some of those norms, such as restitution and reliance, have been familiar territory for contract scholars for a long time. Yet, Professor Fried insists upon leaving them and others outside his closed intellectual system, which he does by analyzing only their interface with that closed system. The artificiality of this suggests that Professor Fried's hierarchy contains some value that is not immediately apparent.

That value, I believe, is rationality for the sake of rationality. Man has an immense desire for order and consistency. This is particularly true of anything affecting his own life.[169] Order, however, is impossible, which frustrates everyone to varying degrees. People respond to this frustration in many ways, depending upon how they wish to live with the real irrationality of life. Many people create or adopt entirely consistent intellectual systems of social order to cope with the discomfort of this aspect of being human. The believers in such systems, including Professor Fried, may or may not value rationality in other aspects of

---

167 Indeed, as suggested *supra* note 162, he is hostile even to including them in thinking about contracts, although if pressed he could hardly deny either the existence or the vast impact of such law, or of the values putatively or in fact implemented. The impact on contract of sovereign imposition of values is treated in some detail *supra* text accompanying notes 83-91 & 99-124.

168 The complex route by which Professor Fried moves from the idea of atomistic individuals to contract-as-promise is set out in C. FRIED, PROMISE, *supra* note 50, at 7-16. The path between the beginning and ending points may be summarized as follows: (1) introduction of the "liberal ideal" that morality requires respect for the person and property of others so that they are free to make their lives as we are; (2) trust in others based on a conviction that they will do what is right, not just what is prudent; (3) the device giving trust its sharpest, most palpable form is promise, its basis being convention; (4) deliberate invoking of the convention by promising establishes the moral obligation. Professor Fried fails to note many of the pitfalls along this route, but his fatal failure lies in not realizing that exactly the same reasoning can be used to provide a moral basis for any of the common contract norms.

169 Were man completely rational, he would have no such desire. Indeed, the need for order would not occur, nor, probably, could he even imagine the need, assuming he could imagine anything. The Star Trek portrayal of human-like animals of complete rationality in the form of the Vulcans is instructive on the subject of such impossible creatures. Even Mr. Spock—half Vulcan, half human—is an impossibility, which is one of the things that makes him so interesting.

their lives more than do other humans. In the areas of their chosen closed systems, however, they value rationality for its own sake above most else, if not above all else. They award this primary value to rationality even at the expense of accepting much artificiality. In doing so, they reify logical systems, giving them a legitimacy they do not necessarily have in reality. Consequently, they often focus their attention on the "wrong" things—wrong in the sense that perception unclouded by this value would lead them to different subjects of concern.[170]

In sum, Professor Fried's contract-as-promise conceptualizing viewed ahistorically reflects the discrete values of precise focus—following through on planning and consent—accompanied by a special concern for choice. Like other systems of discrete analysis, Professor Fried's system sacrifices relational values. Finally, Professor Fried's system reflects the value of rationality for the sake of rationality.[171]

b. Contract-as-Promise Viewed Historically as Current Political Ideology.—In order to consider the values expressed by the political ideology of any particular conceptualizing, that conceptualizing must be put in its historical context. Professor Fried's conceptualizing must be viewed in the context of the advanced Western capitalist-welfare state and its laws, some carefully selected parts of which are the focus of his inquiry. It is surely accurate to assume that Professor Fried wishes other people to think about contracts as he does,[172] with the promise principle in a position of dominance and moral superiority, albeit with a more limited sphere than that attributed to it by many past contract theorists of a related persuasion. The "other people" he wishes to convince most certainly include not only other scholars, but also lawyers, legislators, judges, and particularly tomorrow's lawyers, legislators, and judges. Moreover, it seems reasonable to assume that he wants his way of thinking to affect the structure, substance, and procedure of contract law in favor of choice.[173] Bearing these assumptions in mind, we can now turn to his conceptualizing viewed as ideology.

---

170 The suicide of Inspector Javert in Victor Hugo's, LES MISERABLES, *supra* note 65, illustrates how great the tension can be when reality imposes too heavily on such beliefs.

All conceptualizations are partially closed systems, but the more closed the system, the greater the likelihood that rationality itself will assume particular value in the eyes of its proponents.

171 Although this value is one found especially in conceptualizing about law, it is also found in law itself. Indeed, this value is found in all human behavior and its norms, including internal contract behavior and its principles and rules. Jurisprudents and other conceptualizers have no monopoly on this value.

172 Indeed, Professor Fried says in the preface to his book that he wants to convince his students of the correctness of his position. C. FRIED, PROMISE, *supra* note 50, preface.

173 It is conceivable that Professor Fried simply wants to clarify thinking about contract (in his terms, of course), and the devil take the hindmost whether his views have a beneficial effect on choice. The fervent tone of his book, however, suggests otherwise.

Precise Focus and Following Through on Planning. Although precise focus and following through on planning are values that are inherent in contract-as-promise, Professor Fried does not accord them prominence. If those whom Professor Fried seeks to influence recognize the importance of those values, it will not be because of direct appeal,[174] but for other reasons, such as belated realization that they are a function of the discrete approach. Nonetheless, these values need never become overt in order to be operative.

Anyone observing current difficulties in the management of the modern economy, and particularly the inability of the political-economic establishment to focus precisely on large scale problems and to follow through on planning, might well consider these values more important over the next half century than some of the other values arising from the discrete position. Because these values are covert rather than overt in Professor Fried's thesis of contract-as-promise, however, it is especially difficult to analyze what effect his thesis might have in promoting these values in, for example, the law of contract. Thus, what real political effect Professor Fried's theorizing might have in promoting these values is problematic.

Dominance of Choice. Professor Fried gives primacy to the promise principle because of its origin in choice, upon which he places high value. He is nevertheless stuck with the fact that, for reasons discussed earlier, choice itself is once removed from the promise principle, and, indeed, is so antithetical to it that promise can be justified on choice grounds only by appeal to pragmatic results, not by deduction from the basic liberal principle of autonomy. To the extent that Professor Fried succeeds with his ideology, people will think more highly of the promise principle and, presumably, will try to cause contract law to reflect the promise principle more completely than it otherwise would. Nonetheless, implementing this value will enhance the role of choice *only* to the extent that rigorously enforcing promise will increase individual autonomy. The question remains whether enhancing the role of promise will actually increase individual autonomy. This is a question of factual prediction, not one answerable by reference to abstract analysis. I raise it not to answer it, but only to point out that in terms of ideology, it must be answered affirmatively before anyone, including Professor Fried himself, is in a position to assert that his conceptualizing is ideologically pro-choice.[175]

Sacrifice of Relational Values. Although Professor Fried's closed system has a single focus— promise—it must be remembered that in

---

174 Unlike Professor Fried, neoclassical microeconomic theorists appeal directly to their readers to recognize the importance of these values.

175 Professor Fried obviously wishes his conceptualizing to favor choice.

showing how promise relates to other values, all of them relational, his whole work sacrifices relational values far less than does his closed system itself. Viewed as ideology, we must look at all he does, not just part of it. In this sense, his book might conceivably further such interests as restitution and reliance as much as did Fuller and Perdue's landmark article,[176] although it seems unlikely to have that effect. As noted earlier,[177] however, many relational values, including many imposed by law, are omitted from the book as well as from the closed system itself.[178] Judges and lawyers faced with the manifold complexities of real life contracts, the countless internal norms they engender, and the countless governmental impositions to which they are subject, will, to the extent Professor Fried succeeds in his educational efforts, continue to think of the "law of contract" as a narrow, isolated phenomenon unrelated to the remainder of the great *corpus juris pactae*.

What the effects on judge and jury lawmaking of such a disjointed doctrinal approach to contracts will be I do not know. Certainly, however, such an approach will result in some arbitrary decisions contrary to any worthwhile principle, and some unnecessary inefficiency can be expected. Beyond those things, the law of contract (writ large) may continue to function as the reasonably effective operational system that, on the whole, it has been in the past in spite of existing intellectual discontinuities between these two aspects of contract law.

Rationality for the Sake of Rationality. To the extent that contract-as-promise fosters the values of rationality for the sake of rationality in contract law, it will promote formalism. The most fertile ground for this in American contract law is in neoclassical contract law—the subject areas covered, for example, by the Restatement (Second) of Contracts. Professor Fried's arguments conceivably could lead to more formalism in other aspects of contract law as well—for exam-

176 Fuller & Perdue, *The Reliance Interest in Contract Damages* (pts. 1 & 2), 46 YALE L.J. 52, 373 (1936-37).

177 *Supra* text accompanying notes 164-67.

178 Reducing ideology to more immediate terms, what may be the effect of Professor Fried's book on the substance of contract law, in the grand sense of the word contract? As earlier noted, I take contract law to be all law pertaining to "relations among people in the course of projecting exchange into the future." *See supra* text accompanying note 1. I would guess the effect of Professor Fried's book on contracts in this sense to be close to nil. Legislatures, administrative agencies, and courts will be influenced little, if at all, by their belief in a closed intellectual system of this kind in deciding whether to continue or reduce their impositions of contract and supracontract norms on contracts. Furthermore, lawyers, business people, and others dealing with contracts will be little influenced to change their behavior by such beliefs. That does not mean, however, that Professor Fried's system will have no effect whatever on the law. His conceptualizing will help continue and exacerbate, especially among students, the doctrinal isolation of the traditional areas of contract law—classical, now neoclassical contract law—from the rest of the law relating to contract, except possibly in those areas that Professor Fried does relate to his closed system, such as restitution, reliance, good faith, duress, and so on.

ple, in judicial approaches to complex bureaucratic regulation of contracts. If they had this effect, they might run very much counter to some of Professor Fried's other values, particularly choice. Already burdened by bureaucracy, choice now would become burdened by bureaucracy made worse by enhanced formalism. Nevertheless, the latter effect seems likely to be small, because the very isolation of Professor Fried's closed promissory system may keep whatever respect for formalism it generates within the limited arena of neoclassical contract law.

Cumulative Effect. Although Professor Fried handles the relation between choice and consent more gingerly than do typical neoclassical microeconomists and attributes a binding morality to promise eschewed by at least some neoclassical microeconomists, his conceptualizing is, on the whole, very much like theirs ideologically. That is, efficiency theorists, in advancing almost all legal-political positions, will find support for those positions in the special moral priority Fried gives to promise (and vice-versa). Furthermore, Professor Fried's ideas are not very different from traditional freedom of contract notions, such as those expressed by Sir George Jessel over a hundred years ago.[179]

In sum, the volumes that have been written about the political thrust of individualist works of this general kind, whether from right, left, or middle, apply to Fried's conceptualizing more or less intact. That is to say, in terms of ideology, Fried simply joins long ranks of present and past individualistic ideologists, or in modern terminology, "conservatives." The assessment of what such conservatives "are *really* about" in their conceptualizing varies greatly among manifold and diverse beholders.

4. *Values in Relational Contract Theory*.—

a. Historical and Ahistorical Analysis.—We have thus far proceeded as if the distinction between historical and ahistorical analysis were relatively clear, but it is not.[180] Formal, ahistorical analysis—unless it is nothing but a mathematical game[181]—must sooner or later be

[179] [I]f there is one thing which more than another public policy requires it is that men of full age and competent understanding shall have the utmost liberty of contracting, and that their contracts when entered into freely and voluntarily shall be held sacred and shall be enforced by Courts of justice.

Printing & Numerical Registering Co. v. Sampson, 19 L.R.-Eq. 462, 465 (1875).

[180] It is sufficiently clear, however, for the analysis of a model such as Professor Fried's, which lies at the ahistorical end of the historical-ahistorical spectrum.

[181] *See* Macneil, *Lon Fuller*, *supra* note 41. *See also* Dworkin's remark about "the grip that the formal style has lately had on Anglo-American political philosophy." After giving some examples, including Rawls, he writes: "Such theories seem more at home with mathematics than with politics." Dworkin, Book Review, N.Y. REV. BOOKS, Apr. 14, 1983, at 5.

applied to a *particular* set or sets of circumstances. Such analysis thus has to be put into history somewhere. On the other hand, historical analysis, like ahistorical analysis, inevitably also involves significant processes of ordering and principles transcending historical particulars. For example, Marxist analysis typically includes at least the following formal ideas transcending history: ideas concerning objectivity and human consciousness;[182] dominance of the social relations of production over other human relations; existence of historical forces; various ideas about the relations of men and men and of men and material things, such as reification, alienation, and the like; a notion of powerlessness and all-powerfulness in social relations; theories about class struggle; and various utopian beliefs concerning the malleability of humans and their societies.[183] Do these formal ideas render Marxist analysis ahistorical? No, but their presence as the foundation of a school of thought claiming to be thoroughly historical suggests difficulty in distinguishing what is historical from what is ahistorical.

Complexity. The conflict between "historians" and "ahistorians" is, at one level, a conflict about how complex a formal model must be for use in social analysis. The more human interaction an analyst believes can be reduced to a simple model, the more ahistorical is his analysis. The more the analyst insists on complexity in his models, the more history he inevitably introduces when he uses them. Two of the more important ways in which a model may be complex is in the number of differing elements it includes and in the complexity of the elements themselves. Neoclassical microeconomic analysis which omits transaction costs is the most extreme example of a simple model, because it uses only one element—maximization—and because that element, once all its complex assumptions are made, is eminently simple itself.

The extent of interplay between a model and any situation to which it is applied is an important indicator of how historical the model is. For example, once the assumptions of the neoclassical microeconomic model are made, the subject examined— whether that subject be consumption of betel nuts on a South Pacific island, or sales of oil in international trade, or love relations, or the building of power in a corporate hierarchy or the Politburo—has no impact on the model itself. In a sense, this is true of the formal elements of any model. Interfaces between various elements in more complex models multiply geometrically with the number of elements, however, and each inter-

182 *See supra* text accompanying notes 138-53.

183 These ideas transcend history in varying degrees. Unlike much utilitarianism, the utopian element in Marxism supplies an ultimate utopian future transcending much of the rest of Marxism's ahistorical formalism. See H. COLLINS, MARXISM AND LAW, *supra* note 151, for a full, yet short, account of the formal ideas of Marxism.

face presents the opportunity for particular circumstances to modify the outcome—to introduce history—and, in a very real sense, to modify the model itself. In addition, where the various elements in the model are themselves complex—for example, reciprocity—the facts of any particular situation have a similar effect on the model. Thus, even though the model remains theoretically intact (and, of course, remains the lens through which the analyst sees), it is in a very real sense subject to constant historical modification.

How Historical is Historical? Closely related to the first level of conflict between "historians" and "ahistorians" are differences over how historical an analysis must be in order to be viewed as historical rather than ahistorical. As the foregoing comments suggest, however, the question should not be viewed this way. All social analysis is both historical and ahistorical, a fact that posing the question as a dichotomy obscures.[184] Understanding and communication would be better served by recognizing "historical" as a quantitative rather than a qualitative word—in other words, by recognizing that analyses are either more or less historical rather than historical or ahistorical.

Objectivity. A third level of conflict between "historians" and "ahistorians" involves a range of different views about objectivity. Particularly sharp disputes arise over how much and what kinds of objectivity are possible and about the possible and actual roles of the observer in terms both of his functions as observer and his effect on the persons and events observed. I suppose, for example, that a non-Marxist might be almost entirely in accord with a Marxist about the nature of the class struggle and still differ greatly with the Marxist about his own objectivity and role as observer-reporter-participant.[185] In addition, there are those purporting to reject objectivity in history because they reject the idea of knowing history altogether, from any view.[186]

[184] One may be forgiven, perhaps, for wondering how much of this obscuring may be deliberate by those in both positivist and radical camps who seem more interested in promoting particular positions than in clarifying the nature of the conflict.

[185] The Marxist might be "almost" rather than entirely in accord, because the differences concerning the observer-reporter role would be viewed by the Marxist as inevitably affecting the observer-reporter's views of the class struggle itself. For a discussion of these kinds of issues, see Corrigan, *Dichotomy is Contradiction: On 'Society' as Constraint and Construction. Remarks on the Doctrine of the 'Two Sociologies,'* 23 SOC. REV. 211 (1975).

[186] Consider, for example, the writing of Grant Gilmore and Arthur Leff, whose anarchic intellectual views suggest that there can be no objectivity, and no history, simply because nothing is knowable. For example, Gilmore says that: "So far as we have been able to learn, there are no recurrent patterns in the course of human events; it is not possible to make scientific statements about history, sociology, economics—or law." G. GILMORE, THE AGES OF AMERICAN LAW, *supra* note 134, at 100. Gilmore evidently did not quite mean it. *Id.* at 109-11. Arthur Leff, however, claimed that he, Leff, did. Leff, *Law and ?*, 87 YALE L.J. 989 (1978). As one privileged to know

Substantive Content of History. A fourth level of conflict, one closely related to objectivity, concerns the substantive content of history. In common usage, historical analysis of any subject means no more than paying attention to its past, and ahistorical analysis means an analysis paying no attention to the past of the subject.[187] But another meaning of historical analysis is one proceeding on a particular view of theory and of its effect on the present and future.[188] As Hugh Collins' definition of Marxism suggests, Marxists use the word historical in the latter manner:

> Marxism is a theory about the meaning of history. However aimless the wanderings of mankind may have seemed to others, Marxists have discerned a regular evolutionary pattern controlling the human condition. Behind the complexity and particularity of isolated events human civilization has been gradually moving towards the goal of history. Once the direction of this progress and the reasons for social change are perceived, then the secrets of the future can be glimpsed. According to Marxism the meaning of history is that man's destiny lies in the creation of a Communist society where men will experience a higher stage of being amounting to the realization of true freedom.[189]

Anyone holding a particular theory of history is very likely to use the word "historical" to refer to analysis consistent with that theory of history and the word "ahistorical" to refer to any differing analysis—no matter how concerned it is with the past of the subject. One wishing to understand a discussion of social analysis in which the past is pertinent, or who wishes to make plain what it is he is saying, needs to be alert to these differing usages. As befits a pluralist dogmatist, I use these words in their common, not their radical, sense.[190]

---

that delightful scholar, who until his untimely death brought so much intelligent humor to the law, I do not really believe it.

187 The words "ahistoric" and "ahistorical" do not appear in the original OXFORD ENGLISH DICTIONARY (1933). In the O.E.D. Supplement (1972) the first example given of "ahistorical" is from 1957, and of "ahistoric" is from 1937.

188 For example, see the quotation from Aldous Huxley in 2 O.E.D. Supp. 106 (1972):

> One word is common to all the dictatorial vocabularies and is used for purposes of justification and rationalization by Fascists, Nazis and Communists alike. That word is "historical". . . . The dictatorship of the proletariat is an "historical necessity." The violence of the Communists is justified because it is being used to forward an ineluctable "historical" process.

189 H. COLLINS, MARXISM AND LAW, *supra* note 151, at 2.

190 At least in part because of the success of political movements putatively based on Marxist principles, radicals have been able to capture the high strategic ground in the history vs. ahistory discussion in a very real sense. (Devotees of ahistorical positivism presumably would view it as the low ground—indeed as a murky marsh full of the gases of ignorance.) The Marxist usage of "historical" and "ahistorical"—although unrecognized in the OXFORD ENGLISH DICTIONARY, even in the Supplement, *see supra* note 187—rather than the common meaning, often seems to be the presumed meaning in academic discourse.

There are, not surprisingly, liberal counterparts to such dogmatic capture of a word, the most striking one being the microeconomic use of the word "rational." Neoclassical economists, for example, have managed in considerable measure to reserve this term for a number of very pecu-

b. Interaction of Relational Contract Theory and History.—

(1) Introduction. Examining relational contract theory in terms of these four levels of conflicting views, clearly at the fourth level it is ahistorical in the Marxist or radical sense, since it does not adopt Marxist or other radical history as its base. Similarly, at the third level it

---

liar and elusive meanings, none of which may be found in any general dictionary I have seen. Two of these are "maximization of utility" and "consistency of preferences." The following quotation illustrates how these meanings dance in and out of economic discourse like so many wraiths at a ghostly ball:

> The basic ideas contained in the economic approach to law are those of maximizing behavior (utility maximization), stable preferences and opportunity cost. The economic approach takes the individual as the basic unit of analysis and pictures him as a self-interested egoist who maximizes utility. Its assumptions of utility maximization and rationality have given rise to much criticism and confusion. When an economist says that an individual is acting rationally or maximizing his utility he is saying no more than that the individual is making consistent choices, and that he chooses the preferred alternative(s) from those available to him. The modern economic theory of utility/rationality attempts to describe rigourously the choice process and to draw out the implications of that process for behaviour under different conditions. . . .
>
> The economic approach does *not* contend that all individuals are rational nor that these assumptions are necessarily realistic. The economist's model of man as a rational actor is a fiction, but one that has proved extremely useful in analysing the behavior of groups. . . .The theory allows for irrationality but argues that *groups* of individuals behave as if their members are rational. . . .
>
> A corollary of the rationality postulate is that individuals react to changes in the net benefits received from the alternatives which confront them. . . .
>
> The utility maximization hypothesis is based on a set of axioms that requires preferences to exhibit certain properties which if they do not will refute the *assumption* that choice is rational. . . . But it is true that the utility maximization hypothesis can be rendered into a sterile truism, particularly when used normatively, if actual choices are accepted without qualification as rational and therefore 'good'.

Burrows & Veljanovski, *Introduction: The Economic Approach to Law*, in THE ECONOMIC APPROACH TO LAW 3-4, 15 (P. Burrows & C. Veljanovski eds. 1981).

The reader will note how "rational" dances in and out of economic analysis in the above discussion. In the first sentence, it is impossible to ascertain whether "rationality" is one of the basic ideas in the economic approach. Two sentences later we find "utility maximization *and* rationality," apparently separate concepts. Then we find two phrases in which those concepts are equated: "acting rationally *or* maximizing his utility," and "theory of utility/rationality." Later, the disclaimer of the universality of rational behavior seems to introduce the nonmicroeconomic idea of rational as meaning reasonable or sensible in some broad sense. Finally comes a paragraph where rationality is equated with certain properties of preferences, but *which* of the properties earlier discussed is unclear.

One thing is clear, however: the introduction into the model of a flow of time, although the model is founded on the exercise of choice, which can occur only instantaneously. This is illustrated by the references to stable preferences and consistency. Making *a* choice can never be inconsistent with anything else an individual does except something happening before or after that choice is made, because making a choice is nothing more nor less than what an individual actually does at any instant when he could be doing something else and does not. (For a discussion of the failure of the economic model to deal with the problem of time, see Macneil, *Economic Analysis*, *supra* note 7, at 1021 n.6, 1036-37, 1045-46 n.72.) Only the introduction of time permits the introduction of rationality as adding anything to utility maximization beyond the idea that choice equals any actual behavior. But what it is, if anything, beyond stability of preference, one cannot tell in this excerpt. For a much shorter example of obscurity, see Judge Posner's phrase "rational maximizer," where the phrase seems to mean "maximizing maximizer." R. POSNER, ECONOMIC ANALYSIS OF LAW 3-4 (2d ed. 1977).

would be ahistorical to those—Marxist, radical, or otherwise—who either reject the idea of objective analysis altogether or who reject objectivity except in terms of dogma different from those underlying relational contract theory. To anyone believing in the possibility of some objectivity and disbelieving that the proponents of any particular dogma have a monopoly on history, this leaves unresolved the first two levels of debate: complexity and how historical a model must be to be historical. These issues will be treated in terms of (1) the minimum historical input required for proper application of relational contract theory and (2) the maximum historical input into the theory that is possible or desirable.

Minimum Historical Input. The interplay between relational contract theory and any given historical situation to which it might be applied has to be extensive. The common contract norms form what has been criticized as a "rich classificatory apparatus,"[191] relational contract theory being rich in the sense that the various norms are many and constitute core concepts, rather than theoretically precise, on-off ideas like maximization. These core concepts are, in varying degrees, meaningful only when fleshed out with living history. In addition, relational contract theory postulates ten norms, each of which interfaces with all the others. Thus, its application to particular historical circumstances provides great potential interaction between the model and those circumstances.[192]

The most obviously historical of the common contract norms in this sense is harmonization with the social matrix.[193] There is in that norm nothing but a germ, no matter how vital, until the contractual

---

191 Williamson, *supra* note 68, at 236.

192 If relational contract theory purported to be a social science model, it would be a very messy one indeed.

193 All contracts are in part relational, and one category of relational norms is supracontract norms. Since supracontract norms are always at least partially specific to time and place, they also will always introduce history into the model.

Reiter, *Good Faith*, *supra* note 20, suggests that relational contract theory "stands idle, like a huge machine waiting for current to be switched through it. . . . What drives it will differ by society, and . . . in the end, 'supracontract norms' will determine the place and shape of contract as historical fact." *Id.* This is only partially correct. First, supracontract norms cannot shape contract (other than by destroying it) beyond the limits imposed by the common contract norms. To continue Reiter's analogy, in order for the contract engine to work, the power of the particular circumstances to be added must be the kind of power suited to an operating engine of its design. If one hooks up a high voltage power line to an engine designed to run on gasoline, the result will not be operation of the engine, but either its destruction, or a short circuit in the power line, or both. Similarly, only some kinds of circumstances will power the contractual engine. Where, for example, increasingly high levels of sheer force are used in place of workable levels of reciprocity, the contract engine begins to sputter and finally to fall apart through lassitude, death, social revolt, and the like.

Second, the particular historical circumstances introduced into an analysis remain only partial determinants of "the place and shape of contract as historical fact." Thus, any historical

behavior being studied is examined in the full context of its particular social matrix. Thus, for example, if one were treating Victorian factories in terms of relational contract theory, a proper analysis would treat the impact of the broad Victorian setting that social historians would view as important.[194] Similarly, the norm of propriety of means—the idea that how things are done is a fundamental consideration partially separable from what is done—becomes a useful tool of social analysis only when connected with specific historical circumstances. For example, modern legislation conferring procedural rights on franchisees faced with threatened nonrenewal of their franchises cannot be treated in terms of relational contract theory except against the broad sweep of American history of the past 75 years or more. These two norms merely illustrate the point; one may continue through all the common contract norms and find each to be a useful tool of analysis only when filled with history.[195]

The minimum historical input necessary to use relational contract theory properly is a larger input than it might otherwise seem because each of the nine more formal norms must harmonize with the particular social matrix separately as well as collectively. If, for example, a particular society scorns hard discrete bargaining in certain kinds of relations, the person violating that particular "propriety of means" norm by adopting a trader-role will have difficulty even though all the other norms— for example, adequate levels of reciprocity—might be met. (There is, of course, an interaction among the more formal norms themselves that makes violation of one likely to be violation of some others as well. In the illustration just given, for example, the trader-

---

contract behavior is a product both of its particular historical circumstances and the fundamental nature of contractual behavior as described by relational contract theory.

Reiter goes on to suggest that the institutionalized search for the components of good faith supplies the "power" for relational contract theory. The problem with this is that good faith in the abstract—that is, the good faith of the unidentified "relevant community"—is equally an idle machine waiting for the power of a particular society to turn it on. Thus, it is not "good faith" that can power relational contract theory. Rather, it is what good faith means in a particular context that can power it. In other words, it is the contextualizing of relational contract theory that powers it, not the injection of abstract good faith.

194 That would, of course, include the pre-Victorian flow of history yielding the Victorian setting.

195 It is arguable that consent, being formal, is an exception and hence ahistorical in nature. It is not possible, however, to ascertain when consent has or has not been given or to what it has or has not been given without consideration of the particular historical context. Nor, outside a specific historical setting, is it possible to ascertain the consequences of consenting, since, as pointed out earlier consent is not choice alone, but choice plus the bindingness added by society. Since the bindingness societies give to consent varies greatly, we can speak of the effect of consent only in terms of particular historical contexts.

As I tried to show in Macneil, *Many Futures*, *supra* note 7, at 810-13, the need to consider specific circumstances in no way prevents the theory from being used to analyze very specific rules of law.

role very likely will lead to actual or perceived violations of power and reciprocity norms as well.)

Thus, the interplay of relational contract theory and particular historical circumstances to which it may be applied requires as a minimum a very significant historical input in any given application.

Maximum Historical Input. Subject solely to the limits imposed by the need for any viable contractual relation, large or small, to comply with each common contract norm to sufficient degree, relational contract theory is entirely open to the addition of history.[196] The fact that unlimited quantities of history may be fitted into relational contract theory does not mean that unlimited quantities should be added to it (or any other historical social analysis). Like any model, it becomes more and more an accumulation of particulars and less and less a model as particulars are added. As is the case with any historical analysis, choices must be made between depicting the trees and depicting the forest.

It should also be noted that, in large measure, relational contract theory can accommodate any kind of history as well as any quantity. That is to say, nothing in relational contract theory itself precludes its being used in conjunction with extremely broad spectra of socioeconomic and political views of history.[197]

The foregoing discussions of minimum and maximum quantities and kinds of history that are required to be used with, or that are compatible with, relational contract theory mean relatively little without specification of some of the basic historical facts that are essential to social analysis, the subject I shall now address.

(2) Key Historical Facts. No list of historical facts to be taken into account in any given situation can possibly be complete, but those following seem to me to be among the more important in using relational contract theory. Their importance relative to each other will vary in different settings.[198]

Natural Environment. Variations in natural environment—climate, geography, kind and quantity of natural resources, and the like—

[196] This is not to suggest that history must give way to this, or any other, theory. To the extent that history may reveal durable contractual relations with lower levels of reciprocity than we might like or perhaps than we can quite believe, it is our understanding of the application of the theory that would require adjustment. Moreover, if history showed significant instances in which durable contractual relations occurred in the absence of one or more of the common contract norms, the theory, as one purporting to be as broad as mankind, would be wrong.

[197] See *infra* text accompanying notes 220-37, for a development of this point and also of its limits.

[198] Once again, I am conscious that my inclusion and omission of certain facts and the way in which I describe them are not politically neutral.

have a profound effect on the manner in which the various contract norms operate in given contracts.[199]

Capital. The quantity and form of capital in any given situation is of major importance. I define capital as labor stored in ways that create value for future use. This distinguishes it from natural resources on which no labor has yet been expended, although the two often, if not invariably, become intertwined in the course of storing labor. The fact that a given society, such as a private or state capitalist society, treats a natural resource the same way for many purposes as it treats such stored labor does not, under this definition, convert the natural resources themselves into capital. Under the definition, the question of who controls and benefits from natural resources and capital is separated from the question of what is capital.

Technology. Although the form of capital varies with technology and technology is vastly influenced by other elements in this list, at any given place and time the technological residue is a major variable in determining the ways in which the contract norms operate. Thus, for example, the very existence of a technology that has led to the production of large electric power plants and permits their continued operation determines in part the operation of contract norms in the 20th century world.[200] One of the most important impacts of technology is

---

199 *See* an early (1845-46) statement of Marx and Engels:

> The first premise of all human history is, of course, the existence of living human individuals. The first fact to be established is therefore the physical organization of these individuals and their consequent relation to the rest of nature. We cannot here, of course, go into either the physical characteristics of men, themselves, or the natural conditions found by men—the geological, orohydrographical, climatic, and other conditions. All historical work must start on the basis of these natural conditions and their modification in the course of history through the action of men.

ESSENTIAL WORKS OF SOCIALISM 44 (I. Howe ed. 1976)(quoting Karl Marx and Friedrich Engels). For a slightly different version, see D. MCLELLAN, KARL MARX: SELECTED WRITINGS 160 (1977).

200 The superb historian, Fernand Braudel, states flatly that technology in itself does not exist. He goes on to say that "science and technology are indeed uniting today to dominate the world, but such unity necessarily depends upon the role played by present-day societies, which may encourage or restrain progress, today as in the past." 1 F. BRAUDEL, THE STRUCTURES OF EVERYDAY LIFE: THE LIMITS OF THE POSSIBLE 431 (1981). It is unclear to me just what he means by this. It is clear enough that societies may or may not foster the development of technological knowledge, and that they may or may not use knowledge at hand, that they may or may not let knowledge be forgotten. But when knowledge has become built into existing capital and, as is increasingly the case, technological knowledge itself reflects vast quantities of sunk capital, then "technology in itself," for all practical purposes, exists just as much as does the natural environment and capital in general. Surely societies today, as in the past, "may encourage or restrain progress" in the technological sense. The sunk capital of existing technology, however, may nevertheless be the tracks and a train in which society rides as engineer holding throttle and brake levers, and defective ones at that. Braudel himself recognizes this at the conclusion of this volume of his work when he discusses the different ways in which 15th-18th century societies answered technological questions: "It is a fact that every great centre of population has worked out a set of

on specialization of labor and consequent patterns of exchange, which are key elements in social relations of production. Any given technology imposes minimum requirements for, and perhaps limits on, specialization of labor. Those requirements in turn affect social relations of production.[201]

Social Relations of Production and Consumption. I analyze this element differently than does traditional Marxist theory in at least two respects. First, for me it is only one of many fundamental elements and is deeply affected by the others, and second, I believe the social relations of consumption to be on a plane of theoretical equality with the social relations of production, whereas in traditional Marxist theory, the social relations of consumption are determined by the social relations of production.[202]

---

elementary answers—and has an unfortunate tendency to stick to them out of that force of inertia which is one of the great artisans of history." *Id.* at 561.

It may also be noted that the Habermas-Marcuse views of technology and science as ideology, which seem to me sound in many respects, are not necessarily inconsistent with a belief in the existence of much technological determinism of a nonideological nature. *See* J. HABERMAS, TOWARD A RATIONAL SOCIETY: STUDENT PROTEST, SCIENCE, AND POLITICS 81-122 (J. Shapiro trans. 1970). Any conflict between beliefs in technology as ideology and as an ideologically independent determinant arises only when analysis moves to questions of the causes and social consequences of technology. At this level, the degree of technological independence believed to exist becomes a salient issue. On this level, I am sure I view existing technology as more like the force of gravity and less like a large ship that can be turned by social action (or will be turned by any human "forces of history") than do most members of the various critical schools.

The definition of capital used here is broad enough to encompass all of technology. Under that definition, any existing technology is simply a form of capital. Hence, this historical determinant duplicates part of the preceding one. The impact of existing technology is so often overlooked in social analysis, however, that much is to be gained by stating it separately. Moreover, it is always difficult to keep questions of ownership of capital separate from questions of existence of capital—witness the habit of referring to Western states, but not socialist states, as capitalist—a distinction making sense only if capital is defined entirely in terms of who controls and benefits from it and not at all in terms of what capital is in the first place. Although technology is also controlled by and also benefits members of society differentially, questions of ownership of technology are less often confused with questions of the existence of technology and its impact than is the case of the existence and ownership of capital. The statement, "Both the Soviet Union and the United States are advanced technological states," simply does not require as much explanation for most audiences as the statement, "Both the Soviet Union and the United States are advanced capitalist states."

201 Technology has analogous effects on social relations of consumption.

202 Theoretical equality respecting any of the fundamental factors discussed does not imply practical equality in all historical circumstances. It may well be, for example, that the social relations of consumption become increasingly important determinants of the operation of contract norms relative to social relations of production as consumption becomes more technolgically complex. Certainly, relational contract theory does not exclude the possibility that in any given historical setting, the social relations of consumption may be of more significant social effect than the social relations of production. Indeed, I am by no means convinced that that is not the case in advanced nations now; consider, for example, the social relations of consumption of the military product in both East and West. Which tail is wagging which dog?

Other Social Relations. Just as existing quantity and forms of capital, existing states of technology, and existing social relations of consumption exercise an impact on the operation of the contract norms independent of the social relations of production, so do other social relations. Even though the development of such social relations is, in my view, deeply affected by the social relations of production and of consumption, they have a life of their own that affects not only the total picture, but the social relations of production and the other independent elements as well. While I have in mind particularly such social relations as the family, church, and ethnic, racial, and national groupings, formal relations such as law, sovereign nations, and international organizations must also be viewed as causes, not simply as effects. Perhaps most important of all in modern times are bureaucratic social relations *per se*, irrespective of their putative purposes.[203]

Psychology. The assertions made in this Article about the contract norms postulates a basic human psychology transcending history. Nonetheless, while the Article postulates very distinct limits on the malleability of human psychology, those limits leave a vast range for variations. The psychological residue in individuals in any given set of historical circumstances will, therefore, vary greatly, and will in turn affect the operation of the contract norms. To mention but one example, the sense of alienation is always a situation-specific feeling. Moreover, its nature varies greatly with historical content.

Historical Forces. If there are "historical forces," such as drives or cyclical patterns regarding equality or inequality, they most certainly will affect the operation over time of the contract norms. I mention this not because I have much belief in such forces,[204] but because others do, and I wish to make it plain that relational contract theory is incompatible with such beliefs only if the beliefs in question postulate changes in human nature incompatible with the limits assumed by that theory.

The Residue. No list of this kind can even approach completeness, but beyond that, the unmeasured residue of historical fact I have omitted often may be more important than those I have included combined,

---

[203] One common mistake in social analysis is to assume that because phenomenon *A* was originally caused by *B*, its continued existence is caused by the continued existence of *B*. If modern bureaucracy arose as the product of capitalism (or socialism) it does not follow that capitalism (or socialism) remains the cause of its continuation. Logically, the opposite is just as possible, that the existence of bureaucracy is what causes the continuation of capitalism (or socialism). See the discussion of technology, *supra* note 200.

[204] I do believe, however, in what appears to be a tendency of human relations to evolve—unless they are in substantial measure destroyed, as in the fall of Rome—towards the more complex. This evolution is analogous to biological evolution of organisms, which rarely, if ever, evolve in the direction of simplicity.

and I would not wish to claim otherwise here. The flotsam and jetsam and chance of history exist and are important, even if we often do not know of them or of their hows and whys.[205] Furthermore, I do not think such variables as aesthetics or religious feelings or fundamental joy or guilt or love or hate are either uninfluential on the operation of the contract norms or adequately captured by the listed elements.

c. Relational Contract Theory Viewed as Ahistorically as Possible.—

Limited Positivism. Relational contract theory reflects a belief in the value *per se* of the search for organized knowledge about the nature of man and his institutions, a value partially independent of other purposes for which the search is made. Underlying this belief is a further belief that humans can, to some degree, see and understand in a positivist sense the physical world outside their own psyches, including human behavior and institutions. The theory thus incorporates limited positivism into social analysis.[206] This value is anathema to the stricter Marxist dogmas in which no social analysis can be understood except in its particular political context and in terms of involvement of the observer in the dynamics of the subject of analysis. This value is founded on the underlying belief that such knowledge is obtainable and perceivable in some degree, although never entirely, free of the distortions of the ideology of the observer. It thus falls into the Western social scientific tradition, but subject to serious limitations.

An aspect of this limited positivism is that relational contract theory founds abstractions about humans more closely on concrete perceptions of how they actually behave[207] than on more highly refined concepts such as promise or rationality (in the technical economic sense). Thus, the oughts of the theory are the product of what appears actually to work in social interaction,[208] rather than the result of formulations derived from more theoretical notions. The theory is thus subject to whatever virtues or vices all nature-based theories enjoy or suffer. The most obvious potential criticism concerns the question raised by Professor Fried[209] about the likelihood that the values are imposed by the observer rather than derived from nature. Each reader will have to decide for himself how much relational contract theory suffers or does not suffer from such defects.

205 Herein lies the substantial, albeit limited, germ of truth in the views of Gilmore and Leff, *supra* note 186.

206 *See* W. RUNCIMAN, SOCIAL THEORY, *supra* note 141.

207 The theory's behaviorism does not, however, deny such ideas an introspection, consciousness, mind, or purpose.

208 This is obviously a kind of utilitarian notion, but that word carries too much baggage to apply accurately here.

209 Fried, *supra* note 41.

Holism and the Individual-Communal Conflict. Relational contract theory rejects as unrealistic the examination in fractions of either people or their institutions.[210] It considers humans only as wholes; indeed, it goes farther, as it rejects the very idea of man-outside-society and insists that the smallest unit of social analysis has to be man-in-a-society. On the other hand, relational contract theory also rejects perfectionism, any idea that man can become a totally self-sacrificing animal;[211] hence, it rejects any possibility of total submergence of man-the-individual into man-the-community.[212] Instead, it focuses on and accepts the eternal human schizophrenia in being inconsistently selfish and self-sacrificing at the same time.

Thus, relational contract theory appears to be less individualistic than the liberal model of man exemplified by Professor Fried's model. The appearance, however, is deceiving. The insistence on looking at whole persons even when doing so forces one also to look at society itself often reflects a greater respect for the value of individual autonomy than does the individualist model.[213] Relational contract theory therefore provides what I believe to be a more realistic and better basis for articulating and effectuating individualistic values than discrete systems of analysis provide.

Relational contract theory, however, also can be used as a vehicle for articulating *less* individualistic values, subject to the limits on selflessness it postulates as a basic characteristic of human nature and the resulting limits it postulates respecting human institutions. Here again, I believe that the insistence on looking at whole persons, including their inherent selfishness, can reflect a greater respect for communal values than can any look at society ignoring that inherent individual character of man.

Holism and History. If one believes, as I do, that humans can be viewed holistically only as historical creatures—creatures for whom place and time are essential aspects of their nature—then holism automatically introduces history. Introduction of history into social analysis involves, I believe, placing a value on the past *per se*—even where the motivation for the social analysis is to undo or change the effects of the past on the future. Paying attention to the past introduces the con-

210 This does not, of course, preclude partial analysis for limited purposes; it precludes building global intellectual systems based on fractionating analysis. *See generally* I. Macneil, Exchange Revisited, *supra* note 7.

211 Relational contract theory also rejects any idea that man can become the Ayn Rand opposite, the perfectly selfish animal.

212 This rejection encompasses not only social and political structures aimed at such perfectionist goals, but also intellectual constructs based on such ideas.

213 It is, after all, individualism taken literally that leads to such highly collectivistic, essentially anti-individualist results as those found in B. Ackerman, Social Justice in the Liberal State (1981).

cept of continuity of human events.[214] Obviously, such conclusions, which are inherent in relational contract theory, are inherently conservative in terms of change.[215]

Values of the Common Contract Norms. Since relational contract theory encompasses examination of all the common contract norms, it necessarily implies that there is value in each of them. As those values have been discussed earlier, it is unnecesary to repeat them here. As noted, however, acceptance of those norms precludes the elevation of either individualism or communalism to a position of sole or even dominant importance in intellectual analysis.

Relative Social Neutrality. Subject to the limits just noted, relational contract theory is fundamentally neutral in terms of choice, consent, planning, equality, power, sovereign imposition of norms on contracts, and the like. In terms of policies for positive law of sovereign states, the theory itself offers direct guidance only when imposition of norms on contracts within the state either erodes norms within them beyond viable limits or is essential in order to preserve contract norms at the minimum levels necessary for the contractual relations to continue.[216] Those who read relational contract theory as necessarily or presumptively supporting great sovereign intervention are mistaken.[217]

---

[214] The most obvious "proof" of this is the actions of revolutionaries who invariably seek not only to make changes in the present for the future, but also to wipe out memory of the past itself to the extent that the past conflicts with the revolutionary changes. We are used to seeing this in revolutions from the left, but the same thing occurs in other revolutions. See, for example, Albert Speer's account of the attitudes of typical Nazi Gauleiters towards historical buildings. A. SPEER, INSIDE THE THIRD REICH 314-15 (1970).

[215] Their political direction in terms of class struggle and the like depend upon the time and place to which they are applied. It may be said, however, that most often such views serve the existing power structure.

[216] It offers social analytical guidance, and hence indirect political guidance, in all cases, even though it does not by itself indicate directly what policy direction should be in circumstances not approaching outer viable limits.

[217] Thus, a commentary such as Strasser, *Contract's "Many Futures" After Death: Unanswered Questions of Scope and Purpose*, 32 S.C.L. REV. 501 (1981), is largely misguided. Although I blame myself in significant measure for Professor Strasser's misunderstanding, it is flatly inaccurate to say that I argue "that contract law simply does not regulate much of the commercial behavior it should," *id.* at 503; *see also id.* at 523, 527. The inaccuracy of such a statement arises directly from a failure to distinguish among various definitions of contract law. I have always tried to make plain that my use of the unmodified phrase "contract law" encompasses *all* law affecting contracts—and that means virtually *all law*. Further, I most certainly have never expressed a belief that the total *corpus juris* of the United States fails to "regulate much of the commercial behavior it should." (Professor Strasser's misunderstanding is ironic, because it happens to be my view, and has been all along, that we have far too much sovereign law imposing norms of various kinds on contract.) It is true, in a limited sense, that I believe that contract law defined as only classical and neoclassical contract law fails to "regulate much of the commercial behavior it should and does not regulate properly that which it does," but that failure has nothing to do with total legal regulation of contract. That failure is because neoclassical contract, which is only one of

Rationality for Rationality's Sake. Relational contract theory rejects the value of rationality for the sake of rationality. Indeed, one of its major underlying themes is that in social analysis of any kind, logic corrupts and absolute logic corrupts absolutely. This is not the rejection of rationality of the flower children and their less pleasant cultural descendents. It is a recognition that rationality—logical consistency—can play only a limited role in the analysis of humans and their institutions. Relational contract theory puts a high premium on the acceptance of the partial irrationality of life[218] and on incorporating such partial irrationality into social theories. While there are many circumstances where totally rational analysis is valuable, its sphere must always be limited, and often severely so, if we are not to go seriously astray through omissions and distortions.

It might seem by negative implication that any norms *not* included in the common contract norms are not highly valued in relational contact theory, but this is incorrect. The introduction of history with its particular norms precludes such a result. So too, this theory explicitly provides for the inclusion of other norms, to the extent that supracontract norms become important internally.[219]

d. Relational Contract Theory Viewed Historically as Current Political Ideology.—Like contract-as-promise, relational contract theory must be placed in the context of the advanced Western capitalist-welfare state in order to be viewed as political ideology.[220] Furthermore, its expositor, like the expositor of contract-as-promise, is properly viewed as seeking to influence other people—including scholars, lawyers, legislators, judges, and students—to think about contract in terms of his theory. To what end politically?

---

many sectors of the *corpus juris pactae*, omits, distorts, and interacts poorly with the remainder of the *corpus juris pactae*. It is not because the total *corpus* fails to regulate enough, or indeed "properly," except for the problems caused by the inadequate conceptualistic structure of classical and neoclassical contract law.

Professor Fried makes mistakes similar to Professor Strasser's, C. FRIED, PROMISE, *supra* note 50, at 133, because he confuses contract law and contract conceptualizing. Elliott comes much closer to understanding what I have been saying than either Strasser or Fried in dealing with both the differences and the interactions between contract law and relational contract theory. Elliott, *supra* note 1 at 347-48.

218 Human irrationality is an integral part of all realistic social models. Rationality is not, of course, used here in the technical economic sense, *see supra* note 190, but in its ordinary, more established, and more common sense of reason, logical consistency, and the like.

219 Externally, the supracontract norms are important respecting *all* contracts, no matter how discrete. Nevertheless, it may be that in many historical settings and respecting many contractual relations, discrete and relational, no additional norms beyond those stated as common contract norms need operate in order to achieve the harmonization. To the extent this is true in any given instance, any noncommon norms would be unimportant, not because relational contract theory precludes noncommon norms, but because the particular circumstances would generate none.

220 While the theory as stated has equal applicability in socialist and other states, and to other times, I shall not attempt a broader analysis here.

A narrow formalistic model such as Professor Fried's contract-as-promise lends itself to examination in these terms far more readily than does a broader, pluralistic theory such as relational contract theory. In part, this is the result of history; the ideology of Professor Fried's theory can be examined by looking at Professor Fried's many past and present intellectual bedfellows. In part, it is the result of the simple character of narrow formalistic models and their resulting sharp focus. The possible bedfellows of any relational contract theorist[221] are, however, too diverse to compare in an Article of this kind. Moreover, the breadth of values possible even under the circumscribed umbrella of relational contract theory as it is advanced here provides a basis for a multiplicity of widely diverse ideologies.

The most that can be done in the way of ideological analysis of a theory as pluralistic as this—especially one not established in the intellectual market place—is to examine some of its salient features and put forth a few ideas about the possible ideological consequence of those features in the current historical context. The reader can then draw his own conclusions about the ideological results of thinking about modern contractual relations in these terms.

Among the many limitations of a social participant-observer is the inability fully to comprehend the "true" ideological thrust of his own observations. Conceding that point, the salient ideological features of relational contract theory as advanced here seem to me to be (1) the idea of nature-imposed limits on the viability of contractual relations, (2) the theory's relative social neutrality,[222] (3) the stress on reciprocity, and (4) aspects of the focus on creation and restraint of power.

(1) Nature-imposed Limits on the Viability of Contractual Relations. The basis in nature of relational contract theory, coupled with a limited positivism, suggests a value in seeking further knowledge about the fundamental nature or natures of man. The theory might therefore be seen as giving ideological justification to social, psychological, and biological investigation of various kinds. The direction any such efforts may take is difficult to ascertain in advance, and they most certainly might be directions I would find abhorent. For example, investigations of this kind could very well be undertaken with an eye to modifying the nature of man—for example, modifying him towards a more passive nature—through technology such as genetic engineering.[223] On the

221 In this instance, I am *not* limiting the term to the relational contract theory advanced here.

222 Stress must be placed on the word "relative"; it is, I hope, plain by now that I do not believe in anything close to truly neutral social analysis.

223 Undoubtedly, in real life, the nature of men would be modified in differential ways; elites doubtless will manipulate genetic engineering to their own benefit just as they have used all technological "advances" to their own benefit throughout history. Aldous Huxley's BRAVE NEW WORLD (1932) is infinitely more likely to be the product of genetic engineering than is some new equalitarian Garden of Eden.

other hand, such perfectionism could equally well be resisted consistently with relational contract theory. In short, since the theory is based on man as he is now,[224] the moral questions concerning such genetic engineering lie outside relational contract theory, except inasmuch as they are to be found in its history-specific aspects. While these history-specific aspects of the theory are an integral part of it, we must look to current historical circumstances, not to the remainder of the theory, for their particular content. Nevertheless, theories based on human nature may be of ideological use in legitimizing resistance to such things as human genetic engineering. For example, to whatever extent such theories provide attractive rational summaries of *homo sapiens*, they may be used in support of other reasons why we should not change the species into *homo-manufactured-by-homo*.[225]

In various ways, the idea of natural limits on the viability of human institutions is anathema to a number of current ideologies. The particular limits advanced here certainly do not fit with the thinking of modern unreconstructed individualist-Leviathanists,[226] who postulate an entirely nonsocial individualist beast on the one hand and, on the other, a state powerful enough to make it desirable for him to cooperate with others.[227] Nor does the idea of limits of the kind suggested fit with either common Marxist views or those of that part of the liberal school believing in the possibility, if not of perfecting man, at least of improving man a very great deal, or, if not perfecting or improving him, at least perfecting or improving his behavior, particularly through action of the state.[228] Finally, it certainly does not fit what seems to me to be the prevailing ideology throughout the Western world, the

224 So he will remain in spite of social intervention, barring genetic engineering, mind-control through chemical means, and the like. I offer no predictions about such changes, other than the point made about elites, *supra* note 223.

225 The species already is made by man, of course, in cultural terms, including technology as part of any culture. But the self-manufacture thus far has been subject to genetic limits, or more accurately, subject to phenotypic limits produced by genetic limits. For a sophisticated discussion of what, if any, phenotypic and genetic limits of culture exist, see R. ALEXANDER, DARWINISM AND HUMAN AFFAIRS (1979).

226 Hayek, Friedman, and Fried are examples of such modern unreconstructed individualist-Leviathanists. The adjective "unreconstructed" is used only to distinguish them from reconstructed descendants of Hobbes, such as Ackerman and Tribe, who appear to believe that through human effort—particularly efforts of the state—humans can be made fundamentally less beastly. (It is, of course, often difficult to tell when a person believes this and when he simply believes that the behavior patterns of a given society can be "improved" without "improving" the underlying nature of its denizens.)

227 They ignore, of course, that there never has been such a wild individualist beast in the history of the species, no matter how far back one goes in primate history.

228 *See supra* note 226. I do not mean to suggest that some societies are not far better than others, or that self-improvement is never possible, merely that we must recognize the very real limits nature imposes on us as well as the costs and self-defeat always resulting when we try to exceed those limits in efforts at self-perfection.

growth-at-all-costs school,[229] which urges us to follow blindly wherever increased production and consumption under heavily capitalized modern technology takes us.

Acceptance of natural limits on the viability of human institutions limits feasible political action relating to contractual relations of all kinds. For example, it precludes the long term implementation of supracontract norms that, by their nature, their ubiquitousness, or both in combination, would significantly erode one or more of the common contract norms. Similarly, as I argued in the section on bureaucratization,[230] political action dependent on implementation by bureaucratic processes[231] is subject to extremely serious limits because of its effect on the common contract norms.

(2) Relative Social Neutrality. The neutrality of relational contract theory within broad ranges concerning choice, consent, planning, equality, change, and power, as well as its claim to a limited positivism, also constitutes a rejection of existing ideologies founded on narrow dogmas, such as Marxism and some varieties of liberalism. Thus, to the extent that a Marxist or a liberal dogmatist might insist on effectuating supracontract norms, like equality or choice, to such a degree that essential common contract norms are eroded too much, such a dogmatist would necessarily reject relational contract theory. Adherents to the dogma of "growth-at-all-costs," however, would be untroubled by this neutrality *per se*, because only limits that might inhibit growth would matter to them.[232]

Although the relative neutrality of relational contract theory respecting choice, consent, planning, equality, change, and power, as well as its position on positivism, constitutes a rejection of existing ideologies founded on narrow dogmas, it rejects such ideologies only in very theoretical terms. While liberalism starts in theory from an extreme individualistic analysis rejected by relational contract theory, it rapidly develops into something far different as soon as it is applied in the real political arena. Indeed, it becomes less individualistic long before it is so applied; Professor Fried's work illustrates this. Although Professor

229 This ideology is by no means limited to the Western world. It dominates the socialist world and the thinking of the elites and much of the population of virtually all the underdeveloped world as well.

230 *See supra* text accompanying notes 119-24.

231 Bureaucratic processes are usually the favored processes of advocates of the last three categories of political belief— much of Marxism, liberal perfectionism, and growth-at-any-cost— discussed above. Following the first view—unreconstructed individualism—causes bureaucratization as well, since that view, in the modern context, tolerates massive bureaucratization as long as it is not bureaucratization by the state.

232 My own view is that growth is pushing us beyond the limits into unviable patterns of contractual relations internationally, nationally, and locally. But that is a particular application of relational contract theory, not an element of the theory itself.

Fried sets out a very individualistic closed system, the introduction of the other values he treats produces results that in many ways are practically, although not theoretically, quite compatible with relational contract theory.

A different kind of liberal analysis that not only is consistent with relational contract theory, but also actually incorporates it, is that of Reiter.[233] He has used good faith—relevant-commmunity standards of appropriate behavior—to "power" relational contract theory. The good faith to which he refers is not, however, the abstract good faith of *a* relevant-community; rather, it is the standards of appropriate behavior of the modern liberal capitalist community as the author sees those standards, with an appropriately Canadian slant.[234] Their ideological thrust, while essentially liberal, is a different branch of liberalism from that of Professor Fried, for example.

Similarly, while most Marxist *dogma* is too narrow to fit within an approach like that of relational contract theory, much Marxist writing is not. Futhermore, even some of the dogma fits as well. For example, Tushnet's recognition of what he calls the "humanitarian aspects of slavery," as well as the clash between those humanitarian aspects and the market side of slavery is largely, if not entirely, compatible with relational contract theory.[235] Had he chosen to do so, Tushnet could have embedded his discussion in relational contract theory with little or no change in the substantive content of his discussion.[236]

---

233 Reiter, *Good Faith*, *supra* note 20.

234 Among other things, Reiter seems to assume a relevant-community in which government equals society, a very Hobbesian notion.

235 M. TUSHNET, SLAVERY, *supra* note 147.

236 In his review of Tushnet, Watson expressed very non-Marxist views, which also could have been embedded in relational contract theory. Watson, *Book Review*, 91 YALE L.J. 1034 (1982). Of course, many reasons, including allegiance to dogma, may prevent anyone—liberals of any persuasion and Marxists alike—from wishing to do so.

The foregoing suggests that acceptance of relational contract theory as a useful tool of social analysis might hasten the merger of Marxist and non-Marxist thinking discussed earlier, *supra* text accompanying notes 143-53, leaving the dogmas of each to operate as limited by the outer boundaries of an umbrella relational theory. It is not clear to me whether this would be more of an intellectual revolution in Marxist theory than it would be in pluralist liberal theory. Probably most Marxists would consider even the suggestion of this happening as hopelessly naive; but the Hobbesian, individualistic root of even the most equalitarian liberalism would also have to be revolutionized; *a fortiori* as to the unreconstructed Hobbesian individualism of microeconomic theory.

While I naturally hope the umbrella relational theory would be relational contract theory not unlike that described in this Article, it certainly need not be, and probably will not be. Nonetheless, some such theory is, I believe, likely to develop and to serve this purpose. It may need to be richer than what I propose; richer, for example, in economic analysis, *see* Williamson, *Governance*, *supra* note 68, richer in institutional thinking, *see* Dugger, *Williamson*, *supra* note 155, richer in conflict and decisionmaking theory, *see* Prattis, *Synthesis*, *supra* note 155, and richer in philosophy, *see* R. Lovin, The Revolt Against Positivism: Contemporary Realism and Natural Law Eth-

(3) Reciprocity and (4) Power. These two salient aspects of relational contract theory will be treated together because they are very intertwined ideologically.

Power as an analytical concept is of particular appeal to what may loosely be characterized as the political left.[237] Its manipulation—creation or restraint—will continue to be a focus of social analysis coming from that direction. The ideological thrust of relational contract theory is not to reject that emphasis, but the theory requires that power be put ideologically in its place along with other contract norms, including, among others, reciprocity.

Reciprocity, on the other hand, tends towards antileft analysis. Reciprocity is by no means entirely in conflict with a common desideratum in radical analysis: needs-based distribution. Nonetheless, an idea such as "to each according to his needs" hardly comes automatically to mind when one starts any social analysis with the concept of reciprocity. The great emphasis on the obligation to work coming from the political right, and the right's great reluctance to maintain systems of wealth distribution to those it views as noncontributors, reveal how strongly the right tends to support reciprocity ideas in its ideology. To whatever extent "rightist" analysis recognizes relational contract theory, the reciprocity norm is likely to receive exceptional emphasis compared to other common contract values. Again, the ideological thrust of relational contract theory is not to reject that emphasis, but the theory requires that reciprocity be put in its place along with other contract norms, including, among others, power.

Thus, the ideological thrust of relational contract theory is, in traditional senses, both anti-Marxist and antiliberal (to the extent that the latter is based on a theory of man as an autonomous individual outside of society). Yet, it is capable of absorbing much of the less dogmatic aspects of each.

V. POSTSCRIPT: A PERSONAL APPLICATION OF RELATIONAL CONTRACT THEORY

Although I believe relational contract theory is a useful analytical tool permitting very wide ideological variations, it would be misleading not to reveal something of the ideological direction in which I would use it myself.[238]

For the foreseeable future, the main direction for social develop-

ics (1982)(unpublished manuscript), to mention but four possibilities. It also needs to be far richer in psychology and history.

237 Power is, of course, also one of many subjects of interest in various kinds of liberal analysis, although neoclassical microeconomics slights it.

238 Although my aim in trying to develop a relational theory of contract has been to develop one as ideologically neutral as possible, obviously that effort is colored by the ideological uses to which I would put my theory in specific applications.

ment will come from human dependence on vast quantities of capital sunk into existing technological uses.[239] It is impossible to abandon, or even rapidly to modify, the sunk capital and its accompanying technology without widespread starvation and social disintegration. Even modest steps in such directions are politically unacceptable. The nature of this sunk capital and its accompanying technology demands highly bureaucratic social organization. These bureaucracies, while necessary to keep the current system going, are increasingly unsuccessful in doing so and are increasingly putting various common contract norms in great jeopardy,[240] with an inevitable disintegration of contractual relations as a result.

The response of many equalitarian-minded liberals of adding more and more state bureaucracy simply exacerbates the problems, sometimes in the short run, and almost always in the long run. On the other hand, the willingness of other liberals who purportedly value individual choice to suffer almost any social harm produced by large "private" bureaucracies has similar results, albeit to some extent in different sectors of society. If one views the essential problem as an excessive reliance on bureaucracy as a way of life, neither route offers a way out of the current erosion of common contract norms.

While all the contract norms are in trouble at a great many levels, four seem in particular difficulty: reciprocity, solidarity, power, and propriety of means. Large sections of the populace—in particular, the poor and the old—are in largely nonreciprocal positions *vis a vis* the rest of the population. This leaves them very vulnerable indeed, and also leaves the rest of the population vulnerable to the more vigorous of them, because at such levels of nonreciprocity, solidarity breaks down as well. Even where reciprocity is present at adequate, or even very high levels, however, solidarity is increasingly the solidarity of bureaucracy, generally a rather sterile and humanly unsatisfying kind, even when it works relatively well in accomplishing assigned tasks.[241] Moreover, bureaucratic solidarity is brittle, and tends to break down just

239 Capital continues to mean labor stored in ways that create value for future use. *See supra* text accompanying note 199. Our cities, our highways, our homes, our farms (to the extent that a farm is more than raw land and space warmed and watered by nature), our factories, our huge collection of moveable artifacts, our vast array of individual and social capital stored in individuals (and by no means necessarily created entirely by the labor of the individual in which it is stored), and much more are included. The reader may note again that the word "capital" is used without reference to who controls it or benefits from it.

240 The breakdown is not mainly in bureaucracies performing relatively specific tasks, not even in public bureaucracies of that kind. *See*, for example, J. MASHAW, BUREAUCRATIC JUSTICE: ADMINISTRATIVE LAW FROM AN INTERNAL PERSPECTIVE (1983). Rather, the breakdown is within bureaucracies charged with broad, difficult-to-define tasks, such as welfare, education, and medical care, and at the vital margins between bureaucracies and elsewhere where politics interfaces in complex ways with the bureaucracies.

241 For a discussion of solidarity in the modern state, see I. MACNEIL, THE NEW SOCIAL CONTRACT, *supra* note 1, at 90-102.

when the going gets hard and it is most needed. In wide sectors of life, there is both too much power and too little power: too much dispersed widely, if unequally, among many of the denizens of large bureaucracies[242] and in other people willing and able to ignore contract norms—terrorists, street criminals, juvenile delinquents, embezzlers, shop lifters, tax evaders—and too little power in those supporting those norms—the judicial system, the public decisionmaking processes, the police,[243] and, above all, people working together in small contractual relations, such as the family and very small businesses. Finally, the proliferation of bureaucratic methods throughout life seems to be breaking the outer limits of viable means of accomplishing many mundane essential tasks, especially in the so-called public sector.

A deep political concern for all of these endangered norms in our present historical circumstances can, in my view, lead in only one direction: seeking social and economic smallness, within the relatively narrow limits permitted us by our dependence on our sunk capital and existing technology and their dynamics, which are so largely out of our control. It would be naive in the extreme to think that the modest economic, social, and political forces pushing in the direction of smallness will have significant effect in major parts of modern life, barring a breakup of the world economy because of some kind of cataclysm. The greatest optimism a realistic believer in small-is-beautiful should permit himself is the possibility of sizeable interstices in the superbureaucratic, superpowerful, yet superweak, inadequately reciprocal, and inadequately solidary world social structure one sees stretching drearily on into the future.[244] It is just possible that such interstices will provide opportunities for small contractual relations providing reasonably well-served—not just barely served—common contract norms for some people. It is also just possible that such small structures will be so effective that they might eventually challenge the bureaucratic dinosaurs. I am not counting on either event happening, but such directions are the ideological thrust that I would add to power relational contract theory.

---

242 Outside their particular bureaucracies, these people are often as weak as anyone else.

243 "The law," even law that virtually everyone would agree is sound, is often simply not being enforced. For example, 75% of the parking summonses issued in the City of Chicago result in no further action. When the Illinois legislature inadvertently provided for automatic suspension of drivers' licenses for those with *ten* or more unanswered parking violations, virtually every politician in the state headed for cover and denied responsibility for the legislation or any desire to enforce it. Prisons are being emptied of criminals, not because the sentences should be terminated, but because society is unwilling to supply the facilities to continue imprisonment through the term deemed appropriate by the judicial and normal parole processes.

244 Perhaps the greatest danger is that that structure will meet the common contract norms enough to survive, yet not enough to yield robust contractual relations—ones in which the common norms prosper—in most aspects of the lives of most people. One of the reasons this may happen is fear throughout the bureaucratic system that failure to maintain the minimum levels of these norms will produce a cataclysmic collapse of the whole system.

[6]

CONTRACTS, PROMISES AND THE LAW OF OBLIGATIONS

I

FOR at least 100 years—and in many respects for more like twice that time—common lawyers have operated within a particular conceptual framework governing the law of obligations. Within this framework, the fundamental distinction has been that between obligations which are voluntarily assumed, and obligations which are imposed by law. The former constitutes the law of contract, the latter falls within the purview of the law of tort. There is, in addition, that somewhat anomalous body of law which came to be known as the law of quasi-contract, or in more modern times, as the law of restitution. This body of law was accommodated within the new conceptual framework by the academic lawyers and jurists from the 1860s onwards, and, after a considerable time lag, their ideas came to be part of the accepted orthodoxies. The law of quasi-contract, it came to be said, was part of the law of obligations which did not arise from voluntary acts of the will, but from positive rules of law. Quasi-contract thus took its place alongside tort law on one side of the great divide. Contract alone remained on the other side. Nobody ever paid much attention to the place of the law of trusts in this scheme of things. Equity, after all, was a peculiarly English invention and theorising about the law of obligations was very much a Roman and subsequently a Continental fashion. It is true that much time and trouble was devoted to the problem of fitting equitable obligations into another typically Roman distinction, namely that dividing a *jus in rem* from a *jus in personam*. But nobody seems to have troubled overmuch about the place of equitable obligations in the great divide between voluntarily assumed and legally imposed obligations.

These broad distinctions reflected a set of values, and ways of thought which also exercised a most profound influence on the conceptual pattern which was imposed on Contract law itself. Contractual obligations came to be treated as being almost exclusively about promises, agreements, intentions, acts of will. The function of the law came to be seen as that of merely giving effect to the private autonomy of contracting parties to make their own legal arrangements. It is, of course, well known indeed, has become part of the modern orthodoxy, that the private autonomy, this extreme freedom of contract, came to be abused by parties with greater bargaining power, and has been curtailed in a variety of ways, both by legislative activity and by the judges themselves. That is a familar story and I do not wish to pursue it here. What I do wish to discuss is the conceptual framework of Contract and its place in the law of obligations as a whole. I want to suggest that, despite the increasing attacks upon freedom of contract, and the great divide between Contract and Tort, the conceptual apparatus which still dominates legal thinking on these issues is the apparatus of the nineteenth century. It goes, indeed, far beyond the law itself. Our very processes of thought, our language in political, moral or philosophical debate, is still dominated by this nineteenth-century heritage to an extent which, I venture to suggest, is rarely appreciated. I want to suggest, further, that this conceptual apparatus is not based on any objective truths, it does not derive from any eternal verities. It is the result, quite specifically of a nineteenth-century heritage, an amalgam of classical economics, of Benthamite radicalism, of liberal political ideals and of the law, itself created and moulded in the shadow of these movements. The result, I will argue, is that our basic conceptual apparatus, the fundamental characterisations and divisions which we impose on the phenomena with which we deal, do not reflect the values of our own times, but those of the last century. It is true that they reflect much that many will still think most admirable about the nineteenth century, the liberal tradition, the belief in the value and rights of the individual, adherence to an economic and social system which had the confidence to reward enterprise, initiative and success. But to recognise that many of the values of our society today are opposed to much that was admirable in the last century is not to denigrate our predecessors. And to argue the case for revising our concepts so that they conform more closely to the values of today involves no judgment that those values are better than the values of yesterday. Indeed, the revision may prove useful to those who think otherwise, for it will bring into greater relief precisely what is involved in today's values.

II

It is time to turn away from these generalities, and I propose to begin by spending a few moments on the paradigm of modern contract theory. If we were asked today to indulge in the fashionable exercise of constructing a model of a typical contract, I suspect most common lawyers would come up with something like this. A typical contract is, first, a bilateral executory agreement. It consists of an exchange of promises; the exchange is deliberately carried through, by the process of offer and acceptance, with the intention of creating a binding deal. When the offer is accepted, the agreement is consummated, and a contract comes into existence before anything is actually *done* by the parties. No performance is required, no benefit has to be rendered, no act of detrimental reliance is needed, to create the obligation. The contract is binding because the parties intend to be bound; it is their will, or intention, which creates the liability. It is true that the law has this technical requirement known as the doctrine of consideration, but except in rare and special cases, mutual promises are consideration for each other, and therefore the model, by definition, complies with the requirement of consideration. When the contract is made, it binds each party to performance, or, in default, to a liability to pay damages in lieu. Prima facie these damages will represent the value of the innocent party's disappointed expectations. The plaintiff may, therefore, bring suit on a wholly executory contract, for example, because the defendant has attempted to cancel his offer or acceptance, or withdraw from the contract, and may recover damages for his disappointed expectations even though he has not relied upon the contract in any way, and even though the defendant has received no benefit under it. The whole model is suffused with the idea that the fundamental purpose of contract law is to give effect—within limits of course—to the intentions of the parties. It is their decision, and their free choice, which makes the contract binding, and determines its interpretation, and its result in the event of breach. It is, of course, a commonplace today that all legal obligations are, in the last resort, obligations created or at least recognised by the law, but the classical model of contract is easily enough adjusted to take account of this truism. The law of contract, it is said, consists of power-conferring rules. The law provides facilities for private parties to make use of them if they so wish. Those who wish to create legal obligations have only to comply with a simple set of rules and the result will be recognised by the law.

There is no doubt that this model has been of astonishing power. For 100 years it has had no serious rival. Today many lawyers would probably want to qualify it, or modify it in a variety of respects. Many would admit, perhaps insist, that the model is primarily useful in connection with the business transaction, and it does not fit the consumer transaction, or the family arrangement, or other agreements which cannot be characterised as business deals. Even in transactions among business men, many lawyers will want to qualify this model. At the least many will recognise that the role of free choice on the part of contracting parties has declined, and that courts may, in the interests of justice as they perceive it, sometimes impose solutions in the teeth of contracting parties' intent. But making all allowances for the necessary qualifications, I do not think it would be seriously disputed that this is the paradigm model of contract which we have inherited from nineteenth-century lawyers. Indeed, a glance at the Contract textbooks will confirm that the model is still alive and well.

The pervasiveness of this model is attested by the closely parallel set of ideas and values which underlie social and philosophical ideas about promises. The binding force of promises, the nature of promissory liability, the role of implication, the idea of a background set of conventions and practices enabling promises to be made, all these and many other topics have been the subject of much debate and discussion among moralists and philosophers. Perhaps it is not surprising that the model of promissory theory most widely adhered to among philosophers appears to correspond very closely to the model of contractual liability sketched above.

Before proceeding further to examine the reality of this model of contract, it is worth pausing to consider some of its underlying presuppositions which are rarely made explicit. The first of these is that the classical model assumes that contract law is fundamentally about what parties *intend,* and not about what they *do.* Here again, of course, qualifications, and important qualifications, have to be made. It is the manifestation of intention and not actual intention that matters most; and what the parties *do* is obviously crucial in measuring the extent to which performance falls short of promise. Nevertheless, classical contract theory assumes that contractual obligations are created by the intention of the parties and not by their actions. The classical model is thus concerned with executory arrangements, with forward-looking planning. Contracts have a chronology, a time sequence, as can be seen by looking at the Table of Contents of any Contract textbook published in the last 100 years. They are *created* first, and performed (or not performed) thereafter. In this respect, of course, contractual obligations necessarily differ from those on the other side of the great divide. The law of torts, and the law of quasi-contract are concerned with what parties *do.* It is human action, or inaction, which creates liability in tort, or in restitution. Among other results, this means that Contract lawyers focus on a different time sequence. In tort, or in restitutionary claims, it is the causing of damage or injury on the one hand, or the rendering of benefits on the other, which is the immediate object of interest. In contract, likewise, damage or injury may be caused, or benefits rendered, but it is not these consequences, or the actions giving rise to them which are the focus of attention of the classical model. It is the intention of the parties which (it is assumed) must necessarily precede the causing of the damage or the rendering of the benefits, and which is therefore the source of the obligation. I will suggest later that this difference in the time which is the focus of attention has led, not merely to an exaggeration of the role of intentional conduct in the creation of contractual obligations, but also to a minimisation of the role of intentional conduct in the creation of other forms of obligation.

The second presupposition of the classical model of contract is that a contract is a *thing,* which has some kind of objective existence prior to any performance or any act of the parties.[1] Of all the examples of legal reification, none is surely more powerful than this. A contract is a thing which is " made," is " broken," is " discharged." So powerful is this reification that most lawyers see nothing odd about the notion of anticipatory repudiation, that is, about the idea that a promise can be treated as broken even before its performance is due. The tendency to reify legal concepts is, in the case of contract, given powerful impetus by the fact that so many contractual arrangements are in written form. Even today, lawyers constantly use the words " the contract " to signify both the legal relations created by the law, and the piece of paper in which those relations (or some of them) are expressed. Here again, there is a profound difference in the lawyer's way of looking at legal obligations on the other side of the great divide. A contract may be a " thing " but nobody would conceptualise a quasi-contract or a tort as a thing. One reason why the tendency to reify the concept of contract has had important results is that it has reinforced the respect for the private autonomy of the contractual relationship. If a contract is a thing created by the contracting parties, it is easier to see it as a relationship within defined and limited parameters. Within these parameters, concepts such as fairness, justice, reasonableness have far less room to operate than they do with diffuse concepts like tort or quasi-contract.

The third presupposition of the classical model of contract concerns the function of the court in the enforcement of contracts. I take it as axiomatic that, in principle, the judicial process is designed to serve either or both of two important social ends. The first is, by the threat of penalties or the promise of rewards, to encourage the citizenry to comply with socially desired standards of behaviour. And the second is to provide machinery for the settlement of disputes by peaceful and fair means. Now the classical model of Contract with its emphasis on intentional conduct and future planning, presupposes that the first of these two goals is the primary function of the courts in dealing with contractual litigation. The purpose of

1 See Arthur Leff, " Contract as a Thing," 19 *Am. U. Law Rev.* 131 (1970).

contract law is to encourage people to pay their debts, keep their promises and generally be truthful in their dealings with each other. The enforcement of contracts, like the protection of property and the punishment of crime, is thus perceived as important primarily for its deterrent or hortatory purpose. It is no coincidence that these were historically linked together as the essential functions of the state even by Adam Smith and the classical economists. By contrast, other parts of the law of obligations are more likely to be dominated by the dispute-settlement functions of the courts, rather than by their deterrent or hortatory functions. In the law of quasi-contract, in particular, the court is almost invariably called upon to deal with a problem by resolving a conflict of equities. Some misfire has occurred, some untoward and unplanned benefit has been rendered. Is it right that the beneficiary should pay for it, or are there grounds on which it is more just that he should be permitted to retain an unpaid for benefit? It is not generally regarded as an important function of the court to discourage (for example) people from paying debts twice over, or rendering benefits to another without ensuring that there has been an agreement to pay for them. Similarly with the modern law of torts, the importance of the deterrent function of the law has declined at the expense of the dispute-settlement function. Increasingly, the emphasis is on the function of the court in dealing with what are essentially perceived as accidents. The court must patch up a dispute, pick up the pieces after an accident, resolve a difficult conflict of equities, but the court is primarily concerned with *these* parties in this particular situation, and not with threatening sanctions or offering rewards to future parties. Although some lawyers would still be prepared to defend the idea that the law of negligence has a value in discouraging negligent conduct, there can be no denying the decline in the relative importance of this aspect of the law. In the ordinary running down action, in particular, it has for some years been a commonplace that the presence of third party insurance on the one hand, and of criminal sanctions on the other, have tended to make the law of torts almost exclusively concerned with compensating the plaintiff rather than deterring future defendants.

The fourth presupposition of the classical model of Contract is that there is indeed *one* model, that it is possible and useful to think still in terms of general principles of Contract. The continued vitality of our textbooks and of our university law courses on Contract attest to the faith which lawyers still have in the generalising effect of the concept of Contract. We know, of course, that most contracts fall into particular categories which have their own rules and qualifications derogating from the general law. There are, for example, special rules applicable to contracts of employment,consumer credit contracts, consumer sales, leases, mortgages, insurance contracts, house purchase, matrimonial agreements and many others. Indeed, there are few contracts today which are *not* governed by specific rules which in some measure derogate from the general law. But none of this has shaken the power of the classical model of Contract. This model is, without doubt, based on an economic model, that of the free market. Historically there is every reason to believe that this classical model grew up under the influence of the classical economists and of the philosophical radicals. There is no need to subscribe to the crude and exaggerated myth that these nineteenth century thinkers wanted to reduce all relationships to economic terms, or to encourage a purely materialist approach to all human motivation. But it is true that many of them saw much in the classical contract model which they felt was both admirable and applicable far beyond the commercial sphere. They thought it desirable that men should learn to order their lives according to some definite plan, that they should be encouraged to aim for particular goals, that they should co-operate with others in attempting to seek those goals, that those who let down their fellows should be made to pay the cost of doing so; they thought it desirable that men should be free to develop their skills and ambitions, and they accepted the natural corollary that some would rise and some would sink. It was partly for these reasons (though there were certainly others too) that the classical model of Contract was so unified, and no doubt, it was partly its unity which gave it so much power.

In the law itself, it was the nineteenth century which very largely saw the supercession of the importance of special kinds of contract by the general principles of contract. It was, of course, an Age of Principles—principles of morality, principles of political economy, principles of justice, and principles of law. When Addison published his *Treatise on Contracts* in 1847 he insisted that Contract law was not a mere collection of positive rules but was founded "upon the broad and general principles of universal law." Indeed, he went further: "The law of contracts," he wrote in his Preface, "may justly indeed be said to be a universal law adapted to all times and races, and all places and circumstances, being founded upon those great and fundamental principles of right and wrong deduced from natural reason which are immutable and eternal." Naturally, a concept of Contract which could dismiss all differences of time and place, of circumstances and people, had no need for trivial distinctions between sale and hire-purchase, mortgages and leases, commercial and consumer contracts.

III

It is necessary now to cast a somewhat more critical eye at this conceptual structure. How far does it stand up to more detailed examination? Is it reconcilable with the value systems of the modern world, and in particular, of modern England? Is it even reconcilable with the developments in positive law which have taken place within this conceptual framework? Is it true that contractual obligataions normally arise from agreements or exchanges of promises? How far is it true to suggest that contracts are intentionally made with a view to future performance? To what extent it is correct to regard contractual liability as depending on voluntarily assumed obligations? To what extent is it possible to adhere to the very concept of a single basic model of Contract?

Let me begin with this last question.

If we look at the law as it is stated in the books and the case law we shall see that the concept of contract is applied in a very wide range of situations and to a very large variety of relationships. Before it is possible to construct a model even of a typical or paradigm case of contract it is necessary to have some idea of what it is that we are trying to achieve. Typical of *what*? Paradigm of *what*? Quite apart from the circular nature of the definitional problem, it is hard to understand how one is to measure the typicality of a particular relationship. If we are concerned with the most *numerous* types of transaction then presumably the typical contract would be the bus ride, the train journey, or the supermarket purchase. But even this is somewhat speculative and only empirical research could actually tell us what are the most commonly made transactions. Alternatively, we may be concerned with the *value* of the transactions we are examining. Commercial transactions are doubtless typically of greater individual value than consumer transactions; but it is unlikely that they are of greater aggregate value. And anyhow commercial transactions are so far removed from the ordinary experience of the average person that it is hard to believe a contractual model based on the commercial transaction would today have a wide and pervasive application outside the particular sphere of business. A third possibility is that the typical contract is that of which practising lawyers have the most experience. But here again there are obvious difficulties. If we are concerned with the experience of solicitors, then there can be no doubt that house purchases and mortgages are the most typcial of contracts. If we are concerned with the experience of a barrister in commercial chambers, then the typical contract might be an international sale, an insurance contract, a building contract, and it would almost certainly be a contract made by business parties.

The truth is, I would suggest, that there is no such thing as a typical contract at all. Moreover, modern society has plainly rejected the values of the market outside the increasingly narrow area in which the market is permitted to operate. The classical model of Contract thus continues to exist though with increasingly little content. The *principles* of Contract law sometimes govern new or marginal or residuary situations, but it is hard to see in what sense they can continue to be called *general* principles. They remain general only by default, only because they are being superceded by detailed ad hoc rules lacking any principle.

Let me turn now to a more challenging question. To what extent is it true to say that contractual liabilities arise from agreement or promises or depend on the voluntary assumption of obligation? I want to begin by suggesting that the power of the classical model here derives largely from its stress on the executory contract. If two parties do exchange promises to carry out some performance at a future date, and if, immediately on the exchange of promises, a binding legal obligation comes at once into existence, then it seems inexorably to follow that the obligation is created by the agreement, by the intention of the parties. If they have done nothing to implement the agreement, if no actions have followed the exchange of promises, then manifestly the legal obligation cannot arise from anything except the exchange of promises. Thus far the classical model appears to be impregnable. But closer examination suggests that the area of impregnability is really rather small.

The first point to note is that wholly executory contracts are rarer, more ephemeral in practice, and somewhat less binding than the classical model of Contract would suggest. In the classical model as I have suggested, the executory transaction lies at the very heart of Contract. It is precisely because the classical model largely defines Contract in terms of executory transactions that it necessarily locates the source of contractual liability in what the parties intend rather than in what they do. But large numbers of contracts are regularly made in which the making and the performance, or at least part performance, are simultaneous or practically simultaneous events. Consider such simple transactions as the boarding of a bus, or a purchase of goods in a supermarket, or a loan of money. Is it really sensible to characterise these transactions as agreements or exchanges of promises? Is it meaningful or useful to claim that a person who boards a bus is promising to pay his fare? If so, would it not be just as meaningful to say that when he descends from the bus and crosses the road he promises to cross with all due care for the safety of other road users? I do not, of course, deny that all these transactions involve some element of voluntary conduct. People do not generally board buses, buy goods in a supermarket, or borrow money in their sleep. But they involve much else besides voluntary conduct. They usually involve the rendering of some benefit, or actions of detrimental reliance, or both. A person who is carried by a bus from point A to point B after voluntarily boarding the bus can normally be presumed to have derived some benefit from the arrangements. Does his liability to pay his fare have nothing to do with this element of benefit? A person who borrows money and actually receives the loan is, according to the classical model of Contract, liable to repay the money merely because he promised to repay it. The fact that he received the money appears to be largely irrelevant. It is not, indeed, wholly irrelevant in law, because of the doctrine of consideration, but in the classical model it is the intention or agreement or promise which is the source of the liability and not the consideration. The consideration is either a historical anachronism, a meaningless technicality, or if it has any rational function at all today, it is merely to provide evidence of the seriousness of a promise. Thus a person who borrows £100 is liable to repay it *because* he has promised; the actual receipt of the money is merely evidence of the seriousness of the promise.

If we look at a normative system not encumbered by the doctrine of consideration—say the moral basis of promissory liability—the position is even more starkly clear. An obligation to perform a promise to pay £100 is generally considered to be precisely the same whether the promise is to make a gift or to repay a loan. Since the basis of the obligation lies in the promise in both cases it makes not a particle of difference that in the former case the promisor receives nothing for his money, while in the latter case he has already received full value. Is it not evident that there is some grotesque distortion here?

Consider next the possibility of detrimental reliance by the promisee. Is it not manifest that a person who has actually worsened his position by reliance on a promise has a more powerful case for redress than one who has not acted in reliance on the promise at all? A person who has not relied on a promise (nor paid for it) may suffer a disappointment of his expectations, but he does not actually suffer a pecuniary loss. The disappointment of an expectation may of course be treated as a species of loss by definition, as indeed, the law generally does treat it, if the expectation derives from Contract. But no definitional jugglery can actually equate the position of the party who suffers a diminution of his assets in reliance on a promise, and a person who suffers no such diminution.

But this is not all, for both in morality and in law the rendering of benefits and actions of detrimental reliance can give rise to obligations even where there was no promise at all. The law of quasi-contract is almost entirely concerned with situations in which one party is entitled to recompense for a benefit rendered to another even though the latter made no promise to pay for it. The rendering of a benefit is thus in some cases a sufficient ground for liability even without an agreement or promise to repay. Of course, the law of quasi-contract has " nothing at all " to do with the law of Contract, as classical contract theory tells us. But that is itself, as I shall suggest later, an idea which is quite unacceptable, both historically and analytically. And if the law of quasi-contracts concerns liability for the restitution of uncovenanted benefits, the law of torts and the law of trusts frequently provide redress for acts of reliance performed in the absence of an express promise. Moreover, the law of Contract itself, together with associated parts of the law sometimes characterised as distinct sets of rules, provide many examples of provisions plainly designed for the protection of acts of reasonable reliance, rather than for the imposition of promissory liability. The law of misrepresentations, of warranty, of estoppel and promissory estoppel, no matter how they are conceptualised, provide many illustrations of what can only be rationally regarded as reliance-based liability.

And so far I have said nothing about one of the most obvious bodies of legal doctrine which is not easy to reconcile with the theory that contractual and promissory obligations rest on voluntary obligation. I refer, of course, to the so-called " objective-test " theory of contractual liability. Every law student is taught from his earliest days that contractual intent is not really what it seems; actual subjective intent is normally irrelevant. It is the appearance, the manifestation of intent that matters. Whenever a person is held bound by a promise or a contract contrary to his actual intent or understanding, it is plain that the liability is based not on some notion of a voluntary assumption of obligation, but on something else. And most frequently it will be found that that something else is the element of reasonable reliance. One party relies on a reasonable construction of an offer, or he accepts an offer, reasonably thinking it is still open when the offeror has revoked it but failed to communicate his revocation. All this is standard staff but I suggest that cases of this type have for too long been regarded as of marginal importance only, as not affecting the fundamental basis and theory of liability. In a simple world of simple promises and contracts this might have been an acceptable perspective. But the arrival of written contracts and above all the standard printed forms has surely rendered this approach much less defensible. A party who signs an elaborate printed document is almost invariably held bound by it not because of anything he intended; he is bound in the teeth of his intention and understandings except in some very exceptional cases of fraud or the like. The truth is he is bound not so much because of what he intends but because of what he does. Like the man who is bound to pay his fare because he boards a bus, the man who signs a written contract is liable because of what he does rather than what he intends. And he is liable because of what he does for the good reason that other parties are likely to rely upon what he does in ways which are reasonable and even necessary by the standards of our society.

What I suggest then, is that wherever benefits are rendered, wherever acts of reasonable reliance take place, obligations may arise, both morally and in law. These obligations are by no means confined to cases where explicit promises are given, for they may arise in cases where we would imply a promise, but they also arise in many cases where any attempt to imply a promise would be nothing but a bare fiction. The man who boards a bus without any intention of paying for his fare is bound to pay it though it is difficult to see what reality there can be in claiming that he impliedly promises to pay. The man who signs a document without reading it does not make an implied any more than an express promise in any genuine sense.

Now I want next to suggest that these cases of benefits rendered or of action in reliance, are more common than is suggested by our conventional image of the legal world. In conventional contract theory, the paradigm of contract is the executory arrangement. Executory contract theory has totally subsumed liabilities and obligations which arise from the receipt of benefits or from acts of reasonable reliance. But in practice, the wholly executory transactions is nothing like such a paradigm as it appears in the books. I have already said something of the difficulties involved in the very concept of a paradigm in this context, but the most cursory look at the world and at the law will reveal that many types of transactions do not fit the model of the wholly executory arrangement at all. Vast numbers of transactions are not in any real sense binding prior to something being *done* by one or both of the parties. This may partly reflect the fact that lawyers have traditionally implied promises very easily from transactions, and that in consequence today there are many situations in which the lawyer would assert that an executory arrangement involves implied mutual promises while the parties themselves might very well deny that they had promised anything at all. The language of consumer transactions, in particular, is not couched in terms of promises. People " book " holidays, or air reservations, they " order " goods, they " accept " estimates, and so on. Even in business circles this sort of terminology is more common than the express language of promises and undertakings. Whether language of this kind is treated as creating an obligation is traditionally thought of as depending upon whether the language is tantamount to being promissory. But it is at least arguable that in many cases of this nature the reality is otherwise. Frequently, both in law and in moral discourse we appear to determine whether there should be an obligation first, and then decide how the language should be construed afterwards. And it follows that the existence or non-existence of the obligation is then being decided independently of the existence of any promise.

Much the same occurs where conduct rather than language is in question. Consider a recent example of the creation of what is, in essence, a new species of liability. The courts have recently decided that a local authority which is guilty of negligence in supervising the construction of a house in accordance with the Building Regulations may be liable to an ultimate purchaser of the house.[2] The liability is, of course, a liability in tort. Now that the liability is established as a matter of law, it would not seem unreasonable or odd to say that a local authority impliedly undertakes or promises to exercise due care in supervising the construction of houses. But it would have been difficult to argue for the existence of such an implied undertaking or promise prior to the establishment of legal liability. Here it is clear that the liability is first created on independent grounds, and the implication of a promise can then be read into the conduct which leads to the liability.

It is not always appreciated, I suspect, how easy it is to interpret transactions or arrangements as binding or not binding in their inception, according to the predilections of the interpreter. Consider, from the law, a simple case like *Queen* v. *Demers* which came before the Privy Council in 1900.[3] Here was an arrangement between a colonial government and a printer for printing government publications for eight years. Disputes led to the cancellation of the arrangement by the government whereupon protracted litigation took place in the colonial courts. In the Privy Council the whole case was disposed

[2] *Dutton* v. *Bognor Regis U.C.* [1972] 1 Q.B. 373; *Anns* v. *Merton London B.C.* [1977] 2 W.L.R. 1024.

[3] [1900] A.C. 103.

of in a judgment consisting of one paragraph by the "discovery" that the transaction involved no promise on the part of the government. The only obligation on the government's part was to pay for the work actually done in accordance with the contract. In other words the transaction was viewed not as a binding executory arrangement but as an agreement on the terms which would govern any work actually carried out. The estate agency cases in this century, though they gave rise to more difficulty, involved, in effect, the same considerations. It came ultimately to be held that to appoint a person as an estate agent to sell a property did not create a binding future obligation.[4] The obligation was only to pay for services rendered after they had been rendered. These interpretations were neither necessary nor inevitable. Indeed, in one case they overturned the views of the lower courts and in the other case, the House of Lords departed from a long line of decisions dating back to the mid-nineteenth century. The differing decisions represent, I suspect, a difference in the values attached to the concept of binding executory arrangements on the one hand, and the freedom to change one's mind on the other. It is also worth reflecting on how, once again, the question whether a person has made a promise may depend upon whether he is under an obligation rather than vice versa. Consider the variety of circumstances in which the modern consumer is accorded the right to withdraw from wholly executory arrangements. These rights are sometimes accorded by Statute, but more often by social and commercial custom. Whether a consumer is "bound" by revocable arrangements of this kind depends thus on the law or on such custom; whether he has made a promise, whether his language or conduct can sensibly be interpreted as promissory can only be decided after it has been settled whether he is liable or bound. Even the use of plainly promissory language does not necessarily settle the issue. For, if rights of withdrawal do exist, then a promise can easily be construed as being subject to such rights. There is nothing very odd about such a possibility which closely resembles the common case where a contract provides for unilateral variation of some of its provisions and any promises must be read subject to such variations. Now I must repeat that I am not arguing that consent, promise, intention, voluntary conduct, are irrelevant to the creation of obligations even where an element of reciprocal benefit is present, or some act of reasonable reliance has taken place. In the first place, where liability arises out of conduct rather than from the voluntary assumption of an obligation, the conduct itself is usually of a voluntary character. Even if liability on a part executed arrangement

[4] *Luxor Ltd.* v. *Cooper* [1941] A.C. 108.

can properly be said to be benefit-based rather than promise-based, a man is normally entitled to choose what benefits he will accept—normally, though by no means invariably. Similarly, with reliance-based liability; it is normally open to a person to warn others that they are not to rely upon him, but must trust to their own judgement. Obviously this raises difficulty where a person wants to have his cake and eat it, where he wants to influence others to behave in a certain manner but wants also to disclaim responsibility for their doing so. There is little doubt that in such circumstances the trend is towards insisting on the imposition of responsibility. The striking down of exemption clauses and disclaimers of liability are evidence of the unacceptability of these attempts to have things both ways. This trend may reflect the increased emphasis on reliance and the declining stress on free choice.

But secondly, and much more important, I would argue that even where obligations can be said to be primarily benefit-based or reliance-based, explicit promises may have a valuable role to play. I referred earlier to the conventional wisdom of English common lawyers which some decades ago suggested that the only rational function of the doctrine of consideration was to serve as evidence of the seriousness of a promise. I now want to suggest that the truth lies more closely in the precise converse of this assertion. Where obligations arise out of the rendering of benefits or from acts of reasonable reliance, the presence of an explicit promise may, I suggest, serve valuable evidentiary purposes. Consider the simple example of a loan of money which I referred to earlier as an illustration of a liability which could not, without distortion, be viewed as purely promissory. The presence of an explicit promise may nevertheless serve valuable evidentiary purposes. First, it helps to avoid doubt about the nature of the transaction. The possibility of a gift is ruled out by the express promise to repay. Then it helps clarify who the parties to the transaction may be, for the handing of money by A to B may create a loan from X to Y where A and B are acting as agents or in a transaction of any complexity. An explicit promise may resolve any ambiguities about such matters. Then again an explicit promise may help settle many minor or ancillary terms, and it is worth reflecting on how and why this is the case. Suppose, for example, that the borrower promises to repay the loan with interest at a specified rate. In the sort of society we live in, it can be taken for granted that a loan should normally carry some rate of interest, and in the absence of an agreed rate, the fixing of the rate would fall to the court in the last resort. What would the court do? The court would, of course, endeavour to fix on a just or reasonable rate of interest having regard to all the circumstances. Here again, therefore, the explicit promise to pay a specified rate does not seem to create the obligation, which would exist anyhow, but to give it precision. And the reason why it gives it precision is, surely, that it functions very like a conclusive admission. If the court is to search for a fair and reasonable rate of interest, the rate which the borrower has agreed to pay is good evidence that that is in fact the fair and reasonable rate. Good evidence, but not conclusive evidence. For if the agreed rate of interest is extortionate, or if it has been obtained by fraud or misrepresentation the promise to pay will not bind.

There are, indeed, some cases in which the evidentiary value of promises has already been distinctly recognised by the courts. Naturally enough, given the classical model of Contract, these cases concern situations in which an independent legal obligation already exists. For example, where a person promises to pay for valuable services previously rendered to him—the so-called past consideration cases—the promise may be treated as evidence of the value of those services.[5] And again, where services are rendered in pursuance of a contract which turns out to be invalid for some technical reason, the value of the services may nevertheless be recovered and the contract can be treated as evidence of that value.[6]

It may, of course, be said that these cases are no illustration of the general nature of contractual liability, but on the contrary serve to illustrate the difference between contractual and other forms of liability. For (it may be urged) the whole point of contractual liability is to permit parties to determine conclusively their own obligations. The promise creates the liability, and does not merely evidence it. In non-contractual cases, *per contra,* the duty is in the first instance created by the law; and the promise cannot be treated as creating the obligation. But I suggest that this analysis is the result of treating the executory contract as the paradigm of contract, the heritage of the classical law which I have already criticised. In the part-executed transaction, as I have argued, it is in fact frequently the case that there would be a liability even apart from any express or implied promise. Promises are not a necessary condition of the existence of a liability or the creation of an obligation. The performance by one party of acts which are beneficial to the other, the rendering of services to another, for instance, would normally be thought of as creating some sort of obligatiton even in the absence of a promise. Similarly, acts of reasonable reliance would often create liability in tort, or by way of trust, or other equitable obligation, even

[5] *Stewart* v. *Casey* [1892] 1 Ch. 104.
[6] *Way* v. *Latilla* [1937] 3 All E.R. 759.

where there is no express or implied promise. Indeed, did not the whole law of trusts arise because property was entrusted to other hands, usually no doubt because of some understanding that the trustee would behave in a certain fashion? In circumstances of this kind, therefore, where obligations would normally be thought of as arising from what has been done, rather than from what has been said, there seems to me no difficulty in regarding promises as having primarily an evidentiary role.

Treating explicit promises as prima facie evidence, and as strong prima facie evidence of the fairness of a transaction, of the appropriate price to be paid for goods and services, is an indispensable tool of efficient administration in a free market society. For any other rule would leave it open to a dissatisfied party to any and every transaction to appeal to a judge to upset an agreed price and fix a new one. But the *extent* of the indefeasibility of a promise, the *extent* to which it is to be treated as a conclusive admission of the fairness and reasonableness of the terms of an exchange, is a much less simple proposition. All promises and contracts are defeasible in *some* circumstances. A promise or agreement extorted by violence is no evidence of the fairness of a transaction, and is therefore naturally set aside by the courts. Promises given as a result of certain types of mistake may likewise be set aside. Alternatively, the courts may uphold the validity of the exchange but adjust the obligations of the parties (for example by implying appropriate terms) so as to ensure, so far as possible, that the exchange is a fair or reasonable one, despite the disparity between the literal obligations assumed by the parties.

The extent to which the courts and the law are prepared to go in treating promises as defeasible, or merely as prima facie rather than conclusive evidence of the fairness of an exchange, is obviously something determined by the degree of paternalism which commends itself to the society and the judiciary in question. A society which believes in allowing the skilful and knowledgeable to reap the rewards of their skill and knowledge is likely to have a higher regard for the sanctity of promises than a society which wishes to protect the weak and foolish from the skilful and knowledgeable. As we shall see, this point is a good deal more important in the case of executory transactions.

IV

So far I have been trying to place the part-executed, or the wholly-executed transaction, more firmly back into the central role of Contract, and to suggest that the classical model, based on will theory and the executory transaction, does not fit a large part of law and life.

But in the case of wholly executory arrangements, it may seem that things are different. If a person is liable, morally or legally, on a wholly executory arrangement, if he is liable on a promise prior to the receipt of any benefit, and prior to any act of reliance by the promisee, then it would seem that the liability must be promise-based and nothing else. Morally, few would doubt that, prima facie at least, a promise is *per se* binding; and lawyers, while insisting on the requirement of consideration, would largely agree with the moralists. Now the requirement of consideration or, at least, the satisfaction of that requirement, in the case of the wholly executory contract, is one of the puzzles of the common law. A, let us say, orders goods from B, to be specially made to his requirements. The next day, A discovers he can buy what he wants ready made elsewhere and cancels the order. B, let it be supposed, has so far done nothing whatever under the contract. There is no doubt in law that B can hold A liable and sue him for damages without having to lift a finger to perform his part of the contract. A receives no benefit, B suffers no detriment, no reliance, and yet he is entitled to damages. How can this be so, and how is it that common lawyers have continued to define the doctrine of consideration in terms of benefit and detriment when this definition does not fit the paradigm case of classical contract theory? The answer to this conundrum, which led to a vast quantity of ponderous legal literature, particularly in America, early in this century, lies I suggest, deep in our legal history. The story is long and complex and I have no time to explore it fully. But in essence I believe it is correct to say that until the end of the eighteenth and beginning of the nineteenth century, the recognition and enforcement of executory contracts was a very different thing from what it is today.

In modern law, the plaintiff who sues on a wholly executory transaction obtains damages for his lost expectations, the difference, roughly speaking, between the value to him of the defendant's performance, and the cost to him of his own performance. He makes, in effect, his profit on the transaction without actually having to go through with the transaction. This was not generally the law until very late in the eighteenth century, and it only reached its full development in the nineteenth century. In earlier times the plaintiff who sued on an executory transaction generally remained bound to perform himself, or to pay damages for his own non-performance in the future. The enforcement of an executory contract thus still envisaged an exchange being carried through, benefit for benefit. The defendant might have to pay damages for his non-performance now, but he paid the full value of his performance in the expectation that he would in due course receive the plaintiff's performance. Thus consideration in the form of benefit would always actually pass. If it had not passed before the plaintiff sued, it would still be due afterwards.[7] There was, except in some special and rare instances, no possibility of a plaintiff obtaining damages without any performance himself, without any actual benefit or detriment.[8]

Now as we know, in modern law, all this is different. A plaintiff is unquestionably entitled to expectation damages for breach of an executory contract, without any actual consideration passing. There is no need to show any actual benefit, any detrimental reliance. The modern law is squared with the doctrine of consideration by saying that the mere promises constitute consideration for each other. That indeed was what judges had been saying since the time of Elizabeth I, but it has not generally been perceived what an enormous difference has come over the practical import of this formula. For in the reign of Elizabeth I, a promise was good consideration for a promise precisely because both promises had to be performed. In our modern law, a plaintiff's promise is good consideration for the defendant's promise even though the plaintiff is discharged from performing his promise by the defendant's breach. It is only since these rules grew up, therefore, that liability on the wholly executory contract has truly become promise-based, rather than benefit- or reliance-based.

But although this form of liability must be treated as promise-based, we are entitled to ask how extensive it is in relation to the rest of the law, and whether it deserves to occupy the central role in Contract and even in promissory theory that it occupies today. It is, I think, worth observing that wholly executory contracts are generally nothing like as binding in practice as legal theory might suggest. Consumers and even business men often expect to be able to cancel executory agreements with the minimum of penalty, paying perhaps only for actual expenses laid out in reliance on the promise. And such reliance expenditures would, by definition, not exist if the arrangement were still wholly executory. And even in strict law, it must be stressed that the expectations protected by executory contracts are limited. They are not generally expectations of performance but expectations of profit. Where there is no difference in the market price of the goods or services which are the subject of the contract, and the market price of comparable goods or services, the

[7] These rules were entangled with the independent covenant rules which also remained in the law till late in the eighteenth century. It was because the plaintiff remained liable on his own promise that non-performance by him did not generally prevent him suing the defendant.

[8] Cases of breach of promise of marriage and also wagers were not uncommon exceptions, but these shared the peculiarity that they could not be part executed contracts. Moreover the independent covenant rules could not have applied to them for obvious reasons.

contract may in law be broken with impunity. In practice this must comprise a high proportion of cases in which executory arrangements are broken. Then again, the binding force of wholly executory contracts is normally of an ephemeral nature. Executory contracts do not normally remain executory for very long. Even if made well before the time for performance, the whole purpose of making them is frequently to enable the parties to make preliminary arrangements in confident reliance on reciprocal performance. Thus action in reliance is likely to follow hard on the heels of the making of most executory contracts, and it is only in the rare cases where cancellation is sought very soon after making the contract, or where, despite the lapse of some longer period of time no action in reliance has been commenced, that the source of the obligation has to be rested in the promise alone. Whatever the paradigm of actual Contract may be, there can be no doubt that the paradigm of *a breach of contract* is not the breach of a wholly executory contract. And this surely reflects the intentions of most parties who enter into executory contracts. The primary purpose of making such a contract is usually to agree upon the terms which are to regulate a contemplated exchange, when and if it is carried through; it is surely a subordinate and less obvious purpose that the contract binds both parties to see that the exchange is indeed carried through.

If this is correct, it is not difficult to see how, even in the case of wholly executory arrangements, the principal functions of the promise are evidentiary, as they are in the case of the executed or part-executed arrangement. For when the parties begin to carry through the exchange which they have contracted about, obligations would anyhow arise even in the absence of the contract. The transaction would then become part executed, and as before, there is no reason why obligations should not then arise even in the absence of promises. It is, therefore, only in relation to the bare, unperformed, unpaid for, and unrelied upon promise, or contract, that the evidentiary theory of promissory or contractual liability cannot be supported. Upon what, then, does liability rest in such circumstances? Wherein is the source of the obligation?

V

To stress the limited nature of the issue I must again draw attention to the fact that promises, especially when given as part of some mutual arrangement, do not usually remain unrelied upon for very long. And there are, of course, obvious and complex issues involved in defining what is meant by action in reliance for these purposes. Does it include inaction? Does a sort of generalised action in reliance serve as sufficient to take the case out of the category of the wholly executory arrangement? These are important and difficult questions but I want to put them aside here and face squarely up to the case where there is no reliance of any kind at all; and equally as I have said, where there has been no payment, no benefit rendered.

Perhaps an illustration is in order. Let me take an example discussed by Sir James Fitzjames Stephen in the first number of the *Law Quarterly Review* in 1885.

> " A wanted to take a furnished house, expecting to have to pass the summer in London. He made a verbal agreement to take the house of B, a friend and a man in his own position in life, who was going out of town. The day after the agreement was made, A was ordered to return to his appointment in India instantly. A, being thus prevented from occupying the house, asked B to release him from his agreement, which I think most men in B's position would have done, as nothing had been done under it, and B had been put to no expense or inconvenience. B, however, refused. A reminded B of the Statute of Frauds, but added, that having given his word, he would if required, fulfil his agreement, whatever he might think of B's conduct. In this case,"

Stephen concludes, " I think A did his duty as a man of honour."

To a lawyer, this case is clear. A contract was made, and if it was not for the Statute of Frauds, the contract would be binding. Moreover, the modern lawyer is likely to share the moral perspective of Stephen himself. A contract is morally binding as well as legally binding, even though it is purely executory and nothing has been paid, nothing been done under the arrangement.[9] These conclusions do not appear to me to be as self-evident as they have seemed to most Englishmen at least since the days of the Natural Lawyers. But it is anyhow worth observing that the most celebrated of the Natural Lawyers offered some argument in support of their views about the inherently binding nature of promises and executory contracts. To Grotius,[10] the right to bind oneself by promise or contract necessarily followed from the power to dispose of property. For to bind oneself by a promise was to dispose of a right, to give the promisee here and now a right over the promisor's liberty or future assets. To him, this appeared a less significant form of disposition and therefore necessarily included in the power of presently disposing of property. Today, this argument simply looks fallacious. No doubt the power to bind oneself as to a future disposition of property is similar

[9] An earlier generation of lawyers may not have agreed with this. Cf. Bayley J. in *Ridout* v. *Bristow* (1830) 1 Cr. & J. 231, 235: " It is just that a promise to pay that which I am under no legal or moral obligation to pay should be considered as nudum pactum."

[10] *De Jure Belli ac Pacis*, Book II, chap. XI.

to the power to bind oneself by a present disposition; but the two things are not the same, and there is no logical ground for supposing that one must follow from the other.

Samuel Pufendorf, second only to Grotius himself as the founder of seventeenth-century Natural Law, devoted a good deal more attention to the binding nature of bare promises or executory contracts.[11] Like many a modern philosopher, he argued that the tendency of promises to be relied upon, of men to place their faith in promises, was the principal justification for treating them as binding. But he added that it would be dangerous to argue that a promise was not binding unless and until it was in fact relied upon. Although, in such a case the promisee is no worse off than he would have been if no promise had ever been made, men's duties are not confined to refraining from causing actual harm, actual loss to their fellow-men. Men are, in addition, bound to strive always to further the interests of their fellows, and therefore even a bare unrelied upon promise is naturally binding. It must be said that this looks somewhat thin and unconvincing today. It is hard to relate these generalised duties to one's fellow-men with the particular obligation deriving from a promise. If there is any substance to the argument, it may be thought to support the evidentiary nature of promises. For the argument, is in effect, that the promise gives precision, clarity and individualised shape to the pre-existing general obligation, owed to the world at large.

If we put aside these historical texts and seek more satisfying arguments for the binding nature of bare promises and contracts, we will, I think, be surprised to discover how little attention has been devoted to them by the common lawyers. Apart from the celebrated article by Fuller and Purdue in the *Yale Law Journal* over 40 years ago,[12] little of value has been written on the question. The modern, and perhaps even, by now, the traditional legal view would probably be that promises and executory contracts give rise to reasonable expectations and that it is the function of the law to protect reasonable expectations. But this is itself a somewhat circular justification. We all have a large number of expectations, many of which are perfectly reasonable, but only a few of them are protected by the law. Besides, the reasonableness of an expectation is itself something which turns largely upon whether it is in fact protected. If the law did not protect expectations arising from a wholly executory arrangement, then it would be less reasonable to entertain such expectations, or at any rate to entertain them as entitlements.

[11] *De Jure Naturae et Gentium*, Book III, chap. V, § 11.

[12] " The Reliance Interest in Contract Damages," 46 *Yale Law Journal* 52 and 373 1936).

Then again, the explanation appears to prove too much. For reasonable expectations may arise from assertions or representations of fact as much as from promises. Yet the law seldom or never protects such expectations unless and until they have been acted upon. If we can, as I think we should, conceptually equate the idea of action in reliance on representations with the notion of detrimental reliance as a consideration in the case of promises, then we must recognise that representations can only give rise to a contractual-type obligation in the case of a part-executed transaction. And this remains true even in the extreme case of fraud. No matter what expectations are thereby generated, a person who tells a downright and deliberate falsehood is not subject to legal obligations unless and until someone suffers loss through acting upon it. Indeed, even when it is acted upon, it is widely thought that the measure of any consequent liability is fixed by the extent of the reliance losses and not by the expectations generated. This, at least, is said to be the measure of damages in tort for fraud, although it is certainly not the measure in cases classified as warranty or estoppel. It is, perhaps, possible that the explanation for this otherwise puzzling distinction between the law's treatment of promises and assertions lies in the too ready acceptance of the idea that words or conduct are in practice easily classifiable as the one or the other. Perhaps the reality is that in more cases than lawyers are willing to admit, words or conduct are classified as promises or assertions precisely because in the particular circumstances the expectations aroused are, or are not, felt worthy of protection. But if this is the case, then it is clear that we cannot defend the protection of bare expectations by pointing to the fact that they derived from a promise.

Another puzzling feature of the law's willingness to protect bare expectations is that a disappointed expectation is a psychological rather than a pecuniary injury, and the law is generally sparing in its willingness to award compensation for injuries or losses which are neither physical nor pecuniary. And if it should be urged that, at least in the commercial sphere, expectation damages are more widely justifiable, a problem might then arise about the extent to which companies and other commercial bodies can be said to suffer from a disappointment of their expectations. If disappointment is a psychological phenomenon can a company suffer disappointment? Now I would not suggest that the disappointment of reasonable expectations is no ground at all for holding contracts or promises to be binding. To raise an expectation and then to decline to fulfil it is, in some measure to worsen the position of the promisee, certainly an individual promisee. Prima facie this is something that should be avoided, other things being equal. But I am bound to say that it does appear to me to be a very weak ground for the enforcement of executory contracts, and one that could very easily be counter-balanced by proof that other things are not equal. In the example discussed by Stephen, it might well be thought by most people that the inconvenience to the promisor of being held to his contract would be enough to outweigh the prima facie desirability of not disappointing the promisee.

The second possible argument for upholding executory contracts is the argument from principle. Executory contracts are made so that the parties can rely upon each other and take the necessary preliminary steps to performance. The whole point of such contracts is that they invite reliance. Therefore, it may be urged, *even if there has in fact been no reliance yet,* it is desirable that the principle of upholding the sanctity of contracts should be maintained. Supporters of this argument, however, must explain why a shift in the onus of proof would not meet the case. Certainly, it may be justifiable to throw upon the promisor the burden of showing that the promisee has not yet acted upon the promise; but if in fact he can show this, or if it is conceded, can the argument on principle be maintained? What principle is it that requires contracts to be held binding because they may be relied upon where in fact it is conclusively demonstrated that the particular contract has not been relied upon? Here again, I do not think the argument is as weak as it may look. Contracting parties will not always know whether the other party has relied upon the contract, and it may be undesirable to encourage the promisor to take the chance that the promisee has not yet acted in reliance. And even if, to take the strongest case, as in Stephen's example, the promisor knows that the promisee has not yet acted upon the contract, the argument on principle is not necessarily to be discounted. There *is* a case for saying that the sanctity of a general principle is likely to be better maintained if people are generally persuaded to observe it *as a matter of principle,* without pausing to examine, in every case, whether the reasons justifying the principle cover the case in hand. But it must be admitted that this is not an argument which seems to carry much weight with the public or our legislators in modern times. Given the temper of the times I doubt if it will much longer be possible to blur the line between holding a promise to be binding because it *may* be relied upon and holding it binding because it *has* been relied upon.

The third possible argument in support of the executory contract concerns the case where the contract is a deliberate exercise in risk allocation. Where the primary purpose of a contract is to shift a risk of some future possibility from one party to another, and where, in particular, the risk is thereby shifted to a party who in a commercial sense is better able to take the risk, or to take avoiding action against the risk eventuating, there appears to be a strong economic case for the executory contract. I believe that this argument lies at the heart of the historical development of the binding executory contract in English law, but it is imperative to note the limits upon its application. It is very far from being true that all contracts, even all executory contracts, are exercises in risk allocation. Frequently, it is the interpretation of the law which converts a simple postponed exchange into a risk-allocation exercise, rather than any deliberate intent of the parties. And it is also far from being always the case that the purpose of an executory contract is to shift a risk to a party whose business it is to handle such risks and who can, therefore, be assumed to be generally more efficient at handling them. Indeed, the clearest and most widespread example of a contract of a risk-allocation character is the simple bet. Even business contracts frequently partake of the nature of a bet in so far as they allocate future risks, though in these cases there is a greater likelihood of some social purpose being served inasmuch as the risk is likely to be shifted to a party better able to handle it. In the ordinary bet, of course, this is not so, and that is why there would appear to be no social purpose in investing bets with a binding contractual force.

I suggested earlier that the extent to which promises are treated as conclusive evidence of the fairness of transactions must reflect the degree of paternalism in any society. I must now observe that if the primary justification for the enforcement of executory contracts is that they are risk-allocation devices, then it follows that the enforcement of such contracts raises profoundly value-laden questions. The justification for the executory contract becomes, in effect, an economic justification, an argument for greater economic efficiency. The purpose of enforcing such contracts is that of facilitating the use of greater skill, intelligence, foresight, knowledge and perhaps even resources by those who possess these advantages. To the extent that the law refuses to recognise the binding force of executory transactions in order to protect the weak, the foolish, the improvident or those who lack bargaining power, it must necessarily weaken the incentives and indeed the power of those not suffering these disadvantages. I must not be thought to be arguing for or against developments of this nature in the law. I have in the past had my share of arguing for a greater willingness to protect contracting parties from their own follies and weaknesses. But I have more recently come to appreciate the importance of the inevitable costs associated with such protection.

Let me illustrate the point by referring to the simple case, which has been much discussed in the media lately, of the house-purchase transaction. As everyone knows, the almost invariable practice in England is for such transactions to be entered into, in the first instance, "subject to contract," which means that the initial agreement lacks binding legal force. Of course, as a matter of legal doctrine, this is explained by reference to the intention of the parties, but I have little doubt that the great majority of buyers and sellers regard the result as prescribed by the law and not as subject to their own intentions at all. The substance of the matter is that the legal profession has devised a procedure which prevents parties from binding themselves to an executory arrangement in most instances until they have had ample opportunity to consult their solicitors and make any necessary financial arrangements. The result naturally protects those who are less able and skilful at managing their affairs from making a commitment which turns out to be disadvantageous. But it inevitably does so by depriving those who are perfectly capable of managing their affairs, of the opportunity of using their skills. The dilemma is, I think, inescapable. The economic arguments for the binding executory contract, like those in favour of the institution of property itself, involve a tendency to a perpetuation of existing inequalities. To strike down, or limit the binding force of executory contracts in order to protect some people from their own folly or ignorance is, by contrast, a redistributive device, and like all such devices must impose costs as well as benefits.

The fourth argument, which I have left to the last, for the binding executory contract is the moral argument. It is simple and appealing to argue that promises are morally obligatory, and that this remains the case whether they have been paid for, or relied upon or not. But as the case for the morally binding nature of promises is examined more closely, it bears a curious resemblance to the case for the binding nature of legal contracts rather than offering an independent reason in support of the law. One of the most commonly adduced reasons for arguing that promises are morally binding is that they have a tendency to be relied upon. We then find it being argued that, if that is the only justification, it is a somewhat circular one. For if promises were not binding, they might not be relied upon.[13] And again, it is argued that if the tendency to rely on promises is the source of their binding character, what of the case where reliance is distinctly disproved? The argument on principle, too, has generated a debate among philosophers which closely parallels the legal and social issues hinted at previously. Principles may be useful as rules

[13] See *e.g.* G. J. Warnock, *The Object of Morality* (London, 1971), pp. 99–100.

of thumb but if it is shown that, in some particular case, adherence to the principle produces worse results than non-adherence, is it not merely rule-worship to insist on maintaining the sanctity of the principle?[14] Then, too, there is the legal argument that a promise to do something which the promisor is already bound to do cannot (anyhow in some circumstances) constitute a valid consideration for a contract. A close parallel to this is to be found in the writings of some philosophers who argue, like J. C. Searle,[15] that a promise to do something which the promisor was going to do anyhow is not really a promise at all. And finally, the argument that executory contracts may be risk-allocation devices has its parallel in the writings of philosophers like John Rawls and H. L. A. Hart who argue that to promise is to deliberately take part in a social practice, accepting the benefits of that practice and therefore necessarily subordinating oneself to its burdens.[16]

But when all is said, I do not find the moral contribution to the problem to be a very satisfying one. For moralists and philosophers, like the lawyers themselves, have not generally perceived the need to separate off the wholly executory arrangement for independent justification. Virtually all discussion of the source of contractual and promissory obligation, in law and in morality, has failed to draw the all important distinction between promises and contracts which rest purely in intention, and promises and contracts which depend partly on action. Surely, nobody can doubt that morally speaking promises are more strongly binding where payment has already been received, or where there is a clear and significant act in reliance which would worsen the position of the promisee if the promise were not performed. And just as I have suggested that, in the law of part executed contracts, explicit promises may play a useful evidentiary role, so it may be suggested that promises themselves are frequently of an evidentiary character. The purpose of a promise, far from being, as is so often assumed, to create some wholly independent source of an obligation, is frequently to bolster up an already existing duty. Promises help to clarify, to quantify, to give precision to moral obligations, many of which already exist or would arise anyhow from the performance of acts which are contemplated or invited by the promise. The promise which is given without *any* independent

[14] See *e.g.* J. J. C. Smart, "Extreme and Restricted Utilitarianism," 6 *Phil. Q.* 344, 348–349 (1956).

[15] See "What is a Speech Act?" in *The Philosophy of Language*, ed. J. C. Searle (Oxford, 1971), pp. 49–50.

[16] See *e.g.* J. Rawls, "Two Concepts of Rules," 64 *Phil. Rev.* 1 (1955); *A Theory of Justice* (Oxford, 1972), pp. 342–350, H. L. A. Hart, "Legal and Moral Obligation," in *Essays in Moral Philosophy*, ed. Melden (Seattle and London, 1958); "Are there any Natural Rights?" 64 *Phil. Rev.* 175 (1955). See also J. C. Searle, *op. cit.* (*supra*, n. 15).

reason for it is a peculiarity, just as the wholly executory contract is a legal peculiarity. Is it pure coincidence that the phrase, a " gratuitous promise " means both a promise without payment and a promise without reason? Could it then be that the refusal of English law to recognise the binding force of executory gratuitous promises is not the peculiarity, the idiosyncrasy it has so long been thought to be? Might it not be that the real oddity lies in the belief that a bare promise creates a moral obligation and should create a legal obligation, without any inquiry into the reason for which the promise was given, or the effect that the promise has had?

VI

These arguments, of course, require much greater development than I can give them here; but enough has been said to show that, if they stand up to further examination, they should suffice to dethrone the executory contract from the central place which it occupies in Contract theory. The consequences of this would be to require some drastic redrawing of the lines of the conceptual structure of contractual and promissory obligation. In the first place, the distinction between contract and quasi-contract would surely come crashing to the ground. This distinction was not anyhow indigenous to English law. It is well known that until the middle of the nineteenth century at least, the common lawyers distinguished between express and implied contracts not between contracts and quasi-contracts. To the early common lawyers, the important point in common between express and implied contracts was that both usually involved a claim for payment or reimbursement for a benefit which had been conferred by the plaintiff on the defendant. Whether the defendant had promised to pay for that benefit was a secondary question. In the nineteenth century, when the executory contract became the pivotal key to the law of obligations, when will theory flourished, and when, we may add, renewed study of the classics reminded common lawyers of the Roman law distinctions and terminology, the old common law distinction fell into disrepute. The process began with academics and writers like John Austin, Henry Maine and Martin Leake. Will theory, which emphasised the importance of free choice and the voluntary creation of obligations was plainly inconsistent with the indigenous common law. The newer ideas got into the books and—after the lapse of a couple of generations—into the Law Reports. They passed into orthodoxy. Everybody began to say that quasi-contracts had nothing to do with contracts. I am afraid that I said it myself. The Contract textbooks expelled the subject. Universities even began to run separate courses on the Law of Restitution.

Plainly, if the part-executed contract is to replace the executory contract as the centre piece of Contract theory, we shall have to turn our back on these exciting new ideas. We may then discover that, far from being new, they derive from the intellectual climate of the early nineteenth century. Free choice in all things, rational planning, calculated risk assessment, and the severest limitation of the active role of State and judge, these are the themes which underlie the distinction between contract and quasi-contract. It is scarcely necessary to add that they are the themes of the last century.

A similar fate may well await the distinction between Contract and Tort when once the executory contract is removed from the central place in the law of obligations. I have already suggested that our nineteenth century heritage has led us to place undue emphasis on the extent to which contractual obligations depend upon intentions and the voluntary assumption of liability. But is it not equally true that, perhaps by way of reaction, Tort theory has swung too far in the opposite direction? In their reaction away from Contract, lawyers and judges have tended to stress the positive nature of tortious liability. Tort duties are imposed by law, not assumed by the parties. They are the reflection of society's standards of fairness and reasonableness and not the result of deliberate submission to a mutual binding arrangement, and so on. I want to suggest that all this has tended to draw far too sharp a line between Contract and Tort. It is not true that consent, intention, voluntary conduct is irrelevant to tort liabilities. The modern law of negligence is, in many respects, an offshoot of nineteenth century Contract law. Historically, the tort of negligence which dominates modern Tort law, grew almost entirely out of contractual-type arrangements. Personal injury actions brought against occupiers of premises, against employers, against railway companies were the forerunners of the modern running down case. The road accident between strangers was not the typical tort action of the last century. And even today it remains true that nearly all tort liabilities arise in the course of the performance of voluntary actions. A person who negligently injures another while driving his car is voluntarily on the road, voluntarily driving his car, and may be said to submit himself to the requirements of the law with as much or as little truth as the seller of goods. The liability of the bus company to pedestrians or other road users does not, in this perspective, differ significantly from its liability to passengers inside the bus. In both cases, I suggest, liability arises primarily from what is voluntarily done, from the element of reciprocal benefit and from the fact of reliance. It is, of course, true that the sharp distinctions drawn by the law between tortious and contractual liability have, over the years, led to various accretions of positive law. In particular, contractual liability is often stricter than tortious liability. The seller of defective goods is liable even without proof of negligence for any injury caused by the goods to someone who can claim that he has contracted to buy them. But this distinction is, in a way, an illustration of the theme I am attempting to state. For here too, lawyers and reformers are rejecting the traditional approach. Most lawyers would today prefer to decide what the obligations of a vendor of goods should be, and would then construe his behaviour to support those obligations. Thus if it is thought, as it widely is, that a vendor of defective goods should be strictly liable to anyone who uses the goods and not only to those who buy the goods, the vendor can be said to give an implied warranty that his goods will be safe. But this implied warranty does not necessarily mean that the vendor is thought to voluntarily accept that liability; he voluntarily sells the goods, and the liability is imposed upon him. If we ask, further, why the obligations should be imposed, we will find, in most cases, that the twin elements of benefit and detriment underlie the judgment. In this particular case, for instance, it would be widely agreed that the vendor gets the benefit of the sale, that the purchaser or user relies upon him to distribute goods which are not dangerous, and that these two factors, together with the fact that the sale is a voluntary transaction, suffice to justify the obligation.

It is worth considering another example, where tort law is concerned primarily with the waiver or reduction of legal obligations, rather than its creation. The liability of a car driver to a passenger has, both in this country, and still more overseas, given rise to many shifts and devices for restricting the application of the normal rules of negligence. Whether this has been done by the former legislative exemption from carrying insurance to cover liability to passengers, or by invocation of the maxim *volenti non fit injuria,* or by denial of a duty of care, or by restricting liability to cases of gross negligence, it is surely not far-fetched to see the benefit to the passenger at the heart of the problem. The passenger who is a mere guest (as opposed to the fare-paying passenger) is deriving a gratuitous benefit from being carried in the vehicle. Is it right that he should be permitted to look this gift-horse in the mouth and sue the driver in the event of injury in an accident? The fact that an emphatic affirmative has, at least in this country, now been given to this question, does not, I think, detract from the value of this illustration.

I do not, of course, want to suggest that the whole law of obligations can be rewritten in terms of a few simple principles drawn from the notions of benefit and reliance. Society and social and economic relationships are too complex in the modern industrial world for oversimplifications of this nature. But what I do want to suggest is that the great divide between duties which are voluntarily assumed, and duties which are imposed by law is itself one of these oversimplifications. A more adequate and more unifying conceptual structure for the law of obligations can be built around the inter-relationship between the concepts of reciprocal benefits, acts of reasonable reliance, and voluntary human conduct.

P. S. ATIYAH *

* Professor of English Law, University of Oxford. This paper presents in summary form many conclusions dealt with at much greater length in a study into the theory of contract which has been generously supported by the Social Science Research Council. The first part of this study will be published in 1979 under the title, *The Rise and Fall of Freedom of Contract.*

VOLUME 95 FEBRUARY 1982 NUMBER 4

HARVARD LAW REVIEW

THE BARGAIN PRINCIPLE AND ITS LIMITS

*Melvin Aron Eisenberg**

How far should bargain promises be enforced? The bargain principle — a central thesis of traditional contract law — states that, in the absence of a traditional defense relating to the quality of consent, bargain promises should be enforced to their full extent. Professor Eisenberg argues that it is necessary to rethink the place of that principle in contract law. He first shows that the two justifications of the bargain principle, fairness and efficiency, are entirely persuasive in the classic case of a contract that has been made in a perfectly competitive market and that only one party has performed. Professor Eisenberg maintains, however, that the principle of unconscionability often justifies limitations on the bargain principle when the assumption of a perfect market is relaxed. In particular, he sets out four categories of contracts — involving the exploitation by one party of another's distress, transactional incapacity, susceptibility to unfair persuasion, or ignorance about prices — and shows how the bargain principle falters in those cases because its justifications are not met. Finally, he examines wholly executory contracts and demonstrates how the reach of the bargain principle in such cases depends on a sensitive consideration of the types of parties and commodities involved.

THE institution of contract is central to our social and legal systems, both as reality and as metaphor. At the present time, however, the institution is in conceptual disarray. In the late nineteenth and early twentieth centuries, scholars and courts constructed a philosophical system of contract law characterized in substantial part by logical deduction from received axioms. This system fell into inevitable decline because it failed to recognize that deduction is a means, not an

* Professor of Law, University of California, Berkeley. Columbia University, A.B., 1956; Harvard University, LL.B., 1959.

Portions of this article have been in draft for several years, and over that period I have benefited from the comments of a number of people who have either read the manuscript or discussed the ideas and whom I gratefully thank. I am particularly indebted to Guido Calabresi, Robert Cooter, Peter Diamond, James Gordley, Thomas Jorde, Lewis Kornhauser, Mitchell Polinsky, Albert Sacks, Alan Schwartz, and Jan Vetter, all of whom made comments that materially contributed to the analysis, and to Susan Avitzour, Janet Cooper, and Martina Marshall, who provided valuable help as research assistants.

end, and that the purpose of contract law is not simply to create conditions of liability, but also to respond to the social process of promising.[1] As part of this decline, in the last thirty to forty years there has been a wholesome reaction against logical deduction as a dominant mode of contract reasoning. Unfortunately, that reaction has often been accompanied by a wholesale retreat from any conceptualization of contract law — a retreat represented in its extreme forms by suggestions that contract is being absorbed into tort[2] or that there is no institution of contract as such, but only particular transaction-types.[3] These approaches neglect the possibility of reconceptualizing contract law through the development of principles that are intellectually coherent, yet sufficiently open-textured to account for human reality and to unfold over time. This Article is the second of a series attempting such a reconceptualization.[4]

The subject of this Article is the bargain principle and its limits. By bargain, I mean an exchange in which each party views the performance that he undertakes as the price of the performance undertaken by the other. Although parties may barter bargained-for performances without making any promises, contract law is concerned with those bargains that involve a present promise to render a future performance — that is, that involve an exchange over time. By the bargain principle, I mean the common law rule that, in the absence of a traditional defense relating to the quality of consent (such as duress, incapacity, misrepresentation, or mutual mistake),[5] the courts will enforce a bargain according to its terms, with the object of putting a bargain-promisee in as good a position as if the bargain had been performed. Part I of this Article explores

---

[1] *See, e.g.*, C. LANGDELL, A SUMMARY OF THE LAW OF CONTRACTS § 15, at 20–21 (2d ed. 1880) (in formulating the rule regarding when a mailed acceptance is effective, "substantial justice" is "irrelevant").

[2] *See* G. GILMORE, THE DEATH OF CONTRACT 87–94 (1974).

[3] *See* Mueller, *Contract Remedies: Business Fact and Legal Fantasy*, 1967 WIS. L. REV. 833, 833–34; *cf.* G. GILMORE, *supra* note 2 (arguing general collapse of traditional contract doctrine); Friedman & Macauley, *Contract Law and Contract Teaching: Past, Present and Future*, 1967 WIS. L. REV. 805, 812 (fundamental concepts of contract law "too general and abstract to regulate current, socially significant business problems").

[4] *See* Eisenberg, *Donative Promises*, 47 U. CHI. L. REV. 1 (1979).

[5] The most important of the remaining traditional consensual defenses are palpable unilateral mistake, and misunderstanding in the *Peerless* sense (i.e., subjectively different but equally reasonable interpretations). *See* Raffles v. Wichelhaus, 2 H. & C. 906, 159 Eng. Rep. 375 (Ex. Ch. 1864). Many courts also recognize nonpalpable unilateral mistake as a defense if the promisee has not relied or his reliance can be reimbursed. *See* Elsinore Union Elementary School Dist. v. Kastorff, 54 Cal. 2d. 380, 353 P.2d 713, 6 Cal. Rptr. 1 (1960).

the reasons that support this principle in the context of half-completed bargains. Part II explores the limits that should be placed on the bargain principle under the doctrine of unconscionability. Part III explores the reasons that support the bargain principle in the context of executory bargains and the limits that should be placed on the principle in this context even in the absence of unconscionability.

I. The Bargain Principle

Since the law does not enforce promises as such, a legal analysis of bargain promises must start with the question whether such promises should be enforceable at all. In considering this question, it is easiest to begin with those bargains in which one party's performance is both due and rendered before the other's, so that the bargain has become a half-completed or credit transaction. For convenience, I shall generally call the unperformed promise a half-completed-bargain promise; the party who has already rendered performance the plaintiff; and the party who has bargained for that performance the defendant.

Whether any given type of promise should be legally enforceable turns on both substantive and administrative considerations. As a substantive matter, the state (speaking through the courts) may fairly take the position that its compulsory processes will not be made available to redress every hurt caused by broken promises, but only to remedy substantial injuries, to prevent unjust enrichment, or to further some independent social policy, such as promotion of the economy.[6] As an administrative matter, the state may fairly take into account the extent to which enforcement of a certain type of promise would involve difficult problems of proof. Cutting across both substantive and administrative categories is the question whether the type of promise at issue is normally made in a deliberative manner, so that it fairly reflects the promisor's wants and resources.

Given these considerations, the half-completed-bargain promise presents the strongest possible appeal for legal enforcement. The interests of the plaintiff are typically substantial, because he has incurred the cost of performance and, normally, has seen the defendant enriched to the extent of that performance. The state has independent interests in enforcing such

---

[6] *See* Hays, *Formal Contracts and Consideration: A Legislative Program*, 41 COLUM. L. REV. 849, 852–53 (1941); Willis, *Rationale of the Law of Contracts*, 11 IND. L.J. 227, 230 (1936).

promises. The very strength of the plaintiff's injury may implicate the state's interest in keeping the peace, because a party who has rendered a bargained-but-unpaid-for performance might resort to self-help if the state refused to act on his behalf.[7] Perhaps more important, the nature of the transaction implicates the state's interest in the smooth functioning of its economy. A modern free enterprise system depends heavily on exchanges over time and on private planning. The extent to which actors will be ready to engage in such exchanges, and are able to make reliable plans, depends partly on the probability that promises to render a bargained-for performance will be kept. Legal enforcement of such promises makes it more likely that they will be kept.[8] Other criteria for enforceability point in the same direction. The fact that a valuable performance has been rendered to an unrelated party helps satisfy the criterion of evidentiary security. The fact that a bargain promise is rooted in self-interest rather than altruism tends to ensure that it will be finely calculated and deliberatively made.[9]

The hard question, therefore, is not *whether* half-completed-bargain promises should be legally enforced, but the *extent* to which such promises should be enforced. Three broad possibilities serve as starting points. Such a promise may be enforced: (1) to the extent of the plaintiff's cost, including his opportunity cost (the reliance measure); (2) to the extent of the value conferred upon the defendant (the restitution measure); or (3) to the extent of the value to the plaintiff of the promised performance — that is, the amount required to put the plaintiff in as good a position as if the contract had been performed (the expectation measure). Often these three measures coincide.[10] But what if they do not? Suppose, in

[7] The techniques for enforcing debts to gamblers and loan sharks provide contemporary examples of self-help in cases in which the law will not enforce a promise — although it is conceivable that, because of the social structure of the gambling and loan-shark industries, self-help would be employed even if legal enforcement were available.

[8] Of course, promissory transactions might occur regularly even in the absence of such enforcement, since reasons of reputation and morality may often be more important incentives for promise-keeping than legal sanctions. Those reasons, however, operate so unevenly, and data concerning reputation is so difficult to assemble, that a regime dependent solely on reputation and morality would almost certainly be less fair and efficient than an enforcement regime.

[9] When these conditions are not likely to be satisfied, a different rule might be appropriate. *See infra* pp. 763–78.

[10] For example, assume that *P*, a plumber working at full capacity, does a five-hour job for *Q* at $20/hour, his usual rate and the market price. *Q* fails to pay. *P*'s

particular, that the defendant resists all but restitutionary damages, on the ground that the terms of the bargain were unfair, in the sense that the value of the performance he promised to render exceeded the value he was to receive in exchange.

Generally speaking, the answer of the common law has been to invoke what I have called the bargain principle, which is commonly expressed by such catchphrases as "courts do not inquire into the adequacy of consideration" or "mere inadequacy of consideration will not void a contract."[11] When stated in this way, the principle appears to be substantive, but in large part it is a rule about remedies. What it means is that damages for unexcused breach of a bargain promise should invariably be measured by the value the promised performance would have had to the plaintiff, rather than, and regardless of, the cost or value of the performance for which the defendant's promise was exchanged — a formulation that can be expressed by the concept that a bargain promise should be enforced to its full extent.

If this principle were to be rigorously applied, bargain promises could never be reviewed for fairness of terms. A number of arguments can be made, on the bases of fairness and economic efficiency, that the principle should be so applied, at least in the context of a half-completed bargain.

First. The idea of reviewing a bargain for fairness of terms implies that an objective value can be placed upon a bargained-for performance. It can be argued, however, that objective value of a bargained-for performance is not a meaningful concept, because the value of such a performance is that which the parties assign to it.[12] A related argument is that a

---

expectation is $100; *P*'s reliance is $100 (his opportunity forgone); and *P*'s work will normally enrich *Q* by $100.

Liquidated damages are not considered in this Article, because most contracts do not include a liquidated-damages provision. Specific performance is also not considered, partly because it is usually not a feasible remedy and partly because in those cases in which it is feasible, it is often simply a special technique for putting plaintiff in the position he would have been in if the contract had been performed.

[11] *See, e.g.*, Schweitzer v. Gibson, 321 Ill. 336, 151 N.E. 865 (1926); Batsakis v. Demotsis, 226 S.W.2d 673 (Tex. Civ. App. 1949); Westlake v. Adams, 5 C.B. (n.s.) 248, 265, 141 Eng. Rep. 99, 106 (C.P. 1858); RESTATEMENT (SECOND) OF CONTRACTS § 79 (1979). This rule applies to all bargains, whether or not half-completed.

[12] *See* T. HOBBES, LEVIATHAN *75 (1651) ("The value of all things contracted for, is measured by the Appetite of the Contractors: and therefore the just value, is that which they be contented to give."); 14 J. LOCRÉ, LA LÉGISLATION CIVILE, COMMERCIALE ET CRIMINELLE DE LA FRANCE 65 (1828) (remarks of Berlier before the Conseil d'Etat), *translated in* von Mehren, *The French Doctrine of Lésion in the Sale of Immovable Property*, 49 TUL. L. REV. 321, 325 (1975) ("Things do not in general have a true price, a just price; they are worth less to one person, more to another; the

party who has received a bargained-for performance cannot legitimately object to paying a price that reflects its value to him, and his agreement shows that he valued the performance at least as high as the promised price.

Second. If *A* has rendered a bargained-for performance to *B*, we know that *A* was willing to render that performance to *B* for the agreed-upon price. We cannot know whether *A* would have rendered that performance to *B* for any lesser price. It can therefore be argued that, having rendered the performance, *A* cannot legitimately be required to accept any lesser price. Such a requirement would unfairly convert *A* from a voluntary to an involuntary actor, because had he known in advance that the price would be reduced, he might not have contracted and performed.

Third. The extent to which private actors are willing to engage in credit transactions (that is, bargains involving exchanges over time) and make plans on the basis of those transactions depends partly on the probability that bargain promises will be kept. It can therefore be argued that failure to enforce bargain promises to their full extent would subvert efficiency by diminishing the willingness of private actors to enter into and plan upon the basis of credit transactions.

Fourth. The contract price is normally the most efficient price, in the economist's sense of that term, because permitting the price of a commodity to be determined by the interaction of buyers and sellers will normally move the commodity to its highest-valued uses, as expressed by the amounts competing buyers are willing to pay, and will best allocate the factors necessary for the commodity's production.

These arguments find their fullest justification in what might be called the exemplary case for application of the bargain principle — that is, a half-completed bargain in a perfectly competitive market. Such a market involves four elements: a homogeneous commodity (which may consist of either goods or services); a marketplace at which perfect cost-free information concerning price is readily available (hereinafter referred to as a homogeneous marketplace); productive resources that are sufficiently mobile that pricing decisions readily influence their allocation; and participants whose market share is so small that none can affect the commodity's price, so that each takes the market price as given by outside forces.[13]

degree of luxury, the utility, the varying situations of the parties, there are plenty of reasons for different evaluations: but the price is known only by the agreement itself; it establishes the price, and the price should not be sought elsewhere.").

[13] *See* E. MANSFIELD, MICROECONOMICS 196–97 (3d ed. 1979).

Now assume such a market, and let the parties to a bargain be a plaintiff-seller, *S*, and a defendant-buyer, *B*. Given a homogeneous commodity and a homogeneous marketplace, the contract price will be the market price. A number of reasons support the proposition that this price is fair: (1) The mechanism by which the price is generated, a perfectly competitive market, is generally regarded as a fair mechanism. (2) By normal measures of value, the contract price will be equal to the benefit *S* has conferred upon *B*. (3) *S* would not voluntarily have transferred the commodity to *B* at any lower price, because if *B* had not agreed to pay the market price, *S* could have sold it to another buyer at that price. (4) A party who has performed under a half-completed bargain should usually be entitled at a minimum to enforce the other's promise to the extent of his cost. Because *S* probably could have sold the commodity to another buyer at the market price if *B* had not acquired it, the contract price is likely to equal *S*'s opportunity cost. Given perfect competition, the contract price will also normally approximate *S*'s marginal cost.

The price in a perfectly competitive market is also efficient. If the price does exceed marginal cost, then given that pricing decisions readily influence the allocation of productive resources, the prospect of above-normal profits will provide an incentive to increase supply, leading to an increase in capacity and a new (and lower) equilibrium price that yields only normal profits. In contrast, to the extent the price is kept from rising to the equilibrium or market price, there is an incentive to decrease capacity by reallocating resources to other uses and not replacing depleted capital stock. Moreover, because perfect competition prevails, demand for the commodity would exceed the supply at any price less than the market price. Some mechanism other than price would therefore be required for rationing the supply among competing buyers, and the supply would not be allocated to its highest-valued uses, as measured by the amounts competing buyers are willing to pay — assuming, at least, that income is either distributed optimally or can best be redistributed by techniques other than price, such as taxation and subsidy.[14]

In short, in the exemplary case the bargain principle is supported by considerations of both fairness and efficiency. Indeed, the bargain principle may well have been formulated on the premise that real cases did not materially differ from the exemplary case. In practice, however, such differences frequently arise, and the balance of this Article considers the

[14] *See* 1 A. KAHN, THE ECONOMICS OF REGULATION 67 (1970).

strength of the bargain principle when the assumptions of the exemplary case are relaxed. Part II shows that if the assumption of a perfectly competitive market is relaxed, the stage is set for invoking limits on the bargain principle based on the quality of the underlying bargain. Part III shows that if the assumption of a half-completed bargain is relaxed, the stage is set for invoking limits on the remedial reach of the principle independent of the quality of the bargain.

II. THE PRINCIPLE OF UNCONSCIONABILITY

Each of the arguments supporting the bargain principle has considerable force, even outside the context of the exemplary case. Each, however, overstates its claim when it is extended beyond that case. The argument that objective value is neither a meaningful nor an appropriate concept can be countered by observing that the law often measures objective value in bargains that are not made in a perfectly competitive market. For example, off-market contracts between a beneficiary and his trustee[15] or between a fiduciary and his corporation[16] are customarily subject to review for objective fairness.[17] If the

---

[15] Owens v. Owens, 196 Va. 966, 86 S.E.2d 181 (1955); RESTATEMENT (SECOND) OF CONTRACTS § 173 & illustration 1 (1979); RESTATEMENT (SECOND) OF TRUSTS § 216(3) (1959) (consent of beneficiary to a transaction between trustee and trust is ineffective unless the transaction is fair and reasonable); 3 A. SCOTT, THE LAW OF TRUSTS § 216.3 (1967).

[16] *See, e.g.*, Geddes v. Anaconda Copper Mining Co., 254 U.S. 590, 598–602 (1921); Sisk v. Jordan Co., 94 Conn. 384, 389–90, 109 A. 181, 183 (1919); Globe Woolen Co. v. Utica Gas & Elec. Co., 224 N.Y. 483, 121 N.E. 378 (1918); 3 W. FLETCHER, CYCLOPEDIA OF THE LAW OF PRIVATE CORPORATIONS §§ 918–919 (rev. vol. 1975); Note, *The Fairness Test of Corporate Contracts with Interested Directors*, 61 HARV. L. REV. 335 (1948); *see also* RESTATEMENT (SECOND) OF CONTRACTS § 15 (1979) (review of contracts entered into by incompetents); 2 S. WILLISTON, A TREATISE ON THE LAW OF CONTRACTS § 254 (3d ed. 1959) (same); Green, *The Operative Effect of Mental Incompetency on Agreements and Wills*, 21 TEX. L. REV. 554 (1943) (same); Green, *Proof of Mental Incompetency and the Unexpressed Major Premise*, 53 YALE L.J. 271, 303–04, 306–11 (1944) (same).

[17] We may look farther afield: the French and German Civil Codes both contain provisions of central importance that hinge on disparity between agreed-upon price and objective value. The French Code, CODE CIVIL [C. CIV.] art. 1674 (78e ed. Petits Code Dalloz 1978), provides, in effect, that a seller of real property can demand rescission if the sale price of the property is less than 5/12 of its value. The value must be estimated as of the date of the contract. *Id.* art. 1675. The buyer can defeat the action by paying 9/10 of the "just price" — that is, the objective value — calculated as of the date of payment. *Id.* art. 1681; *see* von Mehren, *supra* note 12, at 324 & n.11. Section 138(2) of the German Civil Code renders a transaction void "when a person [exploits] the distressed situation, inexperience, lack of judgmental ability, or grave weakness of will of another to obtain the grant or promise of pecuniary advantages . . . which are obviously disproportionate to the performance

mechanism by which a contract price was generated is inferior, in a normative way, to some other mechanism available to a court — such as measurement based on market price, cost, or benefit conferred — then resort to the other mechanism may well be in order. This point also helps answer the related argument that a promisor who has received a bargained-for performance cannot legitimately object to paying a price that reflects the value he placed on the performance. A promisee is not necessarily entitled to capture a surplus representing the excess of the promisor's subjective value over a price set in an objectively desirable manner.

The argument that revising a bargained-for price may unfairly convert a party who has rendered a bargained-for performance into an involuntary actor can be countered by a similar objection. If the price was not set by a mechanism that is regarded as fair, such as a competitive market, it may

given in return." A. VON MEHREN & J. GORDLEY, THE CIVIL LAW SYSTEM 1188 (2d ed. 1977) (translating BÜRGERLICHES GESETZBUCH [BGB] § 138(2) (W. Ger.) (Staudinger 1979)). According to von Mehren and Gordley:

> Formerly, Section 138, par. 2 provided that a juristic act is void "when a person takes advantage of the difficulties [sometimes translated 'necessity'], indiscretion, or inexperience of another to obtain the grant or promise of pecuniary advantages for himself or a third party which exceed the value of the performance given in return to such an extent that the disproportion is obvious." The primary change is to replace the words "difficulties, indiscretion, or inexperience" by "distressed situation, inexperience, lack of judgmental ability, or grave weakness of will." The amendment was intended to extend the scope of the statute to kinds of stress which might not amount to objective "difficulties" and kinds of weakness which might not amount to "indiscretion."

Id. at 1209. For a searching exposition and analysis of § 138(2), see Dawson, *Unconscionable Coercion: The German Version*, 89 HARV. L. REV. 1041, 1052 (1976) [hereinafter cited as Dawson, *Unconscionable Coercion*]. For a discussion of both the French and German provisions, see A. VON MEHREN & J. GORDLEY, *supra*, at 822–27, 1024–26; 2 M. PLANIOL, TREATISE ON THE CIVIL LAW NOS. 1076(2)–(5), 1586–1597 (11th ed. 1939); Dawson, *Economic Duress and the Fair Exchange in French and German Law* (pt. 1), 11 TUL. L. REV. 345, 370–75 (1937) [hereinafter cited as Dawson, *Fair Exchange I*]; von Mehren, *supra* note 12, at 323. Similar provisions were adopted in several other civil law jurisdictions. *See* Dawson, *Economic Duress and the Fair Exchange in French and German Law* (pt. 2), 12 TUL. L. REV. 42, 50 n.140 (1937) [hereinafter cited as Dawson, *Fair Exchange II*]; Thayer, *Laesio Enormis*, 25 KY. L.J. 321, 329 (1937).

Article 1674 of the French Civil Code is derived from the Roman and medieval law doctrine of *laesio enormis*, under which performance of a contract could be excused solely on the ground of a large disparity between price and value. Dawson, *Fair Exchange I*, *supra*, at 364–70; Dawson, *Fair Exchange II*, *supra*; von Mehren, *supra* note 12. Consequently, the quality of the seller's consent is not deemed relevant under article 1674. Except where otherwise explicitly provided, however, the French Civil Code expressly rejects the *laesio* doctrine. C. CIV. art. 1313 (78e ed. Petits Code Dalloz 1978). The framers of the German Civil Code also appear to have rejected the doctrine of *laesio*, insofar as it rests solely on a disparity between price and value. *See* Dawson, *Fair Exchange I*, *supra*, at 375–76; Dawson, *Fair Exchange II*, *supra*, at 50–51.

not be unfair or undesirable to revise it judicially. Many rules of law induce some form of involuntary behavior.

The argument based on the need to facilitate credit transactions and private planning depends for its weight on the strength of the policy behind facilitation, which in turn depends in part on the quality of the market in which the contract is made. In any event, not all types of credit transactions are necessarily to be encouraged,[18] not all bargains involve planning,[19] and in some transactions occurring off competitive markets a party might not be deterred from contracting by the prospect of a reduction in price.[20]

The argument based on the efficiency of contract price is fully effective only to the extent that the relevant market does not materially differ from a perfectly competitive market. In fact, however, many contracts are made in markets that are highly imperfect.

In short, while the arguments supporting the bargain principle are weighty and suggest that limits on the principle should be imposed cautiously, they are not conclusive. Always, therefore, there has been a strong countercurrent against the bargain principle.[21] Equity courts have long reviewed contracts for fairness when equitable relief has been sought.[22] Within recent years the principle has emerged — first in section 2-302 of the Uniform Commercial Code,[23] then in the cases,[24] and later in section 208 of the *Restatement (Second) of Con-*

---

[18] *See infra* pp. 763–85.

[19] *See infra* pp. 755–61.

It might also be argued that, if sellers thought that buyers' promises were enforceable according to their terms only if the buyer had received fair value in the eyes of a factfinder, they might sell only for cash. As a practical matter, however, the choice between a cash and a credit transaction is seldom likely to turn on the prospect of judicial review for fairness: businessmen have other things to worry about. Furthermore, if the law can review a price that is yet unpaid, it could also review a price already paid. Indeed, this is precisely the result under C. CIV. art. 1764 (78e ed. Petits Code Dalloz) and BGB § 138(2) (Staudinger 1979), which draw no distinction between executed and executory transactions.

[20] *See infra* pp. 754–63.

[21] *See, e.g.*, Campbell Soup Co. v. Wentz, 172 F.2d 80 (3d Cir. 1948); McClure v. Raben, 133 Ind. 507, 33 N.E. 275 (1893); Richey v. Richey, 189 Iowa 1300, 179 N.W. 830 (1920); Baltimore Humane Impartial Soc'y v. Pierce, 100 Md. 520, 60 A. 277 (1905); Mersereau v. Simon, 225 A.D. 997, 8 N.Y.S.2d 534 (1938); Dawson, *Economic Duress — An Essay in Perspective*, 45 MICH. L. REV. 253 (1947).

[22] *See, e.g.*, Loeb v. Wilson, 253 Cal. App. 2d 383, 61 Cal. Rptr. 377 (1967); Schlegel v. Moorhead, 170 Mont. 391, 553 P.2d 1009 (1976); McKinnon v. Benedict, 38 Wis. 2d 607, 157 N.W.2d 665 (1968). *See generally* Schwartz, *The Case for Specific Performance*, 89 YALE L.J. 271, 273 & n.8, 299–303 (1979).

[23] U.C.C. § 2-302 (1977). The direct forerunner of § 2-302 was introduced in the 1948 draft of the Uniform Commercial Code. *See* Leff, *Unconscionability and the Code — The Emperor's New Clause*, 115 U. PA. L. REV. 485, 494 (1967). The full

tracts,[25] other uniform acts,[26] and the *Restatement (Second) of Property*[27] — that law courts too may limit or deny enforcement of a bargain promise when the bargain is "unconscionable."

To understand the significance of this principle, it is useful to invoke the concept of a paradigm, in the sense developed by Thomas Kuhn in *The Structure of Scientific Revolutions*. As used by Kuhn, a paradigm is a model, principle, or theory that explains most or all phenomena within its scope, but is sufficiently open-ended to leave room for the resolution of further problems and ambiguities.[28] At the time of its formation, a paradigm looks both backward and forward. Looking backward, the paradigm permits and indeed requires the reconstruction of prior explanations. Looking forward, the paradigm will be applied and extended, by further articulation and specification, to resolve additional problems and ambiguities and to uncover new or previously disregarded phenomena. But as the paradigm is applied and extended in this manner, it typically happens that anomalies — phenomena the paradigm does not account for — are uncovered. These anomalies may eventually lead to the formation of an entirely new paradigm.[29]

The history of contract law, read retrospectively, suggests that the bargain principle, while long implicit,[30] at some point emerged as a controlling paradigm in the area of consideration.[31] Since that time, the law of consideration has been

---

text of the then-final version of the Code became available in 1952. *See* Braucher, *The Legislative History of the Uniform Commercial Code*, 58 COLUM. L. REV. 798, 798–800 (1958).

[24] *See, e.g.*, Williams v. Walker-Thomas Furniture Co., 350 F.2d 445 (D.C. Cir. 1965).

[25] RESTATEMENT (SECOND) OF CONTRACTS § 208 (1979).

[26] *See* UNIF. CONSUMER CREDIT CODE § 5.108 (1974); UNIF. CONSUMER SALES PRACTICES ACT § 4 (1971); UNIF. RESIDENTIAL LANDLORD AND TENANT ACT § 1.303(a)(1) (1972).

[27] RESTATEMENT (SECOND) OF PROPERTY § 5.6 (1977) (expansion or contraction of landlord's obligations or tenant's remedies is valid and binding unless unenforceable because unconscionable or significantly against public policy).

[28] T. KUHN, THE STRUCTURE OF SCIENTIFIC REVOLUTIONS 10, 23, 181–87 (2d ed. 1970).

[29] *Id.* at 6, 7, 27, 29, 52–65 & *passim*.

[30] *See* L. FULLER & M. EISENBERG, BASIC CONTRACT LAW 44–47, 81–84 (4th ed. 1981).

[31] Legal paradigms differ from scientific paradigms in a number of respects, although Kuhn himself draws on the model of legal reasoning in explaining his theory. *See* T. KUHN, *supra* note 28, at 23. For example, a scientific paradigm may be formulated by a single person at a discrete point in time. In contrast, legal paradigms, such as the bargain principle, normally must, by their very nature, be developed over long periods by a number of actors.

concerned to a great extent with the articulation and specification of that paradigm. For example, courts and scholars have analyzed over the years such problems as why executory bargains should be enforceable[32] and how to treat bargains involving a performance that was already legally required,[33] transactions that are bargains in form but not in substance,[34] bargains in which one of the promises is illusory,[35] and unbargained-for reliance.[36]

When the concept of unconscionability was first made explicit by the Uniform Commercial Code, the initial effort was to reconcile it with the bargain principle. A major step in this direction was a distinction, drawn in 1967 by Arthur Leff, between "procedural" and "substantive" unconscionability.[37] Leff defined procedural unconscionability as fault or unfairness in the bargaining *process*; substantive unconscionability as fault or unfairness in the bargaining *outcome* — that is, unfairness of terms. The effect (if not the purpose) of this distinction, which influenced much of the later analysis,[38] was to domesticate unconscionability by accepting the concept insofar as it could be made harmonious with the bargain principle (that is, insofar as it was "procedural"), while rejecting its wider implication that in appropriate cases the courts might review bargains for fairness of terms. Correspondingly, much of the scholarly literature and case law concerning unconscionability has emphasized the element of unfair surprise, in which a major underpinning of the bargain principle — knowing assent — is absent by hypothesis.

Over the last fifteen years, however, there have been strong indications that the principle of unconscionability authorizes a review of elements well beyond unfair surprise, including, in appropriate cases, fairness of terms. For example, comment c to section 208 of the *Restatement (Second) of Contracts* states that "[t]heoretically it is possible for a contract to be oppressive

[32] *See, e.g.*, C. LANGDELL, *supra* note 1, §§ 81–89; Ames, *Two Theories of Consideration* (pt. 2), 13 HARV. L. REV. 29 (1899); Langdell, *Mutual Promises as a Consideration for Each Other*, 14 HARV. L. REV. 496 (1901); Williston, *Successive Promises of the Same Performance*, 8 HARV. L. REV. 27 (1894).

[33] *See, e.g.*, RESTATEMENT (SECOND) OF CONTRACTS § 73 (1979).

[34] *Compare* RESTATEMENT [FIRST] OF CONTRACTS § 84 illustration 1 (1932) (form of a bargain sufficient) *with* RESTATEMENT (SECOND) OF CONTRACTS § 71 illustration 4 (1981) (form of a bargain not sufficient).

[35] *See, e.g.*, 1 S. WILLISTON, A TREATISE ON THE LAW OF CONTRACTS § 103B (rev. ed. 1936); Corbin, *The Effect of Options on Consideration*, 34 YALE L.J. 571, 574 (1925).

[36] *See* Eisenberg, *supra* note 4, at 18–31.

[37] Leff, *supra* note 23, at 486–87.

[38] *See, e.g.*, Epstein, *Unconscionability: A Critical Reappraisal*, 18 J.L. & ECON. 293 (1975).

taken as a whole, even though there is no weakness in the bargaining process."[39] Similarly, section 5.108(4)(c) of the Uniform Consumer Credit Code lists as a factor to be considered in determining whether a transaction is unconscionable "gross disparity between the price of the property or services . . . [and their value] measured by the price at which similar property or services are readily obtainable in credit transactions by like consumers."[40] And a number of cases have held or indicated that the principle of unconscionability permits enforcement of a promise to be limited on the basis of unfair price alone.[41]

As these phenomena have accumulated, it has become clear that they constitute anomalies under the bargain principle, and

[39] Restatement (Second) of Contracts § 208 comment c (1979). According to the Uniform Commercial Code:

> The basic test is whether . . . the clauses involved are so one-sided as to be unconscionable under the circumstances existing at the time of the making of the contract. . . . The principle is one of the prevention of oppression and unfair surprise . . . and not of disturbance of allocation of risks because of superior bargaining power.

U.C.C. § 2-302 comment 1 (1977). Although this language is admittedly delphic, *see* Dawson, *Unconscionable Coercion*, *supra* note 17, at 1043, the references to one-sidedness and oppression suggest that a review for fairness of terms is contemplated.

[40] Unif. Consumer Credit Code § 5.108(4)(c) (1974). An illustration in the official commentary indicates that § 5.108 would be applicable in the case of "a home solicitation sale of a set of cookware or flatware to a housewife for $375 in an area where a set of comparable quality is readily available on credit in stores for $125 or less." *Id.* comment 4.

Unif. Consumer Sales Practices Act § 4(c)(2) (1972) and the official comment follow Unif. Consumer Credit Code § 4.108(4)(c) & comment 4; *see also* Unif. Residential Landlord and Tenant Act § 1.303 comment (1972) ("The basic test is whether, in light of the background and setting of the market, the conditions of the particular parties to the rental agreement . . . are so one-sided as to be unconscionable under the circumstances existing at the time of the making of the agreement . . . .").

[41] *See, e.g.*, Murphy v. McNamara, 36 Conn. Supp. 183, 416 A.2d 170 (Super. Ct. 1979); American Home Improvement, Inc. v. MacIver, 105 N.H. 435, 201 A.2d 886 (1964); Shell Oil Co. v. Marinello, 63 N.J. 402, 307 A.2d 598 (1973), *cert. denied*, 415 U.S. 920 (1974); Kugler v. Romain, 58 N.J. 522, 279 A.2d 640 (1971); Toker v. Westerman, 113 N.J. Super. 452, 274 A.2d 78 (Union County D. Ct. 1970); Toker v. Perl, 103 N.J. Super. 500, 247 A.2d 701 (Law Div. 1968), *aff'd per curiam on other grounds*, 108 N.J. Super. 129, 260 A.2d 244 (App. Div. 1970); Vom Lehn v. Astor Art Galleries, Ltd., 86 Misc. 2d 1, 380 N.Y.S.2d 532 (Sup. Ct. 1976); Jones v. Star Credit Corp., 59 Misc. 2d 189, 298 N.Y.S.2d 264 (Sup. Ct. 1969); Central Budget Corp. v. Sanchez, 53 Misc. 2d 620, N.Y.S.2d 391 (Civ. Ct. 1967); State v. ITM, Inc., 52 Misc. 2d 39, 275 N.Y.S.2d 303 (Sup. Ct. 1966); Frostifresh Corp. v. Reynoso, 52 Misc. 2d 26, 274 N.Y.S.2d 757 (Nassau County D. Ct. 1966), *reversed on issue of damages*, 54 Misc. 2d 119, 281 N.Y.S.2d 964 (App. Term 1967). For comparable recent English cases, see A. Schroeder Music Publishing Co. v. Macauley, [1974] 3 All E.R. 616 (H.L.); Clifford Davis Mgmt. Ltd. v. W.E.A. Records Ltd., [1975] 1 W.L.R. 61 (C.A. 1974). The facts in many of these cases suggest that they may have involved some form of high-pressure selling, but most of the cases do not develop the issue and none rests upon it.

can be explained only on the basis of an expanded, paradigmatic concept of unconscionability that is not limited to procedural elements such as unfair surprise. This new paradigm does not replace the bargain principle, which is based on sound sense and continues to govern the normal case. Rather, the new paradigm creates a theoretical framework that explains most of the limits that have been or should be placed upon that principle, based on the quality of the bargain. What lies ahead is to articulate and extend the unconscionability paradigm through the development of specific norms, other than unfair surprise, that can guide the resolution of specific cases.[42] The balance of Part II is devoted to the development of four such norms, relating to exploitation of distress, transactional incapacity, susceptibility to unfair persuasion, and price-ignorance.

It is not the purpose of Part II to exhaust the concept of unconscionability. Quite the contrary: a basic thesis of this Article is that unconscionability is a paradigmatic concept that can never be exhaustively described. It is, however, a major purpose of Part II to suggest a methodology by which specific unconscionability norms should be developed. Accordingly, the norms described in this Part are important not only in themselves, but also as demonstrations of that methodology. Three general propositions underlie the methodology, and should be stated at the outset: (1) Since the bargain principle rests on arguments of fairness and efficiency, it is appropriate to develop and apply a specific unconscionability norm whenever a class of cases can be identified in which neither fairness nor efficiency support the bargain principle's application. (2) The development and application of specific unconscionability norms is closely related to the manner in which the relevant market deviates from a perfectly competitive market. (3) The distinction between procedural and substantive unconscionability is too rigid to provide significant help in either the development or the application of such norms.[43]

A. Distress

Suppose that *A* makes a bargain with *B* at a time when, through no fault of *B*, *A* is in a state of necessity that effectively compels him to enter into a bargain on any terms he can get — a condition that I shall refer to as distress. The condition evokes various images — for example, *A* is stranded in the desert, and *B* comes upon him; *A* needs a lifesaving

[42] *See* Dawson, *Unconscionable Coercion*, *supra* note 17, at 1044.

[43] *See* 1 ONTARIO LAW REFORM COMM'N, REPORT ON SALE OF GOODS 157 (1979).

operation that only *B* can perform. At first glance these images may seem similar. In fact, however, each raises different problems, and together they illustrate most of the major issues raised by the case of distress. I shall therefore analyze those issues through an exploration of hypotheticals built upon these images.

> *The Desperate Traveler. T*, a symphony musician, has been driving through the desert on a recreational trip, when he suddenly hits a rock jutting out from the sand. *T*'s vehicle is disabled and his ankle is fractured. He has no radio and little water, and will die if he is not soon rescued. The next day, *G*, a university geologist who is returning to Tucson from an inspection of desert rock formations, adventitiously passes within sight of the accident and drives over to investigate. *T* explains the situation and asks *G* to take him back to Tucson, which is sixty miles away. *G* replies that he will help only if *T* promises to pay him two-thirds of his wealth or $100,000, whichever is more. *T* agrees, but after they return to Tucson he refuses to keep his promise, and *G* brings an action to enforce it.

Under traditional contract doctrines, *T*'s promise would be enforceable to its full extent. He has made a bargain, and none of the orthodox contract defenses apply. The defense of duress might seem apposite, but traditionally that defense has required not only that the promisor was in distress, but that he was put in distress by a wrongful act or threat of the promisee.[44] *G* did not put *T* in distress, and because the common law imposes no duty on strangers to rescue persons in distress even when life is at stake,[45] *G*'s threat of refusing aid would probably not constitute a wrongful act within the meaning of this rule.

It seems clear, however, that a promise to pay an unfair price, extracted through the promisee's exploitation of the promisor's distress, should not be enforced to its full extent. Neither fairness nor efficiency, the two major props of the

[44] *See, e.g.*, RESTATEMENT [FIRST] OF CONTRACTS § 492 (1932); Note, *Contracts: Restitution and Rescission: Economic Duress and Business Compulsion in California*, 40 CALIF. L. REV. 425, 426 (1952).

[45] *See* Buttersworth v. Swint, 53 Ga. App. 602, 186 S.E. 770 (1936); Hurley v. Eddingfield, 156 Ind. 416, 59 N.E. 1058 (1901); W. PROSSER, HANDBOOK OF THE LAW OF TORTS § 56, at 340 (4th ed. 1971). A different rule obtains in many civil law jurisdictions. *See* Dawson, *Negotiorum Gestio: The Altruistic Intermeddler* (pt. 2), 74 HARV. L. REV. 817, 1073, 1101–06 (1961). For an update on American law and a brief look at the socialist approach, see Note, *Stalking the Good Samaritan: Communists, Capitalists, and the Duty of Rescue*, 1976 UTAH L. REV. 529.

bargain principle, supports its application in such a case. In terms of fairness, our society posits, as part of its moral order, some degree of concern for others. In *The Desperate Traveler*, *G* has acted wrongly in treating *T* as simply an economic object.

The efficiency argument also fails. When a commodity is sold under perfect competition, the doctrine of distress would usually have no application, even to contracts for necessities. A sale at a perfectly competitive price would normally not be regarded as exploitive, because the price is generated by a mechanism that is conventionally regarded as fair, and normally equals the seller's opportunity cost and approximates the seller's marginal cost. Furthermore, traditional economic analysis suggests that such a price normally allocates supply to its highest-valued uses and encourages the appropriate amount of investment in productive capacity. *G*, however, is not a perfect competitor, but a monopolist.[46] Full enforcement of promises like that made by *T* is not required to move rescue services to their highest-valued uses, and would have no measurable effect on the allocation of resources to rescue-capacity, since the rescue is adventitious, there are no other bidders for the rescue services at the time of the rescue, and prior to the accident there was no market on which the victim could have purchased a contingent contract to rescue. Indeed, there is an argument that full enforcement would be inefficient. If it were known that persons in distress could be required to pay the price demanded for adventitious rescue, however high, people either might be reluctant to engage in activity in which rescue is sometimes necessary or might spend on precautions an aggregate amount exceeding the cost of adventitious rescue.[47]

Moreover, while the common law might have enforced *T*'s promise to its full extent, other mature legal systems do allow the courts to review bargains made under distress for fairness of terms. For example, section 138(2) of the German Civil Code provides that a transaction is void "when a person [ex-

---

[46] Technically, the relationship between *G* and *T* is a bilateral monopoly — that is, a market which effectively consists of a single seller and a single buyer. However, the existence of a bilateral monopoly is not inconsistent with extremely disproportionate bargaining power. Here *T* is bargaining for his life, while *G* is bargaining for a windfall profit. A bilateral monopoly characterized by extreme inequality of bargaining power can lead to inefficiency, because the stronger party can induce a price far in excess of cost.

[47] *See* R. POSNER, ECONOMIC ANALYSIS OF LAW 133–34 (2d ed. 1977); Diamond & Mirrlees, *On the Assignment of Liability: The Uniform Case*, 6 BELL J. ECON. & MGMT. SCI. 487, 512 (1975); Landes & Posner, *Salvors, Finders, Good Samaritans, and Other Rescuers: An Economic Study of Law and Altruism*, 7 J. LEGAL STUD. 83, 91–93 (1978).

ploits] the distressed situation, inexperience, lack of judgmental ability, or grave weakness of will of another to obtain the grant or promise of pecuniary advantages . . . which are obviously disproportionate to the performance given in return."[48] French law is in accord.[49] At home, it is well established in admiralty law that a contract for salvage services — that is, a contract to rescue a vessel or its cargo — is reviewable for fairness of terms if entered into while the promisor is in distress. For example, in *Post v. Jones*,[50] the whaling ship *Richmond* had run inextricably aground on a barren coast off the Arctic Ocean. Several days later three other whaling ships came on the scene. These ships did not have full cargoes and the *Richmond* had more whale oil than they could take. At the instance of one of their captains, the *Richmond*'s captain held a sale of his oil in the form of an auction. One captain bid $1/barrel for as much as he needed, the two others bid $.75/barrel, and each took enough oil at the bid price to complete his cargo. The three vessels then returned to port with the *Richmond*'s oil and its crew. In an action by the owners of the *Richmond*, the sale of the oil at the bid prices was set aside:

> The contrivance of an auction sale, under such circumstances, where the master of the Richmond was hopeless, helpless, and passive — where there was no market, no money, no competition — . . . is a transaction which has no characteristic of a valid contract.
>
> . . . Courts of admiralty will enforce contracts made for salvage service and salvage compensation, where the salvor has not taken advantage of his power to make an unreasonable bargain; but they will not tolerate the doctrine that a salvor can take the advantage of his situation, and avail himself of the calamities of others to drive a bargain . . . .[51]

---

[48] A. VON MEHREN & J. GORDLEY, *supra* note 17, at 1188 (translating BGB § 138(2) (Staudinger 1979)); *see* Dawson, *Unconscionable Coercion*, *supra* note 17, at 1054–60; *supra* note 17.

[49] Judgment of Apr. 27, 1887, Cass. Req., Fr., 1888 Recueil Périodique et Critique I 263 note, *translated in* A. VON MEHREN & J. GORDLEY, *supra* note 17, at 1029; 2 M. PLANIOL, *supra* note 17, No. 1076; 1 M. POTHIER, A TREATISE ON THE LAW OF OBLIGATIONS 115–17 (W. Evans trans. 3d ed. 1853); Dawson, *Fair Exchange II*, *supra* note 17, at 353–57 & n.39.

One reason that was given for making article 1674 of the French Civil Code, *see supra* note 17, applicable to sellers but not buyers was that a seller but not a buyer might act out of necessity. *See* 12 J. LOCRÉ, *supra* note 12, at 188–96 (remarks of Bigot-Preameneu), *translated in* A. VON MEHREN, THE CIVIL LAW SYSTEM — CASES AND MATERIALS FOR THE COMPARATIVE STUDY OF LAW 530–32 (1957).

[50] 60 U.S. (19 How.) 150 (1857).

[51] *Id.* at 159–60.

Similarly, in *Magnolia Petroleum Co. v. National Oil Transport Co.*,[52] the barge *Bolikow* had been left anchored at sea by its tug, which had been forced to go back to port for more fuel. The tug had failed to return, the *Bolikow*'s fires were out, its fresh water was gone, and there was a threat of storm. At this point the vessel *Greer* happened by, and the *Bolikow* asked for a tow to port. The *Greer* was itself headed to port, and under the prevailing weather conditions the tow involved a simple operation. After a brief discussion, the master of the *Greer* said he would leave unless the *Bolikow*'s master promised to pay $15,000 for the tow. The latter agreed, afraid to risk vessel and crew by staying out at sea any longer. The court refused to enforce the bargain:

> I think it clear that this case is ruled by the general principle . . . that there is a clear right in the courts to set aside a salvage agreement, when made on the high seas under compulsion or hardship, morally or otherwise, when such agreement is unconscionable and inequitable, as this agreement plainly is.[53]

---

[52] 281 F. 336 (S.D. Tex. 1922).

[53] *Id.* at 340; *see also* The Sirius, 57 F. 851 (9th Cir. 1893); Higgins, Inc. v. The Tri-State, 99 F. Supp. 694 (S.D. Fla. 1951); The Don Carlos, 47 F. 746 (N.D. Cal. 1891); The Jessomene, 47 F. 903 (N.D. Cal. 1891); The Young America, 20 F. 926 (D.N.J. 1884); The Port Caledonia & The Anna, 1903 P. 184 (Adm.); G. GILMORE & C. BLACK, THE LAW OF ADMIRALTY 579 (2d ed. 1975); A. KENNEDY, CIVIL SALVAGE 309–13 (K. McGuffie 4th ed. 1958).

Landes and Posner, *supra* note 47, agree that rescue contracts should be reviewable, but attempt to rest their analysis on efficiency grounds only, arguing that the courts in such cases attempt to reconstruct a putative competitive price. This proposition is unsupported by case law. For example, the authors correctly point out that a court using their analysis would review rescue-at-sea contracts to ensure that the rescuer's price is not too low, and go on to claim that courts do make such a review. *Id.* at 101 n.39. As far as a moderate search could determine, however, neither the reasoning nor the holdings of American admiralty cases support that claim, nor do the English cases with the possible exception of one or two cases decided by Dr. Lushington, an admiralty judge in the mid-19th century. *See* The Phantom, 1 L.R.-Adm. & Eccl. 58 (Adm. 1866); The Henry, 16 L.T.R. 553, 15 Jurist 183 (Adm. 1851). The Landes & Posner approach also fails to explain why, if the law does indeed follow their approach, the courts take into account, in determining the amount of salvage awards, such elements as the value of the property saved and the no cure, no pay rule, which makes a salvage award contingent on success.

For example, Landes and Posner admit that, "in a competitive market, price equals marginal cost rather than the value to the buyer, which will exceed marginal cost for all but the marginal buyer," so that "[i]t might appear that 'fairness' would explain the emphasis on the value saved." Landes & Posner, *supra* note 47, at 103. In response, they argue that fairness could not really explain this element, because "systems of price discrimination — i.e., of making price vary in accordance with value rather than cost — are not generally applauded as fair." *Id.* In the context of

Of course, German, French, and admiralty law provide support for a doctrine of distress only by analogy.[54] The lack of direct common law support is not critical, however, since the very function of the unconscionability principle is to permit the courts to develop new rules of contract law based on sound analysis rather than on authority. Under this principle the courts are therefore free to go beyond the traditional doctrine of duress and deny full enforcement of a promise that results from the exploitation of distress, whether or not that condition was created by the promisee. Where, as in *The Desperate Traveler*, a promisee has adventitiously achieved a monopoly over a commodity essential to relieve a condition of distress, his refusal to deal except on unfair terms is a wrongful threat (in the language of traditional doctrine) or an unconscionable

---

a reward for benefit conferred, however, that argument is completely wrong: think of real estate commissions, tips, rewards for lost property, and finder's fees.

The authors further argue:

> [T]he value of the property saved provides for estimating the level of inputs that would be devoted to the rescue in a competitive market. The law's attempts to monitor the rescuer's inputs directly are bound to be imperfect. Since the optimal purchase of inputs . . . is positively related to the value of the property saved, a court can utilize the latter to approximate the victim's demand for rescue inputs if transactions were feasible . . . .

Id. at 104.

It may be that *before* a ship is in distress the amount an owner would be willing to invest in safety is related to the value of the property. Once rescue is actually necessary, however, the owners would be willing to spend the entire value of the property, minus $1.00, on rescue inputs. In any event, there is no way to reconstruct a hypothetical demand schedule on this basis, and the courts do not try to do so.

Similarly, Landes and Posner attempt to reconcile the no cure, no pay rule with their approach by arguing that, "[b]y limiting salvage awards to successful rescues, the number of legal proceedings may be cut down, while the courts can, by adjusting the award, compensate the salvors for their unsuccessful attempts." *Id.* at 104 (footnote omitted). However, the courts cannot "by adjusting the award, compensate the salvors for their unsuccessful attempts" when the salvors are adventitious rescuers who may very well never engage in rescue again. Landes and Posner also argue that "in rescues at sea, where the award is made after the event, the costs of monitoring effort and energy are obviously high, and here the cost advantage is likely to lie with monitoring the output of which success is a crucial ingredient." *Id.* This contention, however, ignores the fact that other accepted elements of salvage awards, such as the value of the property the salvor employed and the salvor's time and labor, require precisely the monitoring that Landes and Posner argue the no cure, no pay rule is meant to avoid.

[54] Some support for reviewing a contract in a case like that in *The Desperate Traveler* for fairness in the exchange may also be given by RESTATEMENT (SECOND) OF CONTRACTS § 176(2)(c) (1979), which provides that a threat is improper "if the resulting exchange is not on fair terms, and . . . what is threatened is otherwise a use of power for illegitimate ends." *Id.* The comment to this section does not provide much guidance on when a threat constitutes "a use of power for illegitimate ends." *Id.* comment f. According to an illustration, the phrase would cover a threat by a municipal water main company to refuse water to a developer except at a price greatly

exploitation of distress (in the language of the new paradigm).[55]

This still leaves open how to measure the promisee's recovery in such cases. Financial cost is one possibility. Such a solution, however, would often fail to recognize adequately the benefit conferred upon the promisor. Furthermore, a financial-cost rule might not provide a sufficient incentive to act. In *The Desperate Traveler*, for example, *G*'s financial cost is close to zero. Assuming *G* is under no legal duty to rescue *T*, he would have no economic incentive to perform the rescue if his recovery were limited to financial cost. The need for an economic incentive in such cases should not be overemphasized; most individuals in *G*'s position would be likely to rescue *T* whether they had an economic incentive to do so or not. Nevertheless, an economic incentive would probably be helpful at the margin. Admiralty again suggests a solution. Although it will not enforce unfair rescue contracts, it does provide ample compensation for rescuers under the principle of salvage. Recovery under this principle is viewed both as a reward and as an inducement.[56] Accordingly, in measuring recovery the courts take into account the degree of danger to the rescued property; the value of the rescued property; the risk incurred by the salvors; their promptness, skill, and energy; the value of the property the salvor employed; the degree of

---

in excess of that charged to those similarly situated. *Id.* illustration 16. However, a publicly owned utility may be legally obliged not to discriminate between similarly situated customers. (In the case from which the illustration was derived, S.S. & O. Corp. v. Township of Bernards Sewerage Auth., 62 N.J. 369, 301 A.2d 738 (1973), the result was based in large part on a statute that required municipal sewerage authorities to charge equal rates to similarly situated customers.) The illustration therefore leaves ambiguous whether a refusal to deal could constitute "a use of power for illegitimate ends" in the absence of a legal obligation to provide service.

Under § 176(2)(a), a threat is also improper if the resulting exchange is not on fair terms and "the threatened act would harm the recipient and would not significantly benefit the party making the threat." RESTATEMENT (SECOND) OF CONTRACTS § 176(2)(a) (1979). According to the commentary, subsection (a) is concerned with cases in which if, "the maker of the threat were to do the threatened act, it would . . . be done maliciously and unconscionably, out of pure vindictiveness. A typical example is a threat to make public embarrassing information concerning the recipient unless he makes a proposed contract." *Id.* comment f. Subsection (a) therefore may not cover cases like *The Desperate Traveler*, because the "threatened act" is simply to continue a course of conduct that *G* was pursuing in any event (completing his journey in the same way he began — without *T*).

[55] *Cf.* RESTATEMENT (SECOND) OF CONTRACTS § 208 comment d (1979) ("[G]ross inequality of bargaining power, together with terms unreasonably favorable to the stronger party, . . . may show that the weaker party had no meaningful choice, no real alternative . . . .").

[56] *See* The Blackwall, 77 U.S. (10 Wall.) 1, 14 (1869).

danger to that property; and the salvor's time and labor.[57] In more general terms, the recovery in distress cases involving an adventitious rescuer should not only compensate the promisee for all costs, tangible and intangible, but should also include a generous bonus to provide a clear incentive for action and compensation for the benefit conferred. Recovery measured in this way admits of no great precision, but that is not fatal in situations in which, by hypothesis, planning is not important. The viability of this approach is evidenced by the fact that it has stood the test of time in an area in which distress and adventitious rescue are common occurrences.[58]

> *The Desperate Patient.* *P*, a business executive, is dying of a fatal disease. A new operation that will cure him has been developed by *S*, a surgeon, at a cost to *S* of $100,000, measured by forgone opportunities and out-of-pocket costs. At the moment no one but *S* can perform the operation, and by the time others perfect the surgical technique involved, *P* will have died. *P* asks *S* to operate. *S* (who has the capacity to perform many more of these operations than he is currently doing) replies that he will do so only if *P* promises to pay $300,000, his standard fee for the operation. *P* agrees, but after *S* performs the operation, *P* refuses to keep his promise, and *S* brings an action to enforce it.

As in *The Desperate Traveler*, the promisor in *The Desperate Patient* is in distress, and the promisee has exploited that distress by charging an apparently exorbitant price for rescue. However, there is a significant difference between the two cases. The surgeon *S*, unlike the geologist *G*, has achieved his bargaining power not through adventitious circumstances, but through diligence and skill, and the prospect of deriving ex-

[57] *Id.* at 13–14; B.V. Bureau Wijsmuller v. United States, 1979 Am. Maritime Cas. 2331, 2351–52 (S.D.N.Y.); G. GILMORE & C. BLACK, *supra* note 53, § 8-8; A. KENNEDY, *supra* note 53, at 161–225. Overriding these individual elements is the principle that the reward is to be computed generously in the light of "the fundamental public policy at the basis of awards of salvage — the encouragement of seamen to render prompt service in future emergencies." Kimes v. United States, 207 F.2d 60, 63 (2d Cir. 1953) (Clark, J.); *see also* The Telemachus, 1957 P. 47, 49 (Adm. 1956) ("I have to arrive at such an award as will . . . in the interests of public policy, encourage other mariners in like circumstances to perform like services."); The "Industry," 3 Hagg. Adm. 203, 204, 166 Eng. Rep. 381, 382 (Adm. 1835) (in accord).

[58] Indeed, under modern shipping practice salvors typically leave the payment terms of their contracts open, for determination after the event by negotiation or through arbitration. A. KENNEDY, *supra* note 53, at 302. Furthermore, under the Lloyd's form salvage contract that is in almost universal use, if a fixed amount is agreed upon in advance, it may be objected to thereafter, in which event compensation is fixed by arbitration. *Id.*

orbitant gains may have been precisely what led *S* to forgo other opportunities and develop the new operation. It can therefore be argued that promises made to persons like *S* should be enforced to their full extent to encourage desirable investment.

Nevertheless, in this case too, full enforcement is not supported by efficiency considerations. In a perfectly competitive market, the long-run price of a commodity will equal its long-run cost. Accordingly, all consumers who are willing to pay the cost of production will be able to purchase the commodity. Cases like *The Desperate Patient*, however, involve a price in excess of cost, thereby choking off the demand of some consumers who would be willing to purchase the commodity at cost. A practice of nonenforcement of such promises might lead to underinvestment in the capacity to relieve from a condition of a distress, but a practice of full enforcement might lead to overinvestment in rescue-avoidance measures, to choking off demand for relief, or both.[59] Accordingly, a practice of judicial review, coupled with extremely liberal recovery, would not only reflect conventional notions of fairness, but would be just as likely as a practice of full enforcement — and perhaps more likely — to result in a preferable allocation of resources.

Once more, this is precisely the line taken in admiralty. Admiralty courts review salvage contracts for fairness of terms, not only when the promise is made to a nearby vessel whose rescue capacity results from adventitious circumstances, but also when it is made to a professional salvor whose rescue capacity results from planned investment. The two classes of rescuers are treated differently, however, as regards recovery. To encourage the provision and maintenance of rescue equipment, awards for rescue by professional salvors are deliberately set at a higher level than awards to nonprofessionals.[60] In

---

[59] *See* sources cited *supra* note 47.

[60] Thus, in Salvage Chief — S.T. Ellin, 1969 Am. Maritime Cas. 1739 (S.D. Cal. 1966), the court stated:

> [O]ne who maintains an expensive salvage vessel with expensive salvage equipment thereon . . . is entitled to a more liberal salvage award than the mere casual salvor. Were it not so, there would be no encouragement to the owner of such professional salvage vessel to provide such available salvage equipment and to maintain it always in available status. . . . [T]he *Salvage Chief* is called upon to perform salvage services only from time to time as the need arises; nevertheless the cost of maintenance of the *Salvage Chief*, with her crew, and in a state of readiness, goes on, day after day.

Id. at 1740; *see* W.E. Rippon & Son v. United States, 348 F.2d 627 (2d Cir. 1965); The Lamington, 86 F. 675, 683–84 (2d Cir. 1898); B.V. Bureau Wijsmuller v. United States, 1979 Am. Maritime Cas. 2331, 2354–55 (S.D.N.Y.); The "Glengyle," 1898 A.C. 519 (H.L.); A. KENNEDY, *supra* note 53, at 168–73. An interesting recent

more general terms, the recovery in cases like *The Desperate Patient* should parallel that in professional rescue at sea, and therefore should include an appropriate share of the cost of developing and maintaining rescue capacity, together with a premium to reflect the risk that the investment might not have been fruitful and to induce similar risk-taking in the future.

Needless to say, the two hypothetical cases discussed in this Section are intended to be suggestive, not exhaustive. Although both concern human life, the doctrine of distress is clearly applicable when other personal interests are involved,[61] and admiralty law suggests its applicability even when the only interests at stake are economic.

B. Transactional Incapacity

Suppose that we vary the perfectly competitive market by assuming not that the promisor is in a state of distress, but that the subject matter of the bargain is highly complex, rather than homogeneous. The significance of this variation is that an individual may be of average intelligence and yet may lack the aptitude, experience, or judgmental ability to make a deliberative and well-informed judgment concerning the desirability of entering into a given complex transaction. I shall refer to such inability as transactional incapacity.[62] Assume now that *A*, who knows or has reason to know of *B*'s inability to deal with a given complex transaction, exploits that inca-

---

example is Nicholas E. Vernicos Shipping Co. v. United States, 349 F.2d 465 (2d Cir. 1965). Here the services performed by the tugs of a professional salvor consumed only a day and did not appear to involve exceptional hazard, but Judge Friendly approved a generous award calculated as twice the salvor's monthly expenses for maintaining the tugs. *See id.* at 472.

The effect of the rule of liberal salvage awards is that the cost of creating and maintaining professional rescue capacity, which benefits all who engage in hazardous activity, is borne only by the victims. *See* The Glengyle, 1898 P. 97, 102–03 (C.A.) (lower court opinion). Except for the problem of transaction costs, the ideal regime might therefore be to levy a worldwide tax on all carriers and shippers, and pay rescuers out of the proceeds.

[61] For example, in the New York City blackout of July 1977, many taxi drivers asked $50 and $60 for rides from Manhattan to Brooklyn and Queens. Some sellers of candles, flashlights, transistor radios, and batteries also charged many times the normal price. Wall St. J., July 15, 1977, at 1, col. 4.

[62] There is an obvious parallel between the doctrine of transactional capacity and the doctrine of partial or diminished responsibility in the criminal law. Under the latter doctrine, a distinction is drawn between a lack of capacity so complete that it constitutes a defense to any crime, and a lack of capacity to form the mental state constituting an element of a specified crime, such as the premeditation or deliberate intent requisites for first-degree murder. *See* W. LAFAVE & A. SCOTT, HANDBOOK ON CRIMINAL LAW § 42, at 326–28 (1972); Weihofen & Overholser, *Mental Disorder Affecting the Degree of a Crime*, 56 YALE L.J. 959 (1947).

pacity by inducing *B* to make a bargain that a person who had capacity to deal with the transaction probably would not make, as in the following hypothetical:

Artless Heir. *N* is a twenty-two-year-old high-school graduate, employed in a stockroom. *N*'s great-aunt, who owns a commercial building, dies on June 1. In her will she bequeaths to her fifty-year-old sister, *Y*, a life interest in the building. The remainder interest is bequeathed to *Y*'s fifty-year-old husband, if he survives her, otherwise to *N*.

T is a major tenant in the building and holds a third mortgage on it for $370,000 and a second mortgage on a movie theater for $330,000. The third mortgage pays 11% interest and the second pays 9%. Both have fifteen years to run. On June 15, *T*, who has learned of the bequest to *N*, approaches her and offers to make a deal under which *T* will assign the two mortgages to her in exchange for her promise to transfer her contingent remainder. *T* points out that under this agreement *N* will derive an immediate annual income of more than $70,000; that this income will continue for fifteen years, and that in fifteen years she will receive $700,000 cash. In contrast, *N* will get no immediate income from the contingent remainder and may never see a dollar from it. Even if she becomes the owner, that may not happen for a long time, and by then the building may have declined in value.

Most real estate appraisers would agree that, based on life expectancy tables, applicable discount rates, and the building's value, *N*'s contingent remainder has a present fair value of $870,000–$950,000 to a nonspeculative buyer (such as *Y* or her husband); that if no such buyer could be found, a speculative buyer could be readily found in the $650,000–$900,000 price range; and that *T*'s two mortgages have a total present value of not more than $350,000. *T* knows that a person with *N*'s background does not have the ability to value either the contingent remainder or the mortgages, and also knows that no one who had that ability would enter into the deal. *N* signs a contract, and *T* assigns the mortgages to her. Later, the estate's lawyer learns of the deal and advises *N* to refuse to transfer her interest to *T* and to offer to reassign the mortgages to *T*. *N* follows the lawyer's advice.

If traditional contract rules were strictly applied, *N*'s promise would be enforceable to its full extent. She has made a bargain, and none of the traditional contract defenses apply.[63] The defense of incompetence might seem apposite, but traditionally that defense has required what might be called general incapacity (indeed, near-insanity), consisting of an inability to understand the nature and consequences of one's acts.[64] However, it seems clear that the reasons for applying the bargain principle are inapplicable to a case like *Artless Heir*. Fairness does not support the principle's application. A party (the "promisee") who induces another (the "promisor") to make a bargain on unfair terms by exploiting the latter's incapacity has acted in a manner that violates conventional moral standards. This is true even though the promisor has the competence to understand ordinary transactions, and even if his lack of capacity stems from limitations in experience or training rather than from emotional instability or below-average intelligence.

Efficiency considerations also fail to support application of the bargain principle in such cases. The maxim that a promisor is the best judge of his own utility can have little application: by hypothesis, the promisor is not able to make a well-informed judgment concerning the transaction. The promisee, on his part, has engaged in activity that the economic system has no reason to encourage. Indeed, quite the contrary. Economic theory is predicated in large part on the concept that knowledgeable consumers, contracting freely, will move commodities to their highest-valued uses. In cases involving the exploitation of transactional incapacity, the promisee may very well move the commodity, at least temporarily, *away* from the

---

[63] English courts of equity gave special protection to expectant heirs at least through the 19th century, but American courts rejected this approach except in transactions involving pure expectancies. *See* Dawson, *supra* note 21, at 267–76.

[64] *See* 2 S. WILLISTON, *supra* note 16, § 256.

Many cases and authorities describe mental incapacity in language that looks on its face like a doctrine of transactional incapacity. *See, e.g.*, Cundick v. Broadbent, 383 F.2d 157, 160 (10th Cir. 1967) ("[M]ental capacity to contract depends on whether the allegedly disabled person possessed sufficient reason to enable him to understand the nature and effect of *the act in issue*." (emphasis added)), *cert. denied*, 390 U.S. 948 (1968); Peterson v. Ellebrecht, 205 Cal. App. 718, 721, 23 Cal. Rptr. 349, 351 (1962) ("[T]he test is whether or not the party was mentally competent *to deal with the subject before him* with a full understanding of his rights." (emphasis added)); Comment, *Mental Illness and the Law of Contracts*, 57 MICH. L. REV. 1020, 1027–28 (1959). The discussion that follows these statements, however, is almost invariably pitched to the issue whether and how far the party fell below general standards of sanity and lucidity.

knowledgeable consumer who would value it most highly, and thereby frustrate the market mechanism.[65]

The strict nature of the traditional test for incapacity may have stemmed in part from the drastic consequences of its application: general incapacity usually renders the transaction voidable by the promisor. In contrast, while a court may grant rescission in cases of transactional incapacity, the application of this doctrine might merely call for an adjustment in price. Similarly, under one line of authority general incapacity constitutes a defense even if the competent party neither knew nor had reason to know of the incompetent's condition.[66] Transactional incapacity, on the other hand, should not be a defense unless the fully competent party knew or had reason to know of the incapacity, and exploited it.[67] In the absence of these elements there is no unfair conduct and therefore no unconscionability.

Some support for a doctrine of transactional incapacity can be found even in existing legal materials. Abroad, section 138(2) of the German Civil Code, quoted earlier in the discussion of distress,[68] provides such a doctrine. Even in the common law, courts have often avoided the bite of the traditional capacity test by stretching the doctrine of undue influence.[69] As formulated in the first *Restatement of Contracts*, that doctrine makes a transaction voidable "where one party is under the domination of another, or by virtue of the relation between them is justified in assuming that the other party will not act in a manner inconsistent with his welfare, [and the transaction is] induced by unfair persuasion of the latter."[70]

---

[65] *See* Dawson, *supra* note 21, at 281.

[66] *See, e.g.*, Verstandig v. Schlaffer, 296 N.Y. 62, 64, 70 N.E.2d 15, 16 (1946) (per curiam); *cf.* RESTATEMENT (SECOND) OF CONTRACTS § 15(2) (1979) (if the competent party does not know of the incompetent's mental defect and the contract is fair, the incompetent's power of avoidance terminates to the extent that the contract has been wholly or partly performed, or the circumstances have so changed that avoidance would be unjust).

[67] It might be appropriate to restrict the doctrine of transactional incapacity to cases in which the fully competent party had actual knowledge of the transactional incapacity; however, a promisee with reason to know has at least some culpability, and more important, a standard requiring actual knowledge might be too difficult to administer. When the evidence demonstrates a lack of actual knowledge, the lesser culpability might be taken into account in fixing the remedy.

[68] *See* Dawson, *Unconscionable Coercion*, *supra* note 17, at 1060–62; *supra* pp. 756–57.

[69] *See* Green, *Fraud, Undue Influence and Mental Incompetency*, 43 COLUM. L. REV. 176, 190–96 (1943).

[70] RESTATEMENT [FIRST] OF CONTRACTS § 497 (1932); *see infra* note 93.

A striking case along those lines is *Lloyds Bank Ltd. v. Bundy*, decided by the English Court of Appeal in 1974.[71] Herbert Bundy was an elderly man whose home was at Yew Tree Farm. Herbert, his son, and MJB, a corporation owned by his son, all banked at a local branch of Lloyds Bank. MJB had gotten into difficulty, and in 1966 and 1969 Herbert guaranteed loans that Lloyds made to the corporation, and secured those loans by mortgages on Yew Tree Farm. Shortly after the second guarantee and mortgage, MJB's affairs worsened. An assistant bank manager went with the son to see Herbert at his home, and told Herbert that Lloyds would only continue to support MJB if Herbert increased the guarantee and mortgage up to £11,000, which apparently was the full value of Yew Tree Farm. The bank manager had brought guarantee and mortgage forms ready for signature. Herbert signed the papers on the spot, apparently without realizing there was little or no benefit to be derived in return, because there was little or no chance that MJB's affairs would become viable and Lloyds was not promising to stay its hand.

All three judges of the Court of Appeal agreed that the last guarantee and mortgage were unenforceable. Sir Eric Sachs (with whom Lord Justice Cairns concurred) rested his conclusion on the existence of a "confidential relationship" between the bank and Herbert, but made clear that the real vice of the transaction was that the bank had led a relatively unsophisticated person into a transaction with a severe though not readily apparent potential for unfairness, without pointing out the need for expert advice.[72] Lord Denning rested his decision on broader grounds:

> No bargain will be upset which is the result of the ordinary interplay of forces. . . .
>
> Yet there are exceptions to this general rule. There are cases in our books in which the courts will set aside a contract, or a transfer of property, when the parties have not met on equal terms — when the one is so strong in bargaining power and the other so weak — that, as a matter of common fairness, it is not right that the strong should be allowed to push the weak to the wall.
>
> . . . .
>
> Gathering all together, I would suggest that through all these instances there runs a single thread. They rest on "inequality of bargaining power." By virtue of it, the English law gives relief to one who, without independent advice, enters into a contract upon terms which are very unfair or

[71] 1975 Q.B. 326 (C.A. 1974).
[72] *Id.* at 345.

> transfers property for a consideration which is grossly inadequate, when his bargaining power is grievously impaired by reason of his own needs or desires, or by his own ignorance or infirmity, coupled with undue influences or pressures brought to bear on him by or for the benefit of the other.[73]

Moreover, at least a few American cases have adopted a rule very close to the doctrine of transactional incapacity. For example, in *Morgan v. Reaser*,[74] the Reasers, who owned a ranch, entered into a complex three-cornered transaction with Morgan and Morgan's broker, involving the Reasers' ranch, an apartment complex owned by Morgan, and other consideration. It quickly became apparent that the apartment complex was a losing proposition, and when Morgan brought an action for specific performance, the Reasers counterclaimed for rescission. The court held for the Reasers. While the court recognized that "Reaser was not without some experience in the purchase and sale of real estate nor . . . completely lacking in understanding," it concluded that he "was without understanding of a transaction of this nature and magnitude."[75]

Also providing support to the doctrine of unfair persuasion is the Uniform Consumer Credit Code. Section 5.108(1) of this

---

[73] *Id.* at 336–37, 339.

[74] 87 S.D. 138, 204 N.W.2d 98 (1973) (per curiam).

[75] *Id.* at 149–50, 204 N.W.2d at 104. For comparable cases, see Vincent v. Superior Oil Co., 178 F. Supp. 276, 283 (W.D. La. 1959) (applying Louisiana law); Thatcher v. Kramer, 347 Ill. 601, 607–10, 180 N.E. 434, 436–37 (1932); Hinkley v. Wynkoop, 305 Ill. 115, 122, 137 N.E. 154, 158 (1922); Succession of Molaison, 213 La. 378, 397–98, 34 So. 2d 897, 903 (1948).

Two classic cases of the early common law, James v. Morgan, 1 Lev. 111, 83 Eng. Rep. 323 (K.B. 1623), and Thornborow v. Whitacre, 2 Ld. Raym. 1164, 1165, 92 Eng. Rep. 270, 271 (K.B. 1705), appear to turn on exploitation of the promisor's lack of sophistication. *James v. Morgan* was an action to enforce a promise "to pay for a horse a barley-corn a nail, doubling it every nail." 1 Lev. at 111, 83 Eng. Rep. at 323. The promisor defended on the ground that "there were thirty-two nails in the shoes of the horse, which being doubled every nail, came to five hundred quarters of barley." *Id.* Chief Justice Hyde directed the jury to give the plaintiff only the value of the horse in damages. *Thornborow* was comparable to *James*. These cases were discussed in Hume v. United States, 132 U.S. 406, 413 (1889), in which the Court said that they "were plainly cases in which one party took advantage of the other's ignorance of arithmetic to impose upon him." *Id.* at 413.

Such concerns also seem to have lain behind the traditional rule that the courts will review for fairness a contract between seaman and master. "Every court should watch with jealousy an encroachment upon the rights of seamen, because they are unprotected and need counsel; because they are thoughtless and require indulgence; because they are credulous and complying; and are easily overreached." Harden v. Gordon, 11 F. Cas. 480, 485 (C.C.D. Me. 1823) (No. 6047). For modern applications of this rule, see Newton v. Gulf Oil Corp., 1950 Am. Maritime Cas. 624 (3d Cir.); Pioneer, 1955 Am. Maritime Cas. 1366, 1369–70, 1374–76 (S.D. Cal.).

Code is comparable to section 2-302 of the Uniform Commercial Code. Section 5.108(4)(e) provides that:

> In applying subsection (1), consideration shall be given to . . . the fact that the seller, lessor, or lender has knowingly taken advantage of the inability of the consumer or debtor reasonably to protect his interests by reason of . . . mental infirmities, *ignorance*, illiteracy, inability to understand the language of the agreement, *or similar factors*.[76]

While the Uniform Consumer Credit Code is directly applicable only to consumer credit transactions, the principles it embodies, like those of the Uniform Commercial Code, may be applied to other cases by analogy. Furthermore, the language of section 5.108(4)(e) is paralleled in comment d to section 208 of the *Restatement (Second) of Contracts* ("Unconscionable Contract or Term"), which of course is applicable to contracts of all kinds.[77]

In any event, it is not critical whether the doctrine of transactional incapacity is supported by traditional case law or statutes. The unconscionability principle allows the courts to adopt, on analytical grounds alone, a rule denying full enforcement of promises induced by exploitation of the promisor's intellectual, experiential, or judgmental inability to deal competently with the transaction at hand.

It might be argued against the doctrine of transactional incapacity, as applied to cases like *Artless Heir*, that its introduction would lead to uncertainty in contracting. That problem, however, is inherent in every contract defense. Admittedly, the principle of unconscionability introduces somewhat more uncertainty than many other defenses, but in accepting that principle contract law has in effect bargained away some

---

[76] UNIF. CONSUMER CREDIT CODE § 5.108(4)(e) (1974) (emphasis added).

[77] Also instructive is § 16:

> A person incurs only voidable contractual duties by entering into a transaction if the other party has reason to know that by reason of intoxication
>
> (a) he is unable to understand in a reasonable manner the nature and consequences of the transaction, or
>
> (b) he is unable to act in a reasonable manner in relation to the transaction.

RESTATEMENT (SECOND) OF CONTRACTS § 16 (1979).

The *Restatement* reporter states that the approach of § 16 is more akin to unconscionability than to incapacity in the traditional sense "because the critical factor appears to be the conduct of the sober party, rather than the inability of the drunkard." *Id.* note. But having once shifted the spotlight to the promisee in the case of intoxication, must not the light remain there in the case of incapacity? Has the promisee acted any less unconscionably if he has reason to know that the other party is "unable to understand in a reasonable manner the nature and consequences of the transaction" because of ignorance, inexperience, or lack of capacity for good judgment, rather than because of alcohol?

of its certainty to augment its fairness. In reviewing that jurisprudential bargain, as it applies to the doctrine of transactional incapacity, it is therefore important to examine with precision the problem of uncertainty. So examined, the problem seems relatively minor. First, the doctrine would almost never be applicable to contracts between merchants concerning commodities in which they regularly deal, because a merchant can fairly presume that other merchants have capacity to practice their trade. Second, a promisee with a high regard for certainty could normally avoid application of the doctrine by advising an unsophisticated party to a complex transaction that he should get competent advice.[78] Third, if, as seems to be the case, the courts even today often covertly apply something like a doctrine of transactional incapacity (as in *Lloyds Bank*), open recognition of the doctrine could actually increase certainty, by eliminating covert elements in judicial decisionmaking and thereby facilitating prediction by lawyers.

In many and perhaps most cases, the remedy for exploitation of transactional incapacity would be rescission. How should recovery be measured where the competent party has completed his side of the bargain and rescission is not in order? If the competent party transferred a highly differentiated commodity, his out-of-pocket cost is obviously not a very useful measure, since the value of such a commodity often lies in elements such as uniqueness, strategic location, or beauty, which may be completely unrelated to out-of-pocket cost. Instead, recovery should normally be measured by the competent party's opportunity cost — that is, the value of the commodity in its next-best use. This, in turn, will normally be equal to market value — that is, the price at which the commodity would have been sold in a bargain between willing and informed parties of adequate capacity — and market value will normally be equivalent to the benefit conferred.

---

[78] *Cf.* Morgan v. Reaser, 87 S.D. 138, 150, 204 N.W.2d 98, 104 (1973) (per curiam) ("There is such a lack of competency on the part of the defendants as to have made it necessary that they should have had protection and advice . . . ."), *discussed at supra* p. 768; Lloyds Bank Ltd. v. Bundy, 1975 Q.B. 326, 345 (C.A. 1974) (opinion of Sir Eric Sachs) ("Over and above the need any man has for counsel when asked to risk his last penny on even an apparently reasonable project, was the need here for informed advice as to whether there was any real chance of the company's affairs becoming viable if the documents were signed."), *discussed at supra* pp. 767–68.

If a party who is urged, fairly and in good faith, to seek advice fails to do so, the doctrine of transactional capacity would normally not apply, because the element of exploitation would be lacking. A distinction might be drawn, however, when the party lacks even the transactional capacity sufficient to allow him to understand the importance of getting advice.

It might be objected that a highly differentiated commodity typically does not have a market value, since its very differentiation excludes it from the class of commodities actively traded on a market. But "market value" in the legal sense has never been restricted to the latter type of commodity. Legal market value is typically an idealized construct based on extrapolation from the price at which comparable commodities are bought and sold on actual markets. In this sense even the most highly differentiated commodity has a legal market value, consisting of the price that analogous sales suggest a willing and informed buyer would probably have paid to a willing and informed seller.[79] This approach to remedy further moderates the problem of uncertainty. Unless the promisor can show not only that he lacked transactional capacity, but that a person who had such capacity would not have made the contract, he will normally lose. Even if he can make such a showing, the competent party will get back either what he transferred (if rescission is granted) or its fair value.

The doctrine of transactional capacity is not limited to cases where a promisor lacks capacity to understand the value of the performances to be exchanged; it also applies to cases in which the promisor can understand the value of the performance called for but lacks capacity to understand the meaning of contractual provisions governing the parties' rights in the event of nonperformance. This application is most likely to occur in transactions involving form contracts prepared by relatively sophisticated sellers who deal regularly with relatively unsophisticated buyers. Such transactions raise a special problem. A wide range of buyers are likely to use any given form. Some will be capable of understanding virtually any provision, while others will not. Of those who do not, some might have refused to enter into the contract if they had understood the provision, while others would have gone ahead. Because the agent of the seller who deals with a given buyer may not know the category into which the buyer falls, how should the doctrine of transactional incapacity be applied in form contract cases?

The answer is, if a provision changes the rights that a buyer would otherwise have on nonperformance in a manner the seller knows or should know many buyers would probably not knowingly agree to, it is unconscionable to word the provision in language the seller knows or should know many buyers will lack capacity to understand. For example, in the

[79] *See* C. McCormick, Handbook on the Law of Damages § 44, at 166 (1935); *id.* § 46, at 177–178.

well-known case of *Williams v. Walker-Thomas Furniture Co.*,[80] the buyer regularly purchased furniture and home appliances from the seller on installment credit. The purchase agreements were printed contracts in the form of chattel leases, which contained the following provision:

> [T]he amount of each periodical installment payment to be made by [purchaser] to the Company under this present lease shall be inclusive of and not in addition to the amount of each installment payment to be made by [purchaser] under such prior leases, bills, or accounts; and all payments now and hereafter made by [purchaser] shall be credited pro rata on all outstanding leases, bills and accounts due the Company by [purchaser] at the time each such payment is made.[81]

The effect of this provision was that until the buyer was completely out of debt to the seller, no item she had ever purchased from it would be completely paid off, even though the balances due on some of the items might be worked down (as they were in *Williams*) to a few cents.[82] As a result, no such item would be immune from procedures for summary recovery under replevin statutes, or would fall within the protection of statutes exempting defined classes of property from attachment to satisfy judgments. The seller certainly knew or should have known that many (indeed almost all) buyers would lack capacity to understand the effect of this provision, and probably knew or should have known that if buyers had understood that effect, many would have refused to sign. Under traditional legal rules, the provision would probably have nevertheless bound the buyer on the theory that she had a duty to read the contract and be aware of its contents.[83] Indeed, this was just what happened in *Williams* in the lower court.[84] If such a provision was inconspicuous, most modern courts would probably not enforce it, under the unconscionability norm of unfair surprise. Thus, in its opinion remanding the case, the United States Court of Appeals for the District of Columbia Circuit emphasized the importance of determining whether the term was "hidden in a maze of fine print."[85] But such a provision should be deemed unconscionable, under the

---

[80] 350 F.2d 445 (D.C. Cir. 1965).

[81] *Id.* at 447.

[82] *See* Skilton & Helstad, *Protection of the Installment Buyer of Goods Under the Uniform Commercial Code*, 65 MICH. L. REV. 1465, 1476–77 (1967).

[83] *See, e.g.*, Rossi v. Douglas, 203 Md. 190, 199, 100 A.2d 3, 7 (1953); Sardo v. Fidelity & Deposit Co., 100 N.J. Eq. 332, 134 A. 774 (N.J. 1926); Calamari, *Duty to Read — A Changing Concept*, 43 FORDHAM L. REV. 341, 341–42 (1974).

[84] Williams v. Walker-Thomas Furniture Co., 198 A.2d 914 (D.C. 1964).

[85] 350 F.2d at 449.

doctrine of transactional incapacity, even if it is conspicuous to the eye. Thus, in *Gerhardt v. Continental Insurance Cos.*,[86] the court struck down an obscurely worded exception to a comprehensive insurance policy on the ground that it was "neither conspicuous *nor* plain and clear."[87] In *Weaver v. American Oil Co.*,[88] involving a complex and legalistically phrased provision under which the operator of an Amoco gas station indemnified Amoco against Amoco's own negligence, the court said: "The party seeking to enforce such a contract has the burden of showing that the provisions were explained to the other party and *came to his knowledge* and there was in fact a *real and voluntary meeting of the minds and not merely an objective meeting.*"[89]

What should be the remedy in such cases? Ordinarily, the balance of the contract should stand, but the rights of the parties should be those that would have prevailed in the absence of the relevant term — unless the seller shows either that he explained the term, that it was conspicuous and the buyer had the capacity to understand its effect, or, perhaps, that if the buyer had understood it he would nevertheless have signed. The remedy hardly seems severe, since its only effect is that the parties are governed by a presumably fair rule of law, and the seller can avoid even this effect by writing the term in plain English and presenting it in a manner that avoids unfair surprise.

C. Unfair Persuasion

In a perfectly competitive market, persuasion ordinarily plays little or no role in contract formation: buyers and sellers either take the uniform market price of a homogeneous commodity, or they do not.[90] Away from such a market, however, persuasion may play an important role. This opens the possibility that a party who is normally capable of acting in a deliberative manner may be rendered temporarily unable to do so by unfair persuasion.

First, a definition: by "unfair persuasion" I mean the use of bargaining methods that seriously impair the free and com-

---

[86] 48 N.J. 291, 225 A.2d 328 (1966).

[87] *Id.* at 298, 225 A.2d at 332 (emphasis added).

[88] 257 Ind. 458, 276 N.E.2d 144 (1971).

[89] *Id.* at 464, 276 N.E.2d at 148 (emphasis in original); *cf.* N.Y. GEN. OBLIG. LAW § 5-702 (McKinney Supp. 1981) ("plain English" statute).

[90] Comment, *Unconscionability in Standard Forms*, 64 CALIF. L. REV. 1151, 1154 (1976).

petent exercise of judgment[91] and produce a state of acquiescence that the promisee knows or should know is likely to be highly transitory.[92] Suppose, in such a case, that the promisor changes his mind as soon as the unfair influence is removed and he is given scope for deliberation, as in the following hypothetical:

> *Troubled Widow*. *W* owns in her own name, and manages, a small clothing boutique. On January 5, her husband, *H*, dies of a sudden stroke. At the time of his death, *H* owed $60,000 to *D*, represented by a note and secured by all of the stock in *C* Corporation. Although originally prosperous, the corporation had run into major difficulties, and the stock is now worth only $500–$2500. On January 9, *D* goes to *W*'s house, bringing with him the note and the stock, and tells *W* that *H*'s memory will be permanently dishonored unless his debts are paid. *W* says she does not want to talk about such things now, and asks *D* to come back at another time. *D*, however, goes on, talking about *W*'s ethical obligations and pounding away at the repugnance of dying with a dishonored reputation. *W* pleads with him to stop, but *D* relentlessly continues. After two hours *W* agrees that in exchange for the note and stock (which *D* assigns to her) she will pay *D* $60,000. The next day *W* has second thoughts, tells *D* she will not pay the $60,000, and offers to return the note and the stock.

If traditional contract rules were strictly applied, *W*'s promise would be fully enforceable. She has made a bargain, and none of the traditional contract defenses appears to apply. Undue influence, which might otherwise seem in point, traditionally requires a preexisting relationship between the parties.[93] It seems clear, however, that unfair persuasion should be a defense to a bargain promise whether or not the parties

---

[91] This phrase is drawn from RESTATEMENT (SECOND) OF CONTRACTS § 177 comment b (1979).

[92] *See* Cuming, *Consumer Protection — The Itinerant Seller*, 32 SASK. L. REV. 113, 114–15 (1967).

Conceivably, it could be deemed unconscionable to use bargaining methods that seriously impair the free and competent exercise of judgment even though there is no reason to believe the promisor's acquiescence will be merely transitory. However, if individuals are persuaded to form long-term beliefs that they are freely willing to plan and act upon, the courts should probably not become involved in reviewing the quality of the persuasion.

[93] For example, the *Restatement [First]* provided that:

> Where one party is under the domination of another, or by virtue of the relation between them is justified in assuming that the other party will not act

had a preexisting relationship. Application of the bargain principle is not supported by the argument of fairness. A promisee who extracts a promise by the use of a bargaining method that seriously impairs the free and competent exercise of the promisor's judgment and creates a state of acquiescence that the promisee knows or should know is highly transitory, is as much at fault as a promisee who exploits a promisor's transactional incapacity. Indeed, he is more at fault, since he deliberately *creates* a kind of transactional incapacity.

Nor is application of the bargain principle supported by considerations of efficiency. That principle rests in substantial part on the premises that a bargain context induces a deliberative state of mind, and that a promisor cannot complain if he is required to pay a price that at least equals his subjective utility as revealed by the terms of his promise. These premises do not hold, however, when the promisee has used techniques calculated to move the promisor out of a deliberative frame of mind and to change the promisor's utility function in a way the promisee knows or has reason to know is only transitory. There is no efficiency reason for encouraging the production of manipulative talk.

Although the principle of unconscionability allows the courts to adopt the doctrine of unfair persuasion on analytical grounds alone, some support for the doctrine can be found even in existing case law. A good example is *Odorizzi v. Bloomfield School District*,[94] decided by the California District Court of Appeal in 1966. According to the complaint, Odorizzi, an elementary school teacher, had been arrested on criminal charges of homosexual activity. After he had been questioned by the police, booked, released on bail, and gone forty hours without sleep, two school district officials came to his

---

> in a manner inconsistent with his welfare, a transaction induced by unfair persuasion of the latter, is induced by undue influence and is voidable.

RESTATEMENT [FIRST] OF CONTRACTS § 497 (1932). The commentary explained:

> The protection given parties of the class included under the rule stated in this Section is broader than that given where parties bear no such relation to one another. . . . The relationships that ordinarily fall within the rule are those of parent and child, guardian and ward, husband and wife, physician and patient, attorney and client, clergyman and parishioner. In each of these cases, however, it is a question of fact whether the relationship in a particular case is such as to give one party dominance over the other, or put him in a position where words of persuasion have undue weight; and even though none of the relations enumerated above exist, if the relationship in fact was such that there was dominance or justifiable trust and confidence, the result is the same as if it were based on one of the relationships enumerated above.

Id. comment a; *see also* Green, *supra* note 69, at 180 ("Fraud may be practiced upon a perfect stranger. Undue influence can exist only where one party occupies a position of dominance over the other." (footnote omitted)).

[94] 246 Cal. App. 2d 123, 54 Cal. Rptr. 533 (1966).

apartment. The officials advised Odorizzi that if he did not resign immediately he would be dismissed and his arrest would be publicized, jeopardizing his chances of securing employment elsewhere, but that if he resigned at once the incident would not be publicized. Odorizzi then resigned, and the criminal charges were later dismissed. The court held that on these facts Odorizzi was entitled to reinstatement. Undue influence, the court said, involves two aspects — undue susceptibility and undue pressure:

> Undue influence in its second aspect involves an application of excessive strength by a dominant subject against a servient object. Judicial consideration of this second element in undue influence has been relatively rare, for there are few cases denying persons who persuade but do not misrepresent the benefit of their bargain. Yet logically, the same legal consequences should apply to the results of excessive strength as to the results of undue weakness. Whether from weakness on one side, or strength on the other, or a combination of the two, undue influence occurs whenever there results "that kind of influence or supremacy of one mind over another by which that other is prevented from acting according to his own wish or judgment, and whereby the will of the person is overborne and he is induced to do or forbear to do an act which he would not do, or would do, if left to act freely."[95]

Support for a doctrine of unfair persuasion can also be found in rules that permit a buyer who has made a contract in his own home to rescind during a specified "cooling-off" period, typically three days. Such rules have been adopted by a number of state legislatures,[96] by the Commissioners on Uniform State Laws in the Uniform Consumer Credit Code,[97] by the Federal Trade Commission,[98] and by Congress with regard to home improvement contracts.[99] The diverse agencies

---

[95] *Id.* at 132, 54 Cal. Rptr. at 540–41 (quoting Webb v. Saunders, 79 Cal. App. 2d 863, 871, 181 P.2d 43, 47 (1947)); *accord* Keithley v. Civil Serv. Bd., 11 Cal. App. 3d 443, 89 Cal. Rptr. 809 (1970); *see also* Methodist Mission Home v. B, 451 S.W.2d 539 (Tex. Civ. App. 1970) (unwed mother surrendered child for adoption under pressure from officials of home for unwed mothers in which she was residing). In Newman & Snell's State Bank v. Hunter, 243 Mich. 331, 220 N.W. 665 (1928), which served as a loose model for *Troubled Widow*, the court refused to enforce the contract on the ground that there was no consideration.

[96] *See* Hogan, *Cooling-Off Legislation*, 26 BUS. LAW. 875, 878 (1971); Sher, *The "Cooling-Off" Period in Door-to-Door Sales*, 15 U.C.L.A. L. REV. 717 (1968).

[97] UNIF. CONSUMER CREDIT CODE § 3.502 (1974).

[98] 16 C.F.R. § 429.1 (1981).

[99] Consumer Credit Protection Act § 125, 15 U.S.C. § 1635 (1976) (amended, effective Apr. 1, 1982, by Depository Institutions Deregulation and Monetary Control Act of 1980, Pub. L. No. 96-221, § 612(a)(1), (3)–(6), 94 Stat. 132, 175–76 (to be codified at 15 U.S.C. § 1635(a)–(g))). A major rationale of these rules is that a

adopting these rules gave recognition to the problem of a transitory state of acquiescence produced by unfair means, and fixed a reasonable boundary line for determining the time within which such a state may be expected to lapse. The principle underlying these rules supports a comparable rule applicable to transactions outside the home.[100]

Two objections might be made to the doctrine of unfair persuasion, as here defined. First, it might be argued that the doctrine would permit review of any contract induced by advertising, since advertising often relies on an appeal to non-deliberative elements. This argument need not detain us. Unfair persuasion exists only where the promisee creates and exploits a state of acquiescence that he knows or should know is only transitory. In the case of advertising, time must normally elapse between persuasion and purchase. Accordingly, advertisers would normally have no reason to believe that their advertising would be effective unless it produced a more-than-transitory effect.

A second possible objection is that under the doctrine of unfair persuasion the courts could review any consumer transaction entered into as an immediate result of sales talk. This objection has weight, but it must be put in perspective. In the overwhelming bulk of transactions involving sales talk, there is no use of bargaining methods that seriously impair the free and competent exercise of judgment. Application of the doctrine could also be cut down by limiting its scope to cases in which the consumer makes known his change of heart fairly soon after the bargain, both by analogy to the cooling-off rules and because late objection implies that the seller's persuasion had more than a transitory effect.

---

consumer in his own home is subject to much more intense personal influence by the salesman than a consumer in the store: partly because it is often very difficult, in this marketplace, to break off the transaction; partly because the conventions of hospitality work against the consumer; and partly because door-to-door salesmen often specialize in high-pressure selling techniques. *See* UNIF. CONSUMER CREDIT CODE § 3.502 comments 1–2 (1974).

[100] The *Restatement (Second)* provides that:

> Undue influence is unfair persuasion of a party who is under the domination of the person exercising the persuasion or who by virtue of the relation between them is justified in assuming that that person will not act in a manner inconsistent with his welfare.

RESTATEMENT (SECOND) OF CONTRACTS § 177(1) (1979). Section 177 is derived from *Restatement [First]* § 497, *see supra* note 93, and that provision, taken with its comments, admittedly seemed to contemplate a preexisting relationship. The language of § 177, however, might be interpreted to state two disjunctive tests — one hinging on an existing relationship, the other on domination. Under this interpretation, it would not be a very large step from § 177 to the doctrine of unfair persuasion, because often the intent and effect of unfair persuasion is to put the promisor at least temporarily "under the domination of the person exercising the persuasion."

Assume, however, that in some cases it will be difficult to distinguish between normal sales talk and unfair persuasion, so that the doctrine of unfair persuasion would enable some consumers to back out of a transaction in which the persuasion was not actually unfair. Even under this assumption, the problem is not particularly worrisome. Observation suggests that reputable merchants commonly permit consumers to return unused merchandise for refund or credit. Accordingly, erroneous application of the doctrine of unfair persuasion in the consumer context would do no more than produce a result that is often obtainable from reputable merchants even without judicial intervention.

D. Price-Ignorance

One condition of a perfectly competitive market is a homogeneous marketplace in which cost-free information concerning price is readily available. When this condition is not satisfied and marketplaces are differentiated, the price of a homogeneous commodity in a given marketplace may be strikingly higher than the price at which the commodity is normally sold. For example, the *New York Times* recently reported as follows on a group of Manhattan stores, most of them clustered on Fifth Avenue, which apparently specialize in one-shot sales, often to tourists:

> [S]uch shops . . . [offer] $40 radios for $80, $30 calculators for $95 and ivory and jade collectibles, so-called, at similarly inflated prices, according to cases cited by the New York City Department of Consumer Affairs.
>
> . . . .
>
> . . . [A] lawyer representing some of the leading stores . . . acknowledged that marked prices in his clients' stores might be high . . . but he said that a knowledegable [sic] shopper could easily negotiate a better deal. "My clients will not allow customers to walk out unless they insist on paying less than cost," he maintained, suggesting that a store that paid $50 for a radio and marked it to sell for $100 would be willing to sell it to a shrewd customer for $51. . . .
>
> . . . .
>
> In one shop, . . . [a salesman] offered a Sanyo RP-1900 AM radio for $80 (list price $39.95) and an RP-6700 AM-FM model for $100 ($59.95) . . . .[101]

[101] *On Fifth Avenue, Shoppers' Jungle*, N.Y. Times, July 9, 1980, at C1, col. 5, C9, col. 1. For further data, see the companion article, *'Good Price' Proves To Be No Bargain*, N.Y. Times, July 9, 1980, at C9, col. 1. These articles report that New York City adopted consumer regulations that require merchants not only to mark all goods with the current selling price, but also to disclose the manufacturer's list price if it is lower than the selling price.

Similarly, a number of cases have concerned door-to-door sales at a price more than twice as high as that charged for comparable commodities in conventional retail marketplaces. For example, in *Toker v. Westerman*,[102] People's Foods sold a stripped-down refrigerator-freezer for $899.98 plus a credit charge, when the evidence showed that the normal retail price of this model was $350–400 and that the most expensive model of comparable size, equipped with extra features, retailed for only $500. In *Kugler v. Romain*,[103] Romain was engaged in selling door-to-door a set of books bearing a cash price of $249.50, when the usual retail price for comparable books was approximately $108–110.[104]

In analyzing whether the seller has acted wrongfully in such cases, we must first determine what accounts for the disparity between the contract price and the normal retail price. Let us begin with the Fifth Avenue stores described in the *Times* article. These sellers appear to offer little or no advantage over nearby stores that sell the same commodities at list price. Since no consumer would knowingly pay twice that price in the absence of such advantage, it seems clear that the price disparity in this case is based on the ignorance of some consumers concerning normal retail prices and on their assumption that further search is unnecessary because a merchant-seller's price for a homogeneous commodity is almost certainly representative of the prevailing price.

Accordingly, one method for dealing with such transactions would be to adopt a rule that a merchant who offers homogeneous commodities at fixed prices impliedly represents that the offered price is not strikingly disproportionate to its prevailing price at other readily accessible marketplaces — giving

---

[102] 113 N.J. Super. 452, 274 A.2d 78 (Union County D. Ct. 1970).

[103] 58 N.J. 522, 279 A.2d 640 (1971).

[104] Similarly, in State v. ITM, Inc., 52 Misc. 2d 39, 275 N.Y.S.2d 303 (Sup. Ct. 1966), ITM was engaged in an extensive door-to-door business in which it sold appliances at prices two to three times the normal retail price — for example, a Model 200 broiler at a cash price of $499, while its normal retail price was $199; a Model 300 broiler at a cash price of $699, while its normal retail price was $299; a central vacuum cleaner for $749, while its normal retail price was $350–400; and color television sets at an average price of $999, while their average normal retail price was $600–650. In Jones v. Star Credit Corp., 59 Misc. 2d 189, 298 N.Y.S.2d 264 (Sup. Ct. 1969), the seller sold a food freezer for $900 plus a credit charge while the retail price of a comparable unit was $300. *See* J. WHITE & R. SUMMERS, HANDBOOK OF THE UNIFORM COMMERCIAL CODE § 4-5 (2d ed. 1980). A study of door to door sales of cooking utensils which compared three lines sold at retail with three sold door-to-door found that the door-to-door prices were two to three times as high. Although the door-to-door lines were of higher quality than the retail lines, it is unlikely that much of the price differential was accounted for by differences in manufacturing costs. T. Fish, The Direct Sale of Cooking Utensils, 46–47 (1957) (M.A. thesis available in University of California, Berkeley, Graduate School of Business Library).

due weight to the merchant's tangible and intangible advantages over other merchants, its reputation, and the normal range of pricing variations.[105] On every aspect of a sale transaction except price, the old doctrine of caveat emptor has given way to the doctrines that a seller will be held to his express representations and that the very act of sale gives rise to implied warranties. The theory of caveat emptor was that the obligation to ensure quality was on the buyer; to put it differently, that it was the buyer's task to search for defects in the product. The buyer therefore absorbed the loss if he did not search or searched inadequately. The theory of implied warranty, on the other hand, is that holding out a product for sale creates certain expectations in a buyer — for example, that the goods are fit for the ordinary purposes for which such goods are used[106] — and that these expectations should be protected unless the seller has explicitly negated them.

Caveat emptor might be viewed as justified in its day if we assume that when this doctrine prevailed, buyers had little or no confidence in sellers and therefore had no expectation of quality beyond such expectations as arose from their own search. In a modern economy, however, buyers place confidence in merchant-sellers regarding a great variety of product attributes, and most merchants work hard to engender and maintain that confidence. So too with price. At one time, perhaps, buyers viewed every sale transaction as an occasion for haggling and had no expectations concerning price beyond those engendered by their own search. Today, however, haggling is the exception, not the rule, and it seems clear that in most consumer marketplaces the quotation of a price, like other statements made by a seller, is understood to convey information. This information, in turn, raises certain expectations and implicitly gives rise to certain representations.[107] In particular, it would conform to modern understanding to adopt a rule that a merchant who offers a homogeneous commodity at a fixed price impliedly represents that the price is not strikingly disproportionate to that at which the commodity

---

[105] *See* Thayer, *supra* note 17 at 337.

[106] U.C.C. § 2-314(1), (2)(c) (1977).

[107] For example, in an English experiment:

> [I]nvestigators . . . handed to the subject for inspection . . . a good quality plain Wilton carpet, and . . . were instructed to explain that it was of pure wool, available in a wide range of shades and in all sizes. The actual price (not communicated to the investigators) was 72s. per square yard. . . . Whereas prices in the 40s. to 50s. range elicited about 60 per cent of 'buy' responses, only about half of this percentage was still interested in the 20s. to 30s. range.

Gabor & Granger, *Price as an Indicator of Quality: Report on an Enquiry*, 33 ECONOMICA 43, 51 (1966). The obvious conclusion was that "considerable proportions of the subjects trusted price rather more than the evidence of their senses." *Id.*

is normally sold in readily accessible marketplaces, giving due weight to the merchant's relevant advantages, reputation, and normal price variations.

Under such a rule, however, whether the seller knew or had reason to know that the price quotation was strikingly disproportionate would be irrelevant. The rule would therefore not be based on a concept of fault, and accordingly would go beyond the concept of unconscionability. For now, it is not necessary to go that far. Instead, it suffices to adopt the fault-based doctrine that it is unconscionable for a merchant to exploit a consumer's price-igorance by offering a homogeneous commodity at a price he knows or has reason to know is strikingly disproportionate in the stated manner. Application of the bargain principle to such cases is unsupported by either of that principle's two major props. Fairness does not support application of the principle, since the promisee has violated conventional morality by making a kind of misrepresentation and by exploiting the promisor's ignorance of a body of cheaply acquired and readily available knowledge (as opposed to knowledge that is generated by the promisee's own skill and diligence). Efficiency considerations are at worst neutral: since the commodity is by hypothesis selling at a much lower price in comparable marketplaces, it hardly seems likely that the higher price is required to move the commodity to its highest-valued uses or to allocate properly the factors necessary for its production. Indeed, it is arguable that by reducing wasteful search, a prohibition on exploitation of price-ignorance would lead to greater efficiency than would enforcing the bargain to its full extent. A consumer who knows that the law prohibits a merchant from charging a price for a homogeneous commodity that the merchant knows or should know strikingly exceeds the prevailing price in comparable marketplaces can make a more or less informed decision on whether the likelihood of finding a moderately lower price justifies the cost of searching for such a price. In contrast, a consumer who knows that the law does not prohibit such behavior may feel constrained to search several marketplaces for every purchase, lest he be exploited in the first marketplace.

Thus far, no assumption has been made concerning the seller's profits. Is the argument affected if the seller's profits are not above normal? To explore this issue, let us return to door-to-door sales at prices very much higher than those charged for comparable goods at conventional retail outlets, which I shall refer to hereinafter as high-price door-to-door selling. Assume, for purposes of argument, that high-price door-to-door sellers do not earn above-normal profits. In that case, they are recovering their costs but not much more, and their high prices must therefore reflect high costs. This in turn raises two issues. First, can prices be deemed unconscionable if the seller is only covering its costs, including a fair return? Second, if a high-cost seller is making only normal profits, can it not be inferred that the costs are translated into consumer benefits? The two issues are intimately connected, since if the seller's costs are completely translated into consumer benefits, its price can hardly be deemed unconscionable.

To address these issues, consider two possible models of high-price door-to-door selling. Under one model, prices are high because these sellers offer nonprice benefits that consumers value to the extent of the difference between the contract price and the normal retail price. In particular, these sellers may bring to a buyer's attention information the buyer did not previously have — for example, that a certain type of product exists.[108] Under this model the sellers' high prices are justified, since the consumer is paying for both a commodity and a special service. Indeed, it might be argued that any lower price would be economically inefficient. If sellers were forced to charge a lower price, some or all would have to withdraw from the business.[109] To the extent such sellers are engaged in the provision of information, their withdrawal would result in the provision of less information. Potential buyers who would have valued the commodity at an amount as high as or higher than the price actually charged would therefore be deprived of the utility derived from making the purchase.[110]

The second model is much less flattering. Under this model, high-price door-to-door firms are not selling information, but searching out and exploiting price-ignorant buyers.[111] Each completed sale has a very high cost because each salesperson must spend considerable time and effort searching for

---

[108] *See* Comment, *supra* note 90, at 1176. Another type of information provided may concern the attributes of the product; salespersons in conventional retail outlets are uninterested in providing time-consuming demonstrations. *See, e.g.*, M. JONES, THE MARKETING PROCESS — AN INTRODUCTION 167 (1965); T. Fish, *supra* note 104, at 17.

[109] That is, if the prices of a high-price, door-to-door seller just cover its costs (including a fair profit), it could not remain in business if it had to charge lower prices.

[110] *See* Comment, *supra* note 90, at 1176.

[111] The activity of shoppers in conventional retail marketplaces will usually (although not always) keep prices in such marketplaces competitive. *See* Schwartz & Wilde, *Intervening in Markets on the Basis of Imperfect Information: A Legal and Economic Analysis*, 127 U. PA. L. REV. 630 (1979). Sellers therefore have an incentive to try to seek out buyers who do not frequent normal retail marketplaces, and going door-to-door is one way to do this.

uninformed buyers. The cost of that time and effort is subsidized by completed sales.

It seems likely that the second model describes high-price door-to-door selling better than the first. It is hard to believe that a consumer operating from behind the veil would value the benefits of high-price door-to-door selling to the extent the first model presupposes. (That is, if consumers were given a choice between: (1) no visits by high-price door-to-door sellers, at the cost of occasionally missing out on information concerning new commodities; or (2) periodic visits, at the cost of unknowingly paying twice or more the normal retail price of a commodity on occasion, it is hard to believe that many would choose the second alternative.[112]) If this is true, refusing to enforce contracts with high-price door-to-door sellers to their full extent would not necessarily reduce the satisfaction of buyers as a class, even if some sellers were forced out of business. Call a high-price door-to-door seller who is forced out of the market by a rule against exploitation of price ignorance *S1*. By hypothesis, products comparable to the commodity sold by *S1* are available in other marketplaces, and the buyer would purchase in those marketplaces if he had the relevant information. It seems likely that many of the persons who would buy the commodity from *S1* would sooner or later visit one of these marketplaces and discover the commodity and its normal retail price. In effect, *S1* is engaged in intercepting such persons before they have undertaken a price search themselves. For those buyers, at least, the withdrawal of *S1* from the door-to-door market would result in *increased* utility whenever the difference between the price charged by *S1* and the normal retail price exceeded the utility lost by not having the use of the commodity between the date on which the buyer would have purchased it from *S1* and the date on which the buyer actually purchased it. To this differential must be added the amount of wasteful search, by those buyers who would like to deal with door-to-door sellers, that can be forgone under a doctrine prohibiting exploitation of price-ignorance by such sellers.[113]

---

[112] *See* T. Fish, *supra* note 104, at 69 ("It appears . . . [that the] absence of comparative merchandise at the point of sale is one of the most important advantages to the direct-selling cooking utensil companies.").

[113] Another possible service that may be provided by high-price, door-to-door sellers is to aid people who do not like to shop in conventional retail outlets. *See* S. TERKEL, WORKING 132–39 (1974), *Knock, Knock*, FORBES, Aug. 1, 1971, at 26. It seems unlikely that even such people would knowingly pay more than twice the normal retail price. If, however, they would, prohibiting exploitation of price-ignorance would not prevent selling to them at those prices, because they would buy even if the

In short, if, as seems likely, the second model describes high-price door-to-door sales better than the first, the fact that such sellers earn only normal returns becomes irrelevant. In terms of fairness, conduct may be exploitive even if it does not produce above-normal returns. In terms of efficiency, profits are normal only because the seller incurs the socially wasteful cost of searching out and intercepting the price-ignorant. Even if the seller's prices do provide only a fair return on investment, the investment is not one that the law should promote by enforcing a recovery that reimburses those unproductive costs.

A doctrine prohibiting the exploitation of price-ignorance is sufficiently justified by the principle of unconscionability. In addition, it is but a modest extension of section 5.108(4)(c) of the Uniform Consumer Credit Code, which provides that in determining whether a consumer credit sale is unconscionable, consideration shall be given to "gross disparity between the price of the property or services sold . . . and the value of the property or services measured by the price at which similar property or services are readily obtainable in credit transactions by like consumers."[114] The doctrine also finds support in the results of cases involving door-to-door selling. For example, in *Toker v. Westerman*,[115] the buyer had purchased a freezer for $899.98 plus a credit charge. The retail price of comparable units was $350–400. Buyer made payments of $655.85 and then stopped, and seller's assignee sued for the remaining balance. The court held that the seller and his assignee had already received a reasonable sum, and gave judgment to the buyer. Similarly, in *Jones v. Star Credit Corp.*,[116] the buyer had purchased a food-freezer for $900 plus a credit charge of over $400. The retail price of a comparable unit was $300. Buyer paid $619.88 and then brought suit to reform the contract. The court ordered that the contract be reformed by changing the price to the amount the buyer had paid.

Finally, the doctrine is supported by — and helps rationalize — the language of door-to-door cases in which the courts stressed that the contract price far exceeded the retail price in conventional marketplaces, and concluded that "exorbitant price . . . makes this contract unconscionable and therefore

---

seller disclosed the price differential, and disclosure would negate the element of exploitation.

[114] UNIF. CONSUMER CREDIT CODE § 5.108(4)(c) (1974).

[115] 113 N.J. Super. 452, 274 A.2d 78 (Union County D. Ct. 1970).

[116] 59 Misc. 2d 189, 298 N.Y.S.2d 264 (Sup. Ct. 1969).

unenforceable";[117] that it is "unconscionable . . . [to sell] goods for approximately 2½ times their reasonable retail value";[118] or that "the value disparity itself leads inevitably to the felt conclusion that knowing advantage was taken of the plaintiffs."[119]

III. Executory Bargains

Part I showed that in the case of a half-completed-bargain promise, there are normally very strong reasons for applying the bargain principle, which requires the defendant to pay the agreed-upon price for a bargained-for performance that has been rendered and received. Part II considered limits that should be placed upon that principle when the plaintiff acted unconscionably. These limits might be thought of as substantive, in the sense that they relate to the quality of the bargain. In this Part it will be assumed that the plaintiff did not act unconscionably, but that the defendant broke or repudiated a bargain promise while the bargain was wholly executory, that is, when neither party had begun performance.

At least at first glance, the case for enforcement of such promises to their full extent through the award of expectation damages seems weaker than when the bargain has been half-completed. True, deliberativeness is as likely as in the half-completed bargain, and the concern for evidentiary security is at least partially met by the Statute of Frauds and the relative difficulty of fabricating a bargain promise.[120] Unlike the half-completed transaction, however, performance has been neither rendered nor received. Accordingly, both the interests of the plaintiff and the injustice of nonenforcement may seem relatively slight.[121] On closer inspection, however, it can be seen

[117] Toker v. Perl, 103 N.J. Super. 500, 503, 247 A.2d 701, 703 (Law Div. 1968), *aff'd per curiam on other grounds*, 108 N.J. Super. 129, 260 A.2d 244 (App. Div. 1970).

[118] Toker v. Westerman, 113 N.J. Super. 452, 454, 274 A.2d 78, 80 (Union County D. Ct. 1970).

[119] Jones v. Star Credit Corp., 59 Misc. 2d 189, 192, 298 N.Y.S.2d 264, 267 (Sup. Ct. 1969); *see also* State v. ITM, Inc., 52 Misc. 2d 39, 53, 275 N.Y.S.2d 303, 321 (Sup. Ct. 1966) ("These excessively high prices constituted 'unconscionable contractual provisions.'"), *discussed supra at* note 104.

[120] For example, it would be suspicious if there were no record of the bargain at all, if the parties had no reason for coming together in a contract, or if an undocumented bargain was made at a highly disadvantageous price.

[121] Thus, Professor Atiyah argues that the grounds for imposing liability for any "promise based" obligations are weak, and comes close to arguing that wholly executory contracts ought not to be enforceable. P. Atiyah, The Rise and Fall of Freedom of Contract 1–7, 754–64 (1979). The argument is based on a division of enforceable promises into three categories: "benefit-based," in which a price has been

that three strong justifications, based on fairness and efficiency, normally support the application of the bargain principle even to executory contracts.

---

paid for the promise (largely equivalent to what I have called half-completed bargains); "reliance-based," in which a party has acted in reliance on a promise; and "wholly executory," in which the promise has been neither paid for nor relied upon. Although Professor Atiyah's theses are based principally on English law, it is profitable to examine them in light of American contract principles.

(i) In the benefit-based case, Atiyah argues, liability does not rest on promise, but on benefit conferred. The only function of the promise is evidentiary. "If, for example, a price has been agreed this will obviously provide evidence (often conclusive evidence) of what is a fair price and the court will be spared the necessity of fixing the price itself." *Id.* at 753. As a description of American contract law, this argument would certainly be wrong. If it were right, then whenever *A* sued *B* for breach of a half-completed bargain, seeking to measure damages by the agreed-upon price, *B* would be permitted to introduce counterevidence of fair value. The jury would then be instructed to measure *A*'s recovery by the fair value of *A*'s performance on the basis of all the evidence, including the promise. But that is not what happens. Nor should it, *see supra* pp. 745–46, in the absence of unconscionability, and in the case of unconscionability the promise is not even evidence of fair value. (The problem is not dispelled by suggesting that the promise may often be "conclusive" evidence, because that approach is functionally equivalent to saying that liability is based on the promise.)

(ii) In the reliance-based case, Atiyah makes a comparable argument: liability does not rest on the promise, but on reliance. To support this argument, Atiyah points out that conduct alone may give rise to an action based on reliance. "For instance, a person who buys a new house, in reliance on the proper performance by the local authority of its duties of ensuring compliance with the Building Regulations, may have a remedy against the authority for malperformance even though they give no promise." *Id.* at 2. This argument, however, rests on a non sequitur. That the law sometimes grants recovery for reliance on conduct alone in no way demonstrates that liability for a relied-upon promise is not promise-based. When liability rests on reliance, the reliance must be based on a legitimate expectation. If the expectation is based on conduct, it is conduct-based. If it is based on promise, it is promise-based. As a matter of American law, the argument would also be wrong. An examination of promissory estoppel cases will show that, in most such cases, without a promise there would be no liability. Furthermore, in the case Atiyah describes, liability does not seem to rest on reliance at all; would the plaintiff be out of court if he were new in town and did not know the regulations?

(iii) As to executory contracts, Atiyah argues in part that, "[i]f benefit-based and reliance-based liabilities are taken as the paradigm cases of obligation, whether legal or moral, it may be suggested that promise-based liabilities are neither paradigmatic nor of central importance." *Id.* at 4. This argument is also a non sequitur. The fact that a transaction is not "paradigmatic" or "of central importance" provides no guidance concerning how the law should treat the transaction when it does occur. A further argument is that, based on a change in social values, especially in England, as an empirical matter executory contracts are coming to be regarded as unenforceable unless relied upon. *Id.* at 5–6. This argument has force when applied to questions of damage measures in particular transaction-types, *see infra* pp. 792–98. However, for the reasons given below, *see infra* pp. 787–92, it lacks force (at least in the United States) when applied to executory contracts as a class.

It is of course true that the law does not enforce promises as such. If it did, there would be no doctrine of consideration. The law does, however, enforce classes of promises that ought to be enforced for functional reasons. Bargain promises are one such class.

First, fairness normally requires that a promisee should at least be compensated for the cost he incurred in reasonably relying on a bargain promise. As will be shown below, in many transaction-types enforcement of an executory contract to its full extent is desirable on the ground that expectation damages are approximately equal to cost, but much easier to measure.[122] I shall call this justification the surrogate-cost theory.

Second, a contract for forward delivery typically is made with the purpose of enabling the parties to plan their future conduct reliably. Efficiency normally requires that such planning should be facilitated. The award of expectation damages conduces to that end by making breach unprofitable in the normal case.[123] I shall call this justification the planning theory.

Third, when a contract is made for forward delivery at a fixed price, it is frequently a purpose of the contract to allocate the risk of price changes. Efficiency normally requires effectuating this allocation, and that is just what is done by expectation damages. Risk allocation also implicates considerations of fairness. As Sharp observed:

> [T]his is not only an industrial and credit economy, but also a risk taking, profit making, more or less gambling economy. This may mean not only that harmful reliance, in fluctuating markets, is best remedied by expectation damages, but also that the profits dependent on good guesses about the future are generally to be assured to the person who is willing to gamble on his judgment.[124]

To put this differently, when parties gamble on market movements and the market does in fact move, the contract is in a sense half-completed rather than executory, and the breaching promisor is like a gambler who welshes on his bet. I shall call this justification the risk theory.[125]

The balance of Part III will consider the extent to which these theories support the application of the bargain principle

---

[122] *See* Fuller & Perdue, *The Reliance Interest in Contract Damages* (pt. 1), 46 YALE L.J. 52, 60 (1936).

[123] *See* Barton, *The Economic Basis of Damages for Breach of Contract*, 1 J. LEGAL STUD. 277, 278–79 (1972).

[124] Sharp, *Promissory Liability* (pt. 1), 7 U. CHI. L. REV. 1, 21 (1939). This point is developed further in Simon & Novack, *Limiting the Buyer's Market Damages to Lost Profits: A Challenge to the Enforceability of Market Contracts*, 92 HARV. L. REV. 1395, 1436–37 (1979).

[125] The last two theories tend to merge at their margins, but they reflect two operations, risktaking and planning, that operate independently and should be analyzed that way.

to executory contracts, and the conditions under which it is appropriate to place limits on the full reach of that principle even in the absence of unconscionability. These issues will be discussed in the context of selected transaction-types involving four variables — whether the commodities concerned were goods or services; whether they were homogeneous or differentiated; whether the contract was breached by the buyer or the seller; and the nature of the parties. As in Part II, the cases considered are intended to be suggestive, not exhaustive.

A note on the terminology: For ease of exposition, the term "replacement price" will be used to mean the price payable under a substitute contract.[126] Replacement price may be established by extrapolation from prices in similar transactions (market price), by the price actually paid by the buyer in a substitute purchase (cover price), or by the price actually received by the seller in a substitute sale (resale price). The term "forgone price" will be used to mean the best price that was available from an alternative buyer or seller on the date of the contract (or, in appropriate cases, between the contract date and the breach date). It will be assumed in all cases that no performance occurs before the breach.

A. Sale of Relatively Homogeneous Goods by a Dealer to a Business Concern, with Breach by Seller

Take first a contract for the sale of relatively homogeneous goods in which the seller is a dealer, the buyer is a business concern, and the seller breaches, as in the following hypothetical:

> *Paper Buyer I*. Seller is in the business of selling office supplies to large users. Buyer is a financial corporation. On May 1, Seller and Buyer enter into a contract for the sale of one hundred ten-ream cases of a standard grade of typing paper at a price of $4,000, delivery on July 1, payment on August 1. On July 1, Seller repudiates.

The argument for applying the bargain principle in cases like *Paper Buyer I* is very strong. The buyer's expectation damages in such a case are normally measured by the differ-

[126] Ordinarily, replacement price should be figured on the basis of the price, on the date the innocent party learns of the breach, for delivery on the date set under the original contract. The law sometimes appears to deviate from this approach by requiring the replacement price to be measured on the date set for delivery. *See* U.C.C. § 2-708(1) (1977). These deviations, however, do not affect the basic argument in the text and will be disregarded.

ence between the replacement price and the contract price[127] — a type of measure that will hereinafter be called a replacement-price formula. But a recovery that measured the buyer's damages by cost (the reliance measure) would usually be just as great. This is because the market for relatively homogeneous goods normally has continuity and depth — that is, purchases and sales can normally be made at any time, in significant quantities, at a price very close to the price at which the last such transaction was closed. It can therefore normally be presumed that if the buyer had not made his contract with the breaching seller, he would have made a contract on the contract date with some other seller, who would have performed.[128] By contracting with the breaching seller, the buyer lost the opportunity to make that other contract. The buyer's cost, as measured by his forgone opportunity, equals the difference between the replacement price and the forgone price. Given the nature of the market, however, the forgone price will normally equal the contract price. Accordingly, application of the bargain principle can be justified in such cases under the surrogate-cost theory, on the ground that the buyer's expectation damages will normally equal his cost or reliance damages and are much easier to determine.[129]

The planning and risk theories point the same way. Business firms make forward purchase contracts at fixed prices to ensure supply and to shift the risk of price changes from the buyer to the seller. A replacement-price formula helps ensure supply by making breach unprofitable, and effectuates the intended shift of risk.

B. Sale of Highly Differentiated Goods by a Dealer, with Breach by Buyer

Take now the sale of highly differentiated goods by a dealer, with breach by the buyer, as in the following hypothetical:

---

[127] *See id.* § 2-713. The buyer's damages may include other elements, such as incidental damages. However, since this Article is basically concerned with the enforceability of promises, I shall omit discussion of those nuances in the law of damages that do not affect the basic argument.

[128] The presumption that the other seller would have performed is based on two grounds: (1) The reason for breach is often unique to the original seller — for example, his costs may have become peculiarly high, or a supplier may have failed him. (2) Parties to a bargain will normally perform rather than breach, even in the absence of legal compulsion, because of the economic importance of reputation and their altruistic regard for the morality of promise keeping. *See* Eisenberg, *supra* note 4, at 2–3.

[129] *See* Fuller & Perdue, *supra* note 122, at 62–63.

Ulysses. On June 15, Seller, a rare-book dealer, enters into a contract with Buyer for the sale of a mint first edition of *Ulysses*, which Seller owns, at a price of $5000, delivery on July 1. On July 1, Buyer refuses to accept delivery and repudiates the contract.

As in *Paper Buyer I* the seller's expectation damages in such a case are normally measured by a replacement-price formula.[130] The surrogate-cost theory is not quite as strong as in cases like *Paper Buyer I*. Assume that on July 1, the replacement price for a mint first edition of *Ulysses* (measured, say, by resale price) is $4600. Expectation damages ($400) may then exceed the seller's opportunity cost. That cost is measured by the difference between the replacement price and the forgone price at which the book could have been sold between June 15 and July 1. However, because markets for highly differentiated goods often lack both continuity and depth, the forgone price in cases like *Ulysses* will often be highly uncertain. It may be that the forgone price for a mint first edition of the book during the relevant period was $5000, but perhaps it was not, and when the commodity is highly differentiated, it will often be unclear which is the case. Nevertheless, the seller can argue that but for the contract with the buyer he might have made efforts to sell the commodity during the period between contract date and date of breach, and might have been able to make a sale at a price equal to the contract price. The seller may be unable to prove that he would have made this effort or would have obtained that price. This inability, however, results from the very fact that the buyer's promise diverted the seller from probing the market after the contract date. The buyer should therefore bear the consequences of the resulting uncertainty.

Efficiency considerations point the same way, although again not with quite the same force as in *Paper Buyer I*. Parties in the positions of Buyer and Seller normally realize that the price of a commodity like *Ulysses* is uncertain and speculative. When the contract is made, it therefore normally reflects an intent to allocate the risk of misjudgment of market value, changes in market value, or both. Furthermore, firms like the dealer in *Ulysses* must be able to plan on a reliable basis. One element of such planning is the ability to arrange their affairs as if their contracts will be performed. This ability would be seriously diminished if damages for breach in cases like *Ulysses* were based on the difference between contract

[130] *See* U.C.C. §§ 2-706, -708 (1977).

price and forgone price, just because the latter is so difficult to establish.

C. Sale of Relatively Homogeneous Goods by a Dealer to a Business Concern, with Breach by Buyer

Next consider a contract for the sale of relatively homogeneous goods by a dealer to a business concern, as in *Paper Buyer I*, but with breach by the buyer rather than the seller:

> *Paper Buyer II*. Same facts as *Paper Buyer I* (sale of one hundred ten-ream cases of a standard grade of typing paper for $4,000, delivery on July 1), except that Buyer rather than Seller repudiates on July 1.

Although the variation from *Paper Buyer I* may seem minor, it has major implications. As shown above in Section A, when the seller breaches in a case like *Paper Buyer I*, expectation damages measured under a replacement-price formula are almost certain to equal damages based on cost. When the buyer breaches, however, expectation damages measured under this formula may well exceed damages based on cost. When goods are in relatively unlimited supply, as is typical of relatively homogeneous goods, entering into a contract with any given buyer normally does not cause a dealer to forgo an opportunity to make a comparable contract with another buyer. Accordingly, the dealer's opportunity cost is likely to be zero. So too may be its out-of-pocket cost. In contrast, its expectation damages under a replacement-price formula may be substantial if the market is falling.

Nevertheless, such damages may easily be justified. The very purpose of contracts like that in *Paper Buyer* is normally to allocate the risk of changes in market price. Application of the replacement-price formula can therefore be justified on the grounds that it both effectuates this purpose and facilitates the seller's planning. Damages under a replacement-price formula may also be justified under the surrogate-cost theory. The dealer's contracts of sale are likely to play a significant role in his management of his own inventory and his purchase commitments. Therefore, assuming replacement price declines after the contract date (if it does not, there is no problem), the dealer is likely to suffer a directly related loss, of approximately the same amount, in the value of his inventory or under his contracts of purchase. Of course, the two figures may not be precisely equal, and in some cases the dealer may not have any loss at all. Accordingly, the law could simply require the dealer to prove affirmatively both the existence and amount of such a loss. Still, a replacement-price formula is justifiable, because it is quite likely the dealer will suffer a related loss of approximately the same amount, but quite difficult to match that loss with the contract of sale.

However, in a case like *Paper Buyer II* the dealer also has the right to measure his damages by the difference between the contract price and his actual or projected out-of-pocket cost.[131] I shall hereinafter refer to this type of measure as a net-proceeds formula. (I use the term "net proceeds" rather than the more conventional "lost profits," because the formula reimburses for lost contribution to overhead as well as for lost profits. For example, suppose that the one hundred cases of paper, to be sold for $4000, cost Seller $3,000, and that all his other costs are fixed. His recovery under a net-proceeds formula would be $1000, even though a cost accountant would say that his profit is less because some portion of his fixed costs should be allocated to the sale.) This formula must certainly be available to a dealer as a measure of his expectation damages, if such damages are to put him in as good a position as if the contract had been performed. This is because: (1) if the contract had been performed, the dealer would have been ahead by an amount equal to the contract price minus his out-of-pocket cost,[132] and (2) the dealer usually cannot replace this loss by making another contract, since normally any contract he makes after the breach would have been made even if the breach had not occurred.[133]

---

[131] *See id.* § 2-708(2).

[132] *See* Childres & Burgess, *Seller's Remedies: The Primacy of UCC 2-708(2)*, 48 N.Y.U. L. REV. 833, 881–82 (1973) (arguing that a lost profits — i.e., net proceeds — formula is more appropriate than a replacement-price formula in such cases).

[133] *See, e.g.*, Neri v. Retail Marine Corp., 30 N.Y.2d 393, 285 N.E.2d 311, 334 N.Y.S.2d 165 (1972).

Several commentators have argued that, as a matter of economic theory, a net-proceeds formula is not required in order to place the dealer in as good a position as he would have been in had the contract been performed. *See, e.g.*, Goetz & Scott, *Measuring Seller's Damages: The Lost-Profits Puzzle*, 31 STAN. L. REV. 323 (1979). These arguments, however, are based on models that fail to correspond with business reality. For example, Goetz and Scott begin by arguing that, "[i]n a purely competitive market," any sale made by the seller after the buyer's breach "is a replacement for the breached contract," so that the seller will incur no "lost volume" (i.e., lost proceeds) as a result of the breach. *Id.* at 333. (The theory behind the argument is that if a seller can sell only a limited number of units, and is able to sell that number despite the breach, his proceeds are the same with or without the breach. The authors argue that this is the case in a perfectly competitive market, because in such a market a seller will sell only an optimal number of units — specifically, a number such that the seller's marginal cost of the last sale equals the price of the last unit sold. Since

Nevertheless, this application of the bargain principle may seem too extreme. It would normally not be justified by the surrogate-cost theory: a recovery measured under the net-proceeds formula must by hypothesis exceed out-of-pocket cost and must also exceed a recovery under the replacement-price formula, since otherwise the seller would invoke the latter measure. It may be that the seller would not have entered into the contract unless he was assured of a return equal to net proceeds; and at least if the buyer is or should be aware of that fact, it might be said that the parties had allocated not only the risk of movement in the market price, but also the risk involved in assuring such a return. That such an allocation is intended, however, is far from clear. And while application of a net-proceeds formula will admittedly facilitate planning, since the higher the damages the more likely that performance will take place, the added stimulus provided by this formula, in cases like *Paper Buyer II*, might well be deemed excessive. In a somewhat analogous case, a study of the contract practices of nineteen English engineering manufacturers found:

the seller will sell that number with or without a breach, the breach causes no lost proceeds.)

This argument assumes a completely unrealistic level of planning. Goetz and Scott themselves admit that "[t]he perfectly competitive model is too simple for the real world," partly because "a firm's marginal operating costs in many cases may be nearly constant over wide ranges in output." *Id.* at 335–36. Accordingly, they invoke a second model, in which the seller has some power over price. Here again they admit that "a seller operating under constant marginal cost conditions will sustain classic lost volume from a buyer's breach." *Id.* at 340–41. However, they argue, such sellers sell in two distinct markets, one involving fixed contracts for future commitments and the other involving spot sales; buyers may also sell (that is, resell) on the spot market; and if a contract buyer cancels, the risk that he will resell in the spot market is removed. They conclude, "[I]n a frictionless environment [that is, one in which the buyer will be able to resell the purchased goods in the spot market under the same conditions the seller faces, and there are no costs to the buyer associated with the resale] a breach of B units [by a 'contract' buyer] produces a corresponding shift of B units in the seller's demand curve . . . [and] will actually place the seller in a better position than had the buyer performed." *Id.* at 341–42 & n.45. In footnotes, however, the authors make qualifications that almost entirely vitiate the argument. They admit that, "[b]ecause the model is developed in a frictionless environment, it is not surprising that few real-world applications of this phenomenon can be observed. Some positive transaction costs are associated with any breach. It is difficult to estimate how many sellers, in fact, do better by breach plus damages than by performance." *Id.* at 342 n.47. They also admit that "[t]he buyer's ability to resell in the seller's market is a central part of the thesis" and that "the observation may initially seem counter-intuitive." *Id.* at 344 n.50. To defend the observation, they can only observe that "the argument has been made successfully in one lost-volume case," *id.* — a rather thin defense for the fundamental premise of an economic model. For additional qualifications, see *id.* at 344 n.51.

> In practice if a buyer cancelled before any work had been done or money spent on materials that could not be resold or used for other work a few firms would attempt to insist on payment of a cancellation charge, but most would not. In many cases the loss caused by such a cancellation would be slight, unless there was a shortage of work, and where a charge was made it often represented lost overheads, design costs, etc. On the other hand if work on the buyer's order had commenced even if the goods were standardized and could be resold, or if materials would be wasted, some charge would be made by all sellers and the buyers seemed to accept that sellers should be compensated for such a loss. There was less unanimity on whether the charge would include an element of profit, but most said that it would. However, the charge was usually made according to the machine time expended, and while the charge for machine time usually has a built-in profit element, it can only be profit on the work done.[134]

All these issues are brought into sharper focus in the next two transaction-types.

D. Sale of Relatively Homogeneous Services or Goods by a Merchant to a Consumer, with Breach by Buyer

Assume now a contract for the sale of relatively homogeneous services by a merchant to a consumer, as in the following hypothetical:

> *Dance Lessons*. *E*, an electrical engineer, wants to learn to dance. *S* operates a dancing school. On May 1, *E* signs a contract with *S* to take Dancing 1, a group class, which begins on July 1. Dancing 1 meets two hours a week, runs twenty-six weeks, and costs $500. *E* understands all the provisions of the contract and considered the matter in a deliberative frame of mind, but knows nothing about damage rules. On June 15, *E* changes his mind and repudiates.
>
> *S* incurs little or no incremental out-of-pocket costs for group classes, since its instructors work on full-year contracts and it owns its own studios. *S*'s classes usually don't fill to capacity. The capacity of Dancing 1 is twenty students. On June 15, sixteen students had enrolled. No additional students enrolled thereafter.

When the buyer breaches a contract for the sale of services, the seller's expectation damages are normally measured under

[134] Beale & Dugdale, *Contracts Between Businessmen: Planning and the Use of Contractual Remedies*, 2 BRIT. J.L. & SOC'Y 45, 53 (1975) (footnote omitted).

a net-proceeds formula, that is, contract price minus the seller's out-of-pocket cost of performance.[135] On facts like those in *Dance Lessons*, however, performance by the seller does not entail any incremental out-of-pocket cost. Accordingly, the seller's expectation damages under a net-proceeds formula equal the entire contract price, despite the fact that the buyer has received no benefit.[136]

Such a recovery is not easy to justify under the surrogate-cost theory when the seller has incurred no cost in reliance on the buyer's promise. In considering whether it is justified by the risk theory, two related questions must be asked. The first question is, why would *E* make a contract on May 1, rather than wait until July 1? Consumers normally do not make contracts like that in *Dance Lessons* for the purpose of allocating the risk of price changes or speculating in the market for dancing lessons. Rather, the typical purposes of such advance contracting are to ensure supply (that is, to ensure a place in the class) and, perhaps, to make a self-commitment. The second question is, would the parties have agreed to a provision permitting the seller to measure damages under a net-proceeds formula if they had consciously adverted to the issue? Given the buyer's assumed motivation for contracting, the answer pretty clearly seems to be no. It is hard to imagine that a buyer like *E* would realize that damages would be measured this way by the courts. It is even harder to imagine that he would have agreed to a contractual provision measuring damages this way, simply to ensure a place in the class and make a self-commitment. (This conclusion is reinforced by the fact that if the seller can measure damages under a net-proceeds formula, the remedies for buyer and seller are highly disproportionate. If the buyer repudiates, the seller will recover the entire contract price. If the seller repudiates, however, the buyer will normally be limited to a replacement-price formula. Since the market value of dancing lessons is unlikely to change perceptibly over short periods of time, the recovery under this formula would normally be zero.) The seller, on its part, would be unlikely to insist on such a provision, just

[135] *See, e.g.*, Vitex Mfg. Corp. v. Caribtex Corp., 377 F.2d 795 (3d Cir. 1967); RESTATEMENT [FIRST] OF CONTRACTS § 346(2)(a) & comment h (1932) (construction services).

[136] JJ & L Inv. Co. v. Minaga, 487 P.2d 561 (Colo. App. 1971); Leo Foundation, Inc. v. Kiernan, 5 Conn. Cir. Ct. 11, 16, 240 A.2d 218, 221 (App. Div. 1967); Fayman v. Trustees of Burlington College, 103 N.J. Super. 476, 247 A.2d 688 (Ch. Div. 1968). *But see* Educational Beneficial, Inc. v. Reynolds, 67 Misc. 2d 739, 324 N.Y.S.2d 813 (Civ. Ct. 1971) (contract with commercial school charging $600 non refundable enrollment fee and $7 per hour of instruction in uncompleted course held unconscionable).

because very few buyers would then be willing to contract with it.

The final question is whether a net-proceeds formula is required to enable a seller like *S* to plan effectively. This is an empirical issue on which firm evidence is lacking. However, random evidence suggests that firms selling services to consumers can plan effectively without being entitled to damages measured by a net-proceeds formula. For example, the problem raised by *Dance Lessons* is characteristic of any contract for tuition, and such contracts often involve relatively large amounts. Nevertheless, many and perhaps most schools provide for refunding tuition on a declining basis if the student drops out. Indeed, under FTC regulations, if a student in a proprietary vocational school cancels his enrollment contract, the "school shall not receive, demand, or retain more than a pro rata portion of the total contract price" plus a relatively small registration fee.[137] Large retail sellers seem more likely to plan for default under executory contracts through application of statistical forecasting techniques than through a program of litigation to recover damages under a net-proceeds formula. Even small firms seem unlikely to do much planning on that basis.

Most important, even assuming that planning does require a consumer in *E*'s position to suffer some loss, requiring such a consumer to pay damages equal to the entire contract price seems excessive to the task, particularly if it is assumed that the consumer would not have agreed to such damages at the time the contract was made. Rather, the seller's damages should be measured by what might be called a cancellation charge.[138] Such a recovery should be based on the amount necessary to reimburse the seller for incidental costs, to provide enough deterrent to facilitate planning, and to pay for the benefit of having had a place reserved. The measurement required need not be as difficult as it may seem, since the law could leave it to the seller to fix such an amount in the contract

---

[137] 16 C.F.R. §§ 438.0 to.2, .4 (1981). The retained registration fee may be $25 or 10% of the contract price up to a limit of $75, whichever is greater. *Id.* § 438.4(c). Similarly, airlines normally allow individuals who have booked reservations to return their tickets for refund even though they never canceled their reservations. *See Emergency Reservations Practices Investigation*, [1972–1978 Transfer Binder] AV. L. REP. (CCH) ¶ 22,206 (C.A.B. Apr. 13, 1976). For comparable practices in England, see P. ATIYAH, *supra* note 121, at 756–57.

[138] *Cf. Airlines Start Getting Tough on No-Shows*, Wall St. J., Dec. 9, 1981, at 33, col. 3 ($20 fee for failing to cancel reservations at least 30 minutes in advance on New York Air's Boston-Baltimore-Orlando flights reduced no-shows on some Orlando flights to 5% from as high as 30%; United Airlines suggests $10 administrative fee for refunding unused tickets).

by way of liquidated damages, or might treat a deposit by the buyer as a tacit cancellation charge even if the contract does not so provide. In this connection, the courts might draw by analogy on section 2-718(2)(b) of the Uniform Commercial Code, which provides, in effect, that when a seller justifiably withholds delivery of goods because of a buyer's breach, the buyer is entitled to restitution of any amount by which the buyer's payments exceeded twenty percent of the price or $500, whichever is less.

Suppose in a case like *Dance Lessons*, the seller is operating at full capacity. If the seller reserves a place for the buyer, he may then turn away an alternative customer. If the defaulting buyer's place is not filled, the seller will have incurred an opportunity cost equal to the contract price. One way to handle this problem is to permit the seller to recover damages under a net-proceeds formula if he could shoulder the burden of proving these elements. However, if a buyer would probably not agree to this measure in advance, a net-proceeds formula might be inappropriate even in the full-capacity case, at least in the absence of a specific contractual provision to that effect. In any event, the likelihood that a given seller is both operating at full capacity and unable to replace the defaulting buyer may be too slim to justify a special rule for such cases.

Let us now apply this approach to a sale of relatively homogeneous goods by a merchant to a consumer, as in the following hypothetical:

> *Buick Buyer*. *T*, a high school teacher, wants to buy a new Buick. After shopping around, *T* decides to buy at Seller's dealership, since Seller's price matches the lowest price available from competing dealers and Seller has a good reputation for servicing. On October 1, *T* signs a contract to buy from Seller a new Buick, with specified accessories, for $10,000, delivery on December 1. On November 1, before the factory has begun to fill Seller's order for *T*'s car, *T* repudiates the contract. Seller's factory cost for the Buick ordered by *T* is $8,500, and Seller can buy as many new Buicks from the factory as it sells.

Much the same analysis can be made in this kind of case as in *Dance Lessons*. Application of the bargain principle would permit the seller to recover under a net-proceeds formula. This is not as draconian as the application of that formula in cases like *Dance Lessons*: the seller's projected out-of-pocket cost is significant, and the recovery would therefore be well below contract price. Nevertheless, the result is not easy to justify on the surrogate-cost theory, since the seller will have incurred little or no cost at the time of the breach. It is also not easy to justify on the risk theory. Consumers normally do not make contracts like that in *Buick Buyer* for the purpose of allocating the risk of price changes or speculating in the market for new cars, and a contract provision for such damages would probably be neither requested nor agreed to (particularly since the buyer's damages for seller's nondelivery, based on a replacement-price formula, would normally be very small since the market price of consumer goods normally does not change materially over short periods). The result might be justified on the planning theory, but it is doubtful whether full enforcement of executory contracts under a net-proceeds formula is really required for effective planning by sellers of consumer goods. Casual investigation suggests that few such sellers — including few new-car dealerships — bring suit for breach of executory contracts.[139]

It is of course possible that more consumers would breach executory contracts if it were known that a seller could not recover his net proceeds on a buyer's breach. That seems unlikely, however, because most consumers probably don't know that the seller might be entitled to measure damages this way. Damages for breach by a consumer of an executory contract to purchase relatively homogeneous services or goods should normally be measured by a replacement-price or cancellation-charge formula, even though such a rule places another limit on the fullest reach of the bargain principle.

IV. Conclusion

The first great problem of contract law — usually subsumed under the heading of consideration — is what *kinds* of promises the law should enforce.[140] This problem, however, is tightly linked with another: the *extent* to which a certain kind of promise should be enforced. Indeed, on a deep level the two problems are virtually inseparable. The proposition that promises made as part of a bargain ought to be enforced is relatively straightforward; the real question is to what extent.

The traditional answer to this question is embodied in the paradigmatic bargain principle, namely, that damages for the

[139] This assertion is based on a conversation with counsel for a large regional association of automobile dealers. This is not to say that such litigation is unknown.

[140] *See* 1A A. Corbin, Corbin on Contracts § 210 (1963); Eisenberg, *supra* note 4, at 1.

unexcused breach of a bargain promise should invariably be measured by the value that the promised performance would have had to the plaintiff, regardless of the value for which the defendant's promise was exchanged.

This principle, which in the typical case is supported by considerations of both fairness and efficiency, finds its fullest justification in the exemplary case of a half-completed bargain made in a perfectly competitive market. Bargains made in other kinds of markets are not intrinsically suspect. Nevertheless, that a market is less than perfectly competitive does set the stage for transactions in which the bargain principle loses much or all of its force, because it is supported by neither fairness nor efficiency. For example, a market that involves a monopoly sets the stage for the exploitation of distress; a market in which transactions are complex and differentiated rather than simple and homogeneous sets the stage for the exploitation of transactional incapacity; a market in which actors do not simply take a price established by a general market and are susceptible to transient economic irrationality sets the stage for unfair persuasion; a market that involves imperfect price-information sets the stage for the exploitation of price-ignorance.

Until recently, courts have tended either to apply the bargain principle to cases raising such problems, despite the difficulties this application presents, or to deal with these difficulties in covert and unsystematic ways. Over the past thirty years, however, a new paradigmatic principle — unconscionability — has emerged. This principle explains and justifies the limits that should be placed upon the bargain principle on the basis of the quality of a bargain.

Looking backward, the new paradigm enables us to reconstruct prior theory and phenomena by providing a general explanation for a wide variety of contract concepts that heretofore seemed distinct. So, for example, duress may now be seen as simply a special case of the exploitation of distress; undue influence may now be seen as simply a special case of unfair persuasion; and the prohibition against exploiting palpable unilateral mistake may now be seen as a specific norm of unconscionability.[141] Similarly, the apparent anomaly of review for fairness in courts of equity and admiralty can be explained by the new paradigm, while guidelines can now be set for that review; and the doctrine of general incapacity

[141] *See* RESTATEMENT (SECOND) OF CONTRACTS § 153 (1979) (when mistake of one party makes contract voidable).

might be reformulated to apply only when exploitation is present.

Looking forward, the paradigm must be articulated and extended through the development of more specific norms to guide the resolution of specific cases, provide affirmative relief to exploited parties, and channel the discretion of administrators and legislators.[142] In accomplishing this task, it now appears that the distinction between procedural and substantive unconscionability, which may have served a useful purpose at an earlier stage, does not provide much help once the relatively obvious norms of unconscionability, such as unfair surprise, have been articulated. For example, it is both difficult and unproductive to classify as exclusively either "substantive" or "procedural" the problems posed by the extraction of an unduly high price from a person who is in distress, lacks transactional capacity, or is price-ignorant. Development of more specific norms must instead proceed by the identification of classes of cases in which neither fairness nor efficiency supports the application of the bargain principle — an effort that can be guided in part by the reconstruction and extension of existing contract doctrines.

Even where unconscionability is not present, application of the bargain principle may raise problems if the bargain is wholly executory at the time of breach, since in such cases a performance has, by hypothesis, been neither rendered nor received. Even in executory cases the bargain principle can normally be justified, despite the lack of performance, under the surrogate-cost, risk, or planning theories. In some transaction-types, however — particularly those involving breach by consumers in a contract for the sale of relatively homogeneous commodities — application of the bargain principle to its fullest reach, through a recovery measured under a net-proceeds formula, is supported by neither the surrogate-cost nor the risk theories, and results in damages that seem excessive to planning needs. In such cases the bargain principle should be limited by permitting the seller to measure damages only under a replacement-price or cancellation-charge formula.

Placing limits on the bargain principle is not cost-free. A major advantage of that principle, at least in theory, is its conceptual simplicity and the ease with which it can be administered. To apply the principle, it need only be determined whether a bargain was made, and if so, what remedy is required to put the innocent party in the position he would have been in had the bargain been performed. Development of

---

[142] *See* Dawson, *Unconscionable Coercion*, *supra* note 17, at 1044.

specific unconscionability norms and limitations on the full reach of the bargain principle in certain types of executory contracts make doctrine more complex by singling out certain transaction-types for special treatment. Administration is also made more complex and problematical by requiring decisions on such issues as whether a given course of conduct was exploitive or whether a given price was unfairly high.

The simplicity of the bargain principle, however, is partly a mirage. Concepts of fairness were smuggled into contract law even when the principle seemed most secure, through doctrines such as the legal-duty rule and the principle of mutuality. Partly because these doctrines are allowed to achieve their ends only in a covert fashion, they operate in an extremely technical manner and are riddled with legalistic exceptions. Furthermore, an increase in the complexity of some areas of law may be desirable, if it accurately mirrors the increased complexity of social and economic life. Placing limits on the bargain principle involves costs of administration. Failure to place such limits, however, involves still greater costs to the system of justice.

Part II
Interpretive and Default Rules

[8]

CONTRACT LAW, DEFAULT RULES, AND THE PHILOSOPHY OF PROMISING

*Richard Craswell**

Among the topics addressed by moral philosophy is the obligation to keep one's promises. To many philosophers, there is something strange (or, at least, something calling for explanation) in the idea that moral obligations can be created simply by an individual's saying so — yet this is what seems to happen when a person makes a promise. Consequently, there is by now a large body of literature attempting to identify the exact source and nature of this moral obligation.

Contract law, too, has something to do with promises, so philosophers of law (and philosophically minded lawyers) often draw on philosophical theories about promising when writing about contract law. For example, a recent book by Charles Fried purports "to show how a complex legal institution, contract, can be traced to and is determined by a small number of basic moral principles . . . ."[1] In Fried's view, a recognition of the proper philosophical basis of contract law leads to conclusions profoundly different from those that would result from any attempt to rest contract law on other social policies, such as economic efficiency or the redistribution of wealth.[2]

My thesis is that such claims on behalf of philosophical theories of promising are greatly exaggerated. In particular, analyses such as Fried's have little or no relevance to those parts of contract law that govern the proper remedies for breach, the conditions under which the promisor is excused from her duty to perform, or the additional obligations (such as implied warranties) imputed to the promisor as an implicit part of her promise. These doctrines, which serve to define the exact scope of contractual obligations, are often referred to as

---

* Professor of Law, University of Southern California. B.A. 1974, Michigan State University; J.D. 1977, University of Chicago. — Ed. I have benefited from comments by Scott Altman, Ian Ayres, Randy E. Barnett, Richard A. Epstein, John Finnis, John Gardner, Ronald R. Garet, Catharine W. Hantzis, Michael S. Moore, Joseph Raz, Alan Schwartz, W. David Slawson, Christopher D. Stone, and participants in workshops at USC and at Oxford University. I am also grateful for financial support from the USC Law Center Summer Research Fund and the USC-Oxford Legal Theory Institute.

1. C. FRIED, CONTRACT AS PROMISE: A THEORY OF CONTRACTUAL OBLIGATION (1981), at the first (unnumbered) page of the preface. *See also* Barnett, *Contract Scholarship and the Reemergence of Legal Philosophy* (Book Review), 97 HARV. L. REV. 1223 (1984) (applauding what he sees as the growing recognition of the importance of normative philosophy to contract law and to legal scholarship generally).

2. C. FRIED, *supra* note 1, at 4-6, 74-85, 103-11.

"background rules" or "default rules," although the term "default rules" more commonly refers only to those rules which the parties are free to vary by appropriate language in their contract.[3] As not all contract rules can be varied in this way, I will use the term "background rules" to refer to both waivable and nonwaivable rules.

I am not asserting here that philosophical theories about promising can have no implications for any part of contract law. Such theories may well have implications for questions about the proper scope of freedom of contract — that is, questions about whether any given rule ought to be merely a default rule, or whether it ought to be mandatory for all parties. In addition, *certain* philosophical theories may have implications for the proper content of contract law's background rules. For example, theories that justify the enforceability of promises on grounds of economic efficiency, or on the special value of certain kinds of relationships, may imply that the law should adopt those background rules that are most efficient or that best promote the most highly valued kinds of relationships.

Other philosophical theories, however — including the one endorsed by Fried — have no such implications for the content of the law's background rules. These theories ground the enforceability of promises on considerations of individual freedom and autonomy, or on the principle of fidelity to one's prior statements or commitments. In a nutshell, the fidelity principle is consistent with any set of background rules because those rules merely fill out the details of what it is a person has to remain faithful to, or what a person's prior commitment is deemed to be. Thus, while fidelity may dictate that a promisor must live up to the obligations described by any set of background rules the law has adopted, it cannot guide the legal system in deciding which background rules to adopt in the first place. The principle of individual freedom is equally unhelpful, for it implies only that individuals should be left free to change whatever default rule the law adopts as a starting point. Once again, some other value must be invoked to explain why one starting point ought to be picked by the law in preference to another.

If I am right, this means that it is not enough to reject notions such as economic efficiency, or theories that value certain kinds of relationships more highly than others, as insufficient or incorrect justifications for the basic proposition that promises ought to be enforced. Even if

3. The role of "default rules" is discussed at more length in Goetz & Scott, *The Limits of Expanded Choice: An Analysis of the Interactions Between Express and Implied Contract Terms*, 73 CALIF. L. REV. 261 (1985), and Ayres & Gertner, *Filling Gaps in Incomplete Contracts: An Economic Theory of Default Rules*, 99 YALE L.J. 87 (1989).

those theories are rejected at this most basic level, further argument is needed to explain why they are inadmissible bases for selecting the law's background rules or starting points, and, if so, to explain what other values ought to be used instead. Unfortunately, current writings bringing philosophical analysis to bear on contract law have focused almost entirely on the more basic question of why promises ought to be enforced at all, and have tended to overlook this second level of analysis. This frequently leads to careless or ad hoc statements concerning the proper content of contract law's background rules.

Part I of this article presents a more detailed survey of recent philosophical writings about promises, for the benefit of legal readers who may be unfamiliar with that literature. Part II then discusses the role of background rules in contract law, and shows why the content of those rules cannot be derived from philosophical theories based on individual liberty, or on ideals such as fidelity or truthfulness. Finally, Part III examines the writings of Charles Fried and Randy Barnett to illustrate the consequences of attempting to apply philosophy to contract law without addressing these problems. These two authors have supplied the most comprehensive attempts to give contract law a philosophical grounding, yet each falls into exactly this error.

I. Philosophical Theories About Promising

Broadly speaking, there are two kinds of questions that can be asked about the ethics of promising. One category consists of questions that might be asked by someone wondering whether to make a promise — for example, "Should I promise to donate money to the poor?" or "Should I promise to help a friend, if I can do so at little inconvenience to myself?" The other consists of questions facing someone who has already made a promise — for example, "Should I carry out my promise, even though my circumstances or my desires have changed?" The first class of questions asks what kinds of promises ought to be made, while the second asks what follows from having made a promise.

The first class of questions has received little attention in philosophical writings about promising as such. This should not be surprising, for the ethical theories most relevant to questions about what kind of promises to make will usually be theories with implications far beyond the topic of promising. If a person is wondering whether to promise money to the poor, the most interesting question (from the standpoint of ethics) is whether she ought to help the poor at all. The subsidiary question of whether she ought to help them by *promising* money, rather than giving them money without ever having first promised to do so, seems much less important. Thus, ethical theories about what kind of promises to make usually derive from theories about the particular subject matter of the promise (helping the poor, etc.). They do not derive from theories about promising as such.

The same could be true of the second class of questions, concerning the ethical consequences of having made a promise. That is, there would be nothing illogical in believing that the conditions under which it is excusable to break a promise to the poor have no connection (in the sense of being linked by any common theory) with the conditions under which it is excusable to break a business promise, or a promise to a friend. If that were the case, there would be no point in asking questions about the nature of the commitment represented by promises in general. One could speak of the commitment represented by charitable promises, or business promises, but it would be useless to search for any general, unifying theory of promises.

Most people, though, would reject the idea that the obligations imposed by different kinds of promises have nothing in common. The mere fact that we classify certain speech acts as "promises" strongly suggests that they have something in common; otherwise, there would be no point to that classification. Indeed, there is a growing body of philosophical literature which attempts to describe the obligation someone accepts when she promises to do some action ø, regardless of how ø is filled in. That literature presupposes that there are at least some things that can be said about promises without discussing the specific subject matter of the promise.

Contract law, too, is traditionally concerned with the elements that all promises have in common, so it is this literature that is most often invoked by legal scholars in search of a philosophical grounding for contract law. The remainder of this Part describes this literature in more detail. One branch of the literature takes it as given that promises are morally binding and attempts to describe the exact way in which this "bindingness" should constrain the promisor's subsequent conduct. Another branch attempts to articulate the reasons why promises might be morally binding. While these two inquiries are related at many points, it will be convenient to discuss them separately.

A. *What Does It Mean To Be Bound by a Promise?*

Assume that a person has promised to do some action ø. Most people would agree that this does not place the promisor under an absolute duty to do ø — for example, if ø becomes impossible for reasons beyond the promisor's control, she may be excused from her obligation.[4] Most people would also agree that the promisor's freedom has been constrained in some way, so she cannot decide whether or not to do ø with the same freedom she would have had if she had not made the promise. If asked to articulate the exact way in which her freedom is constrained, however, most people would have a great deal of difficulty.

Philosophers have taken two somewhat different approaches to articulating the way in which a promise constrains the promisor. One approach views the promise as creating additional reasons in favor of doing ø; the other views the promise as barring the promisor from considering certain reasons that might otherwise argue against doing ø. Each of these will be discussed below.

1. *Promises as Excluding Reasons for Action*

One view of the way that promises constrain a promisor's subsequent deliberations can be found in a 1955 article by John Rawls.[5] Rawls was only indirectly concerned with promises, as his main objective was to describe the distinction between justifying a social practice and justifying an individual action within such a practice. But because Rawls found the practice of promising to be a useful example, much of what he said is relevant here.

Rawls' point was that some practices, including promising, are defined so as to make certain arguments no longer available to those acting within the practice. More specifically, once a person has promised to do something, it is no longer open to that person to decide not to perform on the ground that, all things considered, nonperformance seems preferable to performance.[6] While such a preference might be a perfectly proper ground on which to refuse to make a promise in the first place, the rules of promising foreclose such an argument once the promise has been made.

Rawls recognized that this did not mean that a promisor was obliged to carry out her promise regardless of the circumstances:

> Is this to say that in particular cases one cannot deliberate whether or not to keep one's promise? Of course not. But to do so is to deliberate whether the various excuses, exceptions and defenses, which are understood by, and which constitute an important part of, the practice, apply to one's own case. Various defenses for not keeping one's promise are allowed, but among them there isn't the one that, on general utilitarian grounds, the promisor (truly) thought his action best on the whole, even

4. For convenience in the use of pronouns, all my examples will assume a female promisor and a male promisee.

5. Rawls, *Two Concepts of Rules*, 64 PHIL. REV. 3 (1955).

6. *Id.* at 16-17.

though there may be the defense that the consequences of keeping one's promise would have been *extremely* severe.[7]

Rawls argued that the practice of promising must rule out an excuse based on a general balance of considerations — otherwise, the point of having the practice would be lost.

More recently, Joseph Raz has developed a similar theory in which promises supply what he calls "exclusionary reasons."[8] According to Raz, a promise to do ø constrains the promisor's options by preventing her from giving any weight to certain arguments that might be relevant if she had not promised. In other words, promises are not themselves reasons for doing ø, but they bar or exclude certain factors which might otherwise be reasons *not* to do ø.

Like Rawls, Raz recognizes that promises do not exclude *all* other considerations, thereby leaving the promisor under an absolute obligation to do ø. If ø would involve actions that were themselves immoral, for example, it might still be permissible for the promisor to choose not to do ø.[9] Indeed, Raz does not attempt to list the precise reasons that are excluded by a promise — though he would at least agree with Rawls that the reason, "all things considered, it seems best not to ø" is one of the excluded reasons.[10] A promise binds a promisor, in Raz's view, by excluding such arguments from the promisor's subsequent calculations.

2. *Promises as New Reasons for Action*

A different class of theories holds that a promise creates new reasons to perform the promised action, which must then be added to any pre-existing balance of reasons for and against the action. For example, a promise may give rise to expectations in the promisee, and the fact that nonperformance would disappoint those expectations may count as a reason favoring performance.[11] If the promisee has relied on the promise in any way, so that nonperformance would leave him worse off than if the promise had never been made, this might provide

7. *Id.* (footnote omitted).

8. *See especially* Raz, *Promises and Obligations*, in LAW, MORALITY AND SOCIETY 210, 222 (P. Hacker & J. Raz eds. 1977). For more general discussions of the concept of "exclusionary reasons" (or "pre-emptive reasons," as he refers to them in his later work), see J. RAZ, THE MORALITY OF FREEDOM 42-69 (1986); J. RAZ, PRACTICAL REASON AND NORMS ch. 1 (1975); Raz, *Authority and Consent*, 67 VA. L. REV. 103 (1981).

9. Raz, *Promises and Obligations*, *supra* note 8, at 211.

10. *Id.* at 222-23.

11. For examples of this theory, see Ardal, *And That's a Promise*, 18 PHIL. Q. 225, 233-37 (1968); Narveson, *Promising, Expecting, and Utility*, 1 CANADIAN J. PHIL. 207, 213-20 (1971). *See also* Downie, *Three Accounts of Promising*, 35 PHIL. Q. 259, 263-64 (1985) (attributing this argument to Adam Smith).

an even stronger reason in favor of performing the promise.[12]

As in the case of the theories discussed in the preceding subsection, these theories do not imply that a promisor must *always* carry out the promise. While the fact that the promisee would be disappointed may be a reason in favor of doing ø, nothing in this theory rules out the possibility of there being other, stronger reasons against ø. If ø is an immoral action, or has become impossible, the reasons against doing ø might well outweigh the reasons in favor of doing ø. Thus, both sets of theories are consistent with the belief that a promise is not binding in all circumstances.

Similarly, both sets of theories are consistent with the belief that a promise somehow militates in favor of performance, in the sense of requiring the promisor to choose ø in at least some cases where, absent the promise, she would otherwise have chosen not to do so. The first set of theories explains such cases by saying that the promise excludes certain reasons that might otherwise have counseled against doing ø, so the promise will have a decisive effect in any case where those excluded reasons would otherwise have been dispositive. The second set explains the promisor's decision by saying that all the old reasons for and against ø remain relevant, but the promise creates new reasons in favor of ø. On this view, the promise will make a difference whenever the balance of old reasons would have counseled against ø, but the addition of the new reasons is enough to tip that balance in favor of ø.

Finally, neither of these theories attempts to explain *why* a promisor is morally bound to limit her subsequent behavior in the way postulated by the theory. Instead, the goal of these theories is simply to illuminate the ordinary understanding of what it means to be under a promissory obligation, by explaining precisely what it is that a promisor is thought to be bound to do. The question of whether (or why) anyone is morally obliged to follow that ordinary understanding is a separate question which requires a separate analysis. Accordingly, the following section surveys some recent philosophical theories addressed to the question of why the rules of promising are or ought to be morally binding.

B. *Why Should Anyone Obey the Rules of Promising?*

The question of why the rules of promising are morally binding is easily confused with the question addressed in the preceding section,

12. Theorists who focus on the promisee's reliance, rather than the bare expectation of performance, include MacCormick, *Voluntary Obligations and Normative Powers*, 46 ARISTOTELIAN SOCY. 59, 62-63 (Supp. Vol. 1972), and Hanfling, *Promises, Games and Institutions*, 75 PROC. ARISTOTELIAN SOCY. 13, 15-18 (1975).

concerning exactly what it is that the rules of promising require. Some of this confusion was unintentionally introduced by a 1964 article by John Searle, provocatively entitled *How to Derive "Ought" from "Is."*[13] Searle's point was that certain kinds of descriptive assertions, or "is" statements, are statements describing "institutional facts." For example, the statement that someone has hit a home run — as distinct from the statement that someone has hit a round object over a fence with a piece of wood — makes sense only within the institutional framework created by the rules of baseball.[14] Similarly (in Searle's view), the statement that someone has made a promise makes sense only within the framework created by the rules of promising. Thus, to say that a person has promised is to describe that person with reference to the rules of promising, and those rules include the normative or "ought" statement that people who promise are bound to act differently in some way as a result of their promise.[15] In this sense, Searle argued, it is possible to move from certain kinds of "is" statements to certain kinds of "oughts."

A number of writers responded by pointing out that this argument, standing alone, does not really show that anyone who promises ought therefore to accept the rules of the practice of promising, or ought to regard those rules as morally binding.[16] As Searle later clarified, the only kind of "ought" that he was discussing was one that was internal to the practice of promising.[17] It would still be open for someone to reject the entire practice of promising, or to argue that some or all of that practice's rules were unjust. Searle's derivation of "ought" from "is" was never intended to supply the answer to this kind of "ought" question.

In consequence, writers have had to look elsewhere for the source of the moral obligation to respect the rules of promising. Here, too, the various explanations can be grouped into two categories, which correspond in some ways to the two theories discussed in the preceding section concerning what the rules of promising actually require. Some writers have argued that the obligations created by a promise can only be explained by positing that individual promisors possess

13. 73 PHIL. REV. 43 (1964).

14. *Id.* at 54-55.

15. *Id.* at 55-56.

16. *See, e.g.*, Carey, *How to Confuse Commitment with Obligation*, 72 J. PHIL. 276 (1975); Hare, *The Promising Game*, 70 REVUE INTERNATIONALE DE PHILOSOPHIE 398 (1964); Jones, *Making and Keeping Promises*, 76 ETHICS 287 (1966); Miller, *Constitutive Rules and Essential Rules*, 39 PHIL. STUD. 183 (1981); Robins, *The Primacy of Promising*, 85 MIND 321, 329-30 (1976).

17. J. SEARLE, SPEECH ACTS 188-89 (1969).

"norm-creating powers," under which they are authorized to create new moral obligations merely by agreeing to do so. Others have argued that no such powers are necessary, and that the moral obligation to keep a promise is merely a particular instance of a more general obligation, such as the obligation not to cause harm to others or the obligation to tell the truth. Each theory will be discussed below.

1. *Promises and Norm-Creating Powers*

Joseph Raz has offered the most complete defense of the position that the moral obligation to respect the rules of promising must rest on some norm-creating power possessed by the promisor.[18] Without being quite as explicit, and without necessarily agreeing with other aspects of Raz's theory, other writers have taken an essentially similar position. For example, Charles Fried has argued that notions of individual freedom and autonomy require that individuals be allowed to bind themselves by promising.[19] Economists have pointed to the social utility of allowing individuals to bind themselves to a future course of conduct, to make it easier for others to arrange their lives in reliance on the promise.[20] In Raz's terms, all of these are arguments that individuals ought to have at least one norm-creating power: the power to create a moral obligation by making a promise.

In a somewhat similar vein, Randy Barnett has argued that promises are best viewed as marking the promisor's consent to the transfer of part of her bundle of property rights.[21] "Property rights" are meant here in the broadest possible sense; they thus include future rights such as "the right to fifty bushels of wheat on August 1," or even disjunctive rights such as "the right to fifty bushels of wheat or their equivalent in money." On this view, if a seller has consented to transfer to a buyer the right to "fifty bushels of wheat on August 1," the seller no longer has any right to control those bushels when August 1 arrives, so her retention of those bushels would constitute the taking of another's property. Barnett's account of promising might seem more parsimonious than Raz's, as Barnett grounds the force of a promise in an already recognized power — the power to transfer prop-

18. Raz, *Voluntary Obligations and Normative Powers*, 46 ARISTOTELIAN SOCY. 79 (Supp. Vol. 1972). For a somewhat similar position, see Robins, *supra* note 16.

19. C. FRIED, *supra* note 1, at 14-17.

20. *See, e.g.*, Goetz & Scott, *Enforcing Promises: An Examination of the Basis of Contract*, 89 YALE L.J. 1261 (1980).

21. Barnett, *A Consent Theory of Contract*, 86 COLUM. L. REV. 269 (1986). As Barnett notes, this view of contract law dates back at least as far as Blackstone's Commentaries. *Id.* at 292 n.98; *see also* P. ATIYAH, PROMISES, MORALS, AND LAW 179 (1981) (attributing this view of promising to Hobbes).

erty — rather than having to posit a separate normative power for promising. Notice, though, that the power to transfer title to property is itself an instance of what Raz would term a norm-creating power. In this sense, Barnett's theory is merely a particular example of the kind of theory that Raz believes necessary to account for the moral force of the rules of promising.[22]

Of course, positing a norm-creating power of this sort merely pushes the normative question back one step: What justifies the existence of this norm-creating power? To this question, many different answers can be and have been given. Economists usually rely on utilitarian justifications, arguing that a rule letting people make enforceable promises is likely (under certain conditions) to lead to the best use of resources. As noted above, Fried justifies the power to bind oneself as a corollary of respect for autonomy and individual freedom. Raz tentatively suggests a somewhat different answer: since promises create a special relationship between the promisor and promisee, the power to create such relationships is morally justified only if those relationships are themselves desirable.[23]

I will argue below that, when it comes to deriving legal implications, it may well make a difference which argument is used to justify these norm-creating powers.[24] In the philosophical literature on promising, though, these differences are less important (and receive less discussion) because all of these arguments lead to the same conclusion: that individuals ought to have the norm-creating power represented by promising. Thus, all of these theorists find themselves on one side of a divide, with the other side occupied by the theorists to be discussed in the next two sections.

2. *Promises and Harm to Others*

A different approach to explaining the moral force of the rules of promising begins with the observation that breaking a promise will

22. Raz occasionally distinguishes between consenting and promising, but his examples suggest that he is simply using "consent" in a sense that is narrower than Barnett's usage. For example, Raz argues that one can consent to give someone a right to some action, but cannot consent to give someone a mere right of recipience, such as the right to be paid a sum of money. Raz, *Authority and Consent, supra* note 8, at 121-22. Thus, where Barnett would say that a tenant has consented to transfer to her landlord the right to $1000 per month for each of the next 12 months, Raz would simply say that the tenant has promised to pay that sum. As nearly as I can tell, nothing turns on this difference in usage.

23. Raz, *Promises and Obligations, supra* note 8, at 227-28. In another context (while discussing consent generally), Raz has also noted the traditional instrumental arguments that letting people make their own promises is likely to lead to the best use of resources, or that promises develop peoples' characters and train them in such useful virtues as cooperation and careful planning. Raz, *Authority and Consent, supra* note 8, at 123-25.

24. *See infra* notes 48-57 and accompanying text.

often harm the promisee, especially if he has relied on the promise in any way. If there is a general principle that one ought not cause harm to others, that might be enough to justify some sort of rule against promise-breaking, at least when breaking the promise would in fact cause harm. In particular, this justification would fit well with the view that the only obligation imposed by a promise is an obligation to take this harm into account, as one reason — not necessarily the only one, or even a dispositive one — in favor of performing the promised action.[25]

Most people, though, are unwilling to equate a general obligation not to harm others with the specific obligation imposed by a promise. Imagine, for example, that a complete stranger walks up to you and says that he has formed the belief that you are about to give him $50,000 — and, moreover, that he has relied on this expectation by incurring various debts and obligations, none of which he would have incurred had he not believed that you were about to give him the money. The stranger's predicament in this case might provide a slight reason for you to help him out by giving him the $50,000 — after all, helping a fellow citizen is almost always a good reason for action — but it will not be a very strong one. Moreover, none of the writers cited above would say that preventing harm to the stranger is as strong a reason for action in this case as it would be if you had *promised* to give him $50,000, and your promise was what led him to incur his additional debts. Thus, some further argument is necessary to explain the particular force of the reason for action that is generated once a promise has been made.[26]

Some writers have tried to explain the additional force generated by a promise by pointing to the fact that a person who makes a promise has thereby *caused* the rise in the other party's expectations, and has likewise been a cause of the other party's reliance on the promise.[27] By contrast, the example in the preceding paragraph involved expectations and reliance which could not be causally attributed to any action of the person charged with the obligation. Thus, these writers rest the moral force of promissory obligations on a narrower form of the harm principle. While there is no obligation, or at best a very weak obligation, to take steps to *prevent* harm to others (these

25. *See supra* note 12.

26. For other criticisms of the bare-reliance argument, using examples similar to the one in the text, see C. FRIED, *supra* note 1, at 10-11; Raz, *Promises in Morality and Law* (Book Review), 95 HARV. L. REV. 916, 924-25 (1982).

27. *E.g.*, MacCormick, *supra* note 12, at 66-67.

writers would say), there is a much stronger obligation not actively to *cause* that harm.

Even this principle may be too broad, however. As a number of writers have pointed out, it is easy to imagine cases where one person has *caused* another to rely in some way, but the resulting obligation does not seem as strong as if the first person had made a promise to the second. Raz suggests the example of someone who informs a friend that she will almost certainly be able to offer the friend a ride into town, and that the likelihood of her being able to do so is sufficiently high that it makes perfect sense for the friend to rely on her rather than making alternative arrangements — but who warns, "remember — I do not promise anything, I am merely advising you."[28] In such a case, the friend presumably would be perfectly justified in relying on the statement by forgoing any alternative arrangements. The friend's lack of alternative arrangements may even be a factor that the speaker ought to consider in subsequently deciding whether to change her plans in some way that would prevent her from offering the ride. However, the force of this reason for going through with the offered ride still does not seem as strong as if the speaker had offered the ride and said, "I promise I'll be there." Thus, a promise still seems to add something to the force of the reasons for action over and above the force that can be attributed to the principle of not causing harm to others.

A closely related objection notes that the notion of "cause" employed in this argument is more than a little problematic.[29] Reliance on a promise is always caused (in a "but for" sense) by the promisee as well as by the promisor, for it is the promisee who chooses to rely. Thus, some further argument is needed to explain why we quickly attribute moral responsibility for another person's reliance to someone who has *promised* a particular action, but are less quick to attribute as much responsibility to someone who has made clear that she is not promising anything. To say that the person who relies assumes the risk of being disappointed if the other person's statement falls short of being a promise, but does not assume that risk if the other person has made an actual promise, is no answer. Such a response simply posits a difference in the extent of the speaker's responsibility in each case, when it is precisely that difference that needs a moral justification.[30]

28. Raz, *supra* note 18, at 99.

29. For an exceptionally clear statement of this objection, see P. ATIYAH, *supra* note 21, at 63-69; *see also* G. WARNOCK, THE OBJECT OF MORALITY 98-100 (1971); Robins, *supra* note 16.

30. Occasionally, the objection discussed in this paragraph is made by asserting that we cannot determine whether the promisee's reliance is reasonable without knowing whether the promise is binding on the promisor. *E.g.*, Barnett, *supra* note 21, at 275. However, Raz's example of

Patrick Atiyah suggested that the greater responsibility of a promisor might be explained by treating the promise as a conclusive admission that responsibility properly rested on the promisor. That is, Atiyah viewed the allocation of responsibility for the promisee's reliance as a question of social policy, which would normally have to be settled by a court or legislature or other lawmaking institution.[31] He then suggested that if an individual promisor *admits* that she should be responsible for the other party's reliance, by making an explicit promise, that sort of admission against interest should usually be treated as conclusively settling the social policy issue.[32] Notice, though, that this argument grants to individual promisors exactly the sort of norm-creating power for which Joseph Raz has argued.[33] If individual promisors have the sovereign-like authority to determine conclusively who should bear responsibility for certain losses, they are exercising a power whose existence must be justified by some principle beyond the general notion of not causing harm to others.

3. *Promises and Misrepresentation*

The attempt to explain why a speaker's responsibility seems greater if she has made a definite promise — even if the harm to the other party is no greater than in an otherwise similar case where no promise has been made — is one of the factors that led many writers to posit a separate, norm-creating power which individuals can exercise by making a promise. Other writers, however, have responded by narrowing the harm principle still further, saying that there is a particularly strong obligation not to cause harm to others *by making false statements.* Alternatively, the "harm" element can be eliminated entirely, if there is an obligation not to misrepresent the truth regardless of whether the misrepresentation causes any actual harm. Under either of these views, which I will refer to collectively as the "misrepresentation theory," the key fact is not that breaking a promise causes harm, but that breaking a promise violates the obligation to tell the truth.[34]

one friend informing another of a possible ride into town is enough to refute this proposition, by showing that there can be cases where it is reasonable for the promisee to rely regardless of whether the promise is binding. For further discussions of this issue, see McNeilly, *Promises Demoralized*, 81 PHIL. REV. 63 (1971); Narveson, *supra* note 11. Assertions such as Barnett's are probably better interpreted as making the argument discussed in the text: that we cannot know whether it is reasonable *to attribute responsibility for the reliance to the promisor* without first deciding whether the promise is binding.

31. P. ATIYAH, *supra* note 21, at 68-69.

32. *Id.* at 184-202.

33. Raz, *supra* note 26, at 926-27.

34. For examples of this approach, see G. WARNOCK, *supra* note 29, at 101-11; Ardal, *Ought*

The misrepresentation theory reaches this conclusion by interpreting all promises as representations about the promisor's future conduct. A person who promises to give a friend a ride has made a definite statement about what will happen in the future. If she then fails to come through with the ride, her failure makes this statement about the future a false one, thereby violating the obligation to tell the truth (in addition to causing harm). By contrast, a person who says that she will probably give her friend a ride, but who reserves the right to change her mind, has made a much weaker probabilistic statement about the future. That person's failure to perform would not make her previous statement false, and therefore would not violate the obligation to tell the truth, even though it might cause the same amount of harm to her friend. According to the misrepresentation theory, this is why a person who promises to give her friend a ride has a stronger reason to do so than does a person who has merely said that she is likely to give her friend a ride, without actually promising.

Admittedly, the obligation to tell the truth appears here in what may be an unfamiliar guise. The obligation has some elements of strict liability, for it is no defense to say that at the time of promising the speaker *thought* that her statement would come true.[35] In addition, the obligation to tell the truth is perhaps more usually thought of as an obligation limiting what one is allowed to say, by obliging people not to say anything that is false. Under this theory, though, the obligation limits what speakers can *do,* by forbidding people from doing anything that will make their prior statements turn out to be false. Rather than requiring people to conform their statements to reality, the misrepresentation theory of promising requires people to act in such a way that reality will conform to their prior statements.[36]

In some respects, then, the misrepresentation theory is not that different from theories based on the notion of norm-creating powers, as discussed above. If the obligation to tell the truth means that an individual, by choosing to making a definite statement about the future, can thereby place herself under an obligation to make sure that her statement comes true, then that individual certainly has the power to create an obligation of some sort. This obligation need not be of the sort discussed above in section I.A.1, however, which obliged the

We To Keep Contracts Because They Are Promises?, 17 VAL. U. L. REV. 655 (1983); Ardal, *supra* note 11, at 225; Fogelin, *Richard Price on Promising: A Limited Defense*, 21 J. HIST. PHIL. 289 (1983); Hanfling, *supra* note 12, at 24-25.

35. Compare the position of Charles Fried, discussed *infra* at note 68.

36. For a more extended discussion of this aspect of the theory, see Fogelin, *supra* note 34, at 296-97.

speaker not to consider certain reasons which might otherwise counsel against doing the promised act. The misrepresentation theory is equally consistent with obligations of the sort described in section I.A.2, which merely add the value of telling the truth as an additional reason in favor of performing the promised action.

II. The Needs of Contract Law

The rules of contract law can be divided into two categories: "background rules" and "agreement rules." As discussed earlier, background rules define the exact substance of a party's obligation, by specifying (among other things) the conditions under which her nonperformance will be excused, and the sanctions which will be applied to any unexcused nonperformance. By contrast, agreement rules specify the conditions and procedures the parties must satisfy in order to change an otherwise applicable background rule. Agreement rules thus include most of the rules governing offer and acceptance, as well as such doctrines as fraud or undue influence, which define the conditions necessary for a party's apparent consent to be counted as truly valid.[37] To be sure, these two categories are not mutually exclusive, for some rules serve both functions simultaneously. For example, the "mailbox rule" defines a procedure by which parties can agree to a contract changing any otherwise applicable background rule. It also provides a background rule of its own, by providing that the offeror's power to retract her offer ends as soon as an acceptance is posted (unless the offer itself provided otherwise). Notwithstanding such instances of overlap, the distinction between background rules and agreement rules is still useful in understanding the relationship between the philosophical theories of promising and the content of contract law.

The philosophical theories discussed above may well have some relevance for contract law's agreement rules. For example, theories that ground the enforceability of promises on individual liberty might argue that the parties should be allowed to overturn nearly all of contract law's background rules by an appropriate agreement, thereby affording a much wider scope for the operation of whatever agreement rules the law adopts. Different philosophical theories might even have different implications for the content of those agreement rules — for example, the degree of force needed to make an individual's consent no longer voluntary, or the amount of information needed to make an

37. If the law does not permit a particular background rule to be varied by the parties, then the set of "agreement rules" available to change that background is of course the null set. For a slightly different classification of contract rules, see Ayres & Gertner, *supra* note 3.

individual's consent sufficiently informed. In this article, I am not concerned with the content of contract law's agreement rules, so I will not explore these implications further.

It is less clear that the philosophical literature discussed above has any implications for the content of contract law's background rules. All of the authors discussed above recognize that any real system of promising would have to include some set of rules governing excuses, remedies, and other details of the promisor's obligation.[38] Their purpose, however, was to analyze the practice of promising at a higher level of abstraction. They were interested in the elements all promises had in common, regardless of the action ø that was promised, and largely regardless of the background rules governing such topics as remedies or excuses. Granted, a sufficiently extreme background rule — *e.g.*, one excusing nonperformance whenever the promisor no longer felt like performing — might deprive a so-called "promise" of any binding force at all, thereby eliminating the very aspect of promising that interested these philosophers, and excluding the practice governed by such a rule from the scope of their analysis. Within those limits, though, the rules governing such topics as remedies and excuses could effectively be treated as just a more complete definition of the exact obligation undertaken by the promisor — in other words, as just another aspect of ø. The goal of the writings described above was to explain how and why a promisor could be bound to live up to any ø, regardless of exactly what that particular ø required.

This indifference to the content of ø should not be taken to mean that these authors believed that the appropriate background rules could be determined simply by looking to the explicit content of a party's promise. At a minimum, the parties' specifications would be relevant only if the rule were one the parties were free to vary — a "default rule" in the terminology I have used here. Not all of the writers discussed above are willing to grant the parties that much power over every aspect of their obligation.[39]

Even when a background rule concerns a topic that everyone agrees the parties should be allowed to vary — say, the extent of the warranty in the sale of a used automobile by a private individual — many parties simply will not address that topic in their agreement, so there will be nothing in the agreement's explicit content to resolve this issue. As a result, some method must be found to *interpret* the parties' agreement, to provide rules governing any topic not explicitly settled

38. See, for example, the passage from Rawls quoted in the text *supra* at note 7.

39. *See, e.g.*, Raz, *supra* note 26, at 932.

by the parties. Indeed, creative interpretation is often needed to determine whether there has been any binding promise at all, for even this fundamental question is not always explicitly settled by the parties.[40] While it is perhaps more common to speak of "interpretation" in cases where parties attempt to resolve an issue but do so with insufficient clarity, and to speak of applying default rules in cases where the parties made no attempt to address an issue, the principle is much the same in either case.[41] Both require an outside agency, such as a court, to choose the exact rules defining the parties' obligations where the parties have not unmistakably chosen some rule of their own.

A. *Possible Sources of Law*

The philosophical literature discussed above does not address these issues of interpretation and appropriate default rules. As that literature is concerned with the question of how promises could bind even in the best of circumstances, its focus is implicitly limited to cases where there is no question that a promise has been made, and no difficulty in determining the exact content of the promised action ø. That literature may still contribute, however, to the law's resolution of these issues. There are many possible ways of resolving questions of interpretation or background rules, and at least two are perfectly consistent with many of the philosophical positions described above. The first involves a sociological inquiry into the actual practices and customs that exist in any particular community, as a guide to interpreting particular utterances and filling in appropriate background rules. The second involves an appeal to the deeper philosophical values used to justify the institution of promising — that is, values such as social utility or individual freedom or encouraging valuable relationships (depending on the theory of promising employed). Each of these will be discussed below.

1. *Existing Expectations*

The frequent references in the philosophical literature to the "practice" or "institution" of promising could be taken to suggest that the exact scope of any promissory obligation is a matter of sociological fact, to be discovered by careful investigation into the practice of

40. For some famous instances of ambiguity in this respect, see United Steel Workers, Local 1330 v. United States Steel Corp., 492 F. Supp 1, 5-6 (N.D. Ohio), *aff'd. in part and vacated in part*, 631 F.2d 1264 (6th Cir. 1980); Embry v. Hargadine-McKittrick Dry Goods Co., 127 Mo. App. 383, 387-92, 105 S.W. 777 (1907).

41. For a more extended discussion of the similarities between interpretation and the selection of default rules, see Goetz & Scott, *supra* note 3, at 264-86.

promising as it exists in the relevant community.[42] For instance, an inquiry into the use of promises in late twentieth-century America might show that promisors were regularly excused whenever performance became commercially impracticable, or it might show that promisors were never excused no matter how difficult performance had become. In either case, the results of that inquiry would define the exact scope of the obligation that any late twentieth-century American had accepted when she made a promise.

Of course, any serious sociological inquiry would very likely identify several different forms of promising, each with different background rules and assumptions, even within a single community.[43] At the very least, it would certainly be *possible* for a society to recognize several different kinds of promises, each with a different set of rules defining the exact scope of the obligation. For example, a society could have one kind of promise that imposes an absolute obligation to perform (in legal terms, one that exposes the promisor to a suit for "specific performance"), another that imposes an obligation to perform or to pay the equivalent in money ("expectation damages"), and a third that imposes an obligation to perform or to make good any losses the promisee may have suffered by relying on the promise ("reliance damages"). The community could also use promises that impose an obligation to perform unless performance became extremely difficult in some unexpected way (in legal terms, promises subject to the defense of commercial impracticability), and promises that permit no such excuse.

The possibility of more than one kind of promise greatly complicates the difficulties involved in interpreting the sociological data about a society's practices. For example, obvious questions arise concerning the number of people who must follow any set of rules for those rules to be accepted as a legally relevant practice. Must an institution be recognized in the community prior to its invocation in any particular transaction, or can any two parties create a custom-made form of promising on the spur of the moment?[44] A related question involves the way we conceive of an individual who appears to be violating the rules of an existing practice: Is she merely an ordinary rulebreaker, or a pathbreaking pioneer in the creation of a new, perhaps

42. I use "sociological" here in its broadest possible sense, to include existing rules of contract law as well as any extra-legal or private promissory practices.

43. As a number of authors have recognized — *e.g.*, J. FINNIS, NATURAL LAW AND NATURAL RIGHTS 308-10 (1980); Jones, *supra* note 16, at 296; Raz, *Promises and Obligations*, *supra* note 8, at 227-28.

44. The latter position is suggested by Raz, *Promises and Obligations*, *supra* note 8, at 214-15.

more desirable form of promising? Other difficulties include the problem of conflicting expectations at different levels of generality — for example, if people expect written contracts to be binding, but they also expect goods to be sold at a fair price, what is their expectation regarding the force of a written contract that sets an unfair price? And what of the potential for circularity that arises when people's expectations are themselves affected by existing legal rules?[45]

These problems in inferring morally relevant categories from purely empirical data are well-known, so I will not pursue them here. Instead, for the remainder of this section I will assume that sociologists can identify the set of promises — call them promise$_1$, promise$_2$, . . . promise$_n$ — available to members of any particular society. However, this identification of the relevant choice set does not exhaust the possible uses of sociology. In order to reach a decision about any particular case, the courts must have some method of determining which kind of promise was actually made by the parties to any given transaction.

One can imagine societies in which this second question would be easy to answer — *e.g.*, societies with a system of formal devices by which individuals could signal their choice of institutions. For example, the society might require all binding promises to be signed with a seal (ignoring for the moment the possibility of different kinds of binding promises), while treating any promises not made under seal as nonbinding. In such a society, the problem of interpreting the parties' utterances would deserve the lack of attention it received in the philosophical writings about promises, for it would be, quite literally, nothing but a formality.

The difficulty, of course, is that most societies do not use this method of interpreting parties' utterances, and for good reason. Even when there are only two kinds of promises from which to choose, many writers have commented on the difficulties of expecting all lay people to understand the use of the seal, and the apparent harshness of enforcing one set of rules against parties who clearly intended a different set to apply but who forgot to use the appropriate formality.[46]

45. *See, e.g.*, Feinman, *Critical Approaches to Contract Law*, 30 UCLA L. REV. 829, 837 (1983) ("The law presumably is one factor shaping standards of social and especially commercial behavior. People's 'expectations' and merchants' notions of 'good faith' are to some extent dependent on the positive, public expression of norms by contract law itself."). *But see id.* at 844-45 ("Contemporary and historical research suggests that people generally don't know or don't care much about the rules of contract law and generally carry out their affairs with little regard for them.").

46. *See, e.g.*, Kennedy, *Form and Substance in Private Law Adjudication*, 89 HARV. L. REV. 1685, 1697 (1976).

These difficulties multiply rapidly if there are more than two kinds of promises — that is, more than two permissible sets of background rules — from which to choose. It would be very difficult to design a different seal for each of one hundred possible sets of promissory rules — and even more difficult to expect everybody to remember which seal they should use for each purpose. As a consequence, courts following this approach may have to appeal to sociology not only to identify the set of promises recognized in any particular society, but also to identify the more complex signals by which different kinds of promises are invoked. For example, a survey to determine what people usually mean when they say "I promise" or "I intend" might tell us what kind of commitment people usually have in mind when they make those noises — or, if the inquiry becomes more particularized, when they make those noises in particular contexts. Indeed, this is part of what courts do under current contract law when they inquire into the "reasonable interpretation" of the parties' language.[47]

Notice, though, that this kind of inquiry takes judges far beyond the "small number of basic moral principles" referred to in the introduction to this article. If we must rely on sociological investigation to identify the set of possible background rules, and also to tell us which set of rules applies in any particular case, then sociology is doing virtually all of the work involved in fulfilling the needs of contract law. This alone is enough to defeat the claim referred to in the introduction that the philosophy of promising can by itself yield definite implications for the content of contract law.

2. *Substantive Moral Values*

A more serious objection to this total reliance on sociological data is that it provides no perspective from which to criticize existing promissory practices, or to propose reforms in those practices. One might criticize particular legal rules for not properly conforming to those practices, but there would be no way to criticize the practices themselves. However, sociology is not the only possible source of content for contract law's background rules. An alternative is to look to the substantive values which justify the binding force of promises in the first place (according to one of the philosophical theories discussed earlier), to see if those values have implications for contract law's background rules.

Economic analysis is the most familiar instance of this method of determining the content of contract law's background rules. From an

47. But not the whole part — see *infra* note 57 and accompanying text.

economic perspective, if society is justified in giving individuals the power to make morally binding promises, it is because such promises will, under certain conditions, lead to the most efficient satisfaction of human wants. This notion of efficiency (or some variant of it) can then be used to choose among various possible background rules, by identifying the rule that would contribute most to efficiency. For example, there is an extensive body of literature analyzing different contract remedies to determine which remedies are most efficient in which situations.[48] Economists have also addressed the question of the most efficient rule for excusing promisors who fail to perform because of unexpected difficulties in performance,[49] and the conditions under which individuals' promises should not be treated as binding because of "market failures" that distort the promisor's incentives.[50]

John Rawls provides another example of how background rules might be chosen in order best to serve the substantive values that justify the binding force of promises in the first place. Rawls argued that the binding force of promises is justified if and only if the rules of promising — the background rules, in the terminology used here — are themselves consistent with principles of justice. For Rawls, this meant that they must lead to an equal distribution of all "primary

48. For nontechnical introductions to this literature, see A. POLINSKY, AN INTRODUCTION TO LAW AND ECONOMICS ch. 5 (1983); Craswell, *Contract Remedies, Renegotiation, and the Theory of Efficient Breach*, 61 S. CAL. L. REV. 629 (1988); Kornhauser, *An Introduction to the Economic Analysis of Contract Remedies*, 57 U. COLO. L. REV. 683 (1986). More technical analyses include Cooter, *Unity in Tort, Contract, and Property: The Model of Precaution*, 73 CALIF. L. REV. 1 (1985); Craswell, *Performance, Reliance, and One-Sided Information*, 18 J. LEGAL STUD. 365 (1989); Craswell, *Precontractual Investigation as an Optimal Precaution Problem*, 17 J. LEGAL STUD. 401 (1988); Kornhauser, *Reliance, Reputation, and Breach of Contract*, 26 J.L. & ECON. 691 (1983); Polinsky, *Risk Sharing Through Breach of Contract Remedies*, 12 J. LEGAL STUD. 427 (1983); Rogerson, *Efficient Reliance and Damage Measures for Breach of Contract*, 15 RAND J. ECON. 39 (1984); Shavell, *The Design of Contracts and Remedies for Breach*, 99 Q.J. ECON. 121 (1984); Shavell, *Damage Measures for Breach of Contract*, 11 BELL J. ECON. 466 (1980).

49. *See, e.g.*, Bruce, *An Economic Analysis of the Impossibility Doctrine*, 11 J. LEGAL STUD. 311 (1982); Goldberg, *Impossibility and Related Excuses*, 144 J. INST. & THEOR. ECON. 100 (1988); Joskow, *Commercial Impossibility, the Uranium Market and the* Westinghouse *Case*, 6 J. LEGAL STUD. 119 (1977); Perloff, *The Effects of Breaches of Forward Contracts Due to Unanticipated Price Changes*, 10 J. LEGAL STUD. 221 (1981); Posner & Rosenfield, *Impossibility and Related Doctrines in Contract Law: An Economic Analysis*, 6 J. LEGAL STUD. 83 (1977); Sykes, *Increased Cost of Performance and the Doctrine of Commercial Impracticability*, 19 J. LEGAL STUD. (forthcoming Jan. 1990); White, *Contract Breach and Contract Discharge Due to Impossibility: A Unified Theory*, 17 J. LEGAL STUD. 353 (1988).

50. *E.g.*, Kornhauser, *Unconscionability in Standard Forms*, 64 CALIF. L. REV. 1151 (1976); Ordover & Weiss, *Information and the Law: Evaluating Legal Restrictions on Competitive Contracts*, 71 AM. ECON. REV. PAPERS & PROC. 399 (1981); Rea, *Arm-Breaking, Consumer Credit, and Personal Bankruptcy*, 22 ECON. INQUIRY 188 (1984); Rose-Ackerman, *Inalienability and the Theory of Property Rights*, 85 COLUM. L. REV. 931 (1985); Schwartz & Wilde, *Intervening in Markets on the Basis of Imperfect Information: A Legal and Economic Analysis*, 127 U. PA. L. REV. 630 (1979); Schwartz, *A Reexamination of Nonsubstantive Unconscionability*, 63 VA. L. REV. 1053 (1977).

social goods" (liberty, wealth, etc.), except to the extent that an unequal distribution would benefit every member of society.[51] This provides a slightly different criterion for judging possible background rules — although one that will overlap with economic analysis when assessing the ways in which different rules benefit the contracting parties.[52]

Other writers have focused on other substantive values, which could lead them to different conclusions about the proper background rules. For example, John Finnis has argued that the binding force of promises is justified because of the way promises can solve coordination problems.[53] This enables him to endorse whatever background rules are most likely to serve this coordination goal.[54] Still another example can be found in Joseph Raz's suggestion that the binding force of promises is justified by the value of the special relationships which promises create.[55] Though Raz does not develop this theory at any length, it might be possible to decide which of all possible relationships were the most valuable and to adopt the background rules that best facilitated those relationships. For example, if relationships that can be terminated at will are less desirable than those that are more difficult to terminate, that might justify a background rule providing for a relatively large measure of damages for breach of contract.

It is important to realize that the selection of background rules designed to promote the substantive values that justify making promises binding is not necessarily inconsistent with freedom of contract. Under a strong version of this approach — that is, a version arguing that the selected background rules should be *mandatory* — freedom of contract would indeed be restricted.[56] But this approach can also be used in a milder version, endorsing the preferred back-

51. J. RAWLS, A THEORY OF JUSTICE 344-48 (1971). The principles of justice themselves are discussed at more length in *id.* at 54-117.

52. *See id.* at 67-83.

53. J. FINNIS, *supra* note 43, at 298-308. See also the discussion of coordination problems in J. RAWLS, *supra* note 51, at 346-48.

54. *See* J. FINNIS, *supra* note 43, at 320-25 (discussing whether contractual obligations should be viewed as giving the promisor a free election between performing and paying damages).

55. *See* Raz, *Promises and Obligations*, *supra* note 8, at 227-28; *see also supra* note 23 and accompanying text.

56. For various perspectives on arguments that might justify the strong version of one of these theories, see Barnett, *Contract Remedies and Inalienable Rights*, 4 SOC. PHIL. & POLY. Autumn 1986, at 179; Kennedy, *Distributive and Paternalist Motives in Contract and Tort Law, With Special Reference to Compulsory Terms and Unequal Bargaining Power*, 41 MD. L. REV. 563 (1982); Kronman, *Paternalism and the Law of Contracts*, 92 YALE L.J. 763 (1983); Radin, *Market-Inalienability*, 100 HARV. L. REV. 1849 (1987). See also the previously cited economics articles, *supra* note 50.

ground rules merely as default rules or methods of interpretation for those cases where the parties have not specified a preference for some other rule.[57] Any system of law, however committed it may be to the idea of freedom of contract, must have some way of resolving those issues on which the parties' contract is silent or ambiguous. A rebuttable presumption in favor of the rule that best serves some substantive moral value is one way to resolve such cases.

B. *Unhelpful Substantive Values*

The preceding section argued that background rules could sometimes be derived from whatever substantive values justified the binding force of promises in the first place. However, only some of the philosophical theories discussed in section I.B rest on substantive values that are of any help in selecting background rules. In this section, I argue that theories which justify the binding force of promises on the basis of the obligation to tell the truth, or on considerations of individual liberty and autonomy, are of no help at all in such an enterprise. Part III then documents this claim by examining writers who attempt to derive implications for contract law from theories based on individual autonomy or the obligation to tell the truth.

1. *Preventing Misrepresentation*

One of the philosophical theories discussed earlier held that promises derive their binding force from the fact that failing to carry out a promise would falsify the promise as a definite statement about the future, thereby violating the obligation to tell the truth.[58] Assume, for the moment, that this theory is sound. The question is what, if anything, it tells us about the proper background rules of contract law.

With respect to the rules governing implied obligations, such as implied warranties, the misrepresentation theory tells us very little. For example, suppose that someone says, "I promise to give you my car in exchange for $5000," and then delivers a car that doesn't run. The misrepresentation theory says that if the speaker can properly be interpreted as saying "I will definitely give you my car, and it will be in good running condition," then the speaker's failure to do so will make her statement false, thereby violating her obligation to tell the truth. On the other hand, the misrepresentation theory also says that

57. *See, e.g.*, Jacob & Youngs, Inc. v. Kent, 230 N.Y. 239, 242, 129 N.E. 889, 891 (1921) ("From the conclusion that promises may not be treated [as one of the parties had urged] without a sacrifice of justice, the progress is a short one to the conclusion that they may not be so treated without a perversion of intention.").

58. *See supra* section I.B.3.

if the speaker is more properly interpreted as saying "I will definitely give you my car, but I guarantee nothing about its condition," the speaker's failure to deliver a working car will not falsify her earlier statement. In other words, the misrepresentation theory leaves the proper outcome entirely dependent on the proper interpretation of the speaker's promise.

There are, of course, any number of ways to resolve this interpretation question. We could look to sociology to tell us how much responsibility most people expect sellers to assume under these circumstances. Alternatively, we could look to other substantive values to try to resolve the interpretation question. For example, if it is more efficient to put responsibility for such problems on the seller, or if relationships that continue over time are for some reason considered more desirable than relationships where each side's involvement ends as soon as the goods change hands, that might justify interpreting such statements as committing the seller to an implied warranty, at least in the absence of explicit statements to the contrary.

Notice, though, that nothing about the misrepresentation theory tells us which method of interpretation we ought to use. The misrepresentation theory is consistent with interpreting promises in accord with whatever default rule most people already expect, or whatever default rule would be most efficient, or whatever default rule best serves some substantive value other than economic efficiency. While the misrepresentation theory of promising tells us that people must live up to the proper interpretation of their promise, it is equally consistent with any of the ways in which the proper interpretation might be identified.[59] Thus, knowing that contracts should be enforced in order to prevent misrepresentation tells us nothing about which method of interpretation ought to be employed, or anything else relevant to deciding whether there should be an implied warranty in this transaction.

For similar reasons, the misrepresentation theory also tells us little about the background rules governing the proper remedy for nonperformance. If the speaker's promise is interpreted as saying, "I will definitely give you this car, rather than any substitute," then only the delivery of the actual car could avoid falsifying that statement, suggesting that a remedy of specific performance would be most appropriate. But other interpretations are also possible — for example, "I will give you this car, or else give you enough money to let you buy an-

59. For a more extensive discussion of this point, with reference to the law of false advertising, see Craswell, *Interpreting Deceptive Advertising*, 65 B.U. L. REV. 657 (1985).

other car just like it." If this is the proper interpretation to place on the speaker's remarks, ordinary market-value damages would be enough to avoid falsifying her statement. Other interpretations are equally possible — *e.g.*, ". . . or else I'll return your purchase price," ". . . or else I'll make good your reliance expenses," or even ". . . or else I'll pay you *X* dollars to make up for it," where *X* could be any number under the sun.

It might be argued that the misrepresentation theory at least establishes that the seller's failure to deliver the car is wrong, and therefore deserves at least *some* sanction. That is, the misrepresentation theory might seem to point us to punishment theory — to principles of deterrence or retribution, or arguments that the severity of the punishment ought to be proportional to the gravity of the offense — to determine the appropriate sanction for nonperformance. However, even this conclusion depends on an implicit resolution of the interpretation issue discussed in the preceding paragraph. If the seller's statement is best interpreted in one of the ways discussed above — say, "I will definitely give you this car, or else I'll return your purchase price" — then there is nothing wrong with the seller's failure to deliver the car, so long as she is at least willing to return the purchase price. Thus, if the quoted language represents the best interpretation of the seller's statement (according to some theory of what makes for the best interpretation), the question of the proper remedy for nondelivery is settled without any need to appeal to punishment theory. To justify looking to punishment theory to determine the sanction, a misrepresentation theorist would first have to establish that the seller's remarks ought to be interpreted as something other than any of the quoted propositions suggested above.

Admittedly, most promisors probably do not explicitly have in mind anything like those quoted propositions.[60] This may be why it seems inherently correct or natural to treat the question of an appropriate remedy as a question for punishment theory, rather than as a question of interpretation. If most promisors have in mind only something like "I will definitely give you this car," then that certainly *could* be interpreted as an agreement that it would be wrong for the seller to fail to turn over the car, thereby calling on punishment theory to determine the appropriate response. At a minimum, it could be argued that such a construction ought to be adopted as the default rule, thereby shifting to any seller who wanted some other remedy the burden of making a more explicit statement to the contrary.

60. *See* O.W. Holmes, The Common Law 237 (1963 ed.) ("when people make contracts, they usually contemplate the performance rather than the breach").

My argument is simply that this construction — the construction that makes the appropriate sanction turn on some theory of punishment — is not in any way entailed by the misrepresentation theory of promising. The value of telling the truth would in no way be compromised by adopting any of the other constructions discussed above, thereby putting the burden of stating otherwise on sellers who object to the chosen construction. Thus, if there is any reason for preferring one possible construction over the others, that reason has to be something more than just the value of telling the truth. It must rest on some belief about what most people already expect, and some argument about why the law ought to fulfill existing expectations; or a belief about what default rule is most efficient, and some argument about why the law should be concerned with efficiency (to cite just two of the possibilities). In other words, the misrepresentation theory settles none of the possible questions about what values the law ought to look to in selecting its background rules.

2. *Individual Autonomy*

Another view of promising justifies the moral force of a promise as a necessary corollary of individual liberty or autonomy.[61] If promises were not binding, it is argued, individual freedom would be unjustifiably restricted, as individuals would be deprived of the freedom to place themselves under a moral obligation respecting their future conduct. While there may be a slight paradox in the notion that freedom must include the freedom to limit one's freedom in the future, advocates of this theory resolve that paradox in favor of allowing individuals to make binding promises.[62]

Autonomy-based theories may well have implications for what I have called "agreement rules," or rules concerning the conditions under which individuals will be allowed to vary the background rules that would otherwise govern their relations. For example, these theorists generally oppose the restrictions on freedom of contract represented by the rule denying enforceability to promises unsupported by consideration, or to promises that are deemed unconscionable.[63] More precisely, they oppose restrictions on the enforceability of promises unless true consent is lacking (*e.g.*, cases of duress), or unless the sub-

61. *E.g.*, C. FRIED, *supra* note 1.

62. *Id.* at 14. *But cf.* 1 M. ROTHBARD, MAN, ECONOMY, AND STATE: A TREATISE ON ECONOMIC PRINCIPLES 153-55 (1962) (offering a libertarian argument that contracts for personal services should never be legally enforceable); *see also infra* note 64.

63. C. FRIED, *supra* note 1, at 28-39, 103-09; Barnett, *supra* note 21, at 313-14.

ject of the promise is not the promisor's to give away.[64] Thus, one necessary part of these theories is a specification of the conditions under which a party's apparent consent will be recognized as valid. As long as these conditions are satisfied, autonomy-based theories hold that any rule or obligation agreed to by the parties should be allowed to govern their relationship.

In cases where the parties have not specified the rule they prefer, however, autonomy-based theories have much less to tell us. In these cases, autonomy-based theories run into the same problem as the misrepresentation theory. Just as any default rule would be consistent with the obligation to tell the truth, any default rule would also be consistent with individual freedom, as long as the parties are allowed to change the rule by appropriate language. Consequently, some other principle must be invoked to decide which of the many possible default rules to adopt. The rule could be chosen by looking to sociological data to determine which rule most parties already expect in various circumstances; it could also be chosen by appealing to some substantive value such as economic efficiency, or Rawls' difference principle, or any other view about what makes some kinds of contractual relationships more valuable than others. Thus, even if those principles have been rejected as valid justifications for the binding force of promises, one or more of them must still be selected to provide the default rules for parties who have not unambiguously specified some other rule in their contract.

The reason that misrepresentation and autonomy-based theories are unhelpful in the selection of default rules is that, of all the philosophical theories discussed earlier in section I.B, these two share the characteristic of being completely content-neutral.[65] They give rea-

64. *Cf.* Barnett, *supra* note 56, at 185-95, 197 (arguing that individuals cannot alienate control over their persons, and thus have no right to provide for the remedy of specific performance in contracts for personal services). Barnett would, however, allow individuals to alienate the disjunctive right to "my personal services or their value in monetary damages, if I subsequently choose not to perform"; he thus would not render contracts for personal services completely unenforceable. *Id.* at 197.

65. A similar concept, "content independence," is employed by Raz, *Authority and Consent*, *supra* note 8, at 114-16 (discussing examples of content independent reasons for action or belief, including promises); *see also* J. RAZ, PRACTICAL REASON AND NORMS, *supra* note 8, at 70 ("[B]oth [decisions and promises] are content-independent reasons: regardless what you promise or decide to do you have a reason to do it because you have promised or decided.").

Raz argued that theories describing the way in which promises constrain a promisor's subsequent deliberations — that is, theories of the sort discussed earlier in section I.A — had to be content-neutral, or else they could not explain the constraint generated by the promise, as opposed to constraints that might argue in favor of doing ø even if no promise had ever been made. However, Raz in no way suggested that theories explaining the moral force of those constraints (theories of the sort discussed *supra* in section I.B) had to be neutral or indifferent with respect to the content of ø. If anything, his suggestions about the special value of certain kinds of relationships suggest the contrary. Raz, *Promises and Obligations*, *supra* note 8, at 228.

sons why an individual who has promised to do ø thereby incurs some form of obligation to do ø, regardless of how ø is filled in. The reason for this neutrality is understandable: To do anything more requires a theory that would tell people what kinds of promises they ought to make. Unfortunately, the theorists' reluctance to advise individuals as to how they ought to exercise their freedom to fill in the content of ø leaves them equally unable to give legal systems any guidance about how to fill in the content of ø when contracting parties fail to specify their preferred content. As a result, these two theories have nothing to contribute to the selection of default rules governing such important topics as implied terms and conditions, excuses, and remedies for breach.

I should stress that this shortcoming in no way undercuts whatever validity these misrepresentation or autonomy-based theories may have in their original capacity, as justifications for the morally binding force of promises. It simply means that if one of these theories is accepted as the justification for the force of promises, some other theory or theories must then be added to provide a basis for selecting appropriate background rules. This other theory must be a theory that is not neutral between the different ways of filling in the exact scope of the parties' obligation — for example, it must provide some reason for preferring promises with an implied warranty to promises without an implied warranty, or vice versa. In other words, this other theory must rely on more than the value of individual autonomy or the value of telling the truth.

III. Two Examples

Part II demonstrated that even if one accepts any of the misrepresentation or autonomy-based theories as justifications for the moral force of promises, there are still important choices to be made concerning the values used to select the law's background rules. Unfortunately, these choices usually receive much less attention from those who write about contract law from the standpoint of misrepresentation or autonomy-based theories. As a result, those authors often end up defending their choice of default rules on an indefensibly ad hoc basis. At other times, they are led to oppose certain default rules unnecessarily, simply because those default rules are supported by certain values that were rivals to the misrepresentation or autonomy-based theory at the level of a justification for the moral force of promises. The final part of this article illustrates the difficulties that such theorists encounter by considering the theories of Charles Fried and Randy Barnett. These two authors have provided the most careful and comprehensive of recent attempts to give contract law a solid philosophical grounding. In addition, each rests his theory of why promises are binding on some version of the value of individual freedom or the obligation to tell the truth.

A. *Charles Fried*

As noted earlier, Fried justifies the obligation to keep a promise primarily by viewing it as a necessary corollary of individual autonomy. "If we decline to take seriously the assumption of an obligation . . . , to that extent we do not take [the promisor] seriously as a person."[66] To be sure, Fried is somewhat ambiguous on this point, for he also emphasizes the injury done to the promisee by the breaking of a promise. For example, he argues that promise-breaking abuses the promisee's trust in the promise, thereby violating the Kantian injunction against treating other people as means rather than as ends.[67] This moves Fried much closer to the misrepresentation theorists: as Fried himself puts it, promise-breaking "is like (but only *like*) lying."[68] But since the autonomy-based and misrepresentation theories are equally unhelpful when it comes to the selection of default rules, an exact classification of Fried's position as between these two theories is unnecessary to my analysis.

1. *Expectation Damages*

On the question of the appropriate remedy for breach, Fried supports the expectation measure of damages, which is designed to give the promisee the same benefits he would have received had the promise been kept. According to Fried, "[i]f I make a promise to you, I should do as I promise; and if I fail to keep my promise, it is fair that I should be made to hand over the equivalent of the promised performance."[69]

A moment's consideration, however, will show that this conclusion cannot be derived solely from the value of individual freedom and autonomy. Fried may well be correct that, in order to give free rein to an

66. C. FRIED, *supra* note 1, at 20-21.

67. *Id.* at 16. I am indebted to John Gardner for pointing out this ambiguity in Fried's position.

68. *Id.* Fried refuses to join the misrepresentation theorists entirely because he interprets the obligation to tell the truth as an obligation not to lie knowingly, thereby imposing no restriction at all on a promisor who at the time of her promise intended to keep the promise. *Id.* at 17. Under the broader version of that obligation endorsed by most misrepresentation theorists, the difference between their theory and Fried's would become very small. *See supra* note 35 and accompanying text.

69. C. FRIED, *supra* note 1, at 17.

individual's autonomy, "[i]t is necessary that I be able to make non-optional a course of conduct that would otherwise be optional for me."[70] But almost any remedy — reliance damages, punitive damages, specific performance, etc. — makes the promised course of conduct non-optional to some degree, depending on the severity of the threatened penalty. There is surely nothing in the idea of individual autonomy that requires the exact degree of non-optionality provided by the expectation measure. The idea of individual autonomy does suggest that individuals should be allowed to make their conduct nonoptional to any extent they choose, by specifying one of these remedies in their contract. But the law must still select one of these remedies as the default rule, and nothing in the notion of individual autonomy gives any reason for favoring the expectation measure over any of the others.[71]

Fried might, of course, have some other value in mind which explains why the expectation measure is to be preferred (unless the parties specify otherwise) over any of the other possible measures. For example, Fried might believe that the expectation measure promotes economic efficiency, or better satisfies Rawls' difference principle, or would better solve most coordination problems. However, no such argument is made anywhere in his book.

Alternatively, Fried might be appealing to data about people's existing beliefs to justify his preference for the expectation measure. He cannot be relying on existing nonlegal practices, for studies of those practices show that people often do not demand (or offer) expectation damages in cases of unexcused nonperformance.[72] However, Fried might be taking existing *legal* practices as his normative benchmark, for Anglo-American law often does employ the expectation measure of damages. That is, Fried's argument might be that because the law adopts liability for expectation damages as one incident of the obligation of promising, anyone who promises thereby accepts that liability as one of the rules of the game. If this is Fried's argument, though, his theory cannot be what *justifies* the law's choice of the expectation measure. The same argument would work equally well to explain why an individual was obliged to respect any other damage rule the law happened to have adopted.

70. *Id.* at 13.

71. For similar criticisms of Fried's autonomy-based argument for expectation damages, see Epstein, *Beyond Foreseeability: Consequential Damages in the Law of Contract*, 18 J. LEGAL STUD. 105, 106-08 (1989); Farber, Book Review, 66 MINN. L. REV. 561, 564-65 (1982).

72. *E.g.*, Epstein, *supra* note 71, at 112-21; Macaulay, *Non-Contractual Relations in Business: A Preliminary Study*, 28 AM. SOC. REV. 55 (1963).

Fried's only other argument in favor of the expectation measure is really an argument against one of the possible alternatives, the reliance measure of damages. When addressing the possible justifications for the binding force of promises, Fried argues against the theory that promises are binding only because promise-breaking would injure those who relied on the promise. Fried goes on, however, to treat his argument against that justification for the binding force of promises as also being an argument against adopting the reliance measure of damages as a default rule.[73] That is, he seems to assume that the reliance measure of damages could only be justified as a default rule if one first accepted the promisee's reliance as an explanation for the binding force of a promise.

If this is Fried's argument, it rests on a *non sequitur.* Granted, one way of arguing for the reliance measure of damages would be to argue that the reason promises are binding is because promise-breaking injures those who rely on the promise. However, it hardly follows that this is the *only* way that the reliance measure of damages can be supported, or that rejection of the reliance justification for the binding force of promises also entails rejection of the reliance measure of damages. This error becomes even more obvious when it is recalled that we are considering the reliance measure of damages as a default rule, which would still leave the parties free to specify the expectation measure (or any other measure of damages) in its place. Adopting the reliance measure merely as a default rule is in some ways inconsistent with the theory that promises are binding only in order to prevent reliance losses, for a default rule lets the parties agree to other damage rules which would effectively make their promise binding even in the absence of any reliance losses. The notion of reliance damages as a default rule seems much more compatible with the views of someone like Fried, who believes that the binding force of promises derives entirely from the freedom of the individual promisors.

In a nutshell, then, the difficulty with Fried's position on expectation damages is the difficulty identified earlier in Part II of this article. Any damage measure is consistent with the ideal of individual autonomy, as long as it is adopted solely as a default rule, since any default rule expands the promisor's options by making it easier for her to make a certain kind of promise. Fried must therefore invoke some other value in order to decide which of the many damage rules to select as a starting point. Moreover, that value will necessarily be one which Fried rejected as a possible justification for the binding force of

73. C. FRIED, *supra* note 1, at 18-19.

promises, for the only value serving that role for Fried — the value of individual autonomy — is equally consistent with all default rules. To choose a default rule, then, Fried has to let one of the other values back into the analysis, and the only question is which one.

2. *Rescission*

Fried encounters a similar problem when he addresses the question of whether a promisee's *only* remedy for nonperformance is to sue for expectation damages, or whether the promisee should also have the option of rescinding the contract and recovering any advance payments. Such an option could be extremely important to the promisee if, for example, the market price of the promised goods had fallen since the time of the contract. In such a case, the promisee would much prefer to get his money back and buy the goods elsewhere (at their new, lower price), rather than merely being allowed to recover from the promisor the market value of any goods that were defective or were not delivered.

Fried initially seems to regard the promisee's right to rescind the contract as being a natural corollary of the binding force of promising. "Parties bind themselves reciprocally. If one party treats himself as not bound, the other may also treat himself as not bound. By breaking his contract, a contractual partner not only opens himself up to claims for damages but releases his opposite number."[74] This argument, though, is subject to the same objections as Fried's argument about the expectation measure. While a system of promising with that default rule would certainly expand a promisor's freedom, so too would an institution of promising with any other rule as its default rule. The quoted passage merely asserts that our system of promising contains rescission as one of its default remedies, without doing anything to justify that rule.

Interestingly, in this case Fried anticipates this very criticism. That is, he acknowledges that it is possible for contracting parties to provide either (a) that nonperformance by one party releases the other party from the contract (in legal terms, making the promises conditional) or (b) that nonperformance by one party does not release the other party from the contract, but only exposes the first party to a suit for damages (in legal terms, making the promises independent). He also notes that such provisions need not be explicitly stated to be effective.[75] In other words, Fried recognizes that there are (at least?) two

74. *Id.* at 117.

75. *Id.* at 118-23.

possible damage rules which parties should be free to invoke, and that the law must somehow decide which rule to treat as invoked in any particular case. As he puts it much earlier in the book, "does your breaking your promise cancel my reciprocal obligation to you or just give me a remedy for my disappointment? There is no obvious a priori reason for one or the other response."[76]

In this case, Fried resolves the dilemma by an explicit appeal to existing expectations, which he reads as supporting a default rule that includes the remedy of rescission. In his words, "[a]ny other outcome would disturb the expectations on which contractual terms *are usually established.*"[77] Unfortunately, Fried says nothing to explain why the expectations of most people in the community should necessarily be dispositive in any individual case. Indeed, at other points in his analysis Fried seems to view the enforcement of community expectations as somehow inconsistent with promissory principles, belonging more to the realm of tort.[78] The problem, of course, is that Fried has to look to *some* outside value to decide whether rescission ought to be accepted as a normal default remedy. In this instance, he "solves" that problem simply by asserting that community expectations ought to govern the matter, without attempting any defense of that position.

3. *Other Default Rules*

Similar difficulties resurface when Fried turns to the rules governing excuse for impracticability, frustration, or mistake. However, Fried takes a somewhat different approach to the selection of the appropriate default rules for these subjects. Fried sees these rules as necessary to fill the "gaps" in the parties' agreement concerning problems which in some sense were unexpected, and for which neither party had agreed to assume responsibility. Because these rules relate to issues outside the scope of the parties' agreement, Fried argues that their justification need not rest on his theory of promises as exercises of individual autonomy. Instead, Fried views these rules as justified by nonpromissory principles such as fault (responsibility for negligently inflicted losses), or what he calls altruism (sharing among members of

76. *Id.* at 46 n.*.

77. *Id.* at 118 (emphasis added). Fried cites no sociological data to support this claim.

78. *Cf. id.* at 4:

> Now tort law typically deals with involuntary transactions — if a punch in the nose, a traffic accident, or a malicious piece of gossip may be called a transaction — so that the role of the community in adjudicating the conflict is particularly prominent. . . . In contrast, so long as we see contractual obligation as based on promise, on obligations that the parties have themselves assumed, the focus of the inquiry is on the will of the parties.

a community).[79] In this context, then, Fried clearly recognizes that he must appeal to substantive, non-content-neutral values.

Fried also believes that many of the rules governing contract formation must depend on values other than individual autonomy. Examples include the common law's "mailbox rule," which provides that an offer cannot be revoked after an acceptance has been posted by the offeree; or the rule that an offer is deemed to lapse (and cannot later be accepted) if it has once been rejected by the offeree. In this area, Fried explicitly recognizes that any number of different default rules are consistent with his theory of promises, and that the offeror should be permitted to specify in her offer whatever rules she wants to apply.[80] Indeed, on the question of which default rule to adopt, he states that "there are no reasons in principle, nothing entailed by the concepts themselves, only considerations of fairness and convenience."[81] In analyzing particular rules, he usually takes the position that the most sensible default rule would be whichever one most offerors would prefer, for that rule saves a majority of offerors the trouble of having to specify a different rule. He then embarks on an analysis of the costs and benefits of each rule to try to determine which rule most offerors would prefer.[82]

In each of these areas, then, Fried is perfectly willing to appeal to some non-content-neutral value such as "fairness and convenience," even though those may not be the values which justify the binding force of promises. Once again, though, Fried never explains why he chooses the particular values he does. For example, why do the rules governing contract formation rest on arguments of "convenience" about the rule that most promisors would prefer, while the rules governing impracticability and mistake rests on principles of "fairness" such as equal sharing? The rules governing impracticability and mistake are always subject to variation by the parties' agreement, so the argument that the law should adopt whatever rule most parties would prefer (in order to save them the trouble of specifying otherwise) would seem just as strong when applied to those issues. Alternatively, if considerations of fairness trump the convenience of the promisor in contracts involving unanticipated risks, why should they not also

79. *Id.* at ch. 5; *see also id.* at ch. 6 (taking a similar approach to the implied obligation of "good faith"). For criticisms of this aspect of Fried's theory, see Atiyah, Book Review, 95 HARV. L. REV. 509, 520-23 (1981), and Reiter, *Good Faith in Contracts*, 17 VAL. U. L. REV. 705, 719-23 (1983).

80. C. FRIED, *supra* note 1, at 47-51.

81. *Id.* at 49.

82. *See id.* at 49 n.* (discussing the rule that an offer lapses once it is rejected by the offeree); *id.* at 52 (discussing the mailbox rule).

trump the convenience of offerors in cases of offers that are delayed in the mail? Without any explicit theory explaining when each of these different values is an appropriate guide, Fried's appeal to different values in different contexts looks more like an *ex post* rationalization of the rules of contract law than a philosophical justification of those rules.

Fried is also on weak ground in explaining his willingness in the areas of impracticability and mistake to make an explicit appeal to values other than individual autonomy, when he was unwilling to allow such appeals in considering the expectation measure of damages. Fried's only justification for looking beyond considerations of individual autonomy when deciding on the rules governing impracticability and mistake is his belief that most parties do not consciously consider the rules they wish to apply to such unexpected contingencies, so enforcing any particular rule can only be justified as a form of involuntary liability.[83] The same is true, however, of parties who make promises without consciously considering what remedies would be available if the promisor fails to perform without an acceptable excuse.[84] If values other than individual freedom and autonomy can be invoked to set the default rules governing impracticability and mistake, it is hard to see why they cannot also be invoked to set the default rules governing remedies for nonperformance.

When all is said and done, then, Fried's theory about what justifies the binding force of promises — the theory which derives promises' force from considerations of individual freedom and autonomy — plays very little role in his derivation of any of the relevant default rules. Unfortunately, Fried's preoccupation with his theory of promising seems to prevent him from developing a coherent theory of the values that *should* play a role in selecting default rules. Sometimes Fried relies on people's existing expectations; sometimes he uses economic arguments; sometimes he rests on principles of "fault" or "altruism"; and sometimes, as in the case of expectation damages, he advances no justification at all. Such a scattershot approach to the selection of default rules does little to advance our understanding of contract law.

B. *Randy E. Barnett*

As noted earlier, Barnett views promises as transferring to the

83. *Id.* at 60.

84. *See supra* note 60. A similar point has been made by Atiyah, *Misrepresentation, Warranty, and Estoppel*, 9 ALBERTA L. REV. 347, 353 (1971).

promisee the promisor's property right in the promised good or service. He therefore treats the obligation to carry out a promise as a specific instance of the more general obligation to respect property rights.[85] While this explanation of the binding force of promises differs from Fried's in some respects, Fried and Barnett are actually very close on the underlying question of why anyone is obliged to respect property rights (in Barnett's case) or promises (in Fried's). Just as Fried defended the obligation to keep a promise on the ground that the power to make binding promises is a necessary corollary of individual liberty, Barnett sees the power to make binding transfers of property as justifiable on essentially libertarian grounds.[86]

Unlike Fried, however, Barnett does not view the obligation to carry out one's promise as binding only when the promisor truly and subjectively agrees to undertake that obligation. Barnett argues that any workable system of property rights must make use of clear signals of entitlement — boundary markers and title recordation in the case of real estate; objective manifestations of consent in the case of contracts — in order to give maximal guidance to those who need to know what their rights are.[87] Thus, in Barnett's view it is not inconsistent with individual liberty to hold individuals liable whenever they manifest their consent to an obligation, even if they subjectively intended to consent to no such thing. According to Barnett, a contrary rule would be inconsistent with the equal liberty of others, who may need to know whether the individual is subject to an obligation or not.[88]

Thus, an important operational difference between Barnett and Fried lies in Barnett's willingness to endorse the objective theory of interpretation as applied to contract law.[89] This frees Barnett from at least one of the difficulties faced by Fried. Fried believed that any background rules pertaining to promissory matters could rest only on

85. *See supra* notes 21-22 and accompanying text.

86. Barnett, *supra* note 21, at 297-99. At least, if one asks why individuals should have the authority to decide whether and when to transfer away their property rights, Barnett's answer is libertarian: Such a right is the best way of "facilitating freedom of human action . . . ." *Id.* at 297. If one asks why freedom of action is itself a desirable thing, his answer sounds closer to economic or utilitarian notions of preference-satisfaction: Liberty is the best way of facilitating individuals' "pursuit of survival and happiness." Barnett, *Pursuing Justice in a Free Society: Part I — Power v. Liberty,* 4 CRIM. JUST. ETHICS 50, 57 (Summer/Fall 1985). Barnett differs from most economists, however, in his willingness to endorse a particular "vision of the good life for men," rather than relying solely on empirical observations about what people happen to prefer. *Id.* at 71 n.49. Since freedom itself is the only aspect of Barnett's vision of the good life that he invokes in his writings about contract law, it seems appropriate to describe his position as resting ultimately on the value of individual freedom.

87. Barnett, *supra* note 21, at 301-07.

88. *Id.* at 305-06.

89. *Id.* at 300-09; *cf.* C. FRIED, *supra* note 1, at 61-67 (criticizing the objective theory of interpretation as inconsistent with individual liberty).

the value of individual autonomy; he therefore had to exclude large areas of contract law (*e.g.*, mistake, impracticability, and offer and acceptance) from the promissory sphere, in order to accept default rules in those areas which were based on other values.[90] Barnett faces no such obstacle to the acceptance of default rules based on other values, for an "objective" interpretation of any given promise will necessarily depend on factors other than the promisor's subjective act of will.

However, Barnett still faces the task of figuring out just which values *should* inform the objective interpretation of any particular action or agreement. Under Barnett's view of promises as marking consent to the transfer of property rights, the rules governing each party's obligations can be described by specifying exactly which rights have been transferred. To use one of Barnett's examples, if a person who agrees to a sale of a car is best viewed as making an unconditional transfer of the right to that car, the buyer would be entitled to specific performance if the seller fails to hand over the property. If the seller is instead viewed as making a conditional transfer of the right to the car *or* the right to damages for nonperformance, the buyer could not sue for specific performance, but only for monetary damages.[91] As Barnett puts it elsewhere, "[m]ost 'real world' contractual disputes involve determining precisely which rights were intended to be transferred by the parties."[92] While this passage could be read as referring to the actual, subjective intentions of the parties, his other writing makes it clear that the only relevant intentions are those indicated by all the objective markers of consent.[93]

Unfortunately, Barnett does not tell us how to decide which rights we should deem transferred by any particular set of objective indicators. In some cases, he looks solely to existing expectations about the obligations normally assumed by parties in similar circumstances. For example, Barnett would usually resolve the issue discussed in the preceding paragraph in favor of the specific performance remedy, treating the parties as agreeing to an absolute transfer of rights (unless the contract specifies otherwise). His principal rationale for this result is that "most people would expect that when the contract is executed [the buyer] has a right to the specified land or car."[94]

90. *See supra* notes 79-84 and accompanying text.

91. Barnett, *supra* note 56, at 195-96.

92. Barnett, *Squaring Undisclosed Agency Law with Contract Theory*, 75 CALIF. L. REV. 1969, 1979 (1987).

93. Barnett, *supra* note 21, at 301-07.

94. Barnett, *supra* note 56, at 195. *But cf. infra* note 95. Barnett also argues that his preferred rule would properly place the burden of arguing against specific performance on the guilty breacher, rather than on the innocent plaintiff. *See* Barnett, *supra* note 56, at 182. However, this

At other times, Barnett relies on economic arguments about the efficiency of various rules. For example, he suggests that his presumption in favor of specific performance might be reversed in cases where specific performance would be extremely difficult for the seller and a fungible replacement good is easily available to the buyer.[95] On another topic, he argues that an employer who hires an employee but then dismisses him before the job has even begun should normally be treated as having assumed responsibility for any reliance losses the employee suffers — for example, if the employee has given up his prior job or incurred significant moving expenses. Barnett's rationale is a straightforward economic one: employers usually have better information about the risk that the employee will not be needed, so employers will usually be the better risk bearer.[96] At other times, though, Barnett seems to view his theory as not requiring any explicit recourse to economic analysis. For example, he asserts that even if his consent theory is consistent with the dictates of economic efficiency, it is still superior because its outcomes can often be determined "without resorting to an explicit efficiency analysis."[97]

Even more troubling, on other occasions Barnett (like Fried) seems to believe that certain default rules are somehow inherent in the concepts employed by his theory and therefore do not require normative justification of any sort. As an example, consider Barnett's analysis of the undisclosed agency problem which arises when an agent *A* buys goods from a third party *T* and turns them over to his undisclosed principal *UP*, whereupon *UP* gives *A* money to pay *T* for the goods, but *A* becomes insolvent and *T* never receives his payment.[98] Barnett concludes that *T* can sue *UP* to collect his payment, even though this will make *UP* pay twice, once to the now-insolvent *A* and once to *T*. Barnett's argument is that the agency agreement between *UP* and *A* authorized *A* to transfer to *T* any of *UP*'s rights. Once *A* entered into the purchase agreement with *T*, then, the transfer to *T* of *UP*'s owner-

argument is clearly incorrect, for we cannot decide whether the seller is guilty of a breach until after we decide how to interpret the transaction. If the transaction is best interpreted as transferring the right to the specified good or to its equivalent in monetary damages, there is nothing "guilty" in the seller paying monetary damages instead of handing over the good.

95. Barnett, *supra* note 56, at 196 n.59 ("Where these circumstances can be shown to exist. . . it may no longer be safe to presume that sellers would have consented to specific relief."). Barnett would also refuse to allow specific performance in contracts for personal services. *See supra* note 64 and accompanying text. But this is because he believes people should not have the authority to limit their future freedom to this extent.

96. Barnett & Becker, *Beyond Reliance: Promissory Estoppel, Contract Formalities, and Misrepresentations*, 15 HOFSTRA L. REV. 443, 478-80 (1987).

97. Barnett, *supra* note 92, at 1976.

98. *Id.* at 1984.

ship of the purchase price became an accomplished fact, and *UP* therefore had no right to resist *T*'s demand for payment.[99]

While this description of the transaction may be consistent with the rules of agency law, it in no way *justifies* or explains those rules. The problem is that Barnett never justifies his construction of the underlying agency agreement between *UP* and *A*, which he reads as empowering *A* to make an unconditional transfer of *UP*'s rights. At least as a matter of logic, that agency agreement could equally well be interpreted as giving *A* the more limited power to make a conditional transfer of *UP*'s rights (conditional on *A*'s not becoming insolvent), thereby putting the risk of *A*'s insolvency on *T* rather than on *UP*. Either arrangement is perfectly consistent with the principle of giving fair notice to *T*, as long as the legal rule is clear in advance so that *T* knows the degree of risk he is being asked to assume. To put the same point slightly differently, either rule would represent a perfectly "objective" interpretation of the agreement. To argue for one rule over the other, Barnett would have to point to some other reason — efficiency, existing expectations, etc. — to explain why it was better to put the risk of *A*'s insolvency on *UP* rather than on *T*, at least as a presumptive matter. He would then have to explain why the reason he selected (efficiency, or whatever) was the appropriate principle to look to in selecting a default rule.

In discussing a more complex problem of undisclosed agency law, Barnett does suggest an awareness of some of these difficulties. In a footnote, he states:

> Developing a consent theory's approach to construing contractual intent when parties are silent on an issue would require a lengthy and separate treatment. Such an effort would involve, among other topics: (1) a discussion of tacit versus expressed knowledge; (2) the presumption that the parties intended what most similarly situated parties would have intended ex ante, thus putting the onus on a minority of parties to express their dissent from the majority by an express term; and (3) the likely incentive effects of the principles of construction on the bargaining behavior of other parties.[100]

Other topics for discussion could easily be added to this list — for example, (4) the conditions under which transaction costs make it difficult for parties to vary the default rule by an express term to the contrary, and (5) the principle that ought to be used to select the default rule in those cases where whatever rule the law selects is likely to

99. *Id.* at 1984-85.

100. *Id.* at 1986 n.71.

remain in force for most parties.[101]

What Barnett does not seem to realize, however, is how little can be accomplished with respect to the content of the law's background rules until this "lengthy and separate treatment" has been completed. Without a theory of interpretation, the only guidance we are left with in selecting default rules is that the law should take an objective approach to interpretation. But to endorse an objective approach is merely to identify one factor — the secret, subjective intention of either party — which should *not* be used as a reason for preferring one rule over another. It says nothing about which factors *should* be considered. It thus leaves unresolved all the debates concerning the role of efficiency as a goal of contract law, or the extent to which contract law should be shaped by redistributional concerns or other values. Barnett may have rejected those values as inadequate explanations for the binding force of promises, but their role in the selection of default rules remains completely open.

Conclusion

Debates over the question of why promises are binding will no doubt continue to occupy the attention of philosophers and legal scholars. Such debates raise issues that are fundamental to western political thought — issues such as individual freedom versus collective control, economic efficiency versus non-economic values, or (more generally) consequentialist systems of ethics versus deontological ones. Any question that offers such a tempting array of topics will always be the subject of frequent visits by scholars, and the question of why promises are binding is no exception.

My thesis is that debates over the question of why promises are binding do much less than is commonly supposed to settle the role to be played by efficiency, non-economic values, or ethical theories generally in selecting contract law's background rules. More precisely, I have argued that certain answers to the question of why promises are binding do nothing to settle these larger issues. Theories that explain the binding force of promises by pointing to the value of individual freedom, or the obligation to tell the truth, may well be valid answers to the question of why promises are binding. But truth and freedom can usually be served equally well by any background rule, so some other value must be introduced to explain why any one rule ought to be chosen over any other. And when we ask *which* values ought to be

101. For a discussion of these issues from an economic perspective, see the articles cited *supra* in note 3.

introduced for this purpose, we thereby reopen the entire debate about the role of efficiency, non-economic values, and other ethical theories. Even if we have rejected any particular value as an explanation of why promises are binding in the first place, that does not settle the question of whether that value can or should be used in selecting a default rule.

In short, much of the current philosophical debate about the binding force of promises is simply irrelevant to contract law's choice of background rules. Legal philosophers who are interested in the content of contract law should direct their energies to this question, and not solely to the question of why promises ought to be binding.

[9]

A BARGAINING THEORY APPROACH TO DEFAULT PROVISIONS AND DISCLOSURE RULES IN CONTRACT LAW*

JULES L. COLEMAN**
DOUGLAS D. HECKATHORN***
Steven M. Maser****

I. THE PROBLEM

Legal rules facilitate as well as constrain human freedom. H.L.A. Hart captures the difference between these two functions of law by distinguishing between primary and secondary rules.[1] Primary rules impose obligations and thereby constrain behavior. Secondary rules empower individuals to create relations that confer rights and impose duties.[2] Thus, the criminal law constrains individual liberty; the law of contracts enhances it.

Within this framework, the foundation of contracting is mutual agreement. Contractual duties are self-imposed. They are consequences of individuals authoritatively exercising their autonomy under private enabling rules. Coercive civil authority is justifiably employed to enforce contractual obligations because the parties have agreed so to constrain themselves. Of course, even if the parties to a contract agree to bind themselves to one another, it does not follow that they have agreed thereby to

* The earlier versions of this article were presented at the University of Virginia and at conferences on Norms (in Delaware), Legal Liability (at Bowling Green State University), and the Calculus of Consent (at Santa Cruz). The article benefited from comments made on every such occasion. The authors are especially indebted to Alan Schwartz and Randy Barnett for comments, criticisms and suggestions on earlier drafts. The authors would also like to acknowledge support provided by the following grants: Guggenheim Foundation Fellowship (Coleman); George A. and Eliza Gardner Howard Foundation (Heckathorn); Atkinson Fund of Willamette University (Maser).

** Professor of Law and Philosophy, Yale Law School.

*** Associate Professor, Departments of Sociology and Economics, University of Missouri-Kansas City.

**** Professor, Atkinson Graduate School of Management, Willamette University.

1. H.L.A. HART, CONCEPT OF LAW (1961).

2. Hart is not always consistent in drawing the distinction. He characterizes secondary rules as power conferring. Some confer power on private individuals, others authorize officials. Unfortunately, the rule of recognition, which for Hart is the signature of a legal system, is a secondary rule, but it confers power on no one.

have their obligations to one another enforced by the state (or by any other third party).[3]

A. *The Default Rule*

On the assumption that contracting parties are narrowly rational and fully informed, a contract between them that foresees and responds to all possible contingencies would be efficient, or Pareto optimal. That is the definition of a fully specified contract. Because a fully specified contract is efficient, it puts the parties to it in a position where neither can improve his or her lot except at the other's expense. A fully specified contract is also an equilibrium, that is, it is self-enforcing in the sense that no party has an incentive unilaterally to defect from its terms.

Although imagining problems in contract design and execution and devising adequate safeguards against all possible sources of contract failure is a logical possibility, it remains (for everyone but the Gods) a practical impossibility. Even were it practically possible, fully specifying a contract might be irrational in that the expected costs of a more complete specification may exceed the expected gains from nailing down a particular solution to an imaginable, but unlikely, possibility.

Unlikely events are not impossible, however. Contingencies arise with which the contractors have not explicitly dealt. Such is the stuff of contracts casebooks. When contingencies arise for which no adequate provisions have been made ex ante, the parties may disagree about their respective rights and duties ex post. Sometimes they are able to resolve the conflict privately. If they are unable to resolve the conflict privately, however, the

3. Randy Barnett (and much black letter law) holds a different view. For him, to contract is to commit oneself to an enforcement mechanism. This view presupposes a conception of contract embedded within legal or other institutions, including those with the authority and power to enforce contractual terms. *See* Barnett, *The Consent Theory of Contract*, 86 COLUM. L. REV. 269 (1986). We can distinguish between two senses of "contract." The first is the legal one in which to contract is to commit oneself to a coercively enforceable set of rights and responsibilities. The other is the ordinary langage or nontechnical sense in which legal enforcement is not presupposed. Our goal here is to understand the legal practice of contracting. To do so, we believe it is helpful to explain the roles of courts in enforcing agreements by asking under what conditions, if any, rational parties would call upon third parties, including courts, to facilitate or to enforce agreements between them. This approach presupposes that we can imagine circumstances of contracting without law. Thus we take the ordinary sense of contracting as basic and the legal or juridical one as derivative. We explain the latter in terms of failures of private contracting, as we define that term later in this article.

parties may find themselves in court. What rights and responsibilities can a judge, legitimately exercising his or her authority, impose upon them ex post?

It is often suggested that a judge should apply the following general rule: confer those rights and impose those duties to which the parties would have agreed ex ante.[4] Thus, when transaction costs make an explicit agreement too costly ex ante, the court should apply a *default* rule that "mimics" the outcome of a hypothetical contract between them.[5] The hypothetical contract is the one the parties would have made had transaction costs not made their doing so irrational.

As a default rule, the ex ante contract raises two distinct kinds of issues. The first concerns the content of the rule. How are we to model or to understand the ex ante contract? The second concerns the justification a court might have for imposing upon litigating parties the rights and responsibilities implied by the ex ante contract. The problem of justification is complicated by the fact that the parties are being held in contract to terms to which they did not explicitly agree. Given the ex post nature of the obligations and rights it distributes, is there any reason to think that one default rule is any more justifiable than another? Is there, in particular, a case to be made for the ex ante contract as the default rule?

B. *Consent and the Default Rule*

One approach to the problem of justifying a default rule is to connect it to a general theory of contractual obligation. What kind of argument might the theory of contractual obligation suggested by Hart's notion of a private empowering rule—that is, a consent theory—offer? What, in other words, is the relevant connection between explicit consent and hypothetical ex ante contracting?

We can distinguish between at least two kinds of arguments a consent theorist might advance to support the claim that an ex ante hypothetical contract is a uniquely appropriate way to es-

4. *See* Schwartz, *Proposals for Products Liability Reform: A Theoretical Synthesis*, 97 YALE L.J. 353 (1988), in which the tort problem of specifying the conditions of liability for defective product is recast as a contracts problem: that is, the terms of liability should be those the parties would have agreed to ex ante.

5. This is, of course, not the only default rule a judge can apply. In the alternative, a court might assign rights and responsibilities according to a principle of social justice, wealth redistribution or insurance.

tablish ex post the terms of incompletely specified contracts. The first argument relies on the justificatory force of hypothetical consent. Roughly, the argument is as follows: the claims the parties have explicitly imposed upon one another are legitimately enforced against the parties because they have actually consented to those terms. The default rule imposes rights and responsibilities to which the parties would have consented. To the same extent and in the same way that consent justifies a court imposing the rights and responsibilities made explicit in a contract, hypothetical consent justifies imposing the rights and responsibilities that are implied by the application of the default rule. Is the argument persuasive?

In the case of explicit consent, we recognize a difference between *unfree* acts and *irrational* ones. A person may consent to conduct detrimental to his interests (irrational, but free), or he may be compelled against his will to promote his interests (rational, but unfree—as in some forms of paternalism). The distinction between consent and rational self-interest becomes murkier in arguments attempting to establish the terms to which a particular person conceived of in a particular way *would* have consented. An example drawn from the economic analysis of law nicely illustrates this problem in arguments from hypothetical consent and the additional, more fundamental problem of justifying the imposition of duties ex post on the grounds that they would have been agreed to ex ante.

Economists evaluate allocations of resources and states of the world by the criterion of efficiency. From the moral point of view, is the efficiency of an allocation or of a social state a desirable property of it? In effect, this question is an invitation to consider the normative underpinnings of economic analysis. Moral arguments in favor of efficiency are of two sorts: utilitarian and consensual.[6] Only the latter concerns us here.

Economists distinguish among three criteria of economic efficiency: Pareto superiority, Pareto optimality and Kaldor-Hicks efficiency. S^1 is *Pareto superior* to S^0 if and only if no one prefers S^0 to S^1 and at least one person prefers S^1 to S^0. S is *Pareto optimal* if and only if there exists no S^i Pareto superior to it. S^1 is *Kaldor-Hicks efficient* to S^0 if and only if S^1 is potentially Pareto superior to S^0. S^1 is potentially Pareto superior to S^0 if in going

6. *See* J. Coleman, Markets, Morals and the Law 95-132 (1988).

from S^0 to S^1 resources could be arranged so that no one prefers S^0 to S^1 and at least one person prefers S^1 to S^0. Because the other efficiency concepts are defined in terms of Pareto superiority, we might ask what the relationship between it and consent could be. The consensual defense of Pareto superiority is very simple, and although it has been employed primarily by Richard Posner in his defense of efficiency, the argument has its roots in Nicholas Kaldor's work some fifty years earlier.[7] The argument is as follows:

(1) S^1 is Pareto superior to S^0 if and only if no one prefers S^0 to S^1 and at least one prefers S^1 over S^0.

(2) Therefore, each person would consent to S^1, that is, would choose S^1 over S^0.

Some Pareto improvements like rational, voluntary market transactions are in fact consented to, though it remains a further question whether typical market transactions are morally defensible because they are Pareto improving or because they have been voluntarily consummated. In any case, many Pareto improvements are not consented to by every person affected. Take the famous case of *Vincent v. Lake Erie Transportation Co.*[8] In this case, a dock owner refused to allow a ship to remain docked beyond the period of time set forth by the terms of a contract between the dock owner and the ship's captain, and ordered it to leave. The captain refused to set his ship free because it would very likely have been lost at sea, a victim of an impending storm. The ship remained docked, the storm came, and the ship repeatedly smashed the dock, resulting in $500 damages to the dock. The court held that even though the ship's captain acted correctly in firmly tying the boat to the dock, he was required to compensate the dock owner. If the ship's captain acted rationally, he was better off taking the risk and compensating the dock owner ex post than he would have been had he set the ship to sea. Provided the dock owner was fully compensated for whatever damages resulted from the ship captain's decision, the dockowner should be indifferent between what actually occurred and what would have occurred had the captain set his ship afloat. Thus, the outcome of the case constitutes a Pareto improvement, but not one to which all the relevant parties consented. In fact, the dock owner made

7. For a discussion of the argument, see *id.* at 115-29.
8. 100 Minn. 456, 124 N.W. 221 (1910).

every effort to express his unwillingness to agree to the captain's decision. Here we have a Pareto improvement that could not be justified on the grounds of consent.[9]

So the consent argument for the legal rule must be that ex ante the parties seeking to maximize overall wealth or utility *would have consented* to it, not that they actually *did* consent. The premise in that argument is simply the one stated above: all the relevant parties are made better off by the Pareto improving state (or at least are made no worse off by it). Thus, they prefer the Pareto improving state to the Pareto inferior one (Premise One). To say that they prefer one state to the other is to say that under normal conditions they *would choose* the former to the latter (Conclusion): thus we have the connection of Pareto superiority to hypothetical consent. The premise in the argument expresses the individual rationality of the proposed change; the conclusion expresses the parties' hypothetical consent to it. From the fact that a social state makes someone no worse off (that is, it is not irrational for him), we are to infer that the agent would have consented to it. Consent follows as a matter of *logic* from considerations of rationality.

Consequently, the concept of hypothetical consent expresses nothing that is not already captured in the idea of rational self-interest. The distinction between consent and rationality central to moral theory apparently evaporates. The claim that imposing obligations ex post is justified because the parties would have consented to them ex ante adds nothing to a defense of such a proposal that is not already expressed by the argument that imposing obligations ex post is justified whenever such obligations would have been *rational* for the parties ex ante. Thus, the reliance on ex ante rational bargaining provides a rationality or welfarist defense of the default rule, not a consensualist one.

A consent theorist needs another way of connecting hypo-

9. Posner has argued that by accepting compensation ex post, one gives consent, *see* Posner, *The Ethical and Political Basis of the Efficiency Norm in Common Law Adjudication*, 8 HOFSTRA L. REV. 487, 491 (1980), which in this case means that in spite of his protestations to the contrary, the dock owner consented to the captain's decision by accepting compensation. Surely this is seriously confused; first, because often people demand compensation not to give their consent to being harmed, but as *redress* for a wrong done to them; second, because if to accept compensation is to give consent, then the only way not to consent is to refuse compensation, which, of course, would ordinarily count *as giving consent*. The argument that compensation constitutes consent has things absolutely backwards.

thetical rational bargaining to hypothetical consent, a way that maintains both the analytic distinction between the two and the significance of both to a full consensual defense of contractual obligation. One approach could rely on the claim that the relationship between hypothetical rational bargaining and hypothetical consent is *epistemic*, not analytic. What it would have been rational for the parties to bargain for ex ante is not *equivalent* to what they would have agreed to, nor does it formally imply their agreement. It is, nevertheless, *evidence*, perhaps the best evidence, of what the parties would have agreed to ex ante. Rather than trying to derive hypothetical consent from rationality, the suggestion is that the former provides presumptive evidence of the latter. In the absence of contradictory evidence, that is, evidence contrary to that derived from the hypothetical rational bargain, it is legitimate to infer that the parties would have consented to that which would have been the outcome of a rational bargain between them.

The consent theorist's first strategy for defending the ex ante contract as a default rule, then, ultimately rests on the fact that what would have been rational for the parties ex ante is extremely strong evidence of the terms to which they would have agreed. What the parties would have agreed to ex ante in turn provides some justification for holding them to the terms ex post. This line of defense is, of course, incomplete pending an account of why it is that something to which individuals would have agreed (though they did not in fact) provides a civil authority with grounds for imposing those conditions upon them now (when they quite explicitly do not agree to those conditions).

The second line of defense open to the consent theorist is designed to obviate this last problem. In this view, by the very act of contracting the parties consent not only to a framework of explicitly created rights and duties, but to a jurisdiction for resolving conflicts that might arise in construing those rights and duties. Should the occasion arise, the jurisdiction to which the parties consent is authorized to impose rights and duties ex post that were not made explicit ex ante. To contract is, among other things, to consent to the relevant default provisions of the law. Thus, the rights and responsibilities allocated by a default rule ex post are, in a suitable sense, consented to ex ante. This line of argument eliminates the need to demonstrate either that the terms imposed by the default rule would have been consented to by the parties, or that what the parties would have consented to ex ante provides a reason for imposing those terms upon them now. The importance of hypothetical consent simply disappears, and with it the need to establish an evidentiary or analytic connection between it and the ex ante rational bargain.

This approach appears to obviate two problems— specifying the relationship (analytic or epistemic) between rational bargaining and hypothetical consent, and arguing for the normative punch of the latter—but at the expense of creating others. The problem is that if this line of argument constitutes a sound consensual defense of the ex ante contract default rule, it also constitutes an equivalently good defense of all default rules. For if by consenting to a contract, one consents to a jurisdiction's default rule, then one consents to whatever rule the court applies—from those rules aimed at reconstructing a hypothetical bargain to those imposing fair terms, to others imposing efficient terms, to those imposing obnoxious terms, and so on. This reconstruction of the consent theory of contractual obligation, in other words, provides no sense in which the ex ante rational contract is special. If the ex ante rational bargain as a default rule has a special attraction for this sort of consent theorist, it cannot be, strictly speaking, a matter of consent.

If this argument works at all, it works too well. The next question is whether it works at all. It makes sense to say that two contracting parties consent to the obligations and rights their contract specifies to the extent each has alternative opportunities, or at least provided that none of the contractual terms are imposed unwillingly upon either of them. It follows, then, that the parties could be said to consent to a relevant authority's default rule only if they willingly, that is, noncoercively, choose it. This is not typically the case, however. The default rule of any jurisdiction is generally a non-negotiable part of their bargain. For that reason, it is questionable whether by consenting to a framework of contractual rights and responsibilities, the parties consent to the application of the operative default rule.

It is no counterargument that the parties could reduce the extent to which they rely upon the default rule. Although it is true that the parties could more fully specify their contract and thereby reduce the scope of the rule's application, this shows only that the parties can agree to reduce or to minimize the rule's impact, not that in doing so they consent to the rule's use in the areas they do not contract around.

To feel comfortable with the claim that by contracting parties consent to the relevant default rule, we would have to assume something like a competitive market in authoritative jurisdictions. Then, the parties would choose jurisdictions based, among other things, on the default rule in effect.

If the consent theorist's claim is that a default rule is justified to the extent that it would be freely chosen in a competitive market for authoritative jurisdictions, then he too ends up relying upon arguments from hypothetical, not explicit consent. Moreover, the argument the consent theorist would very likely employ to defend the ex ante contract as a default rule would be that among all the possible rules, it is the one that is rational for the parties ex ante. In other words, the ex ante contract is individually and collectively rational and, for those reasons, would have been chosen by rational parties free to pick among alternative default rules. The rationality of the default rule follows from the fact that it reduces the costs of contracting. It enables each party to avoid the costs under other rules of contracting out, of ever more fully specifying their contract. Once again, the argument for the ex ante contract ultimately relies on hypothetical consent and a relationship, analytic or epistemic, between what is rational for someone ex ante and what that person would have consented to ex ante. The effort to replace hypothetical with explicit consent does not, in the end, avoid these problems.

In effect we can characterize a kind of research program for a consent theorist bent on defending the ex ante contract as a uniquely appropriate default rule. The program has three components. The first is to specify rigorously the content of the hypothetical rational bargain between the parties. The second is to determine what sort of evidence, if any, exists about what the parties would have agreed to that could ever contradict the evidence supplied by the hypothetical rational bargain. The third problem we have already mentioned. Even if we can specify rigorously the content of hypothetical rational bargains envisaged by the default rule, and can determine successfully in individual cases (or in general) the reliability of this information for demonstrating what the parties would in fact have agreed to, it is a further question whether what they would have consented to provides a court with sufficient justification for imposing those terms upon them, let alone whether it provides the same sort of justification their actual consent would.

C. *Rationality and the Default Rule*

One problem that keeps emerging when we try to develop a hypothetical consent defense of the default rule is that the best evidence we have of what the parties would have agreed to is that to which it would have been rational for them to agree. We are left then to draw inferences from the latter to the former on the apparent assumption that, as between the two, only the former—what the parties would have consented to—provides a justification for allocating rights and responsibilities. Perhaps that assumption is unwarranted; perhaps considerations of rationality have justificatory force on their own. In that case, one could more straightforwardly defend the ex ante contract not on the grounds that parties in fact agree to it or would have agreed to the allocation of rights and responsibilities it sets out, but on the grounds that it or the rights and responsibilities it imposes are *rational*.

In this approach *rationality*, not consent, is the basis of contractual obligation and the foundation of legitimate third party enforcement. Thus, the justification for applying the default rule is not that it constitutes or is presumptive evidence of the parties' consent, but that, when made rigorous, it specifies rights and obligations that are rational for the parties. Such rights and responsibilities, because they are rational, are justifiably imposed on the parties.

This approach, which can also be characterized as a research program, also raises three kinds of problems. First, like the consent theory, the rationality theory must specify rigorously the content of the hypothetical rational bargain between the parties. Second, while the consent theory has an intuitively plausible theory of enforceable claims made explicit in contracts, it lacks a plausible theory of the default rule. That is, it takes consent as justificationally basic and is left to explain the relevance of rationality to consent. In contrast, the rationality theory has a plausible interpretation of the default rule: that is, the default rule provides a specification of the terms to which it would be rational for the parties to have agreed. It must now give a plausible account of the role of actual consent, when such consent is present. In other words, because the rationality theory takes principles of rationality as justificationally basic, it gives an immediate explanation of the relevance of the default rule. It is left, however, with the task of explaining the significance of explicit consent in contract. If rationality carries the moral weight, what significance does consent have? Third, the rationality theory must show why rationality binds. We take it for granted that a state of affairs to which individuals voluntarily agree is, ceteris paribus, morally unobjectionable. But it is not obvious how the moral defensibility of a state of the world can be said to follow from its rationality.

In the rationality view, the relationship between rationality and actual consent cannot be one of entailment. Just as it does not follow logically that people agree to what is in their interests, it cannot follow logically that what they agree to is rational for them. Thus, in the rationality theory, actual consent, when present, does not justify; rather it provides *evidence*, again perhaps the best evidence, of what is rational for the parties. There is an interesting analogy in the relationship of consent to rational bargaining in the consent and rationality theories of contractual obligation. In the consent theory, rationality provides evidence of consent. In the rationality theory, consent provides evidence of rationality. Both theories also face justificatory obstacles. The consent theory may explain how consent justifies, but its adherence to the default rule requires it to explain how hypothetical consent justifies. Similarly, the rationality theory explains the relevance of the default rule, but it needs to explain the moral relevance of rationality.

Common to both strategies, moreover, is the problem of specifying the content of the default rule. The difference between them is the normative use to which the model is put. In the consent theory, the model of the "ex ante bargain" provides evidence of the terms to which the parties would have consented. In the rationality theory, it specifies what in a particular case, is rational, and, given appropriate premises connecting rationality to morality, what morally can be required of the parties.

What we have done so far is sketch out two research programs. Both rely on the ex ante bargain as a default rule, but which gives a better justification of the legitimacy of a court's applying that rule? In this article we do not intend to adjudicate this dispute in the normative theory of contract. Our aims here are in a sense both more modest and more ambitious. We intend to take seriously the concept of the ex ante bargain and give it some flesh. We want to take appeals to the rational bargain that until now have been more abstract than concrete and give them some structure and rigor. It is not our concern here whether in doing so we advance the cause of any particular theory of contractual obligation. Our goal is to make a contribution to contract theory more generally: for without a specification of the parameters and structure of the rational bargain, appeals to it, however attractive in theory, will be empty in practice. Thus, we intend to give a full and rigorous characterization of rational bargaining in a way that will shed considerable light on both the analytic and the normative questions of contractual obligation. In the course of our presentation of this analytic structure, we attempt to explain how a central doctrine of contract law—disclosure—can be usefully illuminated by conceiving of the process of contracting as a scheme of rational bargaining.

If the idea of the contract as a rational bargain is ultimately unpersuasive, or if our efforts to illuminate some contract doctrines in rational choice terms is unconvincing, we nevertheless would have provided a way of giving content to the default rule: a way that is both rigorous and rich. For the idea of a rational bargain is a complex one, far more complex and difficult to apply than either contract theorists or judges have until now grasped.

II. The Rational Contract

A. *Bargaining and Contract: Introduction*

We begin by looking at how two parties engage in a contractual transaction, how they secure a rational bargain, *without law*. Our analysis benefits from recent formal literature on bargaining under both complete and imperfect information, part of the theory of cooperative games. It looks at how people resolve disputes involving elements of both conflict and cooperation. We depict contracting as a divisible prisoners dilemma game. Here, the parties secure no contract unless they agree on a way of enforcing their agreement and of distributing any potential gains. The conditions under which they invoke third-party participation, including judicial or legislative intervention, and the form of that participation, depend on the costs of consummating the deal. Those costs derive from the inherent risks associated with imperfect information concerning the parties' transaction and the resources they devote to minimizing those risks. In sum, we look at contract law in light of what we know about bargaining, rather than vice versa. That is, although we think analytic study of bargaining "in the shadow of the law"[10] is important and useful, the theory of rational bargaining in the absence of law has a claim to analytic priority. It is that claim we mean to stake.

Anyone familiar with the literature on rational bargaining knows that there are different solutions to the bargaining problem, different ways of spelling out the distribution to which rational parties will agree. We employ a form of the theory that relies on the idea of bargaining as consisting of making claims and rational concessions from those claims. We call this concession theory.[11] Our purpose in doing so is not to establish that the specific distributions the concession theory predicts are superior to the distributions predicted by competing theories. Rather, concession theory captures important features of the way people go about bargaining, synthesizes unique features in the other theories, and adopts assumptions common to all. Therefore, it has a lot to say about the rules people would adopt ex ante to encourage contracting.

A bargaining theoretic approach to contract law has four features that recommend it over competing approaches. First, the bargaining approach admits reward-triggering norms as a basis for social control. Typically, economic and sociological theories, especially those based solely on the prisoners dilemma logic, depend on negative reinforcements to induce compliance with norms.[12] But according to bargaining theory, although one might sanction someone for failing to offer concessions or for violating an agreed upon division, the idea is to reward and

10. *See* Mnookin & Kornhauser, *Bargaining in the Shadow of the Law: The Case of Divorce*, 88 YALE L.J. 950 (1979).

11. *See* D. GAUTHIER, MORALS BY AGREEMENT (1986); Heckathorn, *A Unified Model for Bargaining and Conflict*, 25 BEHAVIORAL SCI. 261 (1980).

12. *See* Ellickson, *Of Coase and Cattle: Dispute Resolution Among Neighbors in Shasta County*, 38 STAN. L. REV. 623 (1986).

to encourage concession-making so as to secure cooperation. We can ask whether legal doctrines do that, and if so, in what ways.

Second, a bargaining theoretic approach takes explicit account of fairness as a part of contractual exchange. If people worry about fairness and if in every theory of rational contracting the parties ineluctably confront fairness concerns, then when and how do the courts take account of it? In fact and in theory, fairness matters. Under what conditions, then, will rational contractors require courts to act on that concern—and in what capacities?

Our approach shares with law-and-economics the importance of efficiency. It differs from many forms of economic analysis in virtue of bargaining theory's emphasis upon the division or fairness problem. Our approach shares with the law-and-society tradition, the importance of *context*. Rational decision-making is necessarily sensitive to the context of the decision. The status quo is relevant; contracting always occurs within a pre-existing web of continuing, contractual relationships. The resources parties bring into bargaining are relevant. And the uncertainties peculiar to different contexts are relevant.

Our approach shares with moral theories the importance of fairness and justice to the legitimacy of civil authority. However, unlike other theories, it appeals to criteria of fairness or justice endogenous to transaction relationships. It does not view contracting as necessarily constrained by external standards of fairness; rather it views the process of rational contracting as, in part, specifying the relevant conception of fairness.

Third, bargaining theory takes a unified view of contracting. It dispels the illusion that contract law doctrines are independent of one another. For example, legal scholarship and judicial decisions present damage measures, disclosure rules, and unconscionability as if they have nothing to do with each other. That is wrong. People will have difficulty reaching an agreement not only if they fear it may become uneconomic, which is relevant to establishing damage measures, but also if they fear it might become unfair, which is relevant to recision because of unconscionability. Their estimates of these fears depend in part on their investments in information, including the representations they make to each other, which in turn bears on the appropriateness of disclosure rules.

Fourth, analyzing the process of rational bargaining in the absence of law yields insight into the varying role of the court in contracts, specifically, into the conditions under which people turn to courts, and the defensibility of various contract law doctrines that have emerged in response. Like any other device to safeguard bargains, the court mitigates some of the risks of contracting better than others, but it is imperfect and costly. It can be more efficacious than alternative devices. People choosing among devices aim to minimize the sum of the costs of uncertainty and of safeguarding against it. Specialized doctrines in law emerge when rational bargainers charge the courts with effecting that policy.

B. *Three Problems in Contracting*

The terms of an agreement to cooperate among two or more people, their *contract*, stipulates (1) specific actions by each to be carried out at some time in the future, and (2) rewards and penalties to be meted out following compliance or defection. These terms constitute safeguards crafted to minimize and allocate risk, but in doing so the terms create risks of their own. What are the conditions under which rational actors will agree to cooperate if charged explicitly with designing a policy to cope with risk and uncertainty in their environment?

The decision-making calculus that rational actors use in crafting a contract is relatively complex because it requires resolving three distinct but intertwined problems: (1) coordination, (2) division, and (3) defection. These problems are captured in a type of game termed the divisible prisoner's dilemma. While other types of games (for example, pure coordination or division games, prisoner's dilemmas) typically isolate one feature of rational decision that can come into play in contracting,[13] this game describes *three* such features, the interaction between those features, and their informational requirements.

The divisible prisoner's dilemma involves three principles of rationality: (1) rational cooperation, (2) rational division, and

13. *See* Landa & Grofman, *Games of Breach and the Role of Contract Law in Protecting the Expectation Interest*, in 3 Research in Law and Economics 67 (R. Zerbe ed. 1981).

(3) rational compliance. Failure to satisfy any one of the three demands of rationality leads to contract failure; satisfying all three is necessary and sufficient for agreement and performance on a contract.

An example of the divisible prisoner's dilemma is depicted in matrix (normal) form in Figure One. For the moment, assume

Figure 1: Divisible Prisoner's Dilemma

Player A \ Player B (Performance)	Contract 1	Contract 2	Non Performance
Contract 1	Contract$_1$ 19, 7 C_1	Status quo 9, 2 D	B free rides 3, 11 NP_b
Contract 2	Status quo 9, 2 D	Contract$_2$ 16, 10 C_2	B free rides 3, 11 NP_b
Non Performance	A free rides 22, 1 NP_a	A free rides 22, 1 NP_a	Status quo 9, 2 D

that each player knows both payoffs in all of the cells. Player *A* (row) and player *B* (column) each make a three-dimensional choice. Each must decide whether to contract or not; and if the choice is to contract, whether to seek and honor contract one or contract two. In making this decision each of three problems of rational contracting emerges.

The *coordination problem* is resolved by whether or not the parties share a common interest in contracting over acting individually. To motivate acting in concert, they must identify feasible gains that would otherwise be unobtainable. In our example, the two contracts represented by cells one and five represent higher payoffs for both parties than do the noncontract alternatives. Thus, we would expect the players to solve their coordination problem. Doing so is not sufficient for contracting, however, for two problems remain. A *division problem* arises if player *A* prefers contract one to contract two whereas player *B* has the opposite preference. Consequently, opposed preferences regarding how to contract complicate the common preference for a contract over no contract. A *defection problem* arises if a player gains from unilaterally defecting from a contract once agreement is secured.

The defection problem is illustrated powerfully in the nondivisible or standard prisoner's dilemma in which the dominant strategy for each player is to defect from whatever agreements he or she has made. In our example, *A* gains by defecting to cell seven or eight, and *B* gains by defecting to cell three or six.

C. *Phases in Contracting*

Each problem in the contractual relationship corresponds to a distinct phase of the contracting process and involves a distinct principle of rationality.[14] First, in the *pre-phase* the decision whether to coordinate, that is, whether to seek a contract, is made. If the parties are rational, each predicates an affirmative decision on expectations that joint gains will be attainable under the contract. Second, in the *negotiation phase* the decision of how to contract is made. That is, the parties agree upon the terms of the contract, specifying the manner in which the gains resulting from the contract and the burdens of enforcing it are to be allocated. Finally, in the *post-phase* each party makes the decision to fulfill or to violate the contract and monitors the compliance of others.

Each phase contains a potential pitfall. That is, individuals may fail to contract because (1) one or more of the essential parties prefers to act independently rather than to seek a contract, (2) the parties fail to agree upon the terms of the contract, or (3) the contract collapses owing to a violation of its

14. For the sake of the exposition, we treat each phase in temporal progression and as distinct from the others. In fact, a rational bargainer may treat concerns arising in different phases of the process at the same time or in the reverse order we suggest. Ours is an analytic device, in which the phases of contracting progress in logical space-time.

terms. Each phase is distinct not only in the sense of carrying its own pitfalls to contracting; to succeed at each phase, a contract must meet the demands of distinct but ultimately related rationality conditions. The phases of contracting and their respective rationality conditions are developed below.

1. *Pre-phase: Joint Rationality*

No one can expect another person to engage in contracting unless *each* perceives an opportunity for *mutual* gain. That surely is the operating assumption when a buyer responds to a seller's "for sale" notice and when labor negotiates with management. Indeed, it is such a commonplace that we tend to take it for granted, overlooking its analytical importance.

We can put this obvious fact about contracting in an analytically precise way. A necessary condition for agreeing to a contract is that its expected outcome satisfies what may be termed the *joint rationality* condition. If U_i is the utility that individual *i* expects to secure in contracting; D_i is *i*'s utility from disagreement (that is, the status quo); $U = (U_a,U_b)$ is a given agreement's utility vector; and $U' = (U'_a,U'_b)$ is any other feasible agreement's utility vector, U is jointly rational if for each feasible outcome U',

$$U_a > U'_a, \text{ or } U_b > U'_b. \qquad (1)$$

The joint rationality condition can be clarified by analyzing Figure Two below.

C_1, C_2 represents the contract curve, that is, the set of Pareto optimal outcomes to the northeast of D. D, in turn, represents the disagreement point, the outcome that results if the parties fail to reach agreement. NP_a and NP_b are the non-performance outcomes. NP_a results when *A* and *B* reach agreement with which *B* complies and from which *A* defects. NP_b represents the outcome that results when *A* complies and *B* defects. These are the free-rider outcomes. Both are Pareto optimal in the sense that no points lie to their northeast in the utility-space representation of the game. Though Pareto optimal, they are not Pareto superior to D, and thus, they do not lie on the contract curve C_1, C_2. NP_a, NP_b, and all the points on the contract curve C_1, C_2 are jointly rational or Pareto optimal. Only points on the contract curve, however, are Pareto optimal and Pareto superior to D.

Figure 2: Divisible Prisoner's Dilemma in Utility Space

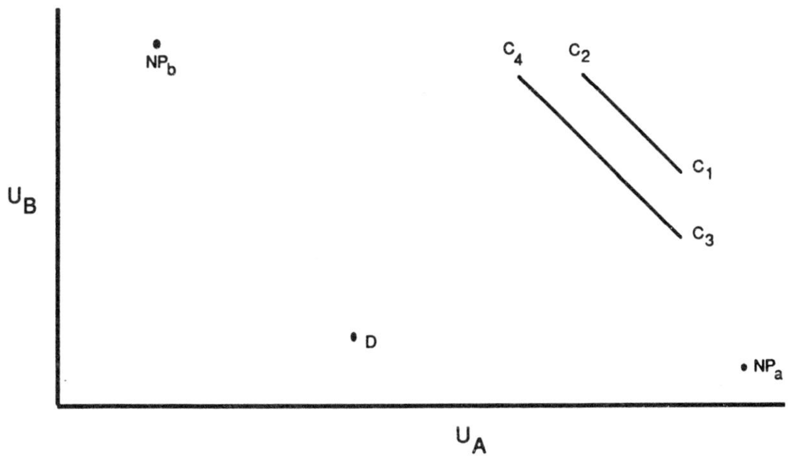

If information is imperfect or incomplete, each party has an incentive to expend resources to inquire whether a bargain with someone else promises to be advantageous. These resources are *transaction resources*. At the coordination or pre-phase, parties may expend transaction resources to identify and secure D at the outset. Everyone wants a referent from which he can evaluate feasible outcomes. Contracting will breakdown and may not even begin without it (as is the case in labor-management negotiations with newly certified unions whose legitimacy is uncertain). Similarly, individuals cannot take for granted the existence of the contract curve, even though opportunities for more efficient cooperation tend to exist in every relationship. If people must expend resources to determine the location of the disagreement point or the contract curve, some or all of the gains from contracting are consumed, that is, in terms of Figure Two, C_1, C_2 moves toward C_3, C_4.

The magnitude of the coordination problem measures the social gains foregone by failing to coordinate.[15] We define the *magnitude of the coordination problem*, M_C, as the *maximum proportion of the gains attainable from contracting that a rational contractor in the system could be motivated to expend on transaction resources to resolve the coordination problem*. This is the ratio of the gain resulting from

15. For an analysis of coordination games, see T. SCHELLING, THE STRATEGY OF CONFLICT 83-118 (1960).

coordination to the maximum gain attainable from contracting over not contracting. The former is the difference between the individual's best hope payoff, B_i, defined as the highest payoff awarded on the contract curve, and the individual's payoff from the noncooperative outcome, N_i, that is, the utility awarded individual *i* by the outcome (or mix of outcomes) resulting if the potential contractors act independently rather than jointly. For example, in Figure One's game if the players sought to contract but failed to correlate their choices between the two alternative contracts (that is, each would choose contract one or two with equal probability), they would contract only fifty percent of the time (cells one or five), and end up at the status quo (cells two or four) the rest of the time. That mixture of outcomes would, on average, award a utility of $N_A = 13.25$ and $N_B = 5.25$.[16] The difference between the best-hope outcome and the noncooperative otucome, $B_i - N_i$, is the gain attributable to coordination. This is the maximum amount that a rational contractor could be motivated to expend to resolve the coordination problem.

Similarly, the maximum gain awarded to the individual as a result of contracting is the difference between the best-hope payoff, B_i, and the disagreement payoff, D_i, that is, $B_i - D_i$. In consequence, the magnitude of the coordination problem for individual *i*, M_{Ci}, is given by the following expression:

$$M_{ci} = (B_i - N_i)/(B_i - D_i) \qquad (2)$$

For example, in Figure One's system, player *A*'s coordination problem is $M_{Ca} = (19 - 13.25)/(19 - 9) = 0.575$, and player *B*'s problem is $M_{Cb} = (10 - 5.25)/(10 - 2) = 0.59$.

The magnitude of the coordination problem faced by a group of individuals can be defined as the maximum problem faced by any of its members, that is,

$$M_C = \mathrm{Max}[M_{Ci}] \qquad (3)$$

For example, in Figure One's system, $M_C = 0.59$. This expression indicates the maximum proportion of contractual gains that any rational group member could be motivated to expend on resolving the coordination problem. This figure is not iden-

16. Alternatively, if the focus of analysis is the problem of coordination in general, rather than the problem of implementing given a prior decision to contract, the noncooperative outcome can be defined as the Nash noncooperative equilibrium. *See* Nash, *Non-cooperative Games*, 54 ANNALS OF MATHEMATICS 286-95 (1951).

tical to actual expenditures to resolve the coordination problem. According to the principles of transactions-cost economics, individuals have incentives to minimize their expenditure of transaction resources, so actual expenditures will tend to fall below that theoretic maximum. Other things equal, actual expenditures on transaction resources will be positively related to the magnitude of the coordination problem.

Contracting to secure mutual gains consumes transaction resources that are scarce and costly to obtain. In the old law-and-economics tradition, transaction costs are assumed to be low in contracting situations, so that parties are able to gather all pertinent information and to assign all relevant risks.[17] Because the old law-and-economics tradition assumes individuals have perfect information, are completely rational, and face no impediments to entering transactions, "[i]t would be surprising if such superhumans were *not able* to manage their own affairs without the intervention of government."[18] As it happens, however, sometimes they are not.

The newer law-and-economics tradition emphasizes transaction costs even in contract (as opposed to "tort" or "stranger") situations. Because this tradition assumes individuals have imperfect information and limited rationality, and encounter substantial impediments in contracting, it would be surprising if such patently imperfect individuals were *able* to manage their affairs without the intervention of government. As it happens, in some cases, they do.

This discontinuity between "prohibitive" and "non-prohibitive" transaction costs is, of course, an analytic artifice begging for elaboration. The private and governmental controls that people craft depend on the relative size of the transaction costs involved. Because each of the three decision-making problems in any relationship involve unique hazards from imperfect information, the undifferentiated, generic treatment of transaction costs is analytically untenable as well.

17. Just think of the Coase Theorem and the long line of Chicago-style law-and-economics that sees itself as driven by Coase's insight that when transaction costs are low, individuals contract around inefficiencies. Thus, we have the identification of contract with low transaction costs. Coase himself did not commit the mistake of identifying contracting with low transaction costs.

18. Farber, *Contract Law and Modern Economic Theory*, 78 Nw. U.L. Rev. 303, 305 (1983).

2. *The Negotiation Phase: Concession Rationality*

Recognizing that contracting would increase efficiency, that it would generate benefits in excess of costs, is not a sufficient condition for contracting to occur.[19] Contracting requires that parties to the negotiations resolve the division problem, either directly by agreeing upon allocations of benefits and costs, or indirectly by agreeing upon a set of procedures by which these allocations are to be determined. The problem is not just the cost of establishing a set of feasible and acceptable outcomes. Even if that cost is nil, the *strategic* nature of the choice may induce a noncooperative outcome.[20] Strategy may require players to disguise their true intentions in pursuit of an agreement, moderating or exaggerating their demands based on their view of how each will respond to the other. Thus, failure to resolve the division problem can complicate the process of contracting even to the point of defeating it.

Returning to Figure Two, the division problem arises because the players have opposite preferences regarding where along the contract curve agreement should occur.[21] Expressed in bargaining theoretic terms, C_1, contract one, is player *A*'s *best-hope outcome* because it is the outcome that is (i) most preferred by *A*, (ii) no worse than disagreement for *B*, (iii) feasible, and (iv) enforceable. Similarly, C_2, contract two, represents *B*'s best hope. The players' best hopes correspond to opposite endpoints of the contract curve. When a *concession* is defined as agreeing to an outcome less preferred than one's own best hope, it is obvious that agreement requires concessions. Either one player makes all the concessions required for agreement by assenting to the other's best-hope outcome, or both players make concessions resulting in agreement at an intermediate point on the contract curve. If bargaining over the allocation of concessions fails, so too does contracting.

Intuitively, we recognize the problem of settling on a division of cooperative gains as endemic in human behavior and know that people resolve it when the conditions are right. Empirical

19. See McClelland & Rohrbaugh, *Who Accepts the Pareto Axiom? The Role of Utility and Equity in Arbitration Decisions*, 23 BEHAVIORAL SCI. 446 (1978).

20. *See* Coleman, *Market Contractarianism and the Unanimity Rule*, SOC. PHIL. & POL'Y, Spring 1985, at 69; Cooter, *The Cost of Coase*, 11 J. LEGAL STUD. 1 (1982).

21. Whereas mixtures between contracts one and two are assumed to be feasible in this game (hence, the C1C2 line), mixtures between other outcomes of this game are assumed not to be feasible. We adopt this convention to simplify the analysis.

studies confirm that standards of "fair division" sometimes guide rational agreement even in the absence of third-party enforcement. In particular, Kahneman, Knetsch and Thaler have shown that when unanticipated events induce unanticipated divisions, they do not necessarily threaten the economic viability of an arrangement.[22] In other words, individuals sometimes appeal to a sense of fairness to solve division problems when failure to reach agreement in division may jeopardize an opportunity for mutual gain. Laboratory experiments testing the Coase Theorem demonstrate as well that parties are able to secure jointly maximizing outcomes, though different methods of assigning property entitlements influence the division of the gains.[23] Other studies confirm (1) the importance of the status quo in choices over division rules, and (2) the heavier weight ascribed to losses than equivalent gains in evaluating outcomes.[24] In short, empirical studies suggest that players are often able to solve their division problem and point to some of the relevant factors in settling on particular divisions: namely, the allocation of initial entitlements, a sense of fairness, the relative disparity in weighting equivalent gains and losses, and so on.

Under a broad range of conditions, then, contracting parties settle on distributions of the gains from trade, which simply means that they allocate concessions. They also have in mind which among the available points on the contract curve they intend to *safeguard* by the terms of any contract. Put analytically, a necessary condition for agreeing to a contract is that its expected outcomes satisfy what may be termed the principle of *concession rationality*.[25]

Each of the formal models in the literature provides a distinct

---

22. *See* Kahneman, Knetsch, & Thaler, *Fairness and the Assumptions of Economics*, 59 J. BUS. 285 (1986).

23. *See* Hoffman & Spitzer, *Entitlements, Rights, and Fairness: An Experimental Examination of Subjects' Concepts of Distributive Justice*, 14 J. LEGAL STUD. 259 (1985).

24. *See* Frohlich, Oppenheimer, & Eavey, *Choices of Principles of Distributive Justice in Experimental Groups*, 31 AM. J. POL. SCI. 606 (1986); Kahneman, Knetsch, & Thaler, *Fairness as a Constraint on Profit Seeking: Entitlements in the Market*, 76 AM. ECON. REV. 728 (1986).

25. Formal theoretic accounts of bargaining have been proposed by economists, game theorists, social psychologists, and strategic analysts. *See* J. HARSANYI, RATIONAL BEHAVIOR AND BARGAINING EQUILIBRIUM IN GAMES AND SOCIAL SITUATIONS (1977); A. ROTH, GAME-THEORETIC MODELS OF BARGAINING (1985); O. YOUNG, BARGAINING: FORMAL THEORIES OF NEGOTIATION (1975); Binmore, Rubinstein, & Wolinsky, *The Nash Bargaining Solution in Economic Modeling*, 17 RAND J. ECON. 176 (1986).

meaning to the concept of concession rationality. No single point-specific solution to the bargaining problem has gained universal acceptance. But we are less concerned with predicting a specific distribution than with identifying the parameters that influence the choice of rules for making it. We want a model that applies to a broad range of contractual settings and incorporates fundamental principles universally accepted as affecting the relative bargaining power of parties.

The problem with many bargaining theories is that while they take account of the parties' relative bargaining strengths, they assume away many of the other problems that lead to bargaining failure, for example, uncertainty. Thus, they typically yield the result that bargainers will secure a cooperative division of the gains that reflects their initial relative bargaining strengths. This outcome is not surprising, but because of all the evidence of noncooperation (wars, strikes, etc.), these models are neither predictive nor descriptive.[26] Again, though all bargaining models view the relative costliness of conflict as affecting relative bargaining power, many do not take into account the parties' best hopes or aspiration levels, which influence the bargainers' willingness to incur costs in reaching agreement. That is inconsistent with a sizable body of experimental evidence indicating that aspiration level is positively related to bargaining power.[27]

In contrast, what we call *resistance theory* renders an explicit account of the conditions under which negotiations break down, treats aspirations as part of the decision making calculus, and describes the information rational contractors require to reach agreement. Thereby, it illuminates the conditions under which people will expend resources to contract.[28] As conceived in resistance theory, bargainers assess the relative strengths of their strategic positions based on the utility structure of the game, for example, based on the location of the disagreement point, on the location and shape of the contract curve, and on their risk and time preferences. The strength with which a bargainer strives to avoid concessions, termed his resistance, de-

26. *See* Cooter, *supra* note 18.

27. *See* S. Bacharach & E. Lawler, Bargaining Power, Tactics, and Outcomes (1981).

28. *See* Heckathorn, *A Formal Theory of Social Exchange: Process and Outcome*, in 5 Current Perspectives in Social Theory 145 (S. McNall ed. 1984) [hereinafter Heckathorn, *A Formal Theory*]; Heckathorn, *supra* note 11.

pends on (1) the costliness to the individual of the concessions required by the agreement (the greater the concession cost, the greater will be the resistance to the agreement); (2) the costliness of conflict (an increase in conflict's cost increases the willingness to make concessions and diminishes resistance); and (3) the aspiration level (higher aspirations enhance resistance). The very existence of opposing proposals reveals conflicting aspirations. They establish concession limits and distributional expectations based on those assessments. Only outcomes in which those limits and expectations overlap satisfy concession rationality.

Formally, if D_i is any bargainer i's utility from disagreement (conflict); B_i is i's aspiration level or best hope—the enforceable outcome on the contract curve that he most prefers, or equivalently, the outcome he most prefers which is enforceable, feasible, and no worse than conflict for any other bargainer; and U_i is i's utility from a given outcome U, i's resistance to outcome U, $R_i(U)$ is defined as

$$R_i = (B_i - U_i)/(B_i - D_i). \qquad (4)$$

During negotiations, each bargainer assesses his own resistance against that of others, which takes into account everyone's strategic position. Under conditions of complete information, each will agree to an outcome only if the concessions it requires are at least matched by the relative concessions of others. On the assumption of equal rationality, each party will make equal relative concessions.[29] It is not rational to be exploited. Expressed in terms of resistances, this means that the bargainer will agree to an outcome if his own resistance to it would equal or fall below the resistances of others. Formally, where $R_i(U)$ is any bargainer i's resistance to outcome U, and $R_j(U)$ is another bargainer's resistance to outcome U, then that outcome lies in the agreement set of i, A_i, if

$$R_i(U) < R_j(U). \qquad (5)$$

Concession rationality requires that an actor's concession behavior fulfill this requirement. Resistance theory posits that in the presence of complete information, people exhibit concession rationality. Under conditions of complete information, rational individuals make equal relative concessions. When

29. This is also David Gauthier's view. *See* D. GAUTHIER, *supra* note 11.

information is incomplete, a bargainer will agree to an outcome if he judges it to be rational in that sense, that is, if his own resistance is matched or exceeded by the expected resistance of everyone else. That is, if *i*'s resistance to U is $R_i(U)$, and i's expectation concerning *j*'s resistance to U is $E_i(R_j(U))$, then the set of outcomes to which *i* would agree, his agreement set A_i, includes outcomes fulfilling the requirement

$$R_i(U) < E_i(R_j(U)). \quad (6)$$

Of course, for an outcome to be agreed upon, it must lie in the agreement sets of each individual with the ability to block an agreement. For example, in a system of bargainers *A* and *B*, the outcome must lie in the intersection of sets A_a and A_b.

The implications of concession rationality for the outcome of bargaining can be illustrated graphically. Consider Figure Three. The outcomes when players' resistances are equal lie on the line connecting the disagreement point D (9,2), where each resistance equals one, to the *ideal point* I (19,10), a nonfeasible outcome where players simultaneously attain their best hope payoffs and resistances are consequently equal to zero. If person *A* exhibits concession rationality as defined in Equation Three, his agreement set lies on or to the right of the line ID; and if person *B* is similarly rational, his agreement lies on or above the line ID. Hence, if both exhibit concession rationality and they possess complete information, their point of agreement must lie on the line ID.

Resistance theory is one way of specifying the content of concession rationality. Concession rationality in turn expresses a condition of rational cooperation or rational contracting. Its domain is the division of the gains from cooperation or the parties' joint stakes in contracting.

The division problem can be more or less troublesome. The magnitude of the division problem in a particular case is a function of the discrepancy between the players' best hopes. If the individuals' best hopes exactly coincide, as in the *nondivisible* prisoner's dilemma game, the contract curve shrinks to a point, and agreement requires no concessions. As the contract curve lengthens, the required concessions increase. That in turn makes divisional bargaining an enterprise with higher stakes. Consequently, expending resources to enhance the strength of one's bargaining position becomes more rational, as do any

Figure 3: Equal Resistance Line

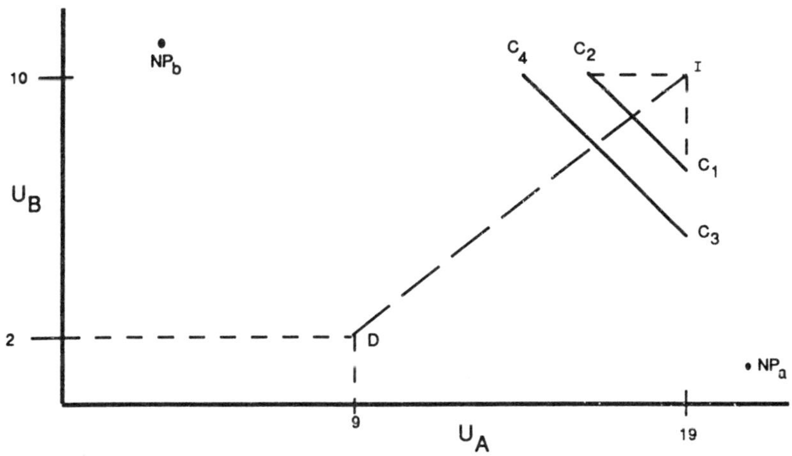

measures to minimize one's own concessions and to maximize those secured from others.

The *magnitude of the bargaining problem*, M_B, can be formally defined in terms of potential expenditures of transaction resources, as the *maximum proportion of the gains attainable from contracting that any rational contractor in the system could be motivated to expend on transaction resources to enhance bargaining power*. As thus defined, the magnitude of the bargaining problem is the ratio of the gain attainable from bargaining to the gain attainable from contracting. The former is the difference between the payoff from the individual's best-hope outcome, B_i, that is, the most preferred point on the contract curve, and the individual's *worst hope*, W_i, that is, the *least* preferred point on the contract curve, which is $B_i - W_i$. This is the maximum amount the individual could be rationally motivated to expend in an endeavor to augment bargaining power. Furthermore, recall that $B_i - D_i$ is the maximum gain attainable from contracting, so the maximum proportion of the gains from contracting that the individual could be motivated to expend on enhancing bargaining power is

$$M_{Bi} = (B_i - W_i)/(B_i - C_i) \qquad (7)$$

For example, in Figure One's system, the magnitude of player

A's bargaining problem is $M_{Ba} = (19 - 16)/(19 - 9) = 0.3$, and player *B*'s problem is $M_{Bb} = (10 - 7)/(10 - 2) = 0.375$.

The magnitude of the bargaining problem, M_B, faced by a *group* of actors is defined as the maximum problem faced by any member of that group, that is,

$$M_B = \text{Max}[M_{Bi}]. \qquad (8)$$

For example, in Figure One's system, $M_B = M_{Bb} = 0.375$. This expression describes the maximum proportion of the gains attainable from contracting that any rational bargainer in the system could be motivated to expend on transaction resources.

3. *Post-phase: Individual Rationality*

We noted above that in the non-divisible prisoner's dilemma, there is no bargaining over the gains from cooperation. The parties' best hopes coincide, and no concessions are required. That is why the prisoner's dilemma is best thought of as illustrating the problem of rational defection, not the problem of rational agreement. The payoffs from cooperation are set; no concessions are required. Once agreement is secured, however, the question remains whether it is in the interest of either or both parties to comply with it.

The defection problem reflects the problematic nature of mutual trust, owing to the presence in most contracts of burdensome provisions and potential loopholes. Frequently, an individual can gain by defaulting upon a contract, often at the expense of those who perform according to its terms. A prerequisite for contracting, then, is a system of enforcement with which to preclude or to deter noncompliance, or to compensate parties injured by others' noncompliance. Not surprisingly, debating whether negotiations are undertaken in "good faith" and carefully scrutinizing contracts for hidden loopholes are prominent features of virtually all contracting.

The compliance or defection problem can be expressed in terms of a third condition of rationality. A necessary condition for rational agreement to a contract is that its expected outcome satisfies *individual rationality*. Neither player will permit himself to be left worse off than the status quo, or disagreement point. That is, when U_i is individual *i*'s expected utility from participating in a contract, and D_i is *i*'s utility from disagreement, *i* is *individually rational* if

$$U_i \geq D_i. \qquad (9)$$

With reference to Figure Three, player *A* prefers defection if point NP_a is to the right of the point on the contract curve at which agreement occurs, and player *B* prefers defection if NP_b is above the contract point. Player *A* would not agree to an outcome lying to the left of point D, such as point NP_b in which *B* free-rides, even though NP_b is jointly rational. Such an agreement would make *A* worse off than he would be were no agreement made, thus violating the individual rationality condition. Nor would player *B* accept any outcome below point D, such as NP_a, for analogous reasons. Hence, if both players are individually rational, neither will tolerate the other's free-riding. The outcomes of Figure Two's game that satisfy each player's requirement of individual rationality include the status quo point, D, and all of the points on the contract curve C_1, C_2. Rational parties will not agree to contracts they expect to make them worse off; thus, they must find a way to eliminate or to minimize the risk of defection. This is no easy task.

A defection problem arises if either player can gain from free-riding. The strength of the incentive to free ride depends on the relationship between each player's unilateral defection payoff and the payoff from points on the contract curve. In general, that incentive is strongest when the utility awarded by contracting is lowest. Thus, driving a hard bargain increases the incentives for others to defect from that contract's terms, and in consequence may be self-defeating. Notice, however, that in Figure One's system a contractor has some incentive for defection even if the agreement represents his best hope or most preferred contract. Every unilateral defection outcome gives him a payoff in excess of *any* cooperative outcome.

Described quantitatively, the *magnitude of the defection problem*, M_D, can be defined as the *maximum proportion of the gains attainable from contracting that a rational individual could be motivated to expend to secure the gains potentially available by defecting*. Recall that the defection problem arises because defection is more rewarding than cooperation. Let NP_i be individual *i*'s *payoff from free-riding*, the payoff awarded a unilateral defector. An actor's incentive to defect is then measured by the difference between that payoff (NP_i), and the payoff from contracting, a payoff that is minimal when the individual attains his worst hope, W_i. Thus, the individual's maximum possible defection incentive is

$NP_i - W_i$, indicating that he could be motivated to expend *up to* $NP_i - W_i$ for the privilege of free-riding with impunity rather than contracting. When the gain from defection ($NP_i - W_i$) is divided by the gains attainable from contracting ($B_i - D_i$), that yields the expression for the magnitude of the individual defection incentive M_{Di}. For any individual *i*, M_{Di} is

$$M_{Di} = (NP_i - W_i)/(B_i - D_i) \qquad (10)$$

For example, in Figure One's system, the magnitude of player *A*'s defection problem is $M_{Ba} = (22 - 16)/(19 - 9) = 0.6$, and player *B*'s problem is $M_{Bb} = (11 - 7)/(10 - 2) = 0.5$.

The magnitude of the defection problem faced by a group of actors is defined as the maximum problem faced by any member of the group, that is,

$$M_D = \mathrm{Max}[M_{Di}]. \qquad (11)$$

For example, in Figure One's system, $M_D = M_{Da} = 0.6$. In sum, the magnitude of the defection problem[30] refers to the strength of the incentive to defect from contracts relative to the gains attainable from contracting.

To resolve the defection problem, each party must reduce the other party's incentive to defect. The power of the incentive to defect can be mitigated in several analytically distinguishable ways. Compliance can be made more rewarding, defection less rewarding, or opportunities to defect reduced or blocked. Of these, the second is the most common because the first tends to be more costly and the third tends to be impractical given the near impossibility of removing all opportunities for nonperformance. In short, no party will rationally agree to comply and to let the other party free ride. But since both parties have at least some incentive to free ride, each party has an incentive to deploy resources to insure the compliance of the other.

Individual rationality, then, requires that an agreement be *enforceable*, not just that an individual be protected against an outcome worse than the status quo.[31] To be an enforceable

30. Heckathorn & Maser, *Bargaining and the Sources of Transaction Costs: The Case of Government Regulation*, 3 J.L. ECON. & ORG. 69, 80 n.4 (1987).

31. At least in the case of cooperating to produce a public good, which can be studied as a prisoner's dilemma game, experimental evidence reveals cooperation rates significantly better when people expect an agreement to be enforceable as compared to when they receive money-back guarantees that they will be no worse off than when they started if the group effort fails. See Dawes, Orbell, Simmons, & Van de Kragt, *Organizing Groups for Collective Action*, 80 AM. POL. SCI. REV. 1171, 1183 (1986).

agreement, the parties must expect that each estimates a cost of violation exceeding the gain from unilaterally defecting. That is, no agreement on C_1, C_2 is enforceable without penalties sufficient to deter defection, termed the *force of agreement*.[32]

Viewed graphically, an enforcement system that penalizes defection displaces the defection points NP_a and NP_b toward the origin, making compliance more rewarding relative to defection. In Figure Three, for example, if each player faces a violation cost that makes him indifferent between defecting and his best-hope outcome, then no points on the contract curve will be enforceable. But if each faces a violation cost that makes him indifferent between defecting and the other party's best hope outcome, then the entire contract curve constitutes a domain of enforceable agreements.

In general, the greater an individual's defection incentive, the stronger must be the penalties that would succeed in making compliance rational. Further, the greater the incentive to defect, the stronger are the incentives for the individual to seek to evade or undermine an enforcement system. Put simply, the more a person wants to defect, the harder and more costly it will be to prevent him from doing so. Although it is not rational to accept a contract that is unenforceable, or one that gives others the opportunity to defect, making a contract enforceable requires expenditure of considerable resources. The greater the incentive to defect, the greater the resources required to prevent it.

C. *Summary of Rational Contracting*

The resistance solution to a bargaining game of complete information can be described in terms of the rationality conditions. Individual and joint rationality, which together comprise the classical notion of economic rationality,[33] together suffice to motivate contracting but not agreement on any unique contract. With reference to Figure Two, they restrict the outcomes of agreement to the portion of the welfare frontier called the contract curve, C_1, C_2. This contains, of course, many feasible outcomes. In classical economic theory, no choice among them can be said to be more or less rational than any other. The

32. *See* Heckathorn, *A Formal Theory*, *supra* note 28, at 153.
33. *See* J. HARSANYI, *supra* note 25, at 141-42.

choice among them cannot be a matter of rationality! Thus, in the usual forms of economic analysis, the choice among Pareto optimal (collectively or jointly) outcomes is said to be a matter of distributive fairness, not a matter of economics (or rationality).

The additional requirement of concession rationality, the signature of the bargaining theory approach we adopt, restricts that outcome to a point on the equal resistance line, ID in Figure Three, so the cumulative effect of these requirements is to specify the intersection of the contract curve and the equal resistance line. For bargainers A and B with complete information, the outcome of the bargaining U satisfies the expression

$$\min[R_a(U) = R_b(U)] \qquad (12)$$

Agreement and performance on a contract occur, then, if and only if it satisfies all three requirement for each party to the transaction. Taken together, then, these conditions are necessary and sufficient; they define a party's interests in a contractual relationship.[34]

Bargaining theory differs from the more common forms of economic analysis precisely by its commitment to a principle of concession rationality. This principle is aimed at explaining and defending some outcomes along the frontier as more rational than others. Concession or bargaining theory thus makes the division of the gains from contracting, that is, the distribution of the game's stakes, a matter of rationality. Unlike forms of economic analysis that set aside questions of distribution, rational bargaining theory takes the division problem to be a part of the problem of rational choice. As a consequence, concession theory not only can explain and defend outcomes of contracting as more or less rational depending on the way in which the gains are distributed; it can explain safeguards in contracting aimed at securing certain divisions, and failures in contracting as often resulting from failures to solve the bargaining or concession problem, or as owing to the high costs of safeguarding agreed upon divisions.

34. The conclusions reached here also hold in the n-person cases and in the dynamic context. We use the static one to simplify the analysis. *See* Heckathorn, *A Formal Theory*, *supra* note 28.

III. Safeguarding the Rational Contract

In the model we have just explicated, bargaining takes place sequentially (at least in logical space-time). First individuals search for potentially advantageous opportunites to cooperate, then they seek agreement on the gains, and finally they monitor compliance with the contract's terms. Each phase leaves plenty of room for contract failure. Thus, guarding against failure is rational—up to a point. That is, one does not want to spend more on preventing failure than failure costs in terms of foregone benefit. The important analytic point is that at least some expenditure of resources to guard against contract failure is rational for all players. We call this process of expending resources to prevent contract failure, "rational safeguarding."

The order in which actors safeguard their interests in contracting reverses the order in which they contract (again in logical space-time). In the divisible prisoner's dilemma, both parties have incentives to defect from unprotected agreements. If it is rational for player A to defect from an agreement, then it cannot be rational for player *B* to bargain with player A over the gains from trade, and *vice versa*. Bargaining without compliance is simply a waste of resources and is, therefore, irrational. If bargaining over the gains from trade is to be rational, the parties must be reasonably confident of one another's subsequent compliance. Thus, the defection problem must be resolved prior to pursuing a division of contract gains.[35] Similar considerations apply regarding the other phases of bargaining. Crafting safeguards to satisfy joint rationality is pointless unless the parties expect both the division and defection problems to be soluble. Early phase decisions are dependent upon expectations regarding decisions in a later phase; anticipating breakdown at a later phase may block affirmative decisions at a prior one.

Each party would prefer that the other bear the full costs of safeguarding. The parties in general cannot insist upon this preference. Concessions are rational, and parties can secure an agreement about distributing the costs of safeguarding. This "contract," that is, the contract over safeguards, has all the same conditions and pitfalls of bargaining over the gains from

35. *See* Kraus & Coleman, *Morality and the Theory of Rational Choice*, 97 Ethics 715 (1987).

trade. So in the complete rational contract, the parties bargain both over the costs of safeguarding and over the gains from trade.

Negotiations over safeguards in a contract comprise a series of nested subgames, corresponding to a type of sequential decision-making that Shubik terms "backward induction."[36] Here, the outcome of one game effects the potential payoffs of the next and issues are analyzed in the reverse of their ultimate behavioral order. Treating the divisible prisoner's dilemma in this way transforms it from a single game in which the defection incentive dominates, so contracting never gets underway, into two cooperative games.

The two cooperative games are then analyzed as follows. The first game involves negotiating over enforcement costs. In this game, we once again assume that the players command resources adequate to enforce an agreement, so that they need not call upon third-party enforcement mechanisms. (This assumption is crucial; otherwise, the account cannot proceed. For otherwise we will generate an infinite regress of nonenforceable contracts.) The only question at this stage—in this game—is, who shall bear which costs in solving the defection problem? If *this* bargaining problem is solved, then the second cooperative game is played. The players' mutual interest is to bargain over points on the contract curve only. The enforceable solutions to the second game therefore lie on the contract curve. Thus, the second bargaining game is over points on the curve.

The first, or enforcement, game is connected to the second, or division-of-the-gains game in three ways. First, solving the enforcement game is a necessary condition for playing the division game; second, any particular solution to the enforcement game will affect solutions to the division game. How much one is willing to concede in bargaining over the gains from trade may well depend on how much one has had to expend in creating safeguards against defection. Third, because they are both bargaining games, the theory of rational bargaining developed above applies to both. In principle there should be equilibrium solutions to the conjunction of these two games that satisfy the rationality conditions.

36. *See* M. Shubick, Game Theory in the Social Sciences: Concepts and Solutions (1982); *see also* T. Schelling, *supra* note 15; Heckathorn, *A Formal Theory*, *supra* note 28.

In general, party *A* will create a safeguard so long as the potential burden imposed on *B* to overcome it exceeds the cost to *A* of creating it; party *A* expects *B* to have a comparable incentive.[37] The equilibrium effect of following these strategies gives rise to an optimizing effect. When parties contract with one another, they bargain so as to minimize the sum of the costs players impose on each other and the costs they must bear to safeguard themselves. Under conditions of *complete information* both cooperative games are solved so that the following is true: a rational contract minimizes the sum of the costs the players impose on one another and the costs they bear to protect themselves.

A. *Safeguarding Against Uncertainty*

Problems in contracting arise when information is not complete, when instead actors are required to behave under conditions of uncertainty. Almost every contract dispute that winds up in litigation turns on a point about an incomplete contract; the traditional reasons for incomplete contracts are matters of information cost: 1) a contingency may be unforeseeable; 2) planning for every foreseeable contingency can be expensive; and 3) some contingencies may involve private information. Indeed, because a complete contract must specify a suitable mechanism for transmitting information to deal with contingencies, it can be particularly costly to devise. Therefore, actual contracts tend to be incomplete and subject to renegotiation.[38]

When bargainers possess less than complete information, failure to identify opportunities for gain or fear of outcomes worse than the status quo can prevent contracting from even getting off the ground. Once it does, agreement can still be blocked or the point of agreement may diverge from the contract curve's equal resistance outcome.[39] For example, if bargainers underestimate one another's resistances, they demand more concessions than the other will grant, and the result is

37. The comparisions here, as with those involved in making concessions, entail no invalid interpersonal comparisions of utility. The calculus for creating safeguards follows the calculus of resistance theory. In resistance theory, people are comparing concessions normalized with respect to each individual's stake in the game. Because the mathematical expressions take the form of the ratio of two utility differences, resistances are validly comparable across individuals. In this way, resistance theory captures a prominent feature of actual bargaining and actual equity judgments.

38. Tirole, *Procurement and Renegotiation*, 94 J. Pol. Econ. 235, 239 (1986).

39. *See* Heckathorn, *A Formal Theory*, *supra* note 28, at 161-68.

conflict. Unresolved conflict does not entail that the rationality conditions are violated. Rather, divergences from the outcome predictable under complete information are predictable consequences of rational actors facing imperfect information. Bargaining with incomplete information can be both rational and unsuccessful.

If uncertainty exists, each party may benefit by manipulating information to create the appearance that conflict has become less costly to him or more costly to others. That makes his threats credible and signals an unwillingness to give in. Similarly, every bargainer possesses incentives to oversell his own preferred contract while denigrating the other's preferred contract. And each possesses incentives to invest in safeguards against precisely this sort of behavior because it threatens the divisions to which they would otherwise agree.

One consequence of this analysis is that the main reason for expending resources in contracting is to overcome some sort of uncertainty, uncertainty that threatens the equilibrium solution to which rational actors would otherwise agree. Because the possible sources of uncertainty differ in each phase of contracting, the logical character of the costs rational bargainers are willing to incur to reduce uncertainty differ as well.

People incur *search costs* because they are uncertain about the feasibility of alternative outcomes. Each bargainer wants information about the group's prospects. To resolve the coordination problem, information about group gains, or the opportunities to secure a Pareto improvement, is necessary. It helps to motivate contracting that satisfies the *joint rationality* condition.

People incur *bargaining and decision costs* because they are uncertain about the acceptability of alternative divisions. Each bargainer wants information about the agreement set. Securing adequate information about one another's resistances is necessary to create an agreement that satisfies the *concession rationality* condition.

People incur *monitoring costs* because they are uncertain about the enforceability of alternative outcomes. Each bargainer wants information about the consequences of the other party's defecting. In that sense, information about the force of the agreement is relevant to creating an enforceable contract that satisfies the *individual rationality* condition.

If an individual need only estimate *his* expected utility for the outcomes *possible* under a proposed contract against that of the status quo to ensure that its terms are no worse than not contracting, then the information required to judge outcomes by this test is the least stringent of all. But because each party needs to estimate the defection incentive and the force of agreement, then, in addition to the information needed to estimate joint and concession rationality, each must estimate NP_a and NP_b.

Significantly, each phase of contracting entails greater risks than the preceding one because, as an inspection of equations (1)-(12) reveals, more terms come into play at each step, so more information is required by succeeding calculations. That means more potential sources of uncertainty exist, more estimates must be made, each with a risk of error. In other words, the mathematics suggests that gathering information sufficient to fashion safeguards against defection is more difficult than securing information sufficient to safeguard against exploitive divisions, and so on. The more general point is that by incurring search, bargaining, and decision costs, individual contractors are able to mitigate *ex ante* risks; by incurring monitoring costs they hope to mitigate *ex post* risks. Thus, one can understand the object of contracting as the joint attempt to minimize the sum of the costs of uncertainty and of its avoidance, when uncertainty afflicts all three dimensions of rationality.[40]

40. This generalizes a formulation found in G. CALABRESI, THE COST OF ACCIDENTS 26-31 (1970), and implied in Cooter's analysis of Coasian versus Hobbesian perspectives on assigning liability, a seminal application of bargaining theory to legal issues, *see* Cooter, *supra* note 18. The Coasian perspective supposes the obstacle to cooperation is the cost of communicating, so courts need only enforce private agreements; Cooter recognizes that the strategic nature of the situation and the absence of a division rule may preclude cooperation, even when communication costs are zero, evoking a more intrusive court. However, Cooter's perspective does not count the cost of concessions as part of the strategic problem to which a court might attend. The Hobbesian perspective supposes that bargainers increase their demands on each other at every opportunity, defeating cooperation unless a third party exists to dictate the terms of a contract. Cooter recognizes that people may adapt their strategies to achieve an agreement, evoking a less intrusive court. He concludes that institutions such as markets serve efficiency without an extraordinarily intrusive state because a market eliminates the power of parties to threaten each other. But the proper standard of efficiency is generating optimal threats, not eliminating threats. Our analysis joins the Coasian and Hobbesian treatments of law, making the court's role contingent on contextual features of social relationships that defeat cooperation.

B. *Factors Affecting Uncertainty*

Different but often related contextual features influence the ability of decision makers to estimate the terms comprising the calculus of contracting; that is, they affect the amount and accuracy of the information that must be acquired, verified, communicated, or processed during the course of contracting.

First, as the *number of principal parties* to the potential contract increases, the number of lines of communication and the amount of information that must be processed during negotiation increases. Opportunities for joint gain can be obscured simply by the noise. Group size affects the defection problem because in larger groups an individual's defection tends to be less noticeable, weakening incentives for individuals to participate in sanctioning defectors.[41] Monitoring compliance in a large group is generally more difficult and more demanding of given resources than in a smaller group. Hence, contracting is riskier.

Second, as *heretogeneity among the principal parties* increases, the bargaining range—if one exists—and defection incentives increase. To be sure, differences of preference are required to provide a basis for exchange and contract, but the less interchangeable the actors, the more difficult the transaction. For example, the commonality among workers at particular job sites facilitiates collective bargaining with management. Only minor adjustments are required to adjust for individual differences in seniority, skill level, and work classification. By contrast, when each party to a contract possesses a wholly unique set of attributes and relations to each other participant, bargaining may prove impossible even in a quite small group. Any bargain ultimately struck will inevitably leave more people disgruntled and, therefore, will create higher, more disparate defection incentives than would an agreement among a more homogeneous assembly.

Third, as the *spatial dispersion* of the group increases, communication costs increase. Bargaining and enforcement systems both require communication. In geographically concentrated groups, oral communication and incidental observations of behavior may suffice, but linking a dispersed group with equally adequate communication between each pair of individuals is

41. *See* M. OLSON, THE LOGIC OF COLLECTIVE ACTION 45 (1965).

technically more difficult. Conversely, improvements in the technology of communication, holding dispersion constant, reduce communication costs, so transaction resources go further.

Fourth, as the *temporal distribution* of the costs or benefits at issue in the transaction increases, they become more difficult to detect and control. For example, delayed defection costs impede monitoring because the adverse consequences become apparent only long after the fact. Similarly, delayed benefits hamper divisional bargaining because bargaining to allocate anticipated gains may appear to be an exercise in wishful thinking.

Fifth, and closely related, as the *level of acceptable risk* decreases, monitoring problems increase. If people engaged in contracting for the sheer thrill of it, then even expending resources in search of opportunities for gain might appear counterproductive. But in classical economics and game theory, the expected utility of a prospect is the product of its probability and utility. An actor who is rational in that sense is indifferent, for example, between the certainty of losing $10, a 1/10 chance of losing $100, and a 1/100 chance of losing $1,000. Yet such outcomes are not equivalent in their implications for contracting. In contrast to defection that imposes a certain cost, "defection" that merely creates a risk of damage can remain undetected unless actual harm occurs. Monitoring is especially difficult when defection results in a very small risk of grave damage (analogous to the 1/100 chance of losing $1000), because only a tiny portion of defections actually impose damage. Just as the absence of damage does not imply that no defection occurred, the presence of a damage does not necessarily prove defection. Risk is simply endemic. That is why so much contract litigation involves assigning liability in the case of an unforeseen contingency that affects the ability of one party to perform.

Sixth, as the *nontransferability of costs and benefits* increases, negotiating becomes more intractable. Bargaining determines how benefits and costs will be allocated, so it requires that at least some benefits or costs be transferable. The problems of quantifying and intersubjectively verifying nontransferable benefits and costs underlie the distinction between fungible and unique goods that has been used, for example, to justify the choice between damages and specific performance in contract disputes.

Seventh, as *instability* increases within a relationship, more transaction resources are required to secure rational outcomes. The best way of understanding how instability increases costs is to understand how stability reduces them. Because decisions themselves convey information about the risks of interacting, frequent and consistent decisions reduce the incentives to expend transaction resources on searching and bargaining over acceptable divisions. Moreover, stability facilitates developing internal systems of enforcement with which to deter defection. For egoists in repeated plays of the same prisoner's dilemma game, cooperation rather than defection can become optimal because defection would disrupt a mutually rewarding pattern of cooperation.[42] If the short-term gains from defection are consistently offset by larger long term losses, a stable pattern of cooperation emerges.

C. *The Rational Expenditure of Transaction Resources*

This is a good time to recap the analysis to this point. (1) Rational contractors seek to create mutually advantageous, enforceable agreement. (2) Doing so requires that they satisfy three independent rationality conditions: joint, concession and individual rationality. (3) These rationality conditions correspond to three phases in the contract process and enable the parties to solve three problems of rational choice: (a) the pre-phase coordination problem (joint rationality), (b) the negotiation-phase division problem (concession rationality), (c) the post-phase compliance problem (individual rationality). (4) A process of rational bargaining can satisfy these conditions but still fail to reach fruition in virtue of uncertainty deriving either from incomplete or imperfect information, or from potential defection. (5) Consequently, it will be rational for parties to create safeguards against contract failure. (6) Creating safeguards requires parties to incur three distinct kinds of cost corresponding to the phases in contracting: (a) search costs (pre-phase), (b) decision costs (negotiation phase), (c) monitoring costs (post-phase). (7) The magnitude of these costs will depend on contextual factors shaping the extent of uncertainty

42. *See* R. Axelrod, The Evolution of Cooperation 174 (1984).

under particular circumstances. (8) In general, the magnitude of uncertainty is greatest in guarding against defection, less great in securing a division and least pressing in safeguarding against coordination failure. (9) Rationality requires that crafting safeguards proceed in the opposite temporal direction from contracting corresponding to the general magnitude of risk of failure. Because the risk of defection dominates in the nondivisible prisoner's dilemma, uncertainty about compliance is greatest and, consequently, crafting safeguards against defection is most pressing. (10) The process of creating safeguards can itself be modeled as a rational bargain over the costs of safeguards. The costs of safeguarding depletes transaction resources.

The capacity of the contractors to employ their own resources to reduce uncertainty and create safeguards can be represented graphically. Figure Four describes the types of

Figure 4: Transaction Space Diagram

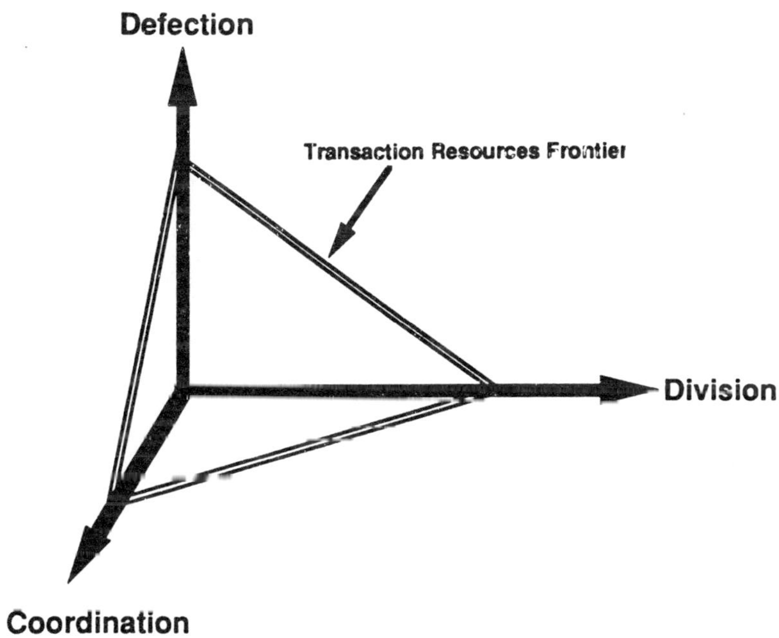

interactions to which contractual arrangements may be matched in the form of a *transaction space diagram*. The vertical axis represents the magnitude of the defection problem. The horizontal axis represents the magnitude of the dividsion problem. And the axis perpendicular to both of these represents the magnitude of the coordination problem.

When a transaction lies near the origin in Figure Four, so that the problems are quite minor, the burden placed upon transaction resources is minimal. In transactions at increasing distances from the origin, indicating that the problems of identifying prospects, of bargaining or of defection are more major, the availability of transaction resources becomes more problematic; the farther any transaction lies from the origin, the greater the transaction costs required for contracting.

In contexts in which the seven factors affecting uncertainty are *favorable* to contracting, only modest resources are required to make contracting possible. For example, small residential groups such as nuclear families possess sufficient endogenous transaction resources with which to develop exceedingly complex systems of mutual understandings. Similarly, conditions in the most hospitable region of transaction space (that is, the area close to the origin) correspond rather well to those identified in any introductory economics text as conducive to private exchange in perfect or near perfect markets. Even in the (otherwise) most inhospitable regions of transaction space, that is, far upward and to the right of the origin but still within the frontier, ingenious safeguards evolve, such as "exchanging hostages" and giving collateral,[43] where people arrive at and enforce contracts independently.

In contexts where the factors affecting uncertainty are unfavorable to contracting, the parties' transaction resources quickly become exhausted. The worst case arises when members of a large, geographically dispersed group with diverse interests consider negotiating an arrangement in which the benefits and costs are delayed, nontransferable, and laden with risk. Locating a national nuclear waste storage facility is an example. Here, the transaction resource frontier will lie close to the origin, indicating that even slight concern over the feasibility of the alternatives or modest division or defection problems exceed the group's ability to contract independently.

43. *See* Kronman, *Contract Law and the State of Nature*, 1 J.L. ECON. & ORG. 5 (1985).

IV. Third-Party Intervention

A. *The Preference for Endogenous Transaction Resources*

We need not presume that a forum external to the original setting of a contract—notably, authoritative experts like judges operating under the auspices of the state—will be more efficacious than private ordering in resolving disputes. This presumption, termed "legal centralism," informs much of the law and economics tradition.[44] That courts or other jurisdictional bodies are necessary to the very idea of contract and are thereby presupposed by the concept itself may simply be an unwarranted theoretical assumption. It does not follow from anything in the analysis presented to this point. To be sure, by assuming that courts exist and stand prepared to enforce whatever agreements private parties make, such a view isolates the problem of breach from those of cooperation and division. In doing so, however, it misleads. For tradeoffs are inevitable among all three problems in contracting. Moreover, judges attempting to make decisions in accord with the theory are denied insights about the constraints rational actors would want on the judges as third-party interveners. Private parties—including social scientists—may find judicial decisions less coherent. Indeed, the resource efficiency of decisions motivated by the paradigm is put in doubt. On grounds of theory, prediction, and policy, the presumption should be struck down in favor of a more realistic one.

Third-party intervention must be explained, not assumed. And it is more plausibly assumed if we start out presuming that people are never without some endogenous transaction resources with which to contract. That means they do not always rely upon or even want a third party to secure agreements.

Endogenous resources, however, are finite. The points in transaction space at which private parties exhaust these resources define what we term the *transaction-resource frontier*. The frontier is simply a way of visualizing the limits to private settlement and the reasons for involving a third party. Attainable gains are lost when contextual features place transactions beyond the frontier and block contracting. That provides an in-

44. *See* O. Williamson, The Economic Institutions of Capitalism (1985); Galanter, *Justice in Many Rooms: Courts, Private Ordering, and Indigenous Law*, 19 J. Legal Pluralism 1 (1981); Llewellyn, *What Price Contract? An Essay in Perspective*, 40 Yale L.J. 704 (1931).

centive for parties to the transaction to seek third-party intervention. When transactions lie outside the transaction-resources frontier, principal parties tend to seek third-party support.

A third party can facilitate contracting in any of three analytically distinct ways. First, it can help to resolve the coordination problem by providing *exogenous transaction resources* to augment the endogenous transaction resources already present in the relationship. If, for example, communication channels are poor, owing to the large number of parties or their geographic dispersion, the centralized channels and *information-processing services* provided by a *mediating* third party may well prove more efficient. Sometimes a mediator recognizes opportunites for mutual gain or audits the status quo more effectively than the principals. Described graphically, this type of intervention moves transactions inside the transaction-resources frontier, or in effect increases the region within which contracting among the principal parties becomes possible. It need not entail granting discretion to the mediator to allocate the gains by defining the terms of an agreement or to enforce one by punishing breach.

Second, third parties can help to resolve the division problem by providing *division services*, for example, a *coalition-building* or *arbitrating* third party may be granted discretion to allocate the gains under the contract, or merely to narrow the range of divisions possible under the contract. Described graphically, this moves the transaction leftward in transaction space, closer to the origin where conditions for contracting are more favorable. It need not entail granting discretion to the arbiter to enforce an agreement, but arbiters, like mediators, need to be a central agent in processing information.

Third, third parties can help to resolve the defection problem by providing *enforcement services*: for example, a *policing* third party may be granted discretion to punish defectors so as to increase the force of contractual agreements. Described graphically, this moves the transaction downward in transaction space, again closer to the origin. It may not entail granting the enforcer discretion to design the terms of an agreement, but to monitor behavior an enforcer needs centralized communication channels like a mediator, and in applying the force of agreement across disputants, the enforcer's judgments may well involve arbiter-like divisioned responsibility.

The existence of finite resources and the need sometimes to expend more than what the parties have available to them creates an incentive for both parties to seek outside help in making and securing contracts. Intervention by a third party, however, may be as problematic as it is promising. First, intervention by a third party complicates the transaction by creating a new contracting problem between it and the principal parties. An n-person game becomes an n+1 person game. The more extensive the intervention, the more powerful the third party can become vis-a-vis the principals.

The third party creates a new coordination problem. The process of searching for a suitable third party and negotiating the terms of its performance is costly. Improperly crafted third party services may prove redundant or unnecessarily intrusive. The greater the intervenor's role in processing information and forging communication channels, the greater too becomes the potential asymmetry between the intervenor and the principals. That can impede the principals' efforts to monitor it as well as each other. In short, the principals may not find it worthwile to involve a third party even when it is a prerequisite to contracting.

Intervention is likely to create a new division problem. How are the residual gains from intervention to be allocated among the principal and third parties? Again, the answer depends on their relative bargaining power. The power of the principals depends on how well they can effect divisions before the intervenor becomes involved. But the more extensive the intervenor's role in determining how contractual gains will be divided, the greater its potential to seize a larger than anticipated share. Greater too is the potential for the intervenor to become embroiled in partisan disputes among the principals and to empower some at the expense of others.

Intervention also creates a new defection problem. The outside party may fear that the principal parties will default on payments after services have been rendered. Alternatively, the more extensive the intervenor's role in establishing enforcement, the greater its potential to punish exploitatively. Indeed, a third party's special access to and control over information makes more difficult the principal parties' problem of preventing its defection by fraud or misrepresentation.

For these reasons, third-party intervention will always strike the principal parties as potentially more threatening than relying on *equivalent* endogenous resources. The implication is that people will prefer using endogenous resources not only because they tend to be less costly, more accessible spatially and temporally, and more readily mobilized than functionally equivalent resources that might be provided by a third party, but also because these resources are less burdened by risk. Moreover, having maximum involvement in shaping the contract helps ensure the principals that it takes efficient account of their preferences and so strengthens their incentives to honor its terms. Studies of arbitration, for example, show that bargainers who succeed in reaching agreement are more likely to honor it than are those who fail and have one imposed by an arbitrator. Finally, even under the simplest conditions, contracting with a third party is asymmetric because the original parties, being more numerous, must bargain among themselves first.

Many of the problems of third-party intervention can be mitigated by competition among providers of the service. Competition gives principals an alternative and, thereby, a safeguard. Thus, it can reduce their bargaining problem and their fear of exploitive mistreatment. This is an important point, because it gives analytic plausibility to suggestions that under conditions in which it is otherwise particularly difficult to constrain a third party, competition among mediators, arbiters, and enforcers may be preferable to a state monopoly on power.[45]

Still, establishing and maintaining a mechanism for third-party intervention is no mere technical exercise by which deficiencies in endogenous transaction resources are corrected. Rather it can be at least as conflictive and politically charged as private contracting. It, too, can fail. Thus, parties have incentives to avoid third-party orderings, such as courts provide, and instead to devise private orderings.[46]

45. *See* Barnett, *Pursuing Justice in a Free Society: Part One—Power vs. Liberty*, CRIM. JUST. ETHICS 50 (Summer-Fall 1985).

46. *See* Galanter, *supra* note 44.

B. *When Only Intervention Will Do*

The existence of uncertainty sufficient to threaten contract failure does not provide a sufficient reason for the parties to call upon third-party intervention. Only when endogenous transaction resources are depleted do the parties have sufficient reason to pursue outside intervention. As we demonstrated above, third-party intervention can create costs in excess of gains. Only if the endogenous resources of the parties are inadequate *and* the expected costs of third-party intervention do not exceed expected gains, would it be rational for contractors to require third-party intervention.

Figure Four depicts the range of cases in which safeguarding against contract failure requires the parties to consume transaction resources.[47] Type I cases fall within the frontier where between them the parties possess adequate resources to resolve whatever problems they face. Moving outward along each axis, endogenous resources prove to be increasingly inadequate. In type II cases, the parties possess internal resources sufficient to solve division and defection problems, but lack resources to identify opportunities for coordination. In type III cases, the parties possess internal resources adequate to identify feasible contracts and to solve the division problem, but are unable by using their own resources to solve the defection problem. In type IV cases, the parties possess internal resources sufficient to solve their defection problem, but are incapable on their own of identifying or solving the division issues. Off the axes, we find a universe of other cases in which the principals in varying degrees lack the resources to resolve combinations of these problems.

This model suggests that we should find that several different types of institutional arrangements emerge in contracting. First, there will exist cases in which private parties are able to

47. The axes and frontier correspond in part to a classification system described in Ellickson, *A Critique of Economic and Sociological Theories of Social Control*, 16 J. LEGAL STUD. 67, 69-71 (1987). Ellickson sees administering positive and negative sanctions as involving rules that divide human behavior into three categories: (1) good behavior triggers rewards; that can have something to do with doctrines encouraging concession-making as well as trust, (2) bad behavior triggers punishment, his concern here is clearly with doctrines discouraging defection; and (3) ordinary behavior that warrants no judicial response; this corresponds to our type I situation where parties have sufficient endogenous resources. As he put it, "The prevalence of tripatite systems is a clue that rulemakers are attuned to an overarching goal of minimizing costs, including administrative costs." *Id.* at 71.

solve their problems without recourse to the intervention of third parties. In fact we find such institutions. The best example is the competitive market. In the market parties are engaged in bilateral agreements, discrete in time and place. A governmental enforcement mechanism is not necessarily a precondition for exchange; self-enforcing convention—sometimes called customary business practices—can work just as well. Markets provide ready sources of alternative exchange opportunities that can be sufficient to safeguard against one party's defecting *before* either performs on an agreement. Without resorting to violence or invoking third-party intervention, private parties can depend on reputational effects and devices like hostage-giving to safeguard against the risks of defection *after* one party acts in reliance on a promised performance.

Transactions along the coordination axis beyond the transaction-resource frontier pose a risk of joint failure sufficient to exhaust the parties' resources for identifying opportunities for mutual gain; that discourages exchange. The simplest convention, like drivers slowing down on approaching an intersection and stopping to wave a crossing vehicle through, break down. More densely settled areas and a more heterogeneous population of drivers will strain the convention, pushing the risks of motorized travel to the point where people begin to forgo its benefits or endure increasing costs. Someone can reduce the strain simply by setting a rule, almost any rule: when two vehicles approach an intersection simultaneously, the vehicle on the *right* proceeds first; where traffic density makes simultaneity increasingly expensive and variable to judge, install a traffic signal.

Contract law has, for example, the mailbox rule: an offeree has power to accept and close a contract by mailing a letter of acceptance, properly stamped and addressed.[48] Little economic justification can be found to support dating the contract from the mailing of the acceptance rather than from its receipt. Its economic justification can be found in the market-expanding properties of having a rule.[49] Like trade associations in various industries that develop consensus standards for product attrib-

48. *See* A. CORBIN, CORBIN ON CONTRACTS 124 (1952).

49. "One of the parties must carry the risk of loss and inconvenience. We need a definite rule; but we must choose one. We can put the risk on either party; but we must not leave it in doubt. The party not carrying the risk can then act promptly and with confidence in reliance on the contract; the party carrying the risk can insure against it if

utes so as to expand the total market for their products, the court expands the resource frontier so that private parties will engage in more transactions.

Beyond the frontier along the division axis, the participants primarily lack resources with which to solve the division problem. The parties would not get to the division problem without having identified an opportunity for productive exchange. Solving the defection problem is less significant, either because of ample internal enforcement resources or because incentives to defect are comparatively weak.

Some scholars have noticed the significance of the division problem in contract doctrine. But almost all of these scholars have confused the rational division problem as a matter of private law with a social or public theory of "fair distribution." For example, Farber suggests that contract law has a mandatory risk sharing system, a social safety net, and it is difficult for parties to bargain around it.[50] Thus, although freedom of contract means the power of parties to allocate risks between themselves, some contract rules reveal a countermanding principle of loss spreading, for example, rules against penalty clauses and warranty disclosure for personal injury to prevent catastrophic losses to one party. Similarly, Dalton has claimed that doctrines such as quasi-contract, duress, and unconscionability police the limits of acceptable bargains by private parties in the name of social (public) norms of fairness.[51] And Cohen claims that court adjudication supplements an original contract as a means of distributing gains and losses from unanticipated events. In this view, contract law consists of rules by which the courts accomplish this according to the equities of such cases. That follows not from the agreement between individuals but as a way of enforcing some kind of distributive justice within the legal system.[52]

These characterizations of the distributive dimensions of contract law may go too far. Our model implies that when courts impose distributive schemes on the parties, their doing so is compatible with the interests of the parties in the contract.

he so desires. The business rule throwing the risk on the offeror has the merit of closing the deal more quickly and enabling the performance more promptly." *Id.* at 126.

50. *See* Farber, *supra* note 18, at 336.

51. *See* Dalton, *An Essay in the Deconstruction of Contract Doctrine*, 94 YALE L.J. 999, 1001 (1985).

52. *See* M. COHEN, LAW AND THE SOCIAL ORDER 101-02 (1967).

No appeal to a global concern for distributive fairness, therefore, is necessary to understand or to justify a court's willingness to impose a distribution of risk among the parties. The legitimate exercise of that authority is restricted to the domain of outcomes the parties would have bargained within, and not to the set of outcomes that would be preferable from the point of view of a principle of social justice or social insurance. However, to the extent that the court, acting as an arbiter, seeks to implement a doctrine likely to resolve a wide range of division disputes efficiently, it may turn to widely accepted principles of social justice for guidance on the grounds that those principles themselves represent an evolved, rational or efficient solution to a wide range of division problems.

Transactions beyond the frontier along the defection axis indicate the defection problem is intractable internally but the cooperation and division problems are soluble. Parties here have relatively abundant internal bargaining resources but deficient internal enforcement resources. Intervention therefore takes the form of an externally applied enforcement system that moves the transactions downward, inside the frontier. Within the constraints of that system, individuals retain control over the terms of the contracts they enter.

The features that make a market such an attractive governance system—anonymity, sponteneity, disaggregated decisions adaptive to local circumstances—exacerbate the endemic risks of defection. Classical economists at least since Adam Smith have foreseen a productive role for a centralized enforcing agent. If third-party intervention diminishes ex post risks, people are freer to expend resources ex ante on searching for and reaching agreements that satisfy joint and concession rationality. Hence, common-law, judicially crafted safeguards that penalize contract breach are widely regarded as promoting economic efficiency.

Of course third-party safeguards designed primarily to reduce the probability of defection can influence the concession rationality of private decisions. That is because the remedies available under contract cannot escape dividing the residual risks of social intercourse and imposing different burdens of proof on the affected parties when one defaults.[53]

53. For examples, see the essays in THE ECONOMICS OF CONTRACT LAW (A. Kronman & R. Posner eds. 1979).

In areas of transaction space away from an axis and outside the frontier, the internal deficit of transaction resources is more profound. Here, assistance is required in solving a combination of problems that afflict contractual relationships. Indeed, even if in absolute terms a relationship is richly endowed with transaction resources, it is virtually assured of falling farthest from the three axes when all of the contextual features we identified impose large obstacles to contracting. Consequently, the degree of third-party intervention is greater because the third party must not only enforce contracts but also specify their terms and bring contractors to the bargaining table.

V. Implications for Contract Law

Our theory implies the following about contractual relationships: (1) not every effort to contract in the absence of law will succeed; (2) contract failure can result from a failure to solve problems of either (a) coordination, (b) division or (c) defection (compliance); (3) these problems are in principle solvable by rational parties negotiating with complete information; (4) contract failure is, therefore, best thought of as owing to some form of uncertainty; (5) parties to an agreement seek to reduce uncertainty by expending endogenous resources; (6) contract failure in the absence of law results when these efforts at safeguarding are inadequate.

That implies the following about law: (1) law as a means of safeguarding can not, therefore, be assumed by a theory of contract, but must be explained instead; (2) the best explanation of it is that law is rational for contractors only if (a) it provides exogenous transaction resources that are necessary to insure a successful contract, and (b) the benefits of appealing to law to enable contracting exceed its costs. (3) Once law is in place, however, it is less costly for individuals to appeal to it to help resolve their contractual disputes than it would have been for them to *create* law for these purposes. (4) In reviewing cases in contract to understand or to criticize developing legal rules, we should inquire into whether uncertainty in coordination, division or compliance is the source of contract failure. We want to know whether the parties are in court because they lack sufficient search, negotiation or monitoring transaction resources. Then we can determine what kind of legal role the court is being asked to play: mediation, arbitration, policing, or all three.

A full rational-choice theory of contract law will demonstrate how different cases can be analyzed as falling into all three categories and the conditions under which rational default rules will call for intervention by courts. (5) The rationality of legal rules, from the point of view of this theory, will not depend on their abstract rationality or efficiency, but on their rationality in the context in which they are to apply.

To this point we have identified the phases of contracting; three associated conditions of rationality that must be satisfied if contracting is to be rational; three related problems rational actors may face in securing a rational contract; the safeguards—endogenous and exogenous—available to protect against contract failure; and the factors that affect the nature and scope of the transaction cost problem. If we are correct, many cases or doctrines in contract law can be assessed as rational responses to problems of coordination, division and defection, corresponding to the three axes defining the transaction resource space. Our long range ambition is to demonstrate the power of the theory in each of these areas where courts have been asked to serve the function of providing exogenous resources.

In this essay, having set forth the general theory for the first time, we attempt a more modest illustration of its relevance. Thus, we take up the role a court might be asked to play in solving coordination problems by playing what we have called a mediating role. In doing so, we analyze in detail a famous case in contract law, *Laidlaw v. Organ*,[54] which in most other accounts is seen primarily as a case creating a property right in information unencumbered by a duty to disclose—a right lauded by proponents of economic efficiency. Contrary to prevailing wisdom, we argue that the court's decision is best understood as serving a coordination function. The decision promotes efficiency, not because a property right in information is efficient, but because the court's authoritative pronouncement reduces uncertainty and provides salience. Thus, we choose the disclosure issue as it arises in *Laidlaw v. Organ* to illustrate both how our theory leads one to think about cases *and* how it may lead to answers different from those suggested by traditional economic analysis.

54. 15 U.S. (2 Wheat.) 178 (1817).

A. *Coordination, Search, and Disclosure*

Nothing could be more fundamental to the notion of a rational bargain than the behavioral presumption that decision makers calculate the relative benefits and costs of alternative contracts predicated upon available information. Because information is costly, it follows that decision makers invest in information to refine their expectations, or in other words, to safeguard themselves. The efficiency of these investments in mitigating risk is always a private and a social concern. It can become a legal concern when one party knows or has reason to know that another is in error about information material to the calculation. When does a contracting party have a duty to disclose, failing which the other party will be excused from performance?

According to Kronman,[55] the nondisclosure doctrine the courts have crafted encourages socially efficient contracting by creating a property right in information. People may retain the benefits of their efforts to secure information relevant to productive exchange opportunities, except in circumstances in which they would have come by the information without effort. When they can come by the information without effort, a disclosure requirement would not reduce the incentive to produce it, and so might not be inefficient. In cases of mistake and disclosure, this argument holds, the court has been called upon as a third-party enforcement agent and it has done so in a way that is at least consistent with the principle of economic efficiency.

Kronman is surely right about the incentives that this doctrine can give individuals to invest in information: "One effective way of insuring that an individual will benefit from the possession of information (or anything else for that matter) is to assign him a property right in the information itself—a right or entitlement to invoke the coercive machinery of the state in order to exclude others from its use and enjoyment. The benefits of possession become secure only when the state transforms the possessor of information into an owner by investing him with a legally enforceable property right of some sort or other."[56]

The more secure the right to information, the more an indi-

55. Kronman, *Mistake, Disclosure, Information, and the Law of Contracts*, 11 J. Legal Stud. 1 (1978).

56. *Id.* at 14.

vidual will be inclined to invest in producing it. The *social* as opposed to the *individual* benefits of such a property right, however, are not as obvious, nor is the distinction between information that results from deliberate search and that which has been casually acquired necessarily decisive in establishing the economic efficiency of the appropriate legal doctrine.

To see where Kronman's argument goes awry, consider the case that is central to his analysis: *Laidlaw v. Organ*. Kronman's recitation of the pertinent facts is illuminating. Organ, a New Orleans commission merchant, had been bargaining with Francis Girault of Laidlaw & Co., also commission merchants, to purchase 111 hogsheads of tobacco. Early in the morning of February 19, 1815, Organ received news that the Treaty of Ghent had been signed, formally ending the War of 1812. Organ obtained the news from a Mr. Shepard, who had a financial interest in the transaction with Laidlaw and whose brother was one of three gentlemen who brought the news from the British fleet. Before 8 A.M., when the news would be made public in a handbill, Organ called on Girault to consummate the purchase. Girault asked "if there was any news which was calculated to enhance the price or value of the article about to be purchased"; the record is not clear on Organ's response other than Laidlaw's attorney alleging "the vendee was silent." Nevertheless Girault and Organ entered into a contract.

The price of tobacco quickly rose by thirty to fifty percent as news of the treaty circulated, signalling an end to the naval blockade of New Orleans and the resumption of exporting. Kronman reports that Laidlaw retained possssion of the tobacco, but the court record indicates that he first transferred it to Organ, then recaptured it by force. In any case, Organ then brought suit for damages and to block Laidlaw from otherwise disposing of the tobacco. The trial judge evidently directed a verdict in Organ's favor, deciding from the testimony that no fraud occurred. On appeal before the Supreme Court, Laidlaw's attorney argued, among other points, that fraud was a matter for the jury to decide.

The Court agreed, reversed the judgment, and remanded with directions for a new trial. Other than noting that Organ's silence may have been fraudulent, Kronman puts aside questions of fraud. He focuses on the *dictum* rather than the holding in the Court's opinion, delivered by Chief Justice Marshall.

Generally regarded as an accurate statement of the law, it reads as follows:

> The question in this case is, whether the intelligence of extrinsic circumstances, which might influence the price of the commodity, and which was exclusively within the knowledge of the vendee, ought to have been communicated by him to the vendor? The court is of opinion that he was not bound to communicate it. It would be difficult to circumscribe the contrary doctrine within proper limits, where the means of intelligence are equally accessible to both parties. But at the same time, each party must take care not to say or do anything tending to impose upon the other.[57]

The attractiveness and subsequent longevity of Marshall's opinion derives, in Kronman's view, from its consistency with the principles of economic efficiency. It gives contracting parties incentives to get valuable information to the market as quickly as efficient investment in producing knowledge permits. Indeed, "[t]he greater the likelihood that . . . information will be deliberately produced [acquired at a cost that would not have been incurred but for the likelihood that the information in question would actually be produced,] rather than casually discovered [by chance], the more plausible the assumption becomes that a blanket rule permitting nondisclosure will have benefits that outweigh its costs."[58] In addition, the administrative costs facing the courts in crafting exceptions are lower compared to the costs of imposing limits on a blanket rule creating a duty to disclose. In sum, a rule of nondisclosure is productively efficient, and a rule of disclosure is too costly to administer.

It is not obvious, however, that a property right in information is productively efficient. Moreover, what is relevant in determining the efficiency of the rule is not the manner in which the information is obtained (casually or deliberately), but its incentive effects (productive or redistributive). Consider, in this regard, an argument by the economist Hirshleifer.[59] Central to Hirshleifer's account is the distinction between foreknowledge—predicting events that nature will autonomously make known to all—from discovery—recognizing something that

57. *Laidlaw*, 15 U.S. (2 Wheat) at 195.

58. Kronman, *supra* note 55, at 18.

59. Hirshleifer, *The Private and Social Value of Information and the Reward to Inventive Activity*, 61 Am. Econ. Rev. 561 (1977).

possibly already exists, though hidden from view until human action extracts it. Information of either sort has value only if it can affect action. From an individual's perspective, the value of new information and hence of investing in generating it, derives from *technology*, gains from allocating resources more efficiently, and *distribution*, wealth transfers that follow from price changes. In the case of technology, information makes the "pie" larger and thus increases ex ante each person's potential share. In the case of distribution, information does not increase the pie's size, only the shares of those who have the relevant information.

From society's perspective, the consequences of technological information are largely salutary, while those of redistributive information are not. As Hirshleifer puts it, "The distributive advantage of private information provides an incentive for information generating activity that may quite possibly be in excess of the social value of the information."[60] The argument is this: all information has a technological as well as a redistributive dimension. In many cases, investment in information will be socially efficient because the technological gains will outweigh the costs of investment. However, in some cases, the technological effects will be less significant than the redistributive ones. In these cases, private investment can exceed social return.

Consider two cases. In one case, Jones and Smith each invest $1 to gather information, the technological effect of which is $10, while the redistributive effect is $1.50. Two dollars are spent to secure $10; $1.50 goes to the discoverer, say Jones, with the net gain of $8 shared among the group (including Jones). In the other case, Jones and Smith again invest $1 to uncover information whose social value is only $.25, but whose redistributive value is $1.50. Jones and Smith each act rationally, spending $1 to seek $1.50, but the net effect is inefficient. Two dollars are spent to create $.25. Thus, giving individuals the full benefit of the information they obtain may lead them to act in socially inefficient ways whenever the redistributive aspect of information dominates its technological dimension.

Kronman recognizes that a rule in favor of nondisclosure can create perverse incentives and, therefore, that the decision to

60. *Id.* at 570.

permit nondisclosure of certain information forces a practical choice between over- and underinvestment. His considered judgment is that because it is "certain" that eliminating property rights will result in underproduction, and "merely a danger" that recognizing them will result in overproduction, the economic case for recognizing them is strong ("but not conclusive"), especially when information is deliberately acquired.[61] Neither alternative is optimal, he notes, but assuming legal rules cannot be more finely tuned, the latter one is better.

Though Kronman relies upon considerations of the sort Hirshleifer summons, his conclusion—that a property right to information that does not require disclosure is, on balance, efficient—is, if Hirshleifer is right, unwarranted. As Hirshleifer sees it, the incentives to secure a distributive advantage "eliminate any *a priori* anticipation of underinvestment in the generation of new technological knowledge."[62] That is, investment in information that is likely to be primarily redistributive with little apparent gain in efficiency may be so great under a rule of nondisclosure that the costs of such a rule in terms of inefficient rent-seeking behavior may outweigh its benefits in terms of the production of net social gains. Thus, Kronman ought not confidently claim, as he does, that "allocative efficiency is best served by permitting one who possesses deliberately acquired information to enter and enforce favorable bargains without disclosing what he knows."[63] Whether the social gains created by a property right in information unencumbered by a requirement of disclosure will outweigh the social costs of investment depends on the relative effect—technological or redistributive—of the information.

Kronman's argument can be read as supporting a property right in information unencumbered by a disclosure rule on the grounds that any more finely-tuned rule will be too costly to administer. Administrative, rather than allocative, efficiency becomes the core of the argument. In order to create an adequate incentive to invest in information, a legal right to the information must be created, and the shape of that right, whether it requires disclosure or not, depends on considerations of ad-

61. Kronman, *supra* note 55, at 17 n.46.
62. Hirshleifer, *supra* note 59, at 573.
63. Kronman, *supra* note 55, at 17.

ministrative cost avoidance. The latter point is emphasized by Chief Justice Marshall.

The foregoing argument rests on three assumptions: first, of course, that a legal property right in information unencumbered by a disclosure rule is *necessary* to secure the benefits of information; second, that such an approach produces benefits in excess of costs; and third, that the property rule in information cannot cost-effectively be more finely-tuned. The truth of none of these assumptions is obvious. First, creating a legally enforceable right is not the *only* means to security. Indeed, people may be able to make the benefits of possession relatively more secure by resorting first to their endogenous transaction resources rather than depending upon legal rules. That was our point much emphasized in Part IV, and, as we shall show, *Laidlaw* in particular was a case in which the parties, commission merchants dealing in a competitive commodities market, were particularly well-suited to secure the gains from information in the absence of legal safeguards. Property rights were neither necessary nor rational. Second, given the risks of third-party intervention we identified in Part IV, action by the state cannot be assumed to secure benefits in excess of costs. Finally, while circumscribing a duty to disclose might be difficult, as Chief Justice Marshall opined, we cannot *a priori* rule out its feasibility in all circumstances.[64]

Even if Kronman's analysis of the problem in terms of the efficiency of a rule of nondisclosure is unpersuasive, he correctly sees the general problem: if the parties to a contract fail to allocate risks and turn to the court for remedy, what default rule makes sense? The answer depends on the risks that will be of concern to rational actors. Kronman takes it that rational actors are primarily concerned with what Hirshleifer called technological risks; in allocating the risk of a mistake, for example,

64. *See Laidlaw*, 15 U.S. (2 Wheat.) at 195. Chamberlin and Scheppele argue that Kronman's approach is wrong because the risk is deeply strategic, a risk that secrets may be employed to influence the actions or feelings of others. The question before the court is how to allocate knowledge between two parties given that one party has it already; the answer turns on the advantage people may be allowed to take of each other. This is something of a distributive risk rather than one of allocative efficiency. Chamberlin and Scheppele effect a Rawlsian solution, analyzing the legal rules as the product of a hypothetical agreement reached among rational actors in advance of knowing whether one or another will be in possession of a deep or shallow secret. *See* J. Chamberlin & K. Scheppele, Fairness and Symmetry in Information Games, Paper Presented at the Meetings of the American Political Science Association (Aug. 1986).

a nondisclosure rule imposes that risk on the mistaken party. The question before the Court in applying that default rule is whether the information required to avoid the mistake is more likely to be generated by chance or by deliberate searching. But what of the redistributive risk that Hirshleifer identified, that is, the risk that private information can be used for redistributive ends? In *Laidlaw*, do technological or redistributive risks dominate?

In bargaining theoretic terms, the default rule embraces both risks: the rule minimize the sum of the costs of uncertainty and of its avoidance. The question before the court is who is in the best position to accomplish that? In some contexts, in which the risks are primarily technological, the court should act in accord with Kronman's formulation of the default rule. When other risks, especially distributive ones, predominate, focusing on whether the information to be disclosed is more likely to be revealed by chance or by deliberate search will not be an appropriate test. In sum, Kronman may be right that the rule is efficient, but for the wrong reasons. Thus, his formula for applying the default rule is misguided.

Examining more closely the context, as well as the holding, in *Laidlaw v. Organ* provides a good illustration of a more rigorous formula consistent with the theory outlined in Sections II through IV. First, the end of the naval blockade, like a drought or a blight, describes a state of nature inevitably to be revealed to the public; information about them is less technological than distributive. So this is *not* the sort of case that, on either Kronman's or Hirshleifer's account, suggests a nondisclosure rule.

Second, the context reveals a network of pre-existing contractual agreements within which the dispute arose. That sheds light on the demand for third-party intervention and sets the stage for Chief Justice Marshall's dictum. The case concerned a contract for a commodity. Conditions in commodity markets represent a close real-world approximation to those found in a theoretical model of a pure exchange economy. Goods are exchanged on the spot, so contracts are well defined in time, place, and purpose. Allowing for readily observable differences in grades, tobacco is a relatively homogeneous and divisible good. Although merchants in a given city who specialize in one commodity might be a relatively small fraternity of members who come to know each other over time, they tend to be sufficiently numerous—or potentially so with relatively low entry costs—so no one sets prices. So long as many exchanges occur, the primary safeguard afforded a tobacco merchant lies in the alternative merchants waiting to deal.

If tobacco merchants buy on their own accounts, as did Organ and Laidlaw, they take on an economic function more than that of sales agents. Commission merchants facilitate market exchange in two ways, both characterized by specializing in *search* activities. First, they collect a transaction fee for bringing buyers and sellers together, narrowing the spread between price bid and price asked. Second, they speculate on extrinsic circumstances, as Chief Justice Marshall phrased it, hedging their exposure to risk by adjusting their inventories. Given the uncertainties, varying initial conditions, and costs of exchange faced by their principals, commission merchants become "market makers," specialists who increase the liquidity and reduce the costs of participating in the commodity trade.[65]

We might expect these merchants to have ample endogenous resources for private contracting. Long before *Laidlaw v. Organ*, they invested in information, making deals and allowing producers to specialize in production. They need no third party to *mediate*; indeed, the merchants are mediators. Moreover, these merchants regularly negotiate over quantity, quality, and price. The risks of unfair divisions are mitigated by transforming the decisions into a sequence solvable within the constraints of available bargaining resources held by private parties. As a consequence these merchants do not normally need a third party to *arbitrate*. Finally, alternative exchange opportunities and reputation effects typically mitigate defection incentives without unduly straining enforcement resources. Thus, the merchants need not risk creating a third-party *enforcer*, except to deal with those categories of defections that are unusually costly to safeguard.

In short, given the theory presented here in which the principal parties are viewed as rational actors embeded in particular

65. "[S]peculation in grain, for example by setting aside a certain class of persons to assume the risks of trade, has the effect of reducing these risks by putting them in the hands of those who have most knowledge, for, as we have seen, risk varies inversely with knowledge." I. Fisher, The Theory of Interest 221 (1930); *see also* S. Khoury, Speculative Markets 169-70 (1984); Williams, *Futures Markets: A Consequence of Risk Aversion or Transaction Costs*, 95 J. Pol. Econ. 1000 (1987).

contexts, it would appear to follow that neither Laidlow nor Organ had sufficient reason to seek any form of third-party intervention. The context, which is so important to our analysis, is one that suggests that the parties in this case possessed easy access to ample endogenous transaction resources.

Two aspects of the case need to be explained. The first is the holding in the case; the second is the dicta. To explain the Supreme Court's holding in the case, we need first to understand how the case came to court, and the question of law the Court was asked to resolve. Recall that we distinguish among three sorts of risks parties will seek to safeguard against, first by deploying endogenous transaction resources, and then by pursuing third-party intervention in the event their resources are inadequate to the task. These are risks of failed coordination, division and defection. When courts are sought to safeguard, we say that they play mediation, arbitration or enforcement roles respectively.

The case comes to court framed as a defection problem in which the principal parties are requesting the court to play an enforcement or policing role. Organ brought the case to court claiming Laidlaw's breach. Laidlaw's defense to the charge of breach rested on Organ's alleged fraudulent misrepresentation of the facts. For his part, Organ sued for possession of the tobacco and for his damages, in effect seeking to employ the power of the state to enforce the contract and, thereby, to punish Laidlaw's breach. The trial judge refused to submit the question of fraud to the jury. The jury refused to award damages, preferring instead to award possession of the tobacco. To be sure, Laidlaw's counsel raised the division problem on appeal: "Though [Laidlaw], after they heard the news of peace, still went on, in ignorance of their legal rights, to complete the contract, equity will protect them."[66]

Because the issue as presented on appeal was that of fraud, the Supreme Court could not avoid addressing the question of defection. It agreed with Laidlaw that the trial judge erred in refusing to submit the question of fraud to the jury and accordingly remanded for a new trial. On the other hand the court did not allow itself to be dragged into protecting against unfair divisions under precisely the conditions where the parties could

66. *Laidlaw*, 15 U.S. (2 Wheat) at 190.

safeguard privately at much lower transaction cost. Division problems are more cheaply solved in a competitive market, as was the context here, than in a court. That accounts in part for Chief Justice Marshall's concern about the administrative costs of judicial intervention: "It would be difficult to circumscribe the contrary doctrine [disclosure] within proper limits, where the means of intelligence are equally accessible to both parties."[67]

Following Kronman's lead, economic analysis ignores the Court's holding, focusing entirely on Chief Justice Marshall's dictum. Our analysis offers a plausible reconstruction of both. Part III shows that safeguarding against defection is the most information-intensive of the three dimensions in rational contracting. The calculus of safeguarding against breach is the most complex. The probability of mistake is greatest and, accordingly, so are the costs of guarding against it.

To see this, consider the difference between errors made in safeguarding divisions and those made in safeguarding against potential defections. If the principals or a court errs in safeguarding against unfair division, the error simply moves the parties from one point along the contract curve to another. The parties remain on the contract curve and, therefore, are better off than both would have been had no contract been made.

In contrast, a mistake in discerning or correcting for an alleged breach can make either party worse off than he would have been in the absence of agreement. Mistakenly determining that no breach has occurred enforces the breaching party's nonperformance payoff. That necessarily makes the other party worse off than he was at the point of no agreement, that is, the status quo. On the other hand, because the force of agreement is aimed at displacing the defection payoff towards the point of no agreement, imposing a penalty when no breach has occurred forces both parties off the contract curve.

Further, when a court as third party determines that a breach has occurred, it sends a message of potential unreliability to other potential cooperators. It thus chills cooperative endeavors. It reminds the parties of the need to expend transaction resources to reduce the probability of nonperformance, and it reminds everyone that sometimes even the optimal expendi-

67. *Id.* at 195.

ture of resources will not foreclose entirely the chance of being victimized by one's partners.

Given this, it is that much more important that courts reduce the probability of error. Court decisions regarding divisions of the gains from trade have no comparable effects on markets. In this sense, mutual trust is more important than is fairness to a scheme of cooperation by contract. In sum, the greatest probability and cost of making a mistake in rational contracting occur in discerning or protecting against defection.

As between a judge and a jury, the jury is better positioned to determine whether a fraudulent "imposition was practiced," that is, whether a defection occured. The reason is rather straight-forward. A finding of fraud typically turns heavily on findings of fact, such as the prevailing practices in the business community (because that delimits what each party can be assumed to have known) and who communicated what, to whom and when. For accuracy, reliability, and community representation in fact finding, a multi-member decision-making body operating under unanimity rule is preferable to a single decision maker, perhaps even an experienced one.[68] Given that the principal parties could no longer resolve the issue privately, remanding for a new jury trial places discretion where the sum of the costs of uncertainty and of safeguarding against it are likely to be least. Thus, our theory provides an extremely plausible account of the case's holding. Now to Chief Justice Marshall's famous dictum.

One supposes that part of what makes commodities markets valuable is their ability to process information—even information about extraordinary events—without recourse to either violent or legal action. However extraordinary an event the signing of a treaty is, it is not more so than is a blight or drought, all of which create opportunities for merchants to use for their personal benefit information not yet available to others.

After having turned over the tobacco, on the day following circulation of the handbill announcing the Treaty, Laidlaw, "by force" retook possession of the tobacco and withheld it from Organ. That action, should it prevail as a practice, would

68. *See* R. Hastie, S. Penrod, & N. Pennington, Inside the Jury (1983); Kaye, *And Then There Were Twelve: Statistical Reasoning, the Supreme Court, and the Size of the Jury*, 68 Calif. L. Rev. 1004 (1980).

threaten the network of communication channels that makes possible market exchange, the specialized normative infrastructure that permits commission merchants to extract payment for their services. The decision to seek to sequester only highlights the extent of the risk, for doing so put at risk whatever gains had been captured by the initial contractual scheme of cooperation.[69]

Think of the problem this way: Laidlaw and Organ are potential cooperators. They disagree about whether individuals who have private information affecting prices should make full disclosure to their contracting partners. That they disagree about disclosure may be unknown to both of them, and in the bulk of the transactions between them their disagreement has no impact. In the circumstances presented by the facts of the case, however, the difference of opinion obviously makes a difference. The important difference between the parties, however, is *not* that one of them is right from either a moral or an economic point of view about the duty to disclose. Rather, what is important is the existence of a *difference*, period. The existence of a difference makes coordination difficult. Bargaining is always easier when property rights are well defined, and it is most difficult when genuine disagreement about them exists.

This disagreement about the norm regarding disclosure or its applicability in the circumstances surrounding the sale is played out in Laidlaw's recapture of the tobacco (or his failing to deliver it—depending on one's reading of the record). This action ultimately invites the Supreme Court to provide an authoritative pronouncement regarding disclosure or misrepresentation. In doing so the Court will play a *mediating* role, specifying authoritatively the norms governing market transactions, thereby reducing the risks and costs of cooperation. To

69. Although two parties always invest in crafting contractual safeguards when allocating risk, it is particularly difficult to craft a force of agreement that will ensure compliance when, as here, the contract entails the small risk of a large loss. Laidlaw lost big. The facts ex post created a circumstance in which reclaiming the tobacco made sense even accounting for possible legal action by Organ and approbation from the community. Whatever privately enforced norms existed among commodity brokers in New Orleans, Laidlaw, who appeared to be performing in accord with the contract long after news of the Treaty circulated, no doubt had to confront his client, a New York merchant who might not have had a stake in those norms. Indeed, whether in the absence of legal action reputation effects would have ultimately punished Laidlaw or Organ for violating a norm could well have been unclear. Given the immediate stakes, each party had ample incentive to seek authoritative affirmation of his view.

see this, we should consider both the context of the case and the longevity of the Court's dictum.

We can distinguish between the coordination and welfare effects of a rule. In circumstances of the sort commission merchants faced, any authoritative rule would have solved their coordination problem. This was, as we noted, a highly competitive market in which the principal parties were repeat players. What Laidlaw and Organ needed was an authoritative characterization of the rule—whatever its content. In that sense, either ruling on disclosure would have sufficed. Thus, from a coordination point of view, the rule expressed in Chief Justice Marshall's opinion has no special efficacy with respect to people investing efficiently in information. Once the rule is in place, negotiations between the parties are easier because the threat of noncoordination is reduced.

If it happens that all negotiating parties discover that they could do better under the alternative rule, then the rule the court announces will be unstable. No party will diverge from it unilaterally but all may be inclined to do so jointly. In the case under discussion, as we already noted, the private information concerned *price changes* and was fundamentally distributive, not productive, in its impact. Thus, there is no reason to think that a norm requiring disclosure would be any less efficient from a welfare point of view than would the rule the court actually advanced. So in the instant case and in competitive or repeat play circumstances generally, either ruling would be efficient in both the coordination and welfare sense.

The point of the Court's opinion, then, is to facilitate communication by providing salience in the form of a nearly arbitrary choice. With respect to all other matters relating to coordination, the Court put the burden of deciding how much to expend on safeguarding squarely on the shoulders of those in the best position to exercise that judgment—the principal parties. That is just as it should be. As Michael Taylor has argued in other contexts, by serving an authoritative coordination role unnecessarily, the state decreases the incentives for parties to devise creative solutions of their own.[70] By substituting legal pronouncements for endogenously devised ones, the state weakens the bonds of community, or, in this case, weak-

70. *See* M. Taylor, Anarchy, Community and Liberty (1982).

ens the market structure. In short, however disinclined they may become to rely upon or to exhaust their transaction resources in favor of a third-party solution, when the principal parties remain in the best position to contract efficiently, courts should place the burdens of safeguarding on them. That is precisely what this case does.

We say that the Court's choice of a rule that does not require disclosure is *nearly*, but not fully arbitrary, for the following reason. Sometimes principal parties will lack endogenous transaction resources sufficient to resolve all conflicts on the terms of cooperation. Perhaps the market in which they transact is inadequately competitive and therefore too few alternatives exist; or the players are contracting on a one-time basis, in which reputational effects are minimized. In these circumstances the parties may rationally call upon the court to mediate. In that event, the rule that does not impose a duty to disclose may be easier to administer than likely alternatives to it. Moreover, if the Court retained discretion to allocate the search and distributive risks involved here, it might incur high direct costs as well as frequently abuse the notions of fair division held by private parties and communities, thereby calling into question the legitimacy of its value as a third-party intervenor.

This is a case about coordination and mediation. As such, either legal rule would have sufficed. Moreover, from the point of view of wealth or welfare maximization, the circumstances of this case provide no argument for nondisclosure as a default rule ex ante. In short, the choice of the nondisclosure rule rests ultimately on considerations of administrative efficiency.

To sum up, Kronman, like much of the law and economics literature that follows his article, reads *Laidlaw* as creating a property right in information, one that can be squared with efficiency. We have argued first that a property right in information may not be generally efficient, and second that a more compelling characterization of *Laidlaw*, one that follows from the theory developed here, sees it primarily as a court resolving a coordination problem by providing salience via authoritative ruling. A court thus mediates rather than arbitrates or polices and, in that way, protects against the transaction-resource frontier shrinking.

Though our analysis of *Laidlaw* is at odds with traditional economic analysis, there are bound to be many areas of overlap. After all, nothing we have said diminishes the incentives associated with protecting the right of one party to realize the gains associated from specialized investments in information. However, it may not be necessary or appropriate to reach the distinction emphasized by Kronman between casual and deliberately acquired information in order to explain the case law. A more plausible explanation, we believe, has the Court distinguishing among the relative efficacy of alternative safeguards—including judicial intervention—given the risks of contract failure involved, and placing responsibility and discretion with the party or parties who are in the best position to safeguard. Perhaps we can further illustrate the force of our theory by comparing the analysis of other cases it suggests with the analysis Kronman offers.

Two lines of cases Kronman explores involve real estate, either the existence of subsurface oil or mineral deposits known by the buyer but not the seller, or the anticipation of a development of some sort that will make the property in question more valuable.[71] In both cases we have speculative, commodity-like markets. Courts would avoid intervening without more compelling reason because the disputants are the most efficient allocators of the risks.[72]

The third line of cases involves distinguishing patent from latent defects. The logic of the standard economic argument merits attention. Suppose the seller can come by the information about a defect without deliberate investigation. If the argu-

71. In the case of Neill v. Shamburg, 158 Pa. 263, 27 A. 992 (1893), a cotenant on an oil lease, Shamburg, discovered a particularly valuable well in the course of developing an adjacent parcel. He did not disclose this when he purchased the interst of his cotentant, Neill. The court rejected Neill's request to set aside the sale. Curiously, Shamburg's information might have been casually acquired in the sense Kronman means; Shamburg was incurring costs to develop the adjacent parcel for oil production anyway.

72. Kronman notes that the courts find a compelling reason in many of these cases because the problem involves breach of a confidential or fiduciary relation between parties to the contract. In these instances, failure to disclose is constructively fraudulent—defection. In other instances, the problem involves discriminating between nondisclosure and positive misrepresentation (fraud). Because these cases center on difficult questions of fact "about which it is difficult to generalize in a way that is theoretically interesting," he elects not to discuss these problems. *See* Kronman, *supra* note 55, at 19. From the perspective of bargaining and transaction costs, interesting generalizations become possible. We should be able to discriminate among these sorts of relationships, that is, guardian and ward, partner and copartners, principal and agent, where market safeguards will be less readily available to mitigate heightened risks, especially ex post risks of defection. In addition, discriminating who is in the best position to ascertain facts and act efficiently with respect to them should prove more tractable than ascertaining the facts themselves.

ment against a disclosure rule applies to information available only through investment in discovery, why do the courts not impose a duty to disclose on the seller as the party able to avoid a mistake at least cost? In fact, the court imposes no such duty. Kronman resolves the inconsistency by saying the "rule that a seller of real property has no duty to disclose *patent* defects makes economic sense where—as is often the case—the seller has no reason to know that the buyer is mistaken."[73] Kronman's resolution does not reach the question whether the seller would come by the information through deliberate investigation for defects, and therefore does not invoke the distinction between casual and deliberate means of obtaining information. Rather, his solution invokes considerations much more amenable to our analysis, for it turns on the question of who should allocate risk when information is public and, hence, has no economic value; that is, information as a safeguard is cheap. And markets provide the most efficient safeguards when no party need invest heavily in information about other parties' knowledge (doing that makes more sense in contexts where the division or defection incentives are particularly high and alternative safeguards are few). So the issue Kronman finds decisive is the same one we find decisive. A court would not intervene so long as market safeguards are available.

On the other hand, courts tend to impose a duty to disclose *latent* defects in products, such as termites in a house for sale. As Kronman says, a disclosure requirement would not be likely to reduce the production of such information.[74] But distinguishing on this score between information about attributes of goods held for sale, as in this case, and information about markets such as demand or supply shifts, as in *Laidlaw*, is not so helpful. For example, availability of product and support services may be attributes affecting price. Most importantly, with latent defects the distributive risks overwhelm the technological risks; ex post costs of remedy for unfair divisions are high, if contractual remedy exists at all.

A reputation for fair dealing helps, but in a fragmented industry such as housing, especially existing housing, reputation is a scarce commodity. Perhaps one motivation for state courts permitting nondisclosure about termites through the mid

73. *Id.* at 23.
74. *See id.* at 25.

1950s and requiring disclosure more frequently thereafter was an explosion in owner-occupied housing likely to generate numerous occasions of defection by failing to disclose latent defects. Indeed, only recently have real estate brokers begun to offer inspection services and guarantees (sometimes because mortgagors require it), in effect acting as a centralized bonding agency.

B. *The Default Rule Revisited*

We close with a brief reconsideration of the default rule. The most powerful implication of our analysis of rational bargaining for contract law concerns the legitimacy of applying the so-called default rule. Courts are often required to fill in the blanks of incomplete contracts by answering the question of what the parties would have agreed to ex ante. Hopefully, one thing we have made perfectly clear is that answering that question is no trivial undertaking—even under the best of circumstances.

Economists of law cite the "ex ante contract" as part of the argument for applying an efficiency interpretation of contract doctrine. Their reason for doing so is clear. The ex ante contract is to be modeled as a rational bargain between the parties and Pareto optimality (joint rationality) is a condition of rational bargaining. Indeed it is.

But so are the conditions of individual and concession rationality. And in all cases, satisfying the demands of rationality in a contract are considerably more complex than the hand-waving response of the legal economist—namely, to find an allocation of rights and responsibilities that is jointly wealth maximizing—would suggest. In fact, any number of distributions of rights and responsibilities between the parties would be jointly profit maximizing. These distributions differ from one another in how they divide the gains from contracting. Thus, to impose any jointly maximizing allocation of rights and responsibilities is incompatible with the lessons of the rational bargaining model developed here. For rational bargainers are as concerned with problems of rational division as they are with joint rationality. It is, therefore, as inappropriate for courts to impose jointly maximizing outcomes on them in the name of efficiency without regard to concession rationality as it would be to impose a distribution of rights and responsibilities that satisfies the concession rationality condition without regard to whether that distribution is jointly rational (or profit maximizing).

More importantly, empty appeals to abstract efficiency or justice ignore the importance of context to rational contractors. What rational parties are prepared ex ante to leave for a court to resolve depends on the transaction resources available endogenously. Attending to those factors enables us to see *Laidlaw* as a case in which the court is being asked to solve a coordination problem by providing an authoritative statement of the norm regarding disclosure. Failing to attend to specific contextual features of disputes in the name of reconstruction in the light of the abstract norms of efficiency and justice makes a mockery of the idea of the ex ante contract as a default rule. For in abstracting from the context, a court is disabled from asking "What would *these* parties have agreed to ex ante?" and asks instead "What would be efficient or just from a global point of view?" We have no doubt that it is an interesting question to ask what is either just or efficient, but it is simply not the question the ex ante contract as a default rule necessarily asks.[75]

---

75. The approach we are developing here takes seriously the idea that in filling out incomplete contracts, courts ought to impose on the parties ex post that to which they would have agreed to ex ante. To do that, courts must reconstruct a hypothetical rational bargain between (or among) the parties. What rational individuals in fact agree to under certain conditions need be neither fair nor efficient. Thus, that to which they would have agreed under those conditions may also be neither fair nor efficient. Do we really mean to suggest that courts should impose a division of rights, responsibilities and risks that merely transmits inequities in the parties' relative bargaining positions, thereby exacerbating, rather than alleviating, whatever injustices between them already exist?

This is a difficult question. Our tentative answer is a qualified "yes." One central aspect of the rational bargaining approach is the importance of conserving transaction resources. To see this, imagine any default rule that sought to rectify pre-existing inequalities by imposing rights and responsibilities ex post in a way that nullified or minimized pre-existing advantages. Because any default rule would be in effect only to the extent that the parties did not contract around it, its net effect would be to encourage as little reliance upon it as would be rational for the parties. In order to protect pre-existing advantages, parties will simply seek more completely to specify their contracts, thus reducing the rule's impact. By doing so, both parties will further deplete their resources, reducing the extent to which those resources can be employed to reduce uncertainty regarding other aspects of negotiations.

Secondly, we should draw a distinction between two concepts of fairness, one endogenous to the transactional framework, the other external to it. We would not want to dispute the possibility of a standard of justice in distribution according to which both pre-existing holding and entitlements that result from the contractual process can be evaluated or criticized. By such a standard, it may well be that a default rule of the sort we are discussing encourages rather than reduces unfairness. Notice, however, that the default rule merely transmits the unfairness of the initial holdings. The unfairness, if there is one, resides in the conditions that comprise the parties' relative bargaining

Whatever one's theory of contractual obligation, whether based on consent, promising or rationality, a minimum condition for justifiably applying the default rule is that it imposes obligations on the parties—including the use of third-party interveners—that reflects what would have been rational for them in the circumstances of their contract. But on any such account, to impose jointly rational outcomes without regard to context is, at the least, to incompletely understand the default rule, and, at worst, to encumber individuals by unjustifiably exercising the coercive authority of the state.[76]

---

positions. To rectify that problem, we should want to preclude *explicit* agreements that take advantage of those inequities, not just those that are imposed in the absence of explicit agreement. There is, in other words, nothing especially objectionable about the default rule itself. Moreover, it is a further question whether these sorts of inequalities are best rectified by courts on a case-by-case basis.

Let us consider the concept of transactional fairness. Any default rule that sought to annul ex post a pre-existing advantage would confer upon the advantaged party less than he could have or would have secured by making the terms of the agreement explicit. In doing so, the rule may treat that party unfairly relative to his trading partners. Not only would such a rule fail the test of rationality by encouraging the use of transaction resources, thereby increasing uncertainty, it may treat the parties, at least from a transactional point of view, unfairly.

76. To examine the role of the court when it is asked to solve division problems by playing what we have called an arbitrating role, one could look to a line of cases and scholarship associated with doctrines such as *laesio enormis* (under Roman law, a standard of equivalence in exchange that, despite its apparent rejection in modern times, arguably has been smuggled into current doctrines under other guises) or unconscionability (a test evaluating one-sided clauses that oppress or unfairly surprise a party). This examination would uncover the guidelines or principles of fairness that may be covert, and should be overt, in common law; and it would assess these in view of the theory of rational bargaining proposed here. *See* Eisenberg, *The Bargain Principle and its Limits*, 95 HARV. L. REV. 741 (1982); Trebilcock, *The Doctrine of Inequality of Bargaining Power: Post-Benthamite Economics in the House of Lords*, 26 TORONTO L.J. 359 (1976).

To examine the role of the court when it is asked to solve defection problems by playing what we have called an enforcing role, one could look at doctrines associated with damage measures or specific performance. For example, the model of behavior posited in the divisible prisoner's dilemma has parallels in the analysis of expectation, reliance, and restitution measures in Fuller & Purdue, *The Reliance Interest in Contract Damages*, 46 YALE L.J. 52 (1936); *see also* Bishop, *The Choice of Remedy for Breach of Contract*, 14 J. LEGAL STUD. 299 (1985); Goetz & Scott, *Liquidated Damages, Penalties, and the Just Compensation Principle: Some Notes on an Enforcement Model and a Theory of Efficient Breach*, 77 COLUM. L. REV. 554 (1977), Goetz & Scott, *The Mitigation Principle: Toward a General Theory of Contractual Obligation*, 69 VA. L. REV. 967 1983); Rubin, *Unenforceable Contracts: Penalty Clauses and Specific Performance*, 10 J. LEGAL STUD. 297 (1981).

Extensions of the analysis could apply to statutory law as well, accounting for conditions under which juducial intervention will tend to prove less satisfactory than legislative action. For example, in the context of administrative processes, see Heckathorn & Maser, *supra* note 30. In the context of constitutional choice, *see* Heckathorn & Maser, *Bargaining and Constitutional Contracts*, 31 AM. J. POL. SCI. 142 (1987).

[10]

CONNECTICUT
LAW REVIEW

VOLUME 22 SPRING 1990 NUMBER 3

THE ABSTRACT CHARACTER OF CONTRACT LAW

*Christopher T. Wonnell**

I. INTRODUCTION

It is difficult to study contract law without being impressed by the extraordinary breadth of subject matter which that corpus of law covers. One need look no further to see this breadth than the standard contracts casebooks from which first-year law students learn the subject. The first ten cases in the book I use as an instructor include an employment/sexual harassment dispute, two land purchase contracts, a brokerage agreement, a construction contract, a promissory note, two intrafamily gifts, a gasoline station lease combined with assignment of accounts receivable, and a company pension program.[1] These cases are used not to study specific substantive areas such as real estate or con-

* Professor of Law, University of San Diego School of Law. B.A., Northwestern University; J.D., University of Michigan. I would like to thank Larry Alexander, Randy Barnett, Kevin Cole, Don Dripps, Paul Horton, Mike Kelly, Evan Lee, Maimon Schwarzschild, and Paul Wohlmuth for their helpful comments.

1. C. KNAPP & N. CRYSTAL, PROBLEMS IN CONTRACT LAW: CASES AND MATERIALS 15-88 (1987).

struction, but to illustrate such general principles of contract law as mutual assent and consideration, which are thought, in some sense, to transcend subject matter boundaries.

It is this feature of contract law—its tendency to abstract from particularities of person and subject matter—that this article seeks to explore. Abstraction runs through virtually the entire taxonomy of the subject. Offer and acceptance, restitution and reliance, interpretation and "gap filling," mistakc and impossibility, fraud and duress—all seem to describe phenomena in a manner one step removed from concrete particulars of the persons and subject matters appearing in the cases. The abstraction is made most complete and vivid by such accounts of the subject as the *Restatement (Second) of Contracts*, with its illustrations of the problems of those personifications of abstraction, *A* and *B*.[2]

One of the questions arising is what justifies this extraordinary abstraction that contract law performs? Is it rational to close one's eyes to precisely who is entering into what kind of contract with whom?[3] Certainly much of the upper level curriculum of law school education retains little of the abstraction of first-year contracts. Labor law, agency law, pension law, corporations and partnerships, real estate law, insurance law, securities regulation, and other courses arise out of contractual relationships but deal with the subjects through their own, more concrete and particularized, set of concepts.[4] These branches of contract law (or perhaps former branches that have snapped off the original tree) are often the product of specialized statutes that alter the common law of contracts to varying degrees. One could envision the end of contracts as an abstract subject as it becomes replaced by specialized bodies of law for each transactional form.[5]

2. *See* Epstein, *A Common Law for Labor Relations: A Critique of the New Deal Labor Legislation*, 92 YALE L.J. 1357, 1364 (1983) ("Legal rules do not refer to flesh-and-blood individuals, but to those lifeless abstractions, A and B, about whom nothing else is known or—more to the point—is relevant.").

3. I have discussed the philosophical issues behind the deliberate refusal to advert to certain ranges of facts in Wonnell, *Problems in the Application of Political Philosophy to Law*, 86 MICH. L. REV. 123, 123-30 (1987).

4. *See* Warren, *Comments on Professor White's Paper*, at the Proceedings of the Conference on Contract Law: From Theory to Practice, in 1988 ANN. SURV. AM. L. 50 ("We no longer embrace some series of abstract principles any place except when we teach them in first year contracts, where we talk about mitigation, liquidated damages, mutuality, consideration, waste, and so on. Instead, it seems to me that contract law has split off into groups of circumstance-specific bodies of law. . . .").

5. *See id.* at 50-51 ("These areas have all split off from general contract law and become

This article offers a defense of the abstract character of contract law. Indeed, it argues that a proper economic analysis of the subject shows the normative indispensability of retaining abstract principles in this area. Specialized bodies of transactional law are desirable only if they serve to concretize those abstract principles, not if they purport to except particular types of transactional law from such principles.

Part II of this article describes the evolution of a conventional wisdom regarding abstraction in contract law. This conventional wisdom suggests that abstraction is a product of a particular historical epoch and that its gradual erosion in the twentieth century is a desirable, perhaps an inevitable, development. Part III argues that this conventional wisdom is wrong to the extent that it claims not merely to observe an erosion of contractual abstraction over time, but to defend it as well. A microeconomic analysis of the problem shows the indispensability of abstraction in contract law, and part of that abstraction is the abstraction from the individuals and subject matters of a particular historical era.

The remainder of the article seeks to apply those insights to contemporary problems of contract law. Part IV examines the problem of formality in contract law from the perspective of the need for contractual abstraction. "Formality" is a term that covers a range of related doctrines, such as the statute of frauds, the parol evidence rule, the plain meaning rule, the objective theory of contracts, and the duty to read. Part V examines the abstract principle of mitigation of damages and its corollary, the concept of "efficient breach," as an illustration of the mistakes that courts can avoid by retaining an essential role for the abstract character of contract law. Finally, Part VI offers some suggestions for future research directions indicated by the focus on contractual abstraction.

II. The Conventional Wisdom: Abstraction as the Product of a Particular Historical Era

One of the first contract scholars to place the phenomenon of abstraction at the center of attention was Lawrence Friedman. In his book *Contract Law in America*,[6] Friedman studied more than 500 con-

---

specific to their very, very different circumstances. . . . 'All of contract law' is all those things that have become specific to their individual circumstances and are no longer decided by abstract, universal principles."); *see also* Unger, *The Critical Legal Studies Movement*, 96 HARV. L. REV. 563, 617 (1983).

6. L. FRIEDMAN, CONTRACT LAW IN AMERICA 20 (1965) ("Contract law is abstraction—what

tract cases decided over a period of more than a century by the Wisconsin Supreme Court. The cases were divided into three historical periods: the frontier era (1836-1861), the progressive period (1905-1915), and the modern era (1955-1958).[7]

Friedman's conclusion was that a working definition of contract law simply had to give pride of place to the judicial tendency of abstraction. In Friedman's words:

> Basically, then, the "pure" law of contract is an area of what we can call abstract relationships. "Pure" contract doctrine is blind to details of subject matter and person. It does not ask who buys and who sells or what is bought and sold. In the law of contract it does not matter whether the subject of the contract is a goat, a horse, a carload of lumber, a stock certificate, or a shoe. . . . When the relationship of parties to land is treated as creating distinctive legal issues, simply because land is involved, this is land law or property law, but not contract.[8]

Friedman found that the first of the three historical periods he studied was "the age of abstraction,"[9] for both factual and ideological reasons. As Friedman writes: "It was fact, not theory, that land was often bought and sold as a colorless commodity. It was fact, not theory, that the residents of Wisconsin were mobile men, not rooted to a particular community or to ancient customs which fixed persons from birth with a given social status."[10] As for ideology, Friedman argued that

> [t]he law of contract is, therefore, roughly coextensive with the free market. Liberal nineteenth-century economics fits in neatly with the law of contracts so viewed. It, too, had the abstracting habit. In both theoretical models—that of the law of contracts and that of liberal economics—parties could be treated as individual economic units which, in theory, enjoyed complete mobility and freedom of decision.[11]

Thus, Friedman concluded that the abstraction of contract law

---

is left in the law relating to agreements when all particularities of person and subject-matter are removed.").

7. *See id.* at 11-12.

8. *Id.* at 20.

9. *Id.* at 186.

10. *Id.*

11. *Id.* at 20-21.

was not a permanently desirable fixture of the law, but a temporary fit with certain historical conditions. Like the models of classical economics, classical abstract contract principles "assumed a frictionless and perfect market, operating instantaneously and universally."[12] And while this lack of realism was tolerable in the wide-open days of the Wisconsin frontier, it became far less so in subsequent periods. As the economy matured into the Progressive Era, all classes clamored for protected niches, and, "in this kind of society, the ideal, abstract law of contract had little to say."[13]

In the second period, Friedman found a tension between the rules of contract doctrine, which were at the height of systematization, and the actual results of cases, which were preoccupied with ideas such as inequality of bargaining power. The abstract rules of formality such as the parol evidence and plain meaning rules seemed to call for one result, but the courts would tend to reach the other by relying on such doctrines as waiver and estoppel.[14]

By the third period, abstraction had declined still further, perhaps under the influence of the legal realists' critique of doctrine. Legislation had taken many important areas entirely out of the ambit of contract principles, and, in the narrow range of cases that remained, courts were free "to tinker and patch, to chip away at the 'rules,' and to do justice in particular cases."[15] "[R]esponsive to their times, . . . [the judges] were abandoning abstraction as a working principle."[16]

The second scholar to articulate what has now become the conventional wisdom on the abstraction of contract was Grant Gilmore in his famous series of lectures published as *The Death of Contract*.[17] Gilmore explicitly embraced Friedman's conclusions on this particular subject:

> Although we shall depart from his analysis at some points, we may retain as central ideas the concept of the general law of contract as a residual category—what is left over after all the "specialized" bodies of law have been added up—highly abstract, in close historical relationship with the free market of classical economic theory, a theoretical construct which, hav-

12. *Id.* at 21.
13. *Id.* at 189.
14. *See id.* at 97-98, 122-24, 191.
15. *Id.* at 213.
16. *Id.*
17. G. Gilmore, The Death of Contract (1974).

> ing little or nothing to do with the real world, would not—or could not—change as the real world changed.[18]

Gilmore's views on this subject are of special relevance because it was his precise objective to abolish contract law as a general category and to analyze cases involving contracts under either a tort framework or a specialized body of rules.[19] Gilmore began by seeking to undermine the idea that abstract contract principles were an ancient idea. There was, he acknowledges, the law of particular kinds of contracts—agency and partnership, promissory notes and bills of exchange, financing and security transactions, and insurance.[20] The general law of contract, however, was the invention of Langdell, Holmes, and Williston, in the late nineteenth and early twentieth centuries. For Gilmore, Langdell was the first to see contract as "a remote, impersonal, bloodless abstraction."[21]

Although Gilmore cites Friedman with approval, their views are not identical, for Friedman places the golden age of abstraction fifty years before Gilmore says it was invented by law professors. Gilmore takes the position—which is indeed quite correct—that economic theory and contractual abstraction are related. His explanation for this isomorphism is that general contract theory was "dedicated to the proposition that, ideally, no one should be liable to anyone for anything."[22] Although complete nonliability was impractical, it explained the preferences of Holmes and Williston for damages over specific performance, and their opposition to reliance- and restitution-based measures of recovery. The analogy to economic theory was clear:

> I suppose that laissez-faire economic theory comes down to something like this: If we all do exactly as we please, no doubt everything will work out for the best. Which does seem to be about the same thing that the contract theory comes down to, with liability reduced to a minimum and sanctions for breach cut back to the vanishing point.[23]

Fortunately, this ideological prison of another era has now been overcome:

---

18. *Id.* at 7-8.
19. *Id.* at 87-88.
20. *Id.* at 8-12.
21. *Id.* at 13.
22. *Id.* at 14.
23. *Id.* at 95.

> It seems apparent to the twentieth century mind, as perhaps it did not to the nineteenth century mind, that a system in which everybody is invited to do his own thing, at whatever cost to his neighbor, must work ultimately to the benefit of the rich and powerful, who are in a position to look after themselves and to act, so to say, as their own self-insurers. . . . No man is his brother's keeper; the race is to the swift; let the devil take the hindmost. For good or ill, we have changed all that.[24]

A large portion of Gilmore's book was devoted to the cases that Langdell, Holmes, and/or Williston chose to treat as "leading" cases, which would illustrate the new abstract general principles. The general tenor of Gilmore's criticism is exemplified by *Stilk v. Myrick*.[25] The case involved two seamen who had deserted a ship that was engaged in a Russian voyage. The ship's master promised to divide the deserter's wages among the remaining crew members, and, when the owner later refused to perform on this promise, the members brought suit. The court ruled for the owners. This case was then treated by Williston as illustrating the following legal proposition:

> Where A and B have entered into a bilateral agreement, it not infrequently happens that one of the parties, becoming dissatisfied with the contract, refuses to perform or to continue performance unless a larger compensation than that provided in the original agreement is promised him.
>
> . . . .
>
> On principle, the second agreement is invalid for the performance by the recalcitrant contractor is no legal detriment to him whether actually given or promised, since, at the time the second agreement was entered into, he was already bound to do the work.[26]

For Gilmore, it was not at all clear that the facts of *Stilk* supported this sweeping rule, or, indeed, fell within its ambit. After all, the seamen did give consideration in the form of working harder to bring the boat back home, now that two of their fellow crew had deserted the ship. The intellectual creators of contract doctrine were reaching for highly ambiguous judicial authority to create a broad rule of universal

24. *Id.*

25. There are two reports of *Stilk v. Myrick*: 170 Eng. Rep. 851 (1809-10), and 170 Eng. Rep. 1168 (1809).

26. 1 S. WILLISTON, A TREATISE ON THE LAW OF CONTRACTS § 130 (3d ed. 1957).

applicability to all future *A*'s and *B*'s.[27]

The merits of the "death of abstraction" thesis will be the subject of Part III of this article. For now, however, it must be noted that many of Gilmore's criticisms concern not the principle of contractual abstraction itself, but the specific abstractions chosen. Promissory estoppel is not obviously less abstract than consideration, nor is specific performance self-evidently less abstract than damage liability. In truth, Gilmore's book is a confused mixture of unrelated criticisms of classical contract doctrine. For purposes of this article, it is only Gilmore's critique of contractual abstraction as such that are in issue and not his views on the proper principles that should govern across-the-board.

The third scholar to solidify the conventional wisdom about abstraction in contract law was Morton Horwitz in his book *The Transformation of American Law: 1780-1860*.[28] Once again, the theme is that abstract principles of contract law were the product of a single, rather short, historical period. Curiously, however, Horwitz dates this period even earlier than Friedman, stating that the abolition of eighteenth-century ideas of finding the just price in each specific transaction gave way shortly after 1820. Early criticisms of the just price doctrine were then "generalized to include all aspects of contract law."[29] Employees were among the principal victims of the new abstract will theory of contract, as in cases where they quit before the full term of their contract and were denied quantum meruit recovery on the basis of the contractual terms.[30] Horwitz offered a somewhat different account than Gilmore of the contribution of Williston to general contract law, but it was no more favorable:

> The emergence of the objective theory, then, is another measure of the influence of commercial interests in the shaping of American law. No longer finding it necessary to enter into battle against eighteenth century just price doctrines, they could devote their energies to establishing in the second half of the nineteenth century a system of objective rules necessary to assure legal certainty and predictability. And having destroyed most substantive ground for evaluating the justice of exchange, they could elaborate a legal ideology of formalism, of which Williston was the leading exemplar, that could not

27. *See* G. GILMORE, *supra* note 17, at 23-28.
28. M. HORWITZ, THE TRANSFORMATION OF AMERICAN LAW: 1780-1860 (1977).
29. *Id.* at 181.
30. *See id.* at 186-87.

> only disguise gross disparities of bargaining power under a facade of neutral and formal rules of contract law but could also enforce commercial customs under the comforting technical rubric of "contract interpretation."[31]

In a sense, then, there were two historical waves of abstracting tendencies. The first was substantive and proposed the general criterion of mutual wills to judge the fairness of all transactions in place of the particular customs and traditions that had severally placed the value of innumerable kinds of transactions. The second wave of abstraction was formalist, disguising what had been done in the first wave by applying "neutral and formal" rules that abstracted from any such bargaining power realities.[32]

Horwitz illustrates the tendency of both courts and treatise writers in the 1840s and 1850s to become " 'seduced' by contractarian 'theory' and 'abstraction' "[33] with cases involving the ability of carriers to disclaim contractually liability for negligence.[34] Rather than return to the earlier idea that common law liabilities were all nondisclaimable, the treatise writers felt obliged to write tentatively that express contracts, and not mere notices, would be necessary to permit such exculpation of liability. The result was that the oppression of the farmers by the railroads was hidden by the abstraction of contract law.[35]

Like Gilmore, Horwitz saw the parallelism between economics and contract doctrine only in terms of the errors they shared. Specifically, both were thought to assume important background equalities that in fact were absent, so that the theoretical errors of economics became the practical errors of abstract contract law: "As contract ideology thus emasculated all prior conceptions of substantive justice, equal bargaining power inevitably became established as the inarticulate major premise of all legal and economic analysis. The circle was completed; the law had come simply to ratify those forms of inequality that the market system produced."[36]

The final author to advocate the conventional wisdom on abstraction in contract law is the English scholar P.S. Atiyah in his book *The*

---

31. *Id.* at 201.
32. *See id.* at 160-201, 253-66.
33. *Id.* at 207.
34. *See, e.g.*, Dorr v. New Jersey Steam Navig. Co., 11 N.Y. 485 (1854).
35. *See* M. HORWITZ, *supra* note 28, at 206-07.
36. *Id.* at 210.

Rise and Fall of Freedom of Contract.[37] The story is again much the same, although the dates are changed. Prior to 1770, there was little support for the enforcement of executory contracts, as opposed to the protection of reliance and restitution interests. The age of freedom of contract, in which promissory liabilities eclipsed these other forms of obligation, began in 1770 and lasted until 1870, which was the time when Gilmore claimed the period was about to begin.[38] Nevertheless, with arresting chapter subtitles, Atiyah presses home the idea that contract was an historical anomaly, e.g., "the decline of principles," "the failure of classical law," "the decline of contract," "the decline of free choice and consent," and the like.[39]

Thus, Atiyah informs us that individualism always was a philosophy only for the few. Working class solidarity was the means for "the weak to unite against the strong."[40] Atiyah traces the nineteenth century intellectual background, which placed great emphasis on the need to preserve long-run principles, not inquiring in each particular case as to their expediency. This intellectual development was coupled with a parallel development in the courts:

> The period 1770-1870 saw the emergence of general principles of contract law closely associated with the development of the free market and the ideals of the political economists. The period saw the shift in emphasis from property law to contract; and within the realm of contract it saw the shift from particular relationships, or particular types of contract, to general principles of contract, and the shift from executed to executory contracts.[41]

Atiyah notes the great influence of the English translation of Pothier's *Law of Obligations*, which appeared in 1806.[42] As Atiyah

---

37. P. ATIYAH, THE RISE AND FALL OF FREEDOM OF CONTRACT (1979).

38. *Id.* at 139-54, 398.

39. These subtitles are taken from Part III of Atiyah's book, which covers "the decline and fall of freedom of contract: 1870-1970." *See id.* at 571-779. Those of a libertarian orientation would be inclined to see Atiyah's tale as bearing a not coincidental relationship to the rise and fall of English prosperity (which, interestingly, has begun to rise once again as Prime Minister Margaret Thatcher took office the year after the book was written and proceeded to reject Atiyah's prescription in its entirety). But there is no doubt where Atiyah stands on the normative questions; he is delighted to see the decline of general principles and the decline of freedom of contract more broadly.

40. *Id.* at 264.

41. *Id.* at 398.

42. R. POTHIER, LAW OF OBLIGATIONS (1806) (2 vols.).

notes, "The central idea that characterized all these writings was the *generality* of contract law, the fact that it could be stated at a high level of abstraction, and the law applied indifferently to all kinds of contracts irrespective of the subject matter."[43] Atiyah does not argue that the abstraction of general contract principles has declined since the nineteenth century. Rather, the principles, as abstract as ever, simply have a much smaller range of applicability given the enormous number of specialized areas of law in twentieth-century England:

> The tendency to believe in general principles of contract law was not seriously affected by the growing evidence that no such general body of contractual principles continued to have any extensive practical application. . . . [S]pecial statutory rules now apply to virtually every type of ordinary contract, for instance, contracts of sale of goods, of hire-purchase, and now of all forms of consumer credit, contracts of employment, leases, shareholding contracts, contracts of carriage, whether of persons or goods, and whether by land, sea or air, and so on.[44]

Professor Atiyah, unlike some of the other authors considered, seeks to reconcile his views with contemporary insights of microeconomic theory. Atiyah observes that the neo-classical economists in England, such as Jevons and Marshall, had themselves lost faith in abstract principles such as those espoused by the earlier classical economists. Ignorance on the part of market participants and/or monopoly power might suggest the inappropriateness of laissez-faire principles in certain contexts. In any event, the modern economists were less concerned with abstract theory and more concerned with empirical evidence than their classical predecessors, such as Ricardo and Mill.[45] For their part, judges in England simply became less and less aware of economics of any kind; they espoused abstract contract principles on narrow legal grounds and watched the contraction of the scope of those principles by legislation with equanimity.[46]

While the four authors studied here do not agree on all the dates and details, the general outline of their story is rather similar. The idea of abstract contract principles applicable generally was the ideology of

43. P. ATIYAH, *supra* note 37, at 400.
44. *Id.* at 686.
45. *See id.* at 602-26.
46. *See id.* at 666-69.

only a relatively brief historical period. It was preceded by case-by-case notions of equity and followed by industry-by-industry legislative action. Moreover, this decline in abstraction is not to be regretted; to the contrary, it is a statement of the bankruptcy (or outdatedness) of classical economic theory.

III. The Economics of Contractual Abstraction

While not purporting to evaluate the historical analysis of the conventional wisdom,[47] this section of the article argues that the conventional wisdom is wrong in claiming that the wisdom of abstract principles has somehow become out of date. Rather, this section presents an argument that abstract principles of contract law serve essential economic functions.

The argument of the section is divided into four parts. Part A explains why contract law, if it is to serve utilitarian or consequentialist aims, must satisfy the same kinds of formal considerations that have been identified in the literature on central planning or socialist calculation. Part B argues that those requirements of sound central planning have an abstract structure that is isomorphic with the principles of abstract contract law. Part C shows how the analysis of central planning fits in with and explains the necessity for the more traditional law-and-economics account of contractual abstraction. Finally, Part D deals with the challenges posed to the economic account of contractual abstraction from redistributive and paternalist motives in contract adjudication.

A. *Contract Law as Central Planning: The Problem*

In a sense, it might be regarded as odd to think of economic analysis as providing an explanation for the abstract character of contract law. Economic analysis is concerned with consequences, and, while economics as a science is in principle value-free,[48] it is clear that its interest to us lies primarily in the part of our normative tradition that can be characterized broadly as utilitarian. There are, however, nonconsequentialist or deontological theories of contractual obligation that might be thought to offer a much simpler account of contractual ab-

47. Since all four books are unquestionably "histories with a contemporary political purpose," i.e. to bury contractual abstraction, they probably carry the suspicion that attaches to any work of that genre.

48. *See* Friedman, *The Methodology of Positive Economics*, in THE PHILOSOPHY OF ECONOMICS 210, 211-12 (D. Hausman ed. 1984).

straction. If contractual obligation stems from the autonomous human will,[49] or from consent,[50] or from the sanctity of promises,[51] then it might seem rather obvious that it does not matter whether one is dealing with land, goods, services, or shares of stock.

Of course, a simplistic economic analysis could also produce a quick theory of contractual abstraction. If two people enter into a contract—any contract—it is because they believe the contract will make them both better off. And since people know their own interests best, they probably are both better off. Thus, utility is maximized by allowing freedom of contract across the board.[52]

The problem with this analysis is that it ignores the interests of third parties. A contract commits scarce resources to particular uses. It, thus, "victimizes" everyone in the society who might have an alternative use for that particular resource. The use of resources pursuant to a contract will also affect those who supply a wide range of commodities including substitutes for those resources, inputs that go into the making of those resources, alternative uses for those inputs in other projects, and outputs that depend on the supply of those resources. Indeed, once the plans and projects of third parties are considered, there is no one who, with confidence it can be asserted, is beyond the ripple effects of a particular contractual placement of resources; the enforcement or nonenforcement of contracts is a kind of unintentional economy-wide central planning of who will be entitled to use what resources for what projects.[53]

The view of the common law as a central planning device is what makes abstraction seem particularly implausible. Surely a centrally planned society would want to create special departments with expertise in housing construction, insurance, labor, industrial machinery, and the like. Surely the "rules" on when too much chromium was going to the automobile industry vis-à-vis the computer industry would bear little relationship to the "rules" on when too much time of mechanical engineers was being spent on office buildings and not enough on amuse-

49. An early statement of this will theory of contract appears in W. Story, A Treatise on the Law of Contracts Not Under Seal 4 (1844).

50. *See* Barnett, *A Consent Theory of Contract*, 86 Colum. L. Rev. 269 (1986).

51. *See generally* C. Fried, Contract As Promise (1981).

52. This is the "victimless crimes" theory of contract that I have criticized elsewhere. *See* Wonnell, *Contract Law and the Austrian School of Economics*, 54 Fordham L. Rev. 507, 511-14 (1986).

53. For further applications of this point, see Wonnell, *Four Challenges Facing a Compatibilist Philosophy*, 12 Harv. J.L. & Pub. Pol'y 835 (1989).

ment rides. Perhaps some unusable formula, such as "free up resources when it would make people happier overall to do so," could be applied to all such decisions, but the actual working rules of the central planning departments could not be considered similar to each other.

The problem is thus squarely presented: given that common law rules, such as the rules of contract, have implications, not merely for the parties to the lawsuit, but for the entire society's use of resources, what role can there be for abstract principles? Are the legal historians not correct in saying that specialized expertise and special rules are now needed in this complex twentieth century, rendering contract principles obsolete from a utilitarian point of view?

B. *The Abstract Character of Central Planning Decisions*

The central planner's role can be conceptualized as having three aspects. The first responsibility is to decide what facts about resources would be relevant to the establishment of a rational plan. The second task is to devise some method for discovering the facts about resource use that have been determined to be relevant. The third requirement is to motivate action by people to employ the resources in the manner factually identified. Let us call these three features the "relevance," "knowledge," and "action" dimensions of the planning process.

The thesis of this section is that abstract principles of contract law are isomorphic with the abstract features of sound central planning. In other words, principles of contract universally applied will direct people's attention to the relevant facts, lead to the discovery of those facts, and motivate action based upon those discoveries. Furthermore, it is contended that, without these abstract features of the decision problem, the central planning process would be essentially hopeless. The rational central planner would, if she continued to care about the happiness of the people, be compelled to turn to abstract contract principles as her method of planning.

1. The Relevance Dimension of Planning

It is convenient to imagine oneself as a central planner, constrained by no capitalist institutions of rights or principles, seeking to use resources in such a way as to maximize social utility. How would one go about such a task? It would not be appropriate simply to envision a useful product, such as a house, that could be made out of a resource, such as a collection of bricks, and order someone to commence the project. This would be wrong for several reasons, and each is important to explore.

First, the resources might be scarce and needed in other projects. If bricks are, and/or the time of bricklayers is, relatively scarce and if there are other useful tasks that could be done with those bricks or bricklayers' time, it might be quite wasteful to construct the house. Let us call this the "scarcity" factor.[54]

Second, there might be other resources available that would serve just as well in the project as bricks and/or bricklayers. The house might be constructed out of limestone or wood, and stone masons or carpenters could be used instead of bricklayers. This might be preferable if wood or carpenters are not as scarce or not as useful in alternative projects. This will be referred to as the "substitutes" factor.[55]

Third, the use of bricks might require certain other resources to be used as well, such as mortar. If mortar is scarce and needed in other projects, this might make it undesirable to use bricks in constructing the house. Indeed, it is possible that the problem of mortar might make it undesirable to build the house, if there were no good substitutes for bricks and their accompanying need for scarce mortar. This problem can be called the "complements" factor, since the fact that mortar is a resource that complements or is used in tandem with bricks is relevant in deciding whether it is wise to use the bricks.[56]

Fourth, the bricks are intended for the use in a house, while the objective is not housing as such, but utility. One would need to know how much utility another individual human being will actually derive from the house and to contrast that with the utility that she or another individual might derive from alternative uses of scarce resources. The need for such information on the happiness (or suffering avoided) that each use of resources would cause for each individual affected can be called the "utility" factor.[57]

Fifth, it has been assumed thus far that the planner already knows all the relevant actual and potential processes for converting resources like bricks and wood into houses. But, of course, it is essential that this information be as accurate as possible. The need for knowledge about productive processes for converting inputs into final products can be

54. The centrality to economic reasoning of the factor of scarcity vis-à-vis human ends is outlined in Robbins, *The Nature and Significance of Economic Science*, in THE PHILOSOPHY OF ECONOMICS, *supra* note 48, at 113-16.

55. On the importance and difficulty of determining substitutability in production and consumption, see T. SOWELL, KNOWLEDGE AND DECISIONS 219-20 (1980).

56. *See* M. LEVI, THINKING ECONOMICALLY 40 (1985) (defining "complements").

57. Strictly speaking, it is marginal utility that is important. *See id.* at 30-33.

called the "technology" factor.[58]

Finally, it would not be enough to know the scarcity and utility of bricks and wood themselves. Since these resources can be augmented by further production, one would need to know facts about the inputs that went into, say, the production of lumber. This might be a ten-stage process or even longer, but it would be necessary to know whether the inputs used at the earlier stages were themselves scarce and needed elsewhere. Let us call this the "inputs" factor.[59]

Should the brick house be built? The answer depends on a complex synergy of all six factors in a specific combination that has been worked out exhaustively in general equilibrium models.[60] The important point to observe here is the *abstract* character of the six factors; they will affect *every* decision on resource use in essentially the same way. The nature of the resources in question affects which other resources will be complements, substitutes, inputs, and the like, but the logical structure of relevant factors in every decision remains the same.

2. The Knowledge Dimension of Planning

The next point to consider is epistemological: by what process can one discover the facts identified as relevant? Specifically, is there a recurrent, abstract structure, not only to the questions that must be answered, but to the method by which they can best be answered?

In this regard, the beginning of wisdom is to see the hideous complexity of the task of central planning. In deciding whether to build a brick house, I am supposed to know about not only the technology of brick houses, but also the scarcity of bricks, the scarcity of brick substitutes and complements, the alternative uses of those substitutes and complements, the inputs employed at prior stages in the making of bricks, the alternative uses of those inputs and their substitutes and complements, as well as the utility innumerable individuals will derive

---

58. *See* T. SOWELL, *supra* note 55, at 220 ("[T]he Soviet machine tool industry alone produces about 125,000 products, involving an estimated '15,000,000,000 possible relations.' ").

59. *See* C. FERGUSON & J. GOULD, MICROECONOMIC THEORY 452-53 (4th ed. 1975). To be precise, this factor could be called the "input/output" factor, since one needs to know not only what went into the making of a product, but what its ultimate destination in the production process was. Outputs are left out of the text since it discusses the planning of a house, which is at the end of the input/output chain.

60. *See id.* Efficiency requires that the "marginal rate of transformation" of any two goods—the rate at which one good can be "transformed" into another by shifting inputs—is equal to the "marginal rate of substitution"—the rate at which consumers would be willing to substitute one good for another. *Id.*

from a house or from other products that these resources could have produced.[61]

The simple truth is that no one has this kind of information. That is especially obvious when one reflects on the fact that all six factors, as they affect each resource, are in a process of continuous change. There is nothing unusual about a brick house in this regard; it is the same problem with any use of scarce resources. The first abstract lesson of epistemology is that there is absolutely no way to supply a direct answer to any question of proper resource use.[62] This supplies an element of urgency to our question of whether abstract contract principles might supply an indirect way of knowing the facts that must be known. Since there is no direct way, the central planner seems destined for a chaotic situation in which she employs resources without having any idea whether her use of the resources represented a contribution to human welfare given what has been sacrificed.

How does one proceed in the face of a problem that requires far more knowledge than any human being can obtain? The problem must be divided into two stages. First, people must discover the relevant facts about resources that *are* within their capacity to discover.[63] Second, those individuals must be placed in a position where their actions, based on the knowledge they can obtain, can be the same *as if* they possessed the remaining relevant knowledge that they cannot directly learn.[64]

a. *Discovering Facts Within One's Learning Capacity*

Some people are capable of learning whether bricks will work as well as wood in building houses in certain parts of the country. Some people are capable of learning that laymen are just as good as trained carpenters at certain tasks but not at others. In all such cases, the people involved must arrive at answers to such questions that are as accurate as possible.[65]

---

61. *See* L. MISES, HUMAN ACTION 699 (2d ed. 1963) ("The director does not simply have to deal with coal as such, but with thousands and thousands of pits already in operation in various places, and with the possibilities for digging new pits, with the various methods of mining in each of them, with the different qualities of the coal in various deposits, with the various methods for utilizing the coal for the production of heat, power, and a great number of derivatives.").

62. *See* Wonnell, *supra* note 53.

63. *See* F. HAYEK, *Competition as a Discovery Procedure*, in THE ESSENCE OF HAYEK 254 (C. Nishiyama & K. Leube eds. 1984).

64. *See* Hayek, *Economics and Knowledge*, 4 ECONOMICA 33, 49-53 (1937).

65. On the importance of entrepreneurial alertness to hitherto unperceived truths about re-

Is there anything that all of these concrete, isolated decisions about resource use have in common? It might be said that all such decisions require expertise, but this simply pushes the problem one step back, for the question then becomes whether there are any abstract characteristics involved in each specific case of expertise. Years of formal schooling and the like are patently more important in some fields than in others; they are not the abstract characteristics one seeks.[66]

Of course, there are certain weaker similarities that all such isolated decisions about resources share. They are all factual inquiries, which seek the truth—or the closest practicable approximations to the truth—about the specific questions that they pose. They, therefore, require human minds that are directed to finding the truth and not distracted by other interests or contented with the first plausible but false answer that comes to mind. Indeed, since change is a constant of all such decisions, they require a mind rather securely fastened to the specific environment, alert to any changes in technology, tastes, or resource availability that might alter the previous conclusions reached or render them irrelevant.[67]

We also have human nature, which, for all its infinite variety, exhibits over time and space certain predictable characteristics. Man has been called the rational animal, but what is eminently clear is that he is, above all, the rationalizing animal. The cognitive psychologists have contributed greatly to our understanding of what might be called the rational roots of irrationality, i.e. the use of mental schemata that can effectively keep new evidence from disrupting a world view one cherishes.[68] A desire to believe that something is true is very difficult to shake; the ability to interpret new evidence that might be inconvenient for the belief as really consistent with it is a constant of all such decision environments.

---

sources, see I. KIRZNER, PERCEPTION, OPPORTUNITY, AND PROFIT (1979); Kirzner, *Uncertainty, Discovery, and Human Action: A Study of the Entrepreneurial Profile of the Misesian System*, in METHOD, PROCESS, AND AUSTRIAN ECONOMICS 139 (I. Kirzner ed. 1982).

66. If the planners could assemble "meta-expertise" in which they knew who was the expert on precisely what matter, the central plan might require nonabstract principles. It is, however, precisely this concrete yet universal knowledge about particulars that the planners lack. What is needed is for individuals to have the incentive to contract for the expertise they severally need, and this is the same problem for all individuals.

67. I have discussed the importance of this "demand for truth" variable elsewhere. *See* Wonnell, *Truth and the Marketplace of Ideas*, 19 U.C. DAVIS L. REV. 669, 696-709 (1986).

68. *See, e.g.*, M. SMITH, PERSUASION AND HUMAN ACTION 30 (1982) (People perceive information through cognitive schemata, which "reflect an idealized view of how things ought to relate," rather than a faithful interpretation of reality.).

Rationalization and complacency may be abstract characteristics that threaten the truth-seeking process in all decision environments, but is there a similarly abstract way of confronting the problem? One thing is clear: rationalization is such a strong and persistent force that modest countermeasures will not do. For example, intellectuals of the left and right are fond of accusing each other of seeking the cover of comforting ideological rationalizations.[69] The implicit assumption is that one's own system of ideas is strong enough to conquer the inherent tendencies of rationalization. But systems of ideas are not that powerful; they are far more capable of assisting the process of rationalization than of breaking it.

There is, however, one force with the persistence, power, and universality to represent a serious rival to the force of rationalization, and that is self-interest. All human beings on this earth are survivors and descendants of a very long line of survivors. The selfish gene will tolerate altruism toward kin, and perhaps to a lesser extent to one's tribe of extended relatives, but there is no evidence that human beings or any other animals can be coaxed into treating every stranger as kin.[70] Our self-interested nature is something civilized society quite properly does not choose to flaunt, but to discipline and confine with cultural and legal constraints. Nevertheless, it would be the height of folly to design legal rules that did not take extremely seriously the strong human predisposition toward self-interest.

The abstract structure of the concrete resource use problem now can be stated in full. We need answers to millions of discrete, very specific and changing factual questions about resources. We need human beings to provide us with those answers, and we need those answers to be true. But human beings are predisposed to complacency and rationalization—not to digging deeply into problems and remaining glued to boring details for insights contradicting one's earlier notions. A very powerful force is necessary to counteract this proclivity, and that powerful force can be found in self-interest. Thus, people must find it in their direct self-interest to come up with true answers to the discrete questions about resource use that they face.

69. On this dynamic, see Wonnell, *Causal and Normative Underpinnings of Legal Controversies: The Constrained Vision of Thomas Sowell*, 21 U.C. DAVIS L. REV. 1009, 1013-17 (1988).

70. I have discussed these points in Wonnell, *Circumventing Racism: Confronting the Problem of the Affirmative Action Ideology*, 1989 B.Y.U. L. REV. 95, 102-10. For sociobiological methodology and conclusions generally, see R. DAWKINS, THE SELFISH GENE (1976); E. WILSON, SOCIOBIOLOGY: THE ABRIDGED EDITION (1980).

b. *Discovering Proxies for Facts Outside One's Learning Capacity*

The other part of the resource problem, it will be recalled, is to find some way of coordinating the discrete insights that such individuals discover about the resources within their ken. Indeed, in a sense, the coordination mechanism logically precedes the discrete questions, since it is only the coordination mechanism that can tell one which problems are worth studying.[71] For example, it may make no sense at all to inquire into the workability of marble houses if marble is extremely scarce and badly needed elsewhere, facts that the designer of houses may have no direct way of knowing.

The coordination mechanism, of course, is the system of market prices. The price of any resource, say zinc of grade *A* at time *B* in place *C*, reflects all of the six abstract characteristics identified above. If substitutes for zinc appear in certain uses, the price of zinc will fall, informing self-interested individuals to begin to study the question of whether zinc might have new, previously unknown, uses. If the inputs used in the mining and production of zinc become more scarce or more useful elsewhere, the price of zinc will tend to rise, encouraging users to study the possibility of doing without zinc in certain uses. In turn, the new uses discovered will place "tugs" on the resources that will change their prices, informing other individuals to begin to uncover still different truths.[72]

For present purposes, the important feature of the system of market prices is the abstract or universal character that it gives to all decisions affecting resources. Bewildering complexity determines the price of zinc of grade *A* at time *B* in place *C*. Equally bewildering complexity, but wholly different in every detail except the six abstract characteristics identified above, determines the price of chromium of grade *X* at time *B* in place *C*. From the perspective of the individual who has to decide whether to build a steel mill with zinc *A* or chromium *X*, however, the decision is greatly simplified. She can acquire her own particularized knowledge, plug in the going prices, and make a self-interested calculation of profits and losses. And the same decisionmaking formula—plugging in market prices, discovering local knowledge, and maximizing—can be employed for any decision affecting any resource. The relevant facts about resource use have been acquired through a single abstract mechanism, which is fortunate because there is no

71. *See* I. KIRZNER, COMPETITION AND ENTREPRENEURSHIP 218-22 (1973).

72. *See* Hayek, *The Use of Knowledge in Society*, 35 AM. ECON. REV. 519 (1945).

known way by which those facts could have been acquired without such an abstract mechanism.[73]

3. The Action Dimension of Planning

The remaining question concerned the abstract character of *acting* on the knowledge acquired. Action, in turn, requires both the willingness to act and the power or capability to act. The contention, once again, is that such an abstract structure does in fact exist and that the principles of contract dovetail with that structure in an important way.

a. *Willingness to Act*

A person may know perfectly well that zinc *A* is a better material for the specific use than chromium *X*, but chooses to keep that knowledge to herself. She may have political or social convictions of her own, or she may simply not wish to be bothered with the hassle of dealing with difficult materials.

It has become commonplace in the literature to deny that capitalist firms are solely motivated by making money but have their own cultural assumptions and political machinations.[74] (And, of course, capitalism is often criticized for the opposite vice of encouraging a money-grubbing ethic.) Perhaps the most accurate observation would be that the rich pluralism of human motivations is substantially, but not completely, suppressed by the widespread desire for money.

The problem is that diversity of motivation is something that must be sharply disciplined in an interdependent world.[75] If people need food, heat for their homes, fuel for their transportation to work, and so forth, then it is imperative that other people set their diversity of motivations aside and devote their energies to supplying these commodities. Factories must have assurances that their inputs will arrive on time and in good condition. Undoubtedly, the producers of those inputs have many goals that are more important to them than the abstract pursuit of economic efficiency. It is the passion for money that keeps their ac-

73. For excellent recent accounts of this problem, the works of N. Scott Arnold are invaluable. *See* Arnold, *Marx and Disequilibrium in Market Socialist Relations of Production*, 3 ECON. & PHIL. 23-47 (1987); Arnold, *Marx, Central Planning, and Utopian Socialism*, 6 SOC. PHIL. & POL'Y 160-99 (1989) [hereinafter Arnold, *Marx, Central Planning*]. The former is especially valuable in refuting the often-repeated hope that some kind of decentralized worker participation variant of socialism can offer a stable solution to the socialist calculation problem.

74. *See, e.g.*, D. HELLRIEGEL, J. SLOCUM & R. WOODMAN, ORGANIZATIONAL BEHAVIOR 359-62 (3d ed. 1983).

75. I have discussed this point at greater length in Wonnell, *supra* note 3, at 134-36.

tions directed toward the needs of others.

Of course, without the passion for money, punishment could serve as a motivator. But, as numerous commentators have noted, it can serve that role only in a very crude sense—to catch shirking that is patent to external observers.[76] Man's capacity for inventing subtle means of shirking responsibilities is thus another universal human trait of greatly underrated importance.

Self-interest, thus, serves two roles in cementing the abstract structure of decisionmaking in a market order. It serves as a force to combat complacency and rationalization as epistemological obstacles in the pursuit of truth. It also serves as a force to combat the tendency to sit on the truths one discovers and to pursue a diversity of goals unrelated to the economic needs of others.[77]

b. *Power to Act*

Action requires not only motivation, but also capability. It is not enough for someone to know that zinc *A* will do a better job than chromium *X*, or to want to act on that information by employing zinc *A*. One must also have access to the resources themselves to make one's knowledge and will effective on the external world.[78]

If one is already the owner of the relevant resources or if one has sufficient money to contract for their purchase, the problem is solved. If not, however, there must be some mechanism for bringing the insight, the motivation, and the resources together. Fortunately, the owners of the resources have an incentive to seek out individuals who have precisely this knowledge and to offer them incentives to act on it. If all the owners are too blind to one's insight to hire one as an employee or independent contractor, one may be able to show a secured lender or investor that one has sufficient insight to justify a loan with which to purchase the resources. None of these mechanisms is perfect, but the important thing is that one who has an insight into resource use has the self-interest of innumerable sources of economic power as his potential allies.[79] Except for those who already own the resources, it is the insti-

---

76. *See, e.g.*, T. SOWELL, *supra* note 55, at 214-17.

77. *See* Arnold, *Marx, Central Planning*, *supra* note 73, at 188-89.

78. The problems arising from gaps between power and knowledge are a major subject of Thomas Sowell's works. *See, e.g.*, T. SOWELL, *supra* note 55, at 11-14.

79. Professor Kirzner, for example, has used the analytical construct of the pure entrepreneur who begins with access to no resources whatsoever. *See* I. KIRZNER, *supra* note 71, at 37-43.

tution of contract that supplies this capacity.[80]

In sum, because contract law affects innumerable third parties, it can serve utilitarian aims only if it satisfies the requirements of sound central planning. Abstract contract principles make sense only if the requirements of sound central planning themselves have a corresponding abstract character. Utilitarian central planning requires the specification of relevant facts to be learned, the knowledge problems that must be overcome to learn those facts, and the motivational problems that must be overcome to induce action on the basis of that knowledge.

Fortunately, these three features of planning, for all the enormity of detail encompassed by the planning regime, do, in fact, share abstract characteristics. Resources should only be used after assessing their scarcity, substitutes, complements, inputs, available technology, and utility. No one has direct access to sufficient relevant information regarding any resource. Thus, for every resource, people must be given an incentive to learn the truths about resources that are within their ken and to receive proxies for the other information that they cannot directly know. Self-interest provides the universal incentive needed to combat complacency and rationalization in the pursuit of truth. The pricing system provides the mechanism for bringing to the attention of each individual using each resource proxies for the information about that resource that they cannot know. Self-interest provides the incentive to act single-mindedly on the available information, and the system of contract rights provides access to the resources on which the agent who discovered some truth must operate.

C. *The Relationship Between a Law-and-Economics Perspective and Abstract Contract Principles*

At this point, it is appropriate to bring the analysis of central planning theory together with the more traditional law-and-economics perspective on contractual abstraction. Professors Kronman and Posner have offered what amounts to an account of abstraction in terms of getting resources into the hands of those who "value" them most highly, which deserves to be quoted at some length:

> The fundamental economic principle with which we begin is that if voluntary exchanges are permitted—if, in other words, a market is allowed to operate—resources will gravitate to-

80. I have applied this idea to the contract doctrines pertaining to the duty to disclose in Wonnell, *supra* note 52, at 528-30.

> ward their most valuable uses. If *A* owns a good that is worth only $100 to him but $150 to *B*, both will be made better off by an exchange of *A*'s good for *B*'s money at any price between $100 and $150; and if they realize this, they will make the exchange. By making both of them better off, the exchange will also increase the wealth of the society (of which they are members), assuming the exchange does not reduce the welfare of nonparties more than it increases *A*'s and *B*'s welfare. Before the exchange—which, let us say, takes place at a price of $125—*A* had a good worth $100 to him and *B* had $125 in cash, a total of $225. After the exchange, *A* has $125 in cash and *B* has a good worth $150 to him, a total of $275. The exchange has increased the wealth of society by $50 (ignoring, as we have done, any possible third-party effects).
>
> *The principle is the same whether we are speaking of the purchase of a string of pearls, a lawyer's time, a machine for making shoes, or an ingot of aluminum.* The existence of a market—a locus of opportunities for mutually advantageous exchanges—facilitates the allocation of the good or service in question to the use in which it is most valuable, thereby maximizing the wealth of society.[81]

The problem with this passage is not, as it might at first appear, its assumption of zero third-party effects. A third individual *C* might have valued the good at $120, in which case she was hurt when her competitor *B* acquired the good instead. But this is consistent with the good having reached the individual who values it most highly, i.e. *B*. Thus, Posner and Kronman have not made the simple "victimless crimes" argument criticized earlier, i.e. that the contract only affects two people in the world and benefits both of them.[82]

Harm to competitors, of course, is not the only significant third-party effect of contracts. The agreement might be one to fix prices, harming consumers, or one to buy high-sulphur coal, harming local breathers of the air. Other principles of law, such as principles against restraint of trade or nuisance, will be required to deal with third-party effects of this nature. As Kronman and Posner acknowledge, abstract

81. A. KRONMAN & R. POSNER, THE ECONOMICS OF CONTRACT LAW 1-2 (1979) (emphasis added).

82. *See supra* note 52 and accompanying text.

principles of contract law were never intended to supplant the equally abstract principles of tort law that shield third parties.[83]

Rather, the problem with the passage is the sense it leaves of how optional the law-and-economics perspective on abstract contract principles is. Why is it so urgent that the good reach the hands of the one who "values" it most highly? Is this really the preeminent social norm, especially when one considers that "value" in economic terms is a product not only of willingness but also of ability to pay?[84] It is not surprising that people come away from reading passages such as these with the view that law-and-economics may occasionally have a few helpful insights into legal problems, but is basically a somewhat right-wing and unnecessary mode of analysis.

The analysis of central planning theory shows how wrong this perspective is. The price of every resource we consider using encapsulates an enormous volume of wisdom about that resource's scarcity, its substitutes and complements, its inputs and their utility in alternative uses, and so forth. If, applying our local knowledge to our particular projects, we value that resource less than its price, that is our only epistemological access to the question of whether our use of that resource would be wasteful.[85] If we give up this indirect doorway onto the world of scarce resources, we are "groping in the dark," using resources without having any idea whatsoever whether the resources we used, including their inputs, were more important in our project or in others.[86]

Of course, all of this assumes that there is some positive correlation between economic "value" and utility, but that can hardly be disputed. People generally part with their money only in return for things that give them utility and part with large amounts of money only in return for things that give them considerable utility. It would be wrong to assume that the wealthier portions of society always outbid the poorer portions of society for resources; that is why there are K-Marts and the rest of the mass society at which the upper classes persistently

83. *See* A. Kronman & R. Posner, *supra* note 81, at 2 n.1.

84. *See id.* at 2 ("[I]t may be argued that since 'value' in this analysis is measured by willingness to pay, which in turn is affected by the distribution of income and wealth (one cannot offer to buy a good without having money or the means to obtain it), the maximization of value cannot be regarded as an uncontroversially proper goal for society to pursue.").

85. *See* L. Mises, *supra* note 61, at 207 (Use of technology, or objective use-value techniques, "ignores the economic problem: to employ the available means in such a way that no want more urgently felt should remain unsatisfied because the means suitable for its attainment were employed—wasted—for the attainment of a want less urgently felt.").

86. *Id.* at 700.

sneer. That is also why, for the first time in history, whole societies exist where fear of hunger and malnutrition is not the general rule, but the cruel exception.

Moreover, the extent of the gap between "value" and "utility" is greatly exaggerated by thinking in static terms. At any one point in time, some resources will flow toward individuals who value them more only because they have more money, but who, in fact, derive less utility from them than others. It is precisely this fact, however, that gives people an incentive over time to strive to improve the financial position of themselves and their children.[87] It is surely the experience of western societies that the concomitant growth of human capital and productivity over time has made it possible for the poorer classes of many generations to live much better than the middle classes of previous generations could have hoped to live.

Finally, it is particularly inappropriate to dwell on the gap between "value" and "utility" in the context of discussing principles of contract law. When a relatively wealthy person bids for a resource, she may indeed be able to acquire it, but only by parting with the money that she was willing to bid. Those dollars are then not available to outbid others in future transactions.[88] If a resource is worth $100 to *A*, $125 to middle-class person *B*, and $150 to upper-class person *C*, it should not be imagined that the position of the middle classes vis-à-vis the upper classes must therefore be improved by a law forbidding *A* to sell the resource to *C* (or fixing its price at $125). *B* wiil be out her $125, and *C* will still have her $150 to outbid other middle-class individuals in future transactions. *C* is clearly worse off because she wanted the resource more than anything else she could envision doing with that specific $150. But *B* may not be better off at all, because she (or another middle-class person *B**) may now be outbid by *C*'s additional $150 for something *B* or *B** wants very badly. It is sensible to worry about the diminishing marginal utility of wealth in the context of discussing tax-and-expenditure rules, but not principles of contract law.[89]

87. *See* F. HAYEK, THE CONSTITUTION OF LIBERTY 61 (1960) ("Even such a celebrated figment as the 'economic man' was not an original part of the British evolutionary tradition. It would be only a slight exaggeration to say that, in the view of those British philosophers, man was by nature lazy and indolent, improvident and wasteful, and that it was only by the force of circumstances that he could be made to behave economically or would learn carefully to adjust his means to his ends.").

88. *See* Coleman, *Efficiency, Utility, and Wealth Maximization*, 8 HOFSTRA L. REV. 509, 521-23 (1980).

89. *See* Wonnell, *Compatibilism and the Controversy over End States: A Reply to Professor*

D. *Redistributive and Paternalist Challenges to Abstraction*

Two challenges to the economic case for abstraction come from other economic motives that some commentators have hoped that contract law can further, i.e., redistributive and paternalist motives. Initially, it will be helpful to explain why these motivations represent a threat to the abstraction thesis. Second, one must show why such purposes of contract law should be rejected as counterproductive. Finally, it will be possible to offer some observations on the implications of these conclusions for the issue of whether contractual obligation is best justified on deontological or consequentialist grounds.

1. Why These Motives Threaten Abstraction

Contract principles abstract from particularities of person and subject matter, i.e. from the question of who is entering into what kind of contract with whom. Abstraction of this character is antithetical to both redistributive and paternalistic ambitions for contract jurisprudence.

In order to use contract law to redistribute contractual incidents from the party with greater bargaining power to the party with less, one needs to know a great deal about the particularities of persons who are entering into the contracts. One would need to know how wealthy they were, how expansive their options were, how badly they needed the specific commodity they were contracting for in the individual case, and the like.[90] Moreover, once one decided to set aside the market results and intervene directly, one would need to know precisely what contractual services ought to be required and prohibited. This substantive task of reconstructing terms would require considerable knowledge about the resources being studied, i.e. the kinds of technical knowledge into substitutes, inputs, and technology that a central planner would be called upon to know.

It might be argued that redistributive motives simply call upon the court to articulate a different abstract rule, i.e. "protect the party with

---

Waldron, 12 HARV. J.L. & PUB. POL'Y 885 (1989).

90. We have, for example, the test for an unconscionable contract articulated in Williams v. Walker-Thomas Furniture Co., 350 F.2d 445 (D.C. Cir. 1965):

> [W]e hold that where the element of unconscionability is present at the time a contract is made, the contract should not be enforced. Unconscionability has generally been recognized to include an absence of meaningful choice on the part of one of the parties together with contract terms which are unreasonably favorable to the other party

Id. at 449.

weaker bargaining power in all cases." This abstraction, however, is rather like the abstract rule imagined earlier for the central planner of "free up resources when it would make people happier overall to do so." The problem with both formulations is that they do so little work in deciding what ought to be done in a particular case. In order to determine "bargaining power," one needs to know a great deal about the persons entering into the contracts and their circumstances. In order to know what "protections" people should be compelled to purchase or prohibited from purchasing, one needs to know a great deal about the subject matter covered by the contracts.

As this article will argue below, it is true that abstract consent-based principles alone cannot do all of the work in contract law.[91] For the sake of predictability, some concretization or formalization of those abstract principles for particular contexts will often be necessary, and to do those concretizations sensibly, one needs to know something about the persons and subject matter of the particular contract. The information required here, however, is sharply constrained by the abstract principle; one is interested in person and subject matter only for their limited evidentiary role in identifying the scope of consent. The kind of sweeping, concrete knowledge of the central planner or the redistributor seeking to replace market terms with "fair" terms is not required. Thus, consent-based principles of contract law are indeed more abstract than redistributive principles in the sense that the abstract statement constrains formalizations more tightly and does more of the work in coming up with results for particular cases.

Paternalist motives are also a challenge to the abstract character of contract law. Paternalism by its very nature cannot be abstractly applied for it asserts that some people are competent to make wise choices for other people, and the only issue that would remain would be a question of "who" is to do it for (or to) "whom." Again, one needs to know a great deal about persons to determine the extent of nondeference that should be accorded to their choices and a great deal about resources to determine how they should be allocated once the allocations of the parties themselves are superseded.

It does not follow from this, however, that all interventions into the terms of a written contract on the basis of differential knowledge are threats to abstraction. The new law-and-economics has made enormous strides in recent years in the development of the crucial concept

91. *See infra* notes 117-45 and accompanying text.

of transaction costs and has come up with many examples of such costs that can be stated as across-the-board, abstract principles that constrain decisionmaking.[92] For example, when a writing that only one party frequently uses purports to place the risk of a low-probability event, the presumption of consent from a signed writing is considerably weaker.[93] Again, it is not to be denied that courts will need to know something about the particular people who are before them to apply this principle (i.e. how frequently they enter this kind of transaction) and something about the subject matter of the particular contract (i.e. which events are low-probability). The abstract principle, however, has done a great deal of work in narrowing sharply the particularized knowledge that is required.

Of course, naked paternalism can be couched in the language of law-and-economics, i.e. different people simply have different "transaction costs" of learning where their own interests lie, given their psychological makeups. It can even be couched in the language of abstraction, i.e. the presumption of consent is reduced for any *A* or *B* for whom their transaction costs of adverting to their own interest is high. As before, however, this abstract statement is only a placeholder for the vast work that would remain in penetrating the psychological makeup of each individual contracting party. The actual working principles of paternalism are not abstract, but quite concrete.

2. The Undesirability of Redistributive and Paternalist Deviations from Contractual Abstraction

The counterproductivity of attempting to use contract rules as a tool for the redistribution of income has been repeatedly shown, and the principal purpose of this section is to organize, in a coherent way, the insights generated by that literature. Indeed, the fact that such redistributive objectives continue to be espoused in the face of that showing, as, for example, by the four legal historians quoted earlier, is one of the things that makes one entertain worries about the futility of rea-

92. For a recent criticism of the concept of "transaction costs," see Goldberg, *Production Functions, Transactions Costs, and the New Institutionalism*, in READINGS IN THE ECONOMICS OF CONTRACT LAW 21-23 (V. Goldberg ed. 1989) [hereinafter READINGS]. Goldberg correctly notes that transaction costs are no different from other costs, unless they are avoidable through alternative institutional arrangements. The defense of the term in the text is not intended as a defense of all examples of avoidable transaction costs that have appeared in the literature, but only some of the most prominent.

93. *See* Rakoff, *Contracts of Adhesion: An Essay in Reconstruction*, 96 HARV. L. REV. 1174, 1180-83 (1983).

son in the face of hope. With this worry noted, however, a brief review of the case against the redistributive use of contract principles is essential for the completeness of the case for contractual abstraction.

It will be helpful to distinguish analytically three types of intervention into the terms of contracts. The first might be called piecemeal substantive intervention, i.e. the striking down of certain contractual clauses, even though fully understood, as substantively harsh, while leaving other clauses, especially thc pricc clause, intact.[94] The second type is comprehensive substantive intervention, regulating all terms of the contract, including the price, on grounds of substantive fairness, rather than lack of understanding. The third type is procedural intervention, striking down clauses on the grounds of their being insufficiently understood or appreciated.

Piecemeal substantive intervention is the easiest of the three to dismiss outright.[95] Barring certain terms while leaving the price term freely adjustable is counterproductive from the point of view of the weaker party.[96] This is completely independent of the question of

94. See *Williams* for the proposition that courts should intervene in unconscionable contracts, where "a party of little bargaining power, and hence little real choice, signs a commercially unreasonable contract with little or no knowledge of its terms, [and] it is hardly likely that his consent, or even an objective manifestation of his consent, was ever given to *all* the terms." *Williams*, 350 F.2d at 449 (emphasis added).

95. *See* Schwartz, *Comments on Professor Harrison's Paper*, in 1988 ANN. SURV. AM. L. 115, 120 ("Now there is actually one of the few things, I suppose, that law and economic analysts do agree on, and that is that it is futile to pursue distributional concerns in bargaining contexts when all of the rules can be altered or avoided.").

96. Professor Ackerman has argued that ideal building codes might work to the benefit of the poor even if rents were not controlled. *See* Ackerman, *Regulating Slum Housing Markets on Behalf of the Poor: Of Housing Codes, Housing Subsidies and Income Redistribution Policy*, 80 YALE L.J. 1093, 1102-05 (1971). His theory is that poor tenants simply will not pay higher rents and that the concomitant increase in landlords' costs will not cause them to abandon the property or cease to rent it out to tenants.

The problem is that the more a market is like this in the short run, the more counterproductive regulation will be in the long run. If an industry is such that capital can be effectively "trapped" for generations, one will undertake great effort to see to it that one's investments cannot be so victimized. People will see to it that they never invest in housing that might someday be useful for the poor, either by investing in less housing or by investing in more elaborate housing in which the poor will never have an interest. Similarly, existing housing will either be abandoned and torn town or, alternatively, rehabilitated to a sufficient quality to attract middle-class tenants.

Ackerman might argue that the supply of housing for the poor will not diminish over the long run because that supply is simply an unintended by-product of housing intended for the upper classes in any event. Three points need to be made here. First, Ackerman's assumption that building codes will be ideal and cost-justified is clearly erroneous given the informational problems identified with planning in the text. Second, if housing does operate in this way, i.e. its supply is totally independent of the cost of supply, it is surely the only product that can be treated as "manna from heaven." Finally, an affirmative incentive to *avoid* having housing become available

whether the industry is perfectly competitive, monopolistic, or somewhere in between.[97] Even a monopolist will not include in the contract a clause that the consumer understands that imposes more cost on the consumer than benefit to the monopolist. It is better from the monopolist's perspective to omit the term and exploit her monopoly power by raising the contract price.[98] For that reason, piecemeal substantive intervention will be aimed at clauses that are efficient, i.e. that confer more benefit on the producer than harm to the consumer. Striking these clauses down will inspire price increases that will leave the consumer worse off than before.[99]

Comprehensive substantive unconscionability tries to regulate the contract in its entirety, including the price term. It is not a priori wrong; in monopolistic conditions, redistribution of income in this manner can be successful. Moreover, it must be admitted that such desirable interventions are in derogation of abstraction—for example, public utility price controls require enormous particularized knowledge about the individual industry in question.[100] In the face of this, why should one continue to adhere to abstract principles of contract law?

The explanation brings one back to the epistemological and action dimensions of the planning problem identified above. Price controls can and almost always have resulted in serious shortages of the commodity being regulated, as prices are set at levels unjustifiable by costs.[101] It is extraordinarily difficult for a court to identify the myriad of factors that go into costs, and the court will be tempted at every stage to rationalize ex post sympathy for the weaker party with its cold empirical observations.[102] By contrast, entrepreneurs have an incentive to spot

---

to the poor can replace a prior indifference to that effect.

97. *See* Wonnell, *supra* note 52, at 535-37.

98. *See* Schwartz, *A Reexamination of Nonsubstantive Unconscionability*, 63 VA. L. REV. 1053, 1072-73 (1977).

99. For a fine demonstration of this point, see Trebilcock, *The Doctrine of Inequality of Bargaining Power: Post-Benthamite Economics in the House of Lords*, 26 U. TORONTO L.J. 359 (1976).

100. *See* Meyer & Leland, *The Effectiveness of Price Regulation*, 62 REV. ECON. & STAT. 555 (1980); Moore, *The Effectiveness of Regulation of Electric Utility Prices*, 36 S. ECON. J. 365 (1970); Stigler & Friedland, *What Can Regulators Regulate? The Case of Electricity*, 5 J.L. & ECON. 1 (1962).

101. *See* Schuettinger, *Four Thousand Years of Wage and Price Controls*, 5 POL'Y REV. 74 (1978).

102. *See* T. SOWELL, *supra* note 55, at 169 ("The costs of an industry are difficult—if not impossible—for third parties to determine. . . . [C]osts are foregone options—and options are always *prospective*. . . . Government regulations and their estimates of 'cost' are based on objective statistical data on actual outlays.").

and act upon genuine cost-price disparities and to see the world in the most rational and heartless of ways.[103] The case for abstraction is not that desirable comprehensive substantive intervention is conceptually impossible; rather, it is based upon an enormous track record of experience with price controls and entrepreneurship as alternative solutions to price-cost disparities.[104]

Finally, courts might consider intervening on the basis of differential knowledge, i.e. that certain terms of the contract or their implications were not fully understood by one party. This is the only one of the three forms of intervention that is not clearly excludable as a general matter on the grounds of either a priori logic or experience.[105] As noted before, however, the most compelling cases for intervention in this area have, in recent years, been encapsulated not by a particularistic paternalism, but by abstract principles of high transaction cost environments. The cruelty of enforcing the invisible terms of standard forms,[106] or of enforcing the semantic meaning of every written term

---

103. Casual empiricism has been one attempt to refute this theory. Mark Kelman has observed that the difference between the full-service and the self-service price of gasoline in Palo Alto has persistently been larger for unleaded than for premium gasoline. Since costs of service cannot vary substantially depending upon the type of gasoline, Kelman concludes, people who buy unleaded gasoline are simply being overcharged for service and would be benefited by regulation fixing the price of service, presumably to the price paid by premium gas users. *See* M. KELMAN, A GUIDE TO CRITICAL LEGAL STUDIES 169-70 (1987).

Kelman fails to discuss two rather obvious reasons for this phenomenon. If people who buy premium gasoline drive cars that, on the average, have larger gas tanks than people who buy unleaded gasoline, then the price-per-gallon of service has to be lower for premium gasoline in order to make the total price of service the same. Moreover, if people who buy premium gasoline desire service more often, the number of services they will require at any given stop will be fewer on the average than unleaded gasoline users, who may demand full service only when they need extensive servicing.

The point here is that *apparent* disequilibrium conditions that persist over time should inspire us to learn more about a particular area, rather than to assume that we have spotted profit opportunities the market is ignorantly overlooking. While my own casual empiricism may be wrong, I am prepared to wager a hefty sum of money that price controls on full-service unleaded gasoline will produce a shortage of full-service stations for unleaded gasoline users.

104. *See* T. SOWELL, *supra* note 55, at 176-82.

105. Duncan Kennedy has thus made open paternalism a major part of his attack against abstract contract law. *See* Kennedy, *Form and Substance in Private Law Adjudication*, 89 HARV. L. REV. 1685, 1749 (1976) ("The altruists demonstrated that no single general analysis could predict the effects of legal intervention in the economy. Everything depended on the structure of the particular market, which in turn depended on the legal system."); *see also* Kennedy, *Distributive and Paternalist Motives in Contract and Tort Law, With Special Reference to Compulsory Terms and Unequal Bargaining Power*, 41 MD. L. REV. 563, 580-83 (1982).

106. *See, e.g.*, Rakoff, *supra* note 93, at 1180-83; Slawson, *Mass Contracts: Lawful Fraud in California*, 48 S. CAL. L. REV. 1, 3-11 (1974); *see also* Goldberg, *Institutional Change and the Quasi-Invisible Hand*, 17 J.L. & ECON. 461 (1974).

even in the face of low-probability events,[107] is not at all indicated by the abstraction thesis.

Open paternalism always has been distasteful, with its pretentious assumption that some people are both willing and able to make accurate judgments, uncontaminated by rationalizations, that other people are systematically ignoring their own interests. Historical experience with paternalism is not encouraging.[108] It is submitted that, when one considers the case for paternalism *minus* the interventions on the basis of differential knowledge that can be stated in the form of working abstract rules, it is not a serious threat to the abstract character of contract law.

3. Implications for the Issue of Deontological vs. Consequentialist Theories of Contract

An interesting feature of the new abstract rules for coping with high transaction cost environments is that such rules bring contractual obligation much closer to the ordinary notion of "consent" than it would otherwise be.[109] It always was fictional to speak of people's having "consented" to all of the implications of a written document's language, including even the low-probability events covered in dense standard form language.[110] The idea that many such words and developments were simply "outside the scope of genuine consent" is what ordinary notions of fairness have always told us.

This confluence of sound economic theory and common sense deontological notions, such as consent, is itself part of the extraordinary general compatibility of these two systems of ideas.[111] Richard Posner has surely been the principal demonstrator of this remarkable parallelism, although what is perhaps most extraordinary is that the places where his principles seem most contrary to common sense fairness almost invariably identify the cases where his economic analysis is

107. *See* A. POLINSKY, AN INTRODUCTION TO LAW AND ECONOMICS 31 (2d ed. 1989).

108. *See generally* P. JOHNSON, MODERN TIMES, THE WORLD FROM THE TWENTIES TO THE EIGHTIES (1983).

109. This increases the importance of consent-based theories of contract, such as that defended in Barnett, *supra* note 50.

110. This is not to deny that courts can err in finding certain terms to be outside the scope of consent. For a finding that consumers respond rationally to warranty terms, see Priest, *A Theory of the Consumer Product Warranty*, 90 YALE L.J. 1297 (1981).

111. *See* Epstein, *The Utilitarian Foundations of Natural Law*, 12 HARV. J.L. & PUB. POL'Y 713 (1989).

shakiest.[112]

The parallelism of these two language systems thus brings the analysis of this long section full circle. It was noted before that deontological ideas, such as the sanctity of consent and the institution of promising that serves to make that consent effective over time, were by their nature abstract.[113] It was consequentialist considerations that caused us to doubt the workability of contractual abstraction, especially after one realized that the consequences of a contract's enforcement or nonenforcement were economy-wide. It is now apparent, however, that the consequentialist analysis brings one back to the abstract ideas of consent and promising, realistically and not fictionally interpreted.

The article previously posed the question of whether economic analysis of contract was necessary.[114] In some sense, this question might seem absurd since contract law and doctrine preceded modern law-and-economics by a considerable number of years. The argument that the socialist calculation problem makes contract principles indispensable seems particularly ironic, since that argument is unquestionably an intellectual discovery of the twentieth century, which none of the historians studied considered to be the high point of freedom of contract.[115]

Recognition of the parallelism between the notion of consent and the abstract principles of modern law-and-economics adds a new level of irony to this problem. Given the centrality of the ordinary concept of consent, it might be said that economic analysis of contract is not necessary after all. Indeed, it might not even be desirable for judges to resort directly to economic analysis to decide contract questions. We have centuries of experience with judges' decisions refining the common sense notion of consent; we have no such experience with unconstrained judicial consequentialist calculation. I have explored elsewhere the difficult question of whether one set of philosophical concepts can be used as a "working philosophy" to promote objectives derived from another set of concepts.[116] Suffice it to say here that we are far more certain that abstract contract principles must be retained for consequentialist reasons than we are that the consequentialist reasoning must be a part

112. *See* Wonnell, *supra* note 52, at 511-14.

113. *See supra* notes 48-51 and accompanying text.

114. *See supra* notes 90-93 and accompanying text.

115. *See* Hayek, *Economic Thought: The Austrian School*, 4 INT'L ENCY. SOC. SCI. 458 (1968).

116. Wonnell, *supra* note 3, at 123-30.

of the conscious decisionmaking of the judges.

IV. Formality in Contract Law

A. *Formality and Abstraction Compared*

Formality is a ubiquitous feature of contract law, as it is of law in general. In this context, "formality" means a tendency of the law to treat as an ultimate fact some demonstrable, externally patent feature of the world, when in strictest theory that external fact is only a more-or-less valid proxy for the variable that is normatively relevant.[117]

In contract law, the most obvious illustrations of formality are those that pertain to the terms of a writing that purports to be a contract.[118] As the prior section noted, in theory, it is consent that is the normatively relevant fact, but contract law often gives great emphasis to the writing itself with doctrines such as the statute of frauds,[119] the parol evidence rule,[120] the plain meaning rule,[121] and the objective theory of contracts.[122]

An extremely important issue is the relationship between the ideas of "formality" and "abstraction." Formality is a device for making legal results turn on predictable, externally patent features of the world. Abstraction is a device for making legal rules invariable with respect to the persons and subject matters of particular transactions. What is the relationship between these two notions?

One similarity of the two doctrines is evident. Both formality and abstraction urge the law to disregard a large range of particulars of individual cases in favor of a narrow subset of facts that appears in innumerable cases. Formality calls upon the court to focus upon the "form" to the exclusion of the totality of circumstances one might call the "substance." Abstraction calls upon the court to focus upon the

117. For a variety of definitions that have been offered to the concepts of formality and formalism, see Phillips, *The Inevitable Incoherence of Modern State Action Doctrine*, 28 St. Louis U.L.J. 683, 686 n.13 (1984).

118. *See generally* Fuller, *Consideration and Form*, 41 Colum. L. Rev. 799 (1941).

119. *See* Restatement (Second) of Contracts §§ 131-32 (1979).

120. *See id.* §§ 209-17.

121. *See* J. Calamari & J. Perillo, The Law of Contracts 118 n.11 (2d ed. 1977) ("The number of cases decided under the plain meaning rule is simply staggering."). The leading modern case rejecting the plain meaning rule is Pacific Gas & Elec. Co. v. G.W. Thomas Drayage & Rigging Co., 69 Cal. 2d 33, 442 P.2d 641, 69 Cal. Rptr. 561 (1968).

122. *See* O.W. Holmes, The Common Law 242 (M. Howe ed. 1963) ("The law has nothing to do with the actual state of the parties' minds. In contract, as elsewhere, it must go by externals, and judge parties by their conduct.").

presence of consent, to use a shorthand word for the set of consent-based contractual principles, to the exclusion of the totality of circumstances pertaining to persons and subject matters.

There is a second similarity between these two ideas that may be somewhat more hidden. Formality focuses upon the externally patent form as a more-or-less valid proxy for the "ultimate" variable of consent. The socialist calculation debate, however, suggests that consent itself is not the ultimate variable, but only a more-or-less valid proxy for the relevance, knowledge, and action dimensions of the utilitarian planning process. As such, abstraction calls upon the court to focus on a proxy variable in much the same way that formality does.

Given these two similarities, it is not surprising that many writers, including Professors Horwitz and Friedman, treat abstraction and formality interchangeably and criticize them together as an outdated relic of nineteenth-century ideology.[123] Consider, for example, the following statement from Professor Friedman:

> There is, therefore, a relationship between the parol evidence rule and the "objective theory" of contracts. Both take as their model of a contract the abstract, impersonal agreement whose meaning is apparent to third persons, and which requires no subjective "interpretation." . . . The parol evidence rule, in its simplest form, fits in well with the abstraction of pure contract law. It demanded similar treatment of similar documents, excluding private, personal, and special features. . . . On the other hand, when the parol evidence rule shuts off enforcement of the "real" agreement, it strikes at the concept of assent, which is basic to contract law. But since assent, abstractly speaking, ought to mean assent evidenced in objectively measurable terms, the parol evidence rule is more in keeping with classical contract law than not.[124]

This tendency to treat the problems of formality and abstraction interchangeably is a very serious error. It is necessary to spell out the basic difference between these two doctrines and then to explain why it is so important not to ignore that difference.

The fundamental difference between the doctrines of formality and abstraction pertains to the *reason* why courts are urged to focus on the narrow set of unitary proxy values. In the case of formality, that reason

123. Horwitz's views on formality are set forth *supra* notes 28-36 and accompanying text.

124. L. FRIEDMAN, *supra* note 6, at 95-97.

pertains to the virtues of form: it can make the law more predictable for parties in advance, less likely to generate expensive factual litigation, and less likely to be manipulated by judges or juries.[125] By contrast, abstraction calls upon the court to ignore person and subject matter so as to create a unitary framework for all persons to fulfill the relevance, epistemological, and action dimensions of planning for all subject matters. The reasons for these superficially similar doctrines could hardly be more dissimilar.

It is essential that this difference in function not be forgotten for it has a direct bearing on the question of whether abstraction is the product of a particular social or historical milieu. The virtues of formality are clearly situation-specific and time-specific. In certain contractual situations—for example, where sophisticated parties represented by counsel bargain at length over each contract term—it may do more harm than good to penetrate the writing in favor of other indicia of consent.[126] By contrast, the formal writing is likely to be a very poor proxy for consent in many contexts, for example, if the literacy of many of the individuals in a particular culture is in doubt. It would be foolish to apply the same formalities to all persons, all subject matters, and all eras. Stated another way, the use of formalities should not be abstract.

By contrast, the formal considerations that make consent such a critical proxy for utilitarian planning are not tied in the same way to historical eras. Different historical periods will have different scarcities, technologies, substitutes, complements, inputs, and tastes, but there is no reason to believe that the logical function of these variables will change. The relationship between abstract consent and utility, although a proxy relationship in form, is so securely cemented in the nature of the human condition that, ironically, its proxy character becomes unimportant.

In other words, given the permanency of the socialist calculation dilemma, it is wise for society to come to regard abstract consent-based principles, not as evidentiary proxies, but as substantive objectives.[127]

125. The evidentiary, cautionary, and channeling functions of formality are discussed in Fuller, *supra* note 118, at 800-03.

126. Even in this context, it may not always be appropriate to view the writing as conclusive evidence of consent. For example, the court brought in trade usage to qualify a seemingly absolute written price term in Nanakuli Paving & Rock Co. v. Shell Oil Co., 664 F.2d 772 (9th Cir. 1981).

127. I have argued elsewhere that we need a philosophy with two levels, one of which regards these intermediate norms as ends in themselves and one of which preserves their proxy character. *See* Wonnell, *supra* note 3, at 123-30.

By contrast, formality must be seen as evidentiary in character and, therefore, as bearing only a contingent and temporary relationship to the ultimate fact that it sometimes evidences, i.e. consent. Above all, criticism of the situation- or era-specific character of formality must not be permitted to spill over into criticism of "abstraction" by wilful or careless use of language equating the two.

The best way to keep this vital distinction clear is to refuse to countenance any attempt to make formality a substantive objective as distinguished from an evidentiary matter, even if, in some contexts, it is thought prudent to regard the formality as conclusive evidence of consent. It is useful, in this regard, to contrast the following statements by Professor Corbin and Judge Learned Hand, interestingly juxtaposed in a leading contracts casebook as if they were saying much the same thing.[128] First, Corbin:

> It may be that some day we may be able to observe a state of mind in the same way that we observe chemical processes and electrical discharges. At present, however, what we observe for judicial purposes is the conduct of the parties. We observe this conduct and we describe it as the expression of a state of mind.[129]

Judge Hand argued in *Hotchkiss v. National City Bank of New York*:[130]

> A contract has, strictly speaking, nothing to do with the personal, or individual, intent of the parties. A contract is an obligation attached by the mere force of law to certain acts of the parties, usually words, which ordinarily accompany and represent a known intent. If, however, it were proved by twenty bishops that either party, when he used the words, intended something else than the usual meaning which the law imposes upon them, he would still be held unless there were some mutual mistake, or something else of the sort.[131]

Although these two views are superficially quite similar, and

128. *See* J. JACKSON & L. BOLLINGER, CONTRACT LAW IN MODERN SOCIETY 310-11 (2d ed. 1980). In fairness, it is probably accurate to say that Corbin and Hand would not have regarded themselves as saying radically different things. Nevertheless, the theoretical differences between their views as stated are enormous.

129. 1 CORBIN ON CONTRACTS 20-21 (1963).

130. 200 F. 287 (D.C.N.Y. 1911).

131. *Id.* at 293.

might, in fact, lead to the same results in a wide range of cases, for our purposes the differences are fundamental. Corbin's position is that external indicators serve as excellent evidence of underlying mental states, the best indicators we have now, but not necessarily the best we will ever have. Hand, on the other hand, suggests that even highly credible evidence (twenty bishops) would not matter because the ultimate fact to be proved is not subjective agreement or mutual consent.[132]

Corbin's theory represents the only tenable starting point for our analysis of formality. On Corbin's evidentiary theory of formality, there will, of course, be pressures to deviate from formality in certain contexts, since the formal terms are much better evidence of actual consent in some settings than in others. This, however, poses no problem for the abstract character of the principles of contract law. To the contrary, it is precisely because the principles of contract are so abstract, so universal,[133] that any one attempt to formalize or concretize them will have evidentiary weight only in certain ranges of the principles' application.

None of this is intended to deny the importance of the evidentiary questions that the various doctrines of formality call to our attention. Is the parties' intent more frequently frustrated by formal rules such as the parol evidence rule, or is it more frequently protected against false claims of oral side agreements? This is an empirical question of considerable importance, the answer to which is likely to vary considerably by context and by the nature of the parties who are contracting. I do not pretend to know the answer to this question, and I am happy to join the chorus of voices protesting the absence of good empirical scholarship in the area of contract law.[134] For now, however, it is sufficient to observe that the logical role of that empirical inquiry is evidentiary; it does not go to the matter of abstraction in the substantive law of contracts.

---

132. I do not deny that, for some purposes, one may wish to disregard uncommunicated subjective intentions. Analytically, the "objective theory of contracts" deals with a series of torts. For example, it deals with the torts of intentionally or negligently failing to communicate one's intentions. It is not clear, however, that the remedy for all such torts should be to enforce the contract as written. Indeed, sometimes the "objective theory" may reward the party guilty of a tort, when she "manifests" *X* in some objective form, knowing that the other party believes not-*X* and will not perceive the "objective" manifestation.

133. "Abstraction" and "universality" are, of course, two sides of the same coin. If the proper legal rules do not depend upon particularities of person or subject matter, then their applicability will transcend particular persons and subject matters.

134. *See, e.g.*, Warren, *supra* note 4, at 52-53.

B. *Contrasting Abstract Contract Principles with Rules for Particular Contract Types*

Formality in contract law reaches far beyond such traditional doctrinal categories as the statute of frauds and parol evidence rule. The various specialized areas of contracts—insurance law, construction law, sales law, and the like—may in themselves be formalizations or concretizations of the general principles of contract. On the other hand, this cannot be taken for granted. Many such bodies of law may be the product of thinly rationalized special interest legislation that seeks to exempt politically powerful interest groups from the constraints of abstract principles.[135] More likely still is that each specialized body of contract law will be a mixture of rules that sensibly concretize abstract principles, rules that try but fail to do so (such as, perhaps, the statute of frauds for service contracts longer than a year), and rules that in no way can be justified on general principles.[136]

For the purpose of contrasting abstract principles of contract with rules for particular contract types, the essential distinction is between rules that seek to concretize the abstract principles of contract law and rules that seek to create exceptions to those abstract principles for particular contexts. Concretization is important; if the law were stated too intangibly it might lose many of the predictability virtues of formality.[137] It would also fail to preserve the "wisdom of the ages" in handling certain types of contracts and their perennial problems. These, however, are justifications for rules that attempt faithfully to apply general principles to particular contexts, modifying them only to the extent necessary to serve the virtues of predictability.

When faced with an abstract contract principle and an apparently inconsistent specific rule for particular types of contracts, the abstraction thesis suggests that something is in need of change. The direction of that change, however, is not immediately evident for an anomaly of this character leaves the court free to consider several intellectual moves. Three such moves deserve particular attention. First, one can defend the specific rule as a sensible concretization of the abstract prin-

135. I have elsewhere argued for a constitutional shield against statutes of this type. *See* Wonnell, *Economic Due Process and the Preservation of Competition*, 11 HASTINGS CONST. L.Q. 91 (1983).

136. On the interesting question of how groups might find it in their interest to deviate from abstract principles that are in their separate individual interests, see Goldberg, *A Relational Exchange Perspective on the Employment Relationship*, in READINGS, *supra* note 92, at 147-51.

137. *See* Alexander, *The Constitution as Law*, 6 CONST. COMMENTARY 103, 106 (1989).

ciple, resulting in a change only in the intellectual background and not in the practical policies pursued.[138] Second, one can criticize the specific rule for its deviation from the abstract principle. Finally, and most daringly, one can use the evident wisdom of the specific rule to show the need to envision a new abstract principle of contract law.

Within this analytical framework, much of the work of Richard Posner can be seen as fulfilling the first function, i.e. showing that particular rules are defensible concretizations of more abstract principles. Consider, for example, his treatment of an apparent anomaly between sales law and construction law on the question of contract conditions. The law of sales allows a buyer to refuse to accept and pay for goods on the grounds of minor defects, subject in many cases to the ability of the seller to cure by substituting a conforming tender.[139] By contrast, construction contract law allows the buyer to refuse to pay for work done only if the deficiency in performance was substantial.[140] For minor breaches, the buyer must pay the contract price but may sue for damages attributable to the contractor's breach.[141]

Posner argues that, in goods contracts, buyer's self-help is generally

> a cheaper remedy, socially as well as privately, than . . . keeping the widgets and suing . . . for damages, or even selling them on [the seller's] account—[the seller] presumably has a better sense of what to do with the defective widgets than [the buyer] (repair them, scrap them, sell them to someone else as 'seconds,' etc.).[142]

By contrast, in the construction area, the resale value of property designed for the buyer's tastes is likely to be quite low, making the ability of the buyer to refuse payment on substantially completed projects inefficient.

In both bodies of law, Posner notes, "The law implicitly compares the cost of the promisee's self-help to the promisor with the promisee's damages, and refuses to allow self-help when the former cost substantially exceeds the latter."[143] Specialized rules for discrete bodies of

138. In other words, a defense of a specific rule as a concretization of a general principle makes the former, in a meaningful sense, a subpart of the latter discipline of law.

139. U.C.C. §§ 2-601, 2-508 (1987).

140. *See, e.g.*, Jacob & Youngs, Inc. v. Kent, 230 N.Y. 239, 129 N.E. 889 (1921).

141. *See id.*

142. R. Posner, Economic Analysis of Law 121 (3d ed. 1986).

143. *Id.* at 122.

transactions are thus argued to be subsets of more general rules for the famous abstract personalities of contract law, *A* and *B*.

The second approach is to criticize specific rules for their deviation from the abstract principles of contract law. Much of the work of Richard Epstein can be understood as performing this function. Epstein has conducted investigations of various specialized areas of contractual relations, including labor law[144] and medical malpractice law[145] and has criticized the specialized rules on the basis of the abstract principles of contract. Since Epstein has characteristically taken on the toughest areas where intuition might suggest the need for deviating from general principles, there is every reason to believe that Epstein's conclusions will have considerable power, on a fortiori reasoning, to other contractual contexts.

Finally, it is always possible that one will find the rules of a specific subpart of contract law so compelling that one may be tempted to envision a new abstract principle that should govern across-the-board. Much of the next section of the article will explore the question of whether something of this nature is indicated for the abstract principles of compensatory damages and the duty to mitigate, or at least for certain versions of those abstract principles.

The basic point behind all of these moves is that scholars' minds should never rest with the idea that different bodies of law for different types of contracts can coexist peacefully for the reason that there are no overarching principles to which they are both accountable. Courts might be justified in "parking" different rules for different transactions for a while until it was clear precisely which concrete rules were in need of change, but the pressure for change in the direction of abstraction should eventually be sufficient to motivate action.

What remains is to employ this research program to the study of each specific principle of contract law. While the analysis of all such principles would be far beyond the scope of an article, the next section will seek to apply this paradigm to two closely related principles: the ideas of compensatory damages and of mitigation of damages. The objective will be to show by example how light can be shed on other principles of contract law by contrasting those abstract principles with concrete rules that appear to conflict with them.

144. *See* Epstein, *supra* note 2.

145. *See* Epstein, *Medical Malpractice: The Case for Contract*, 1 AM. B. FOUND. RES. J. 87 (1976).

V. Contractual Abstraction Illustrated: The Principles of Compensatory Damages and Mitigation of Damages

To better understand the points outlined in the prior sections, it will be helpful to explore specific principles of contract law and to contrast those principles with the treatment of similar issues under bodies of law applicable to particular kinds of transactions. I have chosen two related principles for such analysis. The first principle is the idea that the proper general remedy for breach of contract is a compensatory money damage award,[146] a principle that has been defended in the literature as discouraging inefficient, but not efficient, breaches of contract.[147] The second principle is that damages for breach of contract will be measured on the assumption that the nonbreaching party took reasonable efforts to mitigate damages.[148]

Although the two doctrines have often been treated as distinct, it is clear that they are quite closely related. The "duty to mitigate" damages is a duty to refrain from contractual performances that the other party has signalled, through her own breach, that she no longer values sufficiently to justify their cost. Both doctrines seek to prevent one party from imposing costs on the other party that are unnecessary to secure the benefits of the contract.[149]

Part A of this section analyzes the principle of compensatory damages while Part B discusses the principle of mitigation. Each part is in turn divided into two sections. The first section sets forth and defends a version of the abstract principle in question. The second section identifies and criticizes cases that have deviated from these abstract principles when dealing with particular kinds of contracts.

---

146. *See, e.g.*, Dierickx v. Vulcan Indus., 10 Mich. App. 67, 158 N.W.2d 778, 781 (1968) ("Where a breach of contract occurs, the law aims to make compensation adequate to the real injury sustained, and to place the injured party, so far as money can do it, in the same position he would have occupied if the contract had been fulfilled.") (citations omitted).

147. *See* R. Posner, *supra* note 142, at 105-08.

148. This is sometimes referred to as a "duty to mitigate," although it may not technically be a "duty" since it gives rise to no affirmative liability, its only effect is at the level of damages the party failing to mitigate can claim.

149. The similarity between the ideas of efficient breach and the duty to mitigate is noted in D. Harris, Remedies in Contract and Tort 74-93 (1988).

A. *The Principle of Compensatory Damages*

1. A Defense of One Version of the Abstract Principle

As noted before, the principle that damages for breach of contract are compensatory in nature has been defended as permitting efficient, while discouraging inefficient, breaches of contract. In recent years, however, the "efficient breach" idea has been subjected to a torrent of criticism.[150] The doctrine has been attacked as amoral, disregarding the sanctity of promises. As such, the doctrine presents a challenge for those who hold a compatibilist view that common sense deontological morality and social efficiency are isomorphic.[151]

The striking feature of the concept of "efficient breach" can be seen from the rhetoric it employs. "Efficient" is an explicitly consequentialist notion, while "breach" calls attention to the deviation from an individualist moral code of promissory obligations. Thus, the doctrine seems to be suggesting that private immorality must be tolerated for the greater good, i.e. the doctrine itself is anti-compatibilist. Those who hold that private morality points the way to desirable social consequences can be no more content with the doctrine itself than they can be with its critics, who insist that efficiency must yield to the morality of promise keeping.

The need is to recast the efficiency insight in the proper language of our individualist morality. Toward this end, let us draw a distinction between the "use value" and the "extortion value" of a contractual promise. Contracts contribute to economic efficiency because each party values the performance she is to receive more than the price she is required to pay. The law must, therefore, be scrupulously protective of these use values of contractual performance. The question is whether there is a similar reason to be solicitous of a contract's extortion value.[152]

Consider, for example, as an ideal type that probably has no real world counterpart, a contract whose sole purpose from the perspective

---

150. For criticisms of the concept of "efficient breach," see Linzer, *On the Amorality of Contract Remedies—Efficiency, Equity, and the Second Restatement*, 81 COLUM. L. REV. 111, 138-39 (1981); Macneil, *Efficient Breach of Contract: Circles in the Sky*, 68 VA. L. REV. 947, 951-52 (1982).

151. On the compatibilist thesis, see generally *Symposium on the Compatibility of Rights and Consequentialist Analyses*, 12 HARV. J.L. & PUB. POL'Y 713-888 (1989).

152. The problem of the extortion opportunities that arise in contractual relationships is discussed in Goetz & Scott, *The Mitigation Principle: Toward a General Theory of Contractual Obligation*, in READINGS, *supra* note 92, at 199-200.

of one of the contracting parties was to secure extortion value. I contract to pay $500 to have holes drilled in my driveway. In fact, I prefer my driveway without holes in it and would not pay anything solely for the value of holes as an item of consumption. My entrepreneurial judgment, however, tells me that the land is such that drilling anything in this driveway is going to prove remarkably difficult. Sure enough, although my judgment was based only on an intelligent hunch and not unambiguous fact, the contractor discovers that it is going to cost $5000 to drill the holes.[153]

Should the law allow me to sue for specific performance and/or punitive damages in the case of breach of contract? A remedy that resulted in the contract's actually being performed would be in neither party's interest. As numerous critics of the efficient breach idea have noted, however, this fact should provide an incentive for the parties to negotiate their way out of actual performance.[154] Perhaps the contractor can induce me to drop my suit by paying me $2500, an amount between the value to me of performance ($0) and the cost to the contractor of performance ($5000). Inefficient performance need not occur, and my entrepreneurial gambit will have paid off.

It seems apparent that neither deontological morality nor consequentialist objectives are furthered by such a result. Common sense morality suggests that I have manipulated the system to extort a benefit from the misfortune of another. From an efficiency perspective, resources were dissipated in concocting the scheme, carrying it out, and negotiating for a settlement in a rather high transaction cost "bilateral monopoly" setting.[155]

Let us now drop the assumption that extortion was the motive for a contract's being entered in the first place. I entered into a contract to have holes drilled in the edges of my driveway for $500 because I very much wanted to plant flowers there. Indeed, if forced I would have paid as much as $750 for the work to be done; $250 was consumer surplus. As before, however, it turns out that performance is going to cost $5000. What response should the law take in this situation?

One possibility, of course, is to excuse performance altogether on

153. Making this a matter of entrepreneurial judgment rather than known fact avoids defenses such as fraud or knowingly exploiting a unilateral mistake of fact. *See, e.g.*, E. FARNSWORTH, CONTRACTS 666-67 (1982).

154. *See, e.g.*, Birmingham, *Damage Measures and Economic Rationality: The Geometry of Contract Law*, 1969 DUKE L.J. 49, 69-70.

155. On the problem of strategic behavior generated by conditions of bilateral monopoly, see A. POLINSKY, *supra* note 107, at 18-20.

grounds such as mutual mistake or impossibility. This may be unwise, however, if the contractor was the party who was in the better position to estimate the likelihood of encountering drilling problems.[156] If completely excusing the contractor is rejected, should the law go to the other extreme and impose specific performance and/or punitive damages on the contractor?

Again, the result is likely to be a payment, after considerable bluffing and threatening in negotiations, somewhere between the value to the owner ($750) and the cost to the contractor ($5000), say $2875. As before, it is not apparent that common sense morality would approve this windfall for the driveway owner; the law seems to have lost its bearings in sensible dispute resolution and become a game of its own. From an efficiency perspective, contractors will begin to charge higher prices for their services to compensate them for the transaction and judgment costs of dealing with a few extortionists; work that should be done will be priced out of the market.

If these deontological and consequentialist assessments are correct, why is the idea of efficient breach the subject of so much criticism? One reason has already been noted, i.e. the unfortunate use of consequentialist, rather than deontological, language in which to capture the insight. There is, however, a substantive as well as a rhetorical problem, which is that current legal rules do not adequately protect the use value of a contractual promise, and, moreover, breaching parties are fully aware of that fact.[157]

Above all, litigation costs, such as attorney's fees and the value of parties' time lost to discovery and trial proceedings, are not generally recoverable.[158] Moreover, rules requiring reasonable certainty of proof and disallowing emotional distress or idiosyncratic value contribute to the undercompensation.[159] Commentators, with good reason, simply do not believe that a breaching party who says "see you in court" leaves the nonbreaching party psychologically indifferent vis-à-vis actual per-

156. *See* Posner & Rosenfield, *Impossibility and Related Doctrines in Contract Law: An Economic Analysis*, 6 J. LEGAL STUD. 83 (1977).

157. *See* Farber, *Reassessing the Economic Efficiency of Compensatory Damages for Breach of Contract*, 66 VA. L. REV. 1443 (1980).

158. *See* F.D. Rich Co. v. Industrial Lumber Co., 417 U.S. 116, 126-31 (1974) (Under the so-called "American rule" governing the award of attorneys' fees in federal court litigation, "attorney's fees 'are not ordinarily recoverable in the absence of a statute or enforceable contract providing therefor.' ") (quoting Fleischmann Distilling Corp. v. Maier Brewing Co., 386 U.S. 714, 717 (1967)).

159. *See, e.g.*, RESTATEMENT (SECOND) OF CONTRACTS §§ 352-353 (1986).

formance.[160] In this respect, however, the immorality of the promisor's behavior tracks the problem that the breach may now be quite inefficient, since some of its costs have, as a practical matter, been externalized.[161]

It is now possible to state more fully the abstract principles that ought to govern this area. The privilege of contractual nonperformance must be conditional upon behavior by the breaching party that protects the use value of the promise to the nonbreaching party. Absent countervailing principles, such as that of foreseeability,[162] such full protection must be available as a matter of practical fact, not as the product of legal fictions. If the nonperforming promisor does unambiguously protect the promisee's use value, however, the promisee does not have the right to decline that offer for the purpose of pursuing the extortion value of the promise.

At least when specific performance is a viable remedy, no revolutionary doctrinal changes would be required to implement this abstract ideal. Specific performance is an equitable remedy, and courts of equity have always reserved the power to condition that remedy on the circumstances of the case, including the good or bad faith of the parties to the contract.[163] Specific performance should be available, unless the defendant has already demonstrated, or is now willing to demonstrate, that she is willing to protect unambiguously the plaintiff's full use value.

Such protection at the time of trial would necessarily require compensation for the plaintiff's litigation costs, including attorney's fees and the value of the plaintiff's time consumed in the litigation process. This is simply another way of saying, and meaning, what the courts have said all along—that specific performance will be available if the damage remedy "at law" is inadequate.[164]

On the other hand, if the defendant had earlier made a settlement

---

160. *See* Macneil, *supra* note 150, at 951 & n.19.

161. It is true that "externality" is something of a double-edged sword here. The victim of the breach, if she is allowed to recover damages for all of the effects of that breach, emotional and otherwise, may have an incentive to become overly reliant on the promise because she can externalize the harm of breach. *See* Cooter, *Unity in Tort, Contract, and Property: The Model of Precaution*, 73 CALIF. L. REV. 1-51 (1985). This may provide a reason for limiting plaintiffs to the emotional damages that the person of reasonable firmness would experience.

162. *See id.* at 15 ("It is but a short step to argue that reliance that is excessive in efficiency terms is also unforeseeable.").

163. *See* E. FARNSWORTH, *supra* note 153, at 821-22.

164. *See, e.g.*, Wilson v. Sandstrom, 317 So. 2d 732 (Fla. 1975), *cert. denied*, 423 U.S. 1053 (1976).

offer that, at the time it was made, would have unambiguously protected the plaintiff's use value, there would seem to be no reason to grant the plaintiff either specific performance or legal fees incurred subsequent to the defendant's settlement offer.[165] Such a remedial structure would have the advantage of encouraging early settlement and good faith by both parties and of discouraging the use of the legal system for its extortion value. It would also have the inestimable advantages that come from a legal system that takes its own principles seriously, not as baselines from which to wink at rules and practices that can be made consistent with those principles only through extensive rationalization.

2. A Critique of Deviations from the Abstract Principle

It is now appropriate to consider the interaction between the principle of compensation as defended above and specific areas of contract law. The case selected for analysis is *Foley v. Interactive Data Corp.*,[166] decided by the California Supreme Court at the end of 1988. Plaintiff was an executive employee of the defendant, which marketed computer-based decision-support services. The plaintiff had received steady raises, promotions, and commendations in six years on the job. The defendant then terminated his employment, citing "performance reasons." The plaintiff's complaint alleged that the true reason for his being fired was the fact that he had brought to the attention of his outgoing superior the fact that the superior's replacement was under investigation for embezzling from his prior employer. The complaint asked for punitive damages, alleging, inter alia, that the defendant's breach of contract amounted to a tortious breach of the covenant of good faith and fair dealing.[167]

Foley raised several issues of relevance to the question of contractual abstraction,[168] but the most important of those issues was the ques-

165. An analogy to this principle exists in the concept of an offer of judgment. *See* FED. R. CIV. P. 68.

166. 47 Cal. 3d 654, 765 P.2d 373, 254 Cal. Rptr. 211 (1988).

167. *Id.* at 662-65, 765 P.2d at 374-76, 254 Cal. Rptr. at 212-14.

168. One issue, for example, was whether an employment contract can be implied-in-fact from the conduct of an employer over time, rather than evidenced by formal terms. Consistently with the abstraction thesis defended here, the court held that such an implied-in-fact contract was indeed possible.

> Permitting proof of and reliance on implied-in-fact contract terms does not nullify the at-will rule, it merely treats such contracts in a manner in keeping with general contract law. . . . We see no sound reason to exempt the employment relationship from the ordinary rules of contract interpretation which permit proof of implied terms.

tion of punitive damages for breach of an employment contract.[169] In considering the punitive damage question, the court was faced with insurance precedents allowing the tort claim,[170] lower court employment precedents allowing the claim,[171] and a general rule disallowing punitive damages in contract cases.[172]

The court concluded that punitive damages could not be recovered. Abstraction was the court's approach. The court noted the importance of predictability in contract law and the general rule that contract damages were intended to be compensatory in nature. With regard to the plaintiff's tort claim, it concluded:

> The covenant of good faith is read into contracts in order to protect the express covenants or promises of the contract, not to protect some general public policy interest not directly tied to the contract's purposes. The insurance cases thus were a major departure from traditional principles of contract law. We must, therefore, consider with great care claims that extension of the exceptional approach taken in those cases is automatically appropriate if certain hallmarks and similarities can be adduced in another contract setting.[173]

The court declined to follow the analogy of insurance cases that had permitted punitive damages for breach of the implied covenant of good faith and fair dealing. The court concluded that a greater divergence exists between the interests of insurer and insured than between employer and employee. Once an accident occurs, the insurer is unam-

---

Id. at 681, 765 P.2d at 387, 254 Cal. Rptr. at 225.

169. There was also a question of whether the firing was contrary to public policy for reasons independent of the contract. The court declined to follow cases such as Tameny v. Atlantic Richfield Co., 27 Cal. 3d 167, 610 P.2d 1330, 164 Cal. Rptr. 839 (1980) (employment wrongfully terminated for refusing to fix prices), and Petermann v. International Bhd. of Teamsters, 174 Cal. App. 2d 184, 344 P.2d 25 (1959) (employment wrongfully terminated for refusing to give false testimony). No such overriding public policy was found in *Foley*. 47 Cal. 3d at 667-71, 765 P.2d at 377-80, 254 Cal. Rptr. at 215-18.

I can see no reason why these public policy notions should deviate from abstraction. If it is wrong to terminate an employee for refusing to commit perjury, is it not wrong to terminate a franchisee or a tenant or any contractual relationship on such grounds? In any event, these principles belong primarily to the law of tort rather than contract, for the wrongness of the action inheres in protection of third parties and is independent of the intention of the parties to the contract.

170. Egan v. Mutual of Omaha Ins. Co., 24 Cal. 3d 809, 620 P.2d 141, 169 Cal. Rptr. 691 (1979).

171. Cleary v. American Airlines, Inc., 111 Cal. App. 3d 443, 168 Cal. Rptr. 722 (1980).

172. *Foley*, 47 Cal. 3d at 683, 765 P.2d at 389, 254 Cal. Rptr. at 227.

173. *Id.* at 690, 765 P.2d at 394, 254 Cal. Rptr. at 232.

biguously the adversary of the insured, and the insured can turn to no one else to insure her retroactively. By contrast, employers have a market incentive to retain good employees, and, if they fail to do so, the employees can often cover by seeking alternative employment.[174]

Finally, the court addressed the plaintiff's argument that compensatory damages for a terminated employee were inadequate. After reviewing the work of numerous scholars, the court said:

> These various approaches on the one hand suggest a widespread perception that present compensation is inadequate, but on the other hand vividly demonstrate substantial disagreement about the propriety or even the potential form of tort remedies for breaches of contractual duties or covenants. The multiplicity of solutions advanced underscores the caution with which any attempts to extend such relief must be viewed.[175]

The case evoked angry dissenting opinions. The court should have followed the insurance cases, argued the dissenters, since "[e]mployment is even more important to the community than insurance; most people value their jobs more than their insurance policies."[176] Like insurance, employment implicated peace of mind as well as monetary interests. Indeed, " 'in a modern industrialized economy employment is central to one's existence and dignity.' "[177] Like insurance, employment relations were characterized by adhesion and inequality of bargaining power.[178] Reforming the common law, which was created by judges, is the responsibility of judges, who should not cite complexity as a reason for inaction pending legislative change.[179]

Given the abstraction thesis defended in this article, one might ask whether the majority or the dissenters have the better of the argument. Most of the arguments made by the dissenters can be dismissed rather rapidly. Inequality of bargaining power is as misguided an argument in

---

174. *Id.* at 693, 765 P.2d at 396, 254 Cal. Rptr. at 234.

175. *Id.* at 696, 765 P.2d at 398, 254 Cal. Rptr. at 236.

176. *Id.* at 708, 765 P.2d at 407, 254 Cal. Rptr. at 245 (Broussard, J., concurring and dissenting).

177. *Id.* at 709, 765 P.2d at 408, 254 Cal. Rptr. at 246 (Broussard, J., concurring and dissenting) (quoting Gould, *The Idea of the Job as Property in Contemporary America: The Legal and Collective Bargaining Framework*, 1986 B.Y.U. L. REV. 885, 892).

178. *Id.* at 718, 765 P.2d at 414-15, 254 Cal. Rptr. at 252-53 (Kaufman, J., concurring and dissenting).

179. *Id.* at 719, 765 P.2d at 415, 254 Cal. Rptr. at 253 (Kaufman, J., concurring and dissenting).

this context as it is in others—as always, limited options are no reason to adopt rules whose only effect is to further limit those options. The problem of adhesion contracts might be pertinent if the employer were trying to rely on fine print disclaimers of tenure rights, but nothing of the kind was alleged. The importance of employment in modern society is all the more reason not to tie the employment relation with inefficient rules that discourage employment and decrease wages.

On the other hand, the majority opinion is strangely inconsistent. It begins with a ringing defense of the principle of compensation in contract law, then concedes that almost all commentators consider existing damage rules undercompensatory, and ends with deference to possible future legislative action.[180] It is true that undercompensation is endemic in contract remedies generally, but employment cases show that undercompensation in the most striking way. The contrast between the concrete reality of the terminated employee's litigation plight and the noble abstract principle of full compensation is a striking fact that should have motivated action. The dissenters are surely correct in saying that the judges have an obligation to do the best they can to make real the principles that the common law espouses. If the judges do it wrong, the legislature can attempt its own solution to the problem, but there is no justification for the courts' refusing to try.

Of course, courts in general have been understandably hesitant to resolve this problem by giving juries an open-ended instruction to monetize intangible industries. Lacking objective or formal benchmarks, the jury might bring back damages in amounts that are just as unpredictable as punitive damages, undermining the goal of removing the extortion value of contracts. The existing rule that monetizes at $0 such undeniably real and substantial harms as the emotional distress of wrongful termination and the time consumed in prosecuting lawsuits is, however, an extreme reaction to this legitimate administrative concern. Almost any schedule of damages I can imagine a court or legislature actually adopting would be better than these two extremes. I have set forth in the margin some suggestions for a schedule of damages for emotional distress[181] and the time consumed in litigation.[182] The actual

180. *See supra* notes 173 & 175 and accompanying text.

181. The emotional distress of a firing is presumably related to the magnitude of the loss, although it is likely to reach a plateau at some point. For concreteness, I would suggest an emotional distress award of 25% of lost salary up to a maximum of $25,000.

182. Since attorney's fees will also be recoverable, and since serious opportunities exist for "padding" of time by clients asserting the amount of time they spent in litigation, I would propose the following. Recovery should be limited to time recorded on the attorney's records that was

numbers, however, are far less important than the need to come up with some schedule that is better than the extremes of zero and unlimited damages for serious but finite injuries.

The majority in *Foley* does correctly point to an important difference between insurance cases and employment cases—a difference that suggests the need for an accompanying abstract principle. In the insurance context, one party has already fully performed, and, thus, the other party has a strong incentive to refuse her own performance for reasons that may have nothing to do with the inefficiency of the contractual obligations. By contrast, the termination of employees entails losing their future services as well as one's future duty to pay them and is quite likely to be undertaken in response to efficiency concerns. Of course, this is no justification for breach of contract—the employee bargained for an implied-in-fact assurance of continued employment and is entitled to the full value of that assurance—but it may indeed be relevant on the issue of damages.

What abstract principle might be indicated as a result of this observation? Perhaps it could be said that if *A* and *B* enter into a contract in which *A* has performed first, a breach by *B* will entitle *A* to punitive damages if *B* did not entertain a good faith, reasonable belief either that nonperformance was justified or that cost increases rendered compensatory damages in lieu of performance necessary to avoid extortion. Exploiting the nonsimultaneity of performances is stealing, pure and simple, and, once such exploitation has been identified by excluding other plausible hypotheses, it is eminently appropriate to impose punitive sanctions.[183]

In the case at hand, however, the court was justified in saying that punitive damages were inappropriate. That is the governing abstract principle. It is grounded in sound policy, which is preventing the plaintiff from using a contract to extract its extortion value. That policy is applicable to employment contexts as well as others, since it often is quite costly to retain less productive employees, and that cost can be

actually spent by clients with their billing attorney in discussing interrogatory answers, being deposed, and being in trial. That time should be charged at the employee's former hourly wage rate, figuring that the disutility of litigation is at least as great as the disutility of working. This time would then be scrutinized by the court for reasonableness at the same time that the court scrutinized the award for attorney's fees.

183. *See* R. POSNER, *supra* note 142, at 105 ("If a promisor breaks his promise merely to take advantage of the vulnerability of the promisee in a setting (the normal contract setting) where performance is sequential rather than simultaneous, then we might as well 'throw the book' at the promisor.").

exploited by threatening punitive damage lawsuits. Such exploitation potential works to the detriment of the employee class as a whole, considered ex ante, when the terms of their contracts are up for renegotiation. It works particularly to the detriment of those marginal potential employees who lack the reassuring credentials and track records that make employers feel safe in taking a risk of subsequent litigation or extortionate payoffs.[184]

B. *The Principle of Mitigation*

1. A Defense of One Version of the Abstract Principle

As noted earlier, the principle of mitigation of damages, unlike the idea of efficient breach, is not terribly controversial in the abstract. It is hard not to have sympathy for the doctrine in a case such as *Rockingham County v. Luten Bridge Co.*,[185] where the defendant county decided not to build a road and, therefore, breached its contract with the plaintiff to construct a bridge, but the plaintiff continued to build the bridge anyway in the middle of the forest. It would be economically wasteful to permit recovery for such costs and, thereby, to encourage plaintiffs to provide services that are no longer valued. An abstract principle *against* mitigation of damages in all contexts is certainly unattractive.

In this case, the mitigation required of the nonbreaching party was quite evident and simple—it had only to stop its own performance. In many cases, however, the plaintiff may be called upon to take affirmative steps to mitigate damages by seeking a substitute performance for the one previously coming from the defendant. The difficult question that arises is what burdens can reasonably be imposed on the nonbreaching party in the mitigation process.

One principle, of course, is that any additional burdens reasonably incurred in mitigation are the responsibility of the breaching party.[186] This is necessary to ensure the earlier principle that damage remedies for breach of contract are fully compensatory. If nonbreaching parties incur search costs in looking for new contracting partners, those costs are chargeable to the breaching parties. If the only substitute contracts available are inferior to the first contractual arrangement, some attempt to monetize that inferiority should be made and assessed against

184. *See* Epstein, *In Defense of the Contract at Will*, 51 U. CHI. L. REV. 947, 970-72 (1984).
185. 35 F.2d 301 (4th Cir. 1929).
186. *See* J. CALAMARI & J. PERILLO, *supra* note 121, at 542-43.

the breaching party.

The reimbursement principle alone, however, may not be sufficient. One must ask whether certain burdens should not be imposed upon the nonbreaching party even if she can expect reasonable compensation for assuming those burdens. Specifically, is a nonbreaching party required to relinquish her subjective tastes and to accept a substitute offer that, together with monetary reimbursement, "reasonable" people would regard as the equivalent of the initial contract?

On the one hand, forcing the nonbreaching party to relinquish her subjective or idiosyncratic reasons for preferring the original contract seems to deprive her of that contract's use value. On the other hand, allowing the nonbreaching party to cite idiosyncratic tastes as a justification for refraining from mitigation threatens the principle that contract damages should be reasonably foreseeable.[187]

Let us say, therefore, that a nonbreaching party should behave reasonably in mitigation unless the breaching party was given advanced notice of the nonbreaching party's unusual needs or tastes. A reasonable person would presumably search for an equivalent position for a reasonable time, and then, if necessary, settle for an inferior position with an expectation of reimbursement for that inferiority. Some alternatives, of course, will be so strikingly inferior to the original contract as to be essentially noncomparable, i.e. nonbreaching parties will reasonably believe that the law will not be able to calculate and award an adequate monetary reimbursement.[188] With regard to these alternatives, there would then be no duty to mitigate.

There will, of course, be problems of proof, as there are in implementing all abstract principles. The nonbreaching party will claim that she failed to mitigate because she entertained a good faith, reasonable belief that no opportunities comparable to the original opportunity, even with reimbursement, were available to her.[189] The court or jury, however, may decide that her true reason for failing to mitigate was to increase the damages on the other side by securing the extortion value

---

187. An analogy might be drawn to the duty of buyers to notify sellers of alleged defects in goods if they intend to reject those goods for the seller must be given an opportunity to cure. *See* U.C.C. § 2-605 (1987).

188. In economic terms, it is not a matter of the two offers being literally noncomparable, but of the cost of making the comparison being so high as to justify a belief that it cannot be made accurately. A similar analysis of the doctrine that certain performances are "unique" is provided in Kronman, *Specific Performance*, 45 U. CHI. L. REV. 351 (1978).

189. The "reasonableness" requirement here assumes that the breaching party was not given advanced notice of peculiar, "unreasonable" although good faith tastes of the breaching party.

of her original contract. Analogous evidentiary questions, however, are already handled in contract law in the area of "satisfaction" clauses, where the court is called upon to decide whether a party is genuinely (and, perhaps, reasonably) dissatisfied with contractual performance or is feigning dissatisfaction as a way of escaping a bargain she now regrets having made.[190]

2. A Critique of Deviations from the Abstract Principle

The courts have had a tendency to resist the idea that an abstract duty to mitigate damages should be imposed across-the-board in contracts cases. Both housing and employment contexts have suggested to some courts the need to deviate from such contractual abstraction. The question to be examined is whether such deviations are justifiable.

In *Gruman v. Investors Diversified Services*,[191] the court expressed the traditional view applicable to landlord-tenant situations:

> [A] majority of the courts have held that in a lease such as this the lessor does not have a duty of mitigating damages; may arbitrarily refuse to accept a subtenant suitable and otherwise responsible; and may recover from the lessee the full rentals due under the lease as and when they become due.[192]

The court articulated a number of reasons for this rule. The first justification was derived from property law concepts: "[A] lease is a conveyance of an interest in real property and, when a lessor has delivered the premises to his lessee, the latter is bound to him by privity of estate as well as by privity of contract."[193] The second idea was that the rule was time-honored, and leases had been devised in reliance upon it.[194] The third argument was that lessors exercise a personal choice in the selection of a particular tenant and often expressly provide in their contracts that other tenants will not be suitable without the express consent of the landlord.[195]

None of these arguments is sufficient to justify deviation from the general principle of mitigation of damages. The real property argument

190. On the interpretation of "satisfaction" clauses in contracts, see Morin Bldg. Prods. Co. v. Baystone Constr., Inc., 717 F.2d 413 (7th Cir. 1983); Mattei v. Hopper, 51 Cal. 2d 119, 330 P.2d 625 (1958).

191. 247 Minn. 502, 78 N.W.2d 377 (1956).

192. *Id.* at 505-06, 78 N.W.2d at 379 (collecting cases).

193. *Id.* at 506, 78 N.W.2d at 380.

194. *Id.* at 509, 78 N.W.2d at 381-82.

195. *Id.* at 506, 78 N.W.2d at 380.

is in direct derogation of the idea of abstraction; it asserts that something peculiar about real estate cuts it off from the rest of the law of transactions. But nothing of the kind exists. The justification for the mitigation principle in general is the avoidance of economic waste. There is such waste in allowing rental property to sit idle while someone who no longer values it pays the rents.

Indeed, it was rules of this character—restrictions that confined land in feudal and family bonds and kept it from partaking of the market order—that inspired Sir Henry Maine to observe that the progress of societies had been marked by the movement "*from Status to Contract*."[196] From our twentieth-century perspective, we can add the gloomy observation that the regression of societies has been marked by the extent to which elite opinion in such societies has rejected and ridiculed Maine's dictum.[197]

The reliance argument, to the extent that it deserves serious attention,[198] argues for the prospective overruling of the principle against mitigation.[199] Lease clauses purporting to prohibit subletting are irrelevant when the issue is not whether the tenant is in breach, but what damages ought to be assessed. In addition, standard form leases are a classic example of the high transaction cost environment where the less visible written terms provide highly problematic evidence of consent.[200]

There remains the argument that the landlord personally chose the tenant and should not be compelled to deal with another. Personal choice, however, is a part of all contracts, and there is nothing peculiar about leases in this regard. Rather than raising these burdens to the level of absolute obstacles to a duty to mitigate, it is appropriate to apply the abstract principles of the prior section to the question of what burdens can reasonably be placed on a nonbreaching landlord in mitigation.

A minimal obligation might be for the landlord to have to accept suitable substitute tenants procured by the original tenant. Some courts and commentators have argued for broader rules of mitigation that

---

196. H. MAINE, ANCIENT LAW 165, 295-354 (1864).

197. *See generally* P. JOHNSON, *supra* note 108.

198. It is not clear that it is always desirable to make transitions prospective only. On the general subject, see Kaplow, *An Economic Analysis of Legal Transitions*, 99 HARV. L. REV. 509 (1986).

199. *See generally* Allen, *The Judicial Quest for Penal Justice: The Warren Court and the Criminal Cases*, 1975 U. ILL. L.F. 518, 530 (prospectivity rule encourages the making of new law by reducing some of its social costs).

200. *See supra* notes 106-07 and accompanying text.

would require the landlord, not only to accept a suitable substitute tenant procured by the original tenant, but to actively search for a new tenant.[201] Are burdens of this nature consistent with the abstract principles of mitigation defended in the prior section?

Landlords, like every other *A* and *B*, are entitled to the full use value of their contracts, but not to their extortion value. To protect use value, landlords must be given reasonable time to search for a suitable substitute tenant. Moreover, they must be reimbursed both for the costs of this search (such as advertisements, brokerage fees) and for the costs incurred if they were unable to find equivalent tenants and had to suffer for less (such as wear and tear on the building). Substituting tenants who were so bad that reimbursement could not reasonably be calculated (renting the property to the Hell's Angels) would not be required.

More than this, however, would make leases into an instrument of extortion value, i.e. threatening the tenant with large costs as a means of coercing a favorable settlement. A rule that landlords do not need to conduct any search for tenants, and a fortiori a rule that landlords do not even need to accept substitute tenants procured by the original tenant in mitigation, create such extortion value. Those rules cannot be justified on abstract principles and should be abandoned.

The same problem of the burden of mitigation arises in the employment context. Unfortunately, courts have again flirted with the counterproductive notion that employment is simply different, so that abstract principles of mitigation are inapplicable. Several courts have held that a former employee is not required to seek or accept employment that is more menial or otherwise not comparable or substantially equal to her employment with defendant.[202] On the other hand, the cases generally hold that, if an employee does take such an inferior position, the wages she earns from that position are deductible from the damages she could otherwise recover from the first employer.[203]

When these two rules are juxtaposed, it is obvious that something has gone dreadfully wrong. The terminated employee in effect faces a

201. *See* Vawter v. McKissick, 159 N.W.2d 538 (Iowa 1968) (affirmative duty on landlord to mitigate). The cases are collected in Annotation, *Landlord's Duty, on Tenant's Failure to Occupy, or Abandonment of, Premises, to Mitigate Damages by Accepting or Procuring Another Tenant*, 21 A.L.R.3D 534 (1968).

202. *See, e.g.*, Parker v. Twentieth Century-Fox Film Corp., 3 Cal. 3d 176, 474 P.2d 689, 89 Cal. Rptr. 737 (1970); Streeatt v. Laclede-Christy Co., 409 S.W.2d 691 (Mo. 1966).

203. *See, e.g.*, Rabago-Alvarez v. Dart Indus., Inc., 55 Cal. App. 3d 91, 127 Cal. Rptr. 222 (1976).

100% tax on her earnings from inferior jobs, since anything she makes at those jobs will come dollar-for-dollar out of the reward she could have received from the first employer. If this problem has not proven empirically to create catastrophic work disincentives, that is only because the system of justice is so slow and cumbersome that terminated employees simply had to take second jobs in order to survive. One knows that a terribly wrong turn has been taken when the only thing that makes the legal order tolerable is the practical inability of people to vindicate their legal rights in full.

Nor is it sensible to respond to this problem by refusing to deduct the wages that the employee made from her second job in a suit brought against the first employer. Such a rule would create an enormous extortion value to the employee's contract rights, as the employee could threaten to take a slightly inferior job and to force the employer to pay two salaries to have the work done.

As always, extortion value cannot be defended on the ground that employees are needier people than employers for the extortion value of the job will work to the ex ante detriment of prospective employees who lack reassuring credentials.[204] It might be defended as a crude counterweight to the inadequacy of the employee's damage remedies. There is, however, no reason to believe that these costs would have any tendency to come close to balancing. The sensible thing to do about inadequate compensatory damages is to tackle that problem directly, not to create arbitrary mistakes in the other direction.

The problem, of course, is the tendency to treat employment contracts as sui generis. The general principle of mitigation of damages is designed to prevent economic waste, and that waste is certainly present if a productive employee remains idle, simply waiting for a damage recovery from a former employer. Of course, the employee, like all nonbreaching parties, should be given time to search for an equivalent position, with the amount of time being a function of how long she would have searched on her own account before settling for the inferior position. If the employee finds an equivalent job, the costs of the search for that position are properly chargeable to the breaching employer.

The question is whether an employee should be required to mitigate by taking an inferior job if that is all that is available. As noted before, the existing rule that no such duty is imposed coheres very poorly with the rule that the wages made in an inferior job that the

204. *See supra* notes 95-99 and accompanying text.

employee does take are deductible from the damages chargeable to the breaching employer. How can the box of this 100% tax rate on wages made from inferior positions be avoided?

As before, the law must overcome its tendency to monetize at $0 the genuine psychological harm of having to settle for an inferior employment opportunity.[205] Again, an open-ended jury instruction to monetize such damages might well be less desirable, given the benefits of formality, than a schedule of damages fixed by the legislature[206] or court.[207] The precise nature of any such schedule is far less important than the existence of some schedule that shares the virtue of predictability with the existing $0 rule without the radical undercompensation of that rule.

Once such a schedule is in place, however, the dangerous anomaly of the 100% tax in existing law can be overcome. If the employee accepts the inferior position, her damages against the former employer will be reduced by her subsequent wages, but only by those wages *net* of the disutility of the second position. If the employee fails to mitigate by taking the inferior position despite ample time for search, her damages against the former employer will also be reduced by the amount of wages net of disutility that she would have been able to make in that position. And, of course, employees should never be penalized for refus-

---

205. Section 353 of the RESTATEMENT (SECOND) OF CONTRACTS (1986) provides that recovery for emotional disturbance should be available only when the breach in question was "of such a kind that serious emotional disturbance was a particularly likely result." It is sensible to have some foreseeability limitation on recovery, but there is no reason for the excessive caution indicated in this language.

206. Here I would propose the following schedule. Lower salary is generally, although not always, a proxy for lower status. I would, therefore, propose that in calculating damages, the gap between salaries should be increased by 25%. For example, if one was fired from a job that paid $500 per week and rehired at an inferior job paying $400 a week, damages would be measured at $125 per week (125% of the gap between $500 and $400). Similarly, if one unreasonably refused to accept the second job and remained idle after ample opportunity for search, damages would be measured at $125 per week, establishing the principle of mitigation.

If the employee regards the second job as inferior in status although substantially equal in pay, I would require the employee to prove that fact, perhaps by showing that people take the first job when offered both. If proven, I would permit the plaintiff to reduce the second salary by 10% in calculating damages.

207. Although the use of numerical schedules by courts is uncommon, I can see no principled objection to their use. Such schedules are not taking questions of fact away from the jury. To the contrary, as with all formalities, they are setting a unitary rule of law because the costs of a case-by-case treatment of the issue as one of fact entails more costs than benefits.

The distribution of governmental responsibility between legislatures and courts, however, is peripheral to my essential thesis. If it is felt that the deviation of such schedules from judicial tradition is too great, the same result should be brought about by legislation.

ing to take jobs that they reasonably regard as not being comparable with the original position even with monetary reimbursement—for example, jobs where their physical safety is threatened.

Present law requires employers to prove that employees failed to mitigate and, since the employers are the breaching parties, that allocation of the burden of proof seems sensible.[208] Ordinarily, however, that burden of proof should be satisfied by showing that the second position was sufficiently attractive to a reasonable person in plaintiff's position that she would have taken it had she been acting on her own account. This is not because employees, unlike other contracting parties, are only permitted to derive the use values from contracts that reasonable persons would have derived. Rather, the general principle of foreseeability in contract law would suggest that employers, like other contracting parties, are entitled to notice of idiosyncratic or special needs of their transacting partners.

C. *A Summary of Two Related Principles in Application*

Two abstract principles of contract law are that damages are to be compensatory and that nonbreaching parties have a duty to mitigate those damages. This article has not quarreled with those abstract principles. To the contrary, it has defended them as carving a needed distinction between the use value and the extortion value of contractual promises. The article has also criticized deviations from those principles in favor of landlords, tenants, employers, employees, insurers, and insureds and suggested that careful study of those specific contexts shows that the abstract principles and subprinciples themselves, such as the rules on the reasonableness of burdens that can be imposed on mitigating parties, need to be further refined.

VI. Conclusion: Future Directions for Research

It is customary to conclude many articles of this nature with ideas about directions for future scholarship in the particular area of study. In this case, however, it is critical to conclude the piece in that way, since the areas of future research implicated by the conclusions of this article are so vast.

As noted in the introduction, a large part of the upper level curriculum of modern law schools is concerned with law applicable to partic-

208. *See* Russell v. Barnes Found., 52 F. Supp. 827 (E.D. Pa. 1943); Stewart v. Board of Educ. of Ritenour Consol. School Dist., 630 S.W.2d 130 (Mo. Ct. App. 1982).

ular kinds of contracts, such as agency and partnership contracts,[209] real estate financing contracts, and the like. This article poses a challenge to contrast the specific rules of each such body of law with the corresponding abstract principles of contract law. Tensions between the two could be resolved in any of the ways indicated here: abandoning the context-specific rule, altering the abstract principle, defending the rule as a sensible concretization of the abstract principle, and so on.

Research that starts at the opposite direction—with the abstract principles of contract law—is also needed. The last section of this article began with the principles of compensatory damages and the duty to mitigate and worked from those principles to concrete contexts, shedding light both on the wisdom of the concrete rules and the precise formulations of the principles. There are, of course, many more principles of contract law for which a similar analysis should be provided.

Much of this work can be done simply by applying the underrated tool of common sense, together with the imperative of abstraction, to the available contract materials. These contrasts, however, could be illuminated further both with deontological moral theory and with the consequentialist analysis of modern law-and-economics. An enormous field of inquiry awaits for those who are willing and able to juxtapose abstract contract principles, concrete rules for specific types of contracts, deontological theories of right and wrong, and utilitarian economic insights into the workings of markets.

209. For an excellent piece in this direction, see Barnett, *Squaring Undisclosed Agency Law with Contract Theory*, 75 CALIF. L. REV. 1969 (1987).

Name Index